The Salvation Historical Fallacy?

It is amazing to me that one would go to so much trouble to show that there were actually German theologians who believed the Bible actually presented a unified theology presumably revealed in History.

The

SALVATION HISTORICAL FALLACY?

*Reassessing the History of
New Testament Theology*

Robert W. Yarbrough

deo
PUBLISHING

LEIDEN

History of Biblical Interpretation series, 2
ISSN 1382-4465 (formerly a series by Brill Academic Publishers)

Series Editor: Robert Morgan

Published by Deo Publishing
Scholeksterstraat 16, 2352 EE Leiderdorp, The Netherlands

British Library Cataloguing-in-Publication data
A catalogue record for this book is available from the British Library

NUR 703

ISBN 90-5854-024-3

Contents

Chapter 2
Religion versus Theology: William Wrede and Adolf Schlatter
on New Testament Theology

Chapter 3
The Debate Continues:
Religion versus Theology between the World Wars................118

Chapter 5
Prophet without Honor:
Cullmann's Unseasonable Salvation Historical Synthesis 213

Chapter 6
The Perfect Storm:
Final Assault on Salvation History and Counterinsurgency...261

Preface

This study summarizes two decades of chronic curiosity, sporadic read-ing, and more or less continual reflection. Beginning with a University of Aberdeen doctoral thesis in the mid-1980s,[1] I became fascinated by the disparate interpretive strategies informing New Testament theolo-gies. This is a genre of summary scholarship plied most diligently in Germany. In the last ten years or so, for example, it seems that just one New Testament theology (by G.B. Caird [1994]) has come from Brit-ish or North American circles. Meanwhile, some half-dozen, comprising ten volumes total, have appeared in Germany (by J. Gnilka [1994], F. Hahn [2002], H. Hübner [1990/1993/1995], G. Strecker [1996], P. Stuhlmacher [1992/1999], and U. Wilckens [2003/2003]). New Testament theologies are important because each serves as a syn-thesis of the New Testament's teaching or message. The meaning of the whole, if there turns out to be one, is of obvious importance to anyone striving to understand what to make of the individual parts.

Yet the results at which these summae have arrived since the disci-pline called "New Testament theology" began about two centuries ago vary widely and at times dramatically. Is there a pattern to the variation, and if so how may it be explained? Can we make sense of the disparity? That is the question to which this book seeks to provide some measure of an answer. If it succeeds, a helpful key to synthesizing the syntheses will have been furnished.

This is not a synchronic study. It does not take its stand amidst a cluster of recent New Testament theologies and comparable writings (synthetic volumes by N.T. Wright, J. Dunn, and others come to mind) and assess the past from a set current viewpoint.[2] It is rather a diachronic study. It seeks to enter into key aspects of debates that flared up beginning in the 1800s and to analyze them from the points of view of those who carried on the discussions. It seeks to tell a story more than render a verdict. Those seemingly hoary disputations, and

---

[1] "The *heilsgeschichtliche* Perspective in Modern New Testament Theology," 1985.
[2] H. Räisänen (see p. 1, n. 3 below) has performed that service admirably, though many would view the terrain in a quite different fashion.

the issues that underlay them, are actually still burning questions today. There is every reason to explore them carefully and at length in a little different manner than has been attempted before.

English readers for whom German language works are inaccessible may find this study of particular interest, since many of the primary sources analyzed, and a good number of the secondary studies cited, exist only in German. (Even where translations are available, I have worked most often from the original versions.) It is my hope to contribute to better understanding of and interest in German scholarship, which has led the way in New Testament theology since its inception and will continue to play a leading role in the decades ahead.

This book has been close to publication in past years and earlier recensions. Sometimes publishers delayed, and sometimes I did, conscious of gaps and inadequate treatments and incomplete understanding on my part. How do you do justice to modern scholarship's brilliant and magisterial summations of the theology Jesus brought into the world and the doctrinal activity he set in motion? In the end, you don't. At least I know I haven't. Yet I take heart from Jane Leavy's observation (in her unforgettable *Sandy Koufax: A Lefty's Legacy*): "You don't need to know everything to write the truth. You just need to know enough." Maybe after twenty years I have learned enough to say some valid things about admittedly vast and complex matters. No doubt some readers will detect less truth in my observations than I had hoped. For the limitations and miscues encountered I apologize in advance.

Among research assistants who have labored diligently on aspects of this project, deserving special mention are Dawn Campion Burnett, Stephen Kline, Scott Yoshikawa, and Dong-Won Han. I extend to them all my heartfelt thanks.

I am grateful to the institutional support of Trinity Evangelical Divinity School, and in prior years Covenant Theological Seminary and Wheaton College, for sustaining the research reflected in these pages.

Hans Bayer, Werner Neuer, and Eckhard Schnabel have given me encouragement over the years in my preoccupation with German New Testament scholarship, its leading lights, and its seminal discussions. From them I gleaned, along with much solid counsel, the important insight that sometimes even Germans aren't sure what a Baur, Schlatter, or Bultmann is trying to say. It is to them that I gratefully dedicate this work.

Robert W. Yarbrough   New Year's Day, 2004

Introduction

a bit understated.

Since Christianity generally claims to have some connection with divine revelation that unfolded in history, the relation of the divine to the historical has been of perennial interest[1] in most branches of theological study since critical study of the Bible arose at the time of the Enlightenment.[2] This is especially true in the discipline called biblical theology, an enterprise inaugurated in 1787 in Germany by J.P Gabler.[3] It quickly split into two disciplines, Old and New Testament theology, each still flourishing today.[4] Biblical theology as an attempt to view the Testaments as an integrated whole is receiving attention as well, whether in B. Childs' canonical approach[5] or in what J. Barr has called the pan-biblical proposals of M. Oeming and others.[6]

In Gabler's wake, and as critical study of the New Testament hit its stride in nineteenth-century European (and gradually North Ameri-

---

[1]For a wide-ranging survey and analysis of trends primarily in the domain of philosophical theology see P. Gwynne, *Special Divine Action: Key Issues in the Contemporary Debate (1965–1995)*, 1996.

[2]As mere samples of a vast literature see H. Reventlow, W. Sparn & J. Woodbridge, *Historische Kritik und biblischer Kanon in der deutschen Aufklärung*, 1988; K. Scholder, *The Birth of Modern Critical Theology*, 1990.

[3]See J. Sandys-Wunch & L. Eldredge, "J.P. Gabler and the Distinction between Biblical and Dogmatic Theology: Translation, Commentary, and Discussion of His Originality," *SJT* 33 (1980) 133-158. Helpful analyses include R. Smend, "Johann Philipp Gablers Begründung der biblischen Theologie," *EvT* 22 (1962) 345-357; O. Merk, "Gabler, Johann Philipp (1753–1826)," *TRE* 12, 1–3; B.C. Ollenburger, "Biblical Theology: Situating the Discipline," *Understanding the Word*, 1985, 37-62; R. Morgan, "Gabler's Bicentenary," *ExpT* 98 (1986-87) 164-168; A. Adam, *Making Sense of New Testament Theology*, 1995, 50–63; H. Räisänen, *Beyond New Testament Theology*, [2]2000, *passim*.

[4]See e.g. on (primarily) Old Testament theology H. Sun, *et al.*, eds., *Problems in Biblical Theology*, 1997; B. Anderson, *Contours of Old Testament Theology*, 1999; J. Barr, *The Concept of Biblical Theology*, 1999; R. Murphy, "Questions Concerning Biblical Theology," *Biblical Theological Bulletin* 30/3 (2000) 81–89. For New Testament theology note Adam, *Making Sense of New Testament Theology*; P. Balla, *Challenges to New Testament Theology*, 1997; D. Carson, "New Testament Theology," *DLNT* 796–814; Räisänen, *Beyond New Testament Theology*.

[5]Childs, *Biblical Theology of the Old and New Testaments*, 1993.

[6]Barr, *The Concept of Biblical Theology*, 497–512.

can) Protestantism, the "theology" found in the New Testament was understood increasingly as antiquated tradition that no longer either compelled or deserved assent. "Historical" treatments of the teachings of the New Testament writers arose that self-consciously repudiated or redefined virtually the whole range of cardinal Christian doctrines: the knowability of God, the divinity of Christ (along with his full human-ity), the substitutionary atonement, the bodily resurrection, the authority of Scripture, the historical reality and import of the Bible's reported miracles ... Take any compendium of pre-Enlightenment Protestant doctrine[7] and compare it to, say, the dogmatics of leading theologian Adolf Harnack around the year 1900. It is hard to avoid the impression that in key respects a new religion has arisen.[8] And under-standings of theology yet more caustic than Harnack's were eventually to appear. A novel gospel spread through Western universities, divinity schools, and churches heralding the message that pre-Enlightenment construals of the Bible were, empirically and philosophically speaking, no longer tenable. This trend continued in the twentieth century de-spite notable dissent lodged first from traditional and recently from post-critical quarters. Measured by historic standards, Christianity as articulated in many mainline centers of study had become post-Christian.[9]

New Testament theologians came to read the New Testament in this light, exhilarating or withering depending on one's point of view, over the span of many decades. Three doyens of the discipline stand out in importance: F.C. Baur (1792-1860), W. Wrede (1858-1906), and R. Bultmann (1884-1976). Baur often gets credit for being a sort of father to critical study of the New Testament. Wrede deftly plotted out the hermeneutical tack that New Testament theologians would have to take now that early Christianity was seen as in key respects hardly more unique, true, or binding than any other ancient religious

---

[7]See e.g. K. R. Hagenbach, *A Text-book of the History of Doctrines*, 2 vols., 1861–1862; Heinrich Schmid, *The Doctrinal Theology of the Lutheran Church*, 1876; R. Muller, *Post-Reformation Reformed Dogmatics*, 2 vols., 1987–93.

[8]A point argued at length in J.G. Machen, *Christianity and Liberalism*, 1923. Differ-ent in focus but sounding similar notes more recently is J. Leith, *Crisis in the Church*, 1997.

[9]Typical of this viewpoint is R. Funk, *Honest to Jesus*, 1996. Funk nicely epito-mizes, if at times to an extreme degree, what many biblical scholars and ecclesiastical leaders in the industrial West have believed and passed on to their students for genera-tions. These views are now commonly encountered in the so-called Third World as well. They are, for example, extremely useful to Muslim apologists seeking to discredit the Bible.

manifestation amidst the cultures of humanity. Bultmann in the mid-20th century penned a New Testament theology that has yet to be superseded in its application of critical method to the New Testament corpus to yield a "New Testament theology" palpably foreign to the New Testament writers themselves but intellectually compelling to Bultmann's readers then and since.

Did the revolution in New Testament theology that took place in Gabler's wake occur without a shot? Where were the New Testament theologians who lived alongside Baur and Wrede and Bultmann but did not affirm their radical reconfiguring of Christian faith in the name of post-Enlightenment European conviction? These are questions with no good answers in standard accounts of New Testament scholarship, which do not focus on New Testament theology as a discipline anyway. To shed light on the question from the standpoint of that discipline is the aim of this book.

It is our proposal that a seemingly disparate collection of New Testament scholars—J.C.K. von Hofmann (1810-1877), A. Schlatter (1852-1938), M. Albertz (1882–1956), L. Goppelt (1911-1973), and O. Cullmann (1902–1998)—combine to form an alternative to traditional New Testament theology in the Baur-Wrede-Bultmann mode.[10] What the post-Enlightenment *communis opinio* wrote off as a fallacy—that a particular trajectory within the historical nexus somehow took on normative significance for all history due to God's unique saving presence in and through it—these contrarian-minded scholars pursued as a viable historiographical possibility. Their personal dogmatic orientations vary widely, but their hermeneutical convictions coalesce on the issue of the relation of the Christian faith and history. Whereas Baur-Wrede-Bultmann saw a largely negative relation, so that a "historical" synthesis of New Testament convictions must be fatal to classic Christian belief, these scholars lodge a fascinating minority report. In ways that set them apart from many of their peers, they saw Christian salvation and the world's historical processes as positively related.

It was Hofmann who apparently coined the term that aptly captures this positive relation: *Heilsgeschichte* (salvation history).[11] *Heil* connotes "salvation," the transcendent that encounters the world it created to redeem it, the personal self-disclosure of a God whom Kant

---

[10]G. Ladd (1911–1982) also wrote a New Testament theology from this dissenting viewpoint. But space precludes more than passing mention of him in the discussion below.

[11]A.J. Greig, "A Critical Note on the Origin of the Term Heilsgeschichte," *ExpT* 87 (1976) 118–119.

had declared unknowable.[12] Hofmann, taking his cue from biblical
writers, not only disagreed with Kant but affirmed why: Enlightenment skepticism was called in question by the very history (*Geschichte*)
that figures like G.E. Lessing (1729–1781) appealed to in their move
to debunk the Christian faith.[13]

With Hofmann we can speak of a hermeneutical orientation
within the discipline of New Testament theology for which "critical"
study means to enter into dialogue not only with current but also with
ancient conviction. The effect of the Baur-Wrede-Bultmann approach, we will argue, was frequently to censor the ancients, and any
who dared affirm their testimony in the present, on the basis of
Enlightenment or post-Enlightenment certainties. "Salvation history"
came to be regarded as a pre-critical myth[14] and therefore a methodological fallacy. Since the hegemony of such certainties no longer
commands the respect it did, some may find it refreshing to hear the
story of scholars who were never beguiled by the messianic pretensions
of Western modernist thought to begin with. This is not to say that
the Enlightenment was all bad.[15] But not all of the convictions that
emerged in that era deserve the deference they have commonly enjoyed in critical study of the Bible.

The need for our study is implicit in the fact that none like it exists. Hofmann, Schlatter, Albertz, Goppelt, and to a slightly lesser
extent Cullmann have been underrated as New Testament theologians.
Moreover, while *Heilsgeschichte* (or the somewhat broader concept
"revelation in history") received considerable attention as a *theological*
construct dear to the so-called Biblical Theology Movement in the
years after World War II, its identity and function as a less restrictive,

---

[12]"For even if God were to speak to man, man could never know that it is God
who is speaking to him. It is simply impossible for man to be able to grasp the Infinite
One with his senses, to distinguish Him from sense impressions and thereby know
him" (I. Kant, *Der Streit der Fakultäten*, 1959, 62).

[13]For Lessing "the whole fabric of orthodox Christology was without historical basis" (C. Brown, *Jesus in European Protestant Thought 1778–1860*, 1988, 27). For replies
to Lessing see Adam, *Making Sense of New Testament Theology*, 133–137; M. Williams,
"Crossing Lessing's Ditch," *God and Man*, 1995, 103–126. Lessing is often credited
with the definitive statement of the claim that religious belief cannot be founded on
historical knowledge; "contingent truths of history can never become the proof of
necessary truths of reason" (*Lessings sämmtliche Werke*, vol. 7, 1882, 273). But finding
truth in presumedly ahistorical "reason" had already proven a prominent feature of the
rationalism of figures like Spinoza and Descartes.

[14]Classic is the demolition attempted by D.F. Strauss, *The Life of Jesus Critically Examined*, 1972, 39f.

[15]For a balanced appraisal see J. Byrne, *Religion and the Enlightenment*, 1996.

less culpable *hermeneutical* and *historiographical* posture as reflected in specific New Testament theologies has been overlooked. Redressing that neglect is the aim of this study.

Specifically, we trace the vicissitudes of the *heilsgeschichtliche* or salvation historical perspective (so-called; it is a multiform, not monolithic, entity) since Hofmann as it has functioned in New Testament theology. We proceed in two phases.

Chapters one, two, and six frame the investigation by setting forth distinctives of the outlook in contrast to what we term "critical orthodoxy." That is, we acknowledge New Testament theology's indebtedness to the normative line of inquiry pioneered by Baur, Wrede, and Bultmann. Significantly, Hofmann conceived his New Testament theology as a corrective to Baur; Schlatter wrote in the face of a discipline heavily indebted to Wrede (and Wrede's ideological inspiration E. Troeltsch); Albertz, Goppelt, Cullmann had to reckon with the imposing dominance of Bultmann.

Accordingly, in Chapter 1 we set forth aspects of Baur's views as a foil—which they were historically—to those of Hofmann. Likewise, in Chapter 2, we take up Wrede, who in important respects furthers the tradition Baur established and serves to point up Schlatter's distinctives. Finally, in Chapter 6, Bultmann, whose fundamental affinity to the outlooks of Baur and Wrede is easily demonstrated, serves as the critical constant against which to assess Albertz and Goppelt.

But fixing attention on just a few individual salvation historical New Testament theologians seemed too restricted, considering that the wider and closely related problem of the nature and function of salvation history in New (and Old) Testament theology in the 20th century remains an unchronicled story. Accordingly, Chapter 3 attempts a sketch of where salvation historical perspectives are in evidence in Old and New Testament theology between the world wars. Chapter 4 does the same for the post-World War II period. Without this background it is easy to misconstrue the nature of the salvation historical alternative to critical orthodoxy.

In addition, Chapters 3 and 4 make it possible to see Cullmann in a different light than that in which he is often portrayed. Cullmann wrote no New Testament theology, but he is a major player in salvation historical scholarship of past decades. His views are therefore given attention in Chapter 5. Clarification of Cullmann's contribution then facilitates comparison in Chapter 6 of Bultmann to Albertz and Goppelt, who are not nearly so indebted to Cullmann in their conception of salvation history as might be expected.

We have not (with some minor exceptions) included Roman Catholic studies which incorporate a salvation historical approach, among which is K.H. Schelkle's four-volume New Testament theology.[16] Conceptual developments in post-Vatican II Roman Catholic thought as they impinge on New Testament theology would demand separate treatment.[17] And as J. Levenson has noted, historically speaking biblical theology has been dominated by Protestant rather than Catholic scholars, whose full entrance into critical biblical studies took place only in recent decades.[18]

We have likewise not discussed at length the questions raised by J. Barr regarding "revelation in history" as a theological construct in the Biblical Theology Movement.[19] The problems he cites—"ambiguity about the nature of the revelatory events"; "ambiguity about the sense of 'history'"; "ambiguity about the relation between revelation and history"; and "difficulties in the relation between revelation and the biblical text itself"—are touched on from time to time and are certainly worthwhile questions. But in our view these issues seem intractable because of the impression many harbor that the "revelation in history" impasse of the Biblical Theology Movement was largely brought on by Cullmann. We will argue that this is an oversimplified and unfruitful way of approaching the problem. We thus do not so much neglect Barr's questions as lay the groundwork for their proper

---

[16] *Theology of the New Testament*, 4 vols., 1971-1978. Volume two is subtitled *Salvation History—Revelation*. G. Hasel, *New Testament Theology*, 1978, 77-82, analyzes Schelkle's work as "thematic" rather than "salvation-historical." In fact Schelkle's approach fits under both rubrics.

[17] Excavating the foundations through attention to Johann Adam Möhler and other nineteenth century theologians in the Catholic faculty at Tübingen are M.J. Himes, *Ongoing Incarnation* 1997; D.J. Dietrich & M.J. Himes, eds., *The Legacy of the Tübingen School,* 1997. On developments after Vatican II see E. Stakemeier, "Zur heilsgeschichtlichen Orientierung der Fundamentaltheologie nach Zweiten Vaticanum," *Catholica* 21/2 (1967) 101–126; M. Geisser, "Mysterium Salutis," *TZ* 32 (1976) 159–166; B. Hinze, "The End of Salvation History," *Horizons* 18/2 (1991) 227–245, especially 230 n. 4.

[18] J. Levenson, *The Hebrew Bible, the Old Testament, and Historical Criticism,* 1993, 45. Cf. J. Donahue, "The Changing Shape of New Testament Theology," *TS* 50/2 (1989) 316f.; R. Murphy, *BTB* 30/3 (2000) 81. Levenson also states that Jews have no interest in biblical theology, but see M. Brettler, "Biblical History and Jewish Biblical Theology," *JR* 77/4 (1997) 563–583; A. Bellis & J. Kaminsky, eds., *Jews, Christians and the Theology of the Hebrew Scriptures,* 2000. It is too soon to discern what role, if any, salvation history will play in Jewish biblical theology if it continues to develop.

[19] See Barr, "Revelation in History," *IDBSup* 746-749.

consideration as they relate to the discipline of New Testament theology.

New Testament theology in the Baur-Wrede-Bultmann heritage has overreached in its often swashbuckling conviction that a salvation historical approach must necessarily constitute a fallacy. We will show that the "critical orthodox" hegemony has been more dependent on philosophical, theological, and historiographical convictions intrinsic to the changing times than has been good for either scholarship or religion.[20] At the same time there has been since Hofmann a consistent, if today little remarked, response to Baur-Wrede-Bultmann that appears worthy of a second look. This view has assumed various characteristic forms; it is also fraught with its own philosophical, theological, and historiographical liabilities.

Yet we have before us the story of an outlook committed to doing justice, not only to the demands of modern thought in constructing a New Testament theology, but also to claims and dimensions of the New Testament texts for which critical orthodoxy has never succeeded in giving a universally compelling explanation. New Testament theology has been an enterprise torn between apparent certainties of modernity and now postmodernity,[21] on the one hand, and competing New Testament assertions, on the other. The salvation historical approach in its variegated manifestations has assayed to do justice to both. Just how it undertakes this, and in what respects it works out a critical stance toward both the biblical sources and critical orthodoxy, takes shape as we proceed.

[20] Cf. T. Söding, "Inmitten der Theologie des Neuen Testaments. Zu den Voraussetzungen und Zielen neutestamentlicher Exegese," *NTS* 42 (1996) 184.

[21] For samples of postmodern challenges to the ways of reading the New Testament that gave rise to biblical theology see R. Scroggs, "Can New Testament Theology Be Saved? The Threat of Contextualisms," *USQR* 42 (1988) 17–31 (Scroggs' answer is yes); S. Moore, "History after Theory? Biblical Studies and the New Historicism," *BibInt* 5/4 (1997) 289–299 (Moore is less sanguine).

Hegel - mind concept -
set of contradictions
ultimately - united

dialectic - method of argument -

Hegel - Fichte
Shelling - Id

BAUR (1792-1860)

1

Tübingen versus Erlangen:
F.C. Baur and J.C.K. von Hofmann
on New Testament Theology

One of the first great syntheses of New Testament theology in the Gablerian sense arose from the prodigious labors of the Tübingen university professor F.C. Baur (1792–1860).[1] He is recognized and frequently defended[2] as one of the fathers of modern biblical study. His

[1] On Baur cf. especially B. Weiss, *Lehrbuch der biblischen Theologie des Neuen Testaments*, [2]1873, 24–26; C. Senft, *Wahrhaftigkeit und Wahrheit*, 1956, 47–86; H. Liebing, "Historisch-kritische Theologie. Zum 100. Todestag Ferdinand Christian Baurs am 2. Dezember 1960," *ZTK* 57 (1960) 302–317; P.C. Hodgson, ed. and trans., *Ferdinand Christian Baur on the Writing of Church History*, 1968; H.-J. Kraus, *Die Biblische Theologie*, 1970, 144–150; O. Merk, *Biblische Theologie des Neuen Testaments in ihrer Anfangszeit*, 1972, 226–236; W.G. Kümmel, *The New Testament: The History of the Investigation of its Problems*, 1973, 120–184; H. Harris, *David Friedrich Strauss and His Theology*, 1973, especially 85–116, 274–284; *idem, The Tübingen School*, 1975; C. Senft, "Ferdinand Christian Baur. Methodological Approach and Interpretation of Luke 15:11–32," in *Exegesis. Problems of Method and Exercises in Reading (Genesis 22 and Luke 15)*, Gérald Antoine, *et al.*, trans. D.G. Miller, 1978, 77–96; W.G. Kümmel, "Einführung zum Neudruck von *Vorlesungen über neutestamentliche Theologie*," *Heilsgeschehen und Geschichte*, vol. 2, ed. E. Gräßer & O. Merk, 1978, 101–116; R. Bultmann, *Theologie des Neuen Testaments*, [8]1980, 591ff.; K. Scholder, "Baur, Ferdinand Christian (1792–1860)," *TRE* 5, 352–359; C.K. Barrett, "Quomodo historia conscribenda sit," *NTS* 28 (1982) 303–320; Robert Morgan, "Ferdinand Christian Baur," *Nineteenth Century Thought in the West*, vol. 1, Ninian Smart, *et al.*, eds., 1985, 261–289; E. Ellis, "Die Datierung des Neuen Testaments," *TZ* 42 (1986) 420f.; U. Köpf, "Ferdinand Christian Baur als Begründer einer konsequenten historischen Theologie," *ZTK* 89/4 (1992) 440–461; R. Harrisville & W. Sundberg, *The Bible in Modern Culture*, [2]2002, 104–122; S.J. Hafemann, "Baur, F(erdinand) C(hristian) (1792–1860)," *Historical Handbook of Major Biblical Interpreters*, D.K. McKim, ed., 1998, 376–380; R. Morgan, "Baur, F.C. (1792–1860)," *The Dictionary of Historical Theology*, ed. T. Hart, 2000, 58–59; H. Räisänen, *Beyond New Testament Theology*, 16f.

[2] Cf. H. Rollmann, "From Baur to Wrede: The Quest for a Historical Method," *SR* 17/4 (1988) 443–454; P. Addinall, "Why Read the Bible?" *ExpTim* 105 (1994) 136–140. Räisänen, *Beyond New Testament Theology*, 16, credits Baur with "the first New Testament theology that can be regarded as essentially historical."

approach to New Testament theology was destined to become foundational for the "critical" approach to the discipline that dominated the 20th century through the work of Rudolf Bultmann.

Opposite Baur stands J.C.K. von Hofmann (1810–1877), who lectured for decades at the University of Erlangen. He is generally overlooked in surveys of the history of New Testament scholarship.[3] R. Clements, however, astutely notes that Hofmann "was to become remarkably influential and to establish within the circle of biblical scholarship a new concept: that of *Heilsgeschichte*—a 'History of Salvation.'"[4] Like Baur he pursued the calling of a New Testament theologian in a milieu which had been dramatically influenced by such figures as Kant, Schleiermacher, Hegel, and Strauss. The works of Hofmann and Baur grapple with many of the same questions. But their approaches led them to very different conclusions.

As we will see below, for Baur a salvation historical approach was fallacious because of the nature of the New Testament sources and the largely philosophical certainties that inform "critical" methods used to analyze them. For Hofmann, those same sources remained unintelligible apart from the material influence of a transcendent God who involved himself in the historical process in much the way that biblical writers claim. In the name of the "purely historical science" of New Testament theology Baur puts forth a synthesis intent, as he states in another connection, only on arriving at "historical truth and the pure and impartial investigation of it."[5] In the same name of history, but history less trammeled by the constraints of idealist philosophy, Hofmann arrives at a contrasting construal of identical empirical data.

Baur's conception of New Testament theology

1. Significance and distinctiveness

Baur's book *Vorlesungen über neutestamentliche Theologie*[6] (*Lectures on New Testament Theology*) was recognized by Bultmann as having epochal

---

[3]Räisänen, *Beyond New Testament Theology*, for instance, gives him no independent mention. He is conspicuously absent from T. Hart, ed., *The Dictionary of Historical Theology*, 2000 and receives one sentence in T. Alexander & B. Rosner, eds., *New Dictionary of Biblical Theology*, 14.

[4]R. Clements, "The Study of the Old Testament," *Nineteenth Century Religious Thought in the West*, ed. by Ninian Smart *et al.*, vol. 3, 1985, 126. Carson, *DLNT*, 796–814, also comes closer to giving Hofmann his due.

[5]Baur, *Lehrbuch der christlichen Dogmengeschichte*, 1979 [1868], XII.

[6]1864, edited posthumously by his son Ferdinand Friedrich.

importance. Baur was the first in the discipline of New Testament theology to make the central focus and task of New Testament theology "the conceptual explication of believing self-understanding."[7] New Testament theology for Baur is not greatly concerned with what the New Testament texts record regarding what Jesus and others did and when or in what historical context they did it. New Testament theology is concerned only with those doctrinal ideas or concepts expressed by the New Testament authors.[8]

Now this is in itself not a very controversial assertion. Many New Testament theologies present the doctrine or teaching which they derive from the New Testament texts. But Baur's approach had a new twist. The texts themselves are not sources through which we gain direct access to the message of the New Testament texts. The gospel writings do not, for example, preserve in any considerable measure particular features of Jesus' life; they reflect only "the reflex of the subjectivity of the authors."[9] Thus generally speaking, "Jesus' teaching stands before us at such a historical distance that it defies the attempt of the historian to pull it into focus. Really only the whole rather than the individual component can be envisaged."[10] One must distinguish cause, "the objectively real, as it is in itself,"[11] on the one hand, from the "subjective meaning which it [the objectively real] first took on in the consciousness of the apostles and in their peculiar way of seeing things."[12]

Baur distinguishes, then, between what the texts say and what Baur thinks they are really indicating or what forces they reflect.[13] Baur shifts the focus of New Testament theology from an interpretation of *the texts'* claims—the substantial concern, for example, of a recent ostensibly historical work like P. Barnett's *Jesus and the Logic of History*[14]—to an extrapolation from the texts back to the subjective consciousness of the New Testament writers. What the texts recount is secondary to the light they shed on the beliefs of their composers. The historical context is lost, or at least radically reconstrued so as to signify

[7]Bultmann, *Theologie*, 592.
[8]Baur, *Vorlesungen*, 30.
[9]*Ibid.* 24.
[10]*Ibid.* 122.
[11]*Ibid.* 125.
[12]*Ibid.*
[13]For a defense of Baur here see Senft, *Wahrhaftigkeit*, 68ff.
[14]Grand Rapids 1997.

the processes by which the biblical writers came to express their particular subjective awareness.

2. An example of Baur's approach

It will be illustrative to give an example of Baur's application of this method to a well-known New Testament figure: Paul.

Jesus lay dead in the grave. (Accounts of his resurrection are due only to thoughts which took the form of visions to his shattered devotees, who regarded the visions as "appearances of the resurrected one."[15]) Then with dramatic suddenness the question hit him:

> 'But wait! [Paul exclaimed to himself.] What if it was the destiny of the Messiah to die, and what if his death as an event arranged by God also had a unique religious significance! What other possible significance could it have, however, than this: to be a sacrificial death for the sins of mankind?' But to regard Jesus' death as sacrificial carried within it the presupposition that he would effect that which the entire Old Testament religious establishment had not and could not accomplish. And the more the entire significance of Jesus' messiahship could be seen as tied up exclusively in his death, the more must this new initiative of God appear in opposition to the entire Old Testament religious establishment with its imperfection and insufficiency for the forgiveness of sins, for the justification and the bliss of mankind. Now it was [for Paul] simply a matter of developing dialectically, in the context of its impulses, the relationship of Jesus' death to the Old Testament (or: to the law, as the essential characteristic of the Old Testament) in such a way that it would appear to be something rooted in the inner necessity of the thing itself.[16]

This was "the inner mental process ..., through which the apostle's peculiar viewpoint formed itself and through which his opposition to the law as a matter of principle became the heart of his religious consciousness."[17] In this way Paul came to see Jesus, not as a Jewish national savior, but as one who, by inexorable conceptual processes, had been thrust into "a free, universal, purely spiritual realm."[18] Baur explains a rather central "historical" feature of the New Testament—Paul's belief in Jesus' resurrection—by showing how concepts developed themselves inexorably within him and eventually came to forceful expression. In the end the historical context of the resurrection event is lost. For Paul's thoughts, or those developing themselves

[15]Baur, *Vorlesungen*, 127.
[16]*Ibid.* 130.
[17]*Ibid.*
[18]*Ibid.* 131.

in his consciousness, give rise to Jesus' resurrection, and not a historical event to Paul's thought, as the New Testament writings might be taken on the surface to suggest.

Through this new and original-to-Paul apprehension of the dead Jesus' transcendent import, "all that had been unique to Judaism vanished for Paul in the universalism of Christianity."[19] Above all the law's importance is shattered. Paul realizes that one achieves true ethical integrity only through doing that "of which one is conscious that one ought to do it."[20] This is strikingly similar to Kant's categorical imperative.[21] Only with Paul's insights into the deadness of Judaism has, for the first time in the history of mankind,[22] "a truly spiritual relationship between God and mankind arisen."[23] Vestiges of temporal connections and dependencies are still visible in the view of Christianity set forth by Paul, for whom the faith was "only something supernatural,"[24] inasmuch as he "makes quite visible efforts to grasp it historically."[25] But Christianity as Paul conceives it is in the final analysis "not simply something external which came into mankind, but a stage of religious development which proceeds from an inner principle immanent within man. This principle is the progress of Spirit to the freedom of self-consciousness ..."[26] "Christianity is nothing other than the nullification of everything particular in order that the pure absolute idea of God might realize itself in mankind, or might make its way into mankind's consciousness."[27]

This brief profile of the origin and content of Paul's faith exemplifies Baur's shift of New Testament theology's focus from the information Paul sets forth in his letters (or perhaps this information's relation to reports in Acts or the Gospels) to the subjective consciousness through which the message comes. Significantly, this consciousness is

[19] *Ibid.* 131.

[20] *Ibid.* 136.

[21] Jesus' own basic principle of action also corresponds to a great extent "to the Kantian [categorical] imperative" (*ibid.* 62). Morgan, *The Dictionary of Historical Theology*, 59, notes "a shift to Kant's ethical idealism" in Baur's later work. But the point is that Baur projects it back into a setting where historians might not normally expect to find it.

[22] Baur, *Vorlesungen*, 172.

[23] *Ibid.* 173.

[24] *Ibid.*

[25] *Ibid.*

[26] *Ibid.*

[27] *Ibid.* 205.

in fundamental harmony with the idealisms, whether Hegelian or Kantian or both, of Baur's nineteenth century Germany.[28]

3. The priority of modern understanding in Baur's New Testament theology

We are now in a position to consider Baur's characterization of biblical and hence New Testament theology as "a purely historical science."[29] New Testament theology is concerned "to present the historical, which is New Testament theology's fundamental element, as unadulterated as possible."[30] At the heart of New Testament theology is "the truly historical examination" of the biblical material which wants nothing more than "to allow the life of history in its concrete reality to appear as it objectively is with all its differences and antitheses."[31]

Baur's description of New Testament theology prefigures G. Ebeling's more recent distinction between two views of New Testament theology.[32] It may be seen as an attempt to reproduce the content of the New Testament.[33] But critical study of the Bible has so jeopardized the Bible's theological unity, the concept of canon, and the Bible's status as "theology" in itself[34] that we must today think of New Testament theology as "the scientific explication of the content" of the New Testament.[35]

Baur paved the way for Ebeling's insight. Baur advocated a scientific explication which would take the form of interpreting the New Testament texts within the grid of contemporary understanding. New Testament theology, Baur believes, has finally emancipated "the pure teaching of the Scriptures from the fetters of the dependent relationship which it had come to have in the dogmatic system of the church."[36] The text's statements and theological content cannot, by

---

[28]Defending Baur against the charge of "a naïve apriorism" is H. Rollmann, *SR* 17/4 (1988) 446. Rollmann concedes Hegel's influence (*ibid.* 445) but thinks Baur's commitment to empirical details counterbalances it. Cf. Addinall, *ExpTim* 105 (1994) 136–140, for whom the relativity and arbitrariness of all textual interpretation legitimates Baur's and Hegel's method but calls in question criticisms of it by S. Neill & Tom Wright (*The Interpretation of the New Testament 1861–1986*) and H. Harris (*The Tübingen School*).

[29]Baur, *Vorlesungen,* 1.

[30]*Ibid.*

[31]*Ibid.* 27.

[32]G. Ebeling, "The Meaning of 'Biblical Theology,'" *Word and Faith*, 1963, 79–97.

[33]*Ibid.* 93f.

[34]*Ibid.* 91–93.

[35]*Ibid.* 94.

[36]Baur, *Vorlesungen,* 1. Cf. Harrisville & Sundberg, *The Bible in Modern Culture*, 106f., who cite Baur's antagonism toward the doctrine of Scripture's verbal inspira-

definition of New Testament theology's task, any longer be interpreted in the theological context historically associated with those
texts. Baur finds nothing but radical disunity on the surface of the
New Testament texts anyway, so it is pointless to speak of *a* theological context; at best one could speak of many such contexts. But this
only bears out Baur's methodological contention that New Testament
theology does not take a synthetic theological understanding inherent
to the New Testament texts as the lodestar (much less object) of its
scrutiny. It rather focuses on the various and often mutually exclusive
expressions of religious consciousness which filter something to us.
The composite of this consciousness, what we might call an absolute,
which comes to us in severely refracted form through the utterances
comprising the New Testament texts, is what New Testament theology ultimately presses to explicate.

The New Testament is thus read as witness to the ancient non-
theological religious consciousness which matches the modern non-
theological religious consciousness of the New Testament theologian.
The absolute giving rise to ancient consciousness is explicated so as to
commend it to modern "scientific" religious consciousness. The task
of New Testament theology is thereby given with modern understanding, according to whose non-theological absolute the New
Testament's conceptual content is measured, assessed, and ordered.[37]

4. New Testament theology from and for today

One must be clear, therefore, as to what Baur envisions as the means
to gaining what Kümmel terms "a *substantiated* insight into the temporal context and the inner development of New Testament thought."[38]
This may appear to be simply a reasonable, non-controversial descrip-

---

tion; and Köpf, *ZTK* 89/4 (1992) 459, who notes that for Baur "the critical principle
of Protestantism does not defer even to Holy Scripture."

[37]What comprises this absolute for Baur is unquestionably closely linked with "the
foremost principle of Jesus' teaching in contrast to Mosaic doctrine …, that it is only
the morality of one's beliefs which gives one absolute ethical worth before God"
(*Vorlesungen*, 48). This insight is "the fundamental principle of Christianity" (*ibid.* 51).
Jesus in this view is "himself the concrete contemplation of the importance, which
extends through all eternity, of the absolute truth of his teaching" (*ibid.* 110). God is
"the ethical idea in itself, or the ethical ideal", and we therefore apprehend Jesus "as
the self-manifesting idea" (*ibid.* 117). It seems fair to conclude that the absolute which
Baur thinks informs the consciousness reflected in the New Testament writings is in
large measure the self-actualization of the Hegelian "Geist." This absolute manifests
itself in ethical terms as the categorical imperative inherent in and expressing itself
through human reasoning and response.

[38]Kümmel, "Einführung," *Heilsgeschehen*, 112.

tion of a major intent of any credible New Testament theology. But
what, for Baur, constitutes the "temporal context and the inner development"? It is not the context, perhaps even less the development,
implied in the texts read as historical documents—i.e. documents setting forth at least some semblance of an actual past state of affairs—for
they are only tangentially historical, if at all, as far as New Testament
theology is concerned.[39] From the standpoint of New Testament theology, the texts are the direct means of recovering, not the original
witnesses of something that happened, but many things that were
thought about matters which (as in the case of the resurrection) never
happened at all. For it was not historical occurrences, at least not the
ones related in the New Testament, which gave rise to the concepts in
the New Testament, but to a great extent concepts which led to the
relating of occurrences.

When O. Merk stresses that Baur placed emphasis on "reconstruction," not "interpretation,"[40] one must qualify this by the realization
that Baur's reconstruction is very much an interpretative procedure.
Baur is aware, for example, that he is among the first to understand the
gospels "in the historical-critical, or the pure historical, sense ...,
which alone can give the key to its [the gospel history's] correct understanding."[41] The "historical-critical" or "purely historical sense" is
an approach in which the integrating dynamic or absolute of the New
Testament texts is supplied from the outside by the modern interpreter. The interpreter gives a scientific (i.e. consistent with Baur's
own particular modern perceptions of reality, truth, and ethical values)
explication of the texts. The explicative categories are not those derived from the texts' claims but those inhering in the scientific or
critical outlook of the interpreter.

We can now see why Baur's approach to New Testament theology
as "the conceptual explication of believing self-understanding" is revo-
lutionary. New Testament theology does not presume to set forth
"New Testament theology" derived from the New Testament. The
texts are not "theology"; they are not somehow normative, or even
factually reliable, accounts, descriptions, or interpretations, which the

---

[39]It may be objected here that Baur did in fact structure his theology based on a
rigorously historical ordering of the documents. We agree however with R. Morgan,
The Nature of New Testament Theology, 1973, 14: "Baur's structure is based formally on
the succession of documents, but materially upon the history these were thought to
reflect." This is a purely abstract constellation of ideas.

[40]Merk, *Biblische Theologie des Neuen Testaments in ihrer Anfangszeit,* 235.

[41]Baur, *Vorlesungen,* 20.

theologian in turn analyzes, reflects on, and synthesizes on the way to assembling a holistic picture of "New Testament theology" consistent with them. The texts are rather already "theologizing," and as such are to be regarded as subjective formulations of how unknown ancients developed and expressed their convictions. New Testament theology becomes an extrapolation *from* a comprehensive conceptual framework in which religious consciousness is intelligible to the New Testament theologian (in this case Baur), *to* various believing consciousnesses of some disparate, or even mutually opposed, ancient Christian writers. The determinative starting point is the present, not the past. And the starting point does not affirm theology in any historic sense but a philosophy that understands itself to have superseded Christian doctrine.

Baur's theory of knowledge

Integral to Baur's methodological approach to New Testament theology is his approach to knowing. If New Testament theology is a purely historical discipline, concerned foremost to present the historical, which is its essential element, "as purely as possible in terms of itself,"[42] we must try to grasp how Baur viewed the conditions under which history or the past as such is knowable.

1. The problem and Baur's Cartesian solution

H. Liebing correctly observes that history for Baur

> [had] become problematic. This was the case first because it only led to facts and data which were contingent, without context, lacking sense and significance. But this was also the case methodologically, because between the subject matter of history and the historian lay a gap, a chasm, to which Kant's epistemology had long since called attention.[43]

Baur's own words illustrate this very point:

> Only the crudest empiricism can suppose that one simply surrenders himself to his subject matter, apprehends the objects of historical scrutiny exactly as they lie before us. Since there has been a critical assessment of cognition, a critical epistemology (there has been one, as everyone knows, in any case at least since *Kant*), everyone except him who comes to the historical task bereft of all philosophical training must be aware that there is a distinction to be made. One must distinguish between things as they are in themselves and as they appear to us. One must be aware that they take on the status of

---

[42]Baur, *Vorlesungen*, 1.
[43]Liebing, *ZTK* 57 (1960) 313f.

appearances to us only through the medium of our consciousness. Herein lies the great difference between the purely empirical and the critical outlook …[44]

Baur adopts, to use H. Thielicke's older but still useful taxonomy, a Cartesian[45] understanding of his discipline. This approach accepts the limits on its perception which were established by Kant and thereby essentially endorses a Kantian epistemology,[46] or a modified version of it. It is Cartesian in that it makes "the relevance of the knowing self the center of thought."[47] It is distinctly modern—Thielicke points out that such modernity existed at least as far back as Semler[48]—in that it wants "to bring theological statements into harmony with the sense of truth as this has been transformed by historical and scientific study."[49]

The Cartesian approach may not intentionally set out "to give the modern self-consciousness a dominant position and then to accommodate Christian truth to it as a function."[50] Its concern is rather "to work out the possibilities of understanding Christian truth."[51] But the approach does tilt the interpreter toward focusing on "the possible appropriation of the kerygma rather than its content."[52]

2. The solution's inherent risk

Thielicke concedes that this approach might "do what was not intended and invest the subject of understanding with a normative rank

---

[44]*Ibid.* 314. Liebing quotes Baur's *Lehrbuch der christlichen Dogmengeschichte*, 1847, ix f. Cf. Hodgson, *Baur on Church History*, 364ff., n. 45.

[45]By "Cartesian" Thielicke (*The Evangelical Faith,* vol. 1, 1974) seems *not* to have in mind the (ontologically significant) "'real distinction' between mind and body" but rather Decartes' (epistemologically significant) "egocentric approach which is one of the most characteristic features of his philosophy and which, with its related insistence on epistemology as the starting point of philosophy, serves to distinguish it and much that followed it from most philosophy that preceded it" (B. Williams, "Decartes, René," in *The Encyclopedia of Philosophy*, ed. P. Edwards, vol. 2, 1972, 348, 346). Cf. Thielicke himself, 34f.; also R. Bernstein, *Beyond Objectivism and Relativism*, 1983, 16ff.; 115ff. A. Thiselton, *The Two Horizons*, 1980, 292, possibly fails to note this.

[46]Cf. e.g. D. McKenzie, "Kant and Protestant Theology," *Enc* 43 (1982) 157–167; J. Luick, "The Ambiguity of Kantian Faith," *SJT* 36 (1983) 339–346; P. Fisher, "The Triumph of the Irrational in Postenlightenment Theology," *AUSS* 37 (1999) 5–7.

[47]Thielicke, *Evangelical Faith*, vol. 1, 34.

[48]*Ibid.* 33. Semler lived 1725–1791.

[49]*Ibid.* 32.

[50]*Ibid.* 33.

[51]*Ibid.*

[52]*Ibid.* 41.

for what is understood."[53] And from a different point of view Baur himself voices the same concern: historical work is not possible when "one purposes to find only that which must be believed and dictates to history what it should contain."[54] But the effects of Baur's epistemological starting point as alluded to above may force him to bring the substance of the New Testament under the control of a modern understanding which is foreign, even inimical, to the New Testament texts. Two illustrations point in this direction.

Uncritical acceptance of "new" findings

First, reliance on the latest "historical" studies and viewpoints[55] in order to overturn time-tested assessments of New Testament material calls in question whether Baur was critically balanced—or whether for him "critical" was primarily that which agreed with his own clearly anti-theological outlook.[56] One could argue that he too hastily makes his own iconoclastic[57] understanding the arbiter for assessing the "historical" content of New Testaments texts.

We cite three typical cases:

1. Regarding the New Testament accounts about Jesus, Baur says that "everyone who has followed the course of recent critical research without theological prejudices and presuppositions" must confess that they are far removed temporally from the events they describe.[58] Baur placed the synoptics in the first decades of the second century and John much later.[59] Thus one must insert between the gospels and the time they purport to describe a lengthy interim during which putatively original incidents were fundamentally altered in transmission.[60] It

---

[53] *Ibid.* 33.

[54] Baur, *Vorlesungen*, 33.

[55] A distinctive feature of *Vorlesungen* is a heavy reliance on "the newest investigations" (e.g. 23, 41f.), "the present viewpoint of New Testament criticism" (24; cf. 108, 349), "the basic tenets of the most recent criticism" (28, cf. 85, 99, 104, 312), which Baur consistently pits against that which "until now was the conventional opinion" (25 [referring here to the authorship of the New Testament epistles]). Of course it is desirable that New Testament theology be informed by recent historical findings, but prudence dictates that radically new findings be sifted and tested before they be permitted full acceptance and influence.

[56] Even in Baur's lifetime, "his views and conclusions were almost everywhere rejected by the overwhelming majority of theologians—both orthodox and liberal" (Harris, *Strauss*, 278).

[57] Köpf, *ZTK* 89/4 (1992) 450 notes Baur's "readiness for theological battle."

[58] Baur, *Vorlesungen*, 21.

[59] *Ibid.* 41.

[60] *Ibid.* 21.

is accordingly "simply impossible" to view the gospel writers as "mere ✶✶ lecturers on the teaching and history of Jesus,"[61] and the synoptics (to say nothing of John) are thus not authentic sources of the teaching or life of Jesus.[62]

2. Baur holds that those who view the New Testament as a unity—i.e. as theologically fundamentally harmonious—necessarily do so "because otherwise the content of the writings of the New Testament *true*. could not be treated as a supernaturally revealed revelation which one must simply believe."[63] He alleges, then, a lack of integrity in those for *why?* whom the New Testament conveys a basically unified message. This is a group of notable size and stature in the centuries preceding Baur's work as well as in his own time (and since).

3. Any traces of divinity ascribed to Jesus, or any reports of his miraculous works, are to be rationalized by tracing the gospel material "using the basic principles of the criticism according to which on the whole the gospel history is to be judged" back "to its true and original contents."[64] Similarly, reports of Jesus' resurrection can only be naturalistically (or psychologically) construed for "all who do not accept real, material miracles."[65] Clearly Baur belongs to this group.

In each of these three typical instances, we see that Baur is peremptory in dismissing the general impression which most had obtained for centuries from reading the New Testament. Granted that each gospel writer had his own viewpoint; it is nevertheless something of an overreaction for Baur to adopt such a negative stance toward the temporal proximity of the New Testament texts to the events they relate. (And Baur is inconsistent at this point, for he apparently does regard those parts of the gospels as proximate which preserve what Baur thinks is the true essence—absolute ethical idealism—of the New Testament.)

Again, while there is doubtless more diversity in the New Testament than some of his contemporaries allowed, Baur surely goes too far in attributing views of the New Testament which stress its unity solely to theological prejudice.[66] What would this charge imply for

---

[61] *Ibid.*

[62] *Ibid.* 24. Cf. Harrisville & Sundberg, *The Bible in Modern Culture*, 108f., who stress Baur's skepticism regarding the veracity of any of the four gospels.

[63] Baur, *Vorlesungen*, 32.

[64] *Ibid.* 99. Cf. 298: "Therefore the historical must first be critically separated from the non-historical and the question taken up how we must explain the emergence of the latter." Cf. also 302ff., where Baur ascribes the so-called miracles of the gospels to the "tendency [*Tendenz*] of a traditional idealizing" of Jesus' person.

[65] *Ibid.* 126.

[66] So already B. Weiss, *Lehrbuch*, 26.

Baur's own ultimately unified, one-dimensional reconstruction of New Testament thought?

Finally, Baur's aversion to all miracles and ascription of divinity to Jesus is clearly rationalistic.[67] Of course rationalism is a viable intellectual option. But it may be fairly asked how suitable it is for interpreting and synthesizing the New Testament data.

It seems justified to suggest that Baur did indeed tend to elevate his particular modern outlook to the status of judge of the New Testament.[68] To an extent this is an inevitable feature of the interpretive process. Kant's basic insight that what is known is colored by the subjectivity of the knower would be denied by few. But the hermeneutically vital question arises: Was Baur's understanding, in Thielicke's formulation, "prepared to let itself be revalued and relativized" in view of the data? Or did Baur's understanding seem to have been "determined to assert itself as the normative criterion of the truth addressed to it"?[69] We must conclude that Baur laid cardinal stress on his modern understanding as unerring arbiter. His epistemological starting point seriously reduces his capacity to acknowledge those aspects of the New Testament witness which do not conform to what Baur on largely epistemological grounds is prepared to accept.

---

[67] Barrett, *NTS* 28 (1982) 316, seems to want to deny that Baur worked with rationalist presuppositions. Thus he discounts Harris's claim (*Tübingen School*, 259) that Baur was among those who "made the first comprehensive and consequent attempt to interpret the New Testament and the history of the early Church from a non-supernatural standpoint." Barrett cites Hodgson, *Baur on Church History*, to support an interpretation of Baur as "equally opposed to supernatural and rationalist interpretations of history" (Hodgson, 12–17). This is true in the limited sense Hodgson means it, but it is no less true to say: "It cannot be disputed that Baur never entirely forsook the rationalistic heritage" (Kümmel, "Einführung," *Heilsgeschehen*, 110). Hodgson himself points to Baur's conviction that God "does not impinge upon history as an extrinsic, alien force or personal agency …; he is rather the ground of the process of history itself …" (*Baur on Church History*, 14). Baur expressly rejected miracles conceived as that which occurs when "the hand of God intervenes directly in the affairs of history" (*ibid.*). It is true, then, that Baur has moved beyond pure rationalism and devised a "speculative hermeneutic" with which to view history (*ibid.* 17–36); cf. P. Hodgson, "Hegel's Approach to Religion: The Dialectic of Speculation and Phenomenology," *JR* 64 (1984) 158–172. But it is also true that strong elements of rationalism persist in his work, and this is especially noticeable in his New Testament theology.

[68] Cf. Senft, *Wahrhaftigkeit,* 77, who notes that Baur failed to allow the text freedom to call his own understanding into question.

[69] Thielicke, *Evangelical Faith*, vol. 1, 109. Cf. Morgan, *Nature of New Testament Theology*, 13.

Reads universal religious self-consciousness into NT. (handwritten)

Dubious interpretive grid

Baur seems to hand the substance of the New Testament over to modern understanding to an undue degree in a second way. Commensurate with Thielicke's Cartesian model generally, "general criteria of thought are sought that are present in the pre-Christian and secular consciousness."[70] In the same vein Thielicke shows that in the Cartesian approach the message which Scripture conveys "is given a location in our consciousness."[71] This general outlook is typified in Lessing, for whom "certainty is possible only if the truth that claims me is analogous to what my structure of consciousness contains within it as consciousness of truth."[72] Thus, "I have my own access to truth."[73] In Baur's concept of New Testament theology, largely as a result of his epistemological approach, a conceptual a priori is predicated of universal human religious self-consciousness, which Baur then simply reads into the New Testament texts.

truth is only truth if it matches my truth (handwritten margin)

This feature of Baur's method is clear first of all in his assertion that the teaching of Jesus is "that which lies outside of and precedes all temporal development, that which is unmediated and original."[74] In interpreting the New Testament we must "go back" "to this which is original and unmediated."[75] It is at first mystifying as to how we may do this; Baur has already argued as follows against protests that his method is too preoccupied with abstract concepts rather than full-orbed life ("Leben") itself: such protests erroneously suppose that Christianity "is not something conveyed through concepts but is rather an object of direct experience, actual reality."[76] But this can "not be the case at least for early Christianity, the knowledge of which comes to us through a great deal which lies in between [and obscures its origins]."[77] So Baur has both urged us to recover the "unmediated and original" and then argued that it is inaccessible, at least historically.

We find the solution to this ambiguity in Baur's usage of "Jesus' teaching" as synonymous with the "Christian consciousness."[78] This follows from the observation that Jesus locates "all that gives man his

Discover unmediated original, but it is inaccessible historically. (handwritten)

[70]Thielicke, *Evangelical Faith*, vol. 1, 42.
[71]*Ibid.* 47.
[72]*Ibid.* 70.
[73]*Ibid.*
[74]Baur, *Vorlesungen*, 45.
[75]*Ibid.* 46.
[76]*Ibid.* 31. Cf. 122f.
[77]*Ibid.* 31.
[78]*Ibid.* 62.

ethical-religious worth exclusively in his attitude."[79] And this "attitude" is "that consciousness expressing itself in man directly in its
immanent truth."[80] This attitude is in fact that "to which the entire
content of the Sermon on the Mount may be traced."[81] And for Baur
the Sermon on the Mount is the highest level of New Testament expression.[82]

This shows how Baur has assumed a given ethical human religious
consciousness and elevated it (and its classic supporting text) to the
status of adjudicator of the place, value, and meaning of all other New
Testament texts.[83] This is not just a "canon within the canon" or even
a hypothetical center for the New Testament adopted for pragmatic
reasons in constructing a New Testament theology. It is a serious and
problematic elevation of a philosophical postulate (Kant's categorical
imperative) to normative rank in evaluating the New Testament texts
"historically."

This feature of Baur's procedure surfaces again when he defines the
"original basic outlook of the Christian consciousness" in the New
Testament as "the pure feeling of the need for redemption, containing
within itself the essential opposition of sin and grace, yet remaining
unsullied by it, a feeling which as such contains already within itself
the full reality of redemption."[84] Again it seems that Baur is reading the
New Testament through patently modern lenses, lenses this time still
of Kantian making (here explained with the aid of Hegelian[85] dialectic), but mounted in Schleiermacherian frames.[86] He is locating
redemption in categories immanent to and innate in the religious self-

---

[79] *Ibid.* 60.

[80] *Ibid.*

[81] *Ibid.* 60.

[82] *Ibid.* 64f.: The "moral element" of the Sermon on the Mount is "the really material core of Christianity, to which everything else stands in a more or less secondary
and contingent relationship." See also M. Greschat, ed., *Theologen des Protestantismus im
19. und 20. Jahrhundert I*, 62f.; Harrisville & Sundberg, *The Bible in Modern Culture*, 109.

[83] Cf. *ibid.* 46; also 103, where Baur assesses the authenticity of the concept of Jesus'
propitiatory death in the Last Supper accounts by beginning with the question: "But
how does this stack up against the Sermon on the Mount?"

[84] *Ibid.* 64.

[85] Cf. P.C. Hodgson's sketch of Baur's use of Hegel in the former's doctrine of reconciliation: "Alienation and Reconciliation in Hegelian and Post-Hegelian
Perspective," *Modern Theology* 2 (1985) 42–63, especially, 42–44.

[86] Baur's debt to Schleiermacher is noted by Scholder, *TRE* 5, 353; cf. Sanft,
Wahrhaftigkeit, 48–53. Schelling's influence should however not be overlooked; see C.
Hester, "Gedanken zu Ferdinand Christian Baurs Entwicklung als Historiker anhand
zweier unbekannter Briefe," *ZKG* 84 (1973) 249–269.

consciousness,[87] and it is not at all clear that this is either derived from or appropriate to the texts he is handling. Owing at least in part to the effects of his view of knowing, Baur risks obscuring an understanding of the texts by too facilely championing a modern understanding of understanding.

3. Summary

We have seen that Baur's New Testament theology freely bows to epistemological demands made by the Enlightenment and particularly Kant. Possibly the "purely historical" aspect of Baur's New Testament theological method is conceived in direct parallel to Kant's "pure reason," which may be understood as "reason in so far as it supplies out of itself, independently of experience, a priori elements that as such are characterized by universality and necessity."[88] In many ways Baur treats New Testament history as history "in so far as it supplies out of itself, independently of experience, *a priori* elements that as such are characterized by universality and necessity." The essence of history for Baur is the concept or idea, and "it is intrinsic to the essence of the idea that what it is in itself, it also is in reality."[89] It seems then that the a priori aspect of history, which as a priori is also universal and necessary, reveals itself in a sort of *from* a priori *to* a priori process, i.e. *from* the unconditioned essence which once dynamically constituted human experience of historical reality *to* the unconditioned essence which now dynamically constitutes historical reality as we rethink it.

Important here is that Baur finally locates within the knower a prior-to-all experience knowledge which determines the content of what comprised and comprises historical reality, and thus of what the knower perceives it to be.[90] This greatly influences how Baur handles the New Testament. For if "we impose conditions for receiving messages" as Baur does, "we put them under our control, and openly or secretly we are thus editing them."[91]

[87]Jesus' own relationship to the Father is explained in similar terms: "The divine mission consists in the awakening of this purely moral consciousness, in which he knows himself to be one with the Father" (*Vorlesungen*, 115).

[88]N.K. Smith, *A Commentary to Kant's "Critique of Pure Reason"*, [2]1923, reprinted 1979, 2. It is perhaps also worth noting that, just as Kant seems to have been the first to use the term "Kritik" in German (*ibid.* 1), so Baur first gave the term "historisch-kritisch" wide currency in New Testament studies (Scholder, *TRE* 5, 355). But cf. Merk, *Biblische Theologie des Neuen Testaments in ihrer Anfangszeit*, 199 n. 145.

[89]Baur, *Vorlesungen*, 260.

[90]Cf. Hodgson, *Baur on Church History*, 17ff.

[91]Thielicke, *Evangelical Faith*, vol. 1, 54.

In sum, Baur seems not to avoid the trap of over hastily subordinating the understanding latent in the New Testament texts to a particular understanding of understanding. Scholder aptly characterizes Baur's "historical" method, and thus his New Testament theology, in stating: "Far from withdrawing from the troublesome present into history, Baur sought rather to understand all of history from the standpoint of and for the sake of the present."[92]

Baur's view of history

It was not only Baur's theory of knowledge that decisively shaped his New Testament theology. It was also his view of history. We cannot describe it in its fullness here, but we can survey aspects of it that will help shed light on why his New Testament theology took the shape it did.

1. Basic conception

Baur in a well-known passage describes history in general as "the eternally clear mirror in which the Spirit perceives itself, views its own image, in order to be what it is in itself for itself as well, for its own consciousness, and to know itself as the moving power of historical becoming."[93]

Given this Hegelian conception of history, only the "speculative view of history" is workable.[94] This view—Baur's own—presupposes "that an Absolute truth exists ... and therefore also a consciousness of the Absolute." Baur elaborates: "The Absolute itself must also be the knowledge of the Absolute, for it would not be the Absolute were it not the Absolute for subjective consciousness as well." Thus from Baur's speculative standpoint "the history of dogma," which includes New Testament history, "can be considered only as the movement of Absolute Truth, which in that history discloses itself to subjective consciousness."[95]

It is evident that the "subjective consciousness" to which the absolute is revealing itself is one in which Baur shares. This is clear in his rhetorical question as to whether it is not

---

[92]Scholder, *TRE* 5, 357.

[93]Hodgson, *Baur on Church History*, 365.

[94]*Ibid.* 362ff.

[95]*Ibid.* 364. Baur seems not to allow for the possibility that subjective consciousness might be mistaken.

the nature of history itself that, from every standpoint from which we look anew into the past, there is presented a new image, through which we obtain a truer, more vital and more significant perception of what has happened, even if only in a particular respect.[96]

Baur apparently sees modern critical thought in Germany (and himself along with it[97]) occupying the loftiest peak yet scaled with reference to passing judgment on the reality and meaning of past events. Baur scrutinizes periods "in whose course the Spirit working in the depths and struggling toward the solution of its task has raised itself, at first gradually, to the level on which it stands in the present mode of perception."[98]

This is not just a tentative or peripheral theory on Baur's part but a constitutive factor in his evaluation of historical evidence. Baur assumes he has possession of heretofore unknown keys which can unlock both the specific features and the ultimate meaning of history, including New Testament history and the theology associated with it, in ways long obscured if not totally unprecedented.

2. Historicism's advent in New Testament theology

With Baur we see, then, a profound commitment to a certain conceptualization of history. Harris points out that Baur, like Strauss, wanted a "presuppositionless history," one which did not presuppose "the existence of a transcendent personal God."[99] This is "the base-mark criterion" in assessing Baur's whole critical approach.[100] From Baur's methodological standpoint there was in a sense no God and hence no miracles; conversely, the assumed fact that miracles are impossible is best accounted for on the supposition that there is no God, or at least none who has disclosed knowledge of himself through observable phenomena.

This is already a problematic base from which to approach New Testament theology, but Baur took a further step and identified this

---

[96]*Ibid.* 47.

[97]This sounds shockingly parochial. It must be remembered that Baur spent his entire life in the little German province of Württemberg; his life "was not rich in events from the outside and changes" (Köpf, *ZTK* 89/4 [1992] 441). In Tübingen University parlance of that day, a "foreigner" ("Ausländer") was anyone not from Württemberg (*ibid.* 442).

[98]Hodgson, *Baur on Church History*, 49.

[99]Harris, *Strauss*, 89.

[100]*Ibid.* Barrett, *NTS* 28 (1982) disputes this but offers little evidence.

philosophical principle with the possibility of scientific, critical and historical research. From this time on historical research was to be a presuppositionless investigation whose only allowable presupposition was the
exclusion of every miraculous and supernatural event. All historical criticism not sharing this view was henceforth to be labeled unscientific ...[101]

With Baur's conception of history we see historicism enter the
workshop of New Testament theology.[102]

The possible deleterious effect of this on Baur's interpretation of
specific incidents is self-evident, leading, for instance, to his strained
handling of the resurrection seen above. The broader effects lie in his
reduction of all historical phenomena to a strictly immanent, temporal
plane, developing naturalistically on an organic model, hermetically
sealed from any possible material divine influence or necessary effect
on subsequent times. This platonic dualism makes Senft's characterization of Baur's position correct: "all history, because it is understood
only as a stage to the present, becomes merely the past."[103] Whatever
New Testament theology's historical findings, they are irrevocably
moored to a past forever vanished. The dry bones of history take on
life only as the breath of modernity is breathed into them by the contemporary critic.

3. Baur's idealized salvation history

It would be incorrect, however, to conclude that Baur's historicism
leads him to a fragmented, atomistic conception of New Testament
history. He terms the kingdom of God "that economy of religion
which first came into being with the New Testament," or again speaks
of "the messianic kingdom" as "the period of theocratic world development in which the divine world plan achieves its perfect realization
and reaches the goal toward which it was pointed from the beginning."[104] Baur speaks of "the divine world order"[105] which Paul

---

[101]Harris, *Strauss*, 89.

[102]Cf. H. Schnädelbach, *Philosophy in Germany 1831–1933*, 1984, 36, who mentions
the leading role of Tübingen (the university in which Baur taught) in the advent of
historicistic thinking. With M. Mandelbaum, "Historicism," *The Encyclopedia of Philosophy*, ed. P. Edwards, vol. 4, 24, we take historicism to be "the belief that an
adequate understanding of the nature of anything and an adequate assessment of its
value are to be gained by considering it in terms of the place it occupied and the role
it played within a process of development ... Historicism involves a genetic model of
explanation and an attempt to base all evaluation upon the nature of the historical
process itself."

[103]Senft, *Wahrhaftigkeit*, 77.

[104]Baur, *Vorlesungen*, 69. Cf. Kraus, *Biblische Theologie*, 149.

perceived and "the entire world development."[106] He does not do away with *Heilsgeschichte*. He rather develops a Hegelian version of it. As Kraus notes, these remarks by Baur on the course of history "universalize, in a history of ideas fashion, the traditional concept of the redemptive economy and press this concept into the service of a process of development ..."[107] To say that Baur denied that the New Testament reflects some traditionally conceived salvation history is not to say that there is no legitimate integrated view of the whole New Testament to be had at all. Baur is only saying that such a view is not forthcoming from the New Testament itself but must be elicited from contemporary critical understanding, in which the constantly unfolding definitive assessment of the past reveals itself.

4. Summary: the measure of New Testament history and theology

One can in all fairness characterize the interpretive grid through which Baur draws the New Testament evidence for constructing his New Testament theology as historicistic. Further, he idealizes and universalizes the New Testament history in accordance with a picture of the New Testament "process of development" which is consistent with the historical data primarily on Hegelian assumptions.

Remembering here also Baur's epistemological basis it seems accurate to draw the following conclusion. In Baur's "historical" approach to New Testament theology the measure of what the New Testament documents contain conceptually—i.e., New Testament theology—must finally be (a form of Kantian) critical consciousness of the truth which at all times progressively manifests itself in historical development, immanently understood.

Baur's view of history, then, presupposes that rigorous critical thinking can succeed to a definitive explanation and understanding of the historical process that produced the New Testament. It can do this without recourse to transcendent causation—miracles, propositional revelation, an incarnate God, and so forth. As Hafemann notes, Baur's work was "marked by his willingness to acknowledge the implications of his antisupernaturalist presuppositions and his rejection of divine revelation in the New Testament."[108] Critical thinking is bound to explain the New Testament texts in terms alien to the texts themselves, which confess such transcendent involvement in history as both

---

[105]Baur, *Vorlesungen*, 195.
[106]*Ibid.* 205.
[107]Kraus, *Biblische Theologie*, 149.
[108]"Baur," *Historical Handbook of Major Biblical Interpreters*, 286.

important and real. In Baur's view, however, the ultimate meaning of all reality is latent in and manifests itself only immanently through history. As moderns on the cutting edge of the absolute's current stage of self-unfolding, we are capable of discerning that ultimate meaning. We are bound to move from our contemporary discernment of it to an assessment of all prior history based upon it.[109] This includes, of course, the New Testament and its "theology" as Baur conceives it.

Hofmann and New Testament theology

1. Perceptions of Hofmann

Hofmann[110] (1810–1877) is widely recognized as the father of the salvation historical line of theological inquiry.[111] It seems, however, that his work in New Testament theology has so far been inadequately assessed. Cullmann surprisingly states that in developing his salvation historical outlook he was unaware of any debt to Hofmann; he distances himself from such views as Hofmann's which are alleged to be based, not on exegesis and historical analysis, but on philosophy of history.[112] Ladd mentions Hofmann once and speaks of the "great in-

---

[109]Thus Baur speaks of immersing oneself in historical detail, but always returning to "the universal, to those Ideas that must be the guiding points of view and illuminating starts on the long journey through the centuries" (Hodgson, *Baur on Church History*, 44).

[110]The single best brief treatment of Hofmann is K. Steck's chapter in Greschat, ed., *Theologen des Protestantismus im 19. und 20. Jahrhundert I*, 1978, 99–112. Other significant studies of Hofmann include P. Wapler's biography, *Johannes v. Hofmann*, 1914, augmented by H. Jordan, "Beiträge zur Hofmannbiographie," *Beiträge zur bayerischen Kirchengeschichte* 28/4 (1922) 129–153; Senft, *Wahrhaftigkeit*, 87–123; C. Preus, "The Contemporary Relevance of Von Hofmann's Hermeneutical Principles," *Int* 4 (1950) 311–321; P. Leo, "Revelation and History in J.C.K. von Hofmann," *LQ* 10 (1958) 195–216; F. Kantzenbach, *Die Erlanger Theologie*, 1960, 179–208; idem, *Programme der Theologie*, ²1978, 90–103; G. Merz, *Das bayerische Luthertum*, 1955, 29–42. K. Barth, *Protestant Theology in the Nineteenth Century*, 1972, devotes a chapter to Hofmann. More recently see U. Swarat, "Die heilsgeschichtliche Konzeption Johannes Chr. K. von Hofmanns," *Glaube und Geschichte*, ed. H. Stadelmann, 1986, 211–239; R.A. Harrisville, "Von Hofmann, Johann Christian Konrad," *Historical Handbook of Modern Biblical Interpreters*, 1998, 376–380.

[111]G. Ladd, *A Theology of the New Testament*, 1974, 16; L. Goppelt, *Theologie des Neuen Testaments*, ³1981, 45; O. Cullmann, *Christ and Time*, rev. ed. 1964, 56; idem, *Salvation in History*, 1967, 28.

[112]Cullmann, *Christ and Time*, 8; *Salvation in History*, 55. In both cases Cullmann is trying to evade K. Steck's efforts (*Die Idee der Heilsgeschichte*, 1959) to discredit him by linking him to Hofmann and Adolf Schlatter. Without appearing to have delved into Hofmann or Schlatter himself, Cullmann simply claims that his "basic conception of Heilsgeschichte is essentially different from theirs" (*Salvation in History*, 55). Doubtless

fluence" of the Erlangen school of which Hofmann was part, but then never cites him in his New Testament theology again.

Thus it is surprising when Kantzenbach notes that Hofmann "to an astonishing degree influenced the theologians of the nineteenth century" and pays high tribute to him,[113] and when M. Kähler affirms that Hofmann in his New Testament interpretation and theology "employed all the tools of modern scholarship; in no way does his work breathe the spirit of a narrow literalism" because Hofmann "has contributed greatly to the advancement of New Testament research."[114] Swarat states: Hofmann "was doubtless *the greatest Lutheran theologian of the nineteenth century* and should be placed in the same scientific rank as Schleiermacher, Baur, and Ritschl."[115] Even Karl Barth writes that Hofmann's "exegesis is well worth studying, even now."[116] Similar is Steck's assessment: Hofmann's systematic works are "indispensible" and his biblical interpretation "well worth reading."[117] In their evaluations of Hofmann, Cullmann and Ladd, who are in one sense Hofmann's heirs, seem closer to Bultmann, who omits any reference to him in his sketch of the history of New Testament theology, and to O. Merk, who likewise ignores him.[118]

Negative press
Such negative assessment simply restates the initial negative regard his work received in liberal circles in Germany last century. The longtime doyen of New Testament theology H.J. Holtzmann wrote bitingly of Hofmann:

> The delusion that he was called to halt the critical direction [in New Testament studies] allowed the shrewd man rarely to arrive at a sound

---

Cullmann's position is more nuanced that Steck claims (see discussion of Cullmann below), but the question remains whether it was really possible, or even necessary, for Cullmann to dissociate himself from these earlier figures.

[113]Kantzenbach, *Erlangen Theologie*, 179ff.; cf. J. Wach, "Die Geschichtsphilosophie des 19. Jahrhunderts und die Theologie der Geschichte," *Historische Zeitschrift* 142 (1930) 4.

[114]Kähler, *The So-Called Historical Jesus and the Historic Biblical Christ*, 1964, 116.

[115]Swarat, "Konzeption Hofmanns," *Glaube und Geschichte,* ed. Stadelmann, 211 (his emphasis).

[116]Barth, *Protestant Theology,* 615. U. Kühn gives a practical example of this in "Bemühungen um eine Rückgewinnung des Bekenntnisses," *Bekenntnis und Einheit der Kirche,* M. Brecht & R. Schwarz, eds., Stuttgart 1980, 393–413.

[117]Greschat, ed., *Theologen des Protestantismus im 19. und 20. Jahrhundert I*, 102.

[118]Bultmann, *Theologie,* 585–599; Merk, *Biblische Theologie des Neuen Testaments in ihrer Anfangszeit.*

judgment in questions whose solution requires a sense for historical development, indeed for the actual course of things.[119]

Troeltsch's influential evaluation of nineteenth century theological thought also left no room for Hofmann.[120] As early as 1910 J. Haussleiter lamented that a historicism enchanted "with the magic word 'development'" was unjustly treading Hofmann's contribution underfoot.[121] Perhaps no one championed the concept of development as the key to understanding history more than Troeltsch, who relegated all salvation historical thinking to the status of outmoded, pre-critical orthodoxy. (We will consider him more fully in the next chapter.) He even chided Albrecht Ritschl and Wilhelm Herrmann for advocating theological stances that were too closely tied to history which was, in Troeltsch's view, radically relative.[122]

To the considerable extent that Troeltsch's view of history has affected theology and biblical studies in this century,[123] it has been convenient to regard Hofmann's or similar views of history as antiquated and unscientific.[124] In Troeltsch's wake Hofmannian historical-theological outlooks consistently ran afoul of powerful streams of thinking impinging on the discipline of New Testament theology. These streams, first Barthian, then existentialist, disparaged the idea of

---

[119]Holtzmann, *Lehrbuch der Neutestamentlichen Theologie*, vol. 1, 1897, 18.

[120]Troeltsch recognizes only two legitimate theological positions in the nineteenth century. One is the Herder–Eichorn–Vatke–DeWette–Strauss–Tübingen line, the other the Ritschlian, which Troeltsch characterizes as "the agnostic theology of mediation, strengthened by renewed recourse to Schleiermacher." Thinkers of Hofmann's ilk would appear to be relegated to either "pietistic biblicism" or "the creedal orthodoxy of confessionalism," both untenable according to Troeltsch, although regrettably they "continue to flourish." See Troeltsch, "Half a Century of Theology: A Review," *Ernst Troeltsch: Writings on Theology and Religion*, trans. and ed. R. Morgan & M. Pye, 1977, 53–81, esp. 66f.

[121]*Grundlinien der Theologie Joh. Christ. K. v. Hofmanns in seiner eigenen Darstellung,* 1910, V.

[122]T. Ogletree, *Christian Faith and History,* 1965, 32–37. Ritschl and Herrmann (following Schleiermacher) brought "an absolute into history insofar as" they linked "man's redemption indissolubly to the historical person of Jesus Christ" (*ibid.* 36). Troeltsch viewed this as a grave error.

[123]Morgan noted in 1977 that "no theologian from before the First World War has featured so prominently in the footnotes of learned journals in recent years" (*Troeltsch,* ed. Morgan & Pye, 208). Cf. P. Stuhlmacher, *Historical Criticism and the Interpretation of Scripture,* 1977, 44f. By the end of the 20th century Troeltsch's prominence was more background than center stage, but it was still present.

[124]This point is underscored repeatedly in Swarat, "Konzeption Hofmanns," *Glaube und Geschichte,* ed. Stadelmann.

revelation in history in Hofmann's sense and of past history having any normative significance for contemporary thought, theological or otherwise. Of course the core of this conviction can be found already in Lessing.

Under dialectical theological influence F. Baumgärtel rejects Hofmann for allegedly having a philosophically determined concept of history largely on the grounds of Bultmann's superior existential conception of history.[125] Steck is determined to condemn Hofmann—along with Schlatter and Cullmann, to the vindication of Barthian theology—with a guilt-by-association argument linking Hofmann with Schelling, Hegel, and other discredited idealists.[126] He does this having admitted that Hofmann in his own writings expressly minimized, even denied, these connections.[127]

A comparable anti-salvation history bias animates E. Wendebourg, who wants to chain Hofmann to defunct aspects of the systems of Ranke, Hegel, the later Schelling, and Schleiermacher.[128] Wendebourg devotes a large part of his presentation to admitting that there is little or no demonstrable and culpable direct dependence by Hofmann on these figures. Nevertheless he concludes by rejecting him because "from the point of view of the history of ideas" he was "a child of Romanticism and of idealism's speculative approach to history."[129] No less scathing is Tooman's analysis from a conservative evangelical viewpoint.[130] "The criticisms of von Hofmann are legion."[131] And they have come not only from critical but also from more traditionalist quarters.[132] In his own day he was bitterly opposed for challenging

---

[125]Baumgärtel, *Verheissung*, 1952, 86–91.

[126]Steck, *Idee, passim*, esp. 19–36.

[127]*Ibid.* 18.

[128]Wendebourg, "Die Heilsgeschichte Theologie J.C.K. von Hofmanns in ihrem Verhältnis zur romantischen Weltanschauung," *ZTK* 52 (1955) 64–104.

[129]*Ibid.* 104. W. Lütgert more discerningly argues that while the world of idealist thought marks Hofmann's ideas—how could it not in those decades in Germany?—Hofmann did not share idealism's metaphyisical assumptions; he only took up aspects of its view of history and by no means advocated "the real significance of the logic which was presupposed by the [idealist] method" (*Die Religion des deutschen Idealismus und ihr Ende*, vol. 3, 1925, 177).

[130]See W. Tooman, "The Origin and Development of Heilsgeschichte in Conservative Biblical Theology with Special Attention to the Problem of Revelation and History," 1994.

[131]R.A. Harrisville, *Historical Handbook of Modern Biblical Interpreters*, 380.

[132]See P.I. Johnston, "Reu Reconsidered: The Concept of Heilsgeschichte in the Hermeneutic of J.M. Reu and J.C.K. von Hofmann," *Concordia Journal* 18/4 (October

confessional understandings of the atonement with biblical formulations; in the process he is credited with initiating modern study of
Luther by reading Luther and the Bible against high confessionalism.[133]

Dissenting opinions

Yet R.C. Dentan's contrasting summary points to the controversy
surrounding Hofmann's work: Hofmann "protests against speculative
and philosophical tendencies."[134] Swarat draws attention to the same
lack of consensus: he is seen as the ideological descendent of Coccejus,
Samuel Collenbusch, Bengel, and Oetinger, depending on the critical
study consulted.[135] Tooman roots Hofmann most implausibly in the
thought of Richard Rothe (1799–1867).[136]

While we cannot enter into specifics of this debate, three points
should be made. First, it is certainly true that he was, like virtually all
other German historians of his time, affected by Hegel, if only in that
he reacted against him.

But second, studies such as that of G. Weth[137] and G. Flechsenhaar[138]
suggest that Hofmann's approach to history, in contrast to that of
Hegel, represents "the sharpest rejection of all philosophy of history."[139] We believe that Weth and Flechsenhaar have more accurately
characterized Hofmann's work and would agree therefore with
O. Procksch (trained in the Erlangen school associated with Hofmann's heritage) that "Hofmann is a historical realist,"[140] whatever
tinges of idealism may color his writings. For ultimately, suspicion of
Hofmann's Hegelianism or implication in the romantic-idealist legacy
must be checked to the extent that he opposed F.C. Baur—a considerable extent indeed.

1992) 339-360. Only slightly more positive is G. Maier, *Biblical Hermeneutics*, 1994,
357–359.

[133]Cf. Steck in Greschat, ed., *Theologen des Protestantismus im 19. und 20. Jahrhundert
I*, 102.

[134]R.C. Dentan, *Preface to Old Testament Theology*, [2]1963, 48. Likewise Steck in Greschat, ed., *Theologen des Protestantismus im 19. und 20. Jahrhundert I*, 107.

[135]Swarat, "Konzeption Hofmanns," *Glaube und Geschichte*, ed. Stadelmann, 236 n.
11. Calling attention to scholarship's divided views of Hofmann is also Steck in Greschat, ed., *Theologen des Protestantismus im 19. und 20. Jahrhundert I*, 103.

[136]"The Origin and Development of Heilsgeschichte," 24.

[137]G. Weth, *Die Heilsgeschichte. Ihr universeller und individueller Sinn in der offenbarungsgeschichtlichen Theologie des 19. Jahrhunderts*, 1931.

[138]G. Flechsenhaar, *Das Geschichtsproblem in der Theologie Johannes von Hofmanns*,
1935.

[139]*Ibid.* 103. Cf. 16, 19, 27.

[140]O. Procksch, "Hofmanns Geschichtsauffassung," *ELKZ* 43 (1910) 1035.

Third, G. Schrenk shows convincingly that Hofmann's views are profoundly rooted in the covenant theology of Cocceius mediated to Hofmann through the Reformed Erlangen professor and pastor Christian Krafft.[141] Drawing on his own study of Krafft and comparing it with Hofmann biographer P. Wapler's summaries of Hofmann's outlook, Schrenk draws numerous direct parallels between the two men, among them: (1) "Christ's appearance is the turning point of world history. Christ is history's guiding principle, and the history of Christianity the essential content of all history"; (2) "there is no universal history without a theological principle, but this is furnished by the predictive prophecy of Scripture"; (3) "Christ, as meaning and content of history, as he testifies to himself by the Holy Spirit in the certainty of faith, is the guiding principle of ... theology."[142] Schrenk's study establishes that while Hofmann bears plenty of marks of his own times (e.g. he was affected by the historians Niebuhr and Ranke[143]), he is much more a biblical than an idealist theologian. Hofmann, a chiliast who believed in the restoration of the people of Israel[144] is hardly to be explained by the influence of Romanticism, post-Kantians like Schelling, and Hegel. Ritschl was closer to the mark in his casual comment that "in Pietist circles ... Cocceius ... is actually the rich uncle whose inheritance went to Bengel and Hofmann."[145]

Hofmann as New Testament theologian

What one often seeks in vain in negative assessments of Hofmann, even those made by New Testament theologians, is any cognizance of his sizable contribution to New Testament interpretation, history, hermeneutics,[146] and theology.[147] Even the positive judgments[148] of

[141] G. Schrenk, *Gottesreich und Bund im älteren Protestantismus*, 1967 (= 1923), 322–332.

[142] *Ibid.* 328 n. 2.

[143] *Ibid.* 331.

[144] *Ibid.* 332.

[145] *Ibid.* 331f. n. 1. New appraisal of Cocceius is underway. See W. van Asselt, *The Federal Theology of Johannes Cocceius (1603–1669)*, 2001.

[146] A notable exception: O. Tiililä, "Über die heilsgeschichtliche Schriftauslegung," in *Gedenkschrift für D. Werner Elert*, ed. Hübner, Kinder & Maurer, 1955, 283-287. Hofmann receives but brief mention in E. Schnabel, *Inspiration und Offenbarung*, 1986, 62.

[147] Thus e.g. G. Hasel, *New Testament Theology*, 1978, merely lists Hofmann's *Biblische Theologie* in the bibliography but never cites it, centering rather on his earlier "systematic" works.

[148] Besides Procksch, Kantzenbach, Weth, Flechsenhaar, Tiililä and Swarat (all cited above), see also M. Keller-Hüschmenger, "Das Problem der Gewissheit bei J.Chr.K.

those reading Hofmann more fairly have not been able to remove the
stigma of "nineteenth century idealist philosopher of history" from
one who was in fact not a systematic theologian, certainly not a philosopher,[149] but rather an exegete with theological awareness, i.e., a
biblical theologian. Leo goes so far as to assert: "We can make a clear
distinction between Hofmann the systematician and Hofmann the
exegete."[150] Steck calls him a "theologian of Scripture" who should
not be understood as a systematic theologian or adherent to a particular school.[151]

Hofmann could rightly be called a forgotten son of New Testament
criticism whose work merits renewed attention. He devoted some
eleven volumes (approximately 5500 pages) to analysis and synthesis of
the New Testament.[152] The first eight of these are detailed exegesis of
the thirteen traditional Pauline writings, Hebrews, the Petrine letters,
Jude, James, and Luke.[153] Volume nine is a New Testament introduction which contains a section on the development of the canon.
Volume ten is a history of the New Testament period. Volume eleven
is Hofmann's New Testament theology itself. Hofmann also produced
the last comprehensive treatment of biblical hermeneutics to appear
from 1880 until 1928.[154] This body of largely neglected material, not
his so-called systematic works, should form the basis of assessment of
Hofmann as a New Testament theologian, and it is to this corpus we
look as we bring Hofmann into dialogue with Baur. This will at least

von Hofmann im Rahmen der 'Erlanger Schule'," in *Gedenkschrift für Elert*, 288-295.
Virtually all of these writers take issue with Hofmann at various individual points, yet
see more to praise than to damn in his work.

[149]At least not a Hegelian one. In a letter to F. Delitzsch Hofmann divulges that
hearing Hegel's lectures as a student in Berlin and later reading about his "philosophy
of history completely spoiled my appetite for his philosophy" (Flechsenhaar,
Geschichtsproblem Hofmanns, 19). Cf. J. Rogerson, *Old Testament Criticism*, 1985, 106 n.
6; Harrisville & Sundberg, *The Bible in Modern Culture*, 136: "Hofmann was no philosopher."

[150]Leo, *LQ* 10 (1958) 209.

[151]Greschat, ed., *Theologen des Protestantismus im 19. und 20. Jahrhundert I*, 103.

[152]Hofmann, *Die heilige Schrift neuen Testaments zusammenhängend untersucht*, [2]1869-
1886.

[153]Hofmann died suddenly just as he neared completion of Luke. Volumes 9-11 and
his hermeneutics were edited and published posthumously by W. Volck.

[154]According to Goppelt, *Typos*, 1969 (= 1939), 16. Cf. Hofmann, *Biblische Hermeneutik*, 1880. When citing this work we have used C. Preus's translation: *Interpreting the
Bible*, 1959. The book originated as lectures given by Hofmann at Erlangen in 1860.

inaugurate the unfinished task alluded to by Steck:[155] "A careful comparative study of Hofmann and Baur remains undone as far as I am aware."

2. Hofmann's conception of New Testament theology vis-à-vis Baur

Baur's outlook

We noted already that Baur's New Testament theology is concerned to set forth a "conceptual explication of believing self-understanding." This means primarily that a context for interpreting the texts is not sought within the texts but rather within the categories of understanding acceptable to current scientific thought. New Testament theology frees the New Testament from a theological context and places it within a philosophical or moral-ethical one.[156]

Whereas the New Testament might appear to grow out of the personal exposure of numerous individuals to Jesus' person, work, teaching, or personal followers, whether before or after the resurrection, Baur sees in the New Testament dogmatizing degeneration away from the pure religion of Jesus and his acute ethical self-awareness. The New Testament is largely the product of imaginative, if earnest, literary and religio-philosophical activity, in conjunction with the inexorable self-realization of the absolute in human thinking.

Common ground ...

Hofmann concurs with Baur that New Testament theology's proper focus is the historical development through which the New Testament books, and hence New Testament theology, came into being. It is a historical discipline; "accordingly one must investigate the growth and progressive formation of the doctrine whose documentary monument is Holy Scripture."[157] New Testament theology must take on a genetic form which shows the interrelated rise and development of biblical doctrine—or "Erkenntniss" (knowledge) as Hofmann often styles it— as a complement to the New Testament history. This is why Hofmann's New Testament theology is preceded by a New Testament

---

[155]Steck in Greschat, ed., *Theologen des Protestantismus im 19. und 20. Jahrhundert I*, 112.

[156]Both D.F. Strauss and Baur "carried out the historical examination of the Bible as refutation of its inspiration and authority as word of God" (Swarat, "Konzeption Hofmanns," *Glaube und Geschichte*, ed. Stadelmann, 216.

[157]Hofmann, *Biblische Theologie des neuen Testaments*, 1.

history, *Die biblische Geschichte neuen Testaments.*[158] New Testament
theology does not dispense with but rather grows directly out of the
historical documents comprising the New Testament.

Hofmann, like Baur, is concerned to set forth New Testament theology in its organic development, and he sees this inextricably linked
with history itself. History, not "a systematic schema, within which
individual phenomena from various temporal contexts are arranged,"
provides the framework for presenting New Testament theology.[159]
"Hofmann," no less than Baur, "takes his stand ... unreservedly on the
ground of the modern historical worldview."[160]

... but parting of the ways

But Hofmann and Baur part company decisively on the question: what
then precisely is New Testament theology? Hofmann seems to have
Baur's approach in mind when he laments: "It is still far too often the
case that when individual biblical doctrines are set forth, the explanation of their history is made in such a way that the doctrines appear to
owe their origin to the authors in whose writings we see the doctrines
stated."[161] In contrast, Hofmann denies that New Testament theology
should take the form of "the history of an inquiry"[162] or that its content should be seen primarily as purely a "result of literary activity."[163]
Hofmann does not agree, then, with an approach like Baur's, insofar as
it sees the New Testament writings as little more than the reflections
of a search for a theological rationale for a religion which gradually
came to full expression over the course of more than a century. That
would make the Christian religion a totally immanent human belief-
system which almost gratuitously used Jesus as its founder and primal
mover. Hofmann turns away from what in Baur's view New Testament theology becomes, which is a history of "a search for
actuality."[164]

Instead, the core of Hofmann's New Testament theology will be
the "actuality" which in the New Testament texts "became public and

---

[158]Vol. 10 of his eleven volume investigation of the New Testament. For his view
of how New Testament theology and New Testament history interrelate, see his
Biblische Theologie des neuen Testaments, 7.

[159]Hofmann, *Biblische Theologie des neuen Testaments,* 1, cf. 6f.

[160]Swarat, "Konzeption Hofmanns," *Glaube und Geschichte,* 216.

[161]Hofmann, *Biblische Theologie des neuen Testaments,* 2.

[162]*Ibid.* By this Hofmann appears to mean "a history of (unknown writers' heuristic)
inquiry" to develop a dogmatic system out of Jesus' simple teaching.

[163]*Ibid.*

[164]*Ibid.*

widely comprehended."[165] For Baur New Testament theology reflects a variegated, internally contradictory immanent intellectual process, whereby a simple pure religion was creatively (dialectically) transformed into the basis for a baroque dogmatic superstructure. New Testament theology is in that sense a history of "a search for actuality." Hofmann reverses the process. "Actuality" stands at the historical starting point, not the end. It is this actuality—its effects, its gradual apprehension, its being experienced, appropriated, and proclaimed in the early church—upon which Hofmann places emphasis.

So conceived, Hofmann's New Testament theology falls under Ebeling's definition of a discipline which attempts to set forth the content of the New Testament.[166] Hofmann, unlike Baur, can approach the New Testament in this way because, by his exhaustive reckoning, there *is* a theological (and historical) unity to the New Testament; the canonical books *are* rightfully deemed apostolic in content if not in actual authorship; one *can* still today read the New Testament as theology in itself, and not merely as "the reflex of the subjectivity of the authors"[167] which then must be radically reinterpreted by the modern analyst.

Hofmann is not arguing that "the doctrinal content of Scripture forms a system."[168] But he contends that New Testament theology's task lies in grasping the "Erkenntniss" (doctrinal knowledge) which the texts convey, not in cutting them to fit the size of an alien preunderstanding which the New Testament theologian brings to his work.

Further differences: the structure of New Testament theology
We can see more clearly the difference between Hofmann's and Baur's procedures by looking briefly at how they actually organized their New Testament theologies.

Baur's can be split into two major divisions. After commenting on the history of the discipline,[169] he deals with the "teaching of Jesus."[170] Baur does his best with a topic about which little can be known:

> One finds here nothing that is direct; everything is conveyed through a presentation. And one does not know what sort of an effect the presenta-

---

[165] *Ibid.*
[166] Ebeling, "The Meaning of 'Biblical Theology,'" *Word and Faith*, 79–97.
[167] Baur, *Vorlesungen*, 24.
[168] Hofmann denies this: *Biblische Theologie des neuen Testaments*, 7.
[169] Baur, *Vorlesungen*, 1–44.
[170] *Ibid.* 45–121.

tion has had on the subject matter itself, how much has been added or de-
leted as a result of the presentation.[171]

"The teaching of Jesus" is for Baur much more a somewhat speculative reconstruction of "the teaching about Jesus" than some semblance
of "that which Jesus taught," about which very little is, or can be,
known.

His second major division is "the teaching of the apostles."[172]
Whereas Jesus' teaching in its original form "was very distinct from a
dogmatically developed doctrinal concept," to the apostolic era belongs "the entire historical course of development," or "process of
development," through which "the person of Jesus first acquired the
great importance which it has for the Christian consciousness."[173] Baur
divides this epoch into three periods. In the first he traces the formation of Paul's[174] "doctrinal concepts" (*Lehrbegriffe*) as well as those of
the author of Revelation,[175] which Baur felt was the only New Testament book whose author might actually reflect the viewpoint of one
of Jesus' followers. In the second period, extending well into the second century, he deals with the "doctrinal concepts" of Hebrews, the
shorter (non-) Pauline letters (excluding the Pastorals), James, the
Petrine letters, the synoptics, and Acts.[176] The third period covers the
dogmatic formulating reflected in the Pastorals and Johannine writings.[177]

Hofmann's whole treatment, on the other hand, stands under the
heading of "The Doctrinal Content"[178] of the New Testament writ-
ings. This already bespeaks the fundamental unity he thinks the New
Testament comprises, with no radical rupture to be found between
Jesus and subsequent apostolic teaching. To determine this teaching
Hofmann proposes the following procedure:

One must inquire how the fact of the relationship of God and mankind,
which is transmitted in Christ, presents itself as doctrine in the Scripture;

---

[171] *Ibid.* 122.

[172] *Ibid.* 122-407.

[173] *Ibid.* 122f.

[174] For Baur the only genuine Pauline letters were Romans, Galatians, and 1 and 2
Corinthians.

[175] Baur, *Vorlesungen* , 122-230.

[176] *Ibid.* 230-338.

[177] *Ibid.* 338-407.

[178] Hofmann, table of contents to *Biblische Theologie des neuen Testaments.*

[one must inquire] how this same fact presents itself disparately and yet uniformly according to the progress of salvation history.[179]

Hofmann, like Baur, begins with comments on the task and history of the discipline[180] but adds to this a section on "the Old Testament presuppositions," without which both New Testament history and theology are unintelligible.[181] Here he departs radically from Baur, whose idealist philosophical commitments, it may be surmised, render the Old Testament of only formal significance for New Testament thought as he presents it. As Steck notes, "His interest inclined steadily more to Socrates and Plato than to Moses and the prophets."[182] Hofmann then further describes his modus operandi:

We first observe what new doctrine surfaces through prophetic proclamation about Jesus, then through his own testimony about himself, and finally through his witnesses, who for their part first bore him witness within their own nation and then beyond the boundaries of their nation in the pagan world.[183]

We can perhaps sum up Hofmann's approach as we have seen it thus far by terming it Jesus-Christocentric. In contrast to Baur, for whom the appellation "Christ" was applied to Jesus only long after his death, he takes up the New Testament's own surface preoccupation with Jesus who came to be called Christ virtually in his own lifetime and relates all the appropriate New Testament material, undergirded by the Old Testament background, to the Jesus-Christ word-event complex.

He begins by covering "the prophetic proclamation of the New Testament realization of salvation."[184] This deals chiefly with the material in Luke 1–2 and its Old Testament background. While stylistically this material is highly colored by its author or transmitters, the content is factual.[185] Next comes "the witness of the Baptist."[186] Following that is a lengthy section on "Jesus' witness during his earthly life."[187] This is not just gospel material but also draws on Acts and the epistles. Hof-

---

[179] *Ibid.* 2.

[180] *Ibid.* 1-8.

[181] *Ibid.* 8-22.

[182] Greschat, ed., *Theologen des Protestantismus im 19. und 20. Jahrhundert I*, 62.

[183] *Biblische Theologie des neuen Testaments*, 22.

[184] *Ibid.* 23-30.

[185] *Ibid.* 23.

[186] *Ibid.* 30-37.

[187] *Ibid.* 37-130.

mann, here much exercised to oppose Baurian approaches, wishes to demonstrate that New Testament theology is a confirmation of and organic outgrowth from Jesus' teaching and influence, not an imaginative theological meditation. His concern is indicated as he writes:

> As little as the apostles are teaching novelty when they testify to Jesus' divine sonship, just as little [do they teach novelty] in that which they say concerning his death; and what they say about him is always the same, only applied variously according to the given occasion. Neither here nor there do we find an idea which takes shape in various doctrinal concepts. Rather we find a fact which is the content of the common faith and which is weighed as a possibility according to the particular aspect [of the fact] to which the occasion for pondering it gave rise.[188]

In the same vein he concludes, following lengthy investigation, that in Matthew, James, and Hebrews, we see that "the apostolic preaching introduces no essentially new knowledge; it only applies in peculiar fashion the facts given in Jesus' proclamation and in the Old Testament."[189]

Hofmann is convinced that "the apostolic assertions" are "grounded in Jesus' testimony about himself."[190] This does not however minimize the fact that Jesus' full import only gradually came to be fully appreciated among his followers; e.g. "the fact that Jesus is a divine person [literally: "divine self"] was clearly and fully recognized only after his decease, when the work he was to accomplish on earth was completely finished."[191] The resurrection, then, gives insight into Jesus' past and present, and even future, significance. For next Hofmann comments briefly on "the instruction of the disciples through the resurrected Jesus."[192] Here his openness to the transcendent is evident, as well as his desire to integrate the biblical reports into a history which happened, not merely was thought. The remaining portion of Hofmann's work is divided into nine parts under the heading "the doctrine of Jesus' witnesses."[193]

3. Summary

Baur sees New Testament theology first of all as the theologizing comprising the New Testament writings. It is the dogmatizing activity

---

[188] *Ibid.* 65.
[189] *Ibid.* 180.
[190] *Ibid.* 43.
[191] *Ibid.* 43.
[192] *Ibid.* 130–136.
[193] *Ibid.* 136–328.

which gave rise to them. Accordingly, New Testament theology as a discipline gives a scientific ("speculative"; historical-critical) analysis and synthesis of this activity. It attains to the *real* explanation for the coming into existence of the New Testament writings, an explanation which the New Testament writings themselves largely conceal.

Hofmann, on the other hand, seeks to understand the New Testament texts in their stated context, i.e. as witnesses to the redemptive ministry of the promised Old Testament deliverer/New Testament church founder, his teaching, and his work, and then to his empirical after-effects. He views this method as giving a more credible explanation for these texts, both theologically and historically, than Baur's method can.

Hofmann's theory of knowledge

1. Hofmann as non-Cartesian

We showed above that Baur is strongly influenced by an epistemology which contributes to a subordinating of understanding communicated by the New Testament texts to Baur's own Kantian outlook. We characterized Baur's approach as a Cartesian one.

Hofmann has no clear commitment to one particular formal theory of knowledge. In anticipation of discussion in the final chapter below, however, we might call attention to Hofmann's repeated use of "Erkenntniss" (knowledge) as a term denoting the content of the New Testament. We are dealing here, Hofmann implies, not simply with things believed, subjective impressions, but rather assured facts. We should note that this in itself bespeaks a distinct departure from a Kantian epistemology for which no "Erkenntnis"[194] of things divine or transcendental is accessible to man. Hofmann, then, breaks decisively with Baur's pronounced dualism. This will prove to be a distinctive of the salvation historical perspective in New Testament theology generally.

For now it suffices to understand Hofmann as a non-Cartesian. Thielicke sets forth as a basic tenet of this approach "that while the present situation and its questions have to be considered, they must not become a normative principle nor must they be allowed to prejudice the answer; they must be constantly recast and transcended in the light of the text."[195]

---

[194]Single -s is the modern spelling.
[195]Thielicke, *Evangelical Faith*, vol. 1, 127.

This view "seeks to preserve or reclaim what has come into being historically, not because it is subservient to the law of sloth, but because what has come into being has proved itself."[196] If Cartesian thought risks *accommodation*—making "me" the norm of truth—non-Cartesian method strives for *actualization*, which "always consists in a new interpretation of truth, in its readdressing, as it were."[197]

The non-Cartesian approach runs risks of its own,[198] but in it there is hope that "truth remains intact" and that "the hearer is summoned and called 'under the truth' in his own name and situation."[199] While the two views can be seen as closely related—both are concerned to bring theological insight, or at least religious experience, of ancient times into the contemporary world—in fact "they are as opposite as two antithetical attitudes, namely, loyalty and disloyalty."[200]

2. Hofmann and Scripture

If we are to understand Hofmann as a non-Cartesian, we must what this does *not* mean. It does not mean that he believed in an inerrant Scripture so that an attempted reproduction of its contents demands unthinking, passive acceptance, an allegiance precluding the need for intellectual wrestling with Scripture's contents.[201] Hofmann states unambiguously that "the history recorded in the Bible is not to be understood as an errorless segment of world history."[202] Or again: what the Bible "teaches concerning the history of the origin of mankind rests upon a tradition which may not agree with actual facts."[203] Thus he says that "the Biblical records have this in common with the historiography of antiquity, that they are closer to epics than modern historiography is."[204] With reference to John's gospel it would be false to assume that "Jesus must always really have uttered that which is reported at the juncture and in the form which it appears."[205] Hofmann was no inerrantist, and it would thus be unfair to attribute his

---

[196] *Ibid.* 36.

[197] *Ibid.* 27.

[198] As Thielicke himself recognizes: see *ibid.* 53f., 115ff.

[199] *Ibid.* 27.

[200] *Ibid.*

[201] *Pace* the tone of P. Stuhlmacher's handling of Hofmann in *Vom Verstehen des Neuen Testaments*, 1979, 145-148. See rather Harrisville & Sundberg, *The Bible in Modern Culture*, 129.

[202] Hofmann, *Interpreting the Bible*, 64.

[203] *Ibid.* 72.

[204] *Ibid.* 205.

[205] Hofmann, *Biblische Theologie des neuen Testaments*, 45.

non–Cartesian point of view to an unconscionable commitment to a dogmatic theory.[206]

3. Hofmann and Baur contrasted
Baur: desire to do justice to modern thinking
Hofmann's point of view gains clarity by contrasting it to Baur's. Baur labors to show that the New Testament is a monument, not to the rise and spread of the one true Christian gospel and faith, but to a plethora of partisan religious spokespersons or groups seeking ascendancy for their own points of view.[207] His fundamental hypothesis is that the surface picture offered by the New Testament—Jesus was sent from God in fulfillment of Old Testament promises; he taught followers and worked miracles; he died for the salvation of all persons who would accept him in faith; he rose from the dead; his followers sought to proclaim the gospel of Jesus Christ to the ends of the earth—is materially impossible. Assuming this, Baur attempts to construct an alternate scenario in which the New Testament writings can be placed and understood. Inasmuch as Baur starts with a patently modern worldview and proceeds to give a total picture of the New Testament in accordance with it, his entire program may be seen as a typically Cartesian methodology.

Hofmann: desire to do justice to texts' claims on modern thinking
Hofmann turns Baur's program around. He says in effect, Let us grant that the New Testament writings *could* be substantially trustworthy. This is also a critical approach, because Hofmann remains open to the possibility that portions (and subsequently the whole) of the New Testament could be misguided or misleading. Yet he is at the same time critical in regard to a modern worldview which would too facilely dismiss the New Testament witnesses without a fair hearing. He seeks to determine whether it is possible to give a conceptually coherent, historically plausible account of the rise and interrelatedness of the New Testament's ideological or theological content in accordance

---

[206]This is almost certainly the charge Baur would level against Hofmann: see *Vorlesungen*, 32ff. Baur inveighs against approaches which see a basic unity within the New Testament, attributing them to uncritical acceptance of (or a desire to prove) a theory of biblical inspiration. Any approach which finds conceptual unity in the New Testament wrongly neglects "that which by its very conception is the primary focus of New Testament theology: the real disparity of the doctrinal concepts" (*ibid.* 32).

[207]Köpf, *ZTK* 89/4 (1992) 451 regards this as one of Baur's enduring insights.

with the "surface" context which the documents share. This is Hofmann's main purpose.

Does he have any substantial grounds for declaring Baur's method unsatisfactory? Hofmann thinks so. He notes that in New Testament theology of his day as well as in the study of New Testament history

> the denial of miracle and the criticism of the historical content of the New Testament Scripture for which this denial is decisive had as its consequence that the conception and presentation of that content suffered inner contradiction and bogged down in insoluble riddles which made it incomprehensible.[208]

So then, the non-Cartesian Hofmann observes that those Cartesian attempts to give an account of the New Testament data are unsatisfactory which work from the assumption of "the denial of miracle and the criticism ... for which this denial is decisive." And he specifically questions Baur closely at this point.

He notes that Baur concedes that "Christianity in its historical manifestation would be an impossibility and an inconceivability without the faith in Jesus' resurrection."[209] Yet Baur does not seriously consider the possibility that Jesus really rose; he evades the problem which, by his own admission, the chorus of ancient witnesses raises by asserting that "the factuality of the resurrection narrative" is not at issue, "but rather only that it was believed by his disciples."[210]

Against such a methodological outlook Hofmann protests:

> But just how his disciples are supposed to have come to believe in it Baur leaves unanswered. He thus finally arrives at a question mark which he is unable to get around. Either he must accept a psychological miracle, or he must let the actual and ultimate origin of Christianity stand as an incomprehensible fact. Therefore, either the existence of Christianity is, after all, based on a miracle, namely, that Jesus' disciples came unanimously to the conviction that the one who was crucified is resurrected; or scientific investigation must declare the origin of Christianity to be actually unknown and simply not understandable to it. In the latter case, science concedes that Christianity itself is something inconceivable to it.[211]

---

[208]Hofmann, *Die biblische Geschichte neuen Testaments*, 11.

[209]*Ibid.* 15. Baur makes claims to this effect, e.g., in *Vorlesungen*, 127.

[210]Hofmann, *Die biblische Geschichte neuen Testaments*, 15.

[211]*Ibid.* Hofmann makes a similar point in direct opposition to Baur in *Die heilige Schrift neuen Testaments*, vol. 1, 17. Arguing along the same line at that time was C.A. Auberlen, *The Divine Revelation*, 1867, and some years later E.C. Hoskyns & F.N. Davey, *The Riddle of the New Testament*, [2]1936.

As this citation reveals, Hofmann charges that Baur's assumptions do not explain, or even permit explanation of, that which permeates the New Testament: the assertion that Jesus rose from the dead. This seems to be the ground on which Hofmann justifies an alternative methodological posture toward the New Testament texts in constructing a New Testament theology.

4. Summary: Hofmann's modified critical posture

Hofmann strikes a modified "critical" pose, since he refuses to declare on a priori grounds what can or cannot, must or must not, have been true about the matters to which the New Testament documents testify. This modified critical outlook, which is willing at least theoretically to let its own inherited modern perceptions be challenged by the sources it examines, may be understood in terms as a non-Cartesian approach.

Our earlier examination of Baur concluded that Baur's epistemological starting point too often effectively determines the significance and historical status of the New Testament material he explicates. It privileges a particular modern outlook in interpreting the New Testament. Going back to a quote from Thielicke above, Baur seems willing to grant at the outset that to have intellectual integrity in the modern world one must be "disloyal" to central claims of New Testament.

Hofmann's epistemology is less clearly defined than Baur's. He is obviously aware of and to an extent shares in the modern critical debate. He is no biblical inerrantist. But he wants to make his hypothetical starting point for determining what dynamics gave rise to the New Testament history and theology the New Testament texts themselves, not modern assumptions which determine a priori what *can* have been the case without sufficiently thorough consideration of what actually *was* the case. We can say, then, that Hofmann privileges the New Testament, or to put it differently, a modern understanding of the New Testament which sees its first task as trying to reformulate the content of the New Testament within a context presupposed by the New Testament, not within the context demanded by a worldview inimical to a good deal of its surface claims. Hofmann would seem to hold that no interpretation of the New Testament has intellectual integrity which uncritically—even if paradoxically in the name of criticism—elevates a particular a priori modern understanding to the status of authority over what *can* be true about or *could have* given rise to the New Testament subject matter. In terms of Thielicke's disloyalty-loyalty antithesis set forth above, Hofmann thinks a certain loyalty to the New Testament evidence is the only way to come to a satisfactory apprehension of it.[212]

Hofmann's approach to history

1. *The contemporary dilemma: Strauss, Bauer, and Baur*

Somewhat surprisingly, Hofmann praises Strauss for having helped bring clarity to the debate regarding the New Testament's historicity.[213] Prior to Strauss, says Hofmann, critics like Cölln and de Wette had applied the term "myth" arbitrarily to those parts of Scripture telling (1) of God appearing or speaking to persons and (2) of miracles. They used myth in the sense common to classicists of the day. Strauss was more consistent and precise in declaring the whole history contained in the four gospels as mythical. It is in fact "unintentional fiction."[214] In this way Strauss, following O. Müller, defined myth as "a tale, relating directly or indirectly to Jesus, which and insofar as it does not record fact but rather is the result of an idea of his earliest adherents."[215]

Strauss knows the New Testament to be myth because he believes he has shown it to be unhistorical. Hofmann questions the methods Strauss uses to demonstrate this unhistoricity[216] and finally rejects his approach:

> Thus his extension of the category "mythical" to the entire historical content of the gospels made these themselves incomprehensible. And the origin of Christianity became just as incomprehensible after nothing remained of the history in which its origin lay but the rabbi Jesus of Nazareth who died on the cross. One queried in vain where those ideas came from whose result was supposed to be the gospel history.[217]

---

[212]Cf. Senft, *Wahrhaftigkeit*, 109. Baur himself realizes that his own approach and one like Hofmann's are not simply slightly divergent but fundamentally antithetical. Regarding the possibility of reading the New Testament as a basically unified whole, Baur speaks of "the point at which two totally divergent views part company" (*Vorlesungen*, 124). Views which see a unified or unifiable continuum between Jesus and the New Testament's dogma are automatically illicit. Hofmann is of course of this view.

[213]Hofmann, *Die biblische Geschichte neuen Testaments*, 6.

[214]*Ibid.* 6f.: "absichtlose Dichtung." The word "Dichtung" also has a more purely literary connotation and may then refer to poetry or other creative literature. But the context in which Strauss uses it calls for a more restricted rendering of the word.

[215]*Ibid.*

[216]*Ibid.* 7f.

[217]*Ibid.* 8.

Bruno Bauer (1809–1882) forms a bridge from Strauss to Baur. Bauer argues that there was a well-developed messianic expectation in Jesus' time. He explains the apparently historical content of the gospels, not as "unintentional fiction," but as "deliberate fiction, in which the ideas of the first Christendom took shape with consciousness and design."[218] This is a more intellectually consistent theory than Strauss', says Hofmann, but the question remains, "where does this Christianity which has given expression to its ideas originate, and where have these Christian ideas come from?"[219] This is the question, claims Hofmann, which Baur rightly took up.

In a perceptive summary of Baur's position Hofmann notes: "Baur constructs a history of the development of Christianity by working backward from the materials and conditions of the second Christian century."[220] Hofmann then accurately outlines Baur's celebrated reshuffling, chronologically and conceptually, of the New Testament writings, history, and thought.[221] He says that Baur's work marks progress over that of Strauss and Bruno Bauer "on the way to recognition of the reality of a New Testament history."[222] For Baur singles out of the New Testament certain "established facts … on the basis of which the rest could be assessed."[223] This is the same procedure Hofmann adopts in his investigation of the New Testament.[224] Yet the "history of the development of Christianity" which Baur describes turns out to be unsatisfactory, in Hofmann's view:

> For his entire historical construction, one which construes the history of Christianity as a history of literarily advocated factional tendencies, founders on Paul's own declaration (in Galatians, which Baur himself recognizes as genuinely Pauline) regarding his relationship to those who were apostles prior to him.[225]

---

[218] *Ibid.* 9.

[219] *Ibid.*

[220] *Ibid.* The point of contact with W. Bauer, *Orthodoxy and Heresy in Earliest Christianity*, 1971 (first German edition 1934), is worth noting.

[221] Hofmann, *Die biblische Geschichte neuen Testaments*, 9.

[222] *Ibid.* 9-11.

[223] *Ibid.* 11.

[224] Cf. *Die heilige Schrift neuen Testaments*, vol. 1, 59f.; Hofmann's entire study of the New Testament begins "with an investigation of that portion of Galatians, which gives us that historical information, and with a comparison to Acts to the extent that it treats precisely the same things."

[225] *Die biblische Geschichte neuen Testaments*, 11. Hofmann disagrees with Baur on the strength of his own exegetical study of Galatians (*Die heilige Schrift neuen Testaments*, vol. 2), in which he concludes (235): "He [Paul] argues for the independent, not the

This ambiguity in Baur's case opens up the possibility, indeed the necessity, of an alternate approach.

2. Hofmann's starting point

In laying the foundation for his New Testament theology, which Hofmann does by composing a New Testament history, he concedes that someone like Baur, who "a priori and as a matter of principle declares everything to be impossible which is thought not to have occurred according to the ordinary laws of other occurrence,"[226] will take issue with Hofmann's whole basic perspective. This is despite the fact that his New Testament history grows out of his nine-volume "investigation of the New Testament with reference to its origin and historical authenticity."[227] But, as pointed out above, Baur cannot easily deny Hofmann a working starting point on the basis of which the historical veracity of the New Testament writings can be vindicated. For on Baur's own premises his form of criticism "arrives at either an enigma which it cannot get around or at a question which it cannot answer."[228]

We thus arrive at Hofmann's key methodological declaration:

> In view of this state of affairs it is in any case more justified if we cast off the dogmatic presupposition [which Baur embraces] that whatever is not according to the ordinary laws of occurrence is non-existent. We thus approach the testimony of the history lying before us without this presupposition; in a sense we operate without presuppositions. Yet we are not without presuppositions in the sense of fancying that we stand outside the faith which we cannot renounce throughout. But by virtue of this faith we bring to the solution of our task only this expectation: the [New Testament] history ... will prove itself to be actual fact. With this expectation we proceed to the solution of our task. We accept a priori that here in these historical documents comprising the New Testament there was the intention to recount historical reality and that historical reality will be recounted. In the sense, therefore, that the historical content of the documents is

---

sole, justification of his apostleship, and for the perfect, not the exclusive, truth of heathen [i.e. hellenistic, as opposed to Palestinian] Christianity". Thus Hofmann sees tension but not, like Baur, primarily controversy between Pauline and early Palestinian Jewish Christianity.

[226] *Die biblische Geschichte neuen Testaments*, 14.
[227] *Ibid.*
[228] *Ibid.* 16.

offered to us by the documents, we take it up. Then it becomes for us not merely reality pure and simple, but rather salvation historical reality.[229]

This statement permits a glimpse into Hofmann's approach vis-à-vis Baur at four points: (1) admission of presuppositions, (2) the role of faith in apprehension, (3) the burden of proof question, and (4) the nature of salvation history.

Admission of presuppositions

At the methodological level Baur denied the veracity of reported historical events that defied a basically rationalistic worldview. I am not aware that he actually terms his work presuppositionless, but he certainly gives the impression that his method alone, over against all others, facilitates "the truly historical examination"[230] of the evidence. He does not appear to consider his assumptions—that the New Testament writings are disparate and only negatively (or even polemically) related, with most originating in the second century—to be assumptions, but as proven scientific verities.

Hofmann, on the other hand, while remarking tongue-in-cheek that he is presuppositionless, does not think presuppositionless work is even possible.[231]

In fact "a complete lack of presuppositions" on the part of the interpreter would be unthinkable. It is impossible for the interpreter to be neither Christian nor non-Christian, neither religious nor non-religious, but merely interpreter. He approaches Scripture as a person with a definite character and nature and experience, not as a "blank sheet" upon which Scripture inscribes itself.[232]

Hofmann essentially denies the rationalistic-historicistic base which Baur builds upon. For he calls in question Baur's premise that a "purely historical" method is either possible or necessary, a method whose parameters for historical analysis are already established according to a priori principles. Objectivity is not reached, Hofmann believes, by the scientific sophistication of those

who have no relationship to the content of the Bible ...The question is rather, what is the proper, appropriate-to-the-subject presupposition: one

---

[229] *Ibid.*
[230] Baur, *Vorlesungen*, 27.
[231] It is time for someone besides R. Bultmann to receive credit for this insight.
[232] Hofmann, *Interpreting*, 14.

must have an inner relationship to the Bible and its content if one wishes to understand and interpret it.[233]

Hofmann does not claim absolute supremacy for his own approach; he simply terms it "more justified" in light of the insoluble problems confronting Baur. In the end we see Hofmann rather freely admitting his own presuppositions, while Baur leaves us with the impression that work not following his basic line is simply unscientific, if not willfully obtuse.

The role of faith in apprehension

Hofmann has alleged that every interpreter has assumptions that will color his interpretation. Thus a presuppositionless method is impossible. Now he concedes what his own context in interpreting the subject matter is: that of faith. One cannot evade the effects of such a stance, just as one cannot evade the consequences of a rationalistic or naturalistic (or Baur's "purely historical") method. But what is needed, Hofmann implies, is not attempts at evasion, but rather owning up to assumptions and then rigorous, open-minded, and self-aware research consistent with them, along with a willingness to have assumptions corrected in light of the data.

Hofmann then specifies what he brings to his task by virtue of this faith in which he stands. As Senft points out, it is not an interpretative scheme "regulated externally by means of dogma"; Hofmann does not understand faith "as mere acceptance of the teaching of the church."[234] This faith rather amounts to a qualified expectation that what one as a Christian believer is assured of in faith[235]—the fundamental reality and veracity of New Testament history—will prove itself to correspond to reality in fact.[236] Elsewhere he puts this a bit more clearly. His whole eleven-volume investigation of the New Testament was conceived in the hope that the New Testament might "prove scientifically to be the sacred Scripture that it is to my faith."[237] What Hofmann wishes to do, then, is conduct a historical investigation without blindly endorsing

---

[233]Senft, *Wahrhaftigkeit*, 109.

[234]*Ibid.* 103.

[235]Hofmann (*Die heilige Schrift neuen Testaments*, vol. 1, 54) speaks of the committed believer who trusts Scripture "without as yet having knowledge that and how all the individual parts contribute to the nature of the whole of which he has become generally certain."

[236]There are clear echoes of Hofmann's earlier *Der Schiftbeweis* [2]1857-[2]1860 in this statement.

[237]Hofmann, *Die heilige Schrift neuen Testaments*, vol. 1, 1.

the critical assumptions of historicism. If we agree with Hofmann that historicism involves certain unproved and perhaps unprovable assumptions, then Hofmann says that he prefers to interpret the New Testament from the standpoint of the content of a faith (New Testament Christianity) which can fairly claim to derive from the New Testament rather than to interpret it based on a faith (historicism) which cannot do this very convincingly.

One could object that Hofmann's expectation amounts to an a priori affirmation of what he wants to prove. He is arguing in a circle. To a degree this seems to be the case. But it is hard to see how Baur, either, could avoid this charge. Any synthetic handling of the New Testament involves a mutually complementary relationship of those things which the historian-theologian generally expects he will find there and those things that he actually does find there. We see Hofmann essentially viewing his approach to New Testament theology as a model which will best explain all the facts, or at least many of them, facts (like the resurrection) which he sees no place for in Baur's approach. Of course, from Baur's point of view Hofmann's model is invalid from the start because it leaves room for transcendent cause to explain, whether wholly or in part, contingent event. It is troubled by unexplained facts which are, in the modern view, not facts at all but myth or some other kind of ex post facto construction.[238]

Yet while one can understand philosophically what Baur's objection is, one is less clear on the cogency of his argument from the standpoint of the New Testament data. For it seems that Baur, who wishes methodologically to invalidate all non-historicistic outlooks, must engage in special pleading ("my presuppositions are not presuppositions but scientific fact") with regard to the historical evidence. But is he convincing in explaining the phenomena within his presuppositionless system? Not to Hofmann, and probably not to many today, even among those who are not persuaded by Hofmann.

Hofmann's approach to the New Testament, while it involved something he terms faith, did not in itself necessarily compromise his capacity to do valid exegesis and synthesis of material to any greater extent that Baur's approach compromised his—unless of course we accept Baur's historicistic starting point as our own, which admittedly some are still prepared to do: "There is no way back … from Baur and

---

[238]This seems to be the ground on which Senft, *Wahrhaftigkeit*, 87-123, disparages Hofmann's handling of the miraculous in the biblical narratives.

his school, at least for a Protestant theology claiming scientific legiti-macy."[239]

The burden of proof question

As noted above, Hofmann undertakes to do New Testament history and theology under the assumption that those portions of the New Testament that purport to relate historical reality effectively do so. Inasmuch as these historical portions claim to set forth historical mate-rial, Hofmann is prepared tentatively to accept it as such. It should be noted once more that Hofmann is not a biblical inerrantist; we must take care not to read too much into his "acceptance" of what the New Testament witnesses say.[240] He is not opting for wholesale harmonizing of the gospels as his chosen historical method. He seems rather to mean that it is unduly skeptical to place all the New Testament mate-rial in doubt and then to accept back only that part which commends itself to skeptical thinking. It makes sense to adopt a more open stance to the witnesses, even when they appear to be contradictory and so ostensibly mutually excluding. For as Hofmann points out relative to Strauss' reading of the New Testament:

> When a historical report about something stands in contradiction with itself or with other reports related to it, no one will say: 'What this report indi-cates is unhistorical.' Rather, such an incident demands that one scrutinize the report; yet what is reported can nevertheless be historical reality.[241]

Thus Hofmann wants to assume that the New Testament's historical references are largely trustworthy and authentic. But at the same time he resembles Baur in holding that it is required "to scrutinize the re-port," to engage in some manner of critical historical comparison and reflection, in order to arrive at an accurate understanding of the thing being reported. This is part of Hofmann's concession to the problem caused by the subject-object relation in perception, a problem for which others of his time found an answer largely in Kant.

There are three considerations that could have led Hofmann to this positive assessment regarding the veracity of the New Testament from a historical point of view. He could have invoked biblical inerrancy; but this was not the case. Or as a historian he might have felt com-pelled through extensive research to confer high historical trustworthi-

---

[239]Köpf, *ZTK* 89/4 (1992) 460.

[240]See Hofmann, *Interpreting the Bible*, 64-76, where a number of ambiguities and er-rors in the Bible are cited.

[241]Hofmann, *Die biblische Geschichte neuen Testaments,* 7.

ness to the New Testament texts. This was undoubtedly true to a point, but what Hofmann actually cites as a reason is something else.

He proposes to investigate the New Testament writings as "Christenheit" (Christendom) itself sees them, in order to see if they are historically in line with what "Christenheit" itself claims they are.[242] Hofmann notes that "Christenheit" distinguishes a particular time period—the New Testament era—as that of its primary historical origin. Here lie its roots. The literary monument of this age is, it is argued, above all the New Testament corpus, along with its Old Testament substructure. This group of writings is regarded as a standard for later church writings and thought. Hofmann poses the question, Is the church correct in its assessment and use of these writings? An answer is the goal of his massive investigation of the New Testament. But it would be a dubious undertaking to give an adamant "no" at the outset and then proceed with an investigation that only amassed information to prove the point already decided. Hofmann knows that this is the approach of more radical wings of New Testament criticism. But he demurs.

Instead he gives a tentative "yes" to his question and declares programmatically:

> The historical material presented in the entirety of those documents and treatises which in Christianity bear the title "sacred Scripture of the New Testament" will be assembled together. And it will not be randomly assembled together, but rather, since it would otherwise once more not be biblical history, it will be assembled together scrupulously consistent with the point of view according to which it presents itself in the New Testament Scripture. Now the question will be raised: why are you conceiving of your task in such a fashion instead of, in the manner of other historical research and history writing, using these Scriptures as simply sources for some historical context which suggests itself from some other quarter? Why not therefore always ascertain and assess the value of these [New Testament] sources first through comparing them with other sources? The answer is due to the peculiar relationship in which Christendom stands to this collection of Scripture.[243]

Thus Hofmann takes as his working hypothesis the outlook that Christendom's generally realistic understanding of the New Testament

---

[242]"Christenheit" is conceived of "in such a general manner that no one who is truly a Christian is thereby excluded, and also in such an exhaustive way that everything by which Christians differ from non-Christians is included therein" (*Interpreting the Bible*, 26).

[243]Hofmann, *Die biblische Geschichte neuen Testaments*, 1.

furnishes a workable, fruitful, and ultimately plausible context for critical investigation. It is a context which is at least as promising and
satisfactory as contexts (like Baur's) which are foreign to Christendom's general historic assessment of the sources.

Strictly speaking Hofmann does not claim a priori that this working
assumption has the status of assured fact. It is rather only the hypothesis under which he sets about answering his question. This then is the
ground for his refusal to adopt the position of Baur (and Strauss) with
regard to the historical nature of the New Testament writings. Hofmann seems to want to demonstrate that a cogent picture of the New
Testament's historical origins is best attainable if what the texts say is
regarded cautiously as factual. The burden of proof will then be on
critics to demonstrate that the New Testament in general is mythical
or otherwise only quasi-historical, and not on less skeptical critics like
Hofmann who accept the New Testament's own surface claim to be
referring predominantly to actual states of affairs.

The nature of salvation history

Hofmann states that his qualified acceptance of the New Testament's
historical trustworthiness will have a definite effect: "Then it [the New
Testament's historical content] becomes for us not merely reality pure
and simple, but rather salvation historical reality." This raises the question of just what "salvation historical reality" and salvation history itself
are for Hofmann in his New Testament theology.

On the one hand in Hofmann's New Testament theology we see
him view human history in immanentist terms. He speaks of the "self-
propagating race of man."[244] He refers to "the history of Adam's
race."[245] He refers to "this present world order … in which man's
world is a place of sin and death."[246] Each of these references envisions
man in a historical nexus in which, for the purposes of the context at
hand, Hofmann views man as embedded firmly within an immanent
historical process.

Yet there is also, and concurrently, a transcendent dimension to history, as one can see by scrutinizing the New Testament. Referring to
John the Baptist's proclamation of the kingdom of God, Hofmann
writes:

---

[244]Hofmann, *Die biblische Theologie neuen Testaments,* 39, 41.
[245]*Ibid.* 47.
[246]*Ibid.* 88. The "gegenwärtige Weltlauf" is common in Hofmann to denote history
understood in large measure as immanent process.

The God of Israel is the God of heaven, the God who is transcendent and as such sovereign over mankind. Thus the kingdom that he establishes on earth is a heavenly kingdom, because it—in contrast to earthly kingdoms— is revealed from heaven as that order of things in which God alone is the determinative agent, in which all derives its nature from him and is the realization of his will.[247]

In the same vein Hofmann notes that Jesus seemed to have viewed his ministry in connection with "the Old Testament prophecy which pointed to the end of the present world situation" as well as in connection with the preaching of John the Baptist,[248] an example of the commingling of transcendent and immanent elements. Hofmann states that both the Old and the New Testament speak of a "distinction between the outcome of history for believers and the outcome of history for the race of mankind at large,"[249] a difference that becomes clear on judgment day. In general, then, the New Testament history is the "history of the fulfillment of the hope of Israel, which is rooted in Old Testament prophecy and which points to the termination of world history."[250] Old and New Testament history taken together comprise salvation history.

Hofmann appears to be trying to combine both an immanentist and transcendent perspective[251]—transcendent taken in the sense as that which is thought to be beyond the limits of all possible experience and knowledge within the limits of pure reason. On the one hand he works as any historian, comparing sources and trying to explain phenomena by usual means. One sees this clearly, for instance, in his handling of the Second Temple period.[252] On the other hand, Hofmann does not take up an *a priori* position against Scripture's ubiquitous claims that God's hand was unusually evident or his power overtly present in the lives of persons or the course of certain events. He is open to viewing history not only from an immanent perspective, but also from a perspective which is willing to see in history sovereign, direct, and visible participation of God in the sphere of everyday events.

We may surmise that when Hofmann refers to "mere reality pure and simple," he means an immanentist view of the New Testament's

---

[247] *Ibid.* 30.
[248] *Ibid.* 111.
[249] *Ibid.* 129.
[250] *Ibid.* 17.
[251] Cf. C. Preus, *Int* 4 (1950) 319.
[252] Hofmann, *Biblische Theologie des neuen Testaments*, 17-48.

historical and theological content. Such a view cannot allow for the transcendent as part of historical reality, so it seeks to explain the New Testament without recourse to it. But this results in an impoverished portrait of the New Testament, or at least a highly conjectural one, because the New Testament writings themselves leave no doubt that their authors viewed the transcendent as an integral active component in the events and words they relate. To strip the New Testament of this element one must introduce some other dynamic and then interpret the New Testament on the basis of it. But can such an explanation give a satisfactory account of what gave rise to the New Testament texts and presumably also to the church? Hofmann, we have seen, thinks not.

He wants rather to leave room for what is the only thing that can make sense of the documentary evidence of the New Testament historical process. This permits us to move from a picture of "merely reality pure and simple" to "salvation historical reality." This is reality, not as post-Kantians feel constrained to construe it, but as a non-Cartesian may claim it well must have been, based on observation of the evidence and the continuing experience of many Christians of the reality to which the evidence testifies.

As for the term *Heilsgeschichte*, it does not appear very often in Hofmann's work on the New Testament. This is significant, for it suggests that it may be misguided to ignore his New Testament theology simply because of suspicion created by his earlier systematic works which make more extensive use of the term. It is true that these earlier works inform Hofmann's later ones, so that Wapler is right in saying that none of his writings bears interpreting outside the context of all of them.[253] Yet it is too seldom noted that even Hofmann's "dogmatic" works betray a very strong historical concern and grounding.

It seems that salvation history in Hofmann's New Testament theology would be best understood simply as the affected-by-the-transcendent historical process in its entirety to which the Bible points. A decisive point in this process is marked by Jesus[254] who came to be proclaimed the Christ, whose influence was constitutive of the New Testament history and continues to this day. Since Jesus' lifetime history has comprised a *Zwischenzeit* ("interim period"), "a time of conversion for the pagan world and of repentance for Israel,"[255] the consummation of which has not yet taken place. In this interim pe-

---

[253] Wapler, *Johannes v. Hofmann,* V.
[254] Cf. Hofmann, *Biblische Theologie des neuen Testaments,* 174, 206.
[255] *Ibid.* 121.

riod, which includes the present, persons do not merely look back to a collection of past events having no real present relevance, because God is still present or accessible to mankind through the exalted Jesus[256] and through the Spirit,[257] as well as through Scripture. There remains, too, the abiding expectation of the consummation. Salvation history is not merely past but also bears real present and future significance.

Yet ultimately salvation history is that which gave rise to and is reflected by Scripture:

> We differentiate between past history, which forms the basis for the present existence of the Church, on the one hand, and the actual life of the Church for which Holy Scripture is the standard, on the other; that is, between Holy History [*Heilsgeschichte*] and "saving presence."[258]

He takes Scripture as "the document of Holy History"[259] and pursues New Testament theology using this assertion as a hypothetical starting point. How well the assertion corresponds to exegetical and historical observation is a question that only research can answer. But it is clear that Hofmann thinks salvation history will be best understood as it relates to the New Testament, not by the researcher who methodologically denies history's possible transcendent dimension, but by the one who is open to seeing not only "merely reality pure and simple" but also "salvation historical reality." What Hofmann says about coming to terms with Jesus' person seems to apply as well to his thinking regarding an adequate understanding of history: in relation to that which "has appeared in so pitiable form as the glory of Israel, it will become evident who truly desires the salvation of God and who does not."[260]

Conclusion

History, as the saying goes, is written from the point of view of the victors. This is certainly true of the history of New Testament studies. What synthetic treatments of it exist make little or no mention of

[256] *Ibid.* 171.
[257] *Ibid.* 218.
[258] Hofmann, *Interpreting the Bible*, 28.
[259] *Ibid.*
[260] Hofmann, *Biblische Theologie des neuen Testaments*, 29.

Hofmann.[261] Yet he was comparable to Baur in industry and output, a difference being that Hofmann restricted himself much more to biblical exegesis, while Baur's work increasingly became preoccupied with what is now called historical theology.

In hindsight, far from the partisan discussions of a century and a half ago, it should be possible to acknowledge that however hallowed Baur's memory deserves to be, his positive theological proposals find little echo today—and rightly so. To read the New Testament rigidly in the light of Hegelian critical theory is an interesting hermeneutical strategy but can hardly dignify its construals with the adjective "historical." To adopt prescriptive Enlightenment epistemology in seeking understanding of antiquity may be permissible, but only to the extent that the conceptuality allows itself to be shaped by the realities encountered in the application of it. This Baur was unprepared to do. Historicism as Baur implemented has a hoary heritage but must inevitably prove unfruitful in constructing a New Testament *theology*. There is in fact little in Baur's reading of the theology of the New Testament that would be upheld today as a compelling depiction of the thought of the writers, much less a synthesis holding much ongoing religious relevance. His work made history but in important respects failed the test of time.

Nor is the argument here that we should simply repristinate Hofmann. But the more fundamental issue is whether he should even be remembered, having been relegated to oblivion by the discipline which at one time he did much to nurture. The discussion above suggests a positive answer to this question. If historical and linguistic acumen are the measure, Hofmann was Baur's peer (and in Semitic languages perhaps his superior). If mastery of the ancient sources is the measure, again Hofmann stacks up well.

How about "critical" thinking? If that means conformity to a reigning university philosophy of the day, Baur gets not only the laurel but a scepter and a throne. Baur's approach, in substituting post-Enlightenment beliefs for historic Christian confession, was destined to become sovereign across wide domains of academic study of Scripture. In no small measure due to Baur, "the decision to study Christianity by a historical method which refuses to see the web of history disrupted by supernatural interventions appears the only realistic option

---

[261]O. Merk, "Biblische Theologie II. Neues Testament," *TRE* 6, 461, devotes a few words of a dependent clause to Hofmann's *Schriftbeweis* but ignores his New Testament theology.

for a theology committed to relating Christian faith to the knowledge of the day."[262]

But any suggestion that Hofmann was not "committed to relating Christian faith to the knowledge of the day" is groundless. If, as A. Plantinga has argued, critical thinking needs to preserve the capacity to question not only historical sources but also modern methods and their underpinnings that may prove ephemeral and historiographically counterproductive,[263] then Hofmann's work appears gratifyingly sophisticated. And this is true not only because of what he stood against. His biographer Wapler concludes that while Hofmann's students leaned on Hofmann's work as a repudiation of Baur's Tübingen school, Hofmann himself had a far more constructive goal: not only to correct Baur, and reply to Strauss' rationalism and Hengstenberg's ahistorical supernaturalism, but to arrive at a fresh historical and theological method adequate to the challenges of the time and beyond.[264]

The Bavarian Hofmann's surprisingly competent counterpoint to Baur's reading of the New Testament deserves to be noted as a milestone alongside the Tübingen master's.

But it is time now to turn to another Tübingen master—one who upheld the precedent Hofmann established. He was only eight years old when Baur died. His grave can be found a scant stone's throw from Baur's in a quiet Tübingen cemetery. At the same time, we will see Baur's mantle descend on a new generation of scholars whose "history of religion" method was destined to shake biblical studies down to the present hour.

---

[262]Morgan, "Ferdinand Christian Baur," *Nineteenth Century Thought in the West,* vol. 1, 266.

[263]Plantinga, "Two (or More) Kinds of Scripture Scholarship," *Modern Theology* 14/2 (1998) 243–278.

[264]Wapler, *Johannes v. Hofmann,* 101 n. 1. Cf. the largely positive assessment in Harrisville & Sundberg, *The Bible in Modern Culture,* 137–145.

2

/

Religion versus Theology:
William Wrede and Adolf Schlatter
on New Testament Theology

The Tübingen professor buried near F.C. Baur (see close of previous chapter) is Adolf Schlatter. Their grave sites lie close together, but their viewpoints do not. One clue: Baur's headstone is a bleak craggy boulder. On a recent summer afternoon dense foliage almost concealed the only hint of an epitaph: "Doctor of Theology." Schlatter's is a white stone cross standing as tall as some graveside visitors. Its gleam catches the eye from afar when a shaft of sunshine penetrates the tangled branches overhead. On it are Jesus' words of invitation as rendered in the Luther Bible: "If anyone is thirsty, let him come to me and drink" (John 7:37).

Schlatter (1852-1938) was a contemporary of William Wrede (1858-1906) just as Hofmann was of Baur, though Wrede's work was abbreviated by his untimely death before the age of fifty. Schlatter wrote a methodological treatise on New Testament theology that first appeared in 1909. Wrede had published one in 1897. Schlatter published the first edition of his two-volume New Testament theology shortly after Wrede's death. It therefore makes sense to consider their musings on New Testament theology side by side. Not only do they originate in the same general context: not a little of Schlatter's work comprises a direct rebuttal of certain premises—although not the overall concern—of the history of religion school with which Wrede is associated.[1]

---

[1]On Wrede's view of this "school" see his "Das theologische Studium und die Religionsgeschichte," *Vorträge und Studien*, 1907, 64-83, esp. 66f. Note also G.W. Ittel, "Die Hauptgedanken der 'religionsgeschichtlichen Schule,'" *ZRGG* 10 (1958) 61-78 (72f. deals specifically with Wrede); H. Rollmann, "Theologie und Religionsgeschichte," *ZTK* 80 (1983) 69-84 (contains reflections on Wrede's role in the history of religion movement, in particular in relation to Harnack). See also a pair of valuable

In moving from Baur and Hofmann to Wrede we are conscious that a significant shift has taken place in the reigning approach to New Testament theology.[2] Baur's grandiose "edifice," says Wrede, "was an untenable construction."[3] H.J. Holtzmann's New Testament theology, a highly influential work in Wrede's time, marks an improvement, but an unsatisfactory one.[4] Wrede, as a New Testament scholar rather than a theologian per se, is not nearly so clear as Baur as to what dynamic drives history forward, or in what the absolute within history consists. Baur gives the impression that New Testament theology stands as a monument dominating the religious landscape; Wrede asserts tersely that New Testament theology has no other task than to grasp the religio-intellectual reality behind early Christian documents "objectively, correctly, and sharply as possible. That is all."[5] Baur basks in the light of Hegelian hegemony; Wrede assumes the more discreet (but no less self-assured) standpoint of Troeltschian anti-metaphysics.

Baur and Wrede are agreed, however, that a salvation historical approach to New Testament theology is fallacious judged by the conventions of modern thought unfolding in their respective eras. Wrede is acutely conscious that rules of biblical interpretation were changing rapidly: "Ten years ago, and even before that, there was religious history and history of religion research, but there was little talk about it. Today the term [*Religionsgeschichte*, history of religion] passes from person to person; it has become a slogan, a motto, a battle cry ..."[6] Rollmann says of Wrede's interpretation of the gospels: "Wrede's skepticism toward any doctrinal or literary features as being historical was new, as was his rigorous exclusion of any supernatural

---

essays by G. Lüdemann: "Die Religionsgeschichtliche Schule und ihre Konsequenzen für die Neutestamentliche Wissenschaft," *Kulturprotestantismus*, 1992, 78–107; "Die 'Religionsgeschichtliche Schule' und die Neutestamentliche Wissenschaft," *Die "Religionsgeschichte Schule,"* 1996, 9-22.

[2]Cf. Wrede's own observation in 1898: "Biblical exegesis is something entirely different than it was 150 years ago—indeed one could almost say than it was just 50 years ago" (*Vorträge und Studien*, 42).

[3]Wrede, "The Tasks and Methods of 'New Testament Theology,'" R. Morgan, *The Nature of New Testament Theology*, 1973 (hereafter cited as *NNTT*) 92. The original is "Über Aufgabe und Methode der sogenannten Neutestamentlichen Theologie," *Das Problem der Theologie des Neuen Testaments,* ed. G. Strecker, 1975 (hereafter cited as *PTNT*) 119.

[4]*NNTT*, 93f.; *PTNT*, 120ff.

[5]*NNTT*, 69; *PTNT*, 83.

[6]Wrede, *Vorträge und Studien*, 64.

features in the narrative ...".[7] What is said of Wrede's influential contemporary Ernst Troeltsch (see discussion below) is equally true of
Wrede: he "developed the basis for a theological construction applicable to the modern world which did not evade history but used it
creatively for the future, even though such a construction might prove
threatening to the very survival of traditional Christianity."[8] High on
Wrede's list of enemies of critical New Testament theology was a salvation historical approach to the discipline.

We can approach Wrede fruitfully with the same questions with
which we examined Baur. How does he conceive of New Testament
theology? What is his epistemological starting point? How does he
conceive of New Testament history? The answers will be somewhat
different from those of Baur. Yet a continuity will be evident as well.[9]
A grasp of Wrede will further understanding of the dominant direction
in New Testament theology that has deemed salvation history a misunderstanding that is both unpalatable and untenable to post-
Enlightenment humankind.

Wrede's views are still very much on the table at the present hour;
to read his essay on New Testament theology, Morgan observes, "is
not to move far from the concerns of contemporary New Testament
scholarship."[10] Grasp of Wrede will also facilitate informed appraisal of
the salvation historical riposte and synthesis of Schlatter.

Wrede's conception of New Testament theology: Baur's approach furthered

The importance of Wrede's remarks on New Testament theology is
reflected, not only in his enduring influence through Bultmann, but
also in J.M. Robinson's statement that "we should simply concede
Wrede to have been right and hence deny any future to New Testament theology."[11] Robinson wants to follow Wrede's belief that New

---

[7] H. Rollmann, "Wrede, William (1859–1906)," *Historical Handbook of Major Biblical Interpreters*, 1998, 396.

[8] Mark D. Chapman, "Religion, Ethics, and the History of Religion School," *SJT* 46 (1993) 78. Rollmann, *Historical Handbook of Major Biblical Interpreters*, 396, points out that many members of the history of religion school "expected a revivification of Protestantism" from their "vitalist understanding of biblical religion."

[9] Noted e.g. by Lüdemann, "Die Religionsgeschichtliche Schule und ihre Konsequenzen für die Neutestamentliche Wissenschaft," *Kulturprotestantismus*, ed. K. Müller, 1992, 315.

[10] Morgan, "Re-Reading Wrede," *ExpTim* 108 (1997) 207.

[11] Robinson, "The Future of New Testament Theology," *RelSRev* 2 (1976) 20. On Wrede's significance see also, in addition to works cited in footnotes just above, Hasel,

Testament theology can rightly be no more than the "early Christian history of religion" or perhaps "the history of early Christian religion and theology."[12] States Robinson from his Wredian perspective: "We should surrender any pretense [in doing "New Testament theology"] to be presenting anything that can lay a claim on modern times."[13] This point of view has been articulated more recently by G. Lüdemann: "a history of early Christianity must displace ... a theology of the New Testament."[14] It is also a staple conviction informing Räisänen's *Beyond New Testament Theology*.[15] If the proposals of this school of thought prevail, it appears that not only salvation historical New Testament theology but the discipline in general faces hard times ahead. Investigation of Wrede's proposals are obviously in order.

We limit ourselves below to drawing three lines of comparison between Wrede and Baur. This is not to overlook the significant differences in their respective methods. For example, the "doctrinal concepts" (*Lehrbegriffe*) emphasis which Baur popularized (and which B. Weiss later made the basis of his important New Testament theology) comes in for scathing criticism from Wrede. But is to recognize that certain of Baur's emphases, questioned by Hofmann, are built upon by Wrede and will be called in question by Schlatter. This is part of a continuing bifurcation between two approaches to New Testament theology. Wrede joins those who see salvation history as a construct having no place in the modern discussion.

1. The truth behind the texts

Wrede's position
Wrede, like Baur, focuses not on the New Testament texts but on that which gave rise to them. Wrede wants *"to know what was believed, thought, taught, hoped, required, and striven for"* in the earliest period of Christianity; not what certain writings say about faith, doctrine, hope,

New Testament Theology, 43ff.; Merk, *Anfangszeit*, 245-248; Kraus, *Biblische Theologie*, 163-166; G. Strecker, "William Wrede," *ZTK* 57 (1960) 67-91; H. Boers, *What Is New Testament Theology?*, 1979, 39-66; J. Schreiber, "William Wrede als Aufklärer," *Theologie als Aufklärung*, ed. W. Müller & H. Schulz, Würzburg 1992, 285–297; Adams, *Making Sense of New Testament Theology*, *passim*; Morgan, *ExpTim* 108 (1997) 207–210; Räisänen, *Beyond New Testament Theology*, 13-18.
[12]See Wrede, *NNTT*, 116; *PTNT*, 153f.
[13]Robinson, *RelSRev* 2 (1976) 20.
[14]G. Lüdemann, "Die 'Religionsgeschichtliche Schule' und die Neutestamentliche Wissenschaft," *Die "Religionsgeschichte Schule"*, 20.
[15]Noted, e.g., in N.T. Wright's review of the first edition: *TS* 43 (1993) 626.

etc."[16] In New Testament theology, "with a few exceptions, *the writers' personalities and the writings as such are not important, but very subsidiary matters.*"[17] Taken on their own, the following writings are of only pre-liminary and peripheral interest to New Testament theology: Mark and Matthew ("so far as they do not merely codify the tradition"), Luke-Acts, 1 and 2 Peter, Jude, James, the Pastorals, Ephesians, Reve-lation, and Hebrews.[18] At most they provide *the material with the help of which it is possible to conceive the physiognomy and clarify the historical development of the earliest Christianity which lies behind them.*"[19] This points to the fact that for Wrede "the norms governing the presenta-tion [of a New Testament theology] are ... not the writings but the decisive ideas, problems, and spiritual or intellectual phenomena."[20] This leaves Jesus' preaching, Paul's beliefs, and the Johannine material as the "solid entities" from which to work[21]—although just how "solid" Wrede views the Fourth Gospel to be may be seen in this statement:

> If one views [John's] chief intention as the transmission of actual history, many features of the narrative become practically grotesque and ridiculous. Historically speaking, the following features, and many others, are simply pure impossibilities: that Jesus interacted with the Jews regarding his execu-tion or the Last Supper; that he discussed Johannine theology with the Roman procurator; that his simplest words met with the most massive mis-understanding; that in prayers to God he used dogmatic formulations or reflections on the working of prayer on those who listened to him. How-ever, whoever recognizes that the author is led by intentions entirely different than historical ones, that it is his ideas and biases which reshape and idealize the received material and add numerous traditions to it—that person learns to understand why so much must strike us as strange and odd, so delusional and removed from reality ... The battle over the historical value of the Fourth Gospel may well rage on as previously: nevertheless, we must finally get beyond always looking at the ineptitude of the historical

---

[16]Wrede, *NNTT*, 84f.; *PTNT*, 109. Wrede's emphasis throughout.

[17]*NNTT*, 85; *PTNT*, 109.

[18]*NNTT*, 85-89; *PTNT*, 109-115.

[19]*NNTT*, 89; *PTNT*, 115. Rollmann notes that Wrede's stress on development of religious traditions rather than the doctrine found in documents stemmed from history of religion mentor A. Eichhorn (*Historical Handbook of Major Biblical Interpreters*, 395, 397).

[20]*NNTT*, 90; *PTNT*, 115.

[21]*NNTT*, 87; *PTNT*, 112.

outward form. We must look at that which the author, with grandiose indifference to the actually material, wanted to <u>teach</u> and <u>defend</u>.[22]

Ignatius is "more deserving" than any of these of separate treatment, since he "typifies, and for us in many ways especially embodies, personal Christianity at the beginning of the second century."[23] Wrede's point seems to be that Ignatius' distance from problematic early Christian doctrinal formulation makes his testimony more credible than those writings traditionally linked more directly to Christianity's beginning stages.

Morgan speaks of Wrede's "sharp <u>distinction</u> between the <u>literary sources</u> and the historical subject-matter."[24] Wrede's "chief emphasis" is that the historian of early Christianity "*is concerned with what lies behind the sources*" in terms of the <u>history of religion</u>,[25] not what the texts say on particulars.[26] Traditionally the New Testament texts have lent themselves to being understood as examples of and resources for theological reflection and construction. Their contents are descriptive of God, Jesus Christ, soteriology, and the like and not just traditions tangential to these matters. Theology or theologically significant history is read off the texts. The writers are regarded as referring to realities which, according to their perception, really <u>did exist or function as</u> portrayed. Wrede, like Baur, rejects this <u>conception</u>. There are unquestionably gaps in our knowledge about New Testament theology,[27] but we do know this: the texts are secondary to that which gave rise to them.

Wrede's reasoning here has ostensible grounding in historical fact: "The New Testament writings can by no means be temporally located in the apostolic age."[28] This means that an explanation for the New Testament texts must be sought that goes beyond that given on the

---

[22]Wrede, "Charakter und Tendenz des Johannesevangeliums," *Vorträge und Studien*, 230f.

[23]*NNTT*, 89; *PTNT*, 114f.

[24]Morgan, *NNTT*, 12; cf. Wrede, *NNTT*, 84f.; *PTNT*, 108f.

[25]Morgan, *NNTT*, 12.

[26]J. Schreiber's claim that Wrede practically shared Luther's own high view of Scripture needs more nuancing ("William Wrede als Aufklärer," *Theologie als Aufklärung*, 294f.).

[27]Wrede, *NNTT*, 97; *PTNT*, 126.

[28]*NNTT*, 71; *PTNT*, 86: While Wrede rejects many specifics of Baur's reconstruction, he clings to the basic chronological assumption that the writings are temporally remote from what they report. Cf. more fully Wrede's *Die Entstehung der Schriften des Neuen Testaments*, 1907.

surface of the texts, which might indeed give the appearance to the
unwary reader that apostolic-age phenomena are being referred to.
Scholars plying new methods must supply the rational explanation for
the New Testament writings which they, despite their promising appearance, conceal.

Radical relativization of New Testament data

The New Testament is thus to be read, not in a Christian theological
context, but in the openly anti-metaphysical context of history of religion thinking, (see further discussion below). This entails as a
methodological first step the radical relativizing of all New Testament
data. Thus Wrede speaks of the "proper context" for interpreting a
New Testament writing as being "the whole world of related ideas,"
in which "it is easy to estimate its value and show where it belongs."[29]
He describes his approach to New Testament theology as "always both
genetic and comparative ... Every historical datum is only made comprehensible so far as we are able to set it in the context out of which it
has grown."[30] And for Wrede, there is absolutely nothing distinctive or
unique about the context (or the content) of the early Christian writings, which he understands in terms of "a living plant out of religious
history" which "has grown according to the same inner laws which
today and always govern the emergence of ideas, concepts, and conceptions."[31]

Specifically, this means that "the main presuppositions of all early
Christian intellectual construction... are all the result of development
on Jewish soil immediately prior to Christianity."[32] Wrede underscores
his point by a graphic analogy. He likens the New Testament to a
hypothetical collection of documents discovered in AD 3897—2,000
years from Wrede's own time—relating to the nineteenth century
social democratic movement and consisting of

> two popular biographies of Lasalle, an academic treatise of Marx, a few let-
> ters of Lasalle, Engels and one or two unknown workers active as agitators;
> then a few pamphlets two or three pages long and finally a socialist inflam-
> matory writing describing the socialist picture of heaven upon earth.[33]

[29]Wrede, *NNTT*, 91; *PTNT*, 124.
[30]*NNTT*, 96; *PTNT*, 124.
[31]*NNTT*, 96f.; *PTNT*, 125.
[32]*NNTT*, 114; *PTNT*, 151.
[33]*NNTT*, 82; *PTNT*, 103f.

Conclusion

Wrede in naturalistic fashion posits a closed-system nexus and then assays to explain the life behind the New Testament texts in terms amenable to this premise. This presupposes, as Morgan points out, the Enlightenment juxtaposition of religion and theology.[34] It also assumes that New Testament theology is rightfully conceived as history of religion on the basis that Wrede's "own liberal Protestant systematic position involved the substitution of the history of religion for traditional orthodox theology."[35] Without passing judgment here on the tenability of these bases, we would simply reiterate that Wrede sees New Testament theology's task as eliciting, from what are stubborn and even deceptive sources, the underlying, naturalistically conceived religio-historical factors which brought them into being. In this respect he is not far from the methodological starting point of Baur, the chief difference lying in Baur's stress on the Idea itself over against Wrede's focus on the phenomena or traditions through which the ideal or typical comes into view.

Baur wanted Idea.
Wrede wanted history of religion.

2. Methodological exclusivity

Wrede, like Baur, claims exclusivity for his approach to New Testament theology. This seems to follow from his relativizing of the New Testament documents, which has the effect of making the testimony of the sources of little more weight than our own ideas—if not indeed of somewhat less. The reduction of the New Testament documents to the raw material for an a- or anti-theological "historical" reconstruction enthrones Wrede's critical method and implies dogmatic certainty for its results.

It is unavoidable that the conception of the subject matter of a discipline will in large measure determine the shape of the discipline. It is therefore understandable, given the flattened-out radically contingent nexus in which Wrede places the New Testament, that he finds no theology at all in it and banishes all theological relevance and even interest from New Testament theology as a discipline. Theology in any traditional sense implies some form of revelation, i.e., personal self-disclosure of the transcendent, and personal divine revelation has no place in the kind of philosophically naturalistic system that Wrede assumes.[36]

---

[34]Morgan, *NNTT*, 24.

[35]*Ibid.* 22.

[36]Wrede explicitly excludes all possible divine connection with the New Testament historical phenomena in *Entstehung*, 2. This attitude appears to have been requisite for

To delimit one's scope of analysis and assess data from a particular perspective is not only permissible but necessary. But Wrede does not set forth his as simply one possible starting point. He claims exclusivity for his approach. He recognizes that some will take issue with his conception of New Testament theology as having absolutely no theological interest; yet he is firm that whatever practical store some might set by scripture, the "investigation of historical reality has its own laws."[37] He castigates methods which are, unlike his own, "unable to recognize ... the difference between what is historically important and what is not."[38] Whatever arguments one might advance for ameliorating the apparent inflexibility of Wrede's method, "it does not follow ... that our view of the task is incorrect, or that there are several equally possible and equally necessary methods of doing it."[39]

Wrede adopts a methodological posture to end all methodological posturing. "The *Wredestrasse* ... bills itself as the only road to New Testament theology."[40] This too is reminiscent of Baur.

3. From historicism to positivism

Wrede, like Baur, uncritically accepts a given modern worldview as the criterion by which the New Testament data are to be conceived both in their particulars and in their totality. We showed above how Baur subordinated the testimony of ancient views to his own Kantian, Hegelian, and rationalistic ones. His method is fairly termed historicistic. Wrede, some forty years down the line in a Germany which has rejected Baur's metaphysician Hegel and developed a new taste for Kant,[41] is clearly positivistic. We understand positivism generally in the following terms:

> The characteristic theses of positivism are that science is the only valid knowledge and facts the only possible objects of knowledge; that philosophy [and thus New Testament theology to the extent that it seeks to be philosophically responsible in its method] does not possess a method differ-

being regarded as "critical" and "scientific" in Wrede's university and even ecclesiastical setting; see Schlatter's response to this stance in his essay "Atheistische Methoden in der Theologie," available in English translation in W. Neuer, *Adolf Schlatter*, 1995, 211–225. Wrede attributes this rejection of "supernaturalism" to the history of religion school (*Vorträge und Studien*, 66).

[37] *NNTT*, 73; *PTNT*, 90.

[38] *NNTT*, 81; *PTNT*, 102.

[39] *NNTT*, 94; *PTNT*, 122.

[40] Adam, *Making Sense of New Testament Theology*, 3.

[41] See T. Willey, *Back to Kant: The Revival of Kantianism in German Social and Historical Thought, 1860-1914*, 1978.

ent from science; and that the task of philosophy is to find the general principles common to all the sciences and to use these principles ... Positivism,
consequently, denies the existence or intelligibility of forces or substances
that go beyond facts and the laws ascertained by science. It opposes any
kind of metaphysics and, in general, any procedure that is not reducible to
scientific method.[42]

Some of Wrede's statements already cited point to the positivistic
thrust of his program.[43] His commitment to this outlook is further
demonstrated when he states, "Biblical theology investigates the New
Testament writings first of all *without presuppositions* to find out the
content of the biblical religion."[44] The claim to lack presuppositions
may be the surest proof that one is beholden to them. In any case,
New Testament theology, "like every other real science ..., has its goal
simply in itself, and is totally indifferent to all dogma and systematic
theology."[45] Its task is "to lay out the history of early Christian religion
and theology"[46]; and it is evident that by "history" Wrede is speaking
of critically reconstructed history, "critical" harking back to Kant in
the same fashion that it did for Baur.

The point is that Wrede, like Baur,[47] runs the risk of failing to do
justice to the data he interprets. For his positivistic viewpoint, accom-
plishing much by definition,[48] methodologically rejects the possibility
that the texts are to be read in the theological context felt by many to
be inherent to them.

It is true that in modern times "most New Testament scholars have
allowed their world-view and historical method to be given them by
their culture,"[49] and in this Wrede is neither unusual nor necessarily

[42]N. Abbagnano, "Positivism," *The Encyclopedia of Philosophy,* vol. 6, ed. P. Edwards, 1972, 414-419.

[43]Wrede's positivism is also highlighted in G. Lüdemann, "Das Wissenschaftsverständnis der Religionsgeschichtlichen Schule im Rahmen des Kulturprotestantismus,
Kulturprotestantismus, 82f. with n. 18.

[44]*NNTT,* 183 n. 4; *PTNT,* 83 n. 3. Emphasis mine. Rollmann, *Historical Handbook
of Major Biblical Interpreters,* 395, notes that those holding the history of religion viewpoint "were imbued with the nineteenth century ethos for 'presuppositionless'
historical-critical research."

[45]*NNTT,* 69 *PTNT,* 83.

[46]*NNTT,* 84; *PTNT,* 108.

[47]On the "historicism" as a component of history of religion inquiry see
M. Murrmann-Kahl, *Die entzauberte Heilsgeschichte,* 1992, 8. Wrede does not so much
leave Baur behind as add new rules to his hermeneutic.

[48]M. Noll identifies nineteenth century modes of inquiry that amounted to "science
that seemed to accomplish ... much by definition" (*Between Faith and Criticism,* 1991, 34).

[49]Morgan, *NNTT,* 27; cf. Donahue, *TS* 50/2 (1989) 335.

culpable. It is significant, however, that he so fully identifies with a worldview fundamentally antithetical to the surface testimony of the texts whose "life" he earnestly seeks to grasp. As Reventlow notes, critical tools have their place in biblical interpretation, but they are "wrongly deployed if we use them to nullify the claim that the divine Word in Scripture makes on us by obscuring it with our ideological guidelines."[50]

In what sense is Wrede's standpoint a defensible position from which to arrive at a synthetic grasp of the New Testament? This is a question which we must wait for Schlatter to take up below; for now we turn to pertinent aspects of Wrede's epistemology. This will help explain something of the cause and effect of Wrede's willingness to go along with the *Zeitgeist* under the influence of which he wrote.

Ramifications of Wrede's epistemology

Like Baur Wrede operates very much within the limits of a Kantian, or more properly neo-Kantian, outlook.[51] Wrede does not specify his philosophical leanings in detail, but they are implicit in his participation in the history of religion school, whose systematician[52] was Ernst Troeltsch (1865–1923).[53] Troeltsch "was sure that the criteria of his-

[50]"Wurzeln der modernen Bibelkritik," *Historische Kritik und biblischer Kanon in der deutschen Aufklärung*, 63.

[51]For a definition of neo-Kantianism see e.g. Willey, *Back to Kant*, especially 37, 180. In historical terms we understand it here basically as the "revolt of scientists against discredited idealism and naive positivism" (*ibid.*, 74) which characterized much German thought in the late nineteenth and early twentieth centuries. Cf. Schnädelbach, *Philosophy*, 105f. R.A. Johnson rightly laments: "With few exceptions, modern theology and philosophy have ignored the legacy of Neo-Kantianism. The dearth of philosophical discussion of this tradition represents a great loss for theology. For the philosophical roots of mid-twentieth century theology are firmly embedded in Marburg Neo-Kantianism" (*The Origins of Demythologizing*, 1974, 40f.). Troeltsch's (Wrede's) Kantianism had a social science basis associated with Baden rather than the mathematical basis found in Marburg. But the approaches shared common features.

[52]Murrmann-Kahl, *Die entzauberte Heilsgeschichte*, 353–364, provides extensive discussion of the extent of this appellation's aptness. Murrmann-Kahl documents a powerful tension between Troeltsch, on the one hand, and history of religion exegetes, on the other. Only in a loose sense can exegetes like Wrede be counted in the same "school" as a de facto dogmatician like Troeltsch. But since the term "history of religions" from its inception was a term elastic enough to cover both the movement's exegetes and its philosophers, we understand the term in its extended, if technically imprecise, sense here.

[53]Helpful for introduction to Troeltsch is H.G. Drescher, "Ernst Troeltsch's intellectual development," in *Ernst Troeltsch and the Future of Theology*, ed. J.P. Clayton,

torical interpretation were, owing to the Kantian limits of empirical knowledge, necessarily immanent ones."[54] We wish to show that Wrede's approach to New Testament theology, upholding Baur's precedent, subordinates the content of the New Testament texts to his implicit theory of knowledge.

1. Background
Troeltschian immanent criticism

We must first take a closer look at Troeltsch, for his thought contains the rationale which informs Wrede's program. Troeltsch advocated an "immanent criticism." This means that "historical formations," e.g. the New Testament taken as a whole, are assessed or criticized "in terms of the ideal which lies within their main driving force."[55] In other words: "the historical is measured by the historical, the individual formation is measured against the spirit of the whole conceived intuitively and imaginatively."[56]

Troeltsch conceives of "a theology based upon the history of religion" in the heritage of the Deists, Lessing, Kant, Herder, Schleiermacher, de Wette, Hegel, and Baur. Yet he wants to transcend mere rationalism and dispense with "the Hegelian dialectic of the Absolute."[57] In relation to the New Testament texts (or a history or theology derived from them) this means that "the quasi-history of supernatural interventions must be abandoned in favour of real history, based as this is upon critical evaluation of the sources and reconstruc-

---

1976, 3-32. Succinct, translated primary sources yielding entrée into his thought include Troeltsch, "The Dogmatics of the 'Religonsgeschichtliche Schule'," *AJT* 17 (1913) 1-21; *idem*, "Historiography," *Encyclopedia of Religion and Ethics*, ed. J. Hastings, 1922, 716–723; *idem*, "Historical and Dogmatic Method in Theology," *The Historical Jesus Quest*, ed. G. Dawes, 1999, 29–53.

[54]Willey, *Back to Kant*, 159. This remains true despite Drescher's attempt to show that Troeltsch left room for "divine impulses" to manifest themselves in human activity (Drescher, "Troeltsch's development," in *Troeltsch and Theology*, ed. Clayton, 11). Troeltsch's actual openness to the transcendent in history must be adjudged very limited.

[55]Troeltsch, "What Does 'Essence of Christianity' Mean?" in *Ernst Troeltsch*, ed. Morgan & Pye, 1990, 142.

[56]*Ibid.*

[57]Troeltsch, *Gesammelte Schriften*, vol. 2, 738, cited in Morgan, "Introduction," *Ernst Troeltsch*, ed. Morgan & Pye, 10. Yet Troeltsch speaks positively of "Hegelian ethics and philosophy of history" when it comes to historical value judgments ("Historiography," *Encyclopedia of Religion and Ethics*, 722). See R. Morgan, "Some recent works on Troeltsch," *RelSRev* 17 (1991) 328.

tion with the help of the principle of analogy."[58] Troeltsch casts his hermeneutical lot with a "modern historical reflexion" which "consists, precisely like the modern conception of Nature, in a purely scientific attitude to facts"; this "forms a new scientific mode of representing man and his development and, as such, shows at all points an absolute contrast to the Biblico-theological views of later antiquity."[59] "For Troeltsch the implications of epistemological relativity and historical relativism" required "a reformulation of the central doctrines of the Christian faith; this was Troeltsch's theological project."[60]

In this way Troeltsch effected a "massive critical reduction" of a traditional understanding of the biblical texts.[61] For him "the historical method has eliminated any distinction between a higher and lower order or reality," or "between what is eternal and permanent, and what is changing and conventional."[62] Here Troeltsch defies not only traditional theology but also much of the classical philosophical tradition.[63]

In addition, Troeltsch based understanding of the past on a religious *a priori* of Kantian derivation[64] which

is responsible for all findings and conclusions. In the absence of traditional metaphysical distinctions, the divine is found in the human; there is assumed a presence of the divine in the conscientious search of the individual for meaning. Assuming the presence of the spirit of God in the world, reli-

---

[58]Morgan, "Introduction," *Ernst Troeltsch,* ed. Morgan & Pye, 15, citing Troeltsch, *Das historische in Kants Religionsphilosophie,* 1904, 134.

[59]Troeltsch, "Historiography," *Encyclopedia of Religion and Ethics,* 718.

[60]T. Hogan, "The Quest for the Historical Essence of Ernst Troeltsch," *Pacifica* 7 (1994) 295.

[61]Morgan, "Introduction," *Ernst Troeltsch,* ed. Morgan & Pye, 30.

[62]M. Quigley, "Ernst Troeltsch and the Historical Absolute," *HeyJ* 24 (1983) 23.

[63]Quigley, *HeyJ* 24 (1983) 23. In defense of Troeltsch see G. Rupp, *Culture Protestantism: German Liberal Theology at the Turn of the Twentieth Century,* 1977, 25: "There is ... no tenable alternative to one or another variation of Culture-Protestantism [the rubric under which the views of most Ritschlian, post-Ritschlian, and history of religion thinkers of the time, including Troeltsch, are normally grouped] since there is no theological standpoint divorced from human culture. Accordingly, a comparative and critical version of Culture-Protestantism and its equivalents in other traditions—a position like the one Troeltsch's approach represents—is a matter of conviction also in the positive rather than only in the negative sense of the word."

[64]Troeltsch's Baden Neo-Kantianism was "an attempt to find a basis for historical knowledge in a strictly transcendental philosophy in the Kantian sense" (Schnädelbach, *Philosophy,* 56f.).

gious intuition, rather than what is found objectively in the past, becomes the center of focus.[65]

Morgan states this differently in remarking that "Troeltsch hoped to show that the formation of religious ideas was grounded in the structure of human reason itself."[66] Troeltsch describes this religious absolute, "the philosophical substitute for the dogmatic supernaturalism of the church," as "the perfect self-comprehension of the idea that strives for complete clarity, the self-realization of God in the human consciousness."[67]

All this yields insight into some basic features of his outlook, which Wrede echoes in synthesizing the New Testament. He mirrors Troeltsch's neo-Kantian commitments at significant points with the result that "the modern secular world... determines the way theology should be done,"[68] in this case New Testament theology. Morgan thinks that Troeltsch's drive to arrive at "formulations of the essence of Christianity" ought surely to have been "seeking to preserve as much as possible of what earlier generations considered essential, not jettisoning this wholesale."[69] But neither Troeltsch nor Wrede show much sympathy for or interest in the theology that readers and worshipers for centuries had found in the biblical sources. As L. Johnson notes, "The distinctive and noteworthy virtues of the history-of-religions approach ... were ultimately vitiated by its captivity to the dominant paradigm within which it operated."[70]

Neo-Kantianism's appeal

Before examining Wrede further, we should in all fairness note historical factors in Germany which render his (and Troeltsch's) allegiance to Kantian or neo-Kantian ideology at least partially understandable. In mid-nineteenth century Germany the philosophical scene was comparable to "a battlefield strewn with corpses and debris."[71] Hegelianism had broken down, yielding to a radically empiricist materialism which by the 1850s and -60s "became virtually a metaphysical cult."[72] Many

---

[65]Quigley, *HeyJ* 24 (1983) 23; cf. Drescher, "Troeltsch's Development," in *Troeltsch and the Future*, ed. Clayton, 21.

[66]Morgan, "Introduction," *Ernst Troeltsch*, ed. Morgan & Pye, 20.

[67]Troeltsch, *The Absoluteness of Christianity and the History of Religions,* 1971, 55.

[68]Morgan, "Introduction," *Ernst Troeltsch*, ed. Morgan & Pye, 7; cf. Quigley, *HeyJ* 24 (1983) 23.

[69]*RelSRev* 17 (1991) 329.

[70]*Religious Experience in Earliest Christianity*, 1998, 19.

[71]Willey, *Back to Kant*, 24; cf. Schnädelbach, *Philosophy,* 51.

[72]Willey, *Back to Kant*, 25.

Hegelianism — dialectic
Kant — radical empiricism materialism

thinkers who were not content with this crass new scienticism turned
back to Kant, who, it was thought, had succeeded in harmonizing
science and philosophy.[73] This had been, to be sure, Kant's own contention.[74] From the middle of the nineteenth century onwards Kant's
basic dualism[75] served as an epistemological starting point attractive to
religious thinkers, because

> it preserved an "unknowable" noumenal domain for the regulative ideas of
> God, freedom, and immortality transcending natural laws. Men of scientific
> disposition could have at the same time both their faith and their science,
> because Kant's theory of knowledge gave full justice to the phenomenal
> domain governed by the mechanical principle of causality. Kant's dualism
> was, to many German thinkers, an appealing compromise in an age of tran-
> sition from Christian belief to a wholly naturalistic view of the universe. To
> the extent that Kant had demolished the claims of metaphysics without de-
> nying the ultimate truths of religion, he also appealed to the skeptical
> temper of a generation disenchanted with speculative philosophy and en-
> amored of physical science but not yet ready to jettison its transcendental
> beliefs altogether.[76]

The resulting neo-Kantian option became the major viable alternative for critical thinkers unwilling totally to dispense with at least a
semblance of the Christian faith. Troeltsch himself was heavily indebted to Kant as well as to the early neo-Kantian Lotze, eventually
turning to the Baden neo-Kantians Windelband and Rickert.[77] Wrede
may be seen as explicitly assenting to the same general trend in
thought.

2. Resultant outlook
Absolutizing of modern viewpoint
Wrede's own "immanent criticism" is readily discernible. Historical
significance can be assigned to data only from within a history of religion perspective.[78] Interrelationships between New Testament material

[73]The path of other thinkers (Schopenhauer, Nietzsche, Marx) is sketched by C.
Sutton, "The Aftermath of German Idealism," *The German Tradition in Philosophy*,
1974, 77-110.

[74]See e.g. *Immanuel Kant's Critique of Pure Reason,* trans. N.K. Smith, 1950, 21f., 25f.

[75]Well summarized in Kant's celebrated statement, "I have therefore found it necessary to deny *knowledge* in order to make room for *faith*" (*ibid.* 29, his emphasis).

[76]Willey, *Back to Kant*, 26.

[77]Note Troeltsch's praise of them in pioneering "the return to the Kantian theory
of knowledge" so as to frame "a logic of historical reason" in "Historiography," *Encyclopedia of Religion and Ethics*, 719.

[78]Wrede, *NNTT*, 80f.; *PTNT*, 101.

which "are unimportant for the history of ideas—and that means most of the ones which can be traced [within the New Testament]—are irrelevant" for New Testament theology.[79] E.g. Wrede states that demonstrating

> that Pauline conceptions are echoed in the Gospel of Luke is really of little more interest to a history of early Christian belief than evidence of Schleiermacher's influence upon some third-rate theologian would be in a history of nineteenth-century theology.[80]

insulting

This is apparently because much of the New Testament is deemed unimportant or invalid based on our critical perception of religion.[81] This is in turn the standard by which we evaluate the New Testament texts, indeed religious phenomena of any description. Troeltsch stresses how specific historical data are to be "measured against the spirit of the whole conceived intuitively and imaginatively"; Wrede speaks of "the quintessence of historical understanding" as "being able to take control of [*bemächtigen*] the phenomena."[82]

The problem is that Wrede risks reading a foreign meaning into the New Testament texts by assuming that no meaning can inhere in them except for that furnished in advance by a history of religion or Troeltschian outlook. The New Testament theologian is tempted so to "take control" of the data that they yield the picture to which his absolutized *a priori* most readily corresponds. We recall Kant's dictum that "*objects must be viewed as conforming to human thought, not human thought to the independently real.*"[83] This principle, not historical observation in an empirical sense, may go far toward explaining the "historical" reading of the New Testament Wrede envisions. This would be consistent with Troeltsch's example, who "in his reading of the New Testament" projects the "subjectivist Protestantism of modernity onto Jesus and the early church."[84]

[79] *NNTT*, 81; *PTNT*, 101.

[80] *NNTT*, 187 n. 131; *PTNT*, 107 n. 30.

[81] This is how Troeltsch wished his synthesis to be understood. In reality history of religion "for Troeltsch amounts to the present's normative interest in determining the content of Christianity in comparison with the so-called world religions, namely with Buddhism" (Murrmann-Kahl, *Die entzauberte Heilsgeschichte*, 354.

[82] *NNTT*, 110; *PTNT*, 144f.

[83] Smith, *Commentary to Kant's "Critique,"* 18 (his emphasis); cf. *Kant's Critique of Pure Reason*, 22.

[84] A. Rasmusson, "Historicizing the Historicist: Ernst Troeltsch and Recent Mennonite Theology," *The Wisdom of the Cross*, 1999, 225.

Texts' message potentially repressed

Troeltschian overtones sound in Wrede also when he speaks of "the historically normative views" on a New Testament concept which New Testament theology (history of religion) ought to produce.[85] Take the concept of sin. Wrede differentiates between how sin is spoken of in various New Testament texts on the one hand and what role the concept had "in the early Christian understanding of salvation and of Christian life" on the other.[86] It seems hard to understand how Wrede can be so optimistic about finding a "normative" view by which to evaluate the texts when he at the outset sets aside the literary evidences as being the arbiters, or at least main witnesses, in establishing the normative. But then Wrede sets forth his "presupposition" that "the type is far more important than the variant and that the individual conceptions and interpretations are at most points quite insignificant in comparison with the general, widespread views that influence the individual cases."[87] In another context he speaks of seeing "the frame which supports an entire development, and that is more important than the individual facts within the framework."[88] Wrede feels capable, it seems, of determining, not so much on the basis of the New Testament evidence as on that of modern thought, the typical or general which he can then in turn use to sift and assess the individual and specific.

A very similar procedure is outlined by Troeltsch, who speaks of "comparing the most important elements and values of the main religious orientations, ranking them in accordance with a criterion of value, and subsuming them under the idea of a common goal."[89] Troeltsch concedes that the criterion being used here is "a matter of personal conviction and is in the last analysis admittedly subjective."[90] But he is confident that such subjectivity in historical thinking will not lead to skepticism and nihilism—"as long, at least, as the continuity of our culture endures."[91]

---

[85] *NNTT*, 90; *PTNT*, 117.

[86] *Ibid.*

[87] *Ibid.*; cf. *NNTT*, 77 (*PTNT*, 96f.): "There can be no question here in the New Testament of marking off the meaning of a concept according to every possible individual passage."

[88] *NNTT*, 100; *PTNT*, 129.

[89] Troeltsch, *The Absoluteness of Christianity and the History of Religionss*, 94f.

[90] *Ibid.* 96.

[91] *Ibid.* 94. Troeltsch could not foresee that such culture-optimism in Europe would come to an end so hideously with World War I.

Bearing this in mind, and returning to Wrede, the conclusion is inescapable that his "historical" approach to New Testament theology makes only a limited attempt to let the New Testament texts speak on their own terms. It is predetermined at the methodological level that the texts' subject matter will conform to the understanding from which Wrede begins. His approach subjects the texts to a historical-relativist outlook, which freely applies its modern cultural and ideological understanding as the norm of what the New Testament texts present. As B. Gerrish notes, "historical thinking" in the Troeltschian mode excludes "in principle ... at the outset that Christianity is distinguished from all other religions as the sole recipient of an authoritative revelation, or as the object of a miraculous divine activity that is unparalleled in any other religious history."[93] If the primary sources claim otherwise, so much the worse for the sources.

Summary: historical goals endangered

We are not arguing that Wrede set forth his program for New Testament theology with tomes from Kant and Troeltsch open before him. But the implications of Kantian or neo-Kantian thought, demonstrably mediated to Wrede through the history of religion school, are basic to his presentation. It is fair to say that his utterances on New Testament theology are informed, if not determined, by a theory of knowledge (along with assumptions about religion[94]) whose suitability for application to the New Testament he does not question.

Nor are we arguing that Wrede intentionally set out to subjugate the New Testament to his own whims by neo-Kantian artifices. He simply believed that theological concerns are from the critical standpoint irrelevant to interpreting the New Testament writings as artifacts of "history" properly understood.[95] This means that "historical" analysis must prevail:

> The first thing which must be required of anyone who wishes to engage scientifically in New Testament theology is, accordingly, that he be capable of interest in historical research. He must be guided by a pure disinterested concern for knowledge, which accepts every really compelling result. He

[92]Troeltsch, *ibid.* 85, openly concedes that "the historical and the relative are identical." This fact can be "evaded only by one who has deliberately or instinctively thrown up a bulwark to defend Christianity from the modern study of history."

[93]"Errors and Insights in the Understanding of Revelation: A Provisional Response," *Journal of Religion* 78 (1998) 69.

[94]See Chapman, *SJT* 46/1 (1993) 48.

[95]*NNTT*, 69; *PTNT*, 81f.

must be able to distinguish between the alien modern ideas of his own thought and those of the past. He must be able to keep his own viewpoint, however precious, quite separate from the object of his research and hold it in suspense. Then he will indeed know only what really was.[96]

This is surely a commendable goal, for Wrede as for von Ranke, although one which suffers by not taking into account "the relationship of the historian *himself* to his sources and subject-matter."[97] As Morgan notes more recently,

> Even within the framework proposed by Wrede, and setting aside the idea of revelation and any other theological commitments that the scholar might hold, historians of religion always work with some theory of religion, whether or not it is conscious or made explicit, and this affects their perception of this complex data. Wrede's hermeneutical innocence should be noted.[98]

It turns out that Wrede's involvement in a particular philosophical tradition, which he appears to view more as the self-evident truth of science than as a viewpoint, very much affects his ability to carry out his stated historical goals.

Wrede's approach to history

It would be possible to try to extrapolate more precisely from Wrede's remarks on New Testament theology to Troeltsch's systematic statements regarding history. This could yield some formal conception of Wrede's view of history. But it would also risk overreading Wrede, who does not appear to have self-consciously taken up and implemented a view of history in the same way that Baur is often suspected of doing.[99]

It will be more fruitful to limit ourselves to considering three assumptions Wrede makes, each of which contributes to an understanding of his view of history as it relates to New Testament theology.

[96]*NNTT*, 70; *PTNT*, 84.

[97]Morgan, *NNTT*, 21. Cf. Rollmann, *Historical Handbook of Major Biblical Interpreters*, 396, who includes Wrede among those who "never seriously took into account the subjectivity of the critical historian and interpreter." Cf. Baur in the previous chapter.

[98]*ExpTim* 108 (1997) 208.

[99]Boers rightly calls Wrede's conception of history "very ill defined" (*What Is New Testament Theology?* 57) but fails to probe the ideological background.

First, there is no "view of history" intrinsic to the New Testament texts themselves.[100] The New Testament is concerned far more with religion than with theology.[101] This means that the statements of the New Testament texts are primarily reflections of occasional religious outlook, seldom if ever normative theological deliverances that the scholar might incorporate into his work in order properly to assess the data. It follows that from the New Testament one could never deduce a unified view of history, particularly one that was theologically appraised. From Wrede's conception of the New Testament subject matter, a salvation historical reading of the texts would do violence to them, imputing to the documents a theological awareness, purpose, and inner consistency which, even if present, moderns could not accept as binding on them. The documents' temporal and ideological disparity is simply too great to elicit much unity of any kind from them—even if Wrede's focus as a New Testament theologian were the texts themselves, which, as we saw above, it is not.

Second, Wrede posits the most minimal of connections between the Old Testament and New Testament. He rejects the Old Testament as the primary background source for interpreting the New Testament.[102] Thus he criticizes B. Weiss for his handling of James' concept of election.[103] Wrede implies that Weiss has read far more into James' statement regarding God's election of the poor than the text of James will bear in its history of religion context. One notes that Weiss sees much Old Testament influence in James, and this is the basis for his interpretation of James understanding of election.[104] To Wrede this is simply ridiculous. Weiss' whole exposition of three pages can be "dismissed" and his use of *eklegesthai* in relation to the poor explained, not with the aid of the Old Testament, but by the history of religion observation that "at that time, if not every Christian, then at least all those who could speak like this of election, were angry about the pride and luxury of richness."[105]

Owing to Wrede's desire to read the New Testament without any dogmatic or theological considerations, he systematically cuts off its

---

[100]Contra e.g. I.H. Marshall, "Some Aspects of the Biblical View of History," *Faith and Thought* 110 (1983) 54–68; P. Satterthwaite, "Biblical History," *New Dictionary of Biblical Theology*, ed. T. Alexander and B. Rosner, 2000, 43–51. Cf. F. Watson, *Text and Truth*, 1997, 44.

[101]*NNTT*, 116; *PTNT*, 153.

[102]*NNTT*, 114; *PTNT*, 151.

[103]*NNTT*, 78; *PTNT*, 98.

[104]Cf. Weiss, *Lehrbuch*, 120ff., 184ff. Wrede's criticisms apply to the second passage.

[105]*NNTT*, 78; *PTNT*, 98.

apparent direct links to the Old Testament, even in a writer such as James who reflects many prophetic, wisdom, and other Hebrew or Jewish characteristics hard to account for apart from the Old Testament. The prospects for a fair handling of a corpus that cites and builds so extensively on the Old Testament under this assumption are hardly encouraging. But Wrede is determined to explain the New Testament statements in terms of first or second century religion, not the Old Testament writings (except in a sense determined by his understanding of first century Judaism). This accounts for the striking fact that in Wrede's renowned study of the messianic motif in the gospels, he cites only seven Old Testament references.[106] By way of comparison, he cites Justin Martyr—a second-century figure—some fifteen times.

Wrede asserts that "in a living tradition, almost every significant change of outlook is conditioned by processes in the history of religion and only very slightly by what is read."[107] How accurate this assertion is in relation to first century Palestinian Judaism (especially the synagogue) and early Christianity is disputable; it could be argued that the Old Testament played a formative and normative influence in both. Certainly there are indications that the Old Testament, in many ways over against much first century Judaism, conditioned Jesus' life and teachings.[108] Our point is that a salvation historical perspective is excluded for Wrede by his methodological exclusion of the Old Testament as a primary direct moving force for the development of New Testament belief. If no divine economy is visible from an Old Testament-New Testament connection, obviously none will be visible in early Christian writings themselves.

Third, Wrede assumes that the New Testament represents the fragmentary remains of an organic development rigidly analogous to "the same inner laws which today and always govern the emergence of ideas, concepts, and conceptions."[109] Here Troeltschian or history of religion influence is very much in evidence. The inner dynamic of the New Testament is not unique or even intrinsic to the New Testa-

---

[106] *Das Messiasgeheimnis in den Evangelien*, 1901.

[107] *NNTT*, 81; *PTNT*, 102.

[108] Would Wrede's statement hold true as a valid history of religion principle in view of the influence of the Koran in modern Islam? Laleh Bakhtiar states, "The Koran is really much more than an Islamic bible. Its significance makes it more like the person of Jesus Himself than like the Christian Bible" (cited in *Current Thoughts and Trends* 17/4 [April 2001] 37). For a fascinating account of classical writings' influence on the "living tradition" of English thought and life see R. Ogilvie, *Latin and Greek: A History of the Influence of the Classics on English Life from 1600–1918*, 1964.

[109] *NNTT*, 97; *PTNT*, 125.

ment. It is rather recognizable by, because it is intrinsic to, the modern understanding which perceives (and thereby establishes) the "inner laws" that determine historical development. This again spells the end for any salvation historical understanding of the New Testament, for it posits an immanent developmental reality whose identity, power, and value are a discovery or function of the modern critical mind, not something revealed to persons in past times.

In sum, Wrede's view of history is that common to the history of religion school. More will be said in the next chapter regarding the disrepute into which the concept of salvation history was falling at the time Wrede wrote due to the influence of this school of thought. W. Herrmann once wrote that Troeltsch was too much swayed, not by "the growth of dangerous results" generated by fresh scientific study of the biblical data in his time, but by "the method of science" as he articulated it.[110] Similarly it seems to be Wrede's method that plays a decisive role in excluding a salvation historical reconstruction of the New Testament data. Wrede's methodological remarks stand in direct contradiction to the proposals of Schlatter. We now turn to him in order to probe deeper into the characteristics of a salvation historical approach to New Testament theology, seen over against the views of Wrede which came to enjoy such wide favor within New Testament theology, especially through the work of Bultmann, and more recently through the resurgence of interest in Troeltsch.[111]

Schlatter and New Testament theology

1. The new perspective on Schlatter

In 1975 Schlatter specialist Werner Neuer could assert, "Adolf Schlatter's life and work are in many respects not yet sufficiently researched."[112] Given Schlatter's vast output, that statement may always be true. The Swiss *Neutestamentler* who spent most of his teaching

---

[110]Review of Troeltsch, *Die Bedeutung der Geschichtlichkeit Jesu für den Glauben*, reprinted in *ZTK* 57 (1960) 237.

[111]J.C.G. Greig's statement still holds true for many: "Wrede's *methodology* ... has remained determinative for New Testament work right up to the present" ("Translator's Preface," Wrede, *The Messianic Secret*, 1971, ix). Cf. Morgan, *RelSRev* 17 (1991) 327–331; Hogan, *Pacifica* 7 (1994) 304: "it is time [Troeltsch] was placed back on the curricula of theological colleges." Implicitly he has hardly been taken off.

[112]"Der Idealismus und die Erweckung in Schlatters Jugend," *ZKG* 96 (1975) 62.

career in German universities[113] has more than 440 published items to his credit.[114] Moreover, for many who have regarded themselves as "critical" thinkers "Schlatter had (and in many circles still has) the bad reputation of being a conservative, uncritical biblicistic theologian from whom there is little to learn regarding today's issues and debates."[115] Yet his impact on generations of German pastors and theologians was enormous,[116] and Schlatter's stock seems to be rising in contemporary discussion.[117] P. Stuhlmacher helped revive interest in him as the twentieth century drew to a close,[118] and major studies by Neuer have opened up his life and thought as never before.[119] Once little known in the Anglo-Saxon world[120] there is today fresh interest in his work, in part due to the excellent translations of his two-volume New Testament theology by Andreas Köstenberger.[121] Essays by Köstenberger[122] and Yarbrough[123] in these volumes situate Schlatter in

---

[113]Greifswald 1888–93, Berlin 1893–98, Tübingen 1898–1922. After mandatory retirement in 1922 he continued to exercise his right to give lectures in Tübingen until 1930.

[114]R. Brezger, *Das Schrifttum von Professor D.A. Schlatter*, n.d.; Adolf-Schlatter-Stiftung, ed., *Das Schrifttum Adolf Schlatters: Eine Bibliographie*, 1981. Note also W. Neuer, *Adolf Schlatter*, 1996, 823–841, which lists both unpublished and published sources.

[115]W. Härle, introduction to J. Walldorf, *Realistische Philosophie*, 1999, 5.

[116]Cf. I. Kindt, *Der Gedanke der Einheit*, 1978, 11, 155 n. c; A. Köberle, "Evangelium und Natur. Zur Theologie von Adolf Schlatter," *EvK* 10 (1977) 541.

[117]Note e.g. Walldorf, *Realistische Philosophie*; H.-M. Rieger, *Adolf Schlatters Rechtfertigungslehre und die Möglichkeit ökumenischer Verständigung*, 2000.

[118]Schlatter is the author cited more than any other in Stuhlmacher's *Vom Verstehen des Neuen Testaments*, 1979. See also Stuhlmacher, "Adolf Schlatter als Bibelausleger," *ZTK* Supplement 4 (1978) 81-111, a shorter version of which appears as "Adolf Schlatters Interpretation of Scripture," *NTS* 24 (1978) 433-446; and "Adolf Schlatter als Paulusausleger—ein Versuch," *TBei* 20/4 (1989) 176–190.

[119]In addition to Neuer's two biographies, a popular one translated into English and a critical one in German, both entitled *Adolf Schlatter*, see his *Der Zusammenhang von Dogmatik und Ethik bei Adolf Schlatter*, 1986.

[120]But see from years past W. Strunk, "The Theology of Adolf Schlatter," *The Lutheran Church Quarterly* 11 (1938) 395-402; H. Dymale, "The Theology of Adolf Schlatter with Special Reference to his Understanding of History," University of Iowa dissertation 1966; Morgan, *NNTT*; W. Gasque, "The Promise of Adolf Schlatter," *Evangelical Review of Theology* 4 (1980) 20-30; S.F. Dintaman, *Creative Grace*, 1993.

[121]Vol. 1: *The History of the Christ*; vol. 2: *The Theology of the Apostles*, 1997–99.

[122]"Schlatter's Appeal," *The History of the Christ*, 9–15.

[123]"Modern Reception of Schlatter's New Testament Theology," *The Theology of the Apostles*, 417–431. See also articles on Schlatter by Yarbrough in *Historical Handbook of Major Bible Interpreters*, ed. D. McKim, 1998, 518-522; *Biblical Interpreters of the Twen-*

current discussion. F. Neugebauer has likewise called attention to his importance.[124] Perhaps the best introduction to Schlatter is any of four of his autobiographical works.[125] Schlatter's life itself offers fascinating glimpses of intellectual history: how many other major New Testament scholars learned philosophy at the feet of Friedrich Nietzsche?[126]

Before bringing Wrede and Schlatter into dialogue, we must describe the latter's New Testament theology and selected chief features.

2. *Method of a New Testament theology*
Integration of New Testament life and thought-world into concrete history

REAL
HISTORY

Schlatter approaches New Testament theology with the conviction that the ideas and concepts of the New Testament are components in a concrete and living history. They take on significance and meaning when seen in the context of the lives of those who recorded them. The thoughts, ideas, or traditions lying behind the New Testament— with which both Baur and Wrede are virtually exclusively concerned—must be seen in close connection with the individual events, temporal actions, and actual lives which give them substance. Agreeing with Wrede though not Baur, Schlatter holds that the teaching of the New Testament in the sense of "doctrinal concepts" (*Lehrbegriffe*) cannot serve as the sole focus of New Testament theology. For this teaching is not set forth as a deposit of lore abstracted from the resolve and activity of the individuals through whom the teaching comes. It is not isolated from the concrete situations, both individual and social, from which the teaching comes into view.[127] J.H. Schmid gives sound advice: one must never forget that "for Schlatter history is not mental history."[128] As Schlatter explains, "There is, to be sure, no history

tieth Century: A Selection of Evangelical Voices, ed. W. Elwell & J. Weaver, 1999, 59–72; *The Dictionary of Historical Theology*, ed. T. Hart, 505–507.

[124]"Wer war Adolf Schlatter?" *TLZ* 122/9 (1997) 770–782.

[125]I.e., *Die Entstehung der "Beiträge zur Förderung christlicher Theologie" und ihr Zusammenhang mit meiner theologischen Arbeit zum Beginn ihres 25. Bandes,* 1920; *Erlebtes,* [5]1929; "Adolf Schlatter," *Die Religionswissenschaft der Gegenwart in Selbstdarstellungen,* ed. E. Stange, vol. 1, 1925, 145-171; *Rückblick auf meine Lebensarbeit,* [2]1977.

[126]Neuer, *Adolf Schlatter,* 1996, 64f.

[127]Schlatter, *Die Geschichte des Christus,* [3]1977, 5. This is volume one of his two volume New Testament theology. The first edition (1909), though not the second (1923 = [3]1977), carried the subtitle "Das Wort Jesu." The second edition was considerably altered.

[128]J.H. Schmid, *Erkenntnis des geschichtlichen Christus bei Martin Kähler und bei Adolf Schlatter,* 1978, 161.

without thoughts"; yet the New Testament "shows us what happened, not only what has been thought and what should be thought by us."[129]

Remarks by the Old Testament scholar C. Westermann, in which he politely rebukes New Testament colleagues, show the significance of Schlatter's position at this point. Westermann asks with some irony "whether it might be possible to move from a mental-conceptual structure in New Testament theology back to a verbal or historical structure which presents what takes place between God and man in the New Testament."[130] Westermann rightly sees that New Testament studies has long plied approaches that minimize the concrete historical context of its subject matter and maximize the conceptual categories that are alleged best to explicate it. The same tendency held sway in Schlatter's day. Schlatter moves to correct it.

Especially in the case of Jesus is it impossible to distill a timeless conceptual system from sayings attributed to him or statements made about him. His sayings require interpretation in the context of his acts and cultural surroundings. Jesus' work and word, his personal self-assurance and his inner will coming to expression in his activity, are "a close-knit unity."[131] It is possible to attain an adequate comprehension of this unity if what the gospels record as Jesus' words and deeds are set forth as the "deeds of Jesus which arise [dynamically] out of one another."[132] Here Schlatter inverts the more traditional person-work understanding of christology. This reflects his consistent attempt to understand who Jesus was first of all in light of what he did, and not vice versa, as those for whom christology is determined primarily by dogmatic and not historical considerations are wont to do.

Three major historically secure deeds of Jesus form the nodal points of one variegated sequence of events: his extension of the proclamation of John the Baptist, the summons of his people to repentance in view of the at-hand kingdom of God, and his taking up of the cross. A proper grasp of the gospel reports in the context of these pillars of our knowledge of Jesus' life can make clearly visible to us "the splendid riches of his word along with its integrating basis."[133]

Schlatter regards the gospels as "recollections of Jesus" constructed largely in keeping with the "method of the Palestinian school which

---

[129]Schlatter, "Schlatter," in *Die Religionswissenschaft der Gegenwart in Selbstdarstellungen*, ed. Stange, 161.

[130]Westermann, *Theologie des Alten Testaments in Grundzügen*, 1978, 204.

[131]Schlatter, *Geschichte des Christus*, 6/ET *The History of the Christ*, 19.

[132]*Ibid.*

[133]*Ibid.*/ET *The History of the Christ*, 22.

preserved the memory of the fathers by passing on their 'sayings' and 'deeds.'"[134] He thus places the gospels primarily in the context of the synagogue—contra Wrede, for whom the context was the entire world of related ideas. Schlatter here follows his well-grounded conviction[135] that first century Judaism and particularly the Palestinian synagogue hold important keys for accurate interpretation of the gospel accounts.

These accounts comprise "sayings and anecdotes" which "confront us in every case with a particular concrete incident from the life of Jesus."[136] The sayings express how Jesus "bound his disciples to his will in a particular case."[137] The anecdotes show how for Jesus "a certain circumstance provided an occasion for his activity."[138] The divergences in the gospel accounts indicate that, as was customary in the rabbinic social and literary milieu, chronological order was not the main goal. Schlatter accordingly writes:

> I make no attempt to undertake the fruitless task of producing a chronological sequence of the words and acts of Jesus. For as soon as we begin debating the question whether a saying of Jesus belongs to the earlier or later period, we distance ourselves from the sources. At that point we also, however, step beyond the boundary of history and produce only creative literature. For the sources convey to us the sayings of Jesus because they recognize in them that abiding will which is constantly decisive for him. Inasmuch as they force us to deal with an abundance of individual, clearly discernible incidents, however, they summon us to a scientific enterprise which can be fruitful for this purpose: so to think through the numerous individual sayings and actions of Jesus, that the basis which gives rise to them becomes visible.[139]

In this fashion, and with a desire no less serious than Wrede's to get at the history which becomes visible through the New Testament

---

[134]*Ibid.* 7/ET *The History of the Christ*, 23.

[135]Cf. e.g. such studies as *Zur Topographie und Geschichte Palästinas*, 1893; *Der Chronograph aus dem 10. Jahre Antonins*, 1894; "Die Tage Trajans und Hadrians," BFCT 1/3 (1897) 1-100; "Der Glossator des griechischen Sirach und seine Stellung in der Geschichte der jüdischen Theologie," BFCT 1/5-6 (1897); "Jochanan ben Zakkai, der Zeitgenosse der Apostel," BFCT 3/4 (1899) 1-75; *Geschichte Israels von Alexander dem Grossen bis Hadrian*, ³1925 (= 1977); *Die Theologie des Judentums nach dem Bericht des Josefus*, 1932 (recently reprinted).

[136]Schlatter, *Geschichte des Christus*, 7/ET *The History of the Christ*, 23.

[137]*Ibid.*

[138]*Ibid.*

[139]*Ibid.*

reports, Schlatter undertakes to focus attention on "the internal root" rather than "the visible aspect of the events."[140]

Yet unlike Wrede he does not see New Testament history solely in the context of a "scheme of immanent development" or simply in terms of "immanent historical causality and correlation, which would make it possible to explain and understand one in terms of the other."[141] He seeks rather that context which makes Jesus visible as the Christ, which is how he was ultimately perceived by those who associated with him and also how the gospel documents present him. (Even Wrede eventually admitted this: "Shortly before his death ... Wrede changed his mind about the messianic consciousness of Jesus."[142]) And then, based on his study of first century Palestine, he seeks to reconstruct the "events" (*Ereignisse*) surrounding Jesus so that they form, if not a perfectly complete picture, still something more than a mere abstract conceptual construct. In this way the historically visible events give the framework for "the grasp of internal realities."[143] Schlatter's goal, he concludes, lies "not in the fabrication of colorful images which stimulate the imagination," but rather in "insight into the ground and aim of Jesus' work."[144] Or as he states elsewhere: "If we surround [the New Testament] with pieces of background which contradict its clear statements, we are making historical research into a work of fiction. In my view, New Testament theology only fulfills its obligations by observation, not be free creation."[145]

Contra Wrede, Schlatter argues that interpreting the history of Jesus primarily against first century Palestinian Judaism has great scientific merit (Schlatter anticipated contemporary scholarship's findings that this Judaism was thoroughly flavored by Hellenism). For numerous non-New Testament developments—Schlatter cites "the emergence of Hellenism, the development of the Rabbinate and of Pharisaism, the rule of the Herodians, and the way in which Judaism was integrated

---

[140]*Ibid.*

[141]Schmid, *Erkenntnis des geschichtlichen Christus bei Martin Kähler und bei Adolf Schlatter*, 242.

[142]Rollmann, *Historical Handbook of Biblical Interpreters*, 397.

[143]Schlatter, *Geschichte des Christus*, 8/ET *The History of the Christ*, 23.

[144]*Ibid.*/ET *The History of the Christ*, 24.

[145]Schlatter, "The Theology of the New Testament and Dogmatics," R. Morgan, *The Nature of New Testament Theology*, 1973, 117-166, here 135, hereafter cited as *NNTT*. The original is "Die Theologie des Neuen Testaments und die Dogmatik," in G. Strecker, ed., *Das Problem der Theologie des Neuen Testaments*, 1975 (hereafter cited as *PTNT*) 155-214.

into the [Roman] empire"[146]—are constituent parts of Jesus' life or the milieux of those who finally recorded his story. He stops short, however, of dissolving the gospel statements into a purely ideological background. Historical data should be interpreted in the framework of a history of religion which one finds in the first century, not one which Troeltsch and others claim first to have discerned in the nineteenth or twentieth.

Finally, Schlatter holds that "the knowledge of Jesus is the foremost, indispensable centerpiece of New Testament theology."[147] One will recall that Wrede thought it impossible to write a New Testament theology beginning with the teaching of Jesus. Schlatter however takes as his primary sources the four gospels, addressing an issue still debated today:

> In assessing the sources I concur with the judgment of those men who, in the transition from the first to the second century, established the canon of the four gospels. The opposing positions, which proliferate in contemporary publications, stem from history of religions considerations. They do not stem from observations which are based on the language, topography, historical background, and testimony of the documents. Such positions are refuted when it is possible to derive from the gospel reports a unified and plausible picture of the history of Jesus.[148]

Those who obscure the unique character of the New Testament documents over against those that did not eventually find their way into the canon "come into serious conflict not with a dogma but with history."[149] This contrasts strongly with Wrede, whose program envisioned overthrow of canonical parameters.

Schlatter, Hofmann, and Baur

Schlatter does not consciously align his New Testament theology with Hofmann's work,[150] though there are noticeable similarities.[151] Schlatter

[146]Schlatter, *Die Geschichte des Christus*, 8/ET *The History of the Christ*, 24.

[147]*Ibid.*/ET *The History of the Christ*, 21. These are the pregnant first words of his New Testament theology, which today call Bultmann's contrasting position to mind.

[148]*Ibid.* 8/ET *The History of the Christ*, 24.

[149]Schlatter, *NNTT*, 147; *PTNT*.

[150]To this extent, if no further, E. Güting's contention is justified that the description of Schlatter "as a theologian of *Heilsgeschichte* finds no adequate support in Schlatter's writings" (*Neue Zeitschrift für systematische Theologie* 15 [1973] 147 n. 80). Güting is also correct in questioning K. Steck's misrepresentation of Schlatter (Steck, *Die Idee der Heilsgeschichte*, 1959); here see also G. Egg, *Adolf Schlatters kritische Position,* 1968, 46-50. Güting seems, however, to define *Heilsgeschichte* in a manner so narrow as to preclude its usage as one often finds it in New Testament theology. If Schlatter

far outdistances Hofmann in New Testament background expertise and to a lesser degree in critical self-awareness.[152] It could be argued that no major New Testament scholar was ever more cognizant of the effects of philosophy and contemporary thought on New Testament interpretation than Schlatter; at this point Hofmann simply does not measure up. But then there are even fewer New Testament scholars who have produced the likes of *Die philosophische Arbeit seit Cartesius nach ihrem ethischen und religiösen Ertrag* (Philosophical Study since Descartes according to its Ethical and Religious Result), a work praised by both Rengstorf and Thielicke.[153] And possibly no other *Neutestamentler* of the past two centuries could have produced a work like Schlatter's "Metaphysik."[154] Nor have many New Testament scholars gone to Schlatter's lengths in reflecting the conviction that "scientific exegesis of the New Testament ... is not possible without sufficient regard for and knowledge of the Hebrew."[155]

Schlatter distances himself from Baur in two important ways. First, he outstrips him decisively in knowledge of first century Palestine and biblical history generally. Second, he reads the New Testament documents as sources of a religious history intrinsic to the concrete historical contexts of the documents, as opposed to arraying them along a developmental continuum furnished largely by philosophical

was not a direct ideological descendent of Hofmann, he still leaves no doubt as to his answer to the question: "Can it then become a disputed matter among us whether faith regards salvation history as its object?" (Schlatter, "Heilige Geschichte und der Glaube," *Heilige Anliegen der Kirche*, 1896, 22).

[151] As noted e.g. by Dymale, "The Theology of Adolf Schlatter with Special Reference to his Understanding of History," 298f.; W. Lütgert, *Adolf Schlatter als Theologe innerhalb des geistigen Lebens seiner Zeit*, 1932, 11; L. Goppelt, *Theologie*, 47; J. Behm, *Heilsgeschichtliche und religionsgeschichtliche Betrachtung des Neuen Testaments*, 1922, 9.

[152] Dymale's remark ("The Theology of Adolf Schlatter with Special Reference to his Understanding of History," 48) that "Schlatter at no point discussed his method" is very far from accurate.

[153] The book appeared in 1906; see Rengstorf, "Adolf Schlatter," *Tendenzen der Theologie im 20. Jahrhundert*, ed. H.J. Schulz, 1967, 61; Thielicke, *Evangelical Faith*, vol. 1, 276 n. 25. Both cite the unjustified neglect of this volume.

[154] *ZTK* Beiheft 7, 1987, edited from a previously unpublished manuscript by Werner Neuer.

[155] Schlatter's expert command of Hebrew is noted in P. Katz, "Bedeutung und Vermittlung von Hebräischkenntnissen zum Verständnis des Neuen Testaments," *ZAW* 104 (1992) 420f., 427. It is displayed e.g. in his linguistic commentary *Der Evangelist Johannes*, [4]1975.

idealism.[156] Some major points at which he diverges from Wrede are to be taken up below.

3. Schlatter's critique of Wredian methodology

Schlatter notoriously did not involve himself in extended interaction with his opponents in his writings,[157] although it is a mistake to think him out of touch with contemporary scholarship.[158] Often Schlatter's interaction with disagreeing views, e.g. those of Troeltsch, is between the lines.[159] It is nonetheless not difficult to detect his interaction with Wrede. He responds at length to a foundational assumption of Wrede's *Das Messiasgeheimnis in den Evangelien*.[160] And Schlatter's programmatic statement on New Testament theology is a perfect foil for that of Wrede, as Morgan's *The Nature of New Testament Theology* implies. Schlatter did not, however, indulge in *ad hominem* anti-Wredian polemic, but rather assessed Wrede's approach in the wider context of what Schlatter saw as post-Kantian, positivistic, atheistic historical methodology.[161] Thus much of his criticism touches Wrede indirectly and by implication. Yet by going to the roots[162] of the stream of thought in which Wrede operated, Schlatter probably made his objections more effective than had he accepted Wrede's basic premises and then sought to correct him at individual points. Schlatter rightly recognized that Wrede's position implied a whole thought and belief

---

[156]Cf. Schlatter, *NNTT*, 141; *PTNT*, 183f. He also dismantles Baur's vision theory of the resurrection, a pivotal point in Baur's reconstruction of early church history, in *Die Geschichte des Christus*, 519-525/ET *The History of the Christ*, 377–383.

[157]Schlatter explains this fact variously in *Rückblick auf meine Lebensarbeit* (e.g. 93ff., 117f., 136, 171). He felt that it was necessary to choose between comprehensive mastery of contemporary critical opinion, on the one hand, and devoting himself to ancient languages and their milieux, on the other. While he by no means abandoned the importance of the former ideal, he opted primarily for the latter.

[158]Rightly underscored by U. Luck, "Einführung," Schlatter, *Zur Theologie*, ed. U. Luck, 1969, 8 n. 4, 10f., 22, and often elsewhere in literature treating Schlatter.

[159]As noted by K. Holl in a personal letter to Schlatter, commenting on volume one of Schlatter's New Testament theology; see R. Stupperich, ed., "Briefe Karl Holls an Adolf Schlatter," *ZTK* 64 (1967) 230.

[160]Schlatter, "Der Zweifel an der Messianität Jesu," *Zur Theologie*, ed. Luck, 151-202.

[161]Cf. Schlatter, "Atheistische Methoden in der Theologie," Schlatter, *Zur Theologie*, 134-150/ET Neuer, *Adolf Schlatter*, 1995, 211–225. See also R. Leuenberger, "Adolf Schlatter und die 'atheistischen Methoden in der Theologie,'" *Reformatorio* 15 (1966) 291-299.

[162]Here see especially Schlatter's *Die philosophische Arbeit seit Cartesius* and its many allusions to thought affecting biblical criticism.

system which was virtually unfalsifiable from within its own fundamental assumptions.

It will be instructive to note Schlatter's response to the three basic features of Wrede's approach to New Testament theology which we have already explored above.

We saw earlier that Wrede's method makes the New Testament writings secondary to that which gave rise to them.[163] Ideas and phenomena unfold according to unvarying inner laws, to which modern thought since Kant is privy, which always determine their rise and development. The great temporal distance between the New Testament writings and that which they report, as well as their disparate and random nature, render them only indirectly suitable as historical sources for Christianity's rise. An alternate critical religio-historical continuum is posited in keeping with values derived from modern ethical theory. The New Testament writings fade into the background, radically relativized by the absolute claims of the modern perspective which essentially determines their content in the context of "the whole world of related ideas."

Schlatter makes several moves in response to Wrede.

1. His exhaustive historical work and exegesis of both biblical and extra-biblical writings serve to show that it is possible to conceive of the New Testament documents as being in close contact with that which gave rise to them and comprised their primary impetus.[164] Foremost was Jesus, who came to be called Christ, seen in the concrete social, political, and religious world which he and his followers inhabited. Stuhlmacher notes that Schlatter's basic approach to the thorny Jesus of history/Christ of faith problem was "the proper way" and foreshadows the solutions advanced by Kümmel, Jeremias, and Goppelt.[165] Schlatter's was not necessarily biblicistic or naive:

> Schlatter's use of the gospels, which gives the appearance of being naive in its synoptic presentation of all gospel texts viewed with an eye to their historical unity, may well capture more of that reality of Jesus which engenders belief than our current impoverishment of the biblical portrait of Jesus, conditioned as it is by hermeneutically one-sided considerations.[166]

---

[163] See "1. The truth behind the texts" above.

[164] Cf. e.g. Schlatter, *Der Evangelist Johannes.*

[165] Stuhlmacher, *NTS* 24 (1978) 445; cf. Stuhlmacher, *Jesus of Nazareth, Christ of Faith*, 1993.

[166] Stroh and Stuhlmacher, introduction to Schlatter, *Geschichte des Christus,* ³1977, third (unnumbered) page.

Schlatter meets Wrede's challenge first of all with historical work,[167] instructive still today, which shows that Wrede's fundamental hypotheses do not necessarily follow from the data to which they are applied. He undercuts Wrede's historical base.

② Schlatter responds on a wide front to Wrede's program with counterproposals reflecting a more discriminating use of history of religion method and more integrity in owning up to critical predilections. Schlatter by no means renounced insights from the "history of religion school"; Räisänen oversimplifies in saying Schlatter's attitude toward the school was simply to reject its results.[168] He did however plead for a disciplined and controlled use of them.[169] Schlatter "wanted to interpret from a history of religion point of view; but he wished to do so more effectively than those who counted themselves as members of the 'school' of this name."[170] O. Merk is among those finally recognizing that Schlatter deserves to be listed among history of religion pioneers like Wrede, W. Bousset, and H. Weinel, though his views contrasted with theirs at key points.[171]

This is not so naive assertion as it may sound. Schlatter recognizes that many critics (like Wrede) lay claim to a presuppositionless historiography. Their historical reconstruction involves no judgment of the data, just objective and dispassionate description of data. Counters Schlatter: this is the strongest sort of prejudgment of the data, for it is blind to the effects of the historian's own assumptions or preunderstanding. But we can "get free of and rise above our presuppositions" only as we pay "conscious and rigorous attention to them."[172] Without a continual resolute attempt "to lay aside all personal concerns and the opinions of one's school or party, and seriously to *see*, academic work

---

[167]For detailed description of Schlatter's modus operandi see Schmid, *Erkenntnis des geschichtlichen Christus bei Martin Kähler und bei Adolf Schlatter*, 239-456.

[168]*Beyond New Testament Theology*, 33.

[169]Schlatter's basic affinity for history of religion method is evident from of a reading of his program for New Testament theology (see Morgan's *NNTT*). His objections to certain of its biases are clear in *Die philosophische Arbeit seit Cartesius*; cf. "Atheistische Methoden," *Zur Theologie*/ET Neuer, *Adolf Schlatter*, 1995, 211–225. He defends the history of religion bent to his own research in *Die Religionswissenschaft der Gegenwart in Selbstdarstellungen,* 161. Boers' claim (*Theology*, 72) that Schlatter "considered the New Testament history as a development that had been closed off in itself" is baseless.

[170]P. Althaus, "Adolf Schlatters Wort an die heutige Theologie," *ZST* 21 (1950) 96. Cf. Lütgert, *Adolf Schlatter als Theologe innerhalb des geistigen Lebens seiner Zeit,* 9f.

[171]"Theologie des Neuen Testaments und Biblische Theologie," *Bilanz und Perspektiven gegenwärtiger Auslegung des Neuen Testaments,* 1995, 116.

[172]Schlatter, *NNTT*, 127; *PTNT*, 166.

degenerates into hypocrisy."[173] Schlatter concedes that in one sense "an observer sees with his own eyes only what the certainties which internally determine him allow him to see."[174] He demands therefore that the New Testament and "the content of our consciousness should enter into a discussion and mutually come to terms."[175]

The interpreter unquestionably brings something of significance to the New Testament,[176] but he must be capable of letting his prior convictions be adjusted if he is to succeed in historical work, which "demands wide-open eyes and the sort of whole-hearted surrender which perceives that with which it is presented."[177] Wredian methodology, in elevating history of religion historiographical and developmental postulates, or a certain religious ideal (that of liberal German Protestantism's cultural optimism), to axiomatic status in New Testament interpretation, has failed to heed the caveat:

> If we turn our attention straight away to the connections which exist between our object and our own ideas and will, then there is always the danger that we will break off our observation at the point where our own interest in the object ends. Our perception might be directed exclusively towards what we can at once make our own.[178]

3. In sum, Schlatter declined to endorse a historical method which considers the New Testament documents as merely secondary sources of a religious history whose laws of development are already transparent to us on *a priori* religious or philosophical grounds.[179] Contemporary history shows that history does not develop according to some orderly immanent sequence in keeping with human logic or philosophy: the chaotic history of Kantian thought after Kant demonstrates to Schlatter that "the formation of our thoughts is not determined solely by the logical categories of pure reason."[180] The vast temporal distance between the New Testament documents and that which they relate has disputable historical justification. Not a modern value-schema which subsumes New Testament "ideas" under the heading of "the whole

---

[173]*NNTT*, 122; *PTNT*, 161.

[174]*NNTT*, 123; *PTNT*, 161.

[175]*NNTT*, 131; *PTNT*, 171.

[176]*NNTT*, 132; *PTNT*, 172.

[177]*NNTT*, 121; *PTNT*, 159.

[178]*NNTT*, 127; *PTNT*, 167.

[179]On the Troeltschian (Wredian) philosophy of religion see W. Wyman, Jr., "Revelation and the Doctrine of Faith: Historical Revelation within the Limits of Historical Consciousness," *JR* 78 (1998) 55. See also Chapman, *SJT* 46/1 (1993) 48.

[180]Schlatter, *Die philosophische Arbeit seit Cartesius*, 138.

world of related ideas" but rather the history of which the New Testament documents are by far the most tangible evidence is the methodological starting point of New Testament theology.

4. Schlatter's own methodological rationale
No final New Testament theology possible

We saw above that Wrede claimed exclusivity for his approach.[181] He saw in his methodological proposals the end of New Testament theology as previously conceived and the beginning of a discipline which would once for all bring the New Testament within the purview of modern religious science and out of the dogmatizing grasp of the theological or ecclesiastical interpretation in which it had languished so long.

Schlatter by contrast says at the outset that it should be clear that no one can or will write "the" definitive New Testament theology. The discipline has not been well served by rationales—here Wrede would be implicated—which present a scholar's own aims and imply that "that is the whole of the intellectual task with which the subject matter confronts us." This attitude is a holdover from the nineteenth century and its penchant for all-encompassing speculative undertakings.[182]

Schlatter is not opposing method as such. The sine qua non of scientific work is "careful attention to our methods."[183] Schlatter states almost prophetically: "The question whether the coming decades in Germany will see a decline or progress in our theology depends to a considerable degree on the skill with which we master the methods of scientific work."[184] While Wrede speaks of mastering the historical data, then, Schlatter speaks of mastering or controlling the methods by which the data are analyzed. A method is not to be conceived as a prescriptive formulation which renders all other approaches illicit and threatens to straitjacket evidence.[185]

---

[181]See "2. Methodological exclusivity" above.

[182]Schlatter, *NNTT*, 117; *PTNT*, 155.

[183]Schlatter, "Die Bedeutung der Methode für die theologische Arbeit," *Theologischer Literaturbericht* 31 (1908) 5/ET "Adolf Schlatter's 'The Significance of Method for Theological Work': Translation and Commentary," *The Southern Baptist Journal of Theology* 1/2 (Summer 1997) 65.

[184]*Ibid.*

[185]Cf. in the same general era E. Reuss, *Die Geschichte der heiligen Schriften des Neuen Testaments*, ⁶1887, 14, who argues against F.C. Baur "that as long as we are dealing with the concept and form of science, the particular views of an individual critic can-

It is interesting to note that Schlatter, billed by Merk as the fore-runner of purely theological interpretation of the New Testament who sacrificed historical reconstruction in the interest of theological under-standing,[186] grants legitimacy to any number of approaches to the New Testament.[187] One might have expected the "dogmatic" Schlatter to be exclusivistic, with Wrede, the dispassionate historian, ever seeking new truth, being open to the full range of interpretative possibilities. But whereas Wrede in his approach is committed to the axioms of con-temporary history of religion research, methodologically excluding explanations or assumptions which do not match his own, Schlatter somewhat surprisingly states that every theory about the New Testa-ment has the right to try to vindicate itself from and overcome opposing views based upon the historical data.

In an insightful passage dealing with this issue[188] Schlatter concedes "the close connections between historical work and the convictions by which we live." A historian may certainly on methodological grounds reject any discernible role for God in history, including New Testa-ment history. "One cannot deny from the outset the legitimacy of this account of New Testament theology" any more than one could reject without discussion an account attributing Jesus' messianic sayings to a profound psychological imbalance, an imbalance which nevertheless found a large following because the time was right for one of those "vacuous concepts [the messianic idea] in the history of religion which for a time exercise great power but then burst." Every conception of what the New Testament contains "has the right to test its account by the reality we are given," i.e. the historical evidence, in order to try to verify itself as a basic conception which accurately depicts the data. It rightly attempts to show that this particular conception has "the mark of truth" and thus "is shown to be a principle which shapes the course of history."

Thus Schlatter concedes Wrede's right to see "the world as a closed system containing within itself all the conditions for its unfolding processes."[189] New Testament theology as a discipline must be open to

---

not comprise the absolute standard for him in resolving pertinent special questions." Prescriptive method seems to be a penchant of the "critical orthodox" line of research.

[186]Merk, *Anfangszeit*, 250. Räisänen agrees; Schlatter "remains in the fetters of dog-matics" (*Beyond New Testament Theology*, 34).

[187]In this respect Dintaman's thesis (*Creative Grace*) has merit that Schlatter is a fore-runner of postmodern understanding.

[188]Quotes in this and the following two paragraphs are from Schlatter, *NNTT*, 153f.; *PTNT*, 199f.

[189]See previous note.

the possibility that such a basis might facilitate a compelling synthetic understanding of the data.

Need for critical self-awareness

But Schlatter insists that the historian working from a no–God basis, who insists on a totally "from below" reading of the New Testament, must meet the fundamental demand of science: that he or she "be clear about what factors are influencing him." Otherwise he will not "distinguish between the part of his judgment which comes from observation of past events, and that which rests on his own immanent certainties." Unless he is careful here, he will not see that his reading of the New Testament from the start "annuls its central statement," that there *is* a God and that he *does* inhabit and affect historical reality in more than a purely immanent way. It will escape his notice that in the New Testament, whatever modern systematicians or philosophers of religion say, God is not just a human conceptual construct or religious chimera. At every step his description of New Testament development will contravene those causal, but at times non-contingent, connections attested in the New Testament texts themselves. His presentation of the New Testament will and must become polemic against it. The "historian" will have fallen prey to "the danger of totally reshaping what happened according to the demands of" his own viewpoint.[190]

Summary

For Wrede New Testament theology is a somewhat one-dimensional undertaking which consists of a rigorous assessment of early Christian and related evidence, constructing it through scientific description into a history of religious thought. No other procedure, nor any proceeding along similar lines but with fundamentally antithetical or even competing presuppositions, is defensible or warranted. Here perhaps Schlatter's wry remark could be applied: "Germany has never seen a really liberal liberalism."[191]

Schlatter is more open, at least theoretically. He refuses to absolutize a given worldview and then explain the New Testament so as to conform with it. It could be argued that Wrede's proposal contains the seeds of its own death in itself, since it so stringently delimits the scope of reality with which history of early Christian religion has to deal. If there is no more to the New Testament writings than Wrede's positiv-

---

[190]See previous note.
[191]Schlatter, *Die philosophische Arbeit seit Cartesius*, 80.

ism suggests, why go on expending so much research on it?[192] Robinson's call for the end of New Testament theology and a reversion to pure history of religion, makes sense.[193] Schlatter's open-ended, more inductive perspective leads him to assert that "there is no question of an end being reached even of the first and most simple function of New Testament study; namely, seeing what is there."[194] It is not clear that Wrede's is the superior program for ongoing research of the New Testament data.

We can here only call attention to Schlatter's tracing of the roots of the Greek-rationalistic-Enlightenment definition of *Wissenschaft* ("science") as that which "demands recognition from everyone."[195] Seeing Wrede within this tradition, as Schlatter does, does not necessarily impugn the quality of the former's proposals, but it does suggest that they are not as historically unconditioned and thus unquestionable as he seemed to have supposed. It is from the basis of this critique that Schlatter sets out in a different direction.

5. Subject matter and worldview
Danger of world view to scientific observation

Wrede, as suggested above,[196] accepts the modern scientific worldview familiar to him as the general point of departure for assessing the contents of the New Testament. Consequently he falls in step with the religious studies wing of the dominant contemporary German scientific community, the so-called history of religion school. Although Wrede in some sense wished to remain a churchman—his programmatic treatise on New Testament theology originated as lectures to a

---

[192]In fairness to Wrede, his practical theological and pedagogical sense of mission no doubt came into play here; see Schreiber, "William Wrede als Aufklärer," *Theologie als Aufklärung*, 287f. Whoever sees Wrede merely as "a radical, destructive critic of Scripture and especially of the gospels has not understood him" (*ibid.* 294f.).

[193]Robinson, *RelSRev* 2 (1976) 17–23.

[194]*NNTT*, 136; *PTNT*, 177; cf. Schlatter, "Atheistische Methoden," in *Zur Theologie*, 142/ET Neuer, *Adolf Schlatter*, 1995, 211.

[195]This consistent underlying aspect of Schlatter's outlook surfaces e.g. in *Die philosophische Arbeit seit Cartesius*, 44, 80; cf. *Geschichte des Christus*, 6/ET *The History of the Christ*, 22, where he speaks of the intellectual posture common in liberal idealist religiosity which dates at least from classical times and which regards "only itself as 'science'". Cf. also "Atheistische Methoden," *Zur Theologie*, 143f./ET Neuer, *Adolf Schlatter*, 1995, 213–216. For analysis of Schlatter's reading of Greek thought see "Schlatters Auseinandersetzung mit dem 'Griechentum'" (Walldorf, *Realistische Philosophie*, 214–224).

[196]See "3. From historicism to positivism" above.

pastors' conference—he felt the interests of dogma and truth ought to be regarded as mutually exclusive for the sake of real science.

To such a viewpoint Schlatter rejoins: "'Things are done this way now; therefore I must also do things this way'; that is certainly a brand new theological method. No one spoke like that in the church up till now."[197] He would thus question the legitimacy of Wrede's outlook in the ecclesiastical sphere within which Wrede seeks to operate.

But it is not in the name of the church but of science that Schlatter finally objects to Wrede's approach. The systematic separation of New Testament history from the effects worked by the personal God to which the texts testify, and from the reported deeds, impressions, words, and other effects of Jesus, is not necessitated by the subject matter itself, at least not primarily. This separation is spawned rather by acquiescence to the atheistic presuppositions gaining sway in other disciplines. But "the atheistic conception of the world is not a constitutive category of the process of cognition";[198] it is logically fallacious to assume that it is necessary to adopt an atheistic or even agnostic position to be scientific.

Concludes Schlatter, too much is at stake that theology, and by implication biblical criticism, should descend to "servile acquiescence to contemporary moods."[199] To suppose that the meaning of the New Testament is necessarily subject to the caprice of academic philosophy's (or any other discipline's) theory of God is absurd. There is no such thing (except within the framework of unabashed positivism or scientism) as general methodological laws which affect the interpretation of specific data and which *must* be carried over from one discipline to another. Any such laws must be shown to conform to the data of each discipline in turn.

It is thus a scientific as well as a theological mistake to construe the New Testament along lines dictated by Kantian philosophy's academic imperialism. The most general and "inviolable scientific rule," to be observed by members of the truly responsible university community as "an unbreakable obligation," is that "painstaking observation must precede any judgment; prior to one's own production there must be the act of reception. Without that act, judgment and production fly off into wind and illusion."[200] Schlatter doubts that there are compelling historical reasons for systematic skepticism toward the New Testament

---

[197]"Atheistische Methoden," *Zur Theologie*, 142/ET Neuer, *Adolf Schlatter*, 1995, 218.

[198]*Ibid.* 143f./ET Neuer, *Adolf Schlatter*, 1995, 220.

[199]*Ibid.*

[200]*Ibid.* 142f./ET Neuer, *Adolf Schlatter*, 1995, 219f.

writings. There is accordingly no justification for transforming study of them into a history of religion phenomenology.[201] Such a project is not necessitated by the subject matter but arises from assumptions current in other disciplines which are being applied without sufficient historical warrant in New Testament interpretation.[202]

Need to counteract stultifying "rationalism"

The excesses of the procedure just outlined are no reason to abandon the explicative task, says Schlatter; the challenge is to do a better job. But the existence of such wrong-headed historiography is warning against "rationalism," "a pride of judgment which expects to get the whole of reality into its own intellectual grasp and so reduce it to its own field of vision." Schlatter elaborates:

> Where judgment cuts loose from the perception which is indispensable to it, where the intellect's productive power tries to be in command and play the creator so that what we produce is no longer connected with a prior receiving, where thought circles around one's own self, as though this could create from itself the material from which knowledge comes and the rules by which it is to be judged, there we have rationalism. It stands in irreconcilable hostility to the very basis of the New Testament, because acknowledging God is the direct opposite of rationalism. But this rationalism is at the same time the road to dreamland and the death of intellectual integrity.[203]

This tendency, as we have implied already, is unfortunately operative in Wrede's methodological proposals. Schlatter repeats: historical work taking its bearings at the methodological level, not from observation of its subject matter but from the modern worldview alone, "is the enemy not only of the New Testament, but also of the aims and rules of academic work."[204] The critic must never forget that rationalism as just defined "conflicts with science as well as with the New

---

[201] Not in the broad sense that is inclusive of history and theology but in the narrow sense like that found by L. Johnson in the work of Jonathan Z. Smith; cf. L. Johnson, *Religious Experience in Earliest Christianity*, 182f.

[202] Cf. R. Schmitt, *Abschied von der Heilsgeschichte?*, 1982, 43: "Being 'scientific' at any price in the sense of being dependent on the conditions of another science can therefore not serve as the task and goal of theology as long as it wishes to remain factual and fair to its subject matter. Theology would unavoidably lose touch with its subject and thereby also lose its independence and critical function if it were to strive for that kind of a 'scientific' ideal". Cf. also H.-J. Kraus, *Geschichte der historisch-kritischen Erforschung des Alten Testaments*, ³1982, 525.

[203] Schlatter, *NNTT*, 150; *PTNT*, 194.

[204] Quotations in the paragraph are from Schlatter, *NNTT*, 149f.; *PTNT*, 193f.

Testament; it is irrational as well as impious." When the object of historical study is subjected to theories which even potentially deny its ostensible given reality on non- or quasi-historical *a priori* grounds, "we oppose not only the past, but at the same time the ground and law of our thinking activity, and so our existence. In opposing the object we are also opposing the subject."

Does Schlatter have any constructive alternative? This question will find a partial answer in the next section. We may here simply note Schlatter's conviction that

> the most important factor making a New Testament theology scientifically respectable or worthless is whether a scholar possesses the veracity of the genuine observer in concrete cases, or whether in his work he makes bold to determine the course of history to suit himself. He must protect himself against this in the course of his work by not proceeding to make a judgment before carefully and modestly perceiving, surrendering himself to the data, and never once allowing himself to judge, but first making himself feel the whole range of the conditions which produce the knowledge.[205]

> Whether one speaks of fact-ignoring conservative dogmatism[206] or atheistic dogmatism, no historical account of the New Testament is worthwhile which does not strive ceaselessly and honestly to perceive the given first of all as much as possible apart from points of view, religious or irreligious, foreign to it.

It can be objected that no one, Schlatter included, can get free of his presuppositions. But this would miss the point that Schlatter not only acknowledged this insight: it is a major factor in his hermeneutical practice. What Schlatter insists is that through awareness of and thus allowance for presuppositions, it is possible to make historical interpretation into something more than an assessing and employing of data within a pre-determined scheme foreign to the data, a procedure to which Wrede's method seems to open wide the door. Whether or to what extent Schlatter himself avoids the "elevating of theory over reality"[207] for which he faulted others cannot be examined here; at least

---

[205] *NNTT*, 150; *PTNT*, 195.

[206] Schlatter antagonized not only liberals but also conservatives of his day. This is partly what makes the charge of biblicism against him lack force. Schlatter, "like most good theologians, was having to fight on two fronts"; against many conservatives he defended New Testament theology as a historical discipline, not merely a dogmatic one (Morgan, *NNTT*, 31f.). F.W. Kantzenbach makes a similar point in "Biblizismus und Bekenntnisfrage," ... *und fragten nach Jesus*, ed. U. Meckert, G. Ott, and B. Satlow, 1964, 296.

[207] Schlatter, "Zweifel an der Messianität," *Zur Theologie*, 183.

he made methodological allowance creating room for the possibility of such an avoidance and holds it forth as a scientific and theological ideal. This suggests both an intellectual independence and a critical humility, each checking the other, which do not always characterize New Testament theologians. Certainly from Schlatter's point of view it did not characterize the program for New Testament theology set forth by Wrede.

Schlatter's functional epistemology[208] and its hermeneutical result

1. Schlatter and Wrede

We saw above that Wrede adopts a Troeltschian theoretical posture and thus "immanent criticism."[209] The epistemological base for this lies in the realm of neo-Kantianism. Stuhlmacher rightly describes what Schlatter saw as problematic here:

> With admirable sharpness of vision Schlatter recognized the rationalistic bias inherent in Troeltschian historical criticism. According to this bias the knowing subject seeks to seize control of history and by his own efforts critically transform it, instead of engaging the tradition and allowing himself to be called in question by it.[210]

Schlatter himself spells out what he finds objectionable in Troeltsch's *a priori*:

> This formula is burdened with the notion, Kantian in origin, that that which is *a priori* not only exists in one's reason: it originates in one's reason and is reason's own creation, a creation which reason did not receive [but constructed out of itself]. Until the notion, so widely advocated by rationalism, of a reason which perceives nothing once again disappears, it is desirable to avoid the formula "*a priori*" as a preventative measure against fanciful constructions.[211]

Schlatter thinks that a heavy reliance on an *a priori* of this description can only spell trouble for fruitful historical observation.

It is not feasible here to delve into Schlatter's formidable critique of Kantianism, a project recently accomplished by J. Walldorf in the first-

---

[208]See also the comparison between Schlatter and Goppelt in Chapter 6 below.
[209]See "Troeltschian immanent criticism" above.
[210]Stuhlmacher, *Verstehen*, 157.
[211]Schlatter, *Das christliche Dogma*, [3]1977, 558, n. 18.

ever extended investigation of Schlatter's philosophy.[212] One of Wall-dorf's major conclusions is that

> it would be mistaken to expect from Schlatter's philosophical conception (especially his epistemology ...) a philosophical theory that is conceptually polished and comprehensively worked out in detail. What Schlatter offers are main features that mark out his philosophical position ...[213]

This seems to confirm our impression that Schlatter works with a functional rather than formal theory of knowledge.

In contrasting Schlatter with Wrede, we wish simply to outline the basic differences between their respective starting points in dealing with aspects of the problems posed by knowing. This will help explain their differing approaches to New Testament theology.

2. Schlatter's approach to the problem

The problem of epistemology arises inexorably from issues posed by historical work. Schlatter's conception of the historical task is characterized neither by a certain iron-clad method nor by pre-determined standards of what is historically possible. Schlatter wished to see in and as history "that which was historically real";[214] it is significant that Walldorf's study of Schlatter's philosophy finds him to be a philosophical "realist."

> The measure of the historical is therefore for Schlatter not the more or less rationalistically restricted "historically possible," but rather solely that which is "historically real" and "given." Accordingly, the scientific integrity of a historical reflection is decided for him ultimately not by the standards and categories which one already holds, but rather solely by whether one truly manages to get a view of the incidents and occurrences.[215]

This raises the question of how one can be sure that one "truly manages to get a view" of the historical data, which in turns points to the existence of an epistemological rationale, whether explicit or implicit. Schlatter's was primarily the latter.

Schmid indicates here that Schlatter's approach may do a certain justice to the object of study, the Bible, which "imparts much

---

[212] *Realistische Philosophie*, 1999. Note the dozens of reference to Kant in the index (336).

[213] *Ibid.* 284. Unfortunately Walldorf does not reflect on direct connections between the respective philosophies of Schlatter and Troeltsch.

[214] Schmid, *Erkenntnis des geschichtlichen Christus bei Martin Kähler und bei Adolf Schlatter*, 421f.

[215] *Ibid.* 417.

knowledge, however no theory of knowledge." That is, Schlatter is not a "theorist of knowledge" but a "practitioner of knowledge."[216] Schlatter's own words are illustrative at this point:

> What has happened in the past demands of us, by the very fact that it *has happened*, that we grasp it in its *givenness*. The question here is whether we are all wrapped up in ourselves, or whether we are able to be genuinely open to the past so as to be able to see things other than ourselves. I believe that we are given a capacity for seeing. But this cannot be proved to someone who denies it. The rule "Do it and you will know" applies here. As is the case with all our fundamental convictions, *action* is the potency which shapes our consciousness.[217]

For Schlatter, one might say, an epistemology is as an epistemology does. He does not appear to preface historical observation with the formal determination of whether knowledge is possible or under what conditions. Nor does he set forth a prescriptive definition of precisely what, relative to the subject matter, scientifically defensible conclusions would comprise. He opposes the Kant-derived touchstone of virtually all of his contemporaries, that "reality should conform itself to our mental constructs and be obedient to them"; Schlatter "wants to implement a discernment by which the concepts serve the subject matter" and not vice versa.[218]

Yet it is not true that Schlatter simply ignored the problem of the subject's involvement in its apprehending of the object.[219] Rather his critique of the interpreter's perception or reason "occurs on an ongoing basis in actual practice, where the primary issue is to distinguish fantasy from reality."[220] Nor is Schlatter simply a textbook realist,[221] for in that case he would have operated under defined or readily definable epistemological guidelines. This he did not do, as we shall now see.

---

[216] *Ibid.* 423. Cf. Joest's observation relative to Schlatter's dogmatics: "Zur Neuausgabe," foreword to Schlatter, *Das christliche Dogma*, third (unnumbered) page.

[217] *NNTT*, 127; *PTNT*, 167.

[218] Schmid, *Erkenntnis des geschichtlichen Christus bei Martin Kähler und bei Adolf Schlatter*, 423.

[219] Walldorf, *Realistische Philosophie*, 292, in comparing Schlatter's "realist" thought to its current forms in philosophy today, concludes: "the epistemological positions taken by [Schlatter] fit thoroughly and aptly in today's philosophical and theological discussion."

[220] Schmid, *Erkenntnis des geschichtlichen Christus bei Martin Kähler und bei Adolf Schlatter*, 424.

[221] *Ibid.* Cf. Schlatter, *Die Religionswissenschaft der Gegenwart in Selbstdarstellungen*, 153, where Schlatter denies having a tendency toward a simplistic empiricism or a naive view of knowing based solely on sense perception.

3. Resistance to a priori conditions to knowing

It turns out, concludes Schmid, that Schlatter declines to attempt to formulate a distinctive epistemology of his own.[222] He seems to suspect that this would inevitably impair the observer's potential to be open to the given which confronts him: "We still squander too much energy on the logical training of our thought processes in contradistinction to clear apprehension in close contact with reality."[223] This is illustrated by recalling how Schlatter sees no necessary radical break between Jesus and the Christ.[224] His thinking, or his theological and historical reconstruction, moves

> within the existential relationship of being personally committed, and within this relationship there exists an ultimate force of "the objective" which can finally only be borne witness to. It is doubtful that this force can be attained and seen if, and as long as, one remains within purely theoretical definitions. There comes a point when epistemological musings and scientific determination of objectivity appear no longer to suffice.[225]

Thus it is not possible to reduce by means of *a priori* determinations the knowledge transmitted by the New Testament to the mere formal-conceptual level which a consistent prescriptive epistemology demands. Life, history, truth, and love as people experienced them in New Testament times—and now—consist of more than theoretical reflection can encompass.

Schlatter does not minimize the need for rigorous thinking. To the contrary, he concludes his survey of the history of philosophy with these words: "This necessity, that [the church] must think, stands as one of the bedrock results of the course and outcome of the history of

---

[222]Schmid, *Erkenntnis des geschichtlichen Christus bei Martin Kähler und bei Adolf Schlatter*, 429.

[223]Schlatter, *Die philosophische Arbeit seit Cartesius*, 204.

[224]This does not mean that Schlatter is oblivious to the array of modern theories marshalling against this position. And Schlatter knows that "the work of Jesus is clearly distinct from that of his community," the latter being "the most important causal factor leading to doctrinal formulation in the New Testament" (*NNTT*, 141f.; *PTNT*, 184). But he sees the issue in all its sharpness when he calls it "a dominant question in New Testament theology today whether the religious history of the community can be understood as a development of what was created through Jesus, or whether we have here to draw upon outside forces [*fremde Kräfte*] to make the movement of history comprehensible" (*ibid.*). History of religion research stressed the latter alternative, often to the exclusion of the former; Schlatter stressed the former, attempting nevertheless to pursue primary goals of history of religion inquiry.

[225]Schmid, *Erkenntnis des geschichtlichen Christus bei Martin Kähler und bei Adolf Schlatter*, 427.

philosophy we have surveyed."[226] But he resists thought systems which ground the assured results of knowledge of reality in, and thereby finally generate reality from, the results of thought's own self-contemplation. For this reason a formal epistemology is not a feature of his work; what is given to be known must be granted the opportunity to have precedence over self-imposed, possibly inappropriate (in view of the evidence) conditions for knowing. We are reminded here of the Cartesian/non-Cartesian categories applied to Baur and Hofmann above and recall the danger of imposing *a priori* conditions on what we can know, thereby effectively censoring what data can convey to us. Schlatter addresses this same problem, and his response is not dissimilar to Hofmann's.[227]

4. Epistemology and hermeneutical result

Schlatter is rightly seen as a forerunner of Karl Barth,[228] i.e. as a theologically sensitive exegete. Schlatter's thought and praxis is moreover central to Stuhlmacher's "hermeneutic of consent."[229] Herein lies a clue to characterizing him over against Wrede. The latter has a built-in hermeneutic. As far as the New Testament's content is concerned, Wrede's de facto *a priori* (along with Troeltsch's celebrated criticism-analogy-correlation procedure[230]) predetermines what the texts can and cannot signify as having once been historical reality. As far as the New Testament's applicability to the modern world is concerned, the radical relativizing of all history inherent in Wrede's epistemology settles most questions handily: none of it need be applicable which does not conform to the modern religious consciousness of Wrede's cultural Protestantism.[231]

Schlatter has no such faith in *a priori* reflection. He wants to ground his conception of what once was in what the sources testify to apart

---

[226]Schlatter, *Die philosophische Arbeit seit Cartesius*, 241.

[227]Walldorf, *Realistische Philosophie*, 275–276, points to a difference between Hofmann and Schlatter: the former placed more overt emphasis on the need for regeneration in order to see Scripture's truths.

[228]Stuhlmacher, *ZTK* supplement 4 (1978) 104 n. 37. But see Kraus, *Biblische Theologie*, 283, for an important qualification. Barth biographies indicate several direct or indirect contacts between them: e.g. E. Busch, *Karl Barth*, 1975, 9, 37, 43; J. Hemer, *Karl Barth*, 1962, 217f.

[229]Stuhlmacher, *Verstehen*, 205-255.

[230]Given classic expression in Troeltsch, "Historical and Dogmatic Method in Theology," *The Historical Jesus Quest*, 32ff.

[231]On "cultural Protestantism" note H. Müller, ed., *Kulturprotestantismus*, 1992, especially essays by Lüdemann and Weiß.

from what he feels are strained *a priori* constructs. This is not necessarily naive but "criticism of criticism."[232] As far as the New Testament's content is concerned, it opens Schlatter up to the possibility of seeing that which might not accord with modern critical assumptions regarding what can and cannot have transpired to give rise to the New Testament texts. As far as applicability is concerned, Schlatter's refusal to absolutize any given modern *a priori* understanding—including his own, which altered throughout his life and never presumed to have reduced the New Testament to fully explained or explicable dimensions—leaves the possibility open for knowledge of normative status to inhere in the New Testament texts. Biblical authority takes on more than a metaphorical meaning.

Bultmann praises Schlatter's hermeneutical insight[233] and tries, though by different means, to emulate him in avoiding the "severing of the act of thinking from the act of living."[234] It is well known that Bultmann was a chief impetus behind the hermeneutical debates of recent decades. Schlatter must be given some credit for this development. His consistent sensitive implementation of a working hermeneutic, over against the consistent, often wooden application of *a priori* principles, is a major differentiating feature of his work compared to Wrede's. It recalls Hofmann's practical hermeneutical concern over against the philosophical orientation of Baur.

Schlatter's view of history

We referred above to Wrede's view of history in connection with (1) his devaluation of theology in favor of religion, (2) his rejection of any direct Old Testament-New Testament ties (first-century Judaism mediates primarily only religion of its own century), and (3) his endorsement of a Troeltschian history of religion position which posits a historical dynamic, discernible for the first time to modern eyes, which explains New Testament development along strictly immanent lines. Our handling of Schlatter to this point already indicates his grounds for disagreement with such a scheme.

[232]Schlatter, *Die Religionswissenschaft der Gegenwart in Selbstdarstellungen*, 9.
[233]Bultmann, *Theologie*, 597ff.
[234]*Ibid.* 599.

We wish now to move on to state Schlatter's view of history, so far as this is possible within brief compass.[235] We will also try to clarify what salvation history is in Schlatter's outlook.

1. Revelation and history not antithetical

Schlatter's work as a whole represents a repudiation of a "pessimistic assessment and depreciation of history,"[236] whether from the old Protestant orthodox (or like-minded Pietist) side, which sometimes read biblical statements in an a-temporal doctrinal context, or from the modern side, which ranks New Testament statements in a pantheon of ideas or religious concepts to which the contemporary mind already holds the essential key. Both of these viewpoints basically concur that "divine origin and historical mediation are mutually exclusive."[237] Schlatter's New Testament theology is written with the conviction that this antithesis is false.

> Taken seriously, it tears apart the relation of our own life to God; our own consciousness is cut loose from God as radically as the New Testament is. For we have in our consciousness nothing which is not conditioned by history ... If history is excluded from God's influence on the grounds that it is merely transitory and human, there exists no conscious relationship to God granted to us in our personal life.[238]

Schlatter points out that a fundamental tenet of those who methodologically separate God from history is violated by their own claim to have a consciousness of God. But how can this be, if God cannot penetrate history as persons experience it, since no human experience, not even knowing God, is not historically conditioned?[239]

But the New Testament, too, contravenes the familiar God-history dichotomization. It speaks of God's saving activity through Jesus which became human saving experience; persons received something from God—God acted in cognizable fashion—which shaped not only their thought but their lives. In the New Testament one observes that

> God's creating and giving penetrate man's existence and consciousness in their concrete, historically determined form. It establishes him and becomes

---

[235] On Schlatter's view of history cf. also Dymale, "The Theology of Adolf Schlatter with Special Reference to his Understanding of History"; Egg, *Schlatters kritische Position*, 42ff.; Gütung, *Neue Zeitschrift für systematische Theologie* 15 (1973) 143ff.

[236] Güting, *Neue Zeitschrift für systematische Theologie* 15 (1973) 143.

[237] Schlatter, *NNTT*, 151; *PTNT*, 196.

[238] *Ibid.* (Morgan's translation slightly modified)

[239] Cf. Schlatter, *Das christliche Dogma*, 11.

visible in and through him. God does his work of grace and judgment not outside man and so, too, not beyond history but in and through it.[240]

Thus Schlatter holds that revelation and history are not antithetical, which in turn also speaks against those who see historical inquiry as a denial of revelation. This is not to say that Schlatter advocates a natural theology.[241] He asks rather whether any historical phenomena at all have comprised or can comprise a history in which we may participate, a history "which, to be sure, is not a 'sacred' history, but which surely is nevertheless a history which admits of being sanctified" by God's influence.[242] His answer is clearly affirmative.

2. The christocentric "course of history" (Geschichtslauf): Christ the key to history

Schlatter claims that his New Testament theology arose from a desire to make plain to others the historical unity he discerned in the New Testament texts. This unity was not "a cunning feat of my ability to harmonize." Schlatter's vision rather came about "as the consequence of the most concrete imaginable conception" of the historical evidence relating to the New Testament.[243] The New Testament appeared to him finally as "a firmly integrated history which was produced by the same forces throughout."[244] Schlatter, like Hofmann, was no biblical inerrantist, but he did see a common formative origin and resolve permeating the New Testament books.

We stand here near the center of Schlatter's view of history. There is demonstrably—assuming any considerable degree of veracity in the New Testament accounts—"a divine dispensation [*Geschichtslauf*] which sanctifies humanity."[245] New Testament writers attest that they came into contact with God, and vice versa, through Jesus and the community of faith. The New Testament documents do not spread a conception of Christ, or a concept of some inner awareness of the divine, "equally over the whole course of history"; what is said is largely "localized ... at a particular point."[246]

---

[240] *NNTT*, 152; *PTNT*, 197.

[241] Güting, *Neue Zeitschrift für systematische Theologie* 15 (1973) 145.

[242] Schlatter, "Geschichte und Glaube," *Heilige Anliegen*, 25.

[243] Schlatter, *Rückblick auf meine Lebensarbeit*, 233.

[244] *Ibid.*

[245] *NNTT*, 153; *PTNT*, 198f.

[246] *NNTT*, 147; *PTNT*, 190; cf. Schlatter, *Geschichte des Christus*, 518/ET *The History of the Christ*, 376.

Further, neither the New Testament itself nor the ongoing experience of Christians subsequent to New Testament times warrants making "an absolute contrast ... between the present as utterly deserted by God and untouched by his rule, and a past which was filled with the revelation of God." The New Testament does not suggest that Jesus' saving work is to be "followed by the night of total abandonment by God." The New Testament bequeaths a three-fold legacy with which future generations must come to terms: (1) "an indestructible reconciliation which summons the world to God," (2) "Christ's rule which spans the aeons," and (3) "the presence of the Spirit which leads the believer's knowing and willing from God to God."[247]

We draw close, then, to Schlatter's view of history if we grant that the reading of the New Testament reflected in the preceding paragraph has something to commend it. In this case Schlatter tries to explicate, appropriate, and work out the implications of this forward-looking, particularly-based fact complex—the New Testament and the history which surrounds and comprises it. Is Schlatter's procedure not, however, just theologizing on the basis of faith? Not if Schlatter's reading of the New Testament should turn out to be accurate in any considerable measure. For that would imply that the New Testament gives invaluable insight into the enigma of history. It would be setting forth history, not as an inexorable religio-cultural ascent,[248] but as the God-given and God-sustained medium within which relationship to him may be gained; within which one's personal worth, security, and purpose in life is realized; and within which participation in the community of the redeemed is made possible. People could have saving knowledge of God through his presence in history in Jesus.

This is not a claim that Jesus brings an absolute new beginning, that he is not in any fundamental way connected with prior contingent reality. Rather, affirms Schlatter, what Jesus purposed and did bound him securely with a particular history preceding and following him.[249] In this sense he is indeed enmeshed the first-century historical nexus. But this nexus has longer connecting lines to prior and subsequent history than historicism and positivism tend to permit.

---

[247] *NNTT*, 132; *PTNT*, 173.

[248] Cf. Schlatter, *Das christliche Dogma*, 85: "The concept of 'regress' is just as concretely attested as that of 'progress.'" Troeltsch acknowledges this, too: "Historiography," *Encyclopedia of Religion and Ethics*, 720.

[249] Cf. Schmid, *Erkenntnis des geschichtlichen Christus bei Martin Kähler und bei Adolf Schlatter*, 241f.

With respect to the solid wedge driven between Jesus and "Christ" in New Testament criticism since the Enlightenment, Schlatter responds: if Jesus and the high christology of the apostolic writings are largely severed, if Jesus' "messianic will" is deemed a retrospective projection of later religious thought with only nominal historical grounding, then "a historical riddle" is created, which neither Philo, Mithras, nor Babylonian myths—all put forth seriously in Schlatter's day as the most relevant actual precursors or sources of Christianity—can account for. On the other hand, the historian who methodologically recognizes Jesus as the Christ has that which "he as a historian needs, a cause which produced its effects, a giver who formed his receivers, a will which awakened wills, history which generates history."[250]

3. Integration of immanent and transcendent aspects of history

Late in life Schlatter wrote that early on he had come to hold "neither a theology which forgot the world nor a historical conception which forgot God."[251] A historical conception does not necessarily have to assume a hidden or unknowable God; a theological perspective must not presume to grow out of itself with only nominal attachment to history.[252] Schlatter's conception of history is perhaps best explained along these lines: he seeks to combine a history of religion and an open-to-the-transcendent historiography. This is analogous to the New Testament itself, which presents natural cause-and-effect forces at work in history but also the divine. Schlatter wants to try to grasp past reality and its links to the present by an integration of the truths inherent in two positions often considered methodologically irreconcilable.[253]

The immanent dimension

Schlatter realized that "historical sense" (*geschichtlicher Sinn*) was a feature of modern thought which had arrived to stay. This "sense" Schlatter sees as the recognition "that human action is conditioned by the preceding series of events and is related to these in a tight causal context."[254] There can be no escape, especially for those taking the

---

[250]Schlatter, "Zweifel an der Messianität," *Zur Theologie*, 201f.

[251]Schlatter, *Rückblick auf meine Lebensarbeit*, 32.

[252]*Ibid.* 33.

[253]Cf. Dymale, "The Theology of Adolf Schlatter with Special Reference to his Understanding of History," 307.

[254]Schlatter, *Die philosophische Arbeit seit Cartesius*, 96.

biblical witness seriously, from this insight.[255] One of Schlatter's earlier major programmatic essays is an exposé of sorts questioning the old Protestant-Pietist legacy at key points.[256] Schlatter poses the question whether the Christian faith is rightly understood when God, his grace, and salvation are magnified distortedly to the point of excluding any significant regard for and by persons in their historicality. Is the Christian life just passive acceptance, quietism, acquiescence to timeless spiritual reality, thus an inner experience with no necessary interface, or only a negative one, with the historical process?[257] Is it not rather the case that God not only once worked "for us" but also is able to keep working "through us"?[258] Not just as a concession to the *Zeitgeist* but as a deep personal conviction, Schlatter held it illicit to conceive of theology (or history) as an enterprise which could be undertaken totally "from above."

"Christianity is a human matter. It was so from its inception... forward, and it cannot divest itself of this characteristic without dying."[259] Given the tone of much New Testament criticism in and since Schlatter's time, it is unnecessary to belabor his own criticisms of some orthodox or conservative theology. The point is to underscore his overt commitment to historical thinking. Schlatter states that he possessed a "hungry urge to research that made it impossible for me merely to be 'conservative.'"[260] This drive expresses itself in his desire, not for theological and thus timeless spiritual insight, but for theological understanding through historical clarification and explanation of contingent events.[261]

The transcendent dimension

Yet there is something of a dialectic here. For in affirming the value of historical observation, Schlatter also affirms its limits. "The glory of academic work is not that it knows everything, but that it sees what the witnesses make visible and is silent when they are silent."[262] This

---

[255]Cf. Luck, "Einführung," *Zur Theologie*, 23.

[256]Schlatter, "Der Dienst des Christen in der älteren Dogmatik," *Zur Theologie*, 31–105.

[257]Cf. Schlatter, *Der Aufstieg der evangelischen Kirche von der Reformation zur Gegenwart*, 1931, 16: "Were the footing for Christians restricted to that which takes place internally in our hearts, the church would drop out of sight."

[258]Schlatter, "Der Dienst der Christen in der älteren Dogmatik," *Zur Theologie*, 35.

[259]Schlatter, *Wohin? Eine Frage an unsere Schule und unsere Kirche*, 1929, 29f.

[260]Schlatter, *Rückblick auf meine Lebensarbeit*, 93.

[261]Cf. also especially *NNTT*, 136ff.; *PTNT*, 176ff.

[262]*NNTT*, 143; *PTNT*, 186.

spells the end of a historicist and positivist history of religion method which feels that in giving a "purely historical" description it has exhaustively explained a text. True, there can be dogmatic construal of the New Testament by those who believe its message. But there is also the specter of dogmatic construal of it from the critical orthodox side.

From Schlatter's point of view the transcendent can be expunged from New Testament history only at the expense of both its historical and its conceptual coherence, to say nothing of its theological meaning. Schlatter does not dispute that "purely historical" methods have their place; what he does ask is that the inevitable academic battles fought over New Testament issues be waged "with honorable and clean weapons."[263] (The military metaphor is apt. Recent research confirms that "history of religion" as a term denoted an attack on theology from the start; it had less to do with "history" than with a polemical drive to reduce the complexity inherent in research that admits the validity of theological considerations.[264]) This cannot come about until the a-theological proponent owns up to his own viewpoint's effect on his analysis of the New Testament historical data. For when the avowed history of religion practitioner, working with *a priori* laws or a hypothetical religious essence which is believed to have given rise to human spiritual development in all ages, undertakes ostensibly historical description, "history" may unavoidably become "a useless war between an inflated self and what happened" instead of comprising "judgments that grasp the real core of events."[265]

Undoubtedly Schlatter is justified in claiming: "The only thing I, as a scholarly laborer, pursued was the scrutiny of the history of religion."[266] He is not an enemy of history of religion thought as such, for in an important sense we have no other approach to religion than the historical.[267] But he feels it speculative to affirm that the essence or constituent dynamic in religion can be divorced from history as some-

---

[263] *NNTT*, 156; *PTNT*, 202.

[264] Murrmann-Kahl, *Die entzauberte Heilsgeschichte*, 355 n. 10.

[265] *Ibid.*

[266] Schlatter, *Die Religionswissenschaft der Gegenwart in Selbstdarstellungen*, 17. Cf. Dymale, "The Theology of Adolf Schlatter with Special Reference to his Understanding of History," 138.

[267] This should not obscure the fact that for Schlatter Christian knowledge of God is not *only* a horizontal, contingent process. The "mediation" (*Vermittlung*) of Christ's presence is based upon and operative through a historical nexus (cf. Schlatter, *Die philosophische Arbeit seit Cartesius*, 156, 146), but Schlatter does not carry this to the point of radical historicization of God, so that he becomes active or known only immanently. God both is active in and transcends the historical process.

thing timeless and free from historical contingency, an idea or feeling inhering in mankind's "supra-historical essence."[268] The history of theology since Schleiermacher proves that this line of reasoning can give rise to imaginative theological and historical reconstructions. Schlatter insists that "abstractions cut loose from [observed historical] realities are just as useless in practice as they are vacuous in theory."[269] The historian-theologian must not work with "an image of Christ which merely gives expression to our own wishes, but [with] a knowledge of what the Christ was like."[270] The problems involved in grounding theological thinking in historical reality do not absolve theologians of a perennial responsibility to make the attempt.

4. Schlatter and Heilsgeschichte

If we ask now in what sense Schlatter's outlook constitutes a salvation historical perspective, we must affirm first that he does not see salvation history as some grand system of divine acts.[271] He does not separate out of history as a whole a certain special segment, styling it a salvation history. True, he does stress firmly the biblical and New Testament history. But this is out of deference to the New Testament's own apparent proximity to those events which brought salvation to mankind. The New Testament history becomes a focal point for history as a whole, for it was apparently in this era that a critical juncture in God's redemptive will was reached. For Schlatter this is not a dogmatic postulate but to a considerable degree an observable historical verity.

Moreover, in an important sense what the New Testament relates is meant to be "a blueprint for the future instead of a history of the past."[272] Salvation history is not something that happened once but is now temporally distant and cut off from the present. Schlatter writes that it is fully justified to hold that "the object of our faith can be nothing in the past, rather only that which is present."[273] But that does not minimize the import of the New Testament; it establishes it.

For "the sacred history which the eternal God has brought about is not 'past'; it forms rather, with eternal power, the basis out of which that new act of God arises which now rules, humbles, quickens, re-

---

[268]Schlatter, *Die Religionswissenschaft der Gegenwart in Selbstdarstellungen*, 19.
[269]*NNTT*, 134; *PTNT*, 175.
[270]*Ibid.*
[271]Güting, *Neue Zeitschrift für systematische Theologie* 15 (1973) 147 n. 80.
[272]Schlatter, *The Church in the New Testament Period*, 1961, 324.
[273]Schlatter, "Geschichte und Glaube," *Heilige Anliegen*, 32.

deems us."[274] Salvation history is not just a collection of examples of great past truths and thoughts. The New Testament history is not merely an ideological construct, a self-conscious theological enterprise, whose efficacy lay solely in the creative power of the ideas it advanced. Rather it arose out of the creative power of God through the Old Testament, the ministry of Jesus, and the New Testament community, seen as an integrated whole. "The sacred history is the power which generates life."[275] The life of the New Testament pays tribute to this salvation history; we do the same today in glimpsing that "between that which God [once] did, and does today, and one day shall do, there reigns a causal connection of the most powerful, mightiest form."[276] Salvation history is the totality of reality seen as history which interprets ostensibly immanent phenomena as the historically visible expression[277] of God's personal sovereign purpose.

Schlatter is thus neither a Cartesian in the sense of absolutizing a modern view, nor purely non-Cartesian in the negative sense of jettisoning modernity for the sake of allegiance to a cherished view of the past. He is also not simply a mediating theologian, shrewdly seeking a golden mean by which to reconcile opposing factions. He wants rather to view history in its totality under the assumption—which much of his research sought to establish or to ground—that the New Testament relates a basically reliable account, not of all things, but of those things of which it speaks. Granted that "all observation," even of the New Testament, "remains less than comprehensive in its breadth and depth when conceived over against the infinitude and infathomability of that which has taken place."[278] Nevertheless, as Schlatter never grew tired of repeating, "that which is unknown can never make uncertain that which is known; the invisible can never render unsure our knowledge of that which is visible."[279] "We must not, because of what is withdrawn from our view, underestimate what we can perceive clearly."[280] Schlatter's perspective is echoed in these more recent words:

We do not have to have complete comprehension of every aspect of the being and nature of God in order to make *some* true affirmations about

[274] *Ibid.*

[275] *Ibid.*

[276] *Ibid.* 32f. Cf. Schlatter, *Die philosophische Arbeit seit Cartesius*, 245.

[277] Cf. Dymale, *Theology of Schlatter*, 133: "Since causes become visible in their effects, the processes" by which God has worked in history "are not always hidden."

[278] Schlatter, *Die philosophische Arbeit seit Cartesius*, 12.

[279] *Ibid.* 123.

[280] Schlatter, *Church in the New Testament Period*, 3.

Him. In fact, human beings do not have complete comprehension of every aspect of any reality with which they have to do, but this does not prevent them from making some true statements about many things.[281]

So then, salvation history in Schlatter's case must be understood in terms of an integrated hermeneutical, theological, and historical perspective which at once both informs and is informed by the history of which worship of God through Jesus the Christ has come into existence. It is history seen, not strictly "from below," nor again presumptuously "from above," but from an amalgamated vantage point which places high value on man's capacity to perceive and affirms God's continuing involvement in human lives—"history"— in accordance with observed biblical precedent.

Conclusion

In this and the preceding chapter we have isolated features of the salvation historical outlook in Hofmann and Schlatter regarded especially as New Testament theologians. We agree with R. Herrmann that these two bear inclusion under a similar rubric, even if "in view of both of them" one "can barely speak of followers, much less of a formal school."[282] In comparing them with the "critical orthodox" trajectory of Baur and Wrede, we have uncovered, not so much two slightly contrasting perspectives within a common academic discipline, but two fairly opposite conceptions of what New Testament theology is and how it is to be undertaken.

One side conceives of New Testament theology as phenomenology[283] (though paradoxically for both Baur and Wrede there is a shadowy "absolute" hovering in the background which serves somewhat like the transcendent God whom their method has put to flight[284]). Historicism and positivism are welcomed as essential tools for

---

[281] B. Hebblewaite, "'True' and 'False' in Christology," *The Philosophical Frontiers of Theology,* ed. B. Hebblewaite & S. Sutherland, 1982, 234.

[282] R. Herrmann, "Offenbarung, Worte und Texte," in *Bibel und Hermeneutik,* ed. H. Beintker *et al.,* 1971, 201.

[283] In the sense of phenomenalism, the theory that limits knowledge to phenomena only. Ironically, in terms of phenomenology as a formal philosophy, Walldorf (*Realistische Philosophie,* 281f.) finds points of contact between Schlatter and Husserl.

[284] Cf. Wyman, *JR* 78 (1998): "Troeltsch seeks to ground the human consciousness of divinity in reality itself through his theory of the religious a priori. According to this theory, religion arises necessarily out of an inner predisposition that Troeltsch calls an 'a priori consciousness' ... Revelation occurs universally in the depth of the human spirit" (56).

the task of setting forth a scientific explication of, not so much the New Testament texts as what is behind them. Indicators of thoughts, concepts, or traditions, by virtue of their own inexorable power or critically recognized importance, make their way into the documents of the New Testament corpus. New Testament theology is a delineation of the unfolding of the conceptual processes (Baur) or the rise and development of the historical traditions (Wrede). The ostensibly concrete historical events recorded by the New Testament writers as the basis of their kerygmatic claims and doctrines are for the most part illusionary, since modern consciousness rules out the possibility that many of the events ever took place. Modern criticism rejects the precepts of biblical doctrine in favor of the current reigning doctrinal synthesis (Hegelian, Ritschlian, history of religion) which is then read back into the New Testament where the texts can be stretched to bear the load. New Testament theology is a "historical" account that synthesizes (Baur) or otherwise accounts for (Wrede) the New Testament (non-) events, claims, and doctrines and arrays them in summary fashion or explicates their unfolding.

The salvation historical outlook regards the New Testament writings as evincing substantial theological unity and historical veracity and as enjoying temporal proximity to the events or words they relate. They comprise "theology" as they stand, the theology of Jesus himself (or of Old Testament writers, when these are drawn on) and then of his followers. New Testament theology is thus a discriminating reconstruction and contemporary re-expression of the content of the New Testament seen first its own historical setting, not the setting of a "modern" outlook that *a priori* denies the reality of much of what the New Testament sets forth.

Epistemologically, one side is religiously faithful to Kant. There is evidently not a great deal of thought for the danger that interpretations could thereby "mold the texts in accordance with a preconceived philosophical mindset."[285] The other side fears that *a priori* reason or reasons might not be able in all cases to discern rightly the actuality and full import of historical reality generally and of biblical data in its theological dimensions in particular. A broader and deeper concept of truth and God in history is sought. A merging of openness to the transcendent and careful observation of the phenomenal is attempted. A functional, somewhat flexible epistemology emerges, in which not only the text but also the interpreter are called into question. Schlatter

---

[285]E. Ellis, "Foreword," in L. Goppelt, *Typos*, 1982, xix (referring to Baur).

in particular, but also Hofmann to a considerable degree, is thus open to seeing that which might not accord with "modern" assumptions regarding what can and cannot have transpired to give rise to the New Testament texts. Similarly, the refusal to absolutize modern understanding leaves the possibility for Scripture itself, not just modern thoughts about Scripture, to possess a certain authoritative weight.

As far as views of history, one side brings into New Testament theology a conception of history currently dominant in philosophical thought at large. Baur used Hegel's insights, Wrede affirmed Troeltsch's. Both are heavily if often indirectly indebted to Kant. New Testament interpretation becomes a process of debunking the New Testament's own surface rationale for its origin and development. New Testament theology unfolds along a developmental continuum deemed valid under the auspices of dominant critical theory.

The other side works from the assumption that history is not a totally immanent, closed-system process. God has worked and is working in the historical nexus (though Scripture points to many events, like the incarnation and atonement, that are not expected to happen again). He transcends it, but history generally and especially the data of biblical history are finally inexplicable without recourse to a personal and active God as testified to by the New Testament but ruled out by Baur and Wrede.

Salvation history in the New Testament theologies of both Hofmann and Schlatter is hardly a biblicistic, pietistic, or Romantic idealist schema forced onto the biblical data. It is rather a sequence whose chief supports are, it is argued, compelling to a careful observer of the historical facts. These facts, it is true, are interlocked with theological claims, but these claims are articulated by the same writers who present the facts. So even the theology found in Scripture by Hofmann and Schlatter is derived from the sources they would argue, and not brought to them in the way that Baur and Wrede bring, say, Kant's categorical imperative into the Sermon on the Mount. Rather than to interpret the New Testament as a development strictly discrete from any material involvement by a transcendent God, Hofmann and Schlatter seek to explain it based on the measured assumption that the New Testament writers might know more about that which they tell, and understand what they know more accurately, than secular thinkers of two millennia hence who venerate a movement (the Enlightenment) openly hostile to the writers' surface claims. Perhaps a sympathetic (though not naive) rendering of the New Testament's religious and theological content in its ostensible concrete historical setting can better account for the data at hand than the alternate scenarios demanded by idealist historiography, whether Hegelian or neo-Kantian.

The chief characteristics, then, of the salvation historical perspective as seen in Hofmann's and Schlatter's New Testament theologies may be found in its intentional and carefully grounded distancing from the trajectory epitomized in Baur and Wrede. The salvation historical perspective is not fundamentally reactionary or apologetic; it simply attempts to transcend those aspects of modernity it finds too restrictive to account for the phenomena of antiquity and seeks to set forth more fruitful ways to explain them. In the eyes of some this departure from the critically dominant school is bought at the price of appearing to revert to pre-critical thinking. For Hofmann and Schlatter their justification arises from "critical" thinking's own failure convincingly to account for the historical data, with which Hofmann and Schlatter[286] wrestled as earnestly as Baur and Wrede.

[286]Boer's categorical claim (*Theology*, 75) that Schlatter "allowed present-day dogmatic concerns to predetermine the outcome of the historical inquiry" (1) is somewhat simplistic and too sweeping, on the basis of our study, and (2) begs the question which Schlatter insists must be addressed: what are the nature and (often hidden) ground-rules of "historical inquiry"? The same can be said of Räisänen's complaint about Schlatter's "contemporizing tendency" (*Beyond New Testament Theology*, 36). Wredian "historical" research, to which Räisänen is sympathetic, in some ways epitomizes a "contemporizing" impulse.

3

The Debate Continues: Old and New Testament Theology between the World Wars

Some famous books carry titles that tell us little. You have to read *Gone with the Wind* to realize what is gone (the American Old South) and what the wind was (the Civil War). The best-selling *Flags of Our Fathers* says nothing in the title about its subject matter: U.S. Marines who fought in World War II at Iwo Jima, especially the six men in the famous flag-raising photo.

But the titles of other books say it all. An example would be J. Fest's *Plotting Hitler's Death*. Another transparent title, at least for any with a memory of World War II: *Stalingrad* by A. Beevor. Another is by M. Murrmann-Kahl: *Die entzauberte Heilsgeschichte: Der Historismus erobert die Theologie 1880-1920* (Salvation History Debunked: Historicism Vanquishes Theology 1880-1920)

Murrman-Kahl's study of historiography leading up to the years between the wars has been largely overlooked, it seems, by biblical scholars. But it points to the outcome of the Wrede-Schlatter debate chronicled in the previous chapter. Who won? It wasn't Schlatter. True, something akin to his theological emphasis was carried forth by Barth. But in Barth's formulation the historical grounding of theology so important to Schlatter was jettisoned. And Schlatter's understanding of history of religion method as open to transcendence was embraced by few. So Schlatter's outlook met a two-fold fate: university exegetes tended to affirm a Wredian understanding of historiography, while the Barthian articulation of "theology" had but slight ties to the biblical history Schlatter worked hard to recover. In that respect it was not merely theology but history too that suffered.

Murrmann-Kahl's findings caution us against a headlong jump from Schlatter to the next major salvation historical New Testament theologian, Oscar Cullmann (born 1902). It might seem a reasonable move. After all, Schlatter lived until 1938 and thus almost to the 1946 appearance of Cullmann's influential *Christ and Time*. In strict chronological terms, very little separates Schlatter from the post-World War II era during which the idea of salvation history enjoyed considerable currency in the so-called Biblical Theology Movement. Furthermore, if in some sense Hofmann is a methodological first cousin of Schlatter, one could attempt now to assess Cullmann as a conceptual near-kinsman of his salvation historical predecessors.

But we must follow a different course, for a couple of reasons. First and quite simply, there exists no comprehensive treatment of 20th-century salvation historical approaches in general, much less in New Testament theology specifically.[1] This fact is undoubtedly behind G. O'Collins' remark that "we need a study comparable to G. Weth's *Die Heilsgeschichte*"[2] that updates discussion since Weth's time. This is not the place to fulfill that wish. Yet we need to sketch a fuller understanding than we yet possess of the presence, development, and use of the salvation historical perspective in both Old and New Testament theology if we are to move from Schlatter to Cullmann in an informed fashion.

Second, in past years salvation historical scholarship erroneously came to be regarded, first as an innovation of the mid-20th century Biblical Theology Movement, and then apparently as an irrelevance.[3] In the 1970s J. Clemons called it "a hermeneutical method which has dominated biblical studies ... for more than three decades."[4] In the 1980s R. Gnuse spoke of "Salvation History" as a popular category "among biblical theologians in recent years."[5] By the 1990s, the Biblical Theology Movement had faded to such a distant memory that a history of interpretation textbook could devote a number of pages to the history of religion school and mention many of its members but say nothing at all of a corresponding salvation historical outlook. Astonishingly, given his importance in New Testament studies, Cullmann is not even mentioned, and there is only laconic treatment of Hofmann (whose name is misspelled) and Schlatter (about whom

---

[1] W.G. Kümmel, "Heilsgeschichte im Neuen Testament?" *Heilsgeschehen und Geschichte*, vol. 2, ed. E. Grässer & O. Merk, 157-176, only makes a start.

[2] G. O'Collins, *Foundations of Theology*, 1971, 200 n. 8, referring to G. Weth, *Die Heilsgeschichte. Ihr Sinn in der offenbarungsgeschichtlichen Theologie des 19. Jahrhunderts*, München 1931.

[3] The classic tracing of this movement's contours is J. Barr, "Biblical Theology," *IDPSup*, 104–111. See also J. Hayes & F. Prussner, *Old Testament Theology*, 1985, 209–218.

[4] J. Clemons, "Critics and Criticism of Salvation History," *Religion in Life* 41 (1972) 89.

[5] R. Gnuse, "Authority of the Scriptures: Quest for a Norm," *BTB* 13 (1983) 61f.

facts are skewed).[6] Salvation history is not viewed as a fallacy. It simply disapppears.

How accurate is the perception that focus on salvation history was primarily an interlude within mid-20th century "biblical theology" and thus appropriately now forgotten? Probably not very. It is simply not true that Cullmann "more than anyone ... familiarized the English-speaking world with the concept of *Heilsgeschichte*."[7] Perhaps scholars cloistered in the rarified atmosphere of mid-20th century mainline North American biblical studies departments were startled by Cullmann's voice and happy to stifle it after his retirement, but central aspects of his views were alive and well in post-Reformation theology from Cocceius through Pietism and Bengel right up to Hofmann himself,[8] as well as throughout the 19th century not only in Germany but also in the Princeton theological outlook[9] out of which sprang G. Vos' and later G. Ladd's salvation historical theologies.[10] It would only do the history of New Testament theology further disservice if we failed to investigate factors preceding Cullmann that shed surprising light on his contribution and thus on the salvation historical perspective in New Testament theology.

We turn now therefore to the epoch inaugurated by Karl Barth's Romans commentary. By common consent the time of its appearance marks a decisive point for 20th-century theology and biblical studies alike. For both fields of study, "the nineteenth century did not come to a close until after the first World War, for the first quarter of the [20th] century was actually a continuation ... of tendencies which had their origin ... in the preceding century."[11] We will begin by tracing Old Testament theology's fitful movements toward a salvation histori-

---

[6]G. Bray, *Biblical Interpretation*, 1996. For "Hoffmann" [sic] see 282f. On Schlatter see the eight lines he receives on 339. Contrary to the Schlatter entry, he did not follow Cremer; his New Testament theology was not produced in 1909 (volume 1 of the first edition appeared in that year); and his commentaries on the entire New Testament appeared between 1887 (Romans) and 1910 (Revelation), not between 1930 and his death.

[7]R. Fuller, "Some Further Reflections on *Heilsgeschichte*," *USQR* 22 (1967) 93.

[8]Carefully and fully documented in G. Schrenk, *Gottesreich und Bund im älteren Protestantismus*, 1967 (= 1923).

[9]For an entree into this neglected school of biblical scholarship see D. Calhoun, *Princeton Seminary*, 2 vols., Edinburgh/Carlisle 1994–1996.

[10]G. Vos, *Biblical Theology*, 1948; G. Ladd, *A Theology of the New Testament*, 1973. On the salvation historical heritage of Vos see P. Wallace, "The Foundations of Reformed Biblical Theology: The Development of Old Testament Theology at Old Princeton," *WTJ* 59/1 (1997) 41–69.

[11]Hayes and Prussner, *Old Testament Theology*, 90.

cal emphasis, as opposed to a strict history of religion one, in the time span in view. Discussion will at times appear to have minimal contact with New Testament theology since Old Testament theology, unlike its New Testament counterpart, developed independently of the influence of dialectical theology, at least for a good number of years.[12] But Old Testament theology saw considerable progress in synthetic understanding of the Old Testament during this time and shaped parameters within which New Testament theology later worked. This is particularly true with respect to the history of religion paradigm, in which Old Testament scholarship led the way.[13] We will show that the issues Hofmann and Schlatter raised vis-à-vis Baur and Wrede are debated fiercely, though hardly resolved, by a series of Old Testament theologians.

We will also be concerned to determine the fate, or even the presence, of salvation historical thinking in New Testament theology. Did the view suddenly surface, a recessive Hofmannian gene afflicting a theological child untimely born, in Cullmann's *Christ and Time*? Or were other New Testament critics too pointing toward elements of an outlook for which Cullmann's study would become something of a fresh rearticulation?

Heilsgeschichte versus *Religionsgeschichte:* Old Testament theology 1918-1946

Numerous studies exist which are relevant to Old Testament studies and theology during this time.[14] We must go beyond these, however,

---

[12]W.H. Schmidt, "'Theologie des Alten Testaments' vor und nach Gerhard von Rad," *VF* 17 (1972) 4.

[13]R. Smend, "Beziehungen zwischen alttestamentlicher und neutestamentlicher Wissenschaft," *ZTK* 92 (1995) 10.

[14]Cf. e.g. Kraus, *Geschichte der historisch-kritischen Erforschung des Alten Testaments*, 1956, 358-394; Dentan, *Preface*, 61-71; E. Würthwein, "Zur Theologie des Alten Testaments," *TRu* 36 (1971) 185-208; Schmidt, *VF* 17 (1972) 1-25, especially 4-9; E. Kraeling, *The Old Testament Since the Reformation*, 1955, 164-218; R. E. Clements, *A Century of Old Testament Study*, 1976, 126-134; H.G. Reventlow, *Hauptprobleme der alttestamentlichen Theologie im 20. Jahrhundert*, 1982; Hayes & Prussner, *Old Testament Theology*, 143–209; B. Schroven, *Theologie des Alten Testaments zwischen Anpassung und Widerstand*, 1995; S. Felber, *Wilhelm Vischer als Ausleger der Heiligen Schrift*, 1999; P. House, *Old Testament Theology*, 1998, 28–32. Cf. also A.J. Greig, "Geschichte and Heilsgeschichte in Old Testament Interpretation," 1974, 40-48 (heavily dependent on Kraus and Dentan); G. Hasel, *Old Testament Theology*, [2]1979, 31f. (brief sketch). Less accessible but significant is W. McKane, *A Late Harvest*, 1995.

and show more specifically how salvation history came in for discussion. Not seldom the debate, so novel if seen merely from the standpoint of Old Testament studies, merely echoes issues already broached in chapters one and two above. We will suggest that Old Testament theology in some quarters wished to move away from a pure history of religion approach, but that on the whole it failed to break decisively with a Baur-Wrede (Troeltsch) model of inquiry.

Three features of Old Testament studies prior to 1918 are pertinent to assessing the situation following World War I.

1. Previous salvation historical approaches to Old Testament theology
There is first the simple fact that Old Testament theology had previously hardly attempted to take up and develop salvation history as an integrating center or hermeneutical tool. True, F. Delitzsch (1813-1890) and G. Oehler (1812-1878) were sympathetic to a salvation historical outlook.[15] In their work, as in that of other 19th century interpreters, one may detect basic characteristics of a salvation historical approach. True as well that some of the positive fruits of Hegelianism in nineteenth century Old Testament theology mirror those of thinkers who spoke of salvation history: like the latter, some Hegelian Old Testament specialists rightly concluded (1) that Old Testament theology requires "a certain philosophical mood" without which "its interests are likely to appear merely trivial and antiquarian," and (2) that "Hebrew religion cannot be understood apart from the concept of historical development," such development comprising not merely "chronological successiveness" but more importantly "organic growth."[16] But full-scale Hegelianism typically includes features that are incompatible with most conceptions of salvation history. In the end the 19th century failed to produce a salvation historical synthesis of the Old Testament.[17] As a result, early 20th century Old Testament specialists had opportunity to approach the idea of salvation history with somewhat more openness than their New Testament counter-

[15]On Delitzsch see Kraus, *Geschichte der Erforschung*, 214; Kantzenbach, *Erlanger Theologie*, 213f; S. Wagner, *Franz Delitzsch: Leben und Werk*, 1978; Rogerson, *Old Testament Criticism*, 111-120. On Oehler see e.g. Kraus, *Biblische Theologie*, 99-106; Hayes & Prussner, *Old Testament Theology*, 114–118.

[16]Dentan, *Preface*, 39.

[17]Even though Old Testament scholars like Steudel, Hävernick, and Oehler bear marks of a salvation historical emphasis, they "were unable to achieve consistency between that methodological emphasis and their actual presentation of Old Testament theology" (B. Ollenburger, E. Martens & G. Hasel, eds., *The Flowering of Old Testament Theology*, 1992, 12).

parts; Old Testament theology had had no Hofmann fatally to stigma-
tize salvation history for use in a synthetic treatment of the Old
Testament.[18]

2. Dominance of non-salvation historical approaches

A second noteworthy feature of Old Testament studies prior to 1918
involves new approaches to the study of the Old Testament. These
made it easy, even fashionable, to ignore or denigrate the sort of salvation historical synthesis which Hofmann had projected for the entire
Bible[19] and which Delitzsch and Oehler had foreshadowed. These new
trends were surfacing even before Hofmann passed from the scene: "It
was tragic that, precisely in Hofmann's time, historical study of both
Old and New Testament readily avoided the problems of faith."[20] This
would include the problem of how one should conceive of the relationship between history and God's activity within it. It would be
unjust to suppose that Old Testament research consciously and arbitrarily "avoided the problems of faith." Rather the combined weight
of new discoveries[21] and new methods[22] effectively preempted the
theological dimension of Old Testament theology, as paradoxical as
that might sound.[23]

These new discoveries and methods did not work only against a salvation historical approach. G. Hasel comments rightly that "for over
four decades Old Testament theology" in general "was eclipsed by
Religionsgeschichte."[24] He has in mind the period ca. 1880-1920. During
this time there were numerous efforts to give a synthetic picture of

---

[18]Hofmann did however exert a certain influence on Old Testament theology. See
J. Rogerson, "Geschichte und Altes Testament im 19. Jahrhundert," *BN* 22 (1983)
126-138, and the references to Hofmann in Rogerson, *Old Testament Criticism*.

[19]Noted in Hayes & Prussner, *Old Testament Theology*, 82–84.

[20]O. Procksch, "Die Geschichte als Glaubensinhalt," *NKZ* 36 (1925) 485. In
Procksch's parlance the "problems of faith" and the problems attending a salvation
historical approach would be very nearly synonymous.

[21]Cf. "Die Entdeckungen der Archäologie im Orient," Kraus, *Geschichte der Erforschung*, 265-283; R. Kittel, "Die Zukunft der alttestamentlichen Wissenschaft," *ZAW*
39 (1921) 85ff.

[22]Primarily a new stress on "religion" as opposed to dogmatics. Such religion must
be analyzed with all possible utilization of insights from scientific historiography,
psychology, and sociology. When this quest after Old Testament religion in its purely
phenomenological aspects was wedded with a developmental (*entwicklungsgeschichtliche*)
orientation, the so-called history of religion school was born; cf. Kraus, *Geschichte der
Erforschung*, 289-308; Reventlow, *Hauptprobleme*, 10ff.

[23]Cf. also Kraeling, *OT Since Reformation*, 89-97.

[24]Hasel, *Old Testament Theology*, 30.

Old Testament religion. Wellhausen and Gunkel largely set the tone for Old Testament synthetic analysis.[25] There was a renewed call for Old Testament "theology" to be rigorously historical—this often meant historicistic and positivistic—and to sever radically any lingering traces of interest in "dogmatics," in theology in the classic sense.[26]

W. Eichrodt notes in 1933: "It is significant that, in the twenty-five years since the last appearance of Schultz's theology in 1896, no one else has made the attempt to set forth a similar presentation of the Old Testament faith. The 'historical' approach had completely taken over."[27] In the years prior, and even subsequent, to World War I, Old Testament theology in a sense inclusive of Christian dogmatics had essentially collapsed.[28] "Gunkel felt and predicted that no more Old Testament theologies would be written."[29] By the 1930s some Old Testament scholars were even making common cause with the Nazis in their academic work.[30] In more ways than one Old Testament theology was in serious need of a renewed vision.

3. Search for a *salvation historical perspective*

A third feature of Old Testament theology, or what served as its substitute for many years, was a growing awareness of the need for a salvation historical approach to Old Testament theology. As early as

---

[25]For Gunkel's repudiation of "theological and salvation historical" exegesis see Schroven, *Theologie des Alten Testaments zwischen Anpassung und Widerstand*, 66f. On his break with theology see A. Özen, "Die Göttinger Wurzeln der 'Religionsgeschichtlichen Schule,'" *Die "Religionsgeschichtliche Schule,"* 23f. On Wellhausen see Bray, *Biblical Interpretation*, 380–383; Ollenburger, Martens & Hasel, eds., *The Flowering of Old Testament Theology*, 14 (comments on Gunkel as well).

[26]Cf. B. Stade, "Über die Aufgaben der biblischen Theologie des Alten Testaments," *ZTK* 3 (1893) 31-51, who sets forth a denunciation of traditional Christian convictions still plaguing Old Testament theological inquiry and suggests measures finally to eradicate them.

[27]Eichrodt, *Theologie des Alten Testaments*, vol. 1, [5]1957 ([1]1933), 4.

[28]Dentan, *Preface*. 50, remarks: "The year 1878, in which J. Wellhausen published his *Prolegomena zur Geschichte Israels* marks the beginning of the period which saw the apparent death of Old Testament theology." W. Zimmerli speaks of "the dissolution of the presentation of Israel's faith into a 'history of Israelite religion'" ("Biblische Theologie. I," *TRE* 6, 438). Clements, *Century of Old Testament Theology*, 122f., argues that "the aim of presenting an Old Testament theology was not lost sight of … in the last quarter of the nineteenth century," yet must concede that "the prevailing historicism threatened to engulf even the more religious and theological aspects of Old Testament study."

[29]Hayes & Prussner, *Old Testament Theology*, 147.

[30]F. Crüsemann, "Tendenzen der alttestalmentlichen Wissenschaft zwischen 1933 and 1945," *Wort und Dienst* 20 (1989) 79–103.

the 1890s, "the question of the relation between history and salvation history receives renewed attention."[31] On the one hand in synthetic studies of the Old Testament published around the turn of the century, "the theme '*Heilsgeschichte*' is consciously eliminated."[32] On the other hand several recognized that "the future of Old Testament research" depended on the proper weight being accorded to dimensions of the Old Testament which salvation historical approaches seemed best suited to handle.[33]

J. Köberle (1871-1908) realized this relatively early and clearly.[34] His specific contribution to Old Testament theology is noted elsewhere,[35] though not always quite accurately.[36] He writes:

> The history of religion mode of scrutiny as it is currently in use is not "purely historical" but involves a philosophy of history. It is in a distinct sense dogmatic. The dogma is the development from the lower to the higher. If the presently ascendant outlook high-mindedly or disdainfully dismisses the older salvation historical outlook as "dogmatic," then one

---

[31]Kraus, *Geschichte der Erforschung*, 336. In the broader context of German theological and critical thought at that time, Rupp (*Culture Protestantism*, 25) relates this development to the response of Ritschlian dogmatics to the burgeoning challenge of Troeltschian historigraphy: "Indeed, from the 1890s on the allegedly special character of the history that grounds Christian faith became a renewed focus for systematic attention in apologetic efforts from multiple points on the theological spectrum." But not all who called for salvation historical openness were Ritschlians.

[32]Kraus, *Geschichte der Erforschung*, 344, Cf. the presentations of Old Testament religion by W. Robertson Smith (1899), R. Smend (²1899), F. Giesebrecht (1904), J. Lagrange (²1905), and K. Marti (⁵1907).

[33]Kraus, *Geschichte der Erforschung*, 345.

[34]Köberle, "Heilsgeschichtliche und religionsgeschichtliche Betrachtungsweise des Alten Testaments," *NKZ* 17 (1906) 200-222. Köberle's insights are anticipated at points by M. Reichle's fair but penetrating analysis of Troeltsch: "Historische und dogmatische Methode der Theologie," *TRu* 4 (1901) 261-275, 305-324.

[35]E.g. Kraus, *Geschichte der Erforschung*, 344-347.

[36]Greig, "Geschichte and Heilsgeschichte in Old Testament Interpretation," 37f., follows Kraus (previous note) too closely in failing to stress Köberle's call for attention to (1) an openness to the Old Testament's own belief in revelation as basic to Old Testament theology, and (2) modern criticism's inherent antipathy to many traditional Christian beliefs. Hasel, *Old Testament Theology*, 59 n. 12, is hardly correct in claiming that Köberle "wants to give theological validity only to the real history of Israel as reached by modern methodology." In fact this seems to be denied by Köberle; cf. *NKZ* 17 (1906) 218f.

can justly reply that someone who lives in a glass house ought not throw stones.[37]

In these and similar terms Köberle vents criticism at an excessive history of religion stress, along with its underlying, often unreflected rationale.[38] Yet he admits, citing Hofmann's *Weissagung und Erfüllung*, that the salvation history concept "as it has until now normally been utilized"[39] is no longer tenable. Nevertheless he calls for renewed attention to the potential of salvation history. He wants both history of religion and salvation historical method to be integrated in such a way that no "double method" emerges, a "scientific" on the one hand and an "ecclesiastical" on the other, but that rather "a [single] dual way of confirmation," which makes use of "a different manner of religious assessment," comes into play.[40]

In the end Köberle calls for an Old Testament theology which realizes critical historiography's biases and limitations.[41] This is not to repristinate the "conventional salvation historical mode of inquiry"[42] which at times in Köberle's estimation simply overlooked pressing critical questions or presented the Old Testament in a contrived fashion so as to fit in as desired with the New Testament. Rather it is to let the apparent critical certainties of phenomenological research—"the history of religion mode of inquiry"—come into dialogue with the apparent theological verities derived through reflection on the fundamental given of all Old and New Testament study: the text of the Bible itself, understood from a perspective not in the first place inimical to it.[43] The ensuing discussion could then result in a more balanced and accurate synthetic understanding of the Old Testament.[44] Köberle's insights echo the outlooks of both Hofmann and Schlatter.

---

[37]Köberle, *NKZ* 17 (1906) 209. Cf. Reichle, *TRu* 4 (1901) 322. The tenor of Köberle's remarks here and elsewhere is much in line with the criticisms of and suggested alternatives to history of religions excesses which Schlatter also set forth.

[38]Cf. Köberle, *NKZ* 17 (1906) 210f.: "Since Wellhausen's *Prolegomena* in 1878 nothing new, I mean really new, has come out of the entire school of thought he heads up. Is there then absolutely no further progress to be made beyond Wellhausen?"

[39]*Ibid*. 217.

[40]*Ibid*. 219. Also addressing this issue in the same era is C. Bernoulli, *Die wissenschaftliche und die kirchliche Methode in der Theologie*, 1897.

[41]Cf. J. Goldingay, *Approaches to Old Testament Interpretation*, 1981, 73f.; Ollenburger, Martens & Hasel, eds., *The Flowering of Old Testament Theology*, 15.

[42]Köberle, *NKZ* 17 (1906) 221.

[43]Cf. Reischle, *TRu* 4 (1901) 323.

[44]Köberle, *NKZ* 17 (1906) 221f.

W. Lotz in a thorough study virtually forgotten today pursues a similar line with somewhat greater sophistication.[45] He stresses the positive gains of criticism but insists that modern naturalistic world-views, not demonstrable facts, are the main barriers to a salvation historical understanding of the Old Testament. Lotz defines the Old Testament salvation history as

> the history of the development of the God-consciousness of the chosen people, a development conditioned and effected by God's historical leading of and revelatory interaction with Israel, as the result of this development ... was gathered together, partially in the intellectual possession of the people, partially in the sacred scriptures of the Old Testament.[46]

On this basis he concludes:

> As a theological discipline Old Testament salvation history is the treatment of Israelite history which establishes how, in the course of that history, the presuppositions for the revelation of the entire fullness of the divine salvific truth in Jesus Christ were gradually worked out in historical progression. The primary task here is, however, to grasp the progression in the history of Israel as truly historical, to comprehend the history of Israel as a history in the fullest sense of the word.[47]

Lotz is clearly thinking along Hofmannian lines.[48] His proposals evince a noteworthy grasp of both historical criticism's rightful claims and the implications of the Old Testament's revealed historical-theological truth. Both P. Volz[49] and O. Procksch (discussed below) also deserve mention as preserving, or pioneering, insights aiding a salvation historical understanding of the Old Testament. But neither in Lotz's time exhibits his mastery of fact and argument.

In the years prior to 1918 salvation history was seldom if ever the integrating center of an Old Testament theology. This was not all the result of innocent commitment to a scholarly method; a "virulent anti-

---

[45]Lotz, *Das Alte Testament und die Wissenschaft*, 1905, praised by Kraeling, *Old Testament since the Reformation*, 297 n. 1.

[46]Lotz, *Das Alte Testament*, 50.

[47]*Ibid*.

[48]With the important difference that Hofmann is not a Kantian, either epistemologically or morally/ethically, while Lotz reflects the influence of the neo-Kantian Lotze (cf. Kraeling, *Old Testament since the Reformation*, 297 n. 1). On Lotze see Schnädelbach, *Philosophy*, 169-80, and the still valuable work of L. Stählin, *Kant, Lotze, and Ritschl*, 1889.

[49]Cf. Kraus, *Geschichte der Erforschung*, 347-350.

Old Testament attitude" which "reached its apogee under Nazi propaganda and was joined by many respected biblical scholars"[50] was already fermenting at this time. Yet calls for an openness to a salvation historical perspective of some description kept theological conscience alive at a time when Old Testament studies was seeking to blot out the memory of "dogma" in favor of history of religion's redeeming value.[51] A number of critics, including Köberle and Lotz, take a Hofmannian-Schlatterian tack. They insist that not only modern but also ancient verities be given leave to shape contemporary understanding of the Old Testament texts' message.

4. History and theology after World War I
Detailed studies of Old Testament criticism in this period are available elsewhere.[52] It is not possible here to discuss even every Old Testament theology appearing between 1918 and 1946,[53] much less every Old Testament scholar who deals with the Old Testament and history, theology, or salvation history in his work. We will focus attention on six German theologians whose work is germane to understanding Old Testament theology and salvation history within it.[54] The Anglo-Saxon

---

[50]Hayes and Prussner, *Old Testament Theology*, 149, 151.

[51]See Kraus, *Geschichte der Erforschung*, 379-385, for elaboration.

[52]Besides Kraus, *Geschichte der Erforschung*, Dentan, *Preface*; and Schroven, *Theologie des Alten Testaments zwischen Anpassung und Widerstand*, where ample bibliography may be found, and articles in standard reference works, see also from the British perspective N. Porteous, "Old Testament Theology," *The Old Testament and Modern Study*, ed. H.H. Rowley, 1951, 311-345. From an American point of view see R.A. Bowman, "Old Testament Research between the Great Wars," *The Study of the Bible Today and Tomorrow*, ed. H.R. Willoughby, 1947, 3-31; Ollenburger, Martens & Hasel, eds., *The Flowering of Old Testament Theology*, 3–30. For additional useful background see also E. König, *Theologie des Alten Testaments*, 1922, 1-18.

[53]I.e. those by König (1922), E. Sellin (1933), L. Köhler (1936), W. & H. Möller (1938), and P. Heinisch (1940); cf. Dentan, *Preface*, 62ff.; Zimmerli, *TRE* 6, 438f.

[54]Space limitations require omission of other figures worth attention, among them J. Lindblom and W. Vischer. For Vischer see *The Witness of the Old Testament to Christ*, 1949 (first German edition 1934); "Das Christuswort des Propheten Jeremia," *Das Christuszeugnis des Alten Testaments*, volume 30 of *Beiträge aus der Arbeit der v. Bodelschwinghschen Anstalten in Bielefeld-Bethel*, 1985; Felber, *Wilhelm Vischer als Ausleger der Heiligen Schrift*. Lindblom's relevant study is "Zur Frage der Eigenart der alttestamentlichen Religion," *BZAW* 66 (1936) 128-137.

A. Weiser makes use of salvation historical terminology; relevant works include "Die theologische Aufgabe der alttestamentlichen Wissenschaft" [address to the 1935 meeting of German Ancient Near Eastern scholars in Göttingen], *Glauben und Geschichte im Alten Testament*, 1961, 182-200; in the same volume note "Glaube und Geschichte im Alten Testament" (1931), "Das theologische Gesamtverständnis des

contribution will also be acknowledged. The goal will be to sketch chronologically some main features of the critical discussion regarding the task of Old Testament theology and the role of salvation historical approaches within that task, seen within a debate deeply committed to history of religion principles.

R. Kittel (1921)

In a lecture at an inaugural meeting of German Ancient Near Eastern scholars in Leipzig,[55] Kittel acknowledges that "the demand for a history of religion direction" in Old Testament theology has grown "to a sort of battlecry."[56] He does not disparage this history of religion emphasis as such but bitterly decries[57] the tendency of Harnack and others to devalue or deny the Old Testament's "truth content" and its "abiding worth."[58] Because of the Old Testament's relationship to Christianity, a non-negotiable assumption for Kittel is that "Old Testament history of religion work becomes quite on its own a theological discipline, whether it stands within or without a certain faculty, and whether it goes by the name 'Old Testament' theology or by some other."[59]

Kittel rejects outright the likes of Friedrich Delitzsch (1850-1922),[60] for whom the Old Testament was (to put it mildly) dispensable.[61] On the other hand, he stops short of proposing any salvation historical program. Kittel hopes somehow to overcome the prevailing convic-

Alten Testaments" (1943), and "Vom Verstehen des Alten Testaments" (1948). But he belonged to the German Christian movement and "wanted to be Nazi and Christian at the same time, to believe both Adolf Hitler and the Old Testament" (Crüsemann, WD 29 [1989] 92). Salvation historical language is by no means always faithful to the convictions of its biblical originators.

[55]Published as "Die Zukunft der alttestamentlichen Wissenschaft," *ZAW* 39 (1921) 84-99.

[56]*Ibid.* 85.

[57]*Ibid.* 95-98.

[58]*Ibid.* 97. Ironically, a generation earlier B. Stade, *ZTK* 3 (1893) 51 had speculated that Old Testament theology valuing "only the historical understanding"—something Stade himself nevertheless called for—could so distort the picture of Old Testament faith that there would be a risk of the Old Testament being seen as unnecessary for Christianity.

[59]Kittel, *ZAW* 39 (1921) 97.

[60]*Ibid.* 95, 98. Kittel says he will not deign to speak "of the applause which Delitzsch's dilettantism receives from pseudo-experts."

[61]Cf. Delitzsch's *Die grosse Täuschung*, 1920. Deltizsch outstripped Harnack in calling for removal of the Old Testament from the Christian Bible, foreshadowing Third Reich convictions. See Schroven, *Theologie des Alten Testaments zwischen Anpassung und Widerstand*, 18f.

tion that God is to be regarded as "idea and phenomenon" by insisting that he is "a great living entity."[62] Kittel argues that there exists "not only subjectively a feeling of God's nearness, but also objectively and in full truth a rule and work of God in persons" which should form a constituent part of Old Testament research.[63]

But how this is to be expressed in critical Old Testament study is not really addressed.[64] The conflicting demands of rigorous historicism and theological interpretation are only stirred up, not satisfied, by Kittel's Troeltschian[65] characterization of the abiding worth and relevance of Old Testament piety. There is hardly a place here for *Heilsgeschichte*, at least in the sense called for by e.g. Köberle above.[66]

W. Stärk and C. Steuernagel (1925)[67]

Old Testament theology as envisaged by Kittel (and Gressmann) is rejected by both Stärk and Steuernagel. They view it as lop-sided in emphasis.

Stärk affirms the need for history of religion emphasis but denies that this approach alone can do full justice to the Old Testament.[68] Arguing with awareness of issues not only in Old Testament studies but also in systematics, philosophy of religion, and Kantian philosophy, he declares that history of religion research itself points to the acuity and sophistication of the Old Testament religious consciousness in its historical milieu.[69] One must therefore take seriously the Old Testament's own claims that theological understanding had been revealed, especially to Israel's prophets: "The principle of history is not 'natural,' mechanical development but rather unfolding of an interiority, of a

---

[62]Kittel, *ZAW* 39 (1921) 98.

[63]*Ibid.*

[64]Cf. W.F. Albright, "The ancient Near East and the Religion of Israel," *JBL* 59 (1940) 95f., who touches on related weaknesses in Kittel's proposals.

[65]Cf. Kittel, *ZAW* 39 (1921) 97-99 and Troeltsch, "The Dogmatics of the 'Religionsgeschichtliche Schule,'" *AJT* 17 (1913) 10f.

[66]Much the same could be said of the views of H. Gressmann, "Die Aufgaben der alttestamentlichen Forschung," *ZAW* 1 (1924) 1-33. Kittel at least speaks, even if somewhat awkwardly, of the need for God to be granted a real place in Old Testament study, a notion hardly to be found in Gressmann's essay.

[67]Stärk, "Religionsgeschichte und Religionsphilosophie in ihrer Bedeutung für die Theologie des Alten Testaments," *ZTK* 31 (1923-24) 289-300; Steuernagel, "Alttestamentliche Theologie und alttestamentliche Religionsgeschichte," BZAW 41 (1925) 266-273.

[68]Cf. discussion in Ollenburger, Martens & Hasel, eds., *The Flowering of Old Testament Theology*, 16.

[69]Stärk, *ZTK* 31 (1923-24) 296.

synthesis *a priori* in the center of the soul. And this development is not possible without revelation."[70]

When one inquires after "the conditions of the possibility" of the Old Testament's awareness of God, one is forced to go beyond the "pure historical question."[71] Here is where Old Testament theology's task lies. It must set forth a "more precise systematic and historical determination" of the Old Testament's "idea of God" as "expression of special revelation in the entirety of general revelation."[72] History of religion analysis establishes the "experience of the transcendent" of Old Testament figures, in which God reveals himself (*offenbart sich*) as Yahweh, as "creator of the world and Lord of all historical and natural life" and "biblically speaking as the Lord, the God of *Heilsgeschichte* who with and through Israel should become God of all the world."[73] Somehow therefore Old Testament critical studies must overcome "a falsely oriented theologico-antiquarian historicism";[74] it must like the Old Testament reflect the "transition from seeking God to having found God."[75]

Steuernagel grants that pre-history of religion Old Testament theology with its "proof-text method" is now and forever outdated if used in a way that fails to depict the "overall development of Old Testament religion."[76] But as it was once necessary for Gabler to rescue biblical theology from dogmatics, it is now time "to liberate Old Testament theology from the chains of Old Testament history of religion."[77] Both disciplines share a common object ("Israelite religion"), common sources (the Old Testament and all related literary or

---

[70] *Ibid.* 291.

[71] *Ibid.*

[72] *Ibid.* 299.

[73] *Ibid.*

[74] *Ibid.* 300.

[75] *Ibid.* 299. Cf. Stärk's observations concerning Old Testament theology in *Die Religionswissenschaft der Gegenwart in Selbstdarstellungen*, vol. 5, ed. E. Stange, 1929, 195-203. E.g. Stärk writes that "the way out of the ... difficulty [in contemporary Old Testament studies] can only be found through reflection on the revelatory character of the Old Testament which is ascribed to it in the Christian faith ... The presentation [of Old Testament theology] must therefore lay stress on the specific revelatory character of Old Testament religion and the salvation historical approach to faith based upon it" (196f.).

[76] Steuernagel, BZAW 41 (1925) 266f.

[77] *Ibid.* 266.

other ancient remains), and a common method ("the historical").[78] Each discipline informs the other.[79]

But Old Testament theology has its own explicit and legitimate questions whose answers history of religion method too often obscures or ignores. Steuernagel does not actually call for a new look at salvation history, but he does demand that Old Testament scholars reinstate the theological dimension in Old Testament studies.[80] Like Stärk he sees the absurdity of interpreters of the Old Testament holding themselves "scientifically" aloof from the theology which animates the sources they are handling. On this point Stärk and Steuernagel are in fundamental harmony.[81] Old Testament theology and Old Testament history of religion must be integrated, and this can only come about through a modifying of the prevailing one-sided approach.

O. Eissfeldt (1926)[82]

Eissfeldt is cognizant of the current debate in both Old Testament and New Testament studies regarding "history and revelation."[83] Is Old Testament religion to be conceived and presented

> as Israelite-Judaistic history of religion, or as a religion which is the true religion, God's revelation, even if somehow conditioned, and in that sense—for so I would want the term to be defined—as "Old Testament theology"?[84]

Eissfeldt answers, "Both." But the two manners of presenting the Old Testament are fundamentally different, although equally justified. Therefore (contra Stärk and Steuernagel) they are to be kept separate

---

[78]*Ibid*. 272.

[79]*Ibid*. 272f.

[80]Ollenburger, Martens & Hasel, eds., *The Flowering of Old Testament Theology*, 17, raise the question whether "Steuernagel and his peers did not entirely recognize ... the degree to which assumptions about Old Testament theology's very task had changed since Gabler's programmatic essay."

[81]Thus it is not, as Greig, "Geschichte and Heilsgeschichte in Old Testament Interpretation," 43, reports, O. Eissfeldt who first gives definite "guidelines" for regarding Old Testament history and Old Testament theology, respectively, as each discipline individually warrants.

[82]For a concise characterization of Eissfeldt's life and work see R. Smend, "Otto Eissfeldt 1887–1973," *Understanding Poets and Prophets,* ed. A.G. Auld, 1993, 318–335.

[83]Eissfeldt, "Israelitisch-jüdische Religionsgeschichte und alttestamentliche Theologie," *ZAW* 3 (1926) 1. The essay is accessible in translation in Ollenburger, Martens & Hasel, eds., *The Flowering of Old Testament Theology*, 20–29.

[84]*Ibid*.

as much as possible. Criticizing Stärk and Procksch (see discussion below), Eissfeldt insists:

> The theological mode of inquiry attenuates the diversity of historical phenomena, in that it seeks to interpret these from the dogmatic standpoint of the experience of faith. The historical mode of inquiry flattens the depth of the faith in revelation which the Old Testament permits, in that it ranks this revelation on the same level as all other phenomena. The historical mode, on the one hand, and the theological, on the other, belong to two different levels.[85]

Therefore there is to be both "a historical science" and "a theological analysis of the religion of the Old Testament."[86] They form a unity, "seen from a higher vantage point."[87] It is one and the same truth which history of religion work seeks to explicate and by which faith knows itself to have been apprehended.[88] But for practical purposes—here Eissfeldt defends pure historical work against the dialectical theological encroachments of Thurneysen, Barth, and Procksch—Old Testament history of religion and Old Testament theology are not indiscriminately to be mixed, and theoretically not to be mixed at all.

Eissfeldt would thus grant the validity of a salvation historical reading of the Old Testament as a theological approach, but this could not be confused with scientific historical enquiry. Eissfeldt's proposal has the potential of relegating not only a salvation historical but every theological approach to the Old Testament to a twilight realm of dogmatic musings. To the extent that Eissfeldt demands both theoretical and practical separation of the historical and theological tasks, Old Testament theology threatens to become a critically suspect enterprise, and any salvation historical method would seem to be regarded as bereft of historical grounding.[89] It should be noted that Eissfeldt's actual practice in lectures and later writings was not as bifurcated as this essay,

---

[85] *Ibid.* 6.

[86] *Ibid.* 10f.

[87] *Ibid.* 12. It is thus perhaps not certain that Eissfeldt is as guilty of the extreme dichotomization of faith and knowledge as he is sometimes charged; cf. Hasel, *Old Testament Theology*, 32, 38ff.

[88] Eissfeldt, *ZAW* 3 (1926) 12.

[89] Eissfeldt's stance is not only of historical interest: see J. Barton's statement in "Old Testament Theology," *Beginning Old Testament Study*, ed. J. Rogerson, 1983, 109, that between Old Testament history of religion and Old Testament theology "there is no direct line." In general Barton's agreement with Eissfeldt is striking; Eissfeldt's ideas are by no means irrelevant in subsequent discussion.

which bears marks of polemic against dialectical theology's anti-historicism, might suggest.[90]

W. Eichrodt (1929)

Eichrodt's celebrated essay on Old Testament theology marks a high point of deliberations on the theory of Old Testament theology during the period 1918-1946.[91] He endorses Steuernagel's warning that preoccupation with history of religion analysis of the Old Testament is threatening Old Testament theology in any meaningful sense. Yet like Eissfeldt he sees danger in a "spiritual" (*pneumatische*) or existential manner of regarding the Old Testament.[92] He refers to approaches being adopted in dialectical theology, though he acknowledges that the new movement rightly calls attention to theology's "foundation and simultaneously its central problem, the reality of revelation."[93] Eichrodt sees himself as in large measure carrying on the task envisioned by R. Kittel above.

Assuming that the ultimate goal of Old Testament research is "to gain a deeper understanding of the religious life testified to by the Old Testament,"[94] Eichrodt notes that Steuernagel's proposals are being ignored in the theological interpretations rife in the 1920s. "Pneumatic" exegesis and theologizing carry one "out of the line of empirical historical science and over into the circle of normative science."[95] This Eichrodt wants to avoid. But Eissfeldt's solution—a clear methodological separation of Old Testament history and Old Testament theology—raises the difficult question of how Old Testament theology (in Eissfeldt's sense) can be very different from dogmatics of the Old Testament. Eichrodt concludes: "Thus a methodological question opens up before us whose consequences, not only for Old Testament study but also for theological research generally, demand the most sober attention and fundamental consideration."[96] Eichrodt is wrestling here with issues salient for New Testament theology, too,

---

[90]Smend, *Understanding Poets and Prophets*, ed. A.G. Auld, 330f.

[91]Eichrodt, "Hat die alttestamentliche Theologie noch selbständige Bedeutung innerhalb der alttestamentlichen Wissenschaft?" *ZAW* 6 (1924) 83-91. The essay is accessible in translation in Ollenburger, Martens & Hasel, eds., *The Flowering of Old Testament Theology*, 30–39.

[92]*Ibid.* 83.

[93]*Ibid.* 84.

[94]*Ibid.*

[95]*Ibid.*

[96]*Ibid.* 85.

issues that New Testament theology of that time seems seldom to have addressed with Eichrodt's penetrating clarity.[97]

It is true, Eichrodt concedes, that a historicistic analysis of the Old Testament shuts out regard for "the essence of Old Testament religion,"[98] such essence being thought of in a sense congenial to Christian theology. But what if this essence were defined as "that which the Old Testament actually intends; that in which the essence of its history actually consists; that which comprises the deepest sense of its religious thought-world"?[99] Then it becomes possible to be 1) rigorously historical, yet 2) systematic—i.e., methodologically thorough as well as theologically oriented (as opposed to giving simply a "genetic analysis" in history of religion fashion). This could yield a "cross-section of that which has come into being" in the Old Testament, a sympathetic yet critical presentation of "the inner structure of a religion in the relationship of its various contents to each other."[100]

Arguing very much like Schlatter,[101] Eichrodt concedes that the Old Testament historian-theologian is limited by his own embeddedness in the historical process. But it is fallacious to arrogate for oneself the posture of absolute objectivity by appeal to a presumed impartial method of analysis which gives unimpeachable results by granting omniscience through critical distance. No such method exists.[102] On the other hand it would be needlessly skeptical to infer that all interpretations are hopelessly subjective and relative because of the interpreter's historicality. Eichrodt rather argues that "an inner relatedness [elsewhere he uses the word "congeniality"] must exist between the researcher and his object in order to overcome the distance to the foreign phenomenon [here the Old Testament] and in order rightly to comprehend its essence."[103]

Clearly Eichrodt moves away from "a chemically pure, objective, free-from-every-value-judgment history of Israelite-judaistic relig-

---

[97]Or to consider the field of systematics: as late as 1935 H. Thielicke (*Geschichte und Existenz*, [2]1964 [= 1935], p. viii) could bemoan the shortcomings of his own work and attribute them to the fact that "the theological task of thinking through the problem of history with a steady gaze on the demands of historical reality conceived in naturalistic terms is so great and in its basic manifestation so novel." But this problem had been receiving scrutiny in Old Testament criticism for some time.

[98]Eichrodt, *ZAW* 6 (1924) 85.

[99]*Ibid.*

[100]*Ibid.* 85f.

[101]Cf. e.g. *ibid.* 87f. and Schlatter, *NNTT*, 125.

[102]Cf. Schlatter, *Theologische Literaturbericht* 1 (1908) 7f.

[103]Eichrodt, *ZAW* 6 (1924) 87. Cf. Schlatter, *NNTT*, 125-129.

ion."[104] He even sees his program as being capable of fulfilling the more dogmatically conceived task of Old Testament theology being called for in his time.[105] In sum, he "wants to link closely together the historical and the systematic principle."[106]

Hasel summarizes the problems of Eichrodt's approach as it came to expression later in his Old Testament theology.[107] These center chiefly around his conception of covenant as the unifying theme of the Old Testament.[108] What is significant for our purposes are the following: (1) Eichrodt does not call unambiguously for a salvation historical approach to the Old Testament, yet (2) his proposals are amicable to such an approach if they do not in fact constitute one.[109] This is borne out by our additional study of Eichrodt in the following chapter. For the present we may remark that salvation history of some description is implicit in the concept of an overarching covenant, particularly in view of how Eichrodt sees Old Testament theology as finding its "goal" in the "New Testament thought-world" and the guide for its "selection of individual materials" in the answer to the question: what place does a given item have in making "the preparation of the historical ground for the revelation in Christ clear and understandable, a revelation recognized as possessing utmost value"?[110] It could be argued as well that a certain salvation historical predilection is latent in Eichrodt's assumption that "congeniality" can to a satisfactory degree aid in overcoming the distance between the Old Testament data and current critical observation. His language at least calls to mind the similar positions of Hofmann and Schlatter, who sought (like Eichrodt, though by different means) to bridge the chasm which Kantian epistemology had opened up.

Eichrodt's summons "to a radical new orientation"[111] has at its heart at least some semblance of a salvation historical outlook, though in light of the use of this concept by Procksch (who was Eichrodt's teacher) and its association with the idealism so disparaged in Germany

---

[104]Eichrodt, *ZAW* 6 (1924) 88.

[105]*Ibid.* 95.

[106]Kraus, *Biblische Theologie*, 127f.

[107]Hasel, *Old Testament Theology* ; cf. N. Gottwald, "W. Eichrodt, *Theology of the Old Testament*," in *Contemporary Old Testament Theologians*, ed. R. Laurin, 1970, 53ff., 57ff.

[108]But cf. Gottwald (preceding note), 29f.

[109]Cf. P. House, *Old Testament Theology*, 31: Eichrodt's use of the covenant theme "linked him at least thematically with the best of the salvation history proponents."

[110]Eichrodt, *ZAW* 6 (1924) 88.

[111]Kraus, *Biblische Theologie*, 127.

in the 1920s and beyond, it is little wonder that only the idea, not the
term itself, comes into play in Eichrodt's ground-breaking essay. If
Eichrodt's deliberations mark a high point in the consideration of Old
Testament theology's theoretical basis, then a salvation historical mode
of analysis and synthesis should be seen as part of the key to the solution he proposes.

O. Procksch (1930s)[112]

Procksch's work represents the high point of expressly salvation historical consideration of the Old Testament 1918-1946. His interest in
the theological aspect of history was noted earlier. He was "in the
front rank of exegetes, exact in his philology"; at the same time "he
went far to bring the Old Testament back within theology from which
it had been estranged."[113] His writings on various aspects of Old Testament theology and the need for an appropriate view of history span
and even extend beyond the era under consideration,[114] at the end of
which his posthumously published Old Testament theology appeared.[115] This tome stands alone beside von Rad's more recent two
volumes as the only other full-scale attempt to build an Old Testament
theology expressly focusing on salvation history (though von Rad's
view of salvation history is considerably different from Procksch's). In
critical circles his theology was widely influential, especially among
students,[116] as illustrated on the one hand by Eichrodt (who uses his

[112]Procksch's Old Testament theology consists of lectures he gave in Erlangen during the 1930s. The outbreak of war prevented their publication until 1950.

[113]J.N. Schofield, "Otto Procksch, *Theology of the Old Testament*," *Old Testament
Theologians*, ed. Laurin, 116f.; cf. Eissfeldt, "O. Procksch," in *Kleine Schriften*, vol. 3,
ed. R. Sellheim & F. Maass, 1966, 131.

[114]Cf. his *Die Geschichtsbetrachtung bei Amos, Hosea und Jesaia*, 1901; *Geschichtsbetrach-
tung und geschichtliche Überlieferung bei den vorexilischen Propheten*, 1902; "Hofmanns
Geschichtsauffassung," *Allgemeine Evangelisch-Lutherische Kirchenzeitung* 48 (1915);
"Theologie der Geschichte," *idem* 48 (1915); "Die Geschichte als Glaubensinhalt,"
NKZ 36 (1925) 485-499.

[115]*Theologie des Alten Testaments*, 1950. In the foreword (p. vi) von Rad mentions
that the book was largely completed and checked by Procksch himself before his death
in 1947. Von Rad and A. Alt, among others, edited the work.

[116]According to Schofield, "Otto Procksch, *Theology of the Old Testament*," *Old Testament Theologians*, ed. Laurin, 117; cf. 93. Yet Würthwein claims that Procksch
remained an unknown figure after World War II, because "the generation of students
who acquired their picture of [Old Testament] history out of Noth's history of Israel
could not at the same time assimilate Procksch's theology" (*TRu* 36 [1971] 203). The
truth seems to be that Procksch was well known by and influential among older Old
Testament specialists, some of who studied under him, but not at a popular or student
level for long after the end of World War II.

teacher Procksch's "God and the world/God and [his] people/God and mankind" organization) and on the other by von Rad and his own innovative salvation historical approach.

Kraus brands Procksch as an ineffectively christocentric thinker whose Old Testament theology fails to bring out the christological substance which, Procksch alleges, the Old Testament contains.[117] Yet in beginning his Old Testament theology with the words, "All theology is Christology,"[118] Procksch simply seeks to clear the ground for a theological approach to the Old Testament over against the purely historical one of devout history of religion advocates. A proper and reasonable regard for history's theological aspect demands "the recognition of the revelation in Christ and the participation of faith in historical judgment."[119] Procksch's point is merely to justify a theologically sensitive reading of the Old Testament,[120] something which as we have seen he was not alone in doing. Procksch's theology hardlly deserves the curt dismissal Kraus gives it.[121] In fact, in light of the attention biblical theology of the whole Bible is receiving today,[122] Procksch should rather be commended: most in his time were agreed in strictly separating Old and New Testament theology. Procksch however insisted:

> On the contrary, it is to be insisted that the New Testament must be regarded consistently from the standpoint of the Old Testament, and vice

[117]Kraus, *Biblische Theologie*, 128-130; idem, *Geschichte der Erforschung*, 441f.

[118]Procksch, *Theologie des Alten Testaments*, 1.

[119]*Ibid.* 13. As Schofield points out, this is not to say (as Dentan, *Preface*, 73f., alleges) that Procksch holds "faith" to be "a separate organ of perception." But it is also not clear that Schofield goes deep enough in stating simply that Procksch "believes rather, that for the Christian the only approach to any problem must be from the standpoint of faith" ("Procksch," *Old Testament Theologians*, ed. Laurin, 95).

[120]Cf. Procksch's self-analysis in *Religionswissenschaft in Selbstdarstellungen*, vol. 2, 29f., in which he defends the place of faith in Old Testament criticism: "One cannot term the function of faith in the interpretation of scripture as 'unscientific,' since the full reality of the scripture as truth is first realized through it."

[121]Kraus' criticism—that Procksch does not show how Christ and Old Testament theology actually relate—is called into question further if one (1) notes the use of New Testament citations in his *Theologie*, and (2) considers how he addresses certain issues through Christian eyes (cf. the index to *Theologie*, 757-786, and the entries under e.g. Christ, Christentum, Christus, Paulus, etc.). Perhaps Procksch is at times misguided; nevertheless he does make instructive attempts to relate the Old Testament to the New Testament. Cf. Würthwein, *TRu* 36 (1971) 205, who also takes issue with Kraus.

[122]Merk, "Theologie des Neuen Testaments und Biblische Theologie," *Bilanz und Perspektiven gegenwärtiger Auslegung des Neuen Testaments*, 124-143.

versa; for in this context [of the systematic separation of Old and New Testament theology] the force of biblical theology would be sundered.[123]

One finds in Procksch an unabashed appreciation for Hofmann.[124] He recognizes that in some ways Hofmann's systematic works are deficient, for in his handling of biblical texts

> insufficient attention was paid to the developmental aspect of history. Scripture appeared to him as a direct imprint of history; he was unaware of the diversity of the mediating elements lying between the basic historical form, on the one hand, and the resultant canonical shape of that form, on the other. He fails to apply criticism to the historical tradition.[125]

Nevertheless, in Hofmann's understanding of Scripture, history, and personal faith, "he rightly discerned the fundamental features."[126] Above all Hofmann's merit lies in his realization that any theology, systematic or "biblical," inherently assumes some posture relative to history, automatically constructs some procedure or rationale by which to bring faith and history together, or perhaps force them decisively apart. Every theologian works with a theology or philosophy of history. With this insight Procksch feels that Hofmann, despite his limitations, points a way to deal constructively with the problem—the relation of history and theology—which so exercises Old Testament criticism. Hofmann thereby establishes a solid starting point for subsequent Old and New Testament theology.

> Even if the picture of history that Hofmann gives appears outmoded due to its lack of source criticism; even if the same can be said for his analysis of the life works of the individual prophets; even if the inferences from the content of the Christian consciousness to the course of historical events is exaggerated; it is nonetheless clear that here, finally, a theology of history has been produced on the foundation of which subsequent theology must build.[127]

How do features of a salvation historical approach find expression in Procksch's Old Testament theology? First, he insists that talk of theology is warranted as part of Old Testament historical study. This is a position not held by all, perhaps not even by the majority, in

---

[123]Procksch, *Selbstdarstellungen*, vol. 2, 27.

[124]*Ibid.* 9, 12f., 21, 31ff.; *Theologie des Alten Testaments*, 20, 44ff.; cf. *NKZ* 36 (1925) 485–499; *Allgemeine Evangelisch-Lutherische Kirchenzeitung* 43 (1910) 1034–1038.

[125]Procksch, *Selbstdarstellungen*, vol. 2, 32.

[126]*Ibid.*

[127]Procksch, *Theologie des Alten Testaments*, 45.

Procksch's time and one which grows out of his own modified Hofmannian approach. Second, at the same time and also reminiscent of Hofmann, a historical stress does not fall out of view, despite theological focus. A salvation historical outlook demands all the more careful a regard for history, since "humans always receives the revelation which merges into Christ through the mediation of history."[128] Third, and as a result, Procksch's views lead him, as similar views did Hofmann to some extent and Schlatter to an even greater degree, to a combined history of religion and theological approach. Pure history of religion method alone cannot lead to or substitute for credible Old Testament theology.[129]

Procksch asks Eissfeldt's question, "whether in view of the Bible theology of history and history of religion can coexist as two independent sciences, so that both the theological picture of history and the history of religion picture of history have the same authority."[130]

He then gives Eichrodt's answer: history of religion must be given full consideration *in* Old Testament theology, not apart from it, since "it is the mode in which the content of faith becomes apprehensible."[131]

So much for Procksch's theoretical outlook. Practically, one can take account of history of religion data in Old Testament theology only as one seeks to formulate "one's own historical picture of the Old Testament, a picture in which the connection between the Old and New Testaments which is founded on Christ is not lost."[132] He tries to accomplish this first by explicating the Old Testament's "historical world."[133] This is the horizontal dimension of Old Testament theology: "On the one hand one must comprehend, arrange, and present the divine revelation from its inception in the historical forms of the development of the Old Testament in such a way that the historical world of Old Testament faith in its historical order comes into view."[134] No theological synthesis of the Old Testament is possible "if

---

[128] *Ibid.* 14.

[129] *Ibid.* 15f.; cf. 45–47.

[130] *Ibid.* 17.

[131] *Ibid.* 18.

[132] *Ibid.* 47.

[133] *Ibid.* 48–419. Earlier P. Heinisch, *Theologie des Alten Testaments*, 1940, had envisioned a similar procedure, planning as the first part of his *Theologie* "an overview of the history of Old Testament religion" ("Vorwort"). Space limitations precluded this feat.

[134] Procksch, *Theologie des Alten Testaments*, 18.

one does not unroll the entire historical picture with its figures and events in a longitudinal section."[135]

Procksch's second step is to present the Old Testament "thought world."[136] This builds upon and grows out of the "longitudinal section" but is itself a "cross section."[137] It is a historically painstaking presentation whose structure "presupposes the knowledge of the historical world and must be determined by it."[138] He wishes here to develop a theological profile of the Old Testament: "On the other hand the Old Testament's thought world must be investigated, its midpoint and the horizon which in the course of history expanded and deepened. For in this horizon lie the concepts which have come to possess fundamental importance, as well as to furnish the language, for the entire theological enterprise."[139]

Procksch's Old Testament theology resembles Hofmann's New Testament history and New Testament theology, taken as a unified whole,[140] although Procksch gives no clear indication of being familiar with Hofmann's New Testament theology as such. Both authors try to a lay a critical yet theologically open foundation and then erect a theological yet historically responsible superstructure upon it. Schlatter in a sense does this as well, his dogmatics (*Das christliche Dogma*) growing out of his work on Jesus and the early church[141] (though this volume is more dogmatic and didactic than any of Procksch's critical writings[142]).

Procksch manages a bold and trenchant synthetic presentation of the Old Testament, one which attempts to respond to the call of many who saw Old Testament criticism's poverty and insisted on an openness to some form of a salvation historical approach. Among major

---

[135] *Ibid.* 420.

[136] *Ibid.* 420-713.

[137] *Ibid.* 19.

[138] *Ibid.* Cf. Schofield, "Procksch," *Old Testament Theologians*, ed. Laurin, 93f.: "Procksch's twofold arrangement of his material—religious and theological—causes much repetition but in effect this is a good fault, because theological ideas are seen in different lights. Both sections are really complementary."

[139] Procksch, *Theologie des Alten Testaments*, 18.

[140] See chapter one above.

[141] Cf. Schlatter, *Das christliche Dogma*, 5: "The word of Christendom arises out of Jesus' proclamation, and Christendom's own theology comes out of the theology of the New Testament."

[142] Thus Procksch does not produce anything comparable to Schlatter's *Das christliche Dogma* but contents himself instead with allowing the salvation historical dimension he sees in the biblical text to inform his presentation of the Old Testament faith/history complex.

Old Testament theologians of this period,[143] Procksch perhaps comes closest to emulating Hofmann and Schlatter in the face of an Old Testament guild which tended to regard and handle its subject matter one-sidedly, much as Baur and Wrede had advanced comparable methods previously.[144]

Britain and North America

Commenting on the small number and (in the main) poor quality of works on Old Testament theology published in English before 1920, Dentan suggests: "Perhaps there is something in the Anglo-Saxon temper averse to the kind of large-scale philosophic thinking required for the construction of a complete theology of the Old Testament."[145] Rogerson offers an even more explicit assertion which, in commenting on contemporary tendencies, also implies the way things were in the past:

> ... for whatever reason, there appears to be a strong empirical basis for English theology, probably derived from the empirical tradition of English philosophy. There is a strong desire to test and to evaluate evidence, but less willingness to enter the insecure realm of meddling with the evidence itself. If I may generalize from my own attitudes, English scholarship would prefer to say that it does not know, rather than build elaborate theories upon slender premises.[146]

For whatever reason, the British and North American contribution to Old Testament theology 1918-1946 is not great.[147]

J. Smart in 1943 notes that up till then the English-language effort directed toward "the rewriting of Old Testament theology" is negligible.[148] A Society for Old Testament Study symposium published in 1938 shows a striking lack of interaction with or even awareness of the problems concerning Old Testament theology which had been receiv-

---

[143]Among not-so-major figures one should mention König's *Theologie des Alten Testaments*, which seeks both to critique reigning approaches to the Old Testament and to reinstate a salvation historical method: see e.g. "Vorwort"; also 259ff.

[144]Greatly complicating the dynamics of the discussion by the 1930s was the rise of National Socialism; see F. Crüsemann, *WD* 20 (1989) 79–103.

[145]Dentan, *Preface*, 60.

[146]Rogerson, *Old Testament Criticism*, 292.

[147]Cf. O. Baab, "Old Testament Theology Today: Its Possibility and Methodology," *The Study of the Bible Today and Tomorrow*, ed. by H.R. Willoughby, 1947, 404: "It is impossible to find a single book written in English since World War I which can be called a survey of Old Testament theology," much less an actual theology of the Old Testament.

[148]Smart, "The Death and Rebirth of Old Testament Theology," *JR* 23 (1943) 132.

ing attention in Germany for two decades.[149] H.W. Robinson speaks of Israel's philosophy of history,[150] but his purpose is not really directed toward furthering Old Testament theology; he simply wishes to trace "lines along which Israel's instinct moved in regard to the nature and meaning, not of religion, but of history."[151] In a later book he works from the postulate that history is "a vast redemptive and therefore revealing process."[152] Unfortunately Robinson's insights are again not put into a format readily applicable to Old Testament theology, and his presentation seems to lie largely outside the conceptual world of the Old Testament theological discussions going on in Germany in the 1920s and -30s.[153] This is not to minimize his achievement as an Old Testament researcher but is to recognize that he apparently did not greatly contribute to the synthetic task of Old Testament theology. Among the earlier treatises exhibiting a sympathy for and mastery of the salient issues in German Old Testament theology 1918-1946 is that of N. Porteous of Edinburgh (not published however until 1952).[154]

The polarization of Protestantism in North America between the World Wars through the Modernist-Fundamentalist controversies[155] undoubtedly discouraged Old Testament studies there from moving in a theological direction.[156] C. McCown typifies mainline Old Testament criticism of the day when he suggests that ancient Israel's view of God and history was very much due simply to the weather.[157] Also symptomatic of the state of Old Testament theology are C.T. Craig's comments on, not Old, but New Testament theology in 1938. He

---

[149]H.W. Robinson, ed., *Record and Revelation*, 1938.

[150]Robinson, *The History of Israel*, [2]1964 (= 1938), 169-184.

[151]*Ibid.* 172.

[152]Robinson, *Redemption and Revelation in the Actuality of History*, 1942, xlviii. This "process" however in Robinson's view seems to be far more reminiscent of classic liberalism than of incipient salvation historical theology; cf. his statement that the Old Testament "is a history progressively creative of the great ideas which are the foundation of the Christian faith" (*Religious Ideas of the Old Testament*, 1956 [= 1913], 24). Robinson does not seem to have materially altered this basic orientation in later years.

[153]In much the same vein is C.R. North, *The Old Testament Interpretation of History*, 1946.

[154]Porteous, "Old Testament Theology," *Old Testament and Modern Study*, ed. Rowley, 311-345.

[155]Cf. especially G. Marsden, *Fundamentalism and American Culture*, 1980; D. Beale, *In Pursuit of Purity*, 1986. Other important works are listed in Noll, *Faith and Criticism*, 215 n. 5.

[156]Cf. on this point R. Funk, "The Watershed of the American Biblical Tradition," *JBL* 95 (1976) 21.

[157]McCown, "Climate and Religion in Palestine," *JR* 7 (1927) 536.

argues like Wrede some 40 years earlier that the term "New Testament theology" "should be discarded,"[158] since a synthetic presentation of the New Testament is hardly feasible when "*a major result of biblical research may be that there is no reason for a wide dissemination of its findings.*"[159] Doubtless rather more skepticism affected much Old Testament criticism of the day. It is also Craig who in 1943 confesses that historicism has "run into bankruptcy"[160]—though he warns against "a retreat to dogma"[161]—thus calling attention to a potential major shift in American Old Testament research.

Smart trumpets this potential change most clearly. He insists that Old Testament criticism must comprise "a theological, as well as historical, science."[162] It is evident that he has drunk deeply from German fonts. After considering R. Kittel, Steuernagel, Hempel, Eissfeldt, Eichrodt, Sellin, and Vischer, Smart concludes: "A development has been taking place in Old Testament science which is of the greatest moment ... The question is raised whether a science which is not consciously theological can ever get at the heart of the Old Testament."[163]

Yet even before the changes Smart heralds can take hold in the North American context, impatient calls arise for strict limits to be placed on the encroachment of theology into Old Testament studies.[164] In R. Bowman's lengthy essay "Old Testament Research Between the Wars," Old Testament theology receives one scant paragraph of notice, in which he warns of the dangers attending theological interest in the Old Testament.[165]

In the period 1918-1946 British and North American Old Testament studies excel in analysis and the data-gathering fundamentals of history of religion work. There is however scarcely a notable awareness of the task of Old Testament theology; in critical circles there is virtually no contribution to a salvation historical synthesis of the Old Testament's contents.[166] G. Vos stands nearly alone in doing Old (and

---

[158]C. T. Craig, "Current Trends in New Testament Study," *JBL* 57 (1938) 370f.

[159]*Ibid.*, Craig's emphasis.

[160]Craig, "Biblical Theology and the Rise of Historicism," *JBL* 62 (1943) 294.

[161]*Ibid.*

[162]Smart, *JR* 23 (1943) 125.

[163]*Ibid.* 136.

[164]E.g. W.A. Irwin, "The Reviving Theology of the Old Testament," *JR* 25 (1945) 235-246.

[165]*Study of Bible*, ed. Willoughby, 30f.

[166]This remains true despite Porteous' mention of H.W. Robinson's "emphasis on the interpretation of history as being absolutely central to a theology of the Old Tes-

New) Testament theology from some semblance of a salvation historical standpoint during this general period.[167]

5. Conclusion

In the period between the world wars Old Testament theology grapples with questions fundamentally similar to those exercising Baur-
Hofmann and Wrede-Schlatter in chapters one and two. At the most
basic level there is a marked (and familiar) divergence of opinion regarding just what Old Testament theology should be: phenomenology
(Kittel, Gressmann, Eissfeldt at the historical level, Britain and North
America to a considerable extent); or theology, in some semblance of
the classic sense (Stärk, Steuernagel, Eissfeldt at the supra-historical
level, Eichrodt, Lindblom [?], Procksch), with salvation history consequently coming in for renewed attention.

Just as in chapter one there is an (often implicit) epistemological
question at stake, so above we can detect a tension between those who
feel that post-Kantian thought is the starting point and arbiter in assessing all reality, including Old Testament religion and theology, and
those who speak of salvation historical methods as a means of freeing
the Old Testament from a perceived modernizing history of religion
subjugation.

Third, it is possible to consider Old Testament theology's debate
above as an echo of the discussion in Chapters 1 and 2 involving views
of history generally. For self-evidently the champions of *Religionsgeschichte* would identify with an immanent closed-nexus evolutionary
model of historical progression, while those speaking seriously of salvation history are allowing in real terms for the possibility of divine
involvement in the historical process.

This leads to a second observation. While Old Testament theology
is far ahead of New Testament theology of the day in its perception of
the history-theology problem—dialectical theology, which in many
quarters dominated New Testament interpretation, could be accused
of avoiding it—in another sense Old Testament theology has not yet

---

tament" ("Old Testament Theology," in *Old Testament and Modern Study*, 337). As
noted above Robinson's interest in history is of a different order from that of other
(mainly German) Old Testament theologians.

[167]G. Vos, *Biblical Theology*, 1948. Ladd, *Theology*. 25, marks Vos's "comprehensive
work" but notes that it "is more a long essay on revelation in the Old Testament"—a
burning issue in American evangelicalism at the time—"than a biblical theology." Vos
receives higher marks from M. Karlberg, "Justification in Redemptive History," *WTJ*
43 (1981) 213-246.

come as far as Schlatter or even Hofmann. This is Procksch's point. J. Barr drives Procksch's contention home when, speaking of many of the theories of Old Testament theology which we have treated above, he says: "The synthetic work [of Old Testament theology] accepts without any reservation the priority to itself of philological, literary, and historical research."[168] Such theologies "do not form a radical break with the historical-critical discipline."[169] Old Testament theology does not, like Hofmann and Schlatter, conclude that as the malady, so must be the cure, and therefore propose decisive alterations or adjustments to its critical presuppositions.[170]

In conclusion, we see that Old Testament theology was openly weighing the pros and cons of salvation history when Cullmann had hardly finished his schooling. We also observe that the fundamental adjustment which many call for in the dominant history of religion paradigm never really takes place or enjoys very limited implementation. To the extent that Baur and Wrede respectively foreshadow and embrace history of religion method, synthetic Old Testament study, despite various calls for a salvation historical openness, remains tied to a Baurian-Wredian (Cartesian) model. To the extent that Hofmann and Schlatter, building on historical facts as well as offering theological understanding, in some sense break with Cartesian criticism as we have defined it in earlier chapters, Old Testament theology hardly approaches their level of insight, though Procksch perhaps comes close. There is wisdom in the observation that even the theologically acute Eichrodt, who "casts his *Theology of the Old Testament* explicitly as a repudiation of history of religion," nevertheless "proceeds on assumptions that square exactly with those of his opponents" like Troeltsch.[171] The troubled state of Old Testament studies is underscored by G. von Rad's comment that Nazi calls for rejection of the Old Testament found German "Old Testament scholarship almost completely unequipped" to mount an effective response because of its longstanding preoccupation with purely historical issues.[172]

---

[168]Barr, "The Problem of Old Testament Theology and the History of Religion," *CJT* 3 (1957) 141.

[169]*Ibid.*

[170]There is talk of a radical change in a different direction: see R. Gyllenberg, "Die Unmöglichkeit einer Theologie des AT," *Abhandlungen der Herder-Gesellschaft und des Herder-Instituts zu Riga* 6 (1938) 64–68.

[171]Ollenburger, Martens & Hasel, eds., *The Flowering of Old Testament Theology*, 17.

[172]Von Rad cited in Crüsemann, *WD* 20 (1989) 81.

Salvation history and salvation historical emphases in New Testament theology 1918-1946

1. Background

Remarks in the previous chapter concerning Wrede and Schlatter give a foundation for grasping the background of New Testament theology 1918-1946. This foundation is considerably bolstered by J. Behm's trenchant analysis of the state of affairs obtaining in New Testament theology in 1922.[173] He notes the recent synthetic presentations of New Testament theology by Holtzmann, Wernle, Schlatter, Feine, and Weinel.[174] Scholarship seems agreed that a thoroughly historical approach to the New Testament is called for. But there is no consensus as to what constitutes a proper "historical mode of investigation."[175] Scholars "take different paths. Some call for 'salvation historical,' the others for 'history of religion' investigation." Behm recognizes that New Testament theology is faced not merely with "scholarly questions of methodology," but rather with "fundamental questions concerning the Christian religion in history and the present."

Behm acknowledges the virtues of Hofmann's insights.[176] But over against the salvation historical approach in general "a rival has now arisen in the form of history of religion investigation."[177] Schlatter is able to some degree to hold the two together,[178] but in general a disparity of outlooks has arisen. This is all the more problematic since the history of religion approach with its "evolutionary conception stemming from natural science" has become "a dogma of no less determinative influence than [was the case] with the salvation historical approach."[179] Behm confirms that it is not just the salvation historical outlook that is open to the charge of being dogmatically influenced; the more avant garde history of religion method runs afoul of the same objections, though the dogma is a different one. It is worth noting that even at this early stage of his career Bultmann draws fire on this score.[180] Like other New Testament critics he as adopted such a one-

---

[173]Behm, *Heilsgeschichtliche und religionsgeschichtliche Betrachtung des Neuen Testaments,*.
[174]*Ibid.* 4.
[175]This and subsequent quotations in this paragraph are from *ibid.* 5.
[176]*Ibid.* 5f., 8f., 23.
[177]*Ibid.* 6.
[178]*Ibid.* 9.
[179]*Ibid.* 15.
[180]*Ibid.*

sided methodology "that one can no longer speak of a historical manner of study which remains conscious of its own limitations."[181]

In weighing the strengths and weaknesses of the two orientations, Behm argues that in a sense "neither is correct" while nevertheless "both are correct."[182] To combine the two is "the great task facing New Testament scholarship at the present time."[183] While "the direct way back to Hofmann's approach is cut off once for all,"[184] it is imperative that in considering the New Testament, "investigation from the top down—to put it in blunt terms—takes its place next to investigation from the bottom up."[185] He refers to the salvation historical and history of religion modes of analysis, respectively. For the older salvation historical model, despite its limitations, can be employed in full harmony "with the newer knowledge of accurate history's need to be complemented by an intuitively reconstructive historical investigation."[186] Behm names Köberle, Sellin, Reinhold and Alfred Seeberg, Feine, Jordan, Girgensohn, Hunziger, and Emil Weber as scholars who recognize the poverty of the prevailing method and the need for change.[187] In New Testament theology "the goal remains synthesis,"[188] and at the heart of this aim is a salvation historical emphasis: "To extend and to refine this salvation historical mode of investigation appears to me to be an especially important and worthwhile task of contemporary theology."[189]

Behm thus sketches for New Testament theology a program not unlike that we have seen sketched by various Old Testament theologians in the previous section. Yet a salvation historical mode of investigation largely fades from view in New Testament theology in the years following Behm's essay. Behm unconsciously alludes to a primary reason for this fact when he mentions the new and "interest-

---

[181] *Ibid.* 16.

[182] *Ibid.*

[183] *Ibid.* 17.

[184] *Ibid.* 23.

[185] *Ibid.* 22.

[186] *Ibid.* 23. It would appear that Behm has in mind the historical approach pioneered by Dilthey; cf. e.g. E. Gritsch, "William Dilthey and the Interpretation of History," *LQ* 15 (1963) 58-69. Behm's statement is misquoted and misconstrued in Kümmel, "Heilsgeschichte im Neuen Testament?" in *Heilsgeschehen*, 158 n. 6, so that Behm's whole study is unfortunately excluded from Kümmel's consideration.

[187] Behm, *Heilsgeschichtliche und religionsgeschichtliche Betrachtung des Neuen Testaments*, 24.

[188] *Ibid.* 25.

[189] *Ibid.* 24.

ing demand for a 'spiritual exegesis'."[190] This leads us to consider directly the breakdown of salvation historical consideration of the New Testament—indeed the breakdown of New Testament theology generally[191]—in the post-World War I era.

2. *The dissolution of salvation history / salvation historical outlooks in New Testament theology*

Subsequent to Behm's summons to a salvation historical sensitivity in New Testament theology, the possibility of salvation history serving as a central integrating principle for a unified presentation of the New Testament seems to disappear.[192] Some of the major reasons for this are to be found in the theological upheavals transpiring in Germany beginning in the 1920's.[193]

The story is told elsewhere of the eclipse of classic liberalism following World War I and the dramatic rise of dialectical and related theologies. It is a well known fact that a major whipping boy of post-World War I thinking in Germany was not only liberalism but also its basis in philosophical idealism.[194] In 1931 Weth cites Barth and Brun-

---

[190]*Ibid.* 28 n. 34.

[191]Merk, *Anfangszeit*, 252, notes the "amazing" fact that "the theological understanding gained since the beginning of dialectical theology did not lead to the preparation of a New Testament theology," at least not until Bultmann's New Testament theology appeared. There were New Testament theologies by Zahn (1928), B. Büchsel (1935), and E. Stauffer (1941), but none of these utilized the hermeneutical vantage point of the new theology. Presumably that is why Merk virtually ignores them (but see *Anfangszeit*, 251 n. 137).

[192]Kümmel, "Heilsgeschichte im Neuen Testament?" in *Heilsgeschehen*, 158ff., gives several isolated references to salvation history in New Testament exegetical literature between the wars.

[193]Cf. e.g. J. Moltmann, "Exegese und Eschatologie der Geschichte," *EvT* 22 (1962) 38ff.; also S. Haynes, "Between the times: German theology and the Weimar Zeitgeist," *Soundings* 74 (1991) 9–44.

[194]See e.g. W. Hordern, *A Layman's Guide to Protestant Theology*, 1968, 75–77. Deleterious effects of this were noted by E. Käsemann, who recalled that "the Protestant middle class" at the onset of the Third Reich "was rooted in a Romantic idealism which for its part in Germany combined with a reactionary nationalism. This fact is much too seldom reflected on in the church" ("Was ich als deutscher Theologe in fünfzig Jahren verlernte," *Kirchliche Konflikte*, vol. 1, 1982, 234). Yet this also suggests that an intellectual posture hostile to salvation history (on Käsemann's antipathy toward the concept due to its roots in idealism see Harrisville and Sundberg, *The Bible in Modern Culture*, 257) gains support, not because of the salvation historical outlook itself, but because of dangerous tendencies of the German national outlook. Hofmann's realism was certainly not idealist; Schlatter was highly critical of idealism as the great work of his student W. Lütgert implies (*Die Religion des deutschen Idealismus*, 3

ner as sources of a "radical criticism" which marshalls itself "against the old conventional form of salvation historical thought."[195] Althaus remarks ironically that perhaps the anti-idealism which then pervaded theological thinking was in itself "precisely still no proof" for the veracity of ideas based upon it;[196] he protests that too many current theological outlooks find it fashionable and feasible, given the prevailing intellectual climate, uncritically to ignore "the truth in the idealistic understanding of history."[197] Along with idealism in general, salvation history in particular drops from all but polemical consideration.

Three figures in Germany are especially prominent in shaping thought about history at this time: Brunner, Bultmann, and Barth.[198] Brunner's complex view of revelation as "anti-rationalistic, non-supernatural, a-historical, non-docetic, and anti-mystical"[199] precludes any close affinity to a salvation historical outlook in his theology; the most one could say is that revelation, though "essentially non-historical," somehow remains "definitely related to history in the event of Jesus Christ."[200] Bultmann's rejection of any traditional salvation historical approach becomes clear in his review of Cullmann's *Christ and Time* (see Chapter 5 below);[201] it was latent in his work already in

vols., 1923–1925). At a theology conference Schlatter heard and praised a lecture by Brunner contrasting "the God of the idealists and Scripture" (Neuer, *Adolf Schlatter*, 1996, 659).

[195]Weth, *Die Heilsgeschichte*, 2f. Cf. *ibid*. 232: "Today sharp criticism is directed against all historical activity generally."

[196]Althaus, "Die Gestalt dieser Welt und die Sünde: Ein Beitrag zur Theologie der Geschichte," *ZST* 9 (1932) 325.

[197]*Ibid*. 335. Althaus (*ibid*. 324) is aware, on the other hand, that pure philosophical idealism "irreconcilably contradicts ... the way that faith regards history."

[198]Cf. D. Cremer, "Protestant Theology in Early Weimar Germany: Barth, Tillich, and Bultmann," *Journal of the History of Ideas* 56 (1995) 289–307.

[199]R. Eslinger, "Historicity and Historicality," Boston University dissertation 1970, 50.

[200]*Ibid*. 49; cf. J. Macquarrie, *Twentieth Century Religious Thought*, rev. ed., 1971, 326.

[201]Bultmann, "Heilsgeschichte und Geschichte," *PTNT*, 294–308. Bultmann's own view of history has been under scrutiny at least since H. Ott, *Geschichte und Heilsgeschichte in der Theologie Rudolf Bultmanns*, 1955. It is commonly accepted that Bultmann's radically distinctive ontology is the key to his systematic rejection of any view of time and history predating Heidegger; cf. e.g. Ott, *Geschichte und Heilsgeschichte*, 194–203; cf. D. Cairns, "A Reappraisal of Bultmann's Theology," *RelS* 17 (1981) 469–485. But the issue could as well be one of epistemology: see sections on Bultmann below. In any case Käsemann indicates the ambiguity in Bultmann's outlook when he observes: "In a certain respect his demythologizing was dehistoricizing and as such a testimony to his idealistic heritage" ("Was ich verlernte," *Kirchliche Kon-*

the 1920s. "Human existence ... and not human history, is the realm in which the message ... is to be experienced" for Bultmann.[202] Barth's concern with history and theology is evident from early in his career;[203] his Romans commentary condemns a traditional salvation historical perspective[204] by redefining salvation history to signify that experiential realm in which God's revelatory word effects human redemption.[205] Israel's history is thus salvation history in the same sense that it is "merely the historical demarcation of an unhistorical incident, audible human answers to the inaudible voice of the divine caller."[206] History is necessarily "'weak' in the absolute sense"; it is not fit to serve as a medium of revelation "by virtue of the infinite qualitative distinction between God and man."[207] History is as incapable of positive salvific function as flesh is of inheriting the kingdom of God; history is "flesh, inasmuch as it is a completely human matter. It is flesh, even when it dresses itself up as 'salvation history.'"[208] For Barth, "the severance of faith and rationality was the epistemological equivalent of the doctrine of justification by faith alone";[209] a salvation

flikte, vol. 1, 239). See also Watson's critique of Bultmann's "tacit identification of a modern [Nazi] ideology with Israel's *Heilsgeschichte*" (*Text and Truth*, 165).

[202]Haynes, *Soundings* 74 (1991) 32.

[203]Cf. e.g. Barth, "Der christliche Glaube und die Geschichte," *Schweizerische Theologische Zeitschrift* (1912) 1-18, 49-72, written at a time when "it was still permissible to be" an idealist (Busch, *Barth*, 26).

[204]After the first edition, that is; in the first edition Barth still "viewed revelation as occurring within the bounds of history as a separate *Heilsgeschichte*"(Eslinger, "Historicity and Historicality," 40). It is likely too that Barth's views in later life would be less hostile to the older concept of salvation history; cf. Kraus, *Biblische Theologie*, 282-296. Barth's flight from history was pointed to by Schlatter in his review of Barth's Romans commentary (see J.M. Robinson, ed., *The Beginnings of Dialectical Theology*, 1968, 121–125).

[205]Cf. Barth, *Der Römerbrief*, [2]1922, 32: "There is no special divine history as a particle, a quantity in history generally. All religious and ecclesiastical history takes place entirely in the world. The so-called *Heilsgeschichte* however is only the ongoing crisis of all history, not a history in or alongside of history. There is no 'holy history' among that which is 'unholy.'"

[206]*Ibid.* 110.

[207]*Ibid.* 259.

[208]*Ibid.* Barth's views at this point may have mellowed in later years; cf. K. Bockmuehl, "Die Wende im Spätwerk Karl Barths," *TBei* 14 (1983) 180-188.

[209]P. Fisher, "The Triumph of the Irrational in Postenlightenment Theology," *AUSS* 37 (1999) 14. Cf. B. McCormack, "Revelation and History in Transfoundationalist Perspective: Karl Barth's Theological Epistemology in Conversation with a Schleiermacherian Tradition," *JR* 78 (1998) 19: Barth "was interested in proclaiming the independence of revelation and, with that, an ineradicable difference between the

historical understanding will not fare well under this premise. "The suspicion that Barth was engaged in a flight from history in favour of a dogmatic handling of biblical texts continued to follow him."[210]

To the extent that Barth, Bultmann, and Brunner typify and even decisively influence critical thinking in Germany between the wars[211]—and their great effect on New Testament studies is beyond question—the eclipse or even demise of any salvation historical perspective in New Testament theology is understandable.[212] Yet dialectical theology and its variations were not to have the last word.

3. The re-entry of salvation history in New Testament theology
Had Cullmann's *Christ and Time* suddenly appeared, without warning and without exegetical precedent, in the milieu just described, Bultmann's charge that Cullmann had burst onto the scene with "a Christian philosophy of history"[213] would be highly plausible. A glance at New Testament research prior to *Christ and Time* however calls Bultmann's accusation into question. And we have already noted the intensive discussion surrounding salvation history in Old Testament theology.

The fact is that there was ongoing historical research[214] into questions relating to the relationship of New Testament history to theology and eschatology.[215] Numerous studies draw attention to a consistent

---

knowledge of God and the knowledge of creaturely (empirical or non-empirical) reality."

[210]B. McCormack, "Historical-criticism and dogmatic interest in Karl Barth's theological exegesis of the New Testament," *Lutheran Quarterly n.s.* 5 (1991) 213. But see McCormack's countervailing assertions in *JR* 78 (1998) 32-37.

[211]The effect of their world on them, and not only vice versa, bears mention. Haynes (*Soundings* 74 [1991] 23) writes: "Barth's early post-war work so resonates with the cultural ethos of Weimar that it merits Walter Laqueur's description as 'theological Expressionism.'"

[212]For a Barthian statement on the task of New Testament theology see E. Thurneysen, "Schrift und Offenbarung," *PTNT*, 215-248. Insight into Bultmann's program is available in "Das Problem einer theologischen Exegese des Neuen Testaments," *PTNT*, 249-277.

[213]Bultmann, "Heilsgeschichte und Geschichte," *PTNT*, 301.

[214]A survey of literature is given by G. Bertram, "Neutestamentliche Religionsgeschichte und Theologie," *Deutsche Evangelische Erziehung* 46 (1935) 355-362.

[215]To give only the merest sampling: E. von Dobschutz, "Zeit und Raum im Denken des Urchristentums," *JBL* 41 (1922) 212-223; G. Hölscher, *Die Ursprünge der jüdischen Eschatologie*, 1925; T. Hoppe, *Die Idee der Heilsgeschichte bei Paulus*, 1926; R. Paulus, "Zum Problem 'Glaube und Geschichte'," *ZTK* 7 (1926) 378-399; G. Schrenk, "Die Geschichtsanschauung des Paulus auf dem Hintergrund seines Zeitalters," *Jahrburch des Theologischen Schule Bethel* 3 (1932) 59-86; P. Volz, *Die Eschatologie*

and growing critical awareness that, in the midst of theological currents which said "yes" to radical historical criticism but, problematically, "no" to the relevance of history itself, new direction toward a satisfactory view of history in New Testament theology must come first from the sources themselves. (This reflects or parallels similar concern among Old Testament scholars.) A variety of such studies from both German and British quarters illustrate this burgeoning conviction.

Non-New Testament studies: Schrenk and Weth

The works of two non-New Testament specialists merit consideration in that they make up a tiny portion of the historical bridge between the Hofmann-Schlatter heritage and the overt resurgence of interest in salvation history which begins to characterize New Testament theology from the 1930s onward.[216]

Already in 1923 G. Schrenk produces a monograph which in explicating the history of a conceptual complex also defends it. He lays bare the characteristics and especially virtues of a bibically oriented conception of history as it comes to expression in e.g. Cocceius, Bengel, Collenbusch, Hasenkamp, Mencken, and selected Erlangen theologians, including Hofmann.[217] He does not advocate a repristination of old salvation historical systems, but he gives encouragement "to strive for an integrated overview using the means of our time and our new

der jüdischen Gemeinde im neutestamentlichen Zeitalter, 1934; G. Stählin, "Das Problem der johannischen Eschatologie," *ZNW* 33 (1934) 225-259; K. Bornhäuser, *Zeiten und Stunden im Neuen Testament*, 1937; W.G. Kümmel, *Kirchenbegriff und Geschichtsbewusstsein in der Urgemeinde und bei Jesus*, 1943. Zahn's *Grundriss der neutestamentlichen Theologie*, 1928, 1, proceeds from the assumption: "Therefore the only presentation of biblical theology which is proper and scientific is one which describes the Bible's religious teaching and knowledge in its historical development and which orders its material according to the relative stages of salvation history." Cf. the bibliography collected in P. Feine, *Theologie des Neuen Testaments*, [8]1953, 269.

[216] At a more popular level one might note works by E. Sauer, to which is dedicated H. Stadelmann, ed., *Epochen der Heilsgeschichte*, 1984. See e.g. Sauer, *Der Triumph des Gekreuzigten: Ein Gang durch die neutestamentliche Offenbarungsgeschichte*, 1937.

More broadly see e.g. P. Dessauer, *Der Anfang und das Ende: Eine theologische und religiöse Betrachtung zur Heilsgeschichte*, 1939, or on the Anglo-Saxon side W.J. Phythian-Adams, "The Foundations of Biblical Theology, *CQR* 269 (Oct.-Dec. 1942) 1-24, who stresses "Sacred History" (21). Elements of a salvation historical outlook are present in 1935 in R. Herrmann, "Zur Frage: 'Schrift und Offenbarung'," in *Bibel und Hermeneutik*, 31-37. This is also true of G. Bertram, "Die Aufgabe einer Biblischer Theologie beider Testamente," *Kirche im Angriff* 12 (1936) 416-427.

[217] G. Schrenk, *Gottesreich und Bund im älteren Protestantismus vornehmlich bei Johannes Coccejus*, 1923.

historical knowledge in order to gain something whole from the gospels and the kingdom."[218] Significantly, the *Beiträge zur Förderung christlicher Theologie* series in which this study appears is coedited by Schlatter.

Weth's investigation, to the present day still not superseded, covers what he terms the "'history of revelation' theology of the nineteenth century."[219] He sketches what he sees as various salvation historical outlooks since the Reformation, then focuses on J.T. Beck, Hofmann, and C.A. Auberlen. He is by no means uncritical of the salvation historical perspective which, he stresses, contemporary thought in Germany marshalls against. At the same time, his study is studded with jabs at dialectical theology. Weth maintains:

> If one wishes however really to recognize and bring to expression the presence of God in history—which of course is above all the presence of his word of promise—in its factuality and its character as a personal act, then one can exclude neither the concept of salvation history nor the concept of the history of the consummation or the termination of revelation.[220]

Weth's work had little apparent effect on New Testament studies, but it is a monument to the preservation of insights which, as we have seen, Old Testament theology was also struggling to articulate.

O. Piper (1934ff.)

The early writings of O. Piper lie on the border of New Testament theology with systematic or perhaps historical theology.[221] Yet they merit brief mention here because of Piper's self-confessedly "clear and unambiguously Biblical view" of the problems attending New Testament criticism's views of history between the wars.[222] In 1934 he notes the return of Erlangen-type (cf. Hofmann) views of history into Old Testament theology in the thinking of men like Stärk.[223] This is part of what he calls a "New Realism" which emphasizes the biblical faith's historical orientation[224] contra the outlook of dialectical theology, for

---

[218] *Ibid.* ix.

[219] Thus runs the subtitle of Weth's *Die Heilsgeschichte.*

[220] *Ibid.* 240.

[221] Piper, *Recent Developments in German Protestantism*, 1934; idem, *God in History*, 1939; cf. in later years idem, "Biblical Theology and Systematic Theology," *JBR* 25 (1957) 196-111; idem, "Christology and History," *TToday* 19 (1962) 324-340.

[222] Piper, *God in History*, viii.

[223] Piper, *Developments*, 67; cf. discussion of Stärk and Steuernagel above.

[224] Piper, *Developments*, 143ff.; cf. *God in History* , 164.

which history often appeared secondary.[225] Piper seeks to reformulate for his time the basic approach of Bengel, Hofmann, and Auberlen.[226] He does not produce a New Testament theology but rather a salvation historical analysis of both biblical and world history. One might say that what Cullmann in *Christ and Time* tries to set forth in the way of an exegetical basis for a salvation historical theology, Piper in his earlier works sets forth in the way of an overview which justifies, indeed demands, that modern exegesis and theology take notice of and utilize the Bible's own salvation historical stress.

C.H. Dodd (1935ff.[227])

F.F. Bruce notes Dodd's "solid contribution" in New Testament studies resulting from his "realised eschatology," which stresses Jesus' ministry, "not apart from but crowned by the saving event of his accomplished passion and triumph, as the climax of salvation-history."[228] He goes on to speak of Dodd's similarity to Cullmann on this point.[229]

One may likewise note Dodd's similarity to aspects of the Hofmann-Schlatter heritage. Dodd makes it clear that the facticity of the New Testament is crucial to its spiritual import,[230] a stance which Baur and Wrede in their philosophical idealism could hardly endorse. Again, Dodd asserts that Christianity

> takes the series of events recorded or reflected in the Bible, from the call of Abraham to the emergence of the Church, and declares that in this series the ultimate reality of all history, which is the purpose of God, is finally revealed, because the series is itself controlled by the supreme event of all—the life, death, and resurrection of Jesus Christ. This valuation of the series is not imposed upon it from without, but is an integral part of the history itself.[231]

This statement implies that, were Dodd asked what New Testament theology is, he would reply in something of a Schlatterian fashion;

---

[225]Piper, *Developments,* 61–64.

[226]Piper, *God in History,* xix.

[227]An approach to history with implicit salvation historical elements is articulated by Dodd as early as 1935; see his "Eschatology and History," dating from that year, in *The Apostolic Preaching and its Developments,* [2]1944, first edition 1936, 79–96.

[228]Bruce, "The History of New Testament Study," *New Testament Interpretation,* ed. I.H. Marshall, 1977, 48.

[229]*Ibid.*

[230]Dodd, *History and the Gospels,* 1938, 38.

[231]*Ibid.* 30.

certainly for both Dodd and Schlatter, cognitively apprehensible historical facts are of a piece with God's definitive self-manifestation.[232]

Problematic nevertheless is Dodd's platonic, dualistic conception of
history/eternity.[233] The early Church believed itself to have "transcended" the temporal order.[234] The (a-temporal) *eschaton* is, since the
advent of Christ, impinging on the temporal, but the two are qualitatively distinct.[235] In the end one is left wondering whether it is really
God somehow in and through history, or merely bold human faith,
which bridges the history-eternity chasm.

Dodd's approach to salvation history bears comparison to that of
H.W. Robinson above. Dodd reacts (even more so than Robinson)
against old-line liberal historicism, and he sees flaws in the dialectical-
theological historical outlooks common in New Testament research in
Germany in the 1930s.[236] He foreshadows Cullmann in stressing history's salvific concrete aspects as the New Testament portrays them. If
his salvation historical approach falls short of becoming as hermeneutically central in his work as a whole as it did for Hofmann and
Schlatter, Dodd's stress on at least some form of salvation history
probably prepares the Anglo-Saxon ground (cf. discussion of A. M.
Hunter below) for Cullmann's *Christ and Time* several years later. For
Dodd unquestionably maintains that "the whole of history is in the last
resort sacred history, or *Heilsgeschichte*."[237]

H.D. Wendland (1938)

Wendland presents an exegetical analysis of the New Testament in the
hope that "the New Testament theological foundations" will protect
current reflections on history "from speculation and fanaticism on the
one side and from false apocalyptic on the other side."[238] In the New
Testament he finds distinctive views of the present, past, and future.[239]
These views are rooted above all in the Old Testament "prophetic
knowledge of God as the Lord of history,"[240] but also in the conviction

---

[232] *Ibid.* 37.

[233] Cf. e.g. T. Roberts, *History and Christian Apologetic*, 1960, 6, 11f., 16ff., cf. 86ff.,
162f.; V. Harvey, *The Historian and Believer*, 1967, 101 n. 148.

[234] Dodd, *History and the Gospels*, 151.

[235] Cf. Dodd, *Apostolic Preaching*, 79-96.

[236] Dodd, *History and the Gospels*, 11ff.

[237] *Ibid.* 168.

[238] Wendland, *Geschichtsanschauung und Geschichtsbewusstsein im Neuen Testament*,
1938, 3.

[239] *Ibid.* 11.

[240] *Ibid.* 23.

that, consistent with the Old Testament, the New Testament bases itself on an outlook which regards history (1) as the dimension in which God and God's people enjoy fellowship,[241] and (2) as "movement in the direction of a goal."[242] Wendland stresses the "once-for-all-time sending of Jesus Christ"[243] and believes that in the New Testament view Jesus' presence lends to history a quality which distinguishes it fundamentally from prior, e.g. Old Testament, history,[244] even if there are links between the two. The New Testament presents, not a philosophy of history, but a "message about historical acts of God."[245] It thus remains in all events "concentrated on *Heilsgeschichte* with tremendous boldness and onesidedness."[246]

Viewing the New Testament as a whole Wendland infers from his exegetical results:

> In the New Testament there is no world history which can be detached from *Heilsgeschichte* or separated from Jesus the Christ. World history receives unity and meaning from *Heilsgeschichte*, yet in such a way that it also finds its border and termination in *Heilsgeschichte* and the consummation of it.[247]

Such exegetical deliberations prefigure those of Cullmann's *Christ and Time*. They also implicitly call the assumptions of Bultmann and even Barth into serious question from the standpoint of New Testament exegesis. They also serve notice that in German New Testament studies there is renewed interest in the New Testament's own approach to history. What Wendland finds there leads him to stress the historically concrete and teleological aspects of the temporal order as they should, he argues, affect New Testament interpretation and theology.

[241]Wendland, *ibid.* 14, seeks here to dissociate the New Testament view from the dualism (to be found e.g. in the early Barth as well as in some extra-biblical ancient worldviews) which sought radically to distinguish between God and mundane history.

[242]*Ibid.*

[243]*Ibid.* 23.

[244]At this point Wendland oddly falls into line with Barth's view, as Cullmann, *Christ and Time*, 92 n. 6, notes, adding, "In other respects, however ... [Wendland's study] contains perceptions which are of great value."

[245]*Ibid.* 82.

[246]*Ibid.* 83.

[247]*Ibid.*

E. Stauffer (1938)

Another precursor of Cullmann is E. Stauffer.[248] Cullmann concurs
with him in holding that a New Testament theology ought to take "as
its principle of division the redemptive history," although he "would
have to oppose many details" of Stauffer's work.[249] Today Stauffer's
Theology is generally agreed to be marred by "methodologically
weighty deficiencies."[250] Marshall on the other hand, while conceding
these, sees it as "a work of great power and suggestiveness" which
brings out the broad sweep of New Testament teaching and its unity
in ... a compelling, compact, and vigorous manner."[251]

For our purposes Stauffer's view and use of salvation history is of
primary importance. To capture the core of Stauffer's thrust:

> The theology of the primitive Church was a process of ordering. What
> went on was not the making of metaphysical concepts, nor yet the con-
> struction of a system, but an ordering of thought, that sought to discover
> the actual relationships between the different elements of the world of
> human experience. The answer that was found as a result of the church
> was like this: God ordered all reality in history ... In this sense the theol-
> ogy of history is the primary and canonical form of Christian thinking ...
> But what is the actual place of the Christ-event in the theology of history?
> It is the center of history! The whole of history is ordered christocentri-
> cally ... How did the writers of the NT reach this conclusion? Only by
> taking the fundamental fact of the NT revelation of God, the Christ-
> event, and applying it with a ruthless realism, in spite of all presupposi-
> tions of a metaphysical or pseudo-theological kind.[252]

We see here first a strong semblance of the salvation historical emphasis which Cullmann also finds in the New Testament and for that

---

[248]Stauffer, *New Testament Theology*, 1955. The manuscript of this work was completed in 1938; its first German publication was in 1941.

[249]*Christ and Time*, 26 with n. 9. Cullmann's carefully qualified endorsement of
Stauffer's salvation historical "principle of division" is thus hardly sufficient ground for
tarring the former with the brush Stauffer alone deserves. For this reason the criticisms
leveled against Cullmann by Bultmann and Merk, who exaggeratedly bracket the two,
are considerably weakened; cf. Bultmann, "Heilsgeschichte und Geschichte," *PTNT*,
301; Merk, *Anfangszeit*, 253.

[250]Merk, *Anfangszeit*, 252 with note 141. Cf. Bultmann, *Theologie*, 596; H. Conzelmann, *An Outline of the Theology of the New Testament*, 1969, 7.

[251]Marshall, "New Testament Theology," *The Theological Educator* 9 (1979) 54; cf.
Morgan, NNTT, 58. Also helpful, not only on Stauffer but also on the state of New
Testament theology generally at the time, is O. Michel's review article "Probleme der
neutestamentlichen Theologie," *Deutsche Theologie* (1942) 20-30.

[252]Stauffer, *Theology*, 173f.

reason champions. Modern evaluation of the New Testament should concern itself above all with "the theology of the primitive Church"—this is of course the great task of both New Testament exegesis and New Testament theology. But central to the early church's religious outlook are its convictions about the origin, meaning, and destiny of world events, especially those of which its members' lives are part. History thus comprises a non-negotiable substructure of early Christian thought. At this point Stauffer and Cullmann are in full agreement. The fact that Christ has definitively revealed God, that in his work ultimate redemption is to be found, makes his appearing and ministry the central fact of history, in relation to which other events take their place and derive their meaning. This view of history does not involve a historiographical *a priori* but rises out of the "fundamental fact" of what the New Testament witnesses observed and experienced. This view was in fact—and still is—a tool to debunk pseudo- or quasi-Christian historical outlooks, as it is applied "with a ruthless realism" to overcome "all presuppositions of a metaphysical or pseudo-theological kind." Stauffer's views bear a degree of similarity, if a slight one, to those put forth by Cullmann a few years later.

We note secondly the similarity of Stauffer's argument with certain aspects of Schlatter's approach. Both want to base a synthetic reconstruction of the New Testament first of all on the New Testament's own self-conception,[253] so far as this is possible accurately to determine. Both see the synthetic task of New Testament study as involving, in Stauffer's words, "actual relationships between the different elements of the world of human experience." Both see Christ as history's focal point. Both are optimistic in assuming that we today are in a favorable position accurately to recreate and reconstruct in our theologizing the "fundamental fact of the New Testament revelation of God, the Christ-event."

The conclusion here is three-fold. First, Cullmann's *Christ and Time* is a work of a different nature from Stauffer's *Theology* and would have to be seen in a different light at many points.[254] Yet as indicated there is a certain likeness between the two approaches. It is therefore fair to

---

[253]Nevertheless Schlatter is superior to Stauffer on this score, for he, unlike Stauffer, strives intensely to let each individual New Testament writer be heard on his own terms. For Stauffer's weakness at this point see Goppelt, *Theologie*. 43; Marshall, *The Theological Educator* 9 (1979) 54.

[254]Thus Goppelt, *Theologie*, 43, is justified in placing Stauffer, not in the salvation historical but in the "historical-positive" category in his survey of the history of New Testament theology.

say that in a qualified sense Cullmann was anticipated by Stauffer, though Cullmann neither borrows from nor relies on him.

Second, there is continuity between Stauffer and Schlatter. One may therefore even see in Stauffer, not merely a foreshadowing of Cullmann, but also a continuing of the salvation historical line of thought which Schlatter in the heritage of Hofmann carried on.

Third, Stauffer's *Theology* is clearly concerned, not merely with pure historical questions, but also with matters of dogmatic interest. It is therefore possible to place his work on the continuum of New Testament theologies stretching from Hofmann and Schlatter to Goppelt which have to some degree combined the historical and theological tasks and employed some variation of a salvation historical approach as a component in the attempt. In this sense Stauffer is significant, not only as a precursor to Cullmann, but as another example of a proponent of salvation historical New Testament theology. This remains true despite the fact that his *Theology*, due to its de-emphasis of the New Testament's internal variety[255] and its failure to develop the New Testament world along longitudinal lines, may be fairly adjudged to comprise a methodological dead end.[256]

Out of this very failure arises perhaps the most fateful consequence of Stauffer's work from the point of view of our study: its occasional "historical and methodological untenability" has "doubtless caused the understanding of the New Testament resulting from a salvation historical outlook to appear to have questionable adequacy."[257]

L. Goppelt (1939)

Goppelt sets out to demonstrate "the primary form of the interpretation of Scripture used in the New Testament and thereby at the same time the salvation historical self-understanding" of the New Testament.[258] His study claims to open up "a wide and deep salvation historical view"[259] which develops in the New Testament as it regards the Old Testament. New Testament study of the day in its fixation "above all with parallel history of religion phenomena" has overlooked

[255]In fairness to Stauffer it should be said that at various junctures he does at least indicate the disharmony among the New Testament witnesses. See e.g. *Theology*, 68 (the demonic), 119 (theology of history), 138 (the ascension), 168 (faith), 188f. (the synagogue).

[256]Cf. W.J. Harrington, *The Path of Biblical Theology*, 1973, 188; Kraus, *Biblische Theologie*. 184 with n. 69.

[257]Kümmel, "Heilsgeschichte im Neuen Testament?" in *Heilsgeschehen*, 160.

[258]Goppelt, *Typos*, 1939 (= 1969), Vorwort.

[259]*Ibid.*, 239.

the "salvation historical context in which the New Testament's essence inheres."[260] This statement echoes sentiments not only of Schlatter but also of some in Old Testament theology of the same era.

Goppelt claims to be seizing on and furthering Hofmann's basic insight regarding the importance of salvation history. This can be true only to a point, for as we suggest in chapter six, Goppelt works with a certain history-faith dualism which one can hardly read back into Hofmann. Crudely summarized, Goppelt wants to show that New Testament typology

> does not ask: 'What sense does that Old Testament story or institution have?' It rather compares Jesus and the salvation he manifested with Old Testament parallels and ascertains 1) what this means for the New Testament, and on that basis in certain cases 2) what this means for the Old Testament.[261]

The Old Testament does not in fact "predict" or materially prefigure the New Testament;[262] New Testament typology, for which "the starting point and goal ... is the present reality of salvation,"[263] rather finds the Old Testament a useful vehicle for explicating and legitimizing its own self-understanding. In a statement fraught with post-Kantian, dialectical-theological, and existentialist assumptions, Goppelt explains: "Typology removes the New Testament salvation history from the realm of mere contingent facticity and places it within the eternal redemptive decree of God, who calls however not to complacency but to obedient response."[264]

Goppelt's work attempts to reinstate a positive function for sort of salvation history into New Testament theological vocabulary. It is significant that first in the 1960s Goppelt's case began to be weighed seriously in New Testament studies; until then it affected mainly Old Testament studies, especially through von Rad. As we saw above, Old Testament theology on the whole was already far ahead of New Testament theology in giving attention to salvation history. Goppelt's *Typos* is still another attempt, well in advance of Cullmann, to reintroduce a salvation historical perspective into New Testament theology at

[260] *Ibid.* 248.
[261] *Ibid.* 243.
[262] *Ibid.* 241.
[263] *Ibid.* 243.
[264] *Ibid.*

a time when drastically different outlooks were frequently holding sway.[265]

A.M. Hunter (1943)

The Scottish scholar A.M. Hunter in 1943 feels that "these are great days for theology," since "all are realizing anew the importance of Biblical theology."[266] In the past the contents of the New Testament have been too atomistically conceived.[267] Hunter recognizes the diversity present in the New Testament but argues for its overarching unity.[268] To capture the essence of this unity he takes up the term *Heilsgeschichte.* It is said to be the dominant theme of the New Testament.[269] To take salvation history seriously as the integrating theme of New Testament theology is "to see the New Testament as the fulfillment of the Old" and the whole corpus of scripture as "the story of God's saving purpose for his People begun with the deliverance from Egypt, continued in his later dealings with them recorded in Old Testament history and prophecy, and consummated in the sending of his Son the Messiah."[270]

Hunter in this little book has "no intention to write a complete theology of the New Testament from the synthetic point of view."[271] He seeks merely to elucidate the principle, which he believes critical scholarship in his day has already established, that the different strands of the New Testament witness in the end "all lead to the one centre, the *Heilsgeschichte.*"[272] Hunter believes his work shows "the lines along which the [New Testament] unity is to be found," and he maintains that his "approach is the right one," adding: "We must hope that future textbooks on New Testament theology will be written from this synthetic point of view."[273]

---

[265]Note also the more Bultmannian-leaning monograph by G. Delling, *Das Zeitverständnis des Neuen Testaments*, 1940, and Cullmann's disagreement with Delling (*Christ and Time*, 38 n. 2, 49 n. 25, 86 n. 2, 92 n. 6). Cf. also Bultmann, "Heilsgeschichte und Geschichte," *PTNT*, 308, who praises Delling over against Cullmann. Delling's work is another indicator of the currency of the salvation historical discussion prior to Cullmann.

[266]Hunter, *The Unity of the New Testament*, 1943, 110f.

[267]*Ibid.* 11–19.

[268]Cf. in British research at the same time H.H. Rowley, "The Unity of the Old Testament," *BJRL* 29 (1946) 326–358.

[269]Hunter, *Unity*, 9.

[270]*Ibid.* 10.

[271]*Ibid.* 17.

[272]*Ibid.* 19.

[273]*Ibid.* 109.

Hunter's study is further indication of the pre-Cullmann theological awakening in New Testament theology. Hunter represents yet another who sees how a salvation historical sensitivity could facilitate a synthetic understanding and presentation of the New Testament. The salvation historical center of the New Testament calls for a historically responsible delineation of its content without an irresponsible ignoring or wresting of its own clear self-awareness and purpose.[274]

4. Conclusion

We have succeeded in tracing a continuum from the salvation historical perspectives of pre-Barthian times to comparable perspectives around the time of World War II. This can be done in both Old and New Testament theology. It can be done, moreover, with absolutely no recourse to Cullmann—we show below (chapter five) that he seems not even to use the word "Heilsgeschichte" until 1941. But salvation history and salvation historical views crop up frequently in both Old and New Testament theology long before then.

Second, pre-Barthian salvation historical views are generally not simply taken up and built upon between the wars. They are rather adapted, modified, and rearticulated in distinctively different forms. Especially in New Testament theology, one gets the impression (e.g. in the cases of Dodd, Wendland, Stauffer, Delling, and Hunter) that direct contact with the pre-Barthian salvation historical heritage is being avoided if not repudiated. At times perhaps only the term *Heilsgeschichte* endures. It begins in an altered context to take on somewhat new identity. While views arising in the period between the world wars have points of contact with the earlier salvation historical perspectives, this is not facile repristination or uncritical conservatism. Against modern views of history or reality which rendered Scripture's interface with historical reality problematic, recognizably critical perspectives are set forth which claim to derive from the biblical texts themselves. This is analogous to the responses of Hofmann and Schlat-

---

[274]Cf. T.W. Manson, "The Failure of Liberalism to Interpret the Bible as the Word of God," *The Interpretation of the Bible*, ed. C.W. Dugmore, 1944, 104f., who also calls for renewed emphasis on the New Testament's historical outlook, since "the Christian religion is concerned with a God who reveals himself above all in history." Manson here opposes a liberalism which "was predisposed against a God who intervenes in the world, or in history, whether by deed or word" (*ibid.* 95). Classic liberalism (to which Hunter graciously owns a great debt) is also the target of many of Hunter's statements in *The Unity of the New Testament*.

ter to similar historiographical threats posed by Baur and Wrede, even if there can be no talk of slavish dependence or imitation.

Third, discussion of salvation history between the wars points us both backward and forward in the history of Old and New Testament theology. It points us backward in that the discussion underscores that calls for salvation historical approaches are not novel outcries but familiar protests and counterproposals, echoes of cases argued by Hofmann and Schlatter many decades earlier. The echoes between the wars preserve, at times distinctly, the tones of earlier clashes at key points:

1. What is New (Old) Testament theology? Discussion above revealed that Old Testament theology divided between history of religion devotees (cf. Baur, Wrede), on the one hand, and others preferring to speak more in terms of a God who reveals himself through historically discerned acts and words as Scripture testifies (cf. Hofmann, Schlatter). On the New Testament side, dialectical theology threatens to sever theology from history, but as in Old Testament studies there are protests. Salvation historical viewpoints are put forth as empirically justified alternatives. It is fair to say that while one side insists on construing Old or New Testament history in terms of modern knowledge and belief, a modus operandi reminiscent of the Cartesian approach outlined in chapter one, the salvation historical side want to try to inform modern knowledge and to construe theology in terms of the theologically significant Old and New Testament history.

2. What epistemological stance is warranted with reference to the biblical data? Here the echo is more muted. In neither Old nor New Testament theology are the basic historical-critical ground rules of contemporary biblical criticism questioned in any fundamental way. McCormack significantly laments that "Barth never chose to debate Troeltsch publicly on the subject of theology and history ... To this day, modern theology remains the poorer because that debate never took place."[275] This is symptomatic of a period in which, according to Haynes, Barth and others "were actively involved in a kind of rebellion against" their "intellectual 'fathers' typical among members of the Weimar 'war generation.'"[276] There was sometimes avoidance rather than engagement; Barth debated Harnack,[277] but Schlatter never succeeded in getting Barth to speak at a well-known theology conference

---

[275] *JR* 78 (1998) 36. It never took place in part because Troeltsch died in 1923.
[276] *Soundings* 74 (1991) 22.
[277] Robinson, ed., *The Beginnings of Dialectical Theology*, 163–187.

despite repeated attempts.[278] The level of hermeneutical or methodological awareness of Hofmann and especially of Schlatter is generally
not even approximated; P. Schempp has commented on the superficial
level of much of the debate of the 1920s.[279] The problems inherent in
encountering the biblical data with post-Kantian (or Cartesian) viewpoints are however noticeable with the advantage of hindsight. Even
more noticeable, however, are the blind spots of Old and New Testament theology of that time. Salvation historical proposals are indeed at
least in outline put forth, but they stand little chance of broad support
when the epistemological bases of historical criticism are so thoroughly
moored in the neo-Kantian or Troeltschian modes of understanding
intrinsic to the history of religion interpretation that still dominated
the academy.

3. What view of history should inform Old and New Testament
theology? In 1918-1946 there is clear acceptance of, but concurrently
a noticeable dissatisfaction with, Baurian-Wredian, closed-nexus,
strictly immanentist models of history. This replicates the offsetting
assumptions of Baur and Wrede on the one hand and Hofmann and
Schlatter on the other. The bifurcation of New Testament theology
seen already in Chapters 1 and 2 is carried forward to the time of
World War II.

The above discussion also points us forward in our study. It raises
the question of just how and when Cullmann came to his views, and
what they consisted in. This will be taken up in Chapter 5. It also
raises the question of how salvation historical viewpoints fared in the
post-World War II years. This will be our focus in the following chapter.

---

[278]Neuer, *Adolf Schlatter*, 1996, 642ff.
[279]Robinson, ed., *The Beginnings of Dialectical Theology*, 191–200.

4

Slouching toward Crisis: Salvation History in the Biblical Theology Movement

Both New and Old Testament theology seem to be burgeoning enterprises today, and in many ways they are. But their current forms arose from the slag heap of a meltdown, and they remain a bit disfigured. Time was when each discipline proceeded under the banner of a dominant synthesis, led by the likes of Eichrodt or von Rad in Old Testament and Bultmann in New Testament theology. But a crisis (see below) brought such hegemony to an end. Today Old Testament theologies tend to be disparate in approach. A casual reader might be hard pressed to see how the recent works of P. House[1] and W. Brueggemann[2] even belong to the same genre. In New Testament theology studies like those of Räisänen[3] and Balla[4] openly go head to head. Discussion of biblical theological method is dominated by expressions like changing and shifting paradigms,[5] counterpoints,[6] models and perspectives,[7] problems and proposals and prospects,[8] and changing scenes.[9] This does not suggest even a stable mix, let alone emerging consensus.

[1] *Old Testament Theology*, 1998.

[2] *Theology of the Old Testament*, 1997.

[3] *Beyond New Testament Theology*. The 1990 edition was a major subject of Balla's critical investigation (next note); Räisänen brought out a 2000 edition which replies to Balla.

[4] *Challenges to New Testament Theology*, 1997.

[5] R. Rendtorff, "The Paradigm is Changing: Hopes and Fears," *BibInt* 1 (1993) 34–53; W. Brueggemann, "A Shifting Paradigm: From 'Mighty Deeds' to 'Models,'" *The Papers of the Henry Luce III Fellows in Theology*, vol. 1, ed. G. Gilbert, 1996, 7–47.

[6] N. Gottwald, "Rhetorical, Historical, and Ontological Counterpoints in Doing Old Testament Theology," *God in the Fray*, ed. T. Linafelt et al., 11–23.

[7] G. Hasel, "Recent Models of Biblical Theology: Three Major Perspectives," *AUSS* 33/1 (1995) 55–75.

[8] D.T. Olson, "The Bible and Theology: Problems, Proposals, Prospects," *Di* 37/2 (1998) 85–91.

[9] B. Anderson, "The Changing Scene in Biblical Theology," *BRev* 10 (1994) 17, 63.

The seeds of this disarray were sown long ago. We saw last chapter that prior to World War II, what salvation historical thinkers called for and tried to implement materialized only here and there: fundamental adjustment to the basic parameters of historical criticism which, in the form of history of religion method, became increasingly normative for biblical theology. In this respect Old and New Testament theology between the wars did not really claim, far less preserve, the ground which Hofmann and Schlatter glimpsed and sought to occupy. The extensive questioning of method in Old Testament theology seen in the preceding chapter documented a conviction among many that basic issues ought to be reassessed.

Yet New Testament theology of that time hardly moved beyond discussion of whether salvation historical perspectives are to be found in the New Testament sources. There was a dearth of methodological reflection on New Testament theology. This bespoke either a satisfaction with the status quo[10] or an obliviousness as to how to move forward in a "historical" discipline when not only the older liberal positivism but also a theological new wave (dialectical theology) seemed to render history highly problematic.[11] Add to this the problems posed by Weimar instability and finally the rise of Hitler, which threatened the very identity of the church in Germany where biblical theological discussion was centered. Old landmarks in the study of theology, religion, and much else were shifting.[12]

Through it all, debate about salvation history continued. Following World War II, we will now show, it intensified. But while some clarity and progress emerged, the concept proved to be a casualty in the meltdown that ensued. It was B. Childs who most effectively chronicled the eclipse of salvation historical outlooks and biblical theology generally in the post-war era. To understand the complex, relatively rudderless state of New Testament theology today, and to see what the prospects might be in times ahead for a salvation historical approach, we will interact with some of his major points below. There is need to revisit the matters Childs took up, since "the very expression 'biblical

---

[10]See e.g. the New Testament theology written from a history of religion standpoint by H. Weinel, *Biblische Theologie des Neuen Testaments*, [3]1921. It is subtitled *The Religion of Jesus and Eary Christianity*.

[11]E.g. Zahn's *Grundriss der neutestamentlichen Theologie*, 1928, could very well have appeared in the previous century.

[12]Some of the issues and tensions surface in J. Kippenberg and B. Luchesi, eds., *Religionswissenschaft und Kulturkritik*, 1991, a collection of essays dealing with history of religions research and cultural criticism 1890–1950.

theology'" in the post-World War II sense "has passed out of general
theological usage, to such an extent that anyone whose theological
education began after about 1975 will probably have little idea of what
it once represented."[13] To forget the lessons learned at this time would
be a serious mistake.

In taking up Childs' views we will set the stage for suggesting that
the Hofmann-Schlatter heritage, despite a wealth of rhetoric about
revelation in history after World War II, was generally ignored in both
Old and New Testament theology. There are exceptions in both disciplines, but the Baur-Wrede model of inquiry continues its dominant
status. Neither Old nor New Testament theology takes decisive steps
to bring critical assumptions into serious dialogue with the methodological implications of Scripture's historical and theological claims. Yet
the salvation historical voice, while minority in status and muted in
tone, still emerges clearly, if a little plaintively, from the cacophony of
cries of those tumultuous years.

Biblical theology in crisis?

1. Childs' thesis

Childs posits that a "Biblical Theology Movement" began in the
United States after World War II. It arose "largely in response to certain European influences" but had a "peculiar American stamp."[14]
American scholars disillusioned with the polarities caused by the Modernist-Fundamentalist controversies took up the new German stress on
the theological dimension of biblical literature.[15] "The unity of the
Bible" became axiomatic,[16] "The revelation of God in history" grew
into an interpretative slogan.[17] A "distinctive Biblical mentality" was
presumed to be a vital part in understanding biblical writings and in
interpreting them anew today.[18] The historical environment of the
Bible showed the Bible's utter uniqueness[19] and lent credence to the
Biblical Theology Movement's fuzzy mixing of objective historical
data and its adherents' religious convictions.

---

[13]F. Watson, *Text and Truth*, 18.
[14]Childs, *Biblical Theology in Crisis*, 1970, 13.
[15]*Ibid.* 33-36.
[16]*Ibid.* 36-39.
[17]*Ibid.* 39-44.
[18]*Ibid.* 44-47.
[19]*Ibid.* 47-40.

The Biblical Theology Movement died in the early 1960s, according to Childs. He suggests that there was little exegetical or historical base for its key tenets and that it was plagued by several fundamental ambiguities. Chief among these was that its participants glibly took up the rhetoric of European neo-orthodox theologians but did so with classic liberal presuppositions about the purely non-supernatural nature of the phenomena dealt with in Scripture.[20] The result was an inner tension and lack of clarity as to biblical theology's definition and factual basis. The Biblical Theology Movement as such died when J.A.T. Robinson's *Honest to God*,[21] H. Cox's *The Secular City*,[22] and the criticisms of scholars like J. Barr[23] had the effect of rendering its theological relevance questionable and its historical grounding problematic.

2. The problem of revelation in history

Within the context of Childs' thesis as just outlined, he recounts the demise of "revelation in history" emphases. Childs' treatment here embraces not only the North American but also the European scene.

He chronicles the breakdown as follows.[24] First, Bultmann's use of the word "Heilsgeschichte" obfuscated its meaning and brought it into question. This confusion was compounded by J.M. Robinson and the "New Quest" for the historical Jesus in America. Next J. Branton,[25] W. King,[26] and L. Gilkey[27] voiced their opposition to the concept as it was being utilized, especially by certain American thinkers. Gilkey mentions G.E. Wright and B. Anderson in particular. He claims that, since for modern man it is erroneous and impossible to believe literally that "God acted" or "God spoke," biblical theology which uses such phrases is void of meaning. "Revelation in history" means nothing to us today, since "we are sure" that "most of the acts [of God] recorded in Scripture ... like the miracles of Buddha, did not really happen at all."[28] Therefore it is misleading if not preposterous to go on talking

---

[20]Cf. esp. L. Gilkey, "Cosmology, Ontology, and the Travail of Biblical Language," *JR* 41 (1961) 194-205.

[21]Childs, *Biblical Theology in Crisis*, 85f.

[22]*Ibid.* 86f.

[23]*Ibid.* 65f., 71f., 77.

[24]*Ibid.* 63-66.

[25]Cf. J. Branton, "Our Present Situation in Biblical Theology," *RelL* 26 (1956-57) 5-18. For a telling rebuttal of Branton which Childs neglects to cite see J. Smart, "The Need for a Biblical Theology," *RelL* 26 (1956-57) 22-30.

[26]W. King, "Some Ambiguities in Biblical Theology," *RelL* 28 (1957-58) 95-104.

[27]Gilkey, *JR* 41 (1961) 194-205.

[28]*Ibid.* 200.

seriously about "God acting in history." Finally, Childs adduces J. Barr as the one who dealt "the final blow" to the salvation history concept. Barr incorporates "the full weight of the whole European debate" in successfully debunking a revelation in history emphasis.[29]

Childs captured well the impatience with which some regarded the revelation in history category, as well as about other themes with which interpreters in both North America and Europe occupied themselves in the late 1940s, -50s, and beyond. But his criticisms of revelation in history are in some ways superficial and have a limited bearing on salvation historical approaches in the heritage of Hofmann and Schlatter.

3. Childs' criticism of revelation in history

Childs' general thesis received criticism from, for instance, J. Smart which need not be rehearsed here.[30] If Smart is substantially correct, then Childs' analysis retains limited validity. Childs' criticisms of revelation in history deserve particular rethinking. They can hardly be allowed to serve as grounds for sweeping dismissal of a salvation historical perspective.

First, Childs' criticisms seem to be based in part on a logical miscue that, we have shown, is common in the literature. He associates the whole revelation in history idea too closely with a selection of its representatives during a two-decade time span in the twentieth century, mainly in North America. Setting aside the fact that he really does not succeed in demonstrating specifically why those he criticizes are mistaken—we grant that his goal is to give an overview, not detailed critical analysis—he implies that the failure of Wright, Anderson, Cullmann, Piper, H.R. Niebuhr, Bultmann, and P. Minear to come to an agreement on the meaning of salvation history means that the whole concept is unworkable. But, from the ambiguous use of the term among this multi-national, ideologically disparate grouping, one may not deduce that all use of the term is necessarily invalid or mean-

---

[29]Childs, *Biblical Theology in Crisis*, 67f. Cf. 71: "*The Semantics of Biblical Language* ... struck with such incisive and devastating criticism that the defences appeared like a Maginot line facing a new form of blitzkrieg." Childs is perhaps overstating both Barr's representative stature and the success of his attack; see B. Vawter, review of *Biblical Theology in Crisis*, *Bib* 52 (1971) 568.

[30]Smart, *The Past, Present, and Future of Biblical Theology*, 1979, 22-32. Cf. reviews of *Biblical Theology in Crisis* by B. Anderson, *RelL* 39 (1970) 608f.; Vawter, *Bib* 52 (1971) 567-570. Cf. also W. Ward, "Towards a Biblical Theology," *RevExp* 7 (1977) 371-387, especially 371-375. J. Barr, *Holy Scripture*, 1983, 133, finds Childs' analysis "very good," yet marred by "certain flaws."

ingless, only that the various conceptualizations of it may be contradictory or untenable—and Childs is not very convincing in demonstrating even that point except in a general way.

Second, Childs' criticisms of a revelation in history emphasis are vitiated when he is forced to admit the concept's validity. "The stress on the continuity of redemptive history that binds together the two covenants contains an important insight."[31] Furthermore, Childs' proposed canonical approach to biblical theology as outlined in *Biblical Theology in Crisis* at two points simply shifts verities which once were props for salvation historical approaches to a point underneath his own canonical platform. First note this statement:

> ... the concept of canon as it developed was testimony to the belief that faith in Jesus Christ was grounded upon the witness of both prophets and apostles. God had revealed his will ... in concrete manifestations of himself, restricted in time and space, and testified to by particular witnesses.[32]

Here it is not easy how Childs can sidestep his own strictures against a salvation historical foundation in biblical theology. Second, when he asserts that "the concept of canon was an attempt to *acknowledge* the divine authority of its writings,"[33] one may ask, which is the more foundational "context" for biblical theology: the canon which acknowledges divinely given writings, or the salvation history which comprises the process out of which the canon developed and of which the canonical books claim to be witnesses? Without revelation in history Childs does not have his canon, and when he exposes revelation in history to general criticism he discounts not only some types of biblical theology but his own canonical program as well.

Third, Childs fails to do justice to the profound issues involved in holding "revelation" and "history" in the creative tension one observes in many of the biblical writings. His criticism of revelation in history seems to draw its force from a modern outlook which simply denies the possibility of the former taking place in the latter. But a view which poses the "reality of God" as "the fundamental theological question of the age" and then asserts that "this question must be solved apart from and prior to reference to the Bible"[34] seems to be begging the very question which the salvation historical position seeks to raise. Should Old and New Testament theology, in Baur's and Wrede's

---

[31]Childs, *Biblical Theology in Crisis*, 239 n. 4.
[32]*Ibid.* 105.
[33]*Ibid.*
[34]Childs, *ibid.* 87, referring to Gilkey, *JR* 41 (1961) 194-205.

train, come to the biblical texts with "the fundamental theological questions of the age" already decided apart from the Bible? Or may Scripture and the realities to which they point be allowed to serve as arbiters in answering the philosophical and systematic discussion which has so often steered the course of "historical" research?

There is need to revisit the real core of the impasse which Childs chronicles.

4. The issue at stake

An exchange between R. Pfeiffer and F. Filson epitomizes, perhaps more clearly than Childs' entire study, the essence of the debate.

R. Pfeiffer (1951)

Pfeiffer, in a Society of Biblical Literature presidential address, sets forth an updated version of a Baur-Wrede methodology in handing biblical texts, especially with respect to the question of salvation history.[35]

Pfeiffer cites the Old Testament belief in the divine election of Israel. He admits that if it is regarded as a "historical fact," then "the history of Israel is sacred history." But if it is not a historical fact—if it is just "an article of faith" to assert that "the sole universal God actually selected Israel as his own people"—then "the history of Israel is purely secular and is to be told without regarding divine interventions ... as actual facts but merely as expressions of faith." Pfeiffer then immediately deduces that "the points of view of science [Pfeiffer's positivistic view of Israel's election] and faith [views which accept the veracity of the Bible's surface claim that God really did choose Israel and made this choice known] should be kept distinct" in interpreting biblical history.[36] He backs his assertion with his conviction that Israel's view of election is of a purely naturalistic origin and a quote from "a historian who is a Roman Catholic priest, G. Ricciotti."[37]

Pfeiffer next argues that the Old Testament is a hopelessly tangled, unsuccessful attempt at combining fact and faith. He claims that in much ancient Israelite historiography "the deity is not particularly prominent"[38] and suggests that Old Testament allusions to God's working are largely crude admixtures of religious sentiment. What

---

[35]Pfeiffer, "Facts and Faith in Biblical History," *JBL* 70 (1951) 1-14.
[36]Cf. Eissfeldt's views in Chapter 3 above.
[37]Pfeiffer, *JBL* 70 (1951) 4.
[38]*Ibid.* 5.

about the references to God's earthly activity in the unquestionably ancient J and E documents?

> Divine interventions in human events are characteristic of all ancient epics, and in this respect the J and E documents do not differ from the Iliad, the Odyssey, the Ugaritic Poem of Aqhat son of Daniel, the Niebelungenlied, the Mahabharata, and others. Similarly, some Greek, Roman, and later tragedies (including Goethe's Faust) place gods, or lesser divine beings, on the stage with men. But no thinking man, ancient or modern, took seriously the historicity of such intercourse between gods and men, such as we have in J and the rest of this literature.[39]

Pfeiffer then argues that the first Old Testament writings evincing a salvation historical perspective, "in which God is said to control the course of events for the fulfilment of his purposes," are of post-exilic provenance.[40] The book of Joshua is an example. This "dogmatic history" is a revisionist projection of the thinking of Jews under Persian domination onto an imaginary Israelite past. Regarding the events of which the book of Joshua speaks, "the question of historicity is irrelevant: the whole had to be accepted by faith, and having thus been accepted it became the charter of Judaism."[41] The writings of the Chronicler some two hundred years later are a second example. However, "this sort of sacred history, setting forth God's activity in human affairs, is utterly impertinent—for man cannot know God's mind and work—unless it rests on divine revelation."[42] Pfeiffer entertains no illusions that this might have been the case.

From this reading of the Old Testament Pfeiffer condemns Filson's call (see next section) to take Scripture's theological claims (which Filson sees as having historiographical implications) seriously in historical work. Committed as doggedly to a neo-Kantian model of understanding as Baur or Wrede were to models dominant in their day, Pfeiffer argues from the assumption that any historical data which deal with subject matter related to religious belief by definition deal "not with actual facts, but with articles of faith, taught as if they were historical events."[43] Matters in the Bible pertaining to whatever a believer of the Bible might hold to be true with regard to theological or religious concerns "belong to the realm of faith, and not to the realm

---

[39] *Ibid.* 7.
[40] *Ibid.* 8.
[41] *Ibid.*
[42] *Ibid.* 9.
[43] *Ibid.* 11.

of actual knowledge."[44] He goes on to attack biblical theologies for their combining of "doctrinal or philosophical speculation with ... strictly historical research."[45] This enterprise is illicit.

> The unhappy marriage of history and theology ... was never a true union and only divorce will result in the fruitful development of each of the two disciplines. Long ago it was recognized that historical writing and speculation in the fields of theology and philosophy were utterly different in methods and results. Aristotle contrasts history and poetry as follows ...[46]

Thus Pfeiffer implies on a sweeping scale that Scripture's theological data are categorically speculative and may be likened to poetry as regards factual content. "Faith and facts do not mix," whatever combination of the two might seem to be served up in Scripture. Pfeiffer endorses M. Dibelius' view that "what is asserted by faith cannot be proven historically ... The viewpoints of history and faith cannot be simply combined."[47] It is not clear whether for Pfeiffer there could ever be a biblical theology at all, but in any case there is no room for a salvation historical approach, since from the Old Testament idea of election down to all other theological matters, we are dealing not with historical reality, or empirical reality at all, but with religious imagination. And this is irrelevant and invalid for the purely historical operations to which biblical study ought to confine itself.

F. Filson (1950)

A year previous to Pfeiffer's comments Filson, in his own Society of Biblical Literature presidential address, had set forth the position which would become the object of Pfeiffer's scorn.[48] He argues, in a mode distinctly reminiscent of Hofmann and Schlatter, for the validity of a salvation historical approach.

He begins with a summary of the Old and New Testaments from a salvation historical perspective. He asserts that the biblical writers are not concerned with "pure history" in the modern non- or anti-supernaturalist sense; indeed, "if the idea had been made clear to them they would have denounced it."[49] On the contrary, the biblical writers assume that "no understanding of history is possible" except on the

---

[44] *Ibid.*
[45] *Ibid.* 12.
[46] *Ibid.* 13.
[47] *Ibid.* 14.
[48] Filson, "Method in Studying Biblical History," *JBL* 69 (1950) 1–18.
[49] *Ibid.* 4.

basis of the assumption that "God the righteous redeemer is working out his gracious, just, and wise purpose on the earth."[50]

Filson is not advocating "spiritual" exegesis nor is he setting aside historical criticism. He describes in detail why a historical method which speaks of salvation history must be exceedingly rigorous.[51] And he denies the right of ecclesiastical or doctrinal authority to dictate the results at which "free study" may arrive.[52] But like Hofmann, Schlatter, Köberle, Lotz, and others, Filson notes that thought-restricting dogma comes not only from the side of Christian orthodoxy. He calls into question the "various allegedly objective and scientific standpoints which in reality are world views or interpreting platforms" in their own right and comprise de facto attacks on the Bible's own premises,[53] premises supported by historical evidence felt by some to be difficult to explain away.

Such approaches posit that history must be analyzed through a "rigorous elimination of that divine action which for the Biblical mind is the only factor which makes sense of the process."[54] They reconstruct history with a radical rejection of "the Biblical idea of divine action in fulfillment of divine purpose." "The continual recurrence of" this sort of "an organizing point of view or interpreting platform raises the question of objective method."[55]

In the modern era, Filson notes, biblical research typically embraced a rationalism which recognized only "the working of human and natural factors." "The divine will and action can be taken into account as an idea of man, but not as a functioning and determining factor in the things which occur."[56] In Filson's outlook,

> this raises a basic question of truth. If God does so act [as the biblical writers claim], a method which studies and writes history without putting him at the center is not simply faulty from a theological point of view. It is equally unsatisfactory as a historical method, for it is not telling the story as it really was brought about, as it really happened. I know that it will be said that history can be written as the life story of mankind in the natural world, and then faith will be free to supplement or complete that story if it so chooses. My answer to this is that if man is in fact dealing with God in a responsible

---

[50] *Ibid.* 5.
[51] *Ibid.* 5-8.
[52] *Ibid.* 8f.
[53] *Ibid.* 9.
[54] *Ibid.* 10.
[55] *Ibid.* 11.
[56] *Ibid.* 12.

way, there can be no accurate and complete way of writing history which does not take this into account. For him who thinks of God not in terms of the sum total of human and natural processes but in terms of independent personal will and action, history which ignores the divine action is as incomplete as an automobile without an engine.[57]

Therefore, in biblical theology and the historical work which undergirds it, "to be objective" can legitimately be taken to mean "dealing with life as it really is, and ... this involves taking into account not merely the existence, but far more, the reign and work of God."[58] Through recognizing and affirming the "Biblical view of history" Filson wishes to recover "the fundamental unity which a false standard of objectivity has tended to destroy."[59]

5. Conclusion

While Childs' analysis is insightful in many ways, a revelation in history emphasis in the sense pioneered by Hofmann-Schlatter and rearticulated by Filson is hardly touched by his critique. Childs does too little to face the fundamental question: does modern thought on a priori bases establish parameters to which all data, including biblical, must be made to conform? That was basically the Baur-Wrede line, and that is also Pfeiffer's argument. Childs esteems too lightly that, for all the talk of revelation in history in the post-World War II years, it is Pfeiffer's outlook, not Filson's, which dominates.[60] If biblical theology ran aground, a criticism operating on Filson's premises, and a related openness to salvation history, cannot be expected to bear the blame, since this type of criticism was not ascendant during the years in question.[61]

A two-fold conclusion is in order. First, Filson's presentation, amounting in broad terms to a restatement of at least some of the principles common to salvation historical perspectives seen earlier in this study, is decidedly a minority report. Some share his views, but as we

[57] *Ibid.* 13.

[58] *Ibid.* 15.

[59] *Ibid.* 18.

[60] Smart, *Past, Present, Future*, 15, notes that an American "liberal optimism" discouraged "the raising of theological issues" in academic biblical studies in that country in the years under review.

[61] It should be recalled here that Childs' "crisis" refers to the wedding of neo-orthodox theological rhetoric with liberal, rationalistic assumptions about the nature of reality. But Filson is hardly guilty of this confusion, for he is revolting against the very modernist mindset which in Childs' view helped bring the Biblical Theology Movement crashing down.

will see below, Old and New Testament theology after World War II generally works within the familiar confines of the tenets propounded by Baur, Wrede, and Pfeiffer.

Second, the very real crisis which Childs diagnoses is due less to use of a "revelation in history" category than to criticism's widespread failure to find ways to offset its own historicistic and positivistic assumptions. Pfeiffer's cool exclusivistic claims to scientific accuracy are little short of astounding when one considers his own apparently unreflected, systematic endorsement of a classic Kantian faith-fact dualism, or his recourse to Dibelius' neo-orthodox belief. This is hardly "historical" rigor. In fact Pfeiffer flirts with a flight from history understood as the concrete historico-theological dimension of experienced reality to which much Scripture testifies. It is precisely this dimension that the Hofmann-Schlatter heritage seeks to highlight.

Old Testament theology after World War II

It is now time to characterize how salvation history or salvation historical perspectives were taken up in Old Testament theology. To what extent did either a Hofmann-Schlatter or a Baur-Wrede model play a dominant role?

We center primarily on Eichrodt and von Rad.[62] Most would agree that synthesis of the Old Testament peaked in their presentations, which seemed to approach the limits of Old Testament theology's possibilities in their time.[63] After them followed an analytic phase in both New Testament and Old Testament theology[64] which then broadened into the diversity that characterized the end of the 20th

---

[62]T. Vriezen, *An Outline of Old Testament Theology*, 1958, gives attention to salvation history (see e.g. 30, 125, 136, 169, 174, 228). But his stress is on the Old Testament religious consciousness in terms of "*the reality of an immediate spiritual communion between God, the Holy One, and man and the world* (131, his emphasis). This is a relational rather than a salvation historical emphasis; cf. R.E. Clements, "Theodorus C. Vriezen, *An Outline of Old Testament Theology*, in *Old Testament Theologians*, ed. Laurin, 137; House, *Old Testament Theology*, 33.

[63]J. Barton, "Old Testament Study," in *Old Testament Study*, ed. Rogerson, 100. W. Brueggemann, "A Convergence in Recent Old Testament Theologies," *JSOT* 18 (1980) 2, noted that Old Testament criticism agreed about flaws in Eichrodt and von Rad but made little united progress beyond them.

[64]Cf. B. Childs, "Some Reflections on the Search for a Biblical Theology," *Horizons in Biblical Theology* 4 (1982) 1; Kraus, *Geschichte der Erforschung*, [3]1982, 532-553.

century. Of course progress was made after von Rad.[65] But if Old Testament theology achieved "a remarkable range of creative approach to
the ancient texts," it was also true that "no clear emerging consensus"
was arrived at.[66] From the vantage point of the late 1990s House sees
agreement on "certain overriding principles," yet concludes, "The
current state of Old Testament theology is that little agreement exists
about how to achieve these common goals."[67] Even H. Gese's talk of
salvation history serves primarily to demonstrate "once again the diversity that had arisen in Old Testament theology and biblical theology by
the mid-1980s."[68] Old Testament theology today still lies to some extent in the shadow of Eichrodt and von Rad, much as New Testament
theology until very recently was largely a reaction to Bultmann.[69]

We also treat E. Jacob below because he seems to leave more room
for a salvation historical method in the Hofmann-Schlatter sense than
do Eichrodt and von Rad.[70] For this reason he contributes to the discussion of salvation history in which they are the more major players.

1. W. Eichrodt

Eichrodt's significance even today cannot be doubted. Martens calls
him "a pivotal figure" who "helped set the agenda for subsequent
generations" and adds that his Old Testament theology "stands alongside Gerhard von Rad's ... as a classic."[71] It was pointed out earlier that
salvation history is implicit in Eichrodt's conception of the task and
method of Old Testament theology. His Old Testament theology,[72]
consistent with his programmatic essay, reflects elements of a salvation
historical outlook.[73] Israel's "faith in the covenant God assumes the
existence of a remarkably *interior attitude to history*"; just as Israel's "faith
was founded in the first place on a fact of history, from which it is

[65]E.g. Brueggemann, *JSOT* 18 (1980) 2, noted agreement between Westermann,
Terrien, and Hanson.

[66]B. Birch, "Old Testament Theology: Its Task and Future," *Horizons in Biblical
Theology* 6 (1984) iv.

[67]*Old Testament Theology*, 52.

[68]*Ibid.* 45.

[69]Cf. Räisänen, *Beyond New Testament Theology*, 6.

[70]This is also true, though to a lesser degree, of J.B. Payne, *The Theology of the Older
Testament*, 1962. But this work has not affected critical discussion.

[71]"Walther Eichrodt (1890–1978)," *Historical Handbook of Major Biblical Interpreters*,
486.

[72]*Theology of the Old Testament*, 2 vols., 1961, 1967 (1933–1939 in Germany).

[73]Although Eichrodt's *Theology* was first completed in 1939, its influence on the international level was greatest after World War II. It is thus fitting to deal with Eichrodt
in a discussion of post-war Old Testament theology.

continually rekindled," so also "history provides the field in which" this faith "is worked out in practice."[74] For Israel "history acquires a value which it does not possess in the religions of the ancient civilizations."[75] Isaiah especially taught Israel "to regard history as a process governed by a divine plan, which had prepared it in the long distant past and was now guiding it toward its goal."[76] In fact the concept of covenant, the central unifying motif of Eichrodt's theology, is an expression of "the systematic and beneficent character of God's activity" in history.[77] This salvation history is primarily "aimed at the creation of a consecrated people of God,"[78] or again may be termed "the presence of the transcendent God in the destinies of his people."[79]

A number of other passages in Eichrodt's *Theology* pertain directly to salvation history.[80] His criticisms of von Rad reveal further that at many points Eichrodt's conception of Old Testament theology presupposes a view of salvation history basically similar to that called for by various spokesman treated in the previous chapter.[81] More pertinent here, however, are remarks by Eichrodt which deal directly with salvation history.[82] They date from slightly before the post-war period under consideration, but they illuminate his views on the subject at the time he was completing the first edition of his *Theology*. He does not seem to have altered these views later.[83]

In this essay Eichrodt rebuts the hermeneutic of Vischer and others who in Eichrodt's view overlook the historical character of the Old Testament. The pastor H. Hellbardt is Eichrodt's special target; he has taken Vischer's premises and followed them over-zealously. Hellbardt "in this fashion arrives at the decisive repudiation of the salvation historical viewpoint."[84] To be sure, Hellbardt wants to avoid a docetic

---

[74]Eichrodt, *Theology*, vol. 1, 41.

[75]*Ibid.*

[76]*Ibid.*

[77]*Ibid.* 53.

[78]*Ibid.*, vol. 2, 50.

[79]*Ibid.* 78.

[80]E.g. *ibid.* 50-57, 167-185.

[81]*Ibid.* vol. 1, 512-520, especially 516ff.

[82]Eichrodt, "Zur Frage der theologischen Exegese des Alten Testaments," *TBl* 17 (1938) 73-87.

[83]E.g. Eichrodt cites approvingly the article in the preceding note (as well as his programmatic essay of 1929) ten years after it appeared: see Eichrodt, "Offenbarung und Geschichte im Alten Testament," *TZ* 4 (1948) 330 n. 13.

[84]Eichrodt, *TBl* 17 (1938) 76. Cf. H. Hellbardt, "Die Auslegung des AT als theologische Disziplin," *TBl* 16 (1937) 129-143. On the obscure but important Hellbardt see

Christianity; nevertheless he substitutes for a historical revelation one "which has nothing to do with the causal result of cause and effect here on earth."[85] This results in "a punctiliar revelation," and here salvation history in classic dialectical theological formulation becomes a history

> which takes place between heaven and earth and which leaves its trail in earthly events only in the form of individual imprints. These imprints can in no way be related to a historical continuum, and they actually present only *semeia*, signs for something effected in the heavenly realm, signs which can be understand only through the word of the Scripture.[86]

Eichrodt (here and in his *Theology* generally) concedes a great deal to this neo-orthodox perspective[87] but feels that in Hellbardt's hands it dangerously disregards Scripture's historical substance. At this point Eichrodt takes up the subject of salvation history, beginning by clarifying just what he understands by the term.

Wherever revelation is viewed as God somehow entering history, says Eichrodt, this represents a challenge to the intellectualized, basically timeless conception of revelation as "doctrine" which dominated "the a-historical dogmatics of [Protestant] orthodoxy just as it dominated the rational moralism of the Enlightenment."[88] And Hellbardt is risking just this sort of de-historicization. He is sacrificing the historical aspects of God's self-revelation and with them the reality of God's purpose in history, along with man's role and possibilities under God in that history. This is to dispense with salvation history, since such intellectualized, de-historicized salvation history is a contradiction in terms. In a biblical salvation historical formulation, in contrast,

> we are dealing with a progressive redemptive revelation, proclamation, and knowledge, in short, with a revelatory continuity, a closed system of unique divine redemptive acts which is directed toward a great concluding goal. Whoever speaks of salvation history speaks therefore also of completion of the goal, of eschatology as the new, conclusive, historical act which God

---

Schoven, *Theologie des Alten Testaments zwischen Anpassung und Widerstand*, 235–278. On Eichrodt's critique see *ibid.*, 258–260.

[85]Eichrodt, *TBl* 17 (1938) 76.

[86]*Ibid.*

[87]Cf. N. Gottwald, "W. Eichrodt, *Theology of the Old Testament*," *Old Testament Theologians*, ed. Laurin, 55, 57f. E. Martens, "Walther Eichrodt (1890–1978)," *Historical Handbook of Major Biblical Interpreters*, 486, praises him for providing neo-orthodoxy "biblical foundation" it lacked.

[88]Eichrodt, *TBl* 17 (1938) 78f.

commits for mankind. Through this act he brings his redemptive work to completion.[89]

For Eichrodt revelation, crucial to any theological consideration of Scripture at all, must not be conceived of in strictly a-historical terms, for biblically speaking it is intertwined with the contingent causal nexus to the point that one is justified in speaking of "revelation as salvation history."[90]

Eichrodt anticipates the charge that salvation history as he is defining it is just the imposition of a modern thought scheme onto biblical data. The charge "would be utterly perverse."[91] Salvation history is not an offshoot of an outmoded philosophy of inevitable human development, nor an adapted secular philosophy of some other description. On the contrary:

> Before the philosophers of history apply the idea of organic growth to universal history, it is put to use entirely independently by a few theologians of history with respect to salvation history. For the taproot of the salvation historical perspective goes back into the biblical idea of history, which found its rich development precisely in the Old Testament. And the use of the concept of teleological development as a tool for philosophical idealism in regarding universal history is actually only a secularization of a genuinely biblical perspective, one which may not be discredited because of the dubious results of its transferral into another area.[92]

Salvation history is thus rooted in Scripture itself, not merely in modern reconstructions or philosophies of history. One may not therefore reject it as a mere modern historiographical or theological construct. Even its secular counterfeits have been derived from the biblical outlook indirectly.[93] Eichrodt thus argues that salvation history is not a nineteenth century idealistic innovation—rather it is idealism that takes its cue at this point from biblical salvation history. He goes on to assert that salvation history is not only central to the Old Testament but "is taken up by Jesus and the apostles in the New Testament."[94] It is thus a defensible category for biblical theology today.

---

[89] *Ibid.* 79.

[90] *Ibid.*

[91] *Ibid.*

[92] *Ibid.*

[93] A point debated in W. Jaesche, *Die Suche nach dem eschatologischen Wurzeln der Geschichtsphilosophie*, 1976.

[94] Eichrodt, *TBl* 17 (1938) 79.

Nevertheless it is justified, continues Eichrodt, to critique and move beyond the likes of Hofmann. Two things separate modern historical-theological work from that of Hofmann and his day. The first is "historical criticism in its entirety." The second is our "basic knowledge of the relativity of all historical occurrence. This knowledge has utterly destroyed for us any hope of the construction of an unbroken system of teaching for doctrine and life in which the perfect organism of history could be contemplated."[95]

Eichrodt does not elaborate on the first objection to Hofmann's approach; presumably he means that Hofmann was uncritical, or perhaps that criticism since Hofmann has rendered his relatively open stance to the data indefensible. As to the second objection, Eichrodt is suggesting that our awareness of historical relativity requires, not that we reject salvation history, but that it take on a different meaning theologically (and by implication also historically). Salvation history must be viewed as

> a revelatory occurrence—which can only be understood through faith—which, to be sure, constantly has links with tangible history, but which is never simply identifiable with it. In this sense the demand is justified that one should not confuse salvation history with the history of Israelite religion. We are dealing here ... with a divine action in history whose progressive continuity is comprehensible only to faith and explicable only on the basis of the experience of the revelation of Christ.[96]

Eichrodt's remarks are important in three respects. 1. They succinctly advance the argument that it is misguided to dismiss salvation history as a product of Romanticism or idealistic philosophy. This has considerable weight coming from one not known as a supporter of a salvation historical perspective. 2. They document the surprisingly favorable response of Eichrodt to the call for a salvation historical approch in Old Testament theology. 3. They indicate the direction which Eichrodt took in answering the call: a direction very much influenced by neo-orthodox theology and belief.[97] This is significant, in turn for two reasons.

First, what if neo-orthodox theology as Eichrodt's work reflects it does not always enable a convincing integration of Old Testament history and theology? With the advantage of hindsight we see that

[95] *Ibid.* 80.

[96] *Ibid.* 81.

[97] Cf. Martens, "Walther Eichrodt (1890–1978)," *Historical Handbook of Major Biblical Interpreters*, 482.

many felt it did not. Eichrodt's conception of salvation history turned out to be as suspect as the one which he rejected.

Second, what about Eichrodt's pessimism regarding the devastating effect of historical criticism on the old view of salvation history? Eichrodt's argument here is weakened by his failure to recognize that Hofmann's views, at least on the New Testament, were themselves formulated in a milieu of criticism. A man who wrote so many volumes in interaction with F.C. Baur is hardly oblivious to "historical criticism in its entirety." Moreover, it is not true that historical criticism must totally destroy the Bible's picture of history and thus salvation history: extreme skepticism of the Old Testament's historical veracity, while prevalent today, may be as unfounded as uncritical fundamentalism.[98] Further, there is the question: how critical is "critical"? As G.E. Wright notes, many charged Eichrodt with being uncritical in his belief that the Old Testament has a unifying substructure.[99] Eichrodt's objection to a salvation historical approach to Old Testament theology on this ground has limited cogency.

Still further, what about Eichrodt's pessimism, even skepticism, derived from the realization that we must live with "the knowledge of the relativity of all historical occurrence"? Here it seems likely that Eichrodt is conceding much to the Troeltschian synthesis against which Schlatter (as well as Filson and others) remonstrated and because of which the call originally arose for a salvation historical perspective to be given place in Old Testament theology.

Eichrodt does not break with Hellbardt's quasi-historical approach as decisively as he seems to have wished. He does shift position relative to a pure history of religion approach, and he wants to retain more historical mooring than he sees in Hellbardt. But he is finally unable to escape the implications of his own neo-orthodox orientation. He has dealt with the symptoms but not the cause of the chronic malaise of Old Testament theology in Eichrodt's time: the unresolved dilemma arising from the uncertain relationship of God, or human knowledge of God, and history. Eichrodt's approach to salvation history is burdened from the start by his theological views and the epistemology which circumscribes them.

---

[98] A matter argued from different points of view by e.g. V. Long, *The Art of Biblical History*, 1994; L. Grabbe, ed., *Can a "History of Israel" Be Written?*, 1997; Y. Amit, *History and Ideology*, 1999.

[99] Wright, "Reflections Concerning Old Testament Theology," *Studia Biblica et Semetica*, Vriezen Festschrift, 1966, 376f.; Schroven, *Theologie des Alten Testaments zwischen Anpassung und Widerstand*, 90.

2. G. von Rad

Von Rad's work dates from well before World War II,[100] but it is in the post-war years that his influence as an Old Testament theologian really began and he came to dominate Old Testament theology.[101] We wish to survey features of his salvation historical approach and point to its problematic nature. Despite von Rad's use of the salvation history rubric, his salvation historical view is in fact more remote from that of Hofmann and Schlatter than Eichrodt's was.

Conception of salvation history

Spriggs reports that von Rad "never defined exactly what he meant" by salvation history.[102] Whether this is correct depends on how strictly one takes "exactly." Undeniably tensions and ambiguities plagued von Rad's usage of the term.[103] Yet he does define what he means, at least to his own satisfaction.

For example, he characterizes salvation history as "a course of history that is set in movement by God's word and is formed and led to its goal through an ever renewed word from God."[104] This sets Old Testament theology one of its chief tasks: to trace the "salvation historical dialectical interplay of prophecy and fulfillment" which is the principle dynamic of Old Testament self-understanding.[105]

A decade later von Rad notes: "Israel constantly developed new conceptualizations of history in order to interpret the riddle of its exis-

---

[100]For von Rad's early writings see his *Gesammelte Studien zum Alten Testament*, 1958. Probably his most important work from this period is *Das formgeschichtliche Problem des Hexateuch*, 1938. For a chronological bibliographical survey of the von Rad corpus see Greig, "Geschichte and Heilsgeschichte in Old Testament Interpretation," 313 n. 1.

[101]Cf. W.H. Schmidt, "'Theologie des Alten Testaments' vor und nach Gerhard von Rad," *VF* 17 (1972) 1-25. Eichrodt's theology remains important but as von Rad notes is far too naive, from the standpoint of Nothian Old Testament criticism at any rate, about the unity of the Old Testament documents. See von Rad, "Offene Fragen im Umkreis einer Theologie des Alten Testaments," *TLZ* 88 (1963) 403ff.

[102]D. Spriggs, *Two Old Testament Theologies*, 1974, 34. Taking issue with this claim is A.J. Greig, "Some Formative Aspects in the Development of von Rad's Idea of History," *AUSS* 16 (1978) 320 n. 16.

[103]Cf. Spriggs, *Two Old Testament Theologies*, 34-38; Greig, "Geschichte and Heilsgeschichte in Old Testament Interpretation," *passim*; F. Hesse, *Abschied von der Heilsgeschichte*, 1971; Goldingay, *Approaches to Old Testament Interpretation*, 72.

[104]Von Rad, "Grundprobleme einer biblischen Theologie des Alten Testaments," *TLZ* 68 (1943) 227.

[105]*Ibid.* 229.

tence before God."[106] But the course of history which the Old Testament pictures "is not the golden thread of world history; rather it is here that the hiddenness of the divine redemptive activity is increasingly evident."[107] Again, von Rad speaks of "a peculiarly dialectical interplay of prophecy and fulfillment" and sees in this interplay the main subject of Old Testament theology,[108] which is salvation history. In von Rad's theology salvation history seems to be the "ever reaching-out to and avowal of God's acts which in the end made the old creedal statements grow into ... enormous masses of tradition."[109] The Old Testament "way of looking at history ... which may be called salvatio-historical ... understands each period" of its remembered and transmitted past "as a realm of tension between a promise revealed and its realisation, between a prophecy and its fulfillment."[110] Von Rad notes: "Practically the entire ... Old Testament is attached, in the form of larger or smaller accumulations of tradition, to a few saving institutions ordained by God; and this means that Israel was incessantly at work on making her God's saving acts and institutions actual."[111]

Salvation history is thus the unfolding self-awareness of Israel in the Old Testament that God, who acted redemptively in the dimly recollected past so as still to be influencing the present, would again one day manifest himself decisively in the future. A salvation historical outlook is accordingly one which "understands each respective historical epoch under scrutiny in a quite distinctive sense as an area of tension between a promise that had been made, on the one hand, and the cashing in on this promise, on the other, between a prophecy and a fulfillment."[112]

In weighing von Rad's conception of salvation history, it will be instructive, as it was in Eichrodt's case, to see how he assesses Hofmann. He adopts the common (but even by Eichrodt disputed) position that Hofmann's use of salvation history derives simply from "the philosophic climate of the times."[113] Hofmann believed that the objective nature of the Old Testament events was important to the writers of

---

[106]Von Rad, "Kritische Vorarbeiten zu einer Theologie des Alten Testaments," *Theologie und Liturgie*, ed. L. Henning, 1952, 30.

[107]*Ibid.* 30.

[108]*Ibid.* 33.

[109]Von Rad, *Old Testament Theology*, vol. 1, vi.

[110]*Ibid.* vol. 2, 426.

[111]*Ibid.* 368.

[112]Von Rad, *TLZ* 88 (1963) 415.

[113]Von Rad, *Old Testament Theology*, vol. 2, 362.

the Old Testament,[114] while von Rad considers it established that the
picture of Old Testament history as we have it in the Old Testament is
an increasingly imaginative revisionist construct of a host of authors
and redactors scattered across many centuries.[115] Von Rad "adopted a
skeptical stance toward the facts of history."[116] He opposes Hofmann's
assessment of the basic historicity, and therefore unity, of the Old Testament documents with the contention that Israel had its peculiar
"rational understanding," which was "a critical way of thinking ...
which learned how to select, combine, and even reject, data from the
wealth of tradition."[117] Through "arduous work" done "on the traditions,"[118] the unknown compilers of the Old Testament developed
"the theory that Jahweh accompanied Israel along her road through
history."[119]

It would seem that von Rad and Hofmann both use the term salvation history but that their idea of it is vastly different. This is
attributable mainly to Hofmann's assumption of the Old Testament's
basic reliability and unity over against von Rad's stress on the unreli-
ability and "extreme discontinuity" inhering in the Old Testament
documents.[120] For Hofmann salvation history expresses the Old Testament's link with past historical reality, its inner consistency, and its
close ties to the New Testament. Salvation history comprises a historically concrete (as well as theologically relevant) coherent whole. For
von Rad the unity of the Old Testament is largely "a speculative-
philosophical principle which functions as an unconscious premise"; it
is scarcely a legitimate "concern of historical or theological knowledge."[121] And since the Old Testament for von Rad lacks inherent
internal unity, it follows that the "history" on which von Rad's salva-

---

[114] *Ibid.* vi.

[115] *Ibid.* 99-125. Cf. 413: "Israel constantly fell back on the old traditions connected
with the great saving appointments" and then "actualised them in a very arbitrary,
often novel, way." If we inquire after the accuracy of Israel's apprehension and re-
expression of the tradition, von Rad answers: we cannot know in the end whether
Israel's interpretation of its remembered past was in any way faithful to the facts or
not; cf. *TLZ* 88 (1963) 414.

[116] J. Crenshaw, "Von Rad, Gerhard (1901–1971)," *Historical Handbook of Major Biblical Interpreters*, 526. "Von Rad acknowledged the fictional character of the
descriptions, for the most part," of the putatively historical accounts of Moses, Abraham, Joseph, David and Jeremiah (*ibid.* 529).

[117] Von Rad, *Old Testament Theology*, vol. 2, 108f.

[118] *Ibid.* 412.

[119] *Ibid.* 112.

[120] *Ibid.* 362.

[121] Von Rad, *TLZ* 88 (1963) 405 n. 3a.

tion history is based takes on a distinctly shadowy quality. The "most painful weakness" of his presentation is "his failure to link reliable history and reliable historical theology."[122] He "garnered a theological maximum from a historical minimum."[123]

Von Rad's method and the meaning of salvation history
We may already note von Rad's fundamental similarity to the Baur-Wrede heritage. Like Baur with reference to the New Testament, he rejects any unified conception of the Old Testament as necessarily dogmatically or philosophically motivated. Like both Baur and Wrede, he claims methodological exclusivity for his approach.[124] He criticizes Hofmann because of the latter's belief that the Old Testament reports are substantially congruent with actual past historical phenomena; for von Rad it was the religious imagination of ancient Israel that took up, fleshed out, and passed on random disparate traditions which eventually were reified in Israel's religious consciousness. This conception of how the Old Testament reports came into existence—human thinking gave rise to stories about historical occurrences, rather than the latter to the former—has precedent in Baur and Wrede.

Greig reports that the source of von Rad's view of history is Dilthey.[125] Goldingay sees the influence of Barth.[126] It can hardly be disputed that for von Rad, in marked contrast to Hofmann and Schlatter, "the importance of the historical basis of Israel's faith fades out, and the *kerygma* becomes all important."[127] The historical accuracy of the Scripture's testimony to this kerygma remains a question that is primarily answered in the negative.[128] As House comments, "If history

---

[122]House, *Old Testament Theology,* 36.

[123]J. Crenshaw, "Von Rad, Gerhard (1901–1971)," *Historical Handbook of Major Biblical Interpreters,* 530.

[124]Cf. J. Barr, "Recent Biblical Theologies VI. Gerhard von Rad's *Theologie des Alten Testaments,*" *ExpT* 73 (1961-62) 142.

[125]Greig, *AUSS* 16 (1978) 324-331.

[126]Goldingay, *Approaches,* 70 n. 19; cf. Reventlow, *Hauptprobleme,* 156.

[127]Greig, *AUSS* 16 (1978) 322.

[128]According to W. Pannenberg, "Glaube und Wirklichkeit im Denken Gerhard von Rad's," in *Gerhard von Rad: Seine Bedeutung für die Theologie,* 1973, 40, von Rad's position is somewhat more radical that Bultmann's. Bultmann assumed that we today can rediscover and share at least the believing self-understanding of the biblical writers. For von Rad however "the biblical texts in their complete historical differentness pose a question to the present, because *the same* reality—that of man, the world, and of history—was experienced by the authors of the texts entirely differently than it is today."

matters for theology, then accuracy matters."[129] Von Rad's pessimism about historical veracity discourage confidence in his theological claims.

Kraus states that in von Rad's Old Testament theology "all categories and systems that were normative up till now are exploded."[130] It is certainly true that von Rad's approach to salvation history is incongruous with that of Hofmann and Schlatter.[131] For unlike these two, von Rad in no way develops "a critique of the historical method, nor has he attempted to come to grips with its basic philosophical assumptions."[132] Barr speaks for many in concluding that von Rad's approach, by trying "to make *Heilsgeschichte* control everything ... may only prove the impossibility of letting *Heilsgeschichte* control anything."[133]

Whatever the meaning of salvation history in von Rad turns out to be, it has extremely limited resemblance to salvation history as envisioned in the methodologies of Hofmann and Schlatter.[134]

3. E. Jacob[135]

Theology of the Old Testament

Jacob is not usually thought of as advocating a salvation historical outlook. Yet scrutiny of his writings establishes him as the major post-war Old Testament theologian to utilize a salvation historical approach consistent with the requests sounded earlier in Old Testament studies from Köberle and Lotz to Procksch.

Jacob holds that the Old Testament writers or compilers from the Yahwist down to the Chronicler evince a salvation historical perspective. Old Testament theology does well to "draw inspiration from them so as not to fit the Old Testament into a modern scheme or explain it according to a dialectic that is fundamentally foreign to it."[136] Jacob sees the Old Testament as a unity, without which there could be

---

[129]House, *Old Testament Theology*, 33.

[130]Kraus, *Biblische Theologie*, 138. Cf. House, *Old Testament Theology*, 35: von Rad "attempted to turn Old Testament theology in an entirely new direction."

[131]Cf. Kraus, *Biblische Theologie*, 137 n. 50.

[132]Greig, *AUSS* 16 (1978) 323.

[133]Barr, *ExpT* 73 (1961-62) 145.

[134]Von Rad's citation of Schlatter in *TLZ* 68 (1943) 231 really only underscores the contrast between the two men's outlooks in the light of von Rad's subsequent writings.

[135]For biographical data see J.-G. Heintz, "In Memoriam: Professeur Edmond Jacob (1.XI.1909–17.I.1998)," *ZAW* 110 (1998) 485–488.

[136]Jacob, *Theology of the Old Testament*, 1958, 11f.

no Old Testament theology.[137] These remarks betray Jacob's sympathies with others who have stressed salvation history in Old Testament theology, as well as with Hofmann and Schlatter.

Jacob goes on to commend Irenaeus, the Antiochene school, and Augustine for their insight into the salvation-historical presence and work of God.[138] This praise extends as well to both Luther and Calvin, who manifest keen historical (Luther) and typological (Calvin) insight.[139] Jacob also lauds Cocceius and Bengel.[140] As Jacob sketches the background for his own method it is clear that he is identifying to a considerable extent with advocates of a fairly traditional understanding of salvation history.

Rationalism was integral to Gabler's program for biblical theology, and the rationalistic worldview snuffed out vital features of the Old Testament's self-perception.[141] Faced with new challenges from philosophy and critical historiography, theology had somehow to "make fresh contact with the Scriptures as a normative authority" in order to preserve validity and "autonomy."[142] Here Hofmann is noted. "Despite some eccentricities," his overlooked contributions are, first, that he provides an enduring "solid basis for the construction of a theology of the Old Testament which could take account of history and of salvation." Second, he makes "the highly important discovery that salvation is carried out through the course of history."[143] Jacob, here calling Procksch to mind, takes up Hofmann's insights and thereby takes another step in the direction of a salvation historical approach.[144]

Central to Jacob's method is his rejection of any epistemology that would limit valid cognitive knowledge to the purely phenomenal realm. Further, he denies the viewpoint of those who regard Old Testament theology as a branch of study "depending on pneumatic or existential knowledge," in contrast to other scientific disciplines within Old Testament study which derive rather from "historical knowl-

---

[137] *Ibid.* 12f.

[138] *Ibid.* 13ff.

[139] *Ibid.* 16ff.

[140] *Ibid.* 18ff.

[141] *Ibid.* 20f.

[142] *Ibid.* 21.

[143] *Ibid.* 22.

[144] It is to be noted also that Jacob, along with Hofmann, sees a whole-Bible biblical theology as "the logical outcome of a *heilsgeschichtliche* theology" (Jacob, *Grundfragen Alttestamentlicher Theologie*, 1970, 51). And Jacob follows C. Westermann in endorsing a view of the Old Testament-New Testament relationship which is basically a restatement of Hofmann's own systematic outlook (*ibid.* 47 n. 8).

edge."[145] He calls for critical study but like Schlatter rejects the position that "the terms history and history of salvation are ... mutually exclusive."[146] This is because "theology does not work [merely] with ideas, but with historical facts";[147] he asserts that it is fully as licit to link "objective" with what is historically conditioned, but theological, as with what is "objective" from a conceptual standpoint taking its bearings from some a-historical transcendent absolute. For Jacob "history gives faith objective reality, while faith makes history understandable."[148] History is the stage for theology's unfolding, and theology's verities play leading roles in history's drama. History and salvation history are not mutually exclusive since they have a reciprocal, equally objective status; both are aspects of past reality as it was once experienced and as it now presents itself to us when we study and reflect on it. Jacob concludes that "there is no history without theology and no theology without history."[149] A salvation historical approach in very much the sense advocated by Hofmann and Schlatter ought to give Old Testament theology its basic direction, according to Jacob.

Grundfragen Alttestamentlicher Theologie

Jacob's insight within his *Theology* into the topic of "God the Lord of History"[150] has won high praise,[151] but it will be more to the point now to consider his synthesizing methodological deliberations on Old Testament theology.[152] He regards J. Barr's objections to Old Testament theology of only limited validity.[153] Even J. Albrektson's *History and the Gods*, a vigorous attempt to debunk the notion that the Old Testament view of history constitutes something unprecedented in its Ancient Near Eastern milieu, "only pushes the intensity of the historical revelation in Israel into a more brilliant light."[154] Old Testament theology is in a dangerous situation, with the two major trains of thought having inadvertently jumped the Old Testament theological tracks: von Rad

---

[145] Jacob, *Theology*, 27.

[146] *Ibid*. 27f.

[147] *Ibid*. 28.

[148] E. Laurin, "Edmund Jacob, *Theology of the Old Testament*," *Old Testament Theologians*, ed. Laurin, 147.

[149] Jacob, *Theology*, 30.

[150] *Ibid*. 183-232.

[151] Cf. Laurin, "Edmund Jacob, *Theology of the Old Testament*," *Old Testament Theologians*, ed. Laurin, 147; Wright, "Reflections," in *Studia Biblica*, 378 n. 2.

[152] Jacob, *Grundfragen Alttestamentlicher Theologie*, 1970.

[153] *Ibid*. 9f., 42ff.

[154] *Ibid*. 10 n. 4.

has fallen prey to an exaggerated stress on tradition history, Eichrodt to a chronic and inordinate obeisance to often problematic history of religions findings.[155] Jacob seeks to find a way out of this impasse.

Fundamental to the reassessment of Old Testament theology Jacob calls for is a reappraisal of salvation history. It is not sufficient merely to assert that God is to be found especially in "his acting in history,"[156] because this alone fails to do justice to the personal or relational dimension of knowledge of a God not characterized only by active sovereignty over history: the God of the Old Testament is characterized as well by "his desire to come to man."[157] This divine "coming," which Jacob prefers to more static "presence," is reflected especially in the prophets. The prophet is a person in history, but "as a man of God he interprets this history." The encounter of such men under the influence of the God who seeks to "come" to them "with historical facts transforms history to salvation history."[158]

Jacob does not wish to force the Old Testament into a predetermined scheme for the sake of constructing an Old Testament theology. Yet,

> Old Testament theology remains, in spite of all the restrictions that one must place on this contention, a theology of history,[159] in which revelation occurs through an act and not through ideas—and indeed through an act which is determined, if not by a pre-established plan, then nevertheless by an assured goal.[160]

Jacob has no intention of founding an uncritical school of thought whose members hew close to the lines established by the Old Testament narratives accepted indiscriminately. He is aware of the problems posed by Old Testament saga and tradition. Yet "historical narrative and legend are both rooted in facts,"[161] while tradition as found in the Old Testament "stands in so little opposition to history that it becomes identical with it."[162] The designation salvation history is in the end "not entirely inappropriate" as a description of biblical history, since it

---

[155] *Ibid.* 15.

[156] *Ibid.* 26. Jacob perhaps refers to G. Wright, *God Who Acts.*

[157] *Ibid.* 20.

[158] *Ibid.* 31.

[159] But cf. *ibid.* 36f., where Jacob, citing G.E. Wright, says that instead of "theology of history," "it would be more appropriate to speak of a theology of the acts of God."

[160] *Ibid.* 41.

[161] *Ibid.* 34.

[162] *Ibid.* 39.

bespeaks God's presence and witnesses to his activity in both horizontal and vertical dimensions. Jacob concludes:

> Perhaps it is possible to reduce the various forms of the divine working to two lines. The theology of history in the more narrow sense, as we find it primarily in the prophets and the Deuteronomist, corresponds to the horizontal line: God leads his people to the fulfillment of the prophecies under his unrestricted dominion. The vertical line we designate as that of God's coming. Its roots extend to the time of Israel's origin; however, it left its primary mark in the priestly theology, when Jerusalem became the objective of God's ways. For the most part, though, we find that the two lines intersect.[163]

Summary

Jacob carries the pre-World War II demand for a salvation historical approach into post-war Old Testament theology. His position is that biblical theology worthy of the name[164] cannot without jeopardizing its own existence cave in to modern worldviews which in themselves constitute attacks on the testimony of the Old Testament witnesses. Only a historiography open to the theological claims of the Old Testament, working reciprocally with a keen command of Old Testament history, is capable of perceiving, describing, and eventually interpreting for today the historical-theological significance of its contents. It should not be forgotten that in one sense questions of method in Old Testament theology are "ultimately of lesser importance than the content itself."[165] But inappropriate method can easily trample the fragile substance of the Old Testament's spiritual insight into the divine revelation which was the basic fiber of Israel's historical existence. Historiographically speaking this requires that Old Testament theology take its methodological bearings from the salvation historical nature of its charter documents, and that it also attempt to insure that modern "scientific" approaches which reject the possibility of salvation history be made aware of the problematic suppositions inhering in their own modes of ordering and explaining the Old Testament data.

4. Concluding observations

After Jacob's *Grundfragen* much discussion was devoted to the problem of salvation history in Old Testament theology. Reventlow however if anything understated when he said that it is "still not decisively set-

---

[163] *Ibid*. 37.
[164] Cf. *ibid*. 49.
[165] *Ibid*. 50.

tled" how history relates to Old Testament theology.[166] Hesse's claim[167] that is time to take leave of the whole idea of salvation history was endorsed by G. Fohrer but rejected by Kraus[168] and Goldingay.[169] Schmitt's monograph was a painstaking and exhaustive rebuttal of Hesse's thesis.[170] One may well agree with Kraus' tacit answer to the question he poses: "Have we not arrived at a time when the traditional opposition between historical criticism and salvation historical theology has come to a place of peaceful coexistence, in which a complementary understanding of the two points of view is thoroughly possible?"[171] But Fohrer retorted, "No, there can be no such balance, for a salvation historical theology involves a falsification of the Old Testament."[172] Old Testament theology and theologies since von Rad have hardly succeeded in arriving at much methodological reconciliation.

To summarize our look at Eichrodt, von Rad, and Jacob, in general it is safe to say that salvation history does indeed play a prominent role in Old Testament theology after World War II. Yet it must immediately be added: this is frequently an understanding of salvation history which breaks decisively with a Hofmann–Schlatter model.

Eichrodt seeks to preserve the theological advantage of a salvation historical approach, but his neo-orthodox orientation raises questions about the nature of the concrete historical side of the data he seeks to base his theology upon. He places so much weight on the revelatory nature of salvation history as "a revelatory event which can be understood only through faith"[173] that the status of the historical aspect of the revelation apart from believing apprehension is called into question. His break with Hofmann–Schlatter comes precisely at this point. Eichrodt labors "in the certainty that the real word of God, which in all times and places goes out to the people of God, can only be heard in, with, and in the midst of the historically conditioned word of man."[174] This signals an acceptance of a distance between the historical side of the revelation (necessarily reflected quite imperfectly, so far as

---

[166]Reventlow, *Hauptprobleme*, 30.

[167]Hesse, *Abschied*.

[168]Kraus, *Geschichte der Erforschung*, [3]1982, 567-573.

[169]Goldingay, *Approaches*, 67; cf. his *Theological Diversity and the Authority of the Old Testament*, 1987, 201.

[170]Schmitt, *Abschied?*

[171]Kraus, *Geschichte der Erforschung*, [3]1982, 567, 502.

[172]Fohrer, review of Kraus, *Geschichte der Erforschung*, [2]1969, *TLZ* 99 (1974) 503.

[173]Eichrodt, *TBl* 17 (1938) 81.

[174]*Ibid.* 82.

the historical facts are concerned[175]) and the revelatory content (that which through faith "can be heard") which would be unacceptable to both Hofmann and Schlatter. Eichrodt's proposals are not without their attractiveness, but he seems to introduce and maintain an un-bridgeable gap between the biblical history and its revelatory content.

As for von Rad, the 20th century Old Testament theologian for whom salvation history was most important terminologically did the most to bring the term under suspicion. But his use of the concept, and historiographical skepticism that controls him, clearly separate him from any but a nominal connection to Hofmann and Schlatter.

It is Jacob who actually carried the torch passed from the nineteenth into the twentieth century by Köberle, Lotz, Procksch, and others. He praises Hofmann, despite his limitations. He sees the Old Testament as a historically unified and conceptually unifiable entity. He challenges neo-Kantian epistemology's sufficiency to deal with the Old Testament message's full implications. He accordingly denies the assumption, which crops up in Eichrodt and much more in von Rad, that history and revelation must be fairly radically distinguished. Salvation history is an appropriate rubric under with the Old Testament witness can be arrayed and comprehended, notwithstanding its limitations and the perennial criticisms directed against it. Jacob would concur with W. Lemke: "The concept of revelation through history is not simply a passing theological fad or aberration, but belongs to the core of biblical religion."[176]

Salvation history and salvation historical emphases in New Testament theology after World War II

1. The general situation

Studies on history and its meaning, many of which discuss salvation history in some form or another, proliferated during the postwar years.[177] This wide-ranging discussion, in which New Testament the-

---

[175]Cf. *ibid.* 81ff. Eichrodt's assumption that the historical, i.e. the Scriptures or what they relate, is inherently and categorically inferior to its divine referent—so that all cognitive knowledge of God is ruled out—is one of the most noticeable neo-orthodox features of his work.

[176]W. Lemke, "Revelation through History in Recent Biblical Theology," *Int* 36 (1982) 34.

[177]For entree into a voluminous corpus see e.g. C. North, "Bibliography of Works in Theology and History," *History and Theory* 12 (1972) 57-140. Note also many of the entries in B. Gelderbloom, "Bibliographie," *PTNT*, 439-464.

ology participated and by which it was affected, cannot be examined in detail here. Despite numerous attempts to set forth a synthetic understanding of history's nature or direction, it came to be viewed by many, not as a fertile field for creative and fruitful investigation, but as a vexing and insoluble problem. From philosophy came the verdict: "The problem of history has come to be the unavoidable problem of philosophy."[178] The methodological crisis still gripping biblical criticism and theology today came to full bloom in this period. Paradoxically, many New Testament scholars of the time did not seem to be greatly troubled by questions of historical methodology.[179] Yet it gradually comes to be recognized that there was great need "to clarify the nature of New Testament theology as a theological discipline" through "critical reflection upon the procedures of historiography as such."[180]

Reventlow observes that discussion of salvation history in recent decades was carried on largely among systematicians and then

> primarily by New Testament scholars, while the involvement of Old Testament scholars in the discussion is quantitatively smaller. Also, Old Testament theologians are more often positively inclined to the concept as such, while criticism, especially along the lines pioneered by R. Bultmann, has been carried out most strongly by New Testament criticism.[181]

This statement holds true as we look at discussion of salvation history or salvation historical outlooks since World War II in New Testament theology (and related areas where relevant). We will see an extensive rejection of any salvation historical approach underway. This is in many cases a result of Bultmann's influence. "Many New Testament theologians," and not only these, regard salvation history "with disfavor, if not with angry disgust" in the postwar era.[182] Yet at the same time we will observe that a variety of writers, along with but by no means dependent on Cullmann, argue for the validity of a salvation historical outlook in some form. We will seek, not to survey discussion right up to the present hour, but to parallel the discussion of Old

---

[178]W. Müller-Lauter, "Konsequenzen des Historismus in der Philosophie der Gegenwart," *ZTK* 59 (1962) 226.

[179]Cf. T.A. Roberts, "Some Presuppositions of Gospel Criticism," Texte und Untersuchungen 73 (1959 [= Studia Evangelica I]), 66.

[180]A. Richardson, "What Is New Testament Theology?" Texte und Untersuchungen 112 (1969 [= Studia Evangelica VI]), 465.

[181]Reventlow, *Hauptprobleme*, 108.

[182]O'Collins, *Foundations*, 83.

Testament theology above. We will also furnish background for considering Cullmann in the next chapter.

2. Rejections of salvation historical approaches by Bultmann and others
Of course if by "salvation history" one understands an individualistic "historicality,"[183] then Bultmann's approach is salvation historical. But salvation history in the sense pioneered by Hofmann-Schlatter does not and cannot carry this existentialist connotation.

Bultmann's systematic rejection of salvation history, which can be traced especially to epistemological considerations, will emerge in the next two chapters. His basic position was carried forward by G. Klein, whose opinion is already clear from his article's title.[184] Bultmannian thinking also made its way into Old Testament theology, and not only through the work of von Rad.[185] W. Herberg relates salvation history to human existence in thoroughly existentialist terms.[186] Bultmann's basic position, combined with insights from the later Heidegger and Bonhoeffer, becomes the core of a "new hermeneutic" in which any possibility of adopting views amicable to a salvation historical perspective is implicitly excluded.[187] For the new hermeneutic the Bible's history is largely the object of a historical criticism whose goal in turn is to reach "nothing other than the destabilizing of faith."[188] Then paradoxically true faith becomes a possibility.[189] This is not compatible with a salvation historical standpoint.

---

[183]See e.g. G. Kaufman, "The *Imago Dei* as Man's Historicity," *JR* 36 (1956) 157-168. Here insights from Barth and Collingwood lead to the conclusion that man's divine image consists in his historicity, in which he creates himself anew from a remembered past.

[184]Klein, "Bibel und Heilsgeschichte: die Fragwürdigkeit einer Idee [The Bible and *Heilsgeschichte*: The Dubiousness of an Idea]," *ZNW* 62 (1971) 1-47. For rebuttals see Kümmel, "Heilsgeschichte im Neuen Testament?", *Heilsgeschehen*, 157-176; Schmitt, *Abschied?, passim.* Cf. Goldingay, *Approaches to Old Testament Interpretation*, 92 n. 104.

[185]See e.g. G. Fohrer, "Die zeitliche und überzeitliche Bedeutung des Alten Testaments," *EvT* 9 (1949) 447-460; F. Baumgärtel, "Zur Frage der theologischen Deutung des Alten Testaments," *ZST* 15 (1938) 136-162; *idem, Verheissung,* 1952.

[186]Herberg, "Biblical Faith as Heilsgeschichte," *The Christian Scholar* 39 (1956) 25-31.

[187]Cf. the approach to history evinced in Ebeling, "The World as History," *Word and Faith*, 363-373.

[188]E. Reisner, "Hermeneutik und historische Vernunft," *ZTK* 49 (1952) 233.

[189]Cf. Ebeling, "Jesus and Faith," *Word and Faith*, 240, where "the certainty of faith" signifies "taking sure steps although no road is visible, hoping although there is nothing to look for, refusing to despair although things are desperate, having ground under us although we step into the bottomless abyss."

F. Flückiger surprisingly terms Bultmann's a salvation historical theology[190] but in so doing shows the elasticity of the term in the postwar discussion. Approvingly he notes:

> *Salvation history* in Bultmann is actually totally devoted to this "here and now" of encounter; it becomes salvation-historicality, i.e., the encounter with God in his word which occurs continually in one's existence. God never encounters me objectively ..., therefore there can also no longer be any such thing as historical fact that would be revelation.[191]

E. Dinkler stresses the same aspects of Bultmann's theology[192] and defends Bultmann's analysis of history against that of Cullmann.[193] Cullmann's conception of salvation history does indeed rearticulate a viewpoint arising in New Testament times, but it is one "made up of syncretistic components."[194] For New Testament believers "*the history of our human world remains a riddle*."[195] Salvation, then, is only a matter related to salvation history in the sense "that the Christian is set free with regard to his own past, that he is able to transcend history as a nexus, that he can therefore decide within history for history and actualize his history."[196] Bultmann has led us to see the New Testament's real message about history: that it is to be viewed "not in cosmological or metaphysical terms but in terms of the historicity of man."[197] Augustine and Kierkegaard had glimpsed this insight, but since New Testament times it was otherwise "not taken up *explicitly* until the 20th century."[198]

New Testament theologies also reflect Bultmann's influence. This is perhaps most true in the work of H. Conzelmann.[199] He clearly wants to refine and go beyond Bultmann's insights, yet his basic position is that "salvation does not develop out of the world, say as the meaning

[190]Flückiger, "Heilsgeschichte und Weltgeschichte," *EvT* 18 (1958) 41.

[191]*Ibid.* 43.

[192]Dinkler, "Existentialist Interpretation of the New Testament," *JR* 32 (1952) 87-96.

[193]Dinkler, "Earliest Christianity," *The Idea of History in the Ancient Near East*, ed. R.C. Dentan, 1955, 169-214.

[194]*Ibid.* 207.

[195]*Ibid.* 210, Dinkler's emphasis.

[196]*Ibid.* 213.

[197]*Ibid.* 214.

[198]*Ibid.*

[199]Conzelmann, *An Outline of the Theology of the New Testament*, 1969.

and goal of world history."[200] "Redemption is not a situation in the world, but a determination of the being of the world itself."[201]

J. Jeremias' impressive handling of Jesus' ministry is so anti-Bultmannian as to fail, in some respects at least, to move out from under his adversary's shadow.[202] Jeremias speaks of "The Onset of the Time of Salvation"[203] and even of salvation history,[204] and he sees that "uncritical skepticism can unintentionally lead to the falsification of history."[205] But a salvation historical outlook in the Hofmann-Schlatter sense is not a feature of his presentation. Jeremias' preoccupation with the linguistic dimension of the historical data—by no means lamentable in itself—prevents him from integrating extensive theological interpretation or reflection in his work.

Ebeling's influential essay on biblical theology[206] implicitly rules out salvation history in several ways. First, he denies that either the Old Testament or the New Testament comprises a theological unity to begin with.[207] In addition, the idea of canon is ruled out by "application of the historical method."[208] Therefore a unified salvation historical New Testament theology drawn primarily from the canonical Scriptures would be unscientific. Second, the relatively orthodox picture of biblical history, revelation, and faith common to most proponents of a salvation historical perspective is excluded by biblical theology's own "dogmatic element," which necessarily "adopts a more or less critical attitude to that theological tradition" which comprises or circumscribes Christian belief.[209] Third, salvation history is excluded by definition when Ebeling defines it as "the scientific explication of the content of the Old and New Testament" as opposed to an exposition of "the content of the Old and New Testament."[210] Here Ebeling at the outset privileges modern understanding of reality over that found in the Old or New Testament themselves. Ebeling's formulation is consistent with Bultmann's view of New Testament theology as a presentation of certain New Testament writers' believing self-

---

[200] *Ibid.* 201.

[201] *Ibid.* 200.

[202] Jeremias, *Neutestamentliche Theologie*, 1971.

[203] *Ibid.* 81–123.

[204] *Ibid.* 86f., 266f.

[205] *Ibid.* 272.

[206] Ebeling, "The Meaning of 'Biblical Theology'," *Word and Faith*, 79–97.

[207] *Ibid.* 91f.

[208] *Ibid.* 92f.

[209] *Ibid.* 90f.

[210] *Ibid.* 94.

understanding with reference to a kerygma which is conceptually ineffable and indescribable.[211] A salvation historical perspective is methodologically ruled out by this approach, whatever the historical testimony might yield.

Other systematic rejections of salvation history could be mentioned that reflect direct Bultmannian influence.[212] Among New Testament theologians works by S. Neill, E. Lohse, A. Richardson, O. Betz, and D. Guthrie are critical of a salvation history emphasis or give it limited prominence.[213]

Some reject salvation history for reasons akin to those of Pfeiffer mentioned above. Salvation history is assumed to entail a regularity and goal in history which is alien to the modern worldview. We may assume today that there is rational "order in the universe," but otherwise "critical historical research can brook no theoretical presuppositions" of the sort implied in a salvation historical outlook.[214] McCown adds, obviously not considering these as his own theoretical presuppositions:

> The nature of divine activity, as seen by the ancient world, was arbitrary, deterministic, and miraculous ... Modern science and philosophy have no place for miracles and special providences. History is the result of the complex interaction of natural and social forces and the actions and reactions of men ... God acts only through men. Neither the liberal nor the conservative, neither the historian nor the theologian can afford to neglect this total difference of world-view.[215]

McCown thus excludes the possibility of salvation history on the grounds that it reflects a worldview that he deems unacceptable.

W. Irwin speaks in similar, if slightly more optimistic, terms:

---

[211] I.e. its content is not accessible by cognitive means and does not admit to being either expressed in or apprehended by means of propositional statements. The kerygmatic proclamation does not convey information but opens up relational possibilities. See on Bultmann in Chapter 6 below.

[212] E.g. W.R. Baird, Jr., "Current Trends in New Testament Study," *JR* 39 (1959) 137-153; S. Ogden, "What Sense Does It Make to Say 'God Acts in History'?" *JR* 43 (1963) 1-19.

[213] Neill, *Jesus Through Many Eyes*, 1976; Lohse, *Grundriss der neutestamentlichen Theologie*, 1974; Richardson, *An Introduction to the Theology of the New Testament*, 1958; Betz, "History of Biblical Theology," *IDB* 1:432-437 (dismisses a salvation history approach in four terse lines [436]); Guthrie, *New Testament Theology*, 1981.

[214] C. McCown, "The Current Plight of Biblical Scholarship," *JBL* 75 (1956) 17.

[215] *Ibid.*

The only true *Heilsgeschichte* is *Weltgeschichte*, the entire process of the numberless ages through which "the redemptive forces of the universe" have slowly, and as yet very imperfectly, won man away from his beastly impulses towards the path that leads upward to the perfect day.[216]

In the same vein H. Wieman rejects a salvation historical outlook, because it makes history itself subordinate to a non- or supra-historical reality.[217] "The whole of history has no ... overall direction or pattern," contrary to the assumption of those who propound salvation history, and "the greatest danger" faced by man today is religious outlooks on life and history which prevent an appropriately contemporary and purely secular synthesis of man's basic religious drive with the sovereign findings of science and technology.[218]

In numerous spheres of thought, the salvation historical approach meets opposition. As we have already suggested, it is clear that despite a surfeit of verbiage after World War II about revelation in history, the merits of the salvation historical position are hardly weighed in most quarters. This is due most commonly to the popularity of Bultmann's position but has other explanations too.

It is common to suppose that salvation history in the postwar years was primarily a pet theme of the valiant but eventually vanquished Cullmann, who "introduced the theory of *Heilsgeschichte*" into New Testament research.[219] We have seen already the fallacy of attributing the concept to Cullmann. Moreover, alongside Bultmannian skepticism there was a strong undercurrent of support for salvation historical analysis. This cannot be shown to be primarily the direct result of Cullmann; it is rather the continuing insistence of critics in a heritage stretching back to Hofmann that any reading of the Bible which gives short shrift to salvation historical considerations risks misreading it. Examples of protests against cavilier dismissal of salvation history and a salvation historical approach are surprisingly frequent in the literature of the time.

3. Support for salvation historical approaches
Ancillary responses
By no means all of the postwar rhetoric about revelation in history was liberal-critical theologizing utilizing neo-orthodox terminology, as

---

[216]W. Irwin, "A Still Small Voice ... Said, What Are You Doing Here?" *JBL* 78 (1959) 6.

[217]H. Wieman, "Divine Creativity in History," *RelL* 33 (1964) 57.

[218]*Ibid.* 65.

[219]H. Teeple, *The Historical Approach to the Bible*, 1982, 142.

Childs has contended. Many argued for salvation historical outlooks in a sense more consistent with the Hofmann-Schlatter precedent. A series of investigations representing the various fields of historiography, philosophy, New Testament criticism, theology, historical theology, and apologetics argues, whether implicitly or explicitly, in support of acceptance of a salvation historical outlook. These studies illustrate a general renewed, or perhaps just continuing, interest in a modified historical-critical approach commensurate with both historical and theological evidence of God's overarching purpose and personal involvement in history. We cannot here recount treatments by N. Sykes, I. Ramsey, E. Rust, J.S. Marshall, K. Wennemer, J.W. Bowman,[220] and others.[221]

We can only observe that from a wide range of disciplines and viewpoints there was widespread preoccupation with questions about history's purpose and God's role within it. C.T. McIntire may be correct in diagnosing a postwar renaissance "of a predominately Augustinian Christian view of history" in some intellectual and literary circles.[222] Whatever the validity of a salvation historical approach to New Testament theology, it certainly cannot be dismissed, even in the postwar years, as an idiosyncratic innovation introduced by a radical or reactionary few within that discipline.

New Testament theologians also took up and articulated salvation historical modes of historical-theological interpretation during these years. Much in keeping with the Hofmann-Schlatter precedent, historical-critically astute New Testament theologians argue for the hermeneutical necessity of a salvation history approach to the New Testament data if it is to be understood and heard aright.

---

[220]N. Sykes, "Some Recent Conceptions of Historiography and their Significance for Christian Apologetics," *JTS* 50 (1949) 24-37; I. Ramsey, "History and the Gospels: Some Philosophical Reflections," Texte und Untersuchungen 88 (*SE* III, 1964) 201-217; E. Rust, *The Christian Understanding of History*, 1947; idem, *Towards a Theological Understanding of History*, 1963; J.S. Marshall, "History in the Aristotelian Vein," *ATR* 32 (1950) 245-256; K. Wennemer, "Zur Frage einer heilsgeschichtlichen Theologie," *Scholastik* 29 (1954) 73-79; Bowman, "From Schweizer to Bultmann," *TToday* 11 (1954) 160-178; idem, *Prophetic Realism and the Gospel*, 1955

[221]E.g., O. Tiililä, "Über die heilsgeschichtliche Schriftauslegung," *Gedenkschrift für D. Werner Elert*, ed. Hübner, Kinder, and Maurer, 283-287; A. Bengsch, *Heilsgeschichte und Heilswissen*, 1957; J.W. Montgomery, "Where Is History Going?" *RelL* 33 (1963-64) 238-255;

[222]McIntire, "Introduction," in *Herbert Butterfield: Writings on Christianity and History*, ed. McIntire, 1979, xix.

New Testament theology

We limit ourselves below to five examples of this trend. We want chiefly to depict its main features and to show how it is seldom if ever directly dependent on Cullmann.[223]

1. In 1947 A. Wilder calls salvation history "a datum ... found in Scripture."[224] New Testament theology must be scientific and synthetic,[225] but it can also incorporate a Christian confessional standpoint without sacrificing critical integrity. This is true presumably because the data furnish critical ground for the confession. "The most promising contemporary approach" to New Testament theology "lies along the lines denoted by salvation history and *Geschichtstheologie*." Wilder, who shows only nominal familiarity with Cullmann's work, continues with a precise delineation of the parameters and advantages of a salvation historical approach to New Testament theology. Salvation history embodies "the fundamental conception" of New Testament theology and points toward "the proper manner of presentation."[226] New Testament theology, rightly conceived, accordingly

presents the divine plan and the course of divine action from a point before time, through history, to a point beyond time in a history of salvation which is also a history of the totality of existence. The writings of the New Testament taken together present this world picture, some documenting certain aspects of the whole process, others documenting others, but all the writings in their conceptions belonging within the common world view. This historical realism of the Bible, this sense of the creative and redemptive process, in which providence, history, community, conflict with evil powers, and eschatology have so large a place, forbids presentation in terms of static or conceptual doctrines or phases of religious experience or piecemeal documents. And this view corrects the approach of the dialectical theology; for here revelation is embodied in a thoroughgoing and inextricable way in the process of history—indeed, it is hidden, for the superficial observer, in the context of the relative—and not imposed upon it or abstracted from it. This approach also corrects the method of historicism, which fails to give full recognition to the dramatic and organic unity of the canon and which,

---

[223]We omit such figures as E. Stauffer, J. Daniélou, and O. Piper, who would have borne inclusion had space permitted: see Stauffer, "Der Stand der neutestamentlichen Forschung," *Theologie und Liturgie*, ed. Henning, 35-105, especially 97ff.; Daniélou, "The New Testament and the Theology of History," Texte und Untersuchungen (*SE* I, 1959) 25-34; Piper, "Christology and History," *TToday* 19 (1962) 324-340.

[224]Wilder, "New Testament Theology in Transition," *Study of Bible*, ed. Willoughby, 422.

[225]*Ibid.* 434.

[226]*Ibid.* 435.

in its concern for the morphology of religion and the morphology of the religion of the separate writings and figures, loses sight of the over-all picture of the world process. Such an approach renews the insights of the premodern period, while benefiting by the contributions of modern scholarship, and has the further merit of reading the New Testament more fully in the light of its own presuppositions.[227]

Wilder, like Hofmann, Schlatter, and others, is arguing that the New Testament data will not well admit of reduction to the size or shape typically demanded by dominant critical methods. The realities of which the New Testament speaks spring the constraints of historicism and a-historical theology. A satisfactory full-orbed understanding of the New Testament is not forthcoming as long as modern assumptions about reality are used to stifle the claims of the text itself. With virtually no reliance on Cullmann, Wilder carries into the postwar years the same general convictions about the necessity of a salvation historical approach (and the deficiencies, despite their contributions, of non-salvation historical methods) that we traced earlier in the prewar era.

2. In 1953 B. Reicke addresses the problem of the unity of the New Testament as it surfaces in the theologies of Stauffer, M. Burrows, M. Meinertz, and Bultmann. He notes that these four approach the question quite differently. Reicke suggests that what Bultmann and Meinertz have wrongly rejected, and what Stauffer and Burrows have failed adequately to stress, is that "all New Testament writings relate to the same Jesus Christ and the same event which is wrapped up in him. Precisely here, *in the Christ event, is the essential unity* of the New Testament to be sought."[228]

More specifically, Reicke cites approvingly Hunter's thesis (noted in the previous chapter) that the unity of the New Testament lies "in the salvation history that is proclaimed in it."[229] This is exegetically justified, since "everything that the first Christians proclaim in their writings is revelation of God's act in Christ, thus an ongoing Christ-event."[230] New Testament theology must not allow itself to be dominated by a naturalistic "history of religion-oriented theory of development," for New Testament theology is properly concerned with "proclamation which is to be handled as an existing revelation,"

---

[227] *Ibid.* 435f.

[228] Reicke, "Einheitlichkeit oder verschiedene 'Lehrbegriffe' in der neutestamentlichen Theologie?" *TZ* 9 (1953) 405 (Reicke's emphasis).

[229] *Ibid.* 405 n. 10.

[230] *Ibid.*

to be analyzed "without naturalistic-causal hypotheses."[231] As regards
the synoptics, e.g., one may not legitimately explicate their contents
according to a positivistic developmental theory; New Testament theology "ought to the best of its ability relate the outlook of the
evangelist as it actually presents itself."[232] As to the problem of dogmatic elements which may surface in a New Testament theology
written in harmony with its own presuppositions, Reicke states simply: "Whether one personally accepts his presentation is a matter of
faith."[233]

While it is true that the New Testament's broadest divisions (synoptics, Paul, John) evince somewhat different perspectives, "everywhere
we encounter the same type of savior, one and the same salvation history."[234] The different emphases and modes of expressions of the New
Testament writers do not express mutually exclusive assessments of
Jesus but are rather a basically unified expression "of the unity, which
furnishes the basis for the evangelical faith, between the word-
become-flesh, the resurrected Christ, and the Lord of the Christian
church."[235]

These statements, made with very little reference to Cullmann,
again are reminiscent of Hofmann and Schlatter, Hunter, and others.
Modern worldviews, implies Reicke, must be open to modification
from the New Testament evidence. Diversity of viewpoint and expression must not be construed as necessarily conscious disparity of
conviction. Reicke's salvation historical deliberations seek to do justice
to both the relational and the empirical-factual dimensions of the New
Testament witness; it is a false dichotomy, he implies, when the two
are wrenched apart.

3. Goppelt's earliest extended discussion of a salvation historical approach to New Testament theology comes in a bold speech[236] before a
synodal meeting in Hannover. Historical criticism of the Bible can be
done either "from an exterior vantage point" or "from an interior

---

[231] *Ibid.* 407.

[232] *Ibid.* 412.

[233] *Ibid.*

[234] *Ibid.* 415.

[235] *Ibid.*

[236] Goppelt, "Die Authorität der Heiligen Schrift und die Bibelkritik," *Wort Gottes und Bekenntnis*, 1954, 9–17. Re boldness, Goppelt declares that Bultmann's interpretation of the New Testament comprises "so much of an attenuation of its contents that,
in my opinion, a candidate who without qualifications embraces Bultmann's results
cannot make his ordination vows in a Lutheran church with good conscience" (*ibid.*
12).

vantage point."[237] In the former case criticism is used to serve the interests of the prevailing *Weltanschauung,* while in the latter case criticism "works with modern, precision philological and historical means" but seeks to apply these to Scripture "from the standpoint of the faith of the Christian community."[238] Goppelt calls this the "salvation historical-ecclesiastical"[239] line of research, and he names Hofmann, Beck, Zahn, Schlatter, and Schniewind (along with von Rad on the Old Testament side) as its main representatives. He continues:

> This [salvation historical] research encounters the results of historical criticism not only—although this is part of its response—with historical anticriticism, but most of all with a salvation historical understanding of the [biblical] reports, which disproves the arguments of criticism by showing their simple factual misunderstanding.[240]

Goppelt then gives three principles for proper interpretation of Scripture from this salvation historical perspective. First, interpretation must be "historical-theological."[241] Second, this "historical-theological" interpretation must comprise a unified procedure; "the two [the historical and the theological] cannot be severed from each other in two stages."[242] Goppelt explains: "A biblical text does not take on its ultimate meaning through natural reason, after which it is read in faith; it becomes meaningful rather always and only as it is read with reason illuminated by faith."[243] Third, the sort of faith which will enable an interpreter to push through to the true meaning of the New Testament texts is one which respects the fact that "Scripture is according to its own claim the unique source of primary revelation."[244] This implies that a proper historical-theological handling of the Bible is one in which "Scripture is to be interpreted formally on the basis of Scripture itself."[245] "Whoever does not accept Scripture as that which it claims to be fails to understand it."[246]

[237] *Ibid.* 10.

[238] *Ibid.* 14.

[239] *Ibid.*

[240] *Ibid.*

[241] *Ibid.*

[242] *Ibid.* 15.

[243] *Ibid.*

[244] *Ibid.*

[245] *Ibid.*

[246] *Ibid.* 16.

Chapter 6 below takes up the question of an epistemological rift between Goppelt and Schlatter. In broad terms, however, it may be said that Goppelt, independently of Cullmann, argues for a salvation historical approach in much the same vein as Hofmann-Schlatter and many since. Due apparently not to a philosophy of history as such but rather out of deference to New Testament history (as well as impatience with the spread of Bultmann's views), Goppelt calls for rethinking New Testament theology's sometimes unwise commitment to critical methods which too facilely move from each decade's fleeting assumptions about reality to interpretations of the New Testament evidence. The claims of the New Testament deserve to be allowed to shape the methods applied to them.

4. G. Ladd defines biblical[247] theology as "exegetical theology" which comprises "the description and interpretation of the divine activity which seeks man's redemption."[248] It is thus "the description and interpretation of redemptive history."[249] Because the Bible consists of documents with a historical context and historically-conditioned message, biblical theology "must be fundamentally historical in character" and "must therefore squarely face the question of the relatedness of theology and history."[250] "History" is not however to be naturalistically defined, notwithstanding the fact that much of the Bible is offensive to a secular historiography which insists that "all 'historical' events must be capable of explanation in terms of known and demonstrable causes."[251] If the New Testament is to be taken seriously in the discipline seeking to give a synthetic presentation of it, it must be noted that for many biblical events "there is no natural explanation," even though from the Bible's standpoint "*these events actually happened on the scene of human history.*"[252] God himself at times "intervenes" in history, which is not "unnatural," nor "a violation of the laws of nature," but a "manifestation of the divine power which is also evident in the natural order ... Both the natural and the supernatural are evidences of the divine activity."[253] Ladd asserts finally that "historical facts

---

[247]Ladd, "Biblical Theology, History, and Revelation," *RevExp* 54 (1957) 195-204; cf. *idem*, "The Modern Problem of Biblical Scholarship," *Bethel Seminary Quarterly* 5 (1957) 10-20.

[248]Ladd, *RevExp* 54 (1957) 195.

[249]*Ibid.*

[250]*Ibid.* 197.

[251]*Ibid.* 198.

[252]*Ibid.* 199.

[253]*Ibid.* 198.

and their theological meanings must reinforce each other."[254] Ladd holds that "this question of theology and history is the central problem of modern critical Biblical study."[255]

Ladd denies that "redemptive history is ... the only mode of revelation," nor does he accept that revelation in history is "*by itself* an adequate vehicle of revelation."[256] Here Ladd faults G.E. Wright, who stresses "act-revelation" to the exclusion of "word-revelation."[257] Ladd rather claims that "revelation in Israel includes the historical events plus the inspired prophetic interpretation; and the revelation in Christ includes the *historical event plus the apostolic interpretation.*"[258] Both the historical occurrence and the authoritative interpretation are requisite for a genuine salvation historical outlook.

Ladd advances his position without reference to Cullmann. His basic agreement with others already mentioned above is evident, although Ladd differs from them in affirming the infallibility of Scripture. Thus he wants to avoid the danger of stressing the salvation historical events but not the reports from which we learn of the events. His overall concern to avoid an exaggerated faith-fact or theology-history split and to let critical methods be adapted to the subject matter, as well as his overt advocacy of a salvation historical reading of the New Testament, locate him squarely in the Hofmann-Schlatter heritage.

5. H. Ridderbos, perhaps more carefully than any of the four just above, seeks to establish the historical-exegetical grounds on which the New Testament texts can be spoken of in connection with salvation history. He notes that many agree that the Scripture itself has no authority, but only its content or that to which it points.[259] This is a relationally apprehended entity which transcends Scripture, for most to such an extent that Scripture itself is no longer revelation but only functions as revelatory means. It mediates but does not comprise revelation. In broad terms, this would be the position of neo-orthodoxy. In terms of our study, this position would be somewhat less radical than that held by Baur and Wrede, in regard to whom it is questionable how or even whether one could speak of revelation at all.

[254]Ladd, *Bethel Seminary Quarterly* 5 (1957) 18.

[255]*Ibid.*

[256]Ladd, *RevExp* 54 (1957) 202.

[257]*Ibid.* 203 n. 4.

[258]*Ibid.* 203.

[259]Ridderbos, *Redemptive History and the New Testament Scriptures*, 1988, vii. The original Dutch version appeared in 1955.

But "if Scripture is not itself divine revelation, if it is simply a faulty, human medium, then what standards shall we use to establish the authority of its content?"[260] Most New Testament theologians, if they are open to a theological reading of the New Testament at all, would reply that that in some sense Jesus, or Jesus' teachings, would be the standard. The historical problem that arises here, however, is: "We can know Jesus Christ only in the manner in which He comes to us in the canon of the New Testament."[261]

Ridderbos argues accordingly from New Testament evidence that "*the announcement of redemption cannot be separated from the history of redemption itself.*"[262] This general line of argument is to be found also in Hofmann, Schlatter, and Cullmann, though Ridderbos seems to be relying mainly on his own exegesis. A result of his conclusion is, in contrast to prevalent views in New Testament criticism which separate New Testament faith from its historical moorings, to bring faith and cognitively apprehensible data back into mutual proximity. Just because the New Testament message is theologically appraised, this does not mean that its temporal or historical dress is superfluous or even detrimental to understanding it aright. The message of the New Testament books is bound up inextricably in their time-conditioned mode of transmission. Their theological content is of a piece with the historically conditioned expression of it.

This observation gives rise to what for Ridderbos is partially a historical and not solely a dogmatic question. What gives rise to the New Testament writings? What unifies the canon's parts? Here the "a priori of faith" is introduced, i.e., that which was and is prior to and forms the basis for faith, and thus also for a sympathetic grasp of the New Testament message in its entirety. This is not the human act of faith but the reality of what faith reaches out to grasp. Ridderbos in effect confronts New Testament theology in the Baur-Wrede heritage, which seems to generate theological confession or knowledge out of human reflection while leaving the cognitive ground for such reflection unclarified, bracketed, or perhaps even destroyed. But the canonical writings emerged neither out of human faith nor as a result of groundless mystical or existential experience; the ground for their recognition lies rather

---

[260] *Ibid.*
[261] *Ibid.* 43.
[262] *Ibid.* 15, his emphasis.

solely in the apriori of the canon itself, that is, in the redemptive historical reality that lies at the foundation of the canon as such and from which [faith] springs. That reality precedes faith, the church, and the history of the canon. It lies most deeply in Christ himself and in the nature of His coming and work. The ground for the recognition of the canon is therefore in principle redemptive-historical, that is, Christological.[263]

For Ridderbos Jesus Christ established and upholds (or is the content of) the New Testament writings, but he did and does this

not only as a spiritual reality, not merely as a canon within the canon or as his current divine and infallible speaking in the human and fallible word of Scripture and the church. Rather, Christ establishes the canon in the ascertainable character of apostolic preaching and in the legibility of apostolic writings, in the preservation of the apostolic witness and doctrine.[264]

To that which Jesus established and upholds, there corresponds the historical states of affairs related in the New Testament pertaining to Jesus and his followers, on which the New Testament witnesses and teaching are based and out of which they grew.

The outlines of portions of Ridderbos' argument are ancient, and modern criticism would claim to have destroyed much of what he says. But that is the point of Ridderbos' treatise: it is primarily by reading the New Testament in a context openly and needlessly foreign to it that such disparate, often negative theories and conclusions about it and its contents have arisen. A myopic critical historiography has so arbitrarily handled the New Testament that its internal theological coherence, which is not irreconcilable with known historical facts of the first-century context, is shattered.

But this demolition is really unnecessary. If one recognizes the "salvation historical reality" which undergirds and is the prime mover in the formation of the New Testament and does not over-hastily rule out substantial agreement between this reality in its historical-theological manifestation and the written testimony to it, then it is both possible and necessary to speak of a salvation historical reading of the New Testament. Such a reading is critical but at the same time wary of facilely deployed modern assumptions which too often dominate New Testament interpretation.

We can see in this brief glimpse once again how in the context of postwar New Testament theology a salvation historical outlook is set forth and defended. As elsewhere above, this is done without reference

---

[263] *Ibid.* 36f.
[264] *Ibid.* 37.

to *Christ and Time,* although two of Cullmann's other exegetical works are cited. Clearly Ridderbos would side with a Hofmann-Schlatter approach to New Testament theology. His understanding of how salvation history relates to both the New Testament and to modern apprehension of it serves to extend many of the convictions held by Wilder and others above.

5. Conclusion

The postwar era witnesses a great deal of activity in both Old and New Testament theology. The former discipline is dominated first by Eichrodt and then even more decisively by von Rad. The latter discipline receives decisive impetus throughout from Bultmann. In recent decades many changes have come in both Old and New Testament study. Eichrodt was overshadowed by von Rad, who in turn has been left behind by "a shift in paradigm from historical criticism to literary analysis, from diachronic to synchronic studies," to say nothing of "increasing aversion to anything theological."[265] Bultmann is still a patron saint for some New Testament theologians but no longer their guide. Still, fundamental methodological questions raised by the last generation's leaders remain on the table. Lack of consensus on these questions and many others presently obtains in both fields.

Childs rightly calls attention to a groundswell of support that arose for a revelation in history emphasis in the Biblical Theology Movement. He just as rightly diagnoses its fallacy: it stressed the theological important fact of God's acts in history but typically declined to affirm their concrete historical reality. As Barton summarizes, "the critical method ... shows us not what God is like, but what people *thought* he was like."[266] Postwar biblical theology spoke of what God was *thought* to have done. But this bold sounding statement often concealed a weighty assumption: what the biblical writers said about God cannot actually have been and therefore is not the case in historical retrospect. What they expressed is to be distinguished from what we determine to have been true.[267] Our verdict has far more warrant to be trustworthy.

---

[265] J. Crenshaw, "Von Rad, Gerhard (1901–1971)," *Historical Handbook of Major Biblical Interpreters*, 530.

[266] Barton, "Old Testament Theology," in *Old Testament Study*, ed. Rogerson, 94.

[267] Cf. Wrede's remark concerning the gospel sources: "that which actually lies before us is only the conception of a later narrator of the life of Jesus, and ... this confession [is] not identical with the thing itself" (*Das Messiasgeheimnis in den Evangelien*, 2).

In such a hermeneutic it is very easy for criticism to read its own thoughts about God into the biblical text.

Eichrodt, von Rad, Bultmann, and a host of others work to varying degrees within this matrix of understanding. For them, as for Baur and Wrede, there are gains to such an approach. The obvious advantage is that the demands of theories ascendant in the academy are satisfied, enabling interpreters to assure themselves that the results of their scholarship are critical or scientific. But there are also liabilities. Chief among them is Feuerbach's nagging question: is God then just a projection of human religious aspirations, whether ancient or modern, on an imagined cosmic screen? As J. Fenton wrote, "If God does not act, and cannot be known in his action, then faith is merely an aspect of man's attempt to make this world secure for himself, a compensation technique, an undergirder of social cohesion, and a theory about the meaning of life."[268]

If this is not the case, why would it not have been possible for Old/New Testament theology to move beyond the constraints of historicistic or positivistic descriptive method informed by fervent endorsement of the prevailing philosophical-theological movements of thought (dialectical theology, existentialism)? Postwar Old and New Testament theologians for the most part failed to answer this question, which basically restates the question raised in Chapter 3 above by many who were seeing a need for some sort of a salvation historical approach. The surprising fact is that following World War II talk of salvation history eventually comes to be condemned outright, as if it were in every case a reactionary throwback to nineteenth century philosophy of history. As we have seen, discussion of salvation history, which even Hofmann claimed not to have originated but only to have articulated comprehensively, had never abated since Hofmann's time. And it was not even for him primarily a philosophy of history.

While the postwar era is dominated by non- and anti-salvation historical outlooks, Pfeifferian affirmation of modernity's sovereignty over all reality scrutinized by it—an affirmation mirrored in the historical skepticism of von Rad and Bultmann—is offset by argumentation reminiscent of Filson. Such contrarian insistences echo the calls of Hofmann, Schlatter, and many since. Figures like Jacob, Wilder, Goppelt, Ladd, and Ridderbos argue for critical methods to admit of adjustment in the light of the data to which they are applied. (An additional spokesman, M. Albertz, will be discussed in Chapter 6 below.)

---

[268]Fenton, "The Post-Liberal Theology of Christ without Myth," *JR* 43 (1963) 103.

God's discerning, sifting, informing word which worked mightily in former times—not as something blindly concocted and believed but because compelling grounds for it to be trusted became discernible— must be free to do so today; and this freedom must extend not only to the confessional but also to the cognitive realm. If God really has acted as the biblical writers claim, then a historical method which implicitly but categorically debars the divine from the historical in any but an immanent sense is begging vital questions.

The bifurcation in Old and New Testament theology which dates back several generations persists in the postwar years. Consideration of that era, however, remains incomplete until we have factored in Cullmann's presence and contribution. We turn next to examination of his views.

5

Prophet without Honor:
Cullmann's Unseasonable Salvation Historical Synthesis

In his fascinating study of the influence of Ovid, Horace, Plato, Thucydides, and Homer in successive generations of English life, R. Ogilvie notes that "the determining ideas of a civilization have always been the prerogative of the few."[1] In the micro-civilization of New Testament theology "the few" of the last couple of generations were largely Bultmann and his many students and admirers. Like references to Ambrose, Augustine, and Aquinas in *Catechism of the Catholic Church*,[2] references to Bultmann are predictably frequent in studies representative of late 20th century New Testament scholarship. No one else comes close to matching him, or his allies, in frequency of mention in the 1989 North American anthology *The New Testament and Its Modern Interpreters*.[3] He and his followers are likewise prominent in the index of a recent German New Testament survey, a British-American exegetical handbook, and Räisänen's freshly updated, magisterial survey of New Testament theological scholarship.[4]

On the other hand, Oscar Cullmann (1902–1998), leading proponent of a salvation historical synthesis in the second half of the 20th century, has become odd man out. The first of his major works, *Christ*

---

[1] *Latin and Greek: A History of the Influence of the Classics on English Life from 1600–1918*, 1964, xiv.

[2] *Catechism of the Catholic Church*, 1994.

[3] Ed. E. Epp & G. McRae. Mentioned most frequently in the index of modern authors are, in a tier of their own, Bultmann, Käsemann, and Conzelmann. In the next tier are J.M. Robinson, Kümmel, and Koester. From rival schools of thought only Raymond Brown and Jeremias receive as much attention as members of this second tier.

[4] See U. Schnelle, *The History and Theology of the New Testament Writings*, 1998; S.E. Porter, ed., *Handbook to Exegesis of the New Testament*, 1997; Räisänen, *Beyond New Testament Theology*.

and Time, met the buzz saw of a hostile Bultmann review (to be reviewed below) from which Cullmann's reputation never recovered in
the New Testament theological discussion wherever Bultmann's opinions carried authority, particularly in the German university. His
influence now seems to be minimal[5] even among conservative writers
who might be expected to keep memory of his contribution alive[6] or
to cash in on his insights in their own constructive work, as for instance George Ladd did in his *A Theology of the New Testament.*[7]

Cullmann's waning fortunes give pause. In the context of his own
times, on the issue of salvation history he was Bultmann's antipode and
resolute critic who offered a creative synthesis of his own. His main
works gained an increasingly broad hearing as the Biblical Theology
Movement reached its peak. Still in the 1980s he was named alongside
scholars like von Rad, John Bright, Jeremias, Bultmann, and Barth as
someone who "exerted the dominant influence on your scholarly
work" by members of the Institute for Biblical Research, a scholarly
guild in North America.[8] In the modern author index of *The New
Testament and Its Modern Interpreters* he receives as frequent notice as
C.K. Barrett, G. Bornkamm, N. Dahl, M. Dibelius, J. Fitzmyer,
W. Marxsen, Morton Smith, and C.H. Talbert. His main works taken
as a whole "come close to a total presentation of New Testament theology."[9] Cullmann would seem to have a claim to be regarded as one
of the major New Testament theologians of the second half of the
20th century and his salvation historical emphasis to merit serious regard today as a methodological option.

The limping legacy of Cullmann points to the widespread current
sense that a salvation historical approach to New Testament theology is
a fallacy which to leave increasingly far behind could only mark further progress in the discipline.

---

[5]If we tally references to Bultmann and Cullmann in the indexes of the works mentioned in the previous note, Bultmann prevails by the score of 53–4 in Schnelle, 20–1
in Porter, and 38–7 in Räisänen.

[6]Cullmann's absence in Bray, *Biblical Interpretation*, has already been noted.
Bultmann is cited 34 times, Cullmann just 4, in D. Black & D. Dockery, eds., *Inter-
preting the New Testament*, 2001; he is completely absent from G. Maier's *Biblical
Hermeneutics*, 1994.

[7]1974; revised ed. 1993, 9.

[8]See survey results in M. Noll, *Between Faith and Criticism*, 1991, 221–226.

[9]Räisänen, *Beyond New Testament Theology*, 62. Cf. comparable observations in J.
Barr, "Trends and Prospects in Biblical Theology," *JTS* 25 (1974) 269; K. Fröhlich,
"Die Mitte des Neuen Testaments: Oscar Cullmanns Beitrag zur Theologie der
Gegenwart," *Oikonomia*, ed. F. Christ, 1967, 213.

How justified is this conviction? Is Cullmann justly forgotten for being the repristinator of old ideas that Baur, Wrede, and Bultmann conclusively laid to rest? Or may we see his work as a goad reminding New Testament theologians of unpopular but important insights which met cool receptions in Hofmann's and Schlatter's eras, too? Oscar Cullman: prophet or pariah?

Such questions call for a fresh investigation of those years and works in which Cullmann's outlook emerged. This will include comparison to Schweitzer, Barth, and Bultmann as a means of characterizing Cullmann's position, especially before the appearance of *Christ and Time*, the work that in some ways established his reputation.[10] This will furnish a basis for weighing several significant critiques of Cullmann's outlook. Finally, we will summarize Cullmann's relationship to the approach pioneered by Hofmann and Schlatter and reflect on how his views relate to those of Bultmann, who will receive further attention in the next chapter.

If it was right for Bultmann to be hailed as New Testament theology's mastermind and leader for the last half-century, the discipline does well to weigh whether it was at least visited by a prophet in Cullmann.

Background and content of Cullmann's salvation historical reading of the New Testament

1. Emerging awareness
Early theological position and training
Other studies deal in depth with Cullmann's formative years.[11] He entered the biblical scholar's world in the early 1920s not through religious interest as such but through an intellectual curiosity for the subject matter of theology. We showed earlier that discussion of salvation history was already a prominent feature of both Old and New Testament theology at this time. Where would Cullmann properly be

---

[10]First German edition 1946. We cite the revised English edition of 1964.

[11]Cf. especially Cullmann, "An Autobiographical Sketch," *SJT* 14 (1961) 228-233; Fröhlich, "Die Mitte des Neuen Testaments: Oscar Cullmanns Beitrag zur Theologie der Gegenwart," *Oikonomia*, 203-219; Hermesmann, *Zeit und Heil*, 17-29; D. Wallace, "Oscar Cullmann," *Creative Minds in Contemporary Theology*, ed. P. Hughes, 163-202; M. Arnold, "Interview d'Oscar Cullmann," *FoiVie* 92/1 (1993) 9–17; Dorman, "Cullmann, Oscar (b. 1902)," *Historical Handbook of Major Biblical Interpreters*, 467–471. Suffering from lack of grounding in the formation of Cullmann's thought are Steck, *Die Idee der Heilsgeschichte*, 43-51; Eslinger, "Historicity and Historicality," 1970.

located with reference to this discussion? His early views, he claims, were thoroughly those of classic liberalism; through his earliest experiences and training he was "strengthened" in an "aversion to all orthodoxy."[12] At first he studied classical philology as well as historical theology. Through reading Schweitzer's *The Quest of the Historical Jesus* he began to realize the extent to which liberalism was imbued with ideas derived not from Scripture but from modern philosophy. He saw form criticism as a method which, because of its rigorous historical demands, could protect research from what Cullmann says he strove to counter: "the mingling of modern tendencies of thought" with what purports to be purely historical exegesis.[13]

Cullmann studied in Strasbourg under W. Baldensperger[14] and in Paris with M. Goguel, G. Guignebert, and A. Loisy.[15] None of these was of conservative doctrinal persuasion. His doctoral thesis was a historical-critical investigation of the Pseudo-Clementine literature which, according to Räisänen, was "pioneering."[16] As he began his lecturing career he consciously strove to separate those inherited "modern apprehensions of Christianity which had become dear" to him from his exegesis. Herein lies the germ of the perception of the New Testament characteristic of Cullmann: "It was initially through this purely scientific effort that I gradually attained to a deeper theological understanding of things of which the New Testament speaks but which were then strange to me."[17]

Focus on eschatology and Christology

Fröhlich remarks that Cullmann's early literary output follows no discernible plan. In general it seems that those topics Cullmann chose to write about were determined "by the contemporary scientific discussion and the stimulation of his teachers."[18] Two chief areas of interest

---

[12]Cullmann, *SJT* 14 (1961) 229.

[13]*Ibid*. 232; cf. Fröhlich, "Die Mitte des Neuen Testaments: Oscar Cullmanns Beitrag zur Theologie der Gegenwart," *Oikonomia*, 206; Hermesmann, *Zeit und Heil*, 20, 30, 166.

[14]D. Moessner, "Oscar Cullman: Scholar of Early Christianity, Doctor of the Contemporary Church. The Significance of His Contribution," *TZ* 48/2 (1992) 238.

[15]Cullmann, *SJT* 14 (1961) 230.

[16]*Beyond New Testament Theology*, 63.

[17]Cullmann, *SJT* 14 (1961) 231.

[18]Fröhlich, "Die Mitte des Neuen Testaments: Oscar Cullmanns Beitrag zur Theologie der Gegenwart," *Oikonomia*, 206f.

for contemporary biblical research, and therefore for Cullmann, were eschatology and Christology.[19]

In Cullmann's first published study on this subject (1936) he investigates the problem of *to katechon* in 2 Thess 2:6f.[20] This entails consideration of the wider sphere of New Testament eschatology as well. He deduces from Matt 28:20 that the mission of the early Church was essentially eschatological in nature, for this verse "speaks of the period of time which immediately precedes the end and during which the gospel must be preached to the nations."[21] The preaching of the gospel signified and was a necessary condition of the coming of the messianic age.[22] Paul himself, at least early in his ministry, suspected that Christ would return soon, since the nations were being evangelized. "The time is short"[23] becomes one of Paul's guiding convictions and hints at the centrality of a particular conception of time and history in the early church.

Further light is shed on Cullmann's understanding of New Testament eschatology by his review (1938) of F. Holmström's analysis of twentieth century Protestant theology, which Holmström organizes around the three chief models of eschatology he finds vying for recognition since the turn of the century.[24] There is first the "contemporary historical" stage of regarding eschatology; J. Weiss and A. Schweitzer are the key proponents and the salient years 1892-1913.[25] Second comes the "supra-historical" or even "ahistorical" outlook; Holmström here centers on Barth and P. Althaus and marks 1922-1927 as the period of the view's dominance. Third is the "revelation-historical" perspective (1926-1928), which

> seeks to validate in full compass the Christian revelation *and* history and takes its inspiration, not from heterogeneous categories borrowed from

---

[19]Räisänen, *Beyond New Testament Theology*, 185, notes these are "the two serious alternatives" for a starting point in giving a thematic account of New Testament theology.

[20]Cullmann, "Der eschatologische Charakter des Missionsauftrages und des apostolischen Selbstbewusstseins bei Paulus," *Vorträge und Aufsätze, 1925-1962*, ed. K. Fröhlich, 1966, 305-336.

[21]*Ibid*. 326.

[22]*Ibid*. 331.

[23]*Ibid*. 336; cf. 1 Cor 7:29.

[24]Cullmann, "Das eschatologische Denken der Gegenwart," *Vorträge und Aufsätze*, 337-347; cf. F. Holmström, *Das eschatologische Denken der Gegenwart. Drei Etappen der theologischen Entwicklung des 20. Jhs.*, 1936.

[25]Cullmann, "Das eschatologische Denken der Gegenwart," *Vorträge und Aufsätze*, 338.

some pet philosophical system, but entirely from biblical Christianity. It does this without falling prey to the mistakes of historicism or a-historicism and without losing itself in a fruitless biblicism.[26]

Cullmann commends Holmström for his endorsement of this third view and for his high regard for M. Kähler, whom Cullmann sees as "far ahead of his time."[27] He notes that Holmström is understandably incapable of discerning the final outcome of the still-unfolding debate on eschatology. With the jury still out on where things will lead, Cullmann calls for an

> eschatological theology to develop, one grounded in a *Christian* concept of history. In this theology "eternal life" would at the same time be both a present *and* a future entity—present due to its qualitative character, which distinguishes the future from the present; future due to its predominantly *temporal* character.[28]

Cullmann's plea is for a return to the New Testament sources in formulating views of time and history. To this end he calls for close cooperation between exegesis and New Testament theology: "The starting point must therefore be an objective exegesis and a theology of the New Testament which builds strictly upon it, holding itself aloof from philosophical partisanship."[29] If it is not by now plain that Cullmann has already conceived the need for and basic thrust of *Christ and Time*, it becomes transparent when he speaks of "a later publication" in which the problem with which Holmström grapples will be treated on the basis of New Testament exegesis.[30]

Cullmann furthers these deliberations in three other articles. In 1941 he reiterates much of what he had already worked out earlier.[31] In the same year, apparently, the term "salvation history" first appears in his work. This is significant in that it suggests that Cullmann cannot, barring good evidence to the contrary, be charged with a gratuitous acceptance of salvation historical views and a subsequent reading of them into the New Testament, all due to overt involvement in a dogmatic heritage where the notion of "salvation history" was common coin. One must take seriously his claim that he was led to his

---

[26] *Ibid.* 339.
[27] *Ibid.* 340.
[28] *Ibid.* 344.
[29] *Ibid.* 346.
[30] *Ibid.*
[31] Cullmann, "Eschatologie und Mission im Neuen Testament," *Vorträge und Aufsätze*, 348-360.

stress on salvation history by historical work, not dogmatic or philosophical presuppositions as such. Yet this does not preclude the
possibility that Cullmann's work is comparable to that of Hofmann-
Schlatter in certain respects, even if any direct dependence is firmly
denied by Cullmann as well as absent in his early works.

By 1944 Cullmann is able to give an actual outline of what he takes
to be the New Testament's salvation historical perspective[32] and to
write in terms anticipating *Christ and Time*: "The [ancient] Greek
knows only a cyclical concept of time," while the New Testament
presupposes "linear temporal occurrence" that "as such is determined
by the event worked by God" that takes place in it.[33] It is incumbent
on New Testament interpreters to take courage and "really incorporate the present into the salvation historical time-line."[34] It terms
reminiscent of Schlatter, if slightly overstated, Cullmann concludes:

> Hellenism and Christianity must collide against one another, because in
> Christianity the salvation historical conception of linear time is thought
> through in a consistent fashion. This conception overarches and links past,
> present, and future in such a way that here there is actually an indissoluble
> opposition to all ancient and modern Hellenism.[35]

Thus behind *Christ and Time* stands at least ten years of research into
the nature and significance of New Testament eschatology. Characteristics of Cullmann's method include (1) a marked historical-exegetical
emphasis, and (2) a critical attitude which he does not hesitate to apply, not only to the ancient sources, but also to modern thought when
its assumptions or conclusions seem belied by historical evidence.

Along with eschatology Cullmann's views are informed by christological insights furnished to him by his exegesis.

Cullmann calls attention to the nature and inter-relationship of
Christ's spatial and temporal reign within the kingdom of God "in one
of the most important studies of his earlier years at Basel."[36] Even more

---

[32]"Die Hoffnung der Kirche auf die Wiederkunft Christi nach dem Neuen Testament," *Vorträge und Aufsätze,* 378-402, cf. especially 381, 400.

[33]*Ibid.* 381.

[34]*Ibid.* 402.

[35]*Ibid.* 401f. Cullmann's at times simplistic distinction between biblical and Greek
views would eventually become a point of frequent criticism. He drops the emphasis
in his later work.

[36]Fröhlich, "Die Mitte des Neuen Testaments: Oscar Cullmanns Beitrag zur Theologie der Gegenwart," *Oikonomia,* 209, referring to Cullmann, "The Kingship of
Christ and the Church in the New Testament," *The Early Church,* 1956 (first German
edition 1941), 101-137.

clearly he sets forth the core of *Christ and Time* in a study of the earliest Christian confessions, in which he sought to find out "what was the essence of the faith of the earliest Christians."[37] At the center of this faith, not surprisingly, stands Christ, "who by virtue of His divine mission is near to man" and "who already exercises His divine reign now."[38] For Cullmann "Jesus is Lord" was "the essence of early Christian belief," not an immanent ahistorical absolute as in liberalism.[39]

When the early Christians framed their confessions, Cullmann concludes, they did so with a vivid awareness "of the time when it pleased God to reveal his plan of salvation, the precise time when it was propitious for the once-for-all work of the Saviour to take place."[40] Having established the centrality of Jesus Christ for the New Testament believers and the view of reality in relation to time which Jesus' teaching and ministry thrust on them, Cullmann describes the overall plan at whose center Jesus stood:

> The divine plan of salvation embraces the present, but a present bound to the past and the future ... Christian faith does not reduce to an affirmation about the past alone; this would lead straight to a "historism" which impaired the Biblical conception of linear time. Neither does it reduce to an affirmation about the future alone; this would lead straight to an apocalyptic which, in contrast to the Biblical eschatology, tended to separate hope and faith. Christianity is true to its origins in ascribing first-rank importance in its strictly Christological plan of salvation to the present as a time of grace.[41]
> The danger of isolating past or future is then excluded. The course of the Christian revelation becomes clear: past and future are connected by the present, which is the time intervening between the resurrection and the second coming of Christ, the time in which already Christ invisibly exercises His Lordship.[42]

It is evident once again that Cullmann is anticipating *Christ and Time*. Noteworthy too is that Cullmann does not infer a particular Christology from a predetermined philosophy of history. He rather

---

[37] Cullmann, *The Earliest Christian Confessions*, 1949 (first German edition 1943), 62.
[38] *Ibid.* 63.
[39] Cf. Moessner, *TZ* 48/2 (1992) 238.
[40] *Ibid.* 64.
[41] The concept of a "time of grace," if not the word itself, may well hark back to Cullmann's reading of Holmström noted above. There he cites with approval Holmström's use of this word, as it expresses what Cullmann's exegetical studies also show, i.e., "the eschatological significance of the time between the coming of the historical Jesus and the parousia" ("Das eschatologische Denken der Gegenwart," *Vorträge und Aufsätze,* 347).
[42] *The Earliest Christian Confessions*, 64.

educes from the New Testament texts an underlying common early Christian perception of the bearing of Jesus' past, present, and future reality on the present time. New Testament Christology is so intertwined with this underlying common perception that to minimize either the Christology or the view of time would be to distort and ultimately imperil both.

Cullmann and key contemporaries
The distinctive nature of Cullmann's approach takes further shape in the light of his early and enduring concern to handle the New Testament in a more historically responsible fashion than three notable doyens of his day.
     1. *Albert Schweitzer (1875-1965)*. Cullmann at once both admires and suspects Schweitzer's historical method and its results. He recognized that Schweitzer's New Testament work with its eschatological emphasis embodied "a hypothesis, in itself worthy of consideration, which can be fruitful even if it turns out to be incorrect."[43] Yet the hypothetical nature of Schweitzer's position must always be borne in mind.[44] His great service was to have stressed the importance of eschatology for a proper understanding of the New Testament.[45] But after showing how eschatology was central to the New Testament's and Jesus' own thinking, a truth which liberalism had suppressed, Schweitzer then reaffirmed the liberal position that modern Christianity must to a large degree dispense with the eschatological core content of the New Testament, "although historically speaking that is precisely where the foundation of Christianity would have to be located."[46] At the heart of Schweitzer's position, then, is the error that he "eliminates from the gospel the very eschatology which he recognizes as central to it."[47]
     A study done years later strikingly confirmed Cullmann in his suspicion that Schweitzer's historical method was defective and

---

[43]Cullmann, "Das wahre, durch die ausgebliebene Parusie gestellte Problem," *Vorträge und Aufsätze,* 419f.
     [44]*Ibid.* 420.
     [45]Cf. Cullmann, "Notwendigkeit und Aufgabe der philologisch-historischen Bibelauslegung," *Vorträge und Aufsätze,* 113.
     [46]Cullmann, "Das eschatologische Denken der Gegenwart," *Vorträge und Aufsätze,* 339. Cf. E. Grässer, *Albert Schweitzer als Theologe,* 1979, 243-253, a section which carries the heading "Schweitzer's parodox: through history become free from history."
     [47]Cullmann, "Die Hoffnung der Kirche auf die Wiederkunft Christi nach dem Neuen Testament," *Vorträge und Aufsätze,* 383 n. Cf. *Christ and Time,* 30.

inconsistent.[48] J.L. Thompson speaks of Schweitzer's "Historiography of Ethical Mysticism,"[49] in which, in the liberal hermeneutical tradition, Jesus' religion is made to conform to Schweitzer's ethical philosophy.[50] He amply documents Schweitzer's arbitrary antisupernatural positivism.[51] He shows how history for Schweitzer "is only a vehicle ... for a more timeless truth which transcends it,"[52] a truth which while basically a-historical is nevertheless latent in human ethical or volitional consciousness.[53] "Schweitzer finally dissolves Jesus' historical particularity into mere symbolism."[54]

Schweitzer performed the valuable service of first opening Cullmann's eyes to the threat of dogmatic liberalism to a more measured historical understanding of the New Testament.[55] In this sense Schweitzer figures as a vital starting point and impetus for much of Cullmann's research, particularly on eschatology, which in turn is central in the conception of *Christ and Time*.

2. *Karl Barth (1886–1968)*. Barth also had a notable influence on Cullmann's early work. Cullmann states that his development "was not directly influenced by Barth."[56] Yet, quite apart from eventually serving on the same faculty in Basel, in important respects they occupied the same ground relative to Bultmann and his followers, since Cullmann and Barth alike "do not suppose the occurrence which is the object of the biblical revelation to be one with the experience of faith, but take this experience seriously for what it is,"[57] in contrast to Bultmann.

In addition, as Schweitzer prompted Cullmann to reflect on New Testament eschatology, Barth provides the backdrop against which Cullmann develops his hermeneutical outlook.[58] Cullmann insists on the need for both a historically and theologically appraised exegesis.

---

[48]J.L. Thompson, "History and Reason in Albert Schweitzer's World-View," *Duke Divinity School Review* 45 (1980) 3-30.

[49]*Ibid.* 13ff.

[50]*Ibid.* 15.

[51]*Ibid.* 6.

[52]*Ibid.* 20.

[53]*Ibid.* 19.

[54]*Ibid.* 22.

[55]Cf. Cullmann, *SJT* 14 (1961) 229. Martin Werner also played a role in this respect; cf. e.g. Cullmann, *Vorträge und Aufsätze*, 361-377; *Christ and Time*, xii.

[56]Cullmann, *SJT* 14 (1961) 232.

[57]*Ibid.* 232f. Cullmann and Barth had rightly understood Bultmann; see Bultmann, "Theologie als Wissenschaft," *ZTK* 81 (1984) 455.

[58]Cullmann, "Die Problematik der exegetischen Methode Karl Barths," *Vorträge und Aufsätze,* 90-109 (first published 1928).

Concerned for historical accuracy, yet believing it possible to transcend liberalism without going the way of dialectical theology, Cullmann in the heyday of "pneumatic" and "theological" exegesis seeks to establish "the positive connections" between historical criticism, or its findings, and theological understanding.[59] In pursuing this goal he anticipates subsequent hermeneutical debate by elucidating, as a corrective to Barth, the interpretative process in terms of a "circle" in which historical data and theological insight mutually inform each other.[60] Similarly, cognizant of the danger of a historicistic approach on the one hand and a purely theological on the other, Cullmann in contrast to Barth holds that "the collaboration between the historian and the theologian can not really become fruitful if it does not occur in personal union."[61] Thus he does not object to Barth's theological concern as such but feels that it lacks historical grounding because Barth's theological interests at times disregard, or regard too cursorily, significant historical features that are an inseparable dimension of the texts he explicates.

In the end Cullmann finds points of agreement with Barth, praising him, for instance, for focusing on the substance (*die Sache*) of the New Testament texts,[62] not on human self-understanding (his objection to Bultmann[63]). Yet Barth's method is defective, in Cullmann's estimation, by virtue of its underlying epistemology, which is heavily committed "to the Kantian and neo-Kantian dualism."[64] Barth and his followers to an excessive degree "cling to the absolute separation between believing and knowing."[65] If the way were made clear for Barth's outlook to be more open to corroboration by historical observation and facts, it could "perform outstanding services for historical inquiry and theology."[66]

In attempting to wed historical observation with theological understanding—in trying to stress the positive aspects of the interface

---

[59] *Ibid.* 91; cf. 99f.

[60] *Ibid.* 104f.

[61] *Ibid.* 105. By "personal union" Cullmann appears to mean that both historical and theological expertise are united in an individual scholar. At this same point Cullmann criticizes the Old Testament scholar Gressmann (see previous chapter) for his naiveté about his historicistic assumptions.

[62] Cullmann, "Die Problematik der exegetischen Methode Karl Barths," *Vorträge und Aufsätze,* 92f.

[63] *Ibid.* 94 n. 13, 98 n. 16.

[64] *Ibid.* 101.

[65] *Ibid.*

[66] *Ibid.* 109.

between history and theology—Cullmann is already in implicit agreement with Hofmann-Schlatter. This agreement is underscored by Cullmann's criticisms of Barth's epistemological leanings. Dorman has called attention to Cullmann's analysis of the problem. While Barth has a concern for historical exegesis as a preliminary task, so that "there is some degree of relationship between faith and history," Cullmann senses the "inherent contradiction between Barth's epistemology and concept of revelation on the one hand, and his exegetical method on the other."[67] In H. Lazenby's words, for Barth "revelation becomes history" but in such a way that "history does not become revelation."[68] Where Barth saw a one-way, Cullmann saw a two-way street. This was a major point of disagreement between them in the first decade of dialectical theology. "Cullmann believed that Barth's methodology left too little room for historical control,"[69] a serious weakness to the extent that Barth's massive *theological* exegesis of Scripture affects to have any necessary ties to its *historical* dimensions.

3. *Rudolf Bultmann (1884–1976).* Cullmann was much more critical of Bultmann. The debate between the two which began in earnest with Bultmann's "detailed but extremely critical review"[70] of *Christ and Time* will receive treatment below. Long previous to this Bultmann had greeted Cullmann "as an ally"[71] since they both championed form criticism.[72] Cullmann for his part shows an extensive familiarity with the nature of Bultmann's work in the two decades preceding *Christ and Time.* He applauds Bultmann and form criticism from early on, without failing to take note of Bultmann's radical tendencies.[73] He stoutly defends him as one who "works quite like a historian"[74] and whose historical method is "based exclusively on historical intuition."[75] This would be at a time when Cullmann was

---

[67]Dorman, "The Hermeneutics of Oscar Cullmann," 52.

[68]"Revelation in History in the Theology of Charles Hodge and Karl Barth," 1982, 339.

[69]Dorman, "Cullmann, Oscar *(b. 1902),*" *Historical Handbook of Major Biblical Interpreters,* 466.

[70]Fröhlich, "Die Mitte des Neuen Testaments: Oscar Cullmanns Beitrag zur Theologie der Gegenwart," *Oikonomia,* 209.

[71]Cullmann, *SJT* 14 (1961) 230.

[72]Cf. Cullmann, "Geschichte der Evangelientradition," *Vorträge und Aufsätze,* 51f., who states that "it precisely form criticism which could be destined to lead theology out of the blind alley into which the historicism of the last century has led it."

[73]*Ibid.* 64.

[74]Cullmann, "Die Problematik der exegetischen Methode Karl Barths," *Vorträge und Aufsätze,* 90.

[75]Cullmann, "Geschichte der Evangelientradition," *Vorträge und Aufsätze,* 81 n. 97.

relatively young, still sympathetic to liberalism, yet seeking means to reintroduce theological relevance into critical New Testament interpretation. However, he soon shifts ground to challenge Bultmann at two crucial points.

First, in his eschatology Cullmann sees Bultmann replacing New Testament eschatology with the concept of "decision."[76] But this for Cullmann is unacceptable from a historical standpoint, for in the New Testament "eschatology is in fact an entirely temporal concept. It will not do to conceive of it as 'living always in a state of decision,' as happens in Bultmann's formulations. That would be radically reinterpreting eschatology and dissolving it into metaphysics."[77]

Second, Cullmann agrees with Bultmann that presuppositionless exegesis is impossible,[78] yet finds Bultmann's application of this principle in forging a hermeneutic dangerous. Bultmann regards "the problem of *individual existence* as the object of biblical interpretation."[79] This in turn leads to an overly subjective historiography, for Bultmann ends up emphasizing "the necessity of the personal encounter of the historian with the history he is investigating, as if the truth which opens up through this history cannot be separated from the person of the researcher who grasps it."[80]

These two objections touch on central Bultmannian emphases and form the core of the sometimes sharp polemic that arose and persisted between Bultmannian and Cullmannian outlooks.

Like Schweitzer and Barth, Bultmann forms part of the context in which Cullmann's earlier ideas take shape. Cullmann could easily have followed Bultmann, or the other two, since his own early views were decidedly anything but "conservative." But once again, while recognizing Bultmann's contribution, Cullmann stops short of attaching himself to the growing movement around him, just as he maintained a well-reasoned distance from Schweitzer and Barth. Bultmann's definition of eschatology, Cullmann decides, robs it of historical reference, and thus to a degree of its reality, while his hermeneutic so stresses the role of the subject in the formation of the understanding of the object

---

[76]Cullmann, "Das eschatologische Denken der Gegenwart," *Vorträge und Aufsätze,* 342.

[77]Cullmann, "Die Hoffnung der Kirche auf die Wiederkunft Christi nach dem Neuen Testament," *Vorträge und Aufsätze,* 382.

[78]Cullmann, "Die Problematik der exegetischen Methode Karl Barths," *Vorträge und Aufsätze,* 93.

[79]*Ibid.* 94 n. 13.

[80]*Ibid.* 98 n. 16.

that the object threatens to lose its independent status and with it the potential of informing the subject of that which may be foreign or unacceptable to his or her pre-understanding.

Like Hofmann and Schlatter Cullmann is keenly cognizant of contemporary trends in approaching the New Testament. He endorses their primary intent—to make the New Testament understandable today—and some of their results. Yet, also like Hofmann and Schlatter, he seeks to keep theological interpretation of the New Testament grounded in the biblical history in a fashion which guards against the encroachment of modernizing tendencies that cannot help but distort or disregard the history. It is surely Cullmann's non-Cartesian hermeneutical leanings, not a pre-determined philosophy of history, which led him gradually to the views that he eventually formulated at greater length in *Christ and Time*.

2. Cullmann's major works
Christ and Time (1946)

We now turn more directly to the content of Cullmann's most important writings. This will augment the picture we have already sketched of the development of Cullmann's views, enable informed consideration of his critics below, and facilitate appreciation of Cullmann's independent continuance of the Hofmann-Schlatter heritage.

In *Christ and Time* Cullmann sets out primarily to "determine what is central in the Christian proclamation."[81] His chief finding overall is that "a temporally determined salvific event" belongs "to the essence of the New Testament proclamation."[82] As Dorman puts it, Cullmann argues that central to the New Testament proclamation as a whole is the realization "that *the resurrection of Christ has brought a new division into the Jewish view of history.*"[83] Judaism, or prominent sects within it, looked ahead to a decisive temporal break or mid-point which would mark the passing of the present age into the coming age. Primitive Christianity did not abandon this conviction. Yet the Christ-event is seen as a decisive proleptic incursion of the future age into the present one. The eschatological invades time and, by virtue of its origin in God, assumes a lordship in and over time, a lordship real even if partially hidden.[84]

[81] Cullmann, *Christ and Time*, xi.

[82] A. Vögtle, "Oscar Cullmann," *Tendenzen der Theologie im 20. Jahrhundert*, ed. H.J. Schultz, 1966, 490.

[83] Dorman, "The Hermeneutics of Oscar Cullmann," 142 (Dorman's emphasis).

[84] Cullmann, *Christ and Time*, 82f.

More specifically, Cullmann maintains that in the New Testament one finds recognition of "at least three ages": (1) the age preceding creation, during which "the revelatory process is already being prepared"; (2) the present age, lying between creation and the consummation; and (3) the coming age, which is not a reversion to or repetition of a former aeon but rather a period "in which the eschatological drama falls."[85] Basic to Cullmann's understanding is that in the New Testament this time sequence embraces divinely influenced or superintended events which in God's economy reveal him and his will in chronological succession within and as part of human history. Time is not conceived of as being a mere category of human perception. Events in time do not derive form and content solely or even chiefly by virtue of human philosophical deduction or ascription of religious meaning. The temporality of the New Testament—an integral feature of which is its wedding of "noumenal" theological claims with "phenomenal" historical data—is intrinsic to its message and does not admit of being minimized, rejected, or radically reinterpreted.[86]

In this tripartite scheme the New Testament can best be understood as seeing the Christ event as focal- or mid-point.[87] All three ages are to be assessed with reference to their relationship to this central event. The New Testament sees the resurrection as conferring a decisive significance to all time by virtue of the claims affecting history made in the course of history by the crucified and risen Jesus or his appointed spokespersons. The resurrection is the salvation historical event par excellence as an event in time affecting time; it is not primarily, if at all, a symbol or cipher for a supra-temporal reality—e.g., à la Bultmann, an "eschatological" realization of a new self-understanding—for which imaginative early believers found "resurrection" to be a handy and effective catchword.

Contrary to the assumptions or charges of some readers,[88] Cullmann's concern is not with a philosophy of history, nor even with systematic theology; he has also not written "out of interest in the speculative question concerning time."[89] Rather, building on his work

---

[85] *Ibid.* 67.

[86] Cf. Cullmann, "Notwendigkeit und Aufgabe der philologisch-historischen Bibelauslegung," *Vorträge und Aufsätze,* 115.

[87] Cullmann, *Christ and Time,* 68.

[88] Cf. Cullmann, "Mythos und 'Entmythologisierung' im Neuen Testament," *Vorträge und Aufsätze,* 134 n. 18; "Parusieverzögerung und Urchristentum," *Vorträge und Aufsätze,* 430.

[89] Cullmann, *Christ and Time,* xi.

of the preceding ten years,[90] some of which was touched on above, he
wants to set forth "an exegetical-historical examination of some specific questions of New Testament theology."[91] Time as such is not his
main concern, because it is not the main concern of the New Testament;[92] he wants rather to explicate the underlying "framework"
uniting the various New Testament books, even though this framework "as such never was never an object of serious reflection on the
part of early Christians."[93] He is aware of the inner tensions and divergences or competing strands within various New Testament books but
considers it "highly unscientific" to rule out any possibility of discerning unifying elements in the New Testament simply because of the
existence of apparent differences.[94]

It is unnecessary to set forth a summary of Cullmann's entire book.
But its significance warrants reflection. It lies not only in the matters
already broached but also in the methodological considerations in
which *Christ and Time* is rooted, considerations which do not first crop
up here but are present in Cullmann's writings from the start. He argues that New Testament theology can and should draw its basic
categories from the New Testament itself, not from thought systems
outside the New Testament."[95] This is why he is concerned with the
New Testament attitude toward its theological message. This embraced above all the Christ event, with which at least some of the
New Testament writers had first-hand familiarity but which Bultmann
insisted on understanding eschatologically, i.e., a-temporally. Cullmann
argues that de-temporalization of the Christ event can only risk mis-
representing it. The available sources amply justify the conclusion that
the historical reality which the early church experienced with reference to Christ was of a piece with the theological reality that they
confessed. New Testament theology as a historical discipline can and
should first of all work within the framework of New Testament understanding, if a clear and accurate understanding of the New
Testament message in its own context is really its goal. Accordingly,
Cullmann sees "all Christian theology in its innermost essence" as
"biblical history," so that New Testament theology which does not

---

[90] *Ibid.* xiii.
[91] *Ibid.* 3.
[92] *Ibid.* 9.
[93] *Ibid.* 15.
[94] *Ibid.* 4.
[95] *Ibid.* xif.

adopt the major biblical mode of relating history to theology is inadequate from a methodological standpoint.[96]

Such convictions, not a philosophy of history as such, are the key underlying features of *Christ and Time*. In them we detect the roots of the hermeneutical distance between Cullmann and Bultmann which we explore below. Here too we see continuity between Cullmann and the approaches of Hofmann and Schlatter, just as Cullmann's historical-theological concern basically mirrors that of Filson and others in the previous chapter. Although Cullmann, along with many others, saw *Christ and Time* as a somewhat original work—and in certain respects it surely was—two things should be remembered. First, the book's roots lie in prior specific exegetical investigations. Second, whether consciously or unconsciously, he is in important respects following in the train of others before and contemporary with him.

The Christology of the New Testament (1957)[97]

The next major book of direct relevance to Cullmann's salvation historical outlook is his study of New Testament Christology. This work serves to ground the observation that in the New Testament "the person of Christ is virtually never spoken of apart from his work."[98] Cullmann was taken by many to be arguing for a strictly "functional Christology" which would challenge the christological formulations of the first four ecumenical councils, but Cullmann denies this.[99] Rather, without recourse to post-New Testament data, Cullmann wants to attain to "a total picture of the Christological conceptions of the New Testament."[100] He attempts this by focusing on the New Testament titles applied to Jesus: those referring to his first-century activity,[101] those dealing with his future work,[102] those treating of his present ministry,[103] and those speaking of his pre-existence.[104]

The synthetic picture which emerges comprises a "Christological structure which received its character not from syncretism, not from Hellenism, not from mythology, but from the salvation history" of

---

[96] *Ibid*. 23; cf. 26.

[97] Cullmann, *The Christology of the New Testament*, 1959, first German edition 1957.

[98] Cullmann, "Zur Frage der Erforschung der neutestamentlichen Christologie," *KD* 1 (1955) 135. Cf. *Christology*, 3.

[99] Cullmann, "Antwort an Père Bavaud," *Vorträge und Aufsätze*, 591-599.

[100] Cullmann, *The Christology of the New Testament*, 6.

[101] *Ibid*. 11-107.

[102] *Ibid*. 109-192.

[103] *Ibid*. 193-245.

[104] *Ibid*. 247-314.

which the Bible speaks.[105] Cullmann sees the distinctive trait of this
structure as its conviction "that from the beginning it centres in a real
history,"[106] as opposed to a mythological one, or one constructed according to articles of a modern philosophy whose premises are
intrinsically incompatible with the perspective of the biblical writers.
Since the New Testament "neither is able nor intends to give information about how we are to conceive the being of God beyond the
history of revelation,"[107] it is only in terms of the biblical word-event
complex that thought claiming to be rooted in the New Testament
can think and speak legitimately of God and, when it comes to the
New Testament, the Son of God. For Cullmann this means that this
biblical word-event complex—salvation history—is intimately related
to Christology.[108] Conversely, New Testament Christology finds its
fundamental unity in the salvation history which is one of the most
fundamental components in the combined New and Old Testament
witness.

Salvation in History (1965)[109]

This study restates much the same position as *Christ and Time*, but it
takes a different tack exegetically and "uses a rather different set of
arguments."[110] Cullmann stresses *Salvation in History*'s independence
from the early chapters of *Christ and Time* [111] which with their stress on
a linear (biblical)-cyclical (Hellenistic) distinction between ancient
views of time drew considerable fire. Watson has recently shown that
key elements of this criticism were much overstated;[112] it would be a
mistake today to suppose that Cullmann can be safely ignored because
his synthesis lacked empirical or hermeneutical merit.

Cullmann tries to show exegetically and in depth what *Christ and
Time* by comparison only sketched in outline, namely "the origin of
the salvation-historical perspective, its development in the New Testament books, and its importance for all areas of early Christian faith,

---

[105] *Ibid.* 322.

[106] *Ibid.*

[107] *Ibid.* 327.

[108] *Ibid.* 326.

[109] Cullmann, *Salvation in History*, 1967, first German edition 1965.

[110] J. Barr, "Salvation in History," *IDBSup*, 747.

[111] Cullmann, *Heil als Geschichte*, 1965, IX. The English version seems to mistranslate
here.

[112] Watson, *Text and Truth*, 18-26. Watson specifically shows the untenability of J.
Barr's attack on Cullmann's views of biblical words for time and his contrasting of
Greek and biblical thought.

thought, and activity."[113] After a lengthy analysis of contemporary discussion related to salvation history,[114] he attempts to account for its presence in the biblical writings.[115] He goes on to discuss the "phenomenological characteristics" of salvation history, i.e., the relationship between history and myth, between New Testament salvation history and history generally, and between the New Testament sense of "present" as contrasted to "future."[116] Next he discusses salvation history as it comes to expression in the individual New Testament books.[117] "Only portions of salvation history are discernible" in most New Testament passages where salvation history is in evidence at all, but the presence of these numerous and basically unified texts is best accounted for by the hypothesis that the New Testament writers on the whole "presuppose an overall salvation-historical view."[118] Cullmann attempts in this section to document specifically where this salvation historical perspective becomes visible in the New Testament writings. The book concludes with a section on the relationship of salvation history to post-New Testament times, including the present day.[119]

Criticisms of Cullmann

The essence of Cullmann's position takes on further clarity when it is exposed to the glare of his critics' searchlights. Not every criticism, nor even every important one, can be weighed,[120] any more than we can tally up every treatment that regards Cullmann positively.[121] But our aim is not to mount a comprehensive vindication of Cullmann, just to present his thought more completely than has become customary in the literature of New Testament theology. It is not necessary to interact with all criticisms to achieve this goal.

---

[113] *Salvation in History*, 15.

[114] *Ibid*. 19-83.

[115] *Ibid*. 84-135.

[116] *Ibid*. 136-185.

[117] *Ibid*. 186-291.

[118] *Ibid*. 187.

[119] *Ibid*. 292-338.

[120] E.g. we pass over I.G. Nicol, "Event and Interpretation. O. Cullmann's Conception of Salvation History," *Th* 77 (1974) 14-21; E.L. Miller, "Salvation History: Pannenberg's Critique of Cullmann," *The Iliff Review* 37 (1980) 21-25.

[121] See e.g. W. Stegner, "Recent Religious/Political Developments in a New Testament Theological Perspective," *AsTJ* 45/2 (1990) 73-81; L. Hurtado, "Christ-Devotion in the First Two Centuries: Reflections and a Proposal," *TJT* 12/1 (1996) 17-33.

Specifically, we will show that most criticisms of Cullmann are in fact relatively minor ones, while the major criticisms from Bultmann are primarily systematic or philosophical in nature and beg important historical issues. That is, they are rooted in a worldview or view of reality which rules out salvation history, as Cullmann conceives it, from the start, despite his ability to document the widespread presence of the view in the primary sources. So while Cullmann is charged, e.g., by Eslinger and Bultmann with imposing a philosophy of history on the New Testament, it is even more evident that philosophical commitments, not primarily historical data as such, made Cullmann's salvation historical approach unacceptable to them and others.

1. Minor criticisms: J. Barr and R. Eslinger

J. Barr criticized *Christ and Time*'s reliance on certain linguistic and lexicographical misapprehensions.[122] We have already noted that Barr concedes that *Salvation in History* is based on a different set of arguments;[123] I am not aware that he has disproved these. In addition, as we showed above, Cullmann's main findings in *Christ and Time* are based primarily, not on the linguistic or lexical arguments in that book's opening chapters, but on prior historical-exegetical studies dealing with eschatology and Christology. As Dorman notes, when Cullmann in *Salvation in History* declines to base a "time-concept" on lexicography, this is "not so much a retreat from Barr's criticisms as it is a return to Cullmann's own [pre-*Christ and Time*] approach."[124] Barr's arguments rightly question Cullmann's faulty use of linguistic evidence, but Cullmann's salvation historical reading of the New Testament is not primarily based on such evidence.[125] This tends to minimize the force of Barr's arguments in *Biblical Words for Time* as the ground for an all-embracing critique of Cullmann.

R. Eslinger, in a study apparently overlooked by the three major studies of Cullmann published to date,[126] directs a sharp attack against Cullmann in his 1970 Boston University dissertation. He repeats the charge that Cullmann relies on a predetermined philosophy of history .

---

[122]Barr, *Biblical Words for Time*, especially chapter 3.

[123]Barr, "Revelation in History," *IDPSup*, 747.

[124]Dorman, "The Hermeneutics of Oscar Cullmann," 181.

[125]Cf. Cullmann's own response to Barr in *Christ and Time*, 14-16; also Watson, *Text and Truth*, 18–26.

[126]I.e. Hermesmann, *Zeit und Heil*; Dorman, "The Hermeneutics of Oscar Cullmann"; Schlaudraff, *"Heils als Geschichte"?* 1988. For a review of Schlaudraff see R. Yarbrough, *Critical Review of Books in Religion* (1990) 234-236.

and takes offense at the concept of self implied "in a view which understands revelation in terms of an absolute and temporally endless schematization of the divine plan."[127] Cullmann's work is analyzed as one of "two dominant theological responses to the crisis of revelation created by the advent of historicism."[128] Eslinger is concerned with Cullmann's "theological constructions" and not his "exegetical findings."[129]

It is difficult to reconcile the criticisms of this dissertation, which is, apart from Dorman's dissertation, perhaps the most thorough analysis of Cullmann in English, with Cullmann's viewpoint. It is unfounded, as already shown repeatedly, to dismiss Cullmann for having a philosophy of history, and Eslinger's indignation at Cullmann's view of the self seems to attribute a mistaken a-personal determinism to history as Cullmann thinks the New Testament sees it. And it must be adjudged as arbitrary to read Cullmann's works, not as the exegetically-based deliberations they purport to be, but as modern theologizing. Would it not have been methodologically sounder to heed "Cullmann's request to be judged first of all on this basis," that his concern is with historical reconstruction and not with constructive theology?[130]

Further, Eslinger suggests that for Cullmann, "the Troeltschian model of analogy and relativity is relevant everywhere."[131] But Cullmann's disagreement with Troeltschian historiography is unmistakable if largely implicit.[132] He even makes specific negative reference to Troeltsch.[133] He uses analogy as a tool but, unlike Troeltsch, does not elevate this tool to an absolute standard. Similarly, Cullmann tries to see all history in terms of inter-relatedness (correlation), but he predicates true understanding of history on the fact that history in its relativity is subordinate to God who superintends and reveals himself intelligibly within it. One might say that history for Cullmann is only relatively relative. It is hard to see how this resembles Troeltsch's ap-

---

[127]Eslinger, "Historicity and Historicality: A Comparision of Carl Michalson and Oscar Cullmann," v–vi.

[128]*Ibid.* 9.

[129]*Ibid.* 11.

[130]J.P. Martin, review of Cullmann, *Heil als Geschichte, Int* 20 (1966) 341; cf. Dorman, "Cullmann, Oscar *(b. 1902),*" *Historical Handbook of Major Biblical Interpreters*, 469: Cullmann held that "the subject matter of the New Testament must be understood only in light of the text of the New Testament, rather than the text being understood in light of a previously understood subject matter."

[131]Eslinger, "Historicity and Historicality," 98.

[132]Cf. e.g. Cullmann, *Vorträge und Aufsätze*, 99–106; 110–124.

[133]Cullmann, *Christ and Time*, 22 n.

proach. And when Eslinger deduces that interpretation for Cullmann is "the subjective contribution of significance in the encounter with the events of objective reality,"[134] it seems that Cullmann simply has not been understood. "The vagueness of [Cullmann's] epistemological dualism"[135] is in fact Eslinger's reading of Kantian categories of perception into Cullmann's remarks despite Cullmann's steadfast resistance precisely to this epistemological trajectory. It seems that Eslinger has not noticed the normative value which Cullmann accords the biblical writings because they convey, not perfectly but with substantial historical accuracy and complete soteriological sufficiency, divine revelation. This point of view is questionable but is not vague, hardly dualistic in Eslinger's sense, and by no means reduces interpretation to mere "subjective contribution of significance."

Eslinger's direct criticisms of Cullmann are as follows.

1. He thinks Barr's *Biblical Words for Time* destroys Cullmann's exegetical base.[136] Here he goes back on his earlier claim not to concern himself with Cullmann's exegesis. Apparently Eslinger's strategy is to take note of alleged weaknesses in Cullmann's exegesis but to overlook possible strengths.

2. He is persuaded by Bultmann's critical review of *Christ and Time* and accuses Cullmann of "historical positivism."[137] For Eslinger it is wrong to hold, with Cullmann, "that the proper object of faith is a structure of reality already completed in its meaning and divinely given."[138] This miscue on Cullmann's part is aggravated by his "absence of concern for the existential relevance or even personal relevance of the plan of salvation."[139]

3. Cullmann reduces faith to rationalistic knowing.[140]

4. Cullmann associates saving faith with historical events which are problematic,[141] seemingly relegating such events as the resurrection to a "transcendent meta-history."[142]

5. Cullmann's view of the biblical interpretations as basically reliable and in some sense to be believed today is "unthinkable for the con-

[134]Eslinger, "Historicity and Historicality," 98f.
[135]*Ibid.* 99 n. 1.
[136]*Ibid.* 176ff.
[137]*Ibid.* 178ff.
[138]*Ibid.* 180.
[139]*Ibid.* 180f.
[140]*Ibid.* 182ff.
[141]*Ibid.*
[142]*Ibid.* 188.

temporary secularist who cannot accept ... a world view foreign to his own."[143]

We may regard these objections briefly and in order.

1. Barr's *Biblical Words for Time* has already been alluded to. While Barr's criticism's are noteworthy, they are limited to parts of the argumentation of *Christ and Time* and do not necessarily apply to the rest of Cullmann's work, especially *Salvation in History*. If they do apply, Eslinger has not shown how.

2. Bultmann's review of *Christ and Time* will ~be considered below. We should note that even if it were "historical positivism" to place one's faith in "a structure of reality already completed in its meaning and divinely given," Cullmann has only adopted this position on the basis of what New Testament believers seemed to hold. Unless Eslinger could show either that Cullmann in his exegesis or the New Testament believers in their belief were mistaken, this accusation is not serious from the standpoint of New Testament theology. And it is exaggerated to accuse Cullmann of having no conception of the relevance of salvation history to personal faith, since he devotes a whole section of *Salvation in History* to addressing this very concern.[144]

3. Cullmann does stress that New Testament faith has definite propositional content, and in some circles this is automatically a *500* "rationalistic distortion of faith."[145] But in order truly to be rationalistic, the object of faith would have to be of purely rational creation, discovery, or validation. Theologically, Cullmann holds that, based on the New Testament, the starting point of all theological reflection must be the "conviction that we of our own power can have no knowledge of God, if God does not reveal himself to us. Human rea- *Lord*son as such cannot comprehend God."[146] This would seem to clear Cullmann of Eslinger's theological objection. If he objects on the historical level, it remains again for him to demonstrate either that Cullmann's exegesis is inaccurate, or that New Testament faith wrongly assumed that Christian belief is closely linked with words and events, which are appropriated as objects of faith finally inseparable from the God in whom trust is placed.

Points 4 and 5 may be taken together. Here Eslinger quotes modern authorities such as Van Harvey[147] and charges, in essence, that Cull-

---

[143] *Ibid.* 191; cf. 188.

[144] Cullmann, *Salvation in History*, 292–338.

[145] Eslinger, "Historicity and Historicality," 182.

[146] Cullmann, *Vorträge und Aufsätze*, 23.

[147] Cf. Harvey, *The Historian and the Believer.*

mann's concept's of "event" and "interpretation" are today intellectually unacceptable. He asks modern understanding to subject itself to understandings of biblical phenomena, e.g. the resurrection, which are irreconcilable with modern understanding and not corroborated by Troeltschian historiography. If Cullmann insists on asserting that New Testament faith springs from a historical resurrection, or from Jesus' historical person generally, vouchsafed by apostolic interpretation, none of which modern historiography can affirm, then Cullmann clearly "begs the historian's questions and creates a crisis within the epistemology of faith" by placing the resurrection or the life of Jesus "in a transcendent meta-history."[148]

This is compelling argumentation granted Eslinger's chosen historiographical standpoint. But again we return to the question of whether Cullmann's position is consistent with the New Testament texts which he claims to be explicating. Essentially he is under attack precisely for one of the primary characteristics of the salvation historical perspective as we have already discovered it repeatedly: declining to let itself be dictated to by what it sees as modernistic dogma about what could or could not have been the case with reference to the content of the New Testament. Certainly Eslinger is free to be a "contemporary secularist who cannot accept ... a world view foreign to his own"; but this standpoint, if obdurately adhered to, must surely result in an inability, stemming from its confessed unwillingness, to grant validity to any claim about reality, present or past, "historical" or "theological," which contravenes its own understanding or belief. This is once again the essence of the Cartesian/non-Cartesian disagreement.

Eslinger's study is an informative indicator as to how perhaps a good deal of modern criticism assessed Cullmann and the salvation historical perspective, when it regarded them at all. It is illuminating in this respect. But far from showing the weakness of Cullmann's approach, it serves rather to underscore the gap already repeatedly documented between two ways of regarding the New Testament data in a historico-theological way.

2. Major criticism: Bultmann

The really influential criticism of Cullmann from the standpoint of New Testament theology is that of Bultmann. His analysis continued to wield influence for decades. Its tone and substance undergirded

---

[148]Eslinger, "Historicity and Historicality," 188.

Eslinger's critique (above) as well as that of G. Müller-Fahrenholz.[149] Any serious representation of Cullmann must take the Bultmann broadside into account.

Bultmann's interaction with Cullmann is largely an open-and-shut affair: he subjected *Christ and Time* to withering fire, and it is fair to say that thereafter he hardly takes Cullmann's arguments seriously. He was certainly not swayed by them. We wish now to comment on this critique with regard to its (1) influence, (2) content, and (3) cogency and significance.

The influence of the critique

Bultmann's brief review of *Christ and Time*[150] met remarkable endorsement and exerted powerful influence. Complaints that Cullmann's work was too preoccupied with addressing Bultmann overlooked the extent to which this review came to be seen as a self-authenticating rebuttal of Cullmann, one which precluded the need of stepping outside of Bultmannian hermeneutics to ask whether Cullmann's outlook had more merit than Bultmann at first accorded it.[151] The enduring authoritative status of Bultmann's essay is presupposed to a surprising degree in the studies of Eslinger and Müller-Fahrenholz just mentioned. It is accorded authoritative stature in O. Merk's handling of Cullmann, as well.[152]

Even granting that Cullmann did not write a formal New Testament theology of the sort with which Merk is primarily concerned, one may still question whether it is justified for Merk to follow Bultmann's lead so closely in discrediting Cullmann simply by associating him with Stauffer.[153] The incriminating evidence which Merk and Bultmann can adduce to substantiate this association is one footnote

---

[149]G. Müller-Fahrenholz, *Heilsgeschichte zwischen Ideologie und Prophetie*, 1974, 137-169. On these criticisms see Hermesmann, *Zeit und Heil*, 176-180.

[150]Bultmann, "Heilsgeschichte und Geschichte. Zu O. Cullmann, *Christus und die Zeit*," *Das Problem der Theologie des Neuen Testaments,* ed. G. Strecker, 1975, 294-308, hereafter referred to as "Heilsgeschichte und Geschichte." The review first appeared in *TLZ* 73 (1948) 659-666.

[151]One might also ask what would have been the reaction had Cullmann *not* at every turn located himself relative to Bultmann (or Buri, or Werner, or Barth, etc.). When e.g. Schlatter or later Martin Albertz wrote without constant reference to colleagues' work, they were bitterly criticized or just ignored in return.

[152]Merk, *Biblische Theologie des Neuen Testaments in ihrer Anfangszeit*, 253. Cf. Cullmann's observation that "in the opinion of his devotees, Bultmann's review constituted the sentence of death for my book, and they simply repeated his arguments again and again" (*Christ and Time*, 5).

[153]Merk, *Biblische Theologie des Neuen Testaments in ihrer Anfangszeit*, 253 with n. 143.

from *Christ and Time*.[154] Here Cullmann opines that Stauffer's "principle of arrangement" in his New Testament theology has lasting value,
because it attempts to draw organizing categories from the New Testament salvation history and not from, say, Barth's trinitarian
organizational scheme. In other words, Stauffer's attempts to be a historical and not a dogmatic system of organization. At the same time,
however, Cullmann says he must "oppose many details of Stauffer's
work."

     This is too vague an endorsement for Merk, a quarter-century later,
to be allowed to discount Cullmann merely by recalling his "unfortu-
nate" favorable allusion to Stauffer, an allusion which once for all
"burdens" Cullmann's entire perspective. There is no reason to follow
Merk's acceptance of Bultmann's opinion here. This raises the question: What precisely were Bultmann's objections to *Christ and Time*,
and what cogency do they retain today?

     The question is pressing, because Bultmann's review continued to
be cited four decades after its appearance.[155] Through the influence of
Bultmann's student Käsemann, Bultmannian elements are evident in
Schlaudraff's 1980s criticisms of Cullmann—for example, that his pro-
gram pushes faith away from personal encounter in the direction of
placing oneself in a "horizontal salvation historical continuum."[156]
Cullmann would deny the implied dualism. Recently Harrisville and
Sundberg have restated Käsemann's view that compared to Cullmann,
"Bultmann's program, despite its faults, is far superior."[157] This claim
merits testing.

The content of the critique[158]
Bultmann first gives a synopsis of the book which, Cullmann agrees, is
accurate.[159] Bultmann raises some specific exegetical points which are
of no major consequence.[160] He then proceeds to outline four great
objections.

---

[154]*Christ and Time*, 26 n. 9.
[155]Cf. e.g. E. Lessing, "Die Bedeutung der Heilsgeschichte in der ökumenischen
Diskussion." *Evangelische Theologie* 44 (1984) 227–240.
[156]Schlaudraff, *Heil als "Geschichte"?*, 255.
[157]*The Bible in Modern Culture*, 257. Käsemann's view that Cullmann's "salvation
history" was somehow a reversion to German idealism lacks foundation in Cullmann's
writings.
[158]Cf. Hermesmann, *Zeit und Heil*, 161ff. We take a different tack.
[159]Bultmann, "Heilsgeschichte und Geschichte," 294-299; cf. *Christ and Time*, 4.
[160]Bultmann, "Heilsgeschichte und Geschichte," 302f.

1. Cullmann is guilty of gratuitous harmonizing.[161] Even if some New Testament books evince a salvation history perspective—Bultmann allows that this is the case in Paul's writings, Hebrews, Matthew, and Luke-Acts—they are not uniform in this respect. Cullmann tries to press the "body of Christ" into salvation historical term, when this phrase and "the people of God" are in fact mutually exclusive, the former being the product of gnostic thought. Bultmann concedes that it is possible to write a unified New Testament theology, in which an integrating "theme of believing thought underlying all conceptual formulations" is highlighted.[162] But reminiscent of Baur, he sees the New Testament consisting of "truly very different conceptual formations."[163] Cullmann does not, in the end, contribute to New Testament theology as a historical phenomenon but rather gives "an old-fashioned biblical dogmatics."[164]

CALLS IT DOGMATICS

2. Cullmann ignores history of religions questions.[165] He does not realize that New Testament salvation history is nothing other than adapted Jewish apocalypticism. Features of Cullmann's reconstruction that are not from apocalypticism are traceable to gnosticism. In rapid succession Bultmann raises a welter of questions and makes sweeping assertions about docetism, the Hellenistic church, mystery religions, and myth. Cullmann has failed to see how many Pauline passages which seem to refer to salvation historical matters are actually of gnostic origin and not salvation historical at all.

FALLS TO SEE GNOSTICISM

3. Cullmann has failed to see that Christ is the end of history, not the middle.[166] Jesus' appearance comprises "the eschatological event that sets an end to the old age. From now on there can be no more history."[167] Cullmann does not realize that Schweitzer, Werner, and Buri are right in their assessment of the tremendous problems which the delay of the parousia caused for the early church. Cullmann's illustration that Christians in the New Testament, and therefore now, saw or should see themselves as standing between D-Day and V-Day is unconvincing when "the parousia, which Paul expected in his lifetime, has now delayed some 1900 years."[168] It is only the latter parts of the

CHRIST IS END NOT MIDDLE

[161] *Ibid.* 303f.
[162] *Ibid.*
[163] *Ibid.*
[164] *Ibid.*
[165] *Ibid.* 304ff.
[166] *Ibid.* 306ff.
[167] *Ibid.*
[168] *Ibid.*

New Testament (especially Acts) which really support a salvation historical interpretation, and this only proves that the New Testament generally knows no "consistent development of salvation historical thinking but rather a decrease."[169]

4. Cullmann minimizes the problem of the delay of the parousia, failing to recognize the real New Testament solution which Johns sets forth—for whom "parousia, the resurrection of the dead, and judgment have already taken place," and for whom "the future course of time can only be the further completion of the same sort of eschatological occurrence, but never a salvation history"[170]—is actually the correct one. This error leads naturally to the subsequent one of not perceiving the problem "of the temporality of Christian being."[171]

But precisely herein, Bultmann holds, lies New Testament theology's major object of scrutiny. The early believers did not see themselves in a temporal, salvation historical continuum; they were rather "taken out of the world and transposed into the eschatological mode of being as the *hagioi* [saints]."[172] Our task is to delineate their "eschatological being."[173] If this were just a salvation historical self-consciousness in something of the fashion implied by Cullmann's understanding, it could only mean that their "eschatological being" were "one which is temporally located."[174] But "an existence within time is something different from the temporality of being itself."[175] Hence the question arises: how can this eschatological existence in itself, independent of its ostensible basis in and associations with temporality (history), be discerned and explicated?

Bultmann answers: not through understanding the New Testament view of history as (Cullmannian) salvation history, but by working through the New Testament in light of the fact that early church "temporal existence means ... existence in always new decisions, in always new encounters, whether with persons or whether with fate!"[176] The internal, self-actualizing faith affirmations of New Testament believers are thus the heart of New Testament theology, not external,

[169] *Ibid.*
[170] *Ibid.* 307f.
[171] *Ibid.*
[172] *Ibid.*
[173] *Ibid.*
[174] *Ibid.*
[175] *Ibid.*
[176] *Ibid.*

contingent events or experience in which this faith is (wrongly) supposed to have been placed,[177] or some combination of the two.

5. Bultmann sums up his objections by charging that Cullmann is unaware "in what sense one can theologically and legitimately speak of event and history."[178] He seems to align himself with the "early Christian conception"[179] of history which naively assumed that biblical events actually happened, and that they in some sense serve as a basis for Christian faith. But, as we will show below, for Bultmann real faith can have no necessary factual or historical basis. And still more fundamentally, whether or how things happen is not a question of what the biblical records say but what critical reconstructions establish. This leaves Cullmann with the biblical history, which he calls salvation history, and the real history, the critically reconstructed one. Salvation "history," then, is really not based on facts at all. This is because history, what we reconstruct, and "prophetically interpreted history,"[180] what the Bible contains, are in fact mutually exclusive. Cullmann's uncritical confusion at this point, then, renders his statements about God's acts and revelation in history meaningless.

Bultmann cannot accept that anything which is established historically can be an integral component in New Testament faith.[181] "Theological thinking" is "the unfolding of the knowledge which is given in faith as such."[182] Such cognition is for Bultmann, to use classical terms, of the noumenal and not the phenomenal. As such it must be apprehended in itself and not confused with or by its own or other temporal manifestations. Thus a "salvific event" or salvation history can only be regarded as "an event experienced and apprehended in faith," having no necessary dependence on any contingent event or data. But this means that true salvation history—here Bultmann redefines Cullmann's trademark term—is not concerned with biblical events or their proclamation at all, but rather with an analysis of the "historicality" (*Geschichtlichkeit*) of early believers, or their "concept of

---

[177] J. Schniewind, "A Reply to Bultmann," *Kerygma and Myth*, ed. H.W. Bartsch, 1961, 76, points out how for Bultmann, "'Historic' existence is contrasted with 'nature.' Nature is the sphere of the demonstrable and calculable, the realm of causality. 'Historic' being, on the other hand, is realized in decision and resolve."

[178] Bultmann, "Heilsgeschichte und Geschichte," 300ff.

[179] *Ibid.*

[180] *Ibid.*

[181] *Ibid.* 301ff. Cf. Bultmann, *ZTK* 81 (1984) 456: "For faith is not taking cognizance of the event of the past which historical tradition transmits …"

[182] *Ibid.*

faith" (*Glaubensbegriff*), whose referent must be, by Bultmann's defini-tion, non-cognitive and a-historical.

Cullmann has taken us into philosophy of history, not into New Testament theology, Bultmann charges, by interpreting history and faith's (or knowledge's) relationship to it far outside the bounds of the epistemologically acceptable parameters just outlined.

Just as the "concept of faith" of the New Testament must be estab-lished by radical reinterpretation of the New Testament records as accounts of historical phenomena when it comes to "theological thinking" preserved in them, so must "the concepts of salvation and world be determined" according to appropriate, even rigid epistemo-logical principles if salvation history and world history are to be dealt with critically.[183] All other major biblical concepts must be delimited as to their meaning for New Testament theology in similar fashion. This is the essence Bultmann's demythologizing program. Cullmann's criti-cisms of Bultmann's demythologizing exegesis are, Bultmann admits, "completely correct" from Cullmann's standpoint, but Cullmann's standpoint is precisely the problem.[184] As Bultmann demands, what is meant by "history" in "salvation history"? In what sense, if any, can history be part of salvation?

The cogency and significance of the critique

We may now assess Bultmann's objections. We touch only briefly on the first four. Bultmann's major problem with *Christ and Time*, and with Cullmann generally, comes out in 5) above, and it is here that we must center our attention.

1. Bultmann's charge that Cullmann is harmonizing seems fair. Whether this is gratuitous or not is the question. Both agree that a New Testament theology is possible; the real issue seems to be whether the New Testament comprises "very different conceptual formations," as Bultmann thinks, or whether it can be conceived as a unity, albeit with various and varied facets. This is the perennial ques-tion of New Testament unity and diversity,[185] which stretches back through Wrede-Schlatter to Baur-Hofmann. This fundamental issue is a watershed between the salvation historical perspective generally and

Biggest issue — is the NOT unified a too diverse.

[183]Bultmann, "Heilsgeschichte und Geschichte," 302.
[184]*Ibid.*
[185]Cf. J. Reumann, *Variety and Unity in New Testament Thought*, 1991. Reumann mentions both Bultmann's and Cullmann's view on this issue (*ibid.* 7, 9).

the Baur-Wrede-Bultmann line of analysis. Discussion continues to-day.[186]

We may agree with Bultmann's assessment of which side of the question Cullmann stands. But it is overstated to condemn him outright for it. His criticism of Cullmann is not particularly damaging, unless it could be shown that Cullmann's position is bereft of exegetical support. Bultmann could only show this, however, on the basis of his own problematic exegetical premises. Unless these premises were shown to have good New Testament grounding, which seems unlikely,[187] Bultmann's exegesis by itself is not a compelling refutation of Cullmann, even if it can be a continual reminder of the conviction of many still today that the New Testament is not so much harmonious as "a record of strife and controversy."[188]

2. Certainly Bultmann's stress on history of religions data is superior to Cullmann's, assuming that if one can find a parallel, however slight, to a New Testament concept, the concept has been explained. But it may be questioned whether Bultmann distinguishes sufficiently between genealogical and analogical relationships in comparing canonical and non-canonical data. And it seems risky to disparage the New Testament's salvation historical outlook because it reflects Jewish apocalyptic features. Bultmann's view that "late Jewish apocalyptic" owes much to "a new influx of oriental mythology"[189] is borrowed from Bousset and overstated. Nor has the claim that it was actually gnosticism that some New Testament writers added to Jewish apocalypticism[190] to yield a salvation historical scheme withstood scrutiny

---

[186]Cf. Räisänen, *Beyond New Testament Theology*, 99–102.

[187]Cf. D. Fergusson, "Bultmann, Rudolf *(1884–1976),*" *Historical Handbook of Major Biblical Interpreters*, 455: "While Bultmann's writings represent one of the most significant attempts to resolve many of the problems inherited from liberal theology and biblical criticism, his specific conclusions have ceased to command widespread consent."

[188]C.K. Barrett, "What Is New Testament Theology?" *Horizons in Biblical Theology* 3 (1981) 12. Cf. e.g. B. Ehrman, *The New Testament*, 1997, 3–7. Ehrman's commitment to the stress on diversity theorized in W. Bauer, *Orthodoxy and Heresy in Early Christianity*, 1971 (German original 1934) is evident.

[189]Bultmann, *Primitive Christianity in its Contemporary Setting*, 1956, 217 n. 39.

[190]Cf. Bultmann, "Heilsgeschichte und Geschichte," 304f.: "The Christian philosophy of history which the author [Cullmann] outlines is nothing other than Jewish apocalyptic speculation ... The picture has been, to be sure, augmented with a few new features ... These features do not originate from the tradition of salvation historical thought and are also in no sense distinctly Christian; they derive rather from gnostic thought."

over the years; it was already part of the Judaism[191] to which Bultmann commonly gave short shrift. Perhaps Cullmann has taken too little note of certain Hellenistic background details, but Bultmann has too easily dissolved the New Testament texts into a history of religions environment that is in important respects foreign to them.

His objection, then, has general justification—for that matter *any* synthetic presentation of the New Testament will likely draw fire because of insufficient or inappropriate use of history of religions data—but does not acknowledge its own Troeltschian basis. That is, Bultmann, like Wrede, is reading the New Testament strictly in the light of history of religions ideology uncritically received as "scientific" methodology.

Cullmann helpfully commented on the problem of how New Testament faith relates to other religions:

> It is true that the "history of religions school" has included the other religions; however, in doing so it has not proceeded from the basis of the revelation of salvation in Christ but has rather arrayed all religions on the same level, in order to exhibit that which is common to all and, after this, to identify an advantage at certain points in Christianity. That is not a Christian handling of the problem but a syncretistic one.[192]

It is clear that on this point Bultmann meets the same objection from Cullmann that Wrede met from Schlatter. Bultmann's answer to the history of religions question is hardly less fraught with problems than Cullmann's. This is to say nothing of the opprobrium attaching to Bultmann's reading of the "religion" of Judaism in the wake of E.P. Sanders' critique.[193]

3. There is probably as much to be said against Bultmann's interpretation of Rom 10:4—Christ is the end of history—as there is to be said for it. If one studies Cullmann's responses to Werner and Buri, who largely share Bultmann's views here,[194] it becomes evident that Cullmann may well have at least as much New Testament data on his side as his opponents have. When Bultmann sees salvation history only in Acts and other "late" New Testament books or traditions, he may be accused of assuming the reconstruction of the sequence of tradition which he is in fact trying to establish. Perhaps Bultmann's major prob-

---

[191]Note e.g. E.P. Sanders, *Paul*, 1991, 3.

[192]Cullmann, "Gottes Heilsplan in der Weltgeschichte," *EvK* 12 (1974) 730.

[193]Cf. Sanders, *Paul and Palestinian Judaism*, 1977.

[194]Cf. Cullmann, *Vorträge und Aufsätze*, 361-377, 414-455; Hermesmann, *Zeit und Heil*, 165ff.

lem with Cullmann's approach to eschatology is the fact that over 1900 years have elapsed since Christians, some of them anyway, began to await the parousia. Bultmann thinks that continuing such an expectation today is ridiculous in light of the time lapse.[195]

But this is a matter of modern assessment of the viability of a promise which Jesus is reported to have made, not of New Testament exegesis. While New Testament eschatology is an extremely complex subject, and not even Cullmann claimed to have gotten it all right, Bultmann's criticisms, while noteworthy, are not decisive.

4. Bultmann's own elevation of the alleged true Johannine eschatology, in which time's unfolding is the ongoing realization of self-actualizing eschatological experience in the enlightened consciousness of "taken-out-of-the-world' (*entweltlicht*) believers, must be seen as a questionable alternative to Cullmann's assessment of what living in the light of the eschaton means. Cullmann's "already-not yet" stress seems in retrospect to have been on the right track. It does not seem, on the other hand, either practical or possible to conceive of the ultimate ground of New Testament Christian experience in the first century to have been mainly self-authenticating new decisions and new encounters, such decisions and encounters being bereft of any necessary mooring in historical events and devoid of any normative propositional or ethical content. What Bultmann is driving at is an insistence that early Christian consciousness be analyzed, not in connection with its temporal manifestation, but in terms of its grounding in eschatological (as Bultmann defines it, i.e. a-temporal or noumenal) reality.[196] Bultmann seeks to explicate pure early Christian eschatological consciousness itself under the assumption that "an existence within time," the place Cullmann centers his attention, "is something different from the temporality of being itself," the place Bultmann's method delineates and calls believers to occupy.

This brings us to the heart of Bultmann's disagreement with Cullmann.

5. Bultmann and Cullmann ultimately part company on the question: "in what sense one can theologically and legitimately speak of event and history."[197]

---

[195]For Cullmann's reply to Bultmann here see *Vorträge und Aufsätze*, 454f.

[196]Thus Bultmann writes, "The authentic life ... would be a life based on unseen, intangible realities ... This is what the New Testament means by ... 'life in faith'" ("New Testament and Mythology," *Kerygma and Myth*, ed. Bartsch, 19).

[197]Bultmann, "Heilsgeschichte und Geschichte," 300ff.

Bultmann assumes a radical discontinuity between history and "prophetically interpreted history." It is pointless to try to recover and emulate the "early Christian conception" of history, because it is automatically incongruent with modern knowledge of that history. Further, temporal events cannot be the stuff of pure theological knowledge.[198] An event in the New Testament comes to us as "an event experienced and apprehended in faith," and the noumenal dimension of such an event, not its time-conditioned referent or correlate, must be the object of our scrutiny. Normative for Bultmann, therefore, is the modern understanding of history (and reality generally), not the understanding of history which Cullmann takes over from the New Testament writings.

From Cullmann's perspective, however, it seems strange that Bultmann should accuse him of having a philosophy of history. To Cullmann it is clear that Bultmann's own neo-Kantian epistemology (see Chapter 6 below) is itself a serious limitation in trying to understand the New Testament writers. Cullmann would agree that Scripture is not inerrant and flawless, but he would deny the legitimacy of throwing out all so-called "prophetically interpreted history" and accepting back only that which could squeeze through Bultmann's epistemological and historiographical categories.[199]

If for Bultmann temporal phenomena can never be the basis of necessary redemptive truths, Cullmann finds that for the New Testament believers temporal phenomena, in close connection with personal relationship to God, played an important role.[200] This is a major finding of each of his major works examined above. He would for this reason consider it curious that Bultmann, e.g., explains away the Pauline stress on the historicity of the resurrection.[201] It may be well be hazardous to embark on a "criticism of the content" (*Sachkritik*) of the New Testament writings (a procedure often employed by Bultmann and explained in the next chapter) from the standpoint of an epistemology so decidedly foreign to those writings themselves. Granted that we all have current frames of reference and thus time-conditioned percep-

---

[198] Making historical events the object of or even ground for faith is "sin" (*ibid.*). Or again: "We cannot buttress our faith ... by that of the first disciples" (*ibid.* 42).

[199] E.g. relative to form critical methodology Cullmann assumes that *"it is in principle just as plausible that historical words and deeds of Jesus correspond to the tendencies of the believing [New Testament] community as it passed on traditions as that these tendencies rather amount to modifications and novel creations"* (*Vorträge und Aufsätze*, 149, italicized in original).

[200] Cf. e.g. Cullmann, *Vorträge und Aufsätze*, 133, 136.

[201] Bultmann, *Theologie*, 292ff.

tion, the question is whether we choose to make a virtue of this fact,[202] in which case one must, in the name of critical consistency, adopt and maintain a given current philosophical vantage point. But this is to run the risk of failing to hear what the New Testament has to say in its totality due to a prior commitment to what we already think we understand.

Cullmann thinks this is Bultmann's error. Cullmann's position, which recalls Hofmann and Schlatter, is that no reliable means are at our disposal to isolate the theological elements in the New Testament in contradistinction to the historical ones which convey them. The two things are not, as Bultmann supposes, inimical to begin with. The historical and theological elements must be accepted first in their given unity, which the New Testament gives adequate historical warrant to do. What they already comprise in their givenness, not their noumenal reality abstracted out of their phenomenal shell,[203] is our focus of interest. The totality of this given is never exhausted or completely fathomed. Yet as it is comprehensively researched, regarded, and progressively apprehended, it can and does shape understanding with a content which once was not there. The knowing subject increasingly sees what was really there, not just what his or her "pre-understanding" conditions the subject to receive.

It will be instructive at this point to draw insight from a third party to help identify the crux of the Cullmann-Bultmann disagreement. C.H. Duncan in an overlooked 1959 Cambridge dissertation tellingly traces the roots of Bultmann's thought. While Bultmann accuses Cullmann of being naive in the way he speaks of history, Duncan confirms what Cullmann at least implicitly recognizes, that Bultmann's whole system is governed by a rigid epistemology, "a presupposition which determines his conclusions about anthropology, history, hermeneutics, and New Testament criticism."[204]

If Cullmann is trying to sidestep certain axioms of some modern historiographies, especially that of Bultmann, Bultmann seems to be chained to an epistemology, to which he accords "high, if unconfessed

---

[202]Cullmann argues against this strenuously in *Salvation in History*, 65-74.

[203]A former student of Bultmann, H. Jonas calls attention to the similarity between Bultmann and Kant regarding the phenomenon-noumenon distinction in "Is Faith Still Possible? Memories of Rudolf Bultmann and Reflections on the Philosophical Aspects of His Work," *HTR* 75 (1982) 13f.

[204]Duncan, "Dr Rudolf Bultmann's Epistemology: An Examination of the Epistemological Presuppositions in his Theology," 1959, 1.

status,"[205] rooted in Marburg Neo-Kantianism,[206] so that even as a historian "his mind runs according to certain ingrained principles."[207] One recalls Behm's comments already in 1922.[208] Duncan speaks of Bultmann's "flight, or apparent flight, from the evidential" with regard to the historical bases for New Testament belief, objecting: "If we are not allowed the basis of evidence then we are left to wonder how Christian statements arise in the first place, and what they refer to."[209]

If Cullmann, according to Bultmann, is unscientific in his methodology, so that he violates critical rules in his openness to speaking of history and theology in close connection, Duncan charges Bultmann with a "complete absence of systematic doubt in his epistemology." Bultmann has so much faith in his method that he need not, in its application to the New Testament, systematically call it into doubt, so to speak, by consistently seeking to corroborate it by the full scope of New Testament evidence. He need only rigorously apply it as a tool already complete in itself with reference to the subject matter.

Jonas remarks that "Bultmann shared with Kant an exaggerated conception of the tightness and rigidity of worldly causation."[210] Thus Bultmann's style of presentation "is assertive rather than argumentative,"[211] a fact to which anyone who has worked through his *Theologie* with an eye to how carefully and fairly he deals with opposing views can testify. Bultmann thereby opens himself to the suspicion, expressed by Schlatter so colorfully in response to Wrede and again by Filson in response to positivism generally, that his own approach is at least as closed to the full range of evidence as that of Cullmann whom he criticizes. Duncan's study warrants the conclusion that, with respect to Bultmann's all-determining epistemology, since his approach "leaves knowledge in a ragged state" because "any knowledge outside 'my' knowledge is tacitly ignored,"[212] Bultmann's method of interpreting the New Testament could be fairly termed solipsistic.

Works by R. Johnson, A. Thiselton, and C. Garrett cited in the next chapter corroborate Duncan's observations. For now we wish only to mediate between Bultmann and Cullmann. Wherein lies the

---

[205] *Ibid.* 9.
[206] *Ibid.* 22ff.
[207] *Ibid.* 26.
[208] Behm, *Betrachtung*, 17; see Chapter 3 above.
[209] Duncan, "Bultmann's Epistemology," 296.
[210] Jonas, *HTR* 75 (1982) 14.
[211] Duncan, "Bultmann's Epistemology," 312.
[212] *Ibid.*

fundamental key to their disagreement? Duncan's study at least points toward an answer, one which we can relate to our previous discussion. Bultmann in elevating the a priori demands of modern thought as he reifies it to the arbiter of the meaning of the New Testament texts is taking up a Cartesian approach[213]—it is in relation most of all to Bultmann, in fact, that Thielicke defined and employed the term. Cullmann, on the other hand, while taking cognizance of modernity and conceding the obvious fact that interpretation need not and cannot be hermetically sealed off from it, wishes to ask the New Testament first of all, not Marburg Neo-Kantianism, "in what sense one can theologically and legitimately speak of event and history." Cullmann, like Hofmann and Schlatter, makes use of a non-Cartesian method.

Without minimizing the complexity of the differences between Cullmann and Bultmann, and without denying the exegetical study needed to test the merits of their respective proposals at the microcosmic level, we suggest that Bultmann's rejection of Cullmann to a considerable degree stands on the same footing as Wrede's and Baur's rejection of the sorts of methods and results, typical of Schlatter and Hofmann. The division seen so often previously in New Testament theology between a salvation history approach and a non–salvation historical approach in the Baur–Wrede–Bultmann tradition continues, and for strikingly analogous reasons.

Cullmann as participant in the Hofmann-Schlatter heritage

As Cullmann's work drew increasing attention following World War II, some of his critics sought to discredit it by linking Cullmann to Hofmann and Schlatter. The latter two, as we suggested in Chapters 1 and 2 above, were stigmatized as Hegelian (Hofmann), uncritical, conservative, or biblicistic. If Cullmann could be seen as their ideological descendent, then his arguments could already be nearly rejected or ignored—guilt by association.

If there is little evidence that Cullmann borrowed directly from Hofmann and Schlatter, there is even less to suggest that he delved into their work to see just how warranted was the contemporary distaste for their respective memories. He seems simply to have assumed that they deserved the general rejection they received. Cullmann accordingly chose to separate himself from them and seems to have

---

[213]See Chapter 1 above.

assumed that his use of salvation history represented a distinct departure from its earlier usage. Salvation history, he explains, is a term which theology had long since adopted to denote the unfolding of the divine "economy" or "mystery" within and as part of history, and

> there was a school of thought last century in Protestant dogmatics that designated, but also burdened, itself with this name [salvation history]. Although I can concur with this school at points, I would like to remark emphatically that I do not want my position confused with that held by this school. It takes its bearings from Hegel and appears to me to have incorrectly defined the contrast between history and salvation history. My view wishes to reproduce the theology of the Bible.[214]

We should honor Cullmann's wishes and not view him merely a repristinator, even an unconscious one, of certain ideas also held by Hofmann and Schlatter. "From the standpoint of the history of theology, Cullmann does not stand in the heritage of the salvation historical thought which bloomed in the 19th century ..."[215] Yet there are four senses in which Cullmann, despite his disclaimers, fills a role in the milieu of New Testament theology of his day comparable to that played by Hofmann and Schlatter in theirs.

1. Non-inerrantist view of Scripture

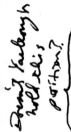

Cullmann remarks: "What I mean by salvation history' is a red flag to many 'modern' theologians. They see in it the rankest conservatism."[216] Doubtless Cullmann has a point here, and correspondingly one recalls the bad press Hofmann and Schlatter have often been subject to, in no small measure because their work has been seen as biblicistic and hence unscientific.

Yet Cullmann asserts that the Bible reflects "distorting influences" which detract from its scientific precision. This is inevitable if "the revelation in salvation history belongs to the incarnation within the human situation," which he feels is the case.[217] Admittedly this distortion is relatively minor and can be minimized through careful historical-critical labor.[218] Nevertheless, the revelation which is transmitted via the New Testament can be termed a *"remembering of revelation, darkened by misunderstanding"*, though "made alive by the

---

[214]Cullmann, *EvK* 12 (1974) 731.
[215]Schlaudraff, *Heil als "Geschichte"?*, 253.
[216]Cullmann, *EvK* 12 (1974) 732.
[217]Cullmann, *Salvation in History*, 97.
[218]Cullmann, *Vorträge und Aufsätze*, 118.

Holy Spirit."[219] Dorman aptly notes Cullmann's neo-orthodox assumption that the historical must in some sense be sinful and flawed, because it is qualitatively inferior to that divine reality which seeks to reveal itself by historical means.[220]

The point is that Cullmann, like Hofmann and Schlatter, stands under the suspicion of uncritical conservatism, while in his writings he nonetheless denies that Scripture is an inerrant deposit of true information. He rejects, by likening to gnosticism, "the theory of the verbal inspiration of the Bible in the strict sense."[221] His "entire view of salvation history owes no debt to any biblicistic concern."[222] All three salvation historical thinkers achieve their synthetic presentations of the New Testament without recourse to a strict view of inerrancy. Yet their work is widely criticized for its conservative leanings. Perhaps this is due in part to a second consideration.

2. Starting point for interpretation

Earlier we suggested that both Baur and Wrede over-hastily subordinate viewpoints latent in the New Testament texts to modern, especially epistemological, considerations which often effectively rule out on a priori grounds the possibility that many central New Testament claims are true or even relevant today from a scientific standpoint. Their starting point in interpretation is a particular reification of current thought. Hofmann and Schlatter take issue with this stance by seeking to allow Scripture at least an equal voice, together with current understanding, in determining the nature of its content and message.

As we will show in Chapter 6, and as Duncan's research noted above suggests, Bultmann follows in the Baur-Wrede train by elevating a patently modern understanding, or amalgamation of understandings, onesidedly over the competing claims of Scripture. For Cullmann, by contrast, "the text takes on absolute priority ... and not the philosophical or even theological theory by means of which a text could be made clear to contemporary understanding."[223] He points out that Jesus reportedly "attacked the scribes precisely because they cut theology loose from its primary base, the revelation given by God

---

[219]Cullmann, *Salvation in History*, 110, Cullmann's italics.
[220]Dorman, "The Hermeneutics of Oscar Cullmann," 302ff.
[221]Cullmann, *Vorträge und Aufsätze*, 118.
[222]Schlaudraff, *Heil als "Geschichte"?*, 254.
[223]Hermesmann, *Zeit und Heil*, 31 n. 6.

himself, and reduced it to human wisdom."[224] Such a caveat represents Cullmann's response to critical approaches which elevate the conceptual constructs of current modes of understanding too quickly over what he sees as the context implied by the empirical given which ought itself to be the starting point for the shaping of New Testament interpretation's conceptual categories: the historical-theological data comprising and relating to the New Testament texts.

Cullmann insists that the critic can and "must be led *by the text* to comprehend in his own consciousness an objective truth existing independently of his consciousness."[225] Or again: "All work on texts of antiquity must proceed from the possibility that they contain objective truths which are new to us."[226] He concedes that any interpretation of texts will be affected by the pre-understanding of the interpreter. What he denies is the legitimacy of giving up the struggle to submit one's own preconceptions, too, to the understanding afforded by texts and other historical data. The interpreter's own views are thus conceded to be an inevitable factor in interpretation, but it is still not true that one can perceive in a text only what he expected or wished to find there, as for instance Cullmann's detractor Steck once suggested.[227]

Criteria for understanding biblical texts can and must therefore "be extracted *out of the text itself.*"[228] Cullmann agrees that non-theological disciplines are indispensable for biblical-theological studies: "God wants us to make use of all knowledge available to us in order to research his word."[229] But it is "a secular science that is aware of its limitations" which can best be of service to the biblical critic.[230] Thus a Wredian or Bultmannian placing of the Bible's theological meaning (and historical veracity) strictly under the control of non-theological disciplines is foreign to Cullmann. He recognized long ago that with

---

[224]Cullmann, *Vorträge und Aufsätze*, 102.

[225]*Ibid.* 94 n. 13.

[226]*Ibid.* 94.

[227]Cf. Steck, *Die Idee der Heilsgeschichte*, 57: "For the person working from a salvation historical understanding, too, comprehends only that, the reality of which he has already believingly recognized …" For a recent refutation of this outlook which upholds Cullmann's viewpoint note J. Barr, "Evaluation, Commitment, and Objectivity in Biblical Theology," *Reading the Bible in the Global Village*, ed. H. Räisänen *et al.*, 2000, 150, 152.

[228]Cullmann, *Vorträge und Aufsätze*, 101.

[229]*Ibid.* 34. Cullmann (*ibid.* 32) specifies: "Philology, archeology, papyrology, textual history, literary and source criticism, secular history, general history of religion, namely of the pagan religions, philosophy, psychology—they all have their significance."

[230]*Ibid.* 94 n. 13.

such an approach the question arises: "Why could the theologians not abandon these disciplines [i.e. the various areas within and tangent to biblical studies] and restrict themselves exclusively to 'practical exegesis'?"[231] It will be recalled that Schlatter, too, saw the danger of New Testament interpretation being distorted through methods or insights unwarrantedly applied to it. Like Schlatter, Cullmann objects. The salvation historical perspective since Hofmann and including Cullmann insists that the starting point for the meaning of the New Testament texts is what the texts themselves say, seen in a context amenable to their message. Elementary as this point sounds, it is not a viewed shared by the Baur-Wrede-Bultmann line of inquiry.

3. Positive relation between revelation and history

Dorman has argued convincingly that Cullmann is best understood as one who "sought to define the relationship between revelation and history in a way which avoids the extreme historicism of Liberalism's 'historical Jesus' on the one hand, and Dialectical Theology's renunciation of a historically-based revelation on the other."[232] That is, Cullmann tries to "articulate a hermeneutics which accurately reflects the *positive* relationship he sees between revelation and history."[233]

We recall that Hofmann opposed Baur's incipient historicism by refusing to relinquish the past and abiding significance, not only of Scripture's ideological or theological, but also its historical, content. Hofmann did not, like Baur, think the two could be separated, at least not in the fashion Baur separated them. Similarly, Schlatter objected to Wrede's Troeltschian attempts to ground the meaning of the New Testament message in an a-historical religious a-priori conveniently compatible with German cultural Protestantism.

Cullmann follows Hofmann and Schlatter here. In contrast to Bultmann's assumption that the New Testament's historical elements as such must often be dissociated from their theological meaning, Cullmann warns of the danger which lurks when "one designates as essential for Jesus and the early church only that in which one feels he himself can believe."[234] It is Cullmann's conviction that the modern theologian is all too often tempted to regard those elements of a text as "time conditioned" which do not comport with his own religious and

---

[231] *Ibid.* 100.
[232] Dorman, abstract of "The Hermeneutics of Oscar Cullmann."
[233] *Ibid.*
[234] Cullmann, *Vorträge und Aufsätze*, 447.

moral conceptions, regardless of the fact that they were of the utmost importance for the author of the text.[235]

Cullmann does not overlook that "part of the biblical revelation is the time-conditioned milieu of language and of the intellectual content of those authors whose peculiarities have left clear traces in the biblical writings."[236] But like his salvation historical predecessors he wants to understand the New Testament evidence in the salvation historical context which is arguably indigenous to it. It is after all possible to see Scripture's time-conditionedness more as unavoidable cultural accommodation than as material error.[237] If "most nineteenth century hermeneutics imposed then-current world-views on Scripture, rather than allowing the Bible to speak for itself,"[238] and if Hofmann and Schlatter each rebelled against this tendency, Cullmann likewise believes that it is imperative to strive for, and possible to attain to, a basically accurate understanding of the phenomena and ideas of which the New Testament speaks, from the standpoint from which the writers viewed them. One must seek in the chiefly historical discipline[239] of New Testament theology to achieve an understanding first of all of the biblical writers' own outlooks. If this is attempted seriously, an adequate understanding of the nature of salvation historical events, as Scripture portrays them, is possible. And in this way the modern interpreter can see the same positive relation between the historical and the revelatory that the biblical witnesses themselves are said to have discerned.

4. Criticism of criticism

Significantly, many reviewers of *Heil als Geschichte* (*Salvation as History*)[240] as well as critics such as Steck and Bultmann concede that Cullmann's reading of the New Testament squares with a good deal of the New Testament itself. This points to a fourth feature of Cullmann's work which, in its relation to critical hegemony of the day, bears comparison to Hofmann and Schlatter seen in the context of a discipline dominated by Baur and Wrede: Cullmann contributes to the

[235] *Ibid.* 102.

[236] *Ibid.* 120.

[237] Dorman, "The Hermeneutics of Oscar Cullmann," 302ff.

[238] *Ibid.* 13f.

[239] Cullmann, *Vorträge und Aufsätze*, 417. Cullmann saw the discipline as primarily a historical, not a dogmatic, enterprise, and arrived at his salvation historical view "on the basis of historical-critical thought" (Schlaudraff, *Heil als "Geschichte"?*, 253).

[240] E.g. D. Braun, *EvT* 27 (1967) 68; L. Goppelt, *TZ* 22 (1966) 51-56; J.P. Martin, *Int* 20 (1966) 340-346.

maintenance of a coherent sense of the New Testament's surface content within a critical discipline for which an understanding of the New Testament texts as an integrated whole has often seemed to be impossible to maintain.

At a time when Baur's reading of the New Testament saw largely strife and fragmentation at the phenomenological level, Hofmann affirmed the historical-theological unity of the New Testament documents. While Wrede saw the New Testament as comprising random and disparate occasional writings, with no more claim to import, and perhaps less to unity, then some non-canonical writings, Schlatter viewed the New Testament "from within in a positive response to the appeal of the Christian proclamation," an approach which is today "considered essential in the case of the study of other world religions."[241] The point is that Hofmann and Schlatter function as contemporary re-articulators of the New Testament message seen from a standpoint not necessarily hostile to its fundamental surface assumptions. By comparison, Baur-Wrede-Bultmann represent a critical position that rejects the possibility of fundamental New Testament surface claims functioning or existing as the texts state. They discount or radically reinterpret such claims to bring them into line with presumed critical certainties that are often avowedly post-Christian.

Perhaps Hofmann, Schlatter, and Cullmann are to New Testament theology what some organisms are said to be to the evolutionary scale: vestiges of a long-past aeon whose existence is an anomaly and whose primary contribution is to afford contemporary observation of an otherwise extinct biological genre—in a word, dinosaurs. Yet as A.N. Wilder once pointed out, "If, indeed, there are impediments or obliquities here or there in the search for the truth" within New Testament research, "these are not confined to the households of faith."[242] Wilder asks whether scholarship would long endure without "these ancient pieties," pieties which the non-Cartesian approaches of the salvation historical group have tend to preserve. In important ways they have upheld tenets of the Augustinian outlook defended by Harrisville and Sundberg.[243] They have likewise showed the extent to which D.

---

[241]Boers, *Theology*, 75.

[242]Wilder, "New Testament Studies, 1920-1950: Reminiscences of a Changing Discipline," *JR* 64 (1984) 445. Cf. Stuhlmacher, *ZTK* 77 (1980) 224, who asserts that in disputes between evangelicals and non-evangelicals in the German Protestant church, "I deem it precarious always to be seeking right answers exclusively in modern theology."

[243]*The Bible in Modern Culture.*

Patte's thesis is apt that "critical" readings are "ordinary" readings, too, subject to correction from those outside the hegemonic guild.[244]

Cullmann, like Hofmann and Schlatter, contributes to the preservation and contemporary restatement of the New Testament's message in a fashion open to the New Testament's own surface claims and open also to the potential unity which many for centuries have found in the New Testament documents. This is not merely an interesting, sentimental, but hopelessly outdated feature of New Testament theology's landscape: Cullmann's salvation historical position, like others before it, can be seen as truly critical by virtue of the fact that *qua* critic Cullmann from his early liberal years was critical not only of the historical sources but of his own inherited critical methods and the contemporary conceptions and convictions which conferred validity on them.

In a word, Cullmann's historical method honors Ebeling's dictum that "it is right for theology to be critical of itself."[245] Cullmann refuses arbitrarily to endorse contemporary views on such difficult questions as God, history, the Bible, knowledge, and their interrelationship. Instead he makes the effort, however inadequate and incomplete, not to disclaim his 20th century location, but nevertheless to bring it into dialogue with to data which seem to have more to commend them than radically reconstructions allow. Cullmann seeks to illumine current understanding by observing, perceiving, and recounting that to which the New Testament points. His attitude in this respect is summed up well in words from Schlatter:

> The more we wish not merely to observe, but to explain; the more the object has to be forced into our already established schema; then all the more graphic becomes the scientific cartoon: all the more surely alleged science is transformed into polemic against its object. What is arrived at is not an account of that which took place but a novel which reveals the historian.[246]

This is a controversial statement, and one could perhaps try to turn it around and apply it to Cullmann.[247] In light of the above discussions, however, one may argue that on the particular issue of salvation history and the salvation historical perspective, figures like Baur-Wrede-

---

[244]See Patte, *Ethics of Biblical Interpretation*, 1995.

[245]Ebeling, *Word and Faith*, 191.

[246]Schlatter, "Atheistische Methoden," in Luck, *Zur Theologie*, 149.

[247]So already not only Bultmann in 1948 but also e.g. W.A. Irwin, "The Interpretation of the Old Testament," *ZAW* 21 (1950) 8: Cullmann "has departed from sound historical method and is merely cramping the facts of history into his preconceived theories."

Bultmann, not Cullmann, have lost critical nerve. They have capitulated to the pressure of contemporary understanding and made insufficient allowance for the possibility that theories dominant among some post-Enlightenment German Protestant circles could stand serious modification from insights—even facts—preserved in documents greatly predating them.

Rather than elaborate, however, on what, from a philosophy of science viewpoint, might seem to be a peculiar obduracy in the face of pertinent data, let us consider only a Christian theological implication, since Baur-Wrede-Bultmann no less than Hofmann, Schlatter, and Cullmann emphatically considered themselves churchmen in some sense. Cullmann refers to

> the danger that one is concerned only to speak in the contemporary idiom, and in doing so does not strive to preserve unadulterated the message itself at every transposition into a modern form of expression. Whenever one does not continually take such pains, it comes about that Christians, instead of proclaiming to the world the message which is strange to it, say to the world only that which they already say, and in part say better. Our witness of salvation in Christ should be understandable to the world, but it should truly remain a witness. In this way the world will more likely prick up its ears than if we say to it that which it already knows apart from us.[248]

This is the same danger to which V. Harvey alludes when he points out that "if the liberal theologian too drastically revises the faith in the direction of modernity, the question arises as to the degree to which his views can legitimately be called Christian."[249] Harvey concludes: "The pathos of the liberal is that, by adopting modernity and accommodating Christianity to it, he is confronted by a solution of his making in which Christianity has lost its 'transcendence' over common experience and is simply a representation of its own self-understanding."[250]

This pathos ought to be felt by many who have so confidently opposed Cullmann and the salvation historical approach. Certainly one gains the impression that objections to Cullmann's outlook are frequently horrified recoilings against his methodological openness to accepting as binding (or even as merely valid) ideas different from those acceptable to and verifiable by modern academics—academics

---

[248]Cullmann, *EvK* 12 (1974) 731.
[249]Harvey, "The Pathos of Liberal Theology," *JR* 56 (1976) 389.
[250]*Ibid.* 390.

who may openly admit to being secularists who cannot accept a world view foreign to their own.

But here a question arises. What has authentic relationship to the Judeo-Christian God—the real possibility of which even Baur-Wrede-Bultmann are uniformly anxious to maintain—always entailed? Did it ever, in either Old or New Testament terms, mean anything other than acceptance of that which is in some respects foreign to unaided human thinking? Has it ever been anything less than a major stumbling block to thinking which (as Harvey intimates) predicates salvation on that which man, apart from God and God's word, already knows or can know, does or can do?

Both the Old Testament prophetic message and the New Testament gospel of the cross and resurrection seem to have demanded a considerable change in basic intellectual posture, along with response in volition and behavior, from their hearers. Cullmann in researching the Old and New Testament corpus is aware of this and allows for it. Many of his critics deny or ignore it. But on what grounds can they deny validity to Cullmann's method? Unless they are calling for renunciation of the Bible (or its message) as the fountainhead of Christian faith, or for a total recasting of the biblical image of God and what constitutes relationship to him, it is fair to surmise that their own platform is a shaky one, from a historical standpoint, from which to attack Cullmann. As Cullmann puts it, the Bultmannian critique leveled against him "absolutely fails to consider the possibility that precisely that aspect of the New Testament which does not appeal to us could have been the essential aspect for the bearers of this witness."[251]

Cullmann is unlikely to have been right in all he affirmed. Yet like Hofmann and Schlatter he set forth a creditable synthetic understanding of the New Testament consistent with a plausible conceptualization of the New Testament's own self-understanding. In doing so he essentially respects the insight voiced by A. Thiselton: "The two poles of the past 'givenness' of the Bible and its present interpretation do not (or at least should not) stand in opposition to each other."[252] In this Cullmann does not neglect but rather enhances the critical function of his discipline. For he engages the New Testament subject matter in a dialogical fashion in which the possibility of the sources being heard in their own terms is likely greater than approaches which fail adequately

---

[251]Cullmann, *Heil als Geschichte*, 4.

[252]Thiselton, "Knowledge, Myth and Corporate Memory," *Belief in the Church*, 1981, 73.

to take into account that a valid interpretative apprehension of the New Testament texts must ply a two way street. In his way he furnishes a model for implementing Thiselton's implied desideratum: "Theology cannot dispense with metacritical reflection."[253]

Is it possible that without Cullmann's and similar contributions, New Testament theology in Bultmann's wake could be in even greater disarray than it already is? Perhaps; and if so, Cullmann's openness to the implications of salvation history and his adaptation of critical methodology to account for it could be less deserving of rejection than the discipline has tended to recognize.

Conclusion

Cullmann should be cleared of the charge of imposing a philosophy of history as such on the New Testament. While he resembles Hofmann and Schlatter in some respects, he did not come to his views in conscious allegiance to them or to schools of thought associated with them.

Cullmann's relative independence as a New Testament interpreter and creative thinker confirms what Chapters 3 and 4 above already imply: 20th century salvation historical approaches to the New (and Old) Testament theology did not grow from a hermeneutical innovation which Cullmann introduced. To a considerable degree it would be possible to write the history of 20th century salvation historical interpretation without reference to him, although he would be a prominent figure in any final picture.

Thus a salvation historical approach to New Testament theology can hardly be thought to stand or fall simply by virtue of Cullmann's success or failure in winning a wider following than Bultmann was able to muster. As a matter of fact, it is not abundantly clear, judging criticisms of Cullmann by their merits, that Cullmann's approach is as problematic as many have charged. In the words of the most recent and complete analysis of Cullmann:

> With its general self isolation from the stimulating effects of Cullmann's salvation historical conception, German New Testament scholarship has done itself harm. Heeding Cullmann's concerns could have protected it from alternatives that are foreign to the Bible: kerygma and history, the

---

[253] *New Horizons in Hermeneutics*, 1992, 550.

eschatological and the historical ... [Salvation history] denotes an objectively indispensable aspect of New Testament as well as biblical theology ...[254]

It is likely that Schlaudraff's findings apply to the discipline beyond German borders.

Moessner well sums up positive aspects of Cullmann's view which New Testament theology should be loath to jettison without very good cause:

> C[ullmann]'s version of Heilsgeschichte thus stresses the essential character of history for biblical revelation vis-à-vis other ancient religions, guards against primarily experiential hermeneutics, and with its theocentricity ensures the fundamental and ongoing importance of Israel while highlighting the functions of Messiah with respect to past, present, and future of God's saving history ...[255]

[254]Schlaudraff, *Heil als "Geschichte"?*, 256.
[255]Moessner, *TZ* 48/2 (1992) 239.

6

The Perfect Storm:
Final Assault on Salvation History and
Counterinsurgency

In his best-selling 1997 novel *The Perfect Storm*, Sebastian Junger reports on a disaster centering around the *Andrea Gail*, a swordfish boat
that went down with all hands somewhere in the Grand Banks of the
Atlantic Ocean in November 1991. Three independent weather systems improbably merged to form one monster low pressure center. In
the temperate latitudes of the northern hemisphere weather generally
moves from west to east, but this system became a rarely seen "retrograde" moving for a time in the opposite direction. Conditions were
"perfect" for a meteorological catastrophe of historic proportions.

   In the latter half of the 20th century, the salvation history approach
to New Testament theology met a fate not unlike that of the *Andrea
Gail*. Baur and Wrede had upheld viewpoints inimical to salvation
history but did not drive all opposition from the field. Salvation historical scholarship survived to see another day. But a "perfect storm"
scenario materialized after World War II, as Rudolf Bultmann combined elements of previous theological outlooks to be discussed below.
The result was his magnum opus *Theologie des Neuen Testaments*. It
cemented his emerging reputation as the leading New Testament
scholar of that generation and perhaps of the century. His outlook,
"retrograde" from the standpoint of historic Christianity since it rejected such Christian truth claims as Jesus' resurrection from the dead,
was widely regarded as the death knell to Cullmann's, the major salvation historical competitor in a sparse post-war field. As Stegemann
observes, in reaction to the frightful realities of the two world wars
that were regarded as "showing every salvation historical interpretation
to be a mythical-illusionary overreading of reality," Bultmann sought

to establish his atemporal "nevertheless" of faith.[1] Current events seemed to demonstrate the fallacy of the notion of a salvation history, and Bultmann's New Testament theology represented a sustained rejection of it.

Bultmann was reckoned by some as an insurgent in the sense that his work, ostensibly unfolding the church's kerygma, countered key Christian affirmations. These scholars were not content to affirm his direction with its drastic implications for historical and theological understanding. Among those who mounted counterinsurgent responses were Martin Albertz (1882–1956) and Leonhard Goppelt (1911–1973). Because they produced New Testament theologies reflecting a salvation historical outlook, they are key players in the final chapter of the story we are tracing.

They failed to stop the Bultmann juggernaut. Albertz never received much press, had his academic work disrupted not only by not only Nazi imprisonment but also Russian occupation of the suburb of Berlin where he lived, and died just as Bultmann's fame was reaching its peak. Goppelt's New Testament theology lay incomplete at his death. The posthumously edited version had the misfortune to appear in the early years of the Biblical Theology Movement's post-crisis funk. It made only slight impact on the field and did little to check the post-Bultmannian hegemony.

Yet by investigating Albertz and Goppelt vis-à-vis the most influential "critical orthodox" synthesis yet to appear, we move closer to the goal of shedding light on the salvation historical "fallacy." Their reading of Bultmann is far from typical potted accounts, and their positive presentations, largely forgotten in a discipline that Bultmann came to dominate, merit at least the dignity of an extended obituary

Counterinsurgent assessments of the Bultmann synthesis: Albertz and Goppelt

Inevitably new theological outlooks justify themselves by putting their spin on past ones. Calvin's *Institutes* does its share of revisioning patristic and medieval exegesis. F.C. Baur and Harnack both produced tomes on historical theology that made their respective syntheses look like the logical next step in the history of theology. The same can be said for Albrecht Ritschl's three-volume history of pietism, Karl

---

[1]E. Stegemann, "Zwischen religionsgeschichtlicher Rekonstruktion und theologischer Interpretation," *TZ* 55/2–3 (1999) 149f.

Barth's brilliant *Protestant Theology in the Nineteenth Century*, and Bultmann's mini-history of New Testament theology appearing as an epilogue in his New Testament theology. Current ideas with any hope for a future must be able to give a credible account of the past.

Albertz and Goppelt hailed from research traditions that understood this well. They therefore are at pains to plot out what they see as the shortcomings of the discipline leading up to—and including—Bultmann.

1. Albertz on the history of the discipline

Albertz seeks to avoid "polemic" and "bitter irony," asking if it were not better "if these bad habits of academic activity did not disfigure our scientific books?"[2] His contemporary E. Fascher testifies: "Chivalry in the assessment of scientific rivals was generally a character trait" of Albertz.[3] We may thus hardly dismiss Albertz's critical reflections on the discipline as unwarranted carping, unfounded exaggeration, or unthinking rejection, however we assess their accuracy.

Albertz's starting point is the observation that New Testament theology from Gabler on can be shown to have subordinated its subject matter "to the thought forms of the opinions of schools of theology, which in the nineteenth and twentieth centuries change like ladies' fashions."[4] That is, he says, the logical outcome of New Testament theology's roots in rationalism. As D. Lange has noted more recently, Bultmann's view of religious language and myth owed much to rationalistic idealism.[5] An integrated understanding of the New Testament might well imply, from the New Testament's own point of view, that in New Testament theology, "one ought to have started from the premise of the living Christ, whose attestation the Bible is."[6]

---

[2]Albertz, *Die Botschaft des Neuen Testaments*, II/2, 13. This is the fourth part of a two-volume, four-part work. Volume one treats "The Rise of the Message" ("Die Entstehung der Botschaft") and comprises two book-length halves: I/1 (1947) "The Rise of the Gospel" ("Die Entstehung des Evangeliums"); I/2 (1952) "The Rise of the Apostolic Canon of Scripture" ("Die Entstehung des apostolischen Schriftenkanons"). Volume two deals with "The Unfolding of the Message" ("Die Entfaltung der Botschaft"), again in two books: II/1 (1954); II/2 (1957). Volume two is actually Albertz's New Testament theology as such, while volume one is his presentation of New Testament introduction. But each volume presupposes and informs the other.

[3]Fascher, "Eine Neuordnung der neutestamentlichen Fachdisziplin?" *TLZ* 83 (1958) 611.

[4]Albertz, "Die Krisis der sogenannten neutestamentlichen Theologie," *Zeichen der Zeit* 8 (1954) 371. Cf. *Die Botschaft des Neuen Testaments*, II/1, 15.

[5]"Was ist verantwortliche Rede von Gott?" *ZTK* 94/4 (1997) 515.

[6]Albertz, *Zeichen der Zeit* 8 (1954) 371.

But as a result of Gabler's rationalistic response to both orthodoxy and pietism, scholars "fell prey, in the foundational stages of our discipline, out of deference to an autonomous philosophy, to an autonomous theology."[7] In other words, not only did Gabler's program rightly invite critical evaluation of the historical artifacts of the Christian tradition; it facilitated an a priori sacrifice of the content of that tradition in favor of some variation of an Enlightenment synthesis. Stegemann has recently confirmed this in observing the sense in which New Testament theology as a discipline from the beginning undermined the Reformation Scripture principle that "distinguished the Bible as *norma normans non normata* from all [merely] human, religious, ecclesiastical tradition."[8]

Accordingly, Albertz identifies five different trends to which New Testament theology "has submitted."[9]

First is the Hegel-Baur line of thought.[10] Second is the "doctrinal concepts" method.[11] Third is the approach of "psychology of religion," in which Albertz was schooled by his teacher A. Harnack.[12] Fourth is the history of religion method.[13]

Fifth is the trend which includes both E. Stauffer and Bultmann.[14] Albertz views their respective New Testament theologies in the light of significant social factors. In both Weimar and Nazi Germany, "worldview" (*Weltanschauung*) was all-important. (Thanks to the Third Reich's total "deification of the 'National Socialist worldview,'"[15] Albertz's activity in "the confessing church for Reformation theology" earned him some two and one-half years imprisonment.[16]) Albertz sees Stauffer's New Testament theology as a courageous rebuttal of Nazi pseudo-Christian revisionism. It constituted a not-too-thinly veiled attack on the National Socialist worldview, as well as a defense of what Stauffer took to be a Christian one. For this Albertz accords Stauffer due credit. Nevertheless, the "message" of the New Testament "is not the presentation of a worldview, not even a Christian one."[17]

---

[7] *Ibid.*

[8] *TZ* 55/2–3 (1999) 137.

[9] Albertz, *Zeichen der Zeit* 8 (1954) 371.

[10] *Ibid.* 371f.; *Die Botschaft des Neuen Testaments* II/1. 15f.

[11] *Die Botschaft des Neuen Testaments* II/1, 16f.; *Zeichen der Zeit* 8 (1954) 372.

[12] *Die Botschaft des Neuen Testaments* II/1, 17; *Zeichen der Zeit* 8 (1954) 372.

[13] *Ibid.*

[14] *Die Botschaft des Neuen Testaments* II/1, 18; *Zeichen der Zeit* 8 (1954) 374.

[15] *Zeichen der Zeit* 8 (1954) 374.

[16] *Die Botschaft des Neuen Testaments* I/1, 12.

[17] *Zeichen der Zeit* 8 (1954) 374; *Die Botschaft des Neuen Testaments* II/1, 18.

He applies this same criticism to Bultmann who, says Albertz, embraces core characteristics of all previous research trajectories from rationalism onward.[18] Following Baur he reduces New Testament theology to an evaluation of Paul and John, deducing the system of both on the basis of a predetermined theological position which, when necessary, reads them even against themselves when their thought does not hew to the lines of Bultmann's convictions. Following the "doctrinal concepts methods," Bultmann's chief concern is with New Testament thought or "theology," while the actual message of the New Testament remains for Bultmann "merely the presuppositions of this theology."[19] Following Schleiermacher and ultimately psychology of religion, Bultmann's New Testament theology comprises the "dismantling of theology in favor of anthropology."[20] Following the history of religions school, Bultmann understands early Christianity as "syncretistic religion."[21] Following social pressure as well as Stauffer's precedent, Bultmann's New Testament theology is "conditioned by a worldview"[22] to a culpable degree.

Albertz concludes with the observation: "Like all his great liberal predecessors he does homage to the absolute demands of the philosophical system he employs. He does the same thing that the theological students following Hegel once did: he does violence to the message using the categories of a modern philosophy."[23] Bultmann's New Testament theology in its "systematic exclusivity" epitomizes the "erroneous development which characterizes all New Testament theological research."[24] From Gabler to Bultmann one travels full circle: now as when Gabler felt constrained to set forth fresh guidelines for New Testament interpretation, New Testament theology does not faithfully explicate the message of its sources but systematically subjects them to reigning modes of philosophical thought. New Testament theology has consistently let "the standards of its criticism" be dictated to it "by the surrounding culture."[25] The result is that "New Testa-

---

[18] *Zeichen der Zeit* 8 (1954) 374; *Die Botschaft des Neuen Testaments* II/1, 18ff. Cf. J. Macquarrie, "The Legacy of Bultmann," *HeyJ* 37/3 (1996) 351: in his exegetical work Bultmann "only reinforced and radicalized the work of predecessors."

[19] Albertz, *Zeichen der Zeit* 8 (1954) 374; *Die Botschaft des Neuen Testaments* II/1, 18ff.

[20] *Ibid.*

[21] *Ibid.*

[22] *Ibid.*

[23] *Zeichen der Zeit* 8 (1954) 374; *Die Botschaft des Neuen Testaments* II/1, 20.

[24] *Ibid.*

[25] *Zeichen der Zeit* 8 (1954) 375.

ment theology" too often amounts to a revisionist enterprise which
loses sight of its subject matter's living reality and message.

Merk asserts that Albertz has in mind a foolish "repudiation of the
historical-critical work of the last century and a half."[26] Yet his remarks, coming from a product of vintage German liberal theological
education and a seasoned veteran of lectern, pulpit, and prison, deserve
a more serious hearing. His concern and elements of his position are
by no means unique; many critics have called attention to similar limitations and flaws in Bultmann's method. Admittedly Albertz was
among the earlier voices to sound such explicit alarm. But he did not
merely critique: he struck out in his own direction. Aspects of his
alternative, salvation historical approach will be sketched below. What
is noteworthy for now is the clarity with which he saw Bultmann's
dependence on earlier schools of thought and the serious implications
of his method for current understanding of the New Testament message. Given Bultmann's increasing dominance in the closing years of
Albertz's life, it is no wonder that he felt compelled to register strong,
if largely unheeded, disagreement.

2. Goppelt on the history of the discipline

Like Albertz, Goppelt responds to Bultmann by describing the history
of New Testament theology in a way that will make his salvation history outlook appear to be compelling. To this end, Goppelt's *Theologie
des Neuen Testaments* begins (as Bultmann's ends) with a lengthy "history and survey of the problems of the discipline."[27] Goppelt notes that
the Enlightenment "set the present at a distance from the past in order
to free the present from the reign of tradition."[28] The Bible is read,
like any other ancient document, as speaking only to another day. Its
significance, if any, is only that which commends itself to "autonomous reason." Interpretation proceeds "from the standpoint of the
respective philosophy of the day, especially its understanding of his-

---

[26] *Biblische Theologie des Neuen Testaments in ihrer Anfangszeit*, 2.

[27] ³1981, 19-57. This edition is cited below. See also, as illustrative of Goppelt's
method, the introduction to his *Christentum und Judentum im ersten und zweiten Jahrhundert*, 1954, 1-15; also Goppelt, "Authorität der Schrift," *Wort*, 9-17. Helpful
discussions of Goppelt's *Theologie des Neuen Testaments* include reviews by T. Holtz,
TLZ 101 (1976) 424-430 and *TLZ* 105 (1980) 599-602; C. Maurer, *TZ* 32 (1976)
107f. and *TZ* 33 (1977) 47f.; D. Guthrie, *JETS* 26 (1983) 238ff. (treats volume one
only). See also W.G. Kümmel, "Ein Jahrzehnt Jesusforschung (1965-1975)," *TRu* 41
(1976) 313ff. (treats volume one only).

[28] *Ibid*. 24.

tory."[29] This insight echoes observations found in Schlatter and Albertz. Goppelt names Semler, F.C. Baur, and Troeltsch as key figures in New Testament theology's beginning phase.

Goppelt stresses positive aspects of their outlook.[30] But he also notes that "'purely historical' study of Scripture" contains within it a serious problematic. As various schools tried to answer the vital question of how the historical evidence of early Christianity is relevant to the present, it became clear over the decades that the answer was emerging simply by reading contemporary convictions and values back into the words of certain portions of the New Testament reports. Rationalism, F.C. Baur, Ritschl, Harnack, Wrede, Troeltsch, Bousset—for all of them "'purely historical' signifies precisely not objective science but rather, as ERNST TROELTSCH himself explained, 'an entire worldview as a conceptual presupposition.'"[31] For Goppelt this raises a fundamental question: "Has historical-critical methodology ultimately freed the study of Scripture from ecclesiastical tradition . . . only to make it all the more dependent on the current philosophy? Is there a way out of this dilemma? Do we not unavoidably share the conceptual presuppositions of our time?"[32]

By way of answer Goppelt turns to a pair of scholars who deserve credit for attempting to break the impasse. First was Karl Barth. True, he only advocated something in which Schlatter had long been engaged: theological interpretation of Scripture. But his discovery was voiced in a way that captured the theological imagination of his generation. Still, from Goppelt's standpoint, Barth's stress on Scripture's contemporaneity too facilely erased the very real historical distance between biblical times and the present.[33]

Next there was Bultmann, who tried to do justice to both the theological and the historical sides of interpretation. And it was primarily Bultmann (not Barth or Tillich[34]) who set the tone for New Testament theology after World War II.[35] He followed Barth in denying that the

---

[29]Goppelt, *Theologie des Neuen Testaments*, 24.

[30]*Ibid.* 24f.

[31]*Ibid.* 31, Goppelt's emphasis.

[32]*Ibid.*

[33]*Ibid.* 32f. Schlatter too called attention to this in his review of Barth's Romans commentary, translated in J. Robinson, ed., *The Beginnings of Dialectical Theology*, 1968, 121–125.

[34]Cf. W. von Meding, "Rudolf Bultmanns Widerstand gegen die Mythologisierung der christlichen Verkündigung," *TZ* 53/3 (1997) 197.

[35]*Theologie des Neuen Testaments*, 33.

New Testament is simply "an expression of human religion."[36] He also grasped the hermeneutical issues involved in New Testament interpretation quite sharply. Further, he rightly saw the need "to integrate historical analysis and theological understanding."[37] But precisely at this point Goppelt wants to improve on Bultmann's focus. Goppelt speaks of three "components that clash" which must be pulled into a workable, mutually supportive (not antithetical) relationship: "1. contemporary conceptual presuppositions, 2. principles of historical analysis, and 3. the original sources' own claim."[38]

Goppelt concludes that Bultmann "makes the first two factors too much into static presuppositions for the third."[39] He deploys the three in sequential fashion; by the time 3. is reached, 1. and 2. have already decisively determined the text's message.

Goppelt maintains 1. and 2. must by brought into dialogue with 3., "namely with the revelatory claim of the original source."[40] For if God himself is not in some definite sense the active integrating dynamic in the New Testament message, "the content of the kerygma threatens to become a 'paradox without content,' and the call to faith response becomes law."[41]

Goppelt notes that a predominant response to "purely historical" scholarship has been the "historical-positive" method, which instead of using "science" to attack Christian tradition seeks by similar means to defend it. "It attempted to view the tradition 'positively' (giving tradition the benefit of the doubt) and to secure, using historical apologetics, the foundations of a theology which took its bearings most of all from the biblical portrait of Jesus and was frequently 'pietistic.'"[42] This school of thought goes back to Neander (1789-1850) and Tholuck (1799-1877) and was continued in updated form by B. Weiss and P. Feine.[43] Stauffer's New Testament theology, despite its surface affinity to a salvation historical outlook, partook of this method to give a unified picture of the New Testament and its teaching seen against

---

[36] *Ibid.* 34.
[37] *Ibid.*
[38] *Ibid.*
[39] *Ibid.*
[40] *Ibid.*
[41] *Ibid.*
[42] *Ibid.* 41.
[43] *Ibid.* 42.

its ostensible historical background.[44] Jeremias too follows this trend in developing "an intensive historical anti-criticism" against Bultmann.[45] Kümmel's New Testament theology is to be seen in a similar light; he attempts "on the basis of a moderately critical exegesis to trace the substance of what the New Testament reports, in a large measure dispensing with contemporary application."[46]

Goppelt's distance from this approach is seen most clearly in his assessment of Jeremias.[47] The latter wishes, out of deference to commitment to the "word's becoming flesh",[48] to reconstruct Jesus' words, or at least message, as the historically-established ground of faith. Goppelt protests that Jeremias

> does not adequately perceive that the word's becoming flesh means not only God's presence in history but also his hiddenness: who Jesus actually is cannot be determined by substantiating historical phenomena. It can only be grasped through an understanding of that which he conveys through discipleship or faith.[49]

It should be stressed that Goppelt is by no means out of sympathy with Jeremias's overall concern. In stark contrast to Bultmann, he devotes a whole volume of his New Testament theology to Jesus. But it is "Jesus' ministry in its theological significance" which Goppelt sets forth.[50] Just what this signifies takes shape as we come now to Goppelt's own position, which he characterizes as salvation historical.

He refers first to Hofmann, who sought with considerable success "to actualize the synthesis between contemporary thought, historical

---

[44]*Ibid.* 43. Herein lies the answer to Marshall's query as to why Goppelt does not assign Stauffer to the salvation historical school of thought; see Marshall, *The Theological Educator* 9 (Spring 1979) 63 n. 13.

[45]Goppelt, *Theologie des Neuen Testaments*, 43.

[46]*Ibid.* 44. See also Goppelt's comments on Kümmel's New Testament theology in "Der Ertrag einer Epoche," *Lutherische Monatshefte* 11 (1972) 97f. Holtz questions whether Kümmel really belongs in this category: *TLZ* 101 (1976) 424.

[47]On Jeremias see also Goppelt, *Lutherische Monatshefte* 11 (1972) 96f. Kümmel, *TRu* 41 (1976) 315 speaks of "the polemic against J. Jeremias" which "dominates" Goppelt's *Theologie des Neuen Testaments*.

[48]Goppelt, *Theologie des Neuen Testaments*, 44. Cf. Hasel, *New Testament Theology*, 106: "The research of Jeremias seeks to serve historical truth and to protect the word from docetic evaporation."

[49]Goppelt, *Theologie des Neuen Testaments*, 44.

[50]This is the title of the first volume of Goppelt's *Theologie des Neuen Testaments*. The (only partially completed) second volume bears the title "Diversity and Unity of the Apostolic Witness to Christ." The similarity to the organization of Schlatter's two-volume New Testament theology is hardly accidental.

research, and theological understanding in the opposite order, as it were, from Bultmann." Hofmann "integrates the historical thinking of modern times into a reformation hermeneutic."[51] Theodore Zahn, with less theological but massive historical-philological expertise, stands in the same tradition, although his work reflects a more ossified "historicizing conservatism."[52]

Schlatter, G. Kittel, and J. Schniewind are in the same heritage. Schlatter seeks to grasp the biblical reports "as witnesses of a self-disclosure of God which overcomes reality," in this respect pursuing a Hofmannian theme.[53] Also like Hofmann, Schlatter refuses to regard New Testament theology merely as an abridged form of dogmatics. He maintained a clear separation between a contemporary systematic theology and biblical theology, thus avoiding biblicistic pietism.[54] Accordingly, Schlatter's New Testament theology does not lay out doctrinal concepts but develops "kerygmatic-theological sketches related to actual historical situations."[55] Neither a "purely historical" nor an anti-purely historical (historical-positive) reading of the New Testament can finally do it justice. E. Lohse sums up Goppelt's outlook: "He does not dispute, to be sure, older historical-critical research its methodological prerogative, but he raises the question whether its outlook is really capable of grasping the early Christian message."[56] He doubts it, and in response he developed his salvation historical approach, one with important points of contact not only with Hofmann and Schlatter but also with Cullmann and von Rad.

Goppelt and Albertz agree that Bultmann's New Testament theology epitomizes, not only the strengths, but also the weaknesses of the discipline as it had developed up to that point. Bultmann left no room for salvation historical thinking. Albertz and Goppelt sought to push the door back open. Specifics of their proposals will emerge below. But to understand what they were up against, and to gauge the significance of what they produced, it will be helpful to revisit Bultmann's New Testament theology. By evaluating aspects of its method in relation to that of his "critical orthodox" forebears Baur and Wrede

---

[51] *Ibid.* 45. Taking a different tack but coming to a similarly positive assessment is H. Thielicke, *Modern Faith and Thought*, 1990, 233–247.

[52] *Theologie des Neuen Testaments*, 46. Questioning Goppelt's assessment of Zahn's perspective is Holtz, *TLZ* 101 (1976) 424.

[53] *Ibid.* 47.

[54] *Ibid.* 47

[55] *Ibid.* 47f.

[56] Lohse, *KD* 21 (1975) 85.

treated in Chapters 1 and 2 above, we can refine our grasp of developments lying behind contemporary New Testament theology. This will facilitate understanding of the salvation historical perspective within it.

Bultmann and New Testament theology

Obviously Bultmann is not just an extension of Baur and Wrede. He sees himself, for instance, as avoiding and even transcending Baur's historicism.[57] Merk speaks of this "turning aside from F.C. Baur" as a methodological move to reverse Baur's reading of "early Christian history as a phenomenon of the past";[58] Bultmann prefers rather to press historical data into serving contemporary theological reconstruction. He likewise rejects Baur's idealistic understanding of Pauline righteousness.[59] He accuses Wrede of sundering the "connection between the act of living and the act of thinking";[60] Wrede rightly understands the New Testament theological material "as the expression and not the object of faith" but wrongly construes such expression as "subsequently added conceptual reflection on the objects of faith" rather than "the unfolding of the believing self-understanding."[61] Dahl notes that Bultmann stresses "the doctrine of justification" to a greater extent than would be acceptable to Wrede.[62] And Bultmann's allegiance to the history of religions school implies a break "with the older Baurian construction of history" as adopted e.g. by Goguel.[63] In several ways Bultmann is to be distinguished from these earlier figures.

Nevertheless, similarities between Baur, Wrede, and Bultmann are readily apparent.

---

[57]Bultmann, *Theologie des Neuen Testaments*, 592f.
[58]Merk, *Biblische Theologie des Neuen Testaments in ihrer Anfangszeit*, 257.
[59]Bultmann, *Theologie des Neuen Testaments*, 278.
[60]*Ibid.* 594.
[61]*Ibid.*
[62]Dahl, *TRu* 22 (1954) 39.
[63]*Ibid.* 30. On Bultmann's allegiance to history of religion premises see D. Lührmann, "Rudolf Bultmann and the History of Religion School," *Text and Logos,* ed. T. Jennings, Jr., 1990, 3–14.

IN Bultmann

1. Features reminiscent of Baur

Reviews or studies of Bultmann's New Testament theology allude to numerous points of contact with Baur.[64] We are concerned only to show similarity at three junctures: (1) the quasi-historical nature of New Testament theology as Bultmann understands it, (2) his subsequent failure to come to grips with historical phenomena of the New Testament, and (3) his functional sacrifice of the New Testament message to a particular modern mode of self- understanding.

Quasi-historical character

We noted in Chapter 1 that Baur's New Testament theology is not primarily concerned with New Testament history in the sense of something that happened in ancient times. It rather presses the New Testament texts into the service of a theological-philosophical reconstruction of the ultimate conceptual reality to which the New Testament points.

It was long argued that Bultmann's work is rigorously historical. Cullmann maintained this in the 1920's,[65] and assessments similar to his have echoed ever since.[66] Classic here are F.C. Grant's words: Bultmann's New Testament theology reflects a "thoroughly historical point of view ... The reader can trust him, for he does not have some ulterior motive ..., and he writes with stark, scientific accuracy and precision."[67] In a slightly broader vein Grässer writes of "the unerring objectivity that characterizes all his works,"[68] while Merk asserts that Bultmann held himself aloof from "ephemeral formulations of questions and theological fashion trends."[69]

It is nevertheless undeniable that Bultmann's New Testament theology's historical basis is very tenuous. Stuhlmacher speaks of the extremely weak foundation on which the whole is constructed.[70] Morgan has argued convincingly that Bultmann's New Testament theology

---

[64]E.g. Dahl, *TRu* 22 (1954) 26f.; Hasel, *New Testament Theology*, 87; Morgan, *NNTT*, 37; Stuhlmacher, *Vom Verstehen des Neuen Testaments*, 173; Albertz, *Die Botschaft des Neuen Testaments*, II/1, 1954, 18.

[65]Cullmann, *Vorträge und Aufsätze*, 90.

[66]Cf. G. Harbsmeier, "Die Theologie Rudolf Bultmanns und die Philosophie," *Zeit und Geschichte*, ed. E. Dinkler, 1964, 472; G. Klein, "Rudolf Bultmann: ein unerledigtes Vermächtnis," *ZTK* 94/2 (1997) 186.

[67]Grant, review of Bultmann, *Theologie des Neuen Testaments*, *JBL* 69 (1950) 69.

[68]Grässer, "Rudolf Bultmann zum Gedächtnis," *ZNW* 75 (1984) 1.

[69]Merk, "Vorwort zur 8. Auflage," of Bultmann's *Theologie des Neuen Testaments*.

[70]Stuhlmacher, *Vom Verstehen des Neuen Testaments*, 188.

seriously and consistently departs from sound historical method.[71] Thielicke states: "Consciousness, not history, is what takes place in Bultmann."[72] Käsemann's conviction that Bultmann's approach cut New Testament interpretation off "from all engagement with history" led to a rift between teacher and student that never healed.[73]

The problem here is that Bultmann systematically devalues the first century context which gave rise to the New Testament text. This is in part due to his existentialist understanding of authentic existence: historical criticism can serve fruitfully to rob faith of all external security and thereby, in Bultmann's view, strengthen it.[74] It is also related to his "Kantian-Ritschlian exclusion of the world from serious concern by theology."[75]

Most of all, however, we see Bultmann handling New Testament history in this way. What is vital is what is vital to all history, namely the self-understanding of the persons who experienced it.[76] "We" (the modernist hegemony in which Bultmann consistently took his stand) now know wherein this self-understanding consists.[77] This means that

---

[71]Morgan, *NNTT*, 33-67; he suggests that Bultmann's legitimate theological interest is allowed to override and thus seriously compromise his historical observation. This was however already noted in 1922; see Behm, *Heilsgeschichtliche und religionsgeschichtliche Betrachtung des Neuen Testaments*, 15f.

[72]Thielicke, *The Evangelical Faith,* vol. 1, 58. Thiselton, *The Two Horizons*, 292, questions the aptness of this charge but may give inadequate attention to the meaning of Thielicke's term "Cartesian." See above, Chapter 1. Thielicke's statement must be read in its whole context (*The Evangelical Faith*, vol. 1, 54-65), and when it is, one sees that Thielicke's point is not so very different from that made by Thiselton himself— that Bultmann's hermeneutic often distorts the most likely meaning of the New Testament texts. Thielicke means that Bultmann's "historical" descriptions of New Testament data tend to become descriptions of what commends itself to Bultmann's highly selective, neo-Kantian historical consciousness. When we read Bultmann's New Testament interpretation, we are often not reading a historical-exegetical account as such at all, but rather an account of the data as they pass through a "sieve" which will bring them into connection with Bultmann's existing self-understanding, or "consciousness" (*ibid.* 58).

[73]P. Zahl, "A New Source for Understanding German Theology: Käsemann, Bultmann, and the New Perspective on Paul," *Sewanee Theological Review* 39/4 (1996) 417.

[74]Dahl, *TRu* 22 (1954) 31.

[75]Morgan, *NNTT*, 54.

[76]The New Testament documents can make a claim to have contemporary significance only when seen "as an expression of an understanding of human existence which is a possible self-understanding for a contemporary person" (*Theologie des Neuen Testaments*, 599).

[77]Bultmann, "New Testament and Mythology," *Kerygma and Myth*, ed. Bartsch, 24f.

New Testament statements—say, words attributed to Jesus—are understood to reflect not primarily temporal, contingent past reality; they present rather clues to reality's enduring essence as we have finally come to apprehend and articulate it with the aid of contemporary categories of understanding. In the New Testament, accordingly, "the thoughts" which Jesus' words express are understood as describing the concrete situation of a person living in time: they express the individual's existence in transition, in uncertainty, in decision; they articulate a possibility of comprehending this existence; they attempt to understand the possibilities and necessity of one's own being.[78]

Thus, while the Bible clearly speaks "about revelatory events in the public world of power structures and politics,"[79] as well as admittedly about individual spiritual or existential encounter, Bultmann exclusively "focuses attention on the theology of the New Testament as statements about believing existence."[80] As Dahl goes on to note: "That is, however, a skewed reading of the sources."[81] It becomes problematic "when Bultmann assumes that human existence remains constant throughout changing views of the world, so that provided the interpreter asks about *this,* he will get at the real meaning of the text."[82] Bultmann is not able, nor is he often even concerned, to demonstrate this postulate with reference to a wide selection of New Testament evidence. Kraus can even charge that in Bultmann "the historical dimension has vanished from view."[83] This is a reasonable

---

[78]Bultmann, *Jesus*, 1929, 14f. For reconsideration of this important book see G. Stanton, "Biblical Classics: XII. Rudolf Bultmann: *Jesus and the Word,*" *ExpT* 90 (1978-79) 324-328. It is fair to cite Bultmann's earlier works in connection with his *Theologie des Neuen Testaments*, since all his works from the 1920s on feed directly into it; see Dahl, *TRu* 22 (1954) 22. Bultmann's dogged consistency over the decades is a commonplace in Bultmann scholarship. His *Theologie des Neuen Testaments* itself refers often enough to his earlier writings, just as *Jesus* (17) presupposes his earlier *Die Geschichte der synoptischen Tradition.*

Still, one must also see in Bultmann "an intermingling of continuity and discontinuity," because while it is true that "Bultmann made up his mind on some essential issues at the beginning of his career ..., on other issues he appears to have changed his mind more than once before he finally settled into his classic position from 1926-1930 ..." (C. Garrett, "The Development of Rudolf Bultmann's Views of Christology and Revelation: 1903–1930," 1979, 347). This same point is made by P.-G. Müller, "Altes Testament, Israel und das Judentum in der Theologie Rudolf Bultmanns," *Kontinuität und Einheit*, ed. Müller & W. Stenger, 1981, 442.

[79]D. Kelsey, *The Uses of Scripture in Recent Theology*, 1975, 84.

[80]Dahl, *TRu* 22 (1954) 84.

[81]*Ibid.*

[82]Morgan, *NNTT*, 41.

[83]Kraus, *Biblische Theologie*, 191.

inference given Bultmann's statement in a letter from 1965: "Man is not, like a creature of nature, subject to the causal setting of natural events."[84] Man is freed from Troeltschian historical determinism but at the price of material connection to contingent events.

In a word, "history" for Bultmann in the conceptual analysis comprising New Testament theology is fundamentally distinct from the ancient "history" which gave rise to the New Testament texts. Bultmann's New Testament theology is not interested in ancient events as such but in ancient "eschatological incidents in the strict sense" (which ultimately correspond to contemporary experience of authentic existence): these are "incidents with which the old way of the world and history in general cease."[85] But a problem arises precisely here, since it is arguably doubtful "whether [earliest] Christianity understood eschatological events in the same sense as B[ultmann] does, as the end of history."[86] For Bultmann "the revelatory and saving event is located in the subjectivity of the man of faith"[87] and is not a matter of history in a more normal sense at all. But this approach both to salvation and to history is foreign to a good deal of the New Testament itself. What warrant is there, other than a pre-determined dogmatic or philosophical one, for declaring this particular self-understanding the measure of the total message and underlying historical background of the New Testament texts? M. Barth is justified in claiming about Bultmann's theology that "it turns out to be more a form of religious philosophy or doctrine of faith than an exegetical work."[88]

Bultmann's *Theologie des Neuen Testaments*, in this respect like Baur's, squares with its ostensible literary-historical basis only in a very qualified sense. And this feature seems to have been built into his approach at the methodological level. While no New Testament theology can ever hope to satisfy everyone in its handling of historical data,[89] his New Testament theology, which for many still enjoys the status of methodological pacesetter in the discipline, is nevertheless fraught with the same liability as Baur's at this point. "Purely histori-

---

[84]Zahl, *Sewanee Theological Review* 39/4 (1996) 417.

[85]Bultmann, *Theologie des Neuen Testaments*, 25.

[86]Dahl, *TRu* 22 (1954) 35.

[87]Kelsey, *Uses of Scripture*, 84. Klein, *ZTK* 94/2 (1997) 184 rightly speaks of Bultmann's "ground-shaking revision of the understanding of revelation."

[88]M. Barth, "Die Methode von Bultmanns *Theologie des Neuen Testaments*," *TZ* 11 (1955) 26.

[89]This was seen already by Schlatter, *NNTT*, 155. See also Morgan, *NNTT*, 45; Guthrie, *New Testament Theology*, 27.

cal" in important respects means not historical at all. At best, from Baur to Bultmann stretches "a line which regards everything pertaining to 'world' as ultimately the thing to be transcended ..."[90]

Unsatisfactory handling of historical data

We noted earlier that Baur's method contributed to an artificial handling of data which did not fit in with his predetermined scheme. No miracles, and certainly not the resurrection, could be taken seriously.[91] As Hofmann and many since have argued, this is unsatisfactory. In Baur's case, it undoubtedly led, for example, to an unconvincing explanation of the resurrection reports. Moreover, New Testament studies since Baur has long since severely qualified the dialectical dynamic of strife[92] which Baur saw as the key to unlock the mystery of New Testament history. True, his basic insight into what he perceived as early church internecine feuding contains an element of truth—but hardly as vital as Baur alleged. And his extreme, and for his reconstruction extremely important, late-dating of most New Testament books has in most cases proven to be unfounded.[93]

In a similar way, Bultmann's one-dimensional handling of the New Testament results in a distortion of historical evidence at more than a few points. Some of the major areas of controversy which would support the argument that Bultmann's method has contributed to a systematic mishandling of data include: (1) the celebrated and contested "Hellenistic church before and contemporary with Paul,"[94] very probably for the most part "Hellenistic castles in the air;"[95] (2) the gratuitous attributing of those Johannine texts confuting Bultmann's idea of Johannine eschatology to a later redactor,[96] as well as the ex-

[90]Stegemann, *TZ* 55/2–3 (1999) 143.

[91]See Chapter 1. Cf. similarly Bultmann, "Zur Frage des Wunders," *Glauben und Verstehen*, vol. 1, 1933, 214-228.

[92]Bultmann largely follows Baur here; see *Theologie des Neuen Testaments*, 59f.

[93]Cf. Ellis, "Dating the New Testament," *NTS* 26 (1980) 487-502; *idem*, "Die Datierung des Neuen Testaments," *TZ* 42 (1986) 409–430.

[94]Bultmann, *Theologie des Neuen Testaments*, 66–186.

[95]T.W. Manson, review of Bultmann, *Theologie des Neuen Testaments*, part 1, *JTS* 50 (1949) 203. But Manson also says: Bultmann's theology is "a book to be read and reread. There is hardly a page on which one will not find original and fruitful suggestions" (*ibid*. 202). Manson reviewed part 2 in *JTS* [new series] 3 (1952) 246-250.

[96]Bultmann, *Theologie des Neuen Testaments*, 181 n.1; cf. 391 n. 1; 393 n. 1; 401 n. 1; 403 n. 1; 407 n. 1, also Bultmann's commentary on John. Cf. also D. Nineham, review of Bultmann's *Theology of the New Testament*, *ExpT* 67 (1955-56) 98.

plaining away of other awkward texts;[97] (3) Bultmann's considerable skepticism regarding our knowledge of Jesus,[98] yet his confidence in reconstructing the personal intent of Jesus' preaching insofar as it expresses a certain proto-gnosticism, so we *do* know e.g. that "Jesus' idea of God" is "radically dehistoricized, and man as regarded on the basis of this idea of God is likewise dehistoricized";[99] (4) Bultmann's "ignoring of the Gospels as theological documents,"[100] and thereby a serious interpretative miscue with wide-ranging implications for his handling of the history which gave rise to them; (5) Bultmann's over-reliance on a fully developed, well-defined pre-Christian gnosticism[101] which provided the basic conceptual framework for whatever in the New Testament does reflect a true-to-existentialism grasp of authentic existence;[102] and (6) his view of myth, built on an antiquated worldview that is no longer tenable.[103]

Other areas might be mentioned,[104] but the above suffices to indicate that Bultmann's handling of historical data raises serious questions. It is not that Bultmann had nothing to substantiate his ostensibly his-

---

[97]We refer to Bultmann's similar handling of Paul (*Theologie des Neuen Testaments*, 206 n. 1), as well as to the assumption that words attributed to Jesus can hardly ever have been his own but rather are "put into his mouth ... by the church" (*ibid.* 47; cf. 16, 19, 51, 58, 85). Bultmann fails to establish the corporate amnesia (or connivance) which could explain such a total lack of memory of Jesus' words. He disposes of much of the synoptic sayings material through such labels as "secondary," "legends," "back-projected," and "vaticinia ex eventu." Analogous reasoning in K.L. Schmidt's *Der Rahmen der Geschichte Jesu* has been shown to be largely without foundation: see D. Hall, *The Gospel Framework: Fiction or Fact?*, 1997.

[98]Cf. Bultmann, *Jesus*, 12: "For I am of the opinion that we can now know as good as nothing about the life and personality of Jesus, since the Christian sources were not interested in this, and are, furthermore, very fragmentary and overgrown with legends ..." Cf. *Theologie des Neuen Testaments*, 38: "Every attempt" to attain "a picture" of Jesus' "personality ... remains a game of subjective imagination."

[99]Bultmann, *Theologie des Neuen Testaments*, 25.

[100]Marshall, *The Theological Educator* 9 (Spring 1979) 55; cf. already Dahl, *TRu* 22 (1954) 29.

[101]Cf. M. Barth, *TZ* 11 (1955) 6f.; K. Prümm, *Gnosis an der Wurzel des Christentums?*, 1972 (to be used with caution); E.M. Yamauchi, *Pre-Christian Gnosticsm. A Survey of the Proposed Evidences*, [2]1983; Macquarrie, *HeyJ* 37/3 (1996) 349, 351.

[102]Bultmann, *Theologie des Neuen Testaments*, 166-186; 479; cf. 365: "So then, the Jesus figure in John is generally sketched in the forms offered by the gnostic redeemer myth ... which had already influenced the christological thinking of hellenistic Christianity prior to Paul and during Paul's time."

[103]E. Grässer, "Notwendigkeit und Möglichkeiten heutiger Bultmannrezeption," *ZTK* 91/3 (1994) 274f.

[104]See e.g. Thiselton, *The Two Horizons*, 263-275.

torical reconstructions, nor that theologically or philosophically Bultmann is unjustified in shaping ancient data to suit the needs of his own reconstruction.[105] But his methodology—an approach in which he could e.g. continue "to hold the theory of the pre-Christian origins of the Heavenly Redeemer myth even after the textual evidence had been thoroughly disproven"[106]—is suspect in a discipline which affects to place a high value on historical integrity. The cogency of Bultmann's New Testament theology, like Baur's, is vitiated by a systematic tendency to mishandle empirical data.

Soon after the initial appearance of Bultmann's *Theologie des Neuen Testaments*, O. Michel queried: "In Bultmann's theology has the truth of the New Testament message come to valid expression, or is it once more bound up with a construction which again and again must be overcome through exegesis itself?"[107] On the whole one could probably make a stronger case for Michel's latter option.[108]

Sacrifice of New Testament message

It has been claimed that Bultmann "certainly does not want to elevate the modern interpreter's understanding of existence so that it becomes the very censoring norm of history."[109] Bultmann states that he, unlike "the older liberals [who] used criticism to *eliminate* the mythology" of the New Testament, wants "to use criticism to *interpret* it."[110] He did not "declare the New Testament to be outmoded, just the mythological interpretation of it."[111] So then, the basis for assessing the New Testament cannot be taken "from modern thought."[112]

The problem here is that Bultmann goes on to state that this basis is to be derived "from the understanding of human existence which the

---

[105]Cf. Morgan, *NNTT*, 61.

[106]Johnson, *The Origins of Demythologizing*, 1974, 56 n. 4; 114ff.; cf. V. Taylor, review of Bultmann, *Theology of the New Testament*, vol. 1, *SJT* 6 (1953) 198, who noted that Bultmann is unmoved by "the many criticisms by which his assertions and denials have been riddled."

[107]Michel, review of Bultmann, *Theologie des Neuen Testaments*, vol. 1, *TLZ* 75 (1950) 31f.

[108]Thiselton, *The Two Horizons*, speaks of the need for correcting Bultmann "at the level of painstaking exegesis" (283).

[109]Kantzenbach, *Programme*, 205. Cf. Thiselton, *The Two Horizons*, 223.

[110]Bultmann, "New Testament and Mythology," *Kerygma and Myth*, ed. Bartsch, 12. Cf. Schmithals, *TRE* 7, 393: "Existentialist interpretation of the New Testament seeks to understand what is mythological existentially, not to eliminate it."

[111]Meding, *TZ* 53/3 (1997) 199.

[112]Bultmann, "New Testament and Mythology," *Kerygma and Myth*, ed. Bartsch, 12.

New Testament itself enshrines."[113] Many have suspected that Bultmann hands over historical claims of the New Testament to a modern understanding which necessarily misinterprets much of the data it treats. For in the end it has proven much easier to see this "understanding of existence which the New Testament itself enshrines" as a product of Bultmann's own peculiar explication of the New Testament in terms of its self-understanding, or of Bultmann's "peculiar" view of eschatology,[114] rather than as the result of a more balanced exegetical inquiry into the actual first century world of thought and activity.[115]

We saw in chapter one that this was one of the effects of Baur's method. Baur can be understood, using Thielicke's rubric, as a Cartesian, in that he is concerned with the "possible appropriation of the kerygma rather than its content."[116] This is a further point of similarity between Baur and Bultmann. "The prominent problematic of Bultmann's theology is ... the verification of the Christian proclamation."[117] Both Baur and Bultmann absolutize a patently modern understanding of reality and then draw the New Testament data through this interpretative grid. This effects a "verification" of many New Testament passages (along with an invalidation of many others), in that it explicates them within a contemporary conceptual framework. Naturally what the New Testament says, inasmuch as it reinforces what scientific or contemporary religious opinion currently affirms, is rendered conceptually coherent and in that sense acceptable.

But is this the real point of historical interpretation? It would be, if it were certain that Bultmann's "understanding of existence" had some absolute validity. And that is in fact what Bultmann repeatedly argued: he avails himself, not of a time-conditioned "worldview" (*Weltanschauung*),[118] but of an unalteringly valid perception of authentic human existence which explicitly aims at "nothing more or less than the conceptual clarification of the structure of human existence and its historical character."[119] In this sense the New Testament text is "not a

---

[113] *Ibid.*

[114] Cf. Stegemann, *TZ* 55/2-3 (1999) 148f.

[115] Raising similar objections to the proposition that Bultmann does not seek to explain away, but merely to reinterpret existentially, is Stuhlmacher, *ZTK* 77 (1980) 225f.

[116] Thielicke, *The Evangelical Faith*, vol. 1, 41.

[117] Schmithals, *TRE* 7, 388.

[118] But see Dahl, *TRu* 22 (1954) 25. Bultmann's argument is highly questionable.

[119] F. Gogarten, *Demythologizing and History*, 1955, 61. This small volume is an eloquent defense of Bultmann's "demythologizing" program. Bultmann, following W.

source about the past; it rather speaks about me."[120] Bultmann has found a way to render the (pre-critical) New Testament message intelligible in the (post-critical) modern world, and moreover to have made it intelligible personally to the modern "me." In what sense does this constitute an unacceptable subordination of the New Testament to modernity?

Not in the sense, certainly, that existential interpretation comprises modernization. For "we all modernize, especially if we preach or pursue dogmatics."[121] But we can go farther and note that history itself "is not value-free,"[122] that "historical criticism is never based on historical fact [alone] but always has roots in the critic's dogma, too."[123] Modernization is to some degree inherent in all interpretation. Nevertheless, if we understand New Testament theology as a historical discipline, it must not only have a firm grasp of modern human believing self-understanding but must also be able to justify its reconstructions in the light of the historical data comprising the New Testament on which it claims to be based. Since Bultmann's "hypotheses and the constructions based on them have been severely criticized by his fellow historians,"[124] Bultmann's form of modernization renders his New Testament theology suspect. Bultmann's failure at this critical point puts him in the same company as Baur.[125]

2. Features reminiscent of Wrede

At issue here are not surface interrelationships, for instance that Bultmann's *Theologie des Neuen Testaments* both explicitly and implic-

---

Herrmann, clearly derives his own understanding of natural reality in terms of "regularity according to naturalistic principles," which is not a matter of worldview at all but is *"given with our existence in the world"* (his emphasis). All our earthly dealings presuppose "this idea of [all] occurrence taking place according to naturalistic principles." Thus, "we recognize in the world only those things as actual which admit of verification in this framework governed by naturalistic principles. And we regard claims which do not pass the scrutiny of this idea to be phantasies." See Bultmann, "Zur Frage des Wunders," *Glauben und Verstehen*, vol. 1, 215.

[120]Kantzenbach, *Programme*, 206.

[121]Dahl, *TRu* 22 (1954) 49.

[122]Morgan, *NNTT*, 60.

[123]Schlatter, *NNTT*, 155.

[124]Morgan, *NNTT*, 52.

[125]Cf. M. Evang, *Rudolf Bultmann in seiner Frühzeit*, 1988, 211, who speaks of Bultmann's closeness to Baur in terms of understanding New Testament theology as presenting the gradual emergence of a unified "religious principle."

itly takes up many Wredian critical positions;[126] that his method generally resembles Wrede's;[127] that he assumes the veracity of Wrede's
messianic secret theory;[128] that like Wrede he systematically devalues
the Old Testament in an important sense;[129] that like Wrede and perhaps for similar reasons he has high regard for Ignatius.[130] Rather we
want to show how Bultmann's method, like Wrede's, makes bold to
penetrate deep beneath the textual superficiality of the New Testament
message to its underlying truth, by means of a critical approach which
claims priority over all others.

The truth behind the texts

Much of what we said in Chapter 2 about Wrede's intention to get
behind the texts to the real subject (*die Sache*) applies *mutatis mutandis*
to Bultmann.

Of course Bultmann's approach to New Testament interpretation
and theology goes well beyond Wrede and the history of religion
school,[131] in which he saw theological deficiency.[132] But at this one
important point there is profound similarity. We saw that Wrede differentiates sharply between the literary sources and the historical

[126]Bultmann, *Theologie des Neuen Testaments*, 1ff., 27ff., 29 n. 1, 33f., 111ff., 167,
188, 190, 296, 469f., 477f., 507, 547f., 563.

[127]Hasel, *New Testament Theology*, 86; Barth, *TZ* 11 (1955) 5; Dahl, *TRu* 22 (1954)
22, 28f. Dahl (39) also points out a difference in that Bultmann stresses the Pauline
"doctrine of justification" beyond what Wrede did.

[128]Dahl, *TRu* 22 (1954) 31; cf. Nineham's comment on Bultmann in *ExpT* 64
(1952-53) 97: "The shade of Wrede still haunts German criticism."

[129]Barth, *TZ* 11 (1955) 4, 7; cf. Kraus, *Biblische Theologie*, 192, 317. This is borne
out by the exceedingly small role played by the Old Testment in Bultmann's *Theologie
des Neuen Testaments* ; cf. his "Die Bedeutung des Alten Testaments für den christlichen Glauben," *Glauben und Verstehen*, vol. 1, 313-336. In defense of Bultmann see
however Müller, "Altes Testament in der Theologie Bultmanns," *Kontinuität und
Einheit*, ed. Müller und Stenger, 430-472. Muller confirms that "the Old Testament—
in keeping with liberal tradition from F.D.E. Schleiermacher to Adolf von Harnack
and Albert Schweitzer—plays only a modest role in Bultmann's hermeneutic" (*Neue
Zeitschrift für Systematische Theologie und Religionsphilosophie* 35/1 [1993] 1).

[130]Barth, *TZ* 11 (1955) 25.

[131]Bultmann points this out in *Theologie des Neuen Testaments*, 594f.; cf. "Autobiographical Reflections of Rudolf Bultmann," *The Theology of Rudolf Bultmann*, ed. C.W.
Kegley, 1966, xxiv. He is critical of the school in *ZTK* 81 (1984) 452f. But his dis-
claimer needs to be weighed against e.g. Johnson, *The Origins of Demythologizing*, 87-
126; also Bultmann, *Theologie des Neuen Testaments*, 598f.; Thiselton, *The Two Horizons*, 218ff.

[132]H. Hübner, "Rudolf Bultmanns Her-Kunft und Hin-Kunft. Zur neueren
Bultmann-Literatur," *TLZ* 120/1 (1995) 6.

subject matter. The New Testament text gives clues as to what "New Testament theology" comprises but is not itself the major source for interpretation of the data. More significant is contemporary insight into the nature of the phenomena of religion in its "historical" mani-festation and development. This supplies both the framework and much of the actual content of New Testament theology understood as early Christian history of religion. Stegemann points to the influence of Bousset here.[133]

Relatively early Bultmann makes it clear that the New Testament text is secondary to New Testament theology's ultimate subject mat-ter. In 1925 he maintains that exegesis is concerned with the text in its historical setting only in a certain sense:

> The exegete is, therefore, ultimately not interested in the question, "What is the meaning of the thing stated (as mere statement) in its contemporary setting, in its contemporary historical context?" His ultimate question is rather, "What *subjects* are being spoken of; to what realities does the thing stated point?"[134]

Bultmann goes on to advocate a "subject exegesis" (*Sachexegese*) which conceives of a given historical area as "so to speak transparent. It desires to comprehend the light gleaming through, light which abides on the far side of the realm of temporal history, and it feels that in this way, and only in this way, can what is conveyed [by the sources] be grasped."[135] This "subject exegesis" in turn implies a "sub-ject criticism" (*Sachkritik*) which "distinguishes between what is stated and what is meant, and assesses what is said in the light of what is meant."[136]

"What is stated" for Bultmann is what the texts say. "What is meant" is the enduringly valid perception of or response to reality, the authentic self-understanding, which portions of the New Testament, mainly in parts of the Pauline and Johannine writings, preserve. The whole New Testament is interpreted by means of applying this stan-dard to the various texts. Thus it is ultimately not the texts which dictate the parameters and content of New Testament theology but the perception of or response to reality, the believing self-understanding, to which parts of some of the texts are believed by

---

[133] *TZ* 55/2-3 (1999) 144f.

[134] Bultmann, "Das Problem einer theologischen Exegese des Neuen Testaments," PTNT, 253.

[135] *Ibid.* 254.

[136] *Ibid.* 256. Cf. Bultmann, *Theologie des Neuen Testaments*, 586f.

Bultmann to testify. It may be asked, however, whether this self-understanding is not first of all a component of a certain strand of modern thought, not necessarily an intrinsic feature of the texts, since it is such a small portion of the texts that lends itself to Bultmann's interpretation (on which more below).

Now much of the New Testament, even those parts preserving testimony of authentic self-understanding, is written in mythological language. New Testament language for Bultmann "only *appears* to describe objective events, and insofar as it does so, this obscures and impedes its intention."[137] To succeed to a true apprehension of these texts they must be "demythologized." What they mean to say must be extricated from the time-bound mode of expression which obscures their true message, a message not about objective or actual states of affairs related in the texts but about human existence as it understands itself in its relationship to God.[138] This is not, Bultmann thinks, explaining the texts away, but is rather interpreting them in view of their own actual intent.[139]

Bultmann, like Wrede, sees the New Testament texts and a great deal of their surface message as secondary to the real subject matter of New Testament theology. He works against any hermeneutical tendency "to take the textual form [*Sprachgestalt*] of the texts ... as indicative of their material substance [*Sachgehalt*] and to dispense with demythologization."[140] The New Testament texts must be transcended and their message radically recast if they are to be read aright.[141] When M. Barth, then, speaking of Bultmann's handling of Paul in his *Theologie des Neuen Testaments*, writes: "to the extent that Bultmann's viewpoints are normative and objective, the church's proclamation and New Testament studies over many hundreds of years must, totally and without further ado, do penance,"[142] he is not over-dramatizing; he is

---

[137]Thiselton, *The Two Horizons*, 262.

[138]Cf. Bultmann, "Problem einer theologischen Exegese," *PTNT*, 272.

[139]Cf. J. Dunn, "Demythologizing—The Problem of Myth in the New Testament," *New Testament Interpretation*, ed. Marshall, 298f.: Bultmann "wishes to affirm the gospel and to 'defend' faith by setting it free from ... first century conceptualizations."

[140]Grässer, *ZTK* 91/3 (1994) 283.

[141]Cf. Bultmann, *ZTK* 81 (1984) 462: New Testament "research ... is *bound* to the witnesses and yet at the same time *free* from them; it is liberated from them by the witnesses themselves."

[142]Barth, *TZ* 11 (1955) 13.

merely indicating the extent to which Bultmann's modus operandi[143] diverges from previous explications of the New Testament texts. Novelty is not necessarily folly. Yet Bultmann's "subject exegesis" and "subject criticism"—his methodological departure from the New Testament writings in constructing his New Testament theology—must be adjudged as problematic, much as a similar tendency in Wrede gives pause.

Methodological exclusivity

Wrede's total relativization of the New Testament data gives rise to the conviction that his method is the only defensible one for understanding the New Testament. Bultmann has often been understood to be methodologically open—"There may be better ways of interpretation. Bultmann expressly holds himself open to them"[144]—but this is an exaggeration.[145] Like Wrede, Bultmann relativizes the New Testament data through an absolutist method.[146] Admittedly he proceeds in a different fashion, especially at the theological level.

For Wrede there is practically no theological level; he dissolves data into a "history of development" in which they are assigned their respective a-theological values by the sovereign researcher, regardless of the claims the data themselves might make. Bultmann for his part sees the New Testament material, at the theological level,[147] in the light of the overarching fact that in it no decisive word from or about God is revealed. God's word is "a veiled word spoken to man ..., so that the

---

[143]One is at a loss as to how to identify Bultmann's procedure since he states emphatically ("Problem einer theologischen Exegese," *PTNT*, 267f.): "We are *not dealing with the proclamation of a new method.*"

[144]Harbesmeier, "Theologie Bultmanns," *Zeit und Geschichte*, ed. Dinkler, 473. Cf. Bultmann, "Reply to John Macquarrie," *Theology of Bultmann*, ed. Kegley, 275.

[145]Cf. M. Barth's comment (*TZ* 11 [1955] 1; cf. (6) regarding Bultmann's *Theologie des Neuen Testaments*: Although it is "the most important product of New Testament theological labor in many years," in it "the only ones who appear on the scene are Bultmann's actual forerunners, mentors, and loyal students. Bultmann's interest does not lend itself to discussion." Cf. Thiselton, *The Two Horizons*, 265; B. Vawter, review of Bultmann's *Theologie des Neuen Testaments*, ³1958, *CBQ* 21 (1959) 399f. If as D. Lose, "The Historical Jesus and the So-Called Crisis of Christology," *Dia* 37/1 (1998) 43, states, "Bultmann was convinced that methodological confidence could be dangerously misleading," he did to little to avoid the danger himself.

[146]Cf. J. Runzo, "Relativism and Absolutism in Bultmann's Demythologizing Hermeneutic," *SJT* 32 (1979) 401-419.

[147]At the phenomenological level Bultmann in fact operates very much like Wrede; cf. Johnson, *The Origins of Demythologizing*, 96.

revelation present in the scripture is a veiled revelation."[148] The New Testament is not, then, information about God or theological truth but about (what is lacking in) human experience: "If it is asked how talk about God is possible, it must be answered: only as talk about ourselves."[149] While much of Scripture can be seen as claiming to be revelation from, or true statements about, God,[150] Bultmann discounts this by interpreting the New Testament strictly "in light of contemporary experience,"[151] experience in which much of what the New Testament says is rejected, whether outright or via radical reinterpretation.

From this follows Bultmann's methodological exclusivity. Dahl feels this to be a major weakness of Bultmann's *Theologie*.[152] Since the New Testament's own surface statements are misleading and often flatly erroneous in contemporary opinion, Bultmann demythologizes to get at the real meaning. The problem here is that "in demythologizing, it is the discipline of philosophy, rather than that of history, which provides both the presuppositions and context for its usage."[153] The effect of Bultmann's procedure is thus not surprisingly to set forth a radically new program for understanding the New Testament, one which as Bultmann rightly prophesied "will tax the time and strength of a whole theological generation."[154] But the high cost is worth paying, for his approach constitutes "the only solution" to a suitable understanding of the New Testament in the modern world.[155] Notoriously, however, the picture which one gets of the New Testament when one views it through Bultmann's interpretative lens is a picture substantially foreign to the New Testament itself.

For Bultmann, this is a point in his favor, for it allows the central parts of the New Testament, those Pauline or Johannine passages reflecting authentic self-understanding, to shine all the more brightly. Many however question an interpretative scheme for which literally

[148]Bultmann, "Problem einer theologischen Exegese," *PTNT*, 274. Cf. Bultmann, *ZTK* 81 (1984) 461.

[149]Bultmann, "Welchen Sinn hat es, von Gott zu reden?" *Glauben und Verstehen*, vol. 1, 33. Cf. Bultmann, *ZTK* 81 (1984) 452, 455ff.

[150]Asserted at length by e.g. W. Grudem, "Scripture's Self-Attestation and the Problem of Formulating a Doctrine of Scripture," *Scripture and Truth*, ed. D. Carson and J. Woodbridge, 1983, 15-59, 359-368.

[151]Morgan, *NNTT*, 42; cf. 54.

[152]Dahl, *TRu* 22 (1954) 49.

[153]Johnson, *The Origins of Demythologizing*, 126.

[154]Bultmann, "New Testament and Mythology," *Kerygma and Myth*, 15.

[155]*Ibid.*

most of the New Testament reflects an inferior or false theological understanding. One may raise the question whether Bultmann's approach interprets New Testament claims and imagery with the validity, cogency, and comprehensiveness which it claims. Does it interpret the New Testament *"exhaustively and without remainder"*?[156] For "when insights which have been articulated through a conceptuality drawn from a particular philosophy are regarded as a comprehensive interpretation of the theology of the New Testament,"[157] problems arise. This is a weakness of Bultmann's method, one which he shares with Wrede.

Summary

In general terms Bultmann resembles Baur in that the respective approaches of both (1) may be termed quasi-historical, (2) contribute at numerous points to inadequate handling of data, and (3) tend to subordinate the New Testament message to modern understanding in a problematic fashion. Bultmann is comparable to Wrede in that both interpret the New Testament texts by means of a truth found primarily not in the texts but in the mind of the self-consciously modern interpreter. This might not present a difficulty, except that what they say the New Testament texts testify to is often remote from what the New Testament texts claim. New Testament theology for Bultmann has the task of presenting the bona fide conceptual understanding present in portions of some of the texts, and conversely of showing how much of the New Testament fails to meet the high standards attained in the thought of the loftier passages. Both Bultmann and Wrede claim a methodological exclusivity which Schlatter proleptically criticized as being deleterious to New Testament theology: they both "have simply described the aim of their work and suggested that this is the whole of the intellectual task with which the subject matter confronts us."[158]

Our discussion of Bultmann's method to this point has served three purposes. First, it has helped round out the significant aspects of the overall picture, begun in chapter one, of the dominant Baur-Wrede-Bultmann trajectory in New Testament theology. It is against this trajectory that the salvation historical understanding of New Testament theology must be understood. Second, it has sketched highlights of Bultmann's approach, against which the work of Albertz and Goppelt will be compared below. But third, it raises a question. We have de-

---

[156]Thiselton, *Two Horizons*, 271 (his emphasis).

[157]*Ibid.* 291.

[158]Schlatter, *NNTT*, 117.

scribed certain features of Bultmann's method, but we have hardly moved beyond hints at a satisfactory explanation for his procedure. We have dealt with what he does, but not really with why. Before moving further a comment is in order regarding this point.

Bultmann's epistemology

1. Neo-Kantian roots

We have seen in chapters one and two that epistemology, whether implicit or explicit, is a telling category in a New Testament theologian's method. This proves to be even truer for Bultmann. But he presents a particular challenge to the analyst. Historical distance is requisite for accurate appraisal of influential thinkers. Bultmann's wide-ranging effects will continue to be felt for decades to come, as recent publications imply, and are therefore in continual flux.[159] He is a moving target. Moreover, it is striking how many basic issues seem still to be unresolved in scholarly assessment of him: the ultimate origin of his thought;[160] his demythologizing program;[161] his life in general, of which no full biography exists;[162] his preservation of the once-for-all-time "myth" of the Christ event, in which he inconsistently preserved something ruled out by the "modern" thought he affirmed;[163] and even his relation to Heidegger.[164] It may still be too early for final as-

[159]See e.g. B. Jaspert, "Sachkritik und Widerstand: das Beispiel Rudolf Bultmanns," *TLZ* 115 (1990) 161–182; O. Bayer, "Entmythologisierung? Christliche Theologie zwischen Metaphysik und Mythologie im Blick auf Rudolf Bultmann," *Neue Zeitschrift für Systematische Theologie und Religionsphilosophie* 34/2 (1992) 109–124; E. Grässer, *ZTK* 91/3 (1994) 272–284; M. Pottner, "Die Einheit von Sachkritik und Selbstkritik," *ZTK* 91/4 (1994) 396–423; H. Hübner, *TLZ* 120/1 (1995) 3–22; W. Schmithals, "Zum Problem der Entmythologisierung bei Rudolf Bultmann," *ZTK* 92/2 (1995) 166–206; G. Klein, *ZTK* 94/2 (1997) 177–201; W. Meding, *TZ* 53/3 (1997) 195–215; D. Lose, *Di* 37/1 (1998) 38–45; E. Stegemann, *TZ* 55/2-3 (1999) 137–155.

[160]Hübner, *TLZ* 120/1 (1995) 22

[161]Meding, *TZ* 53/3 (1997) 194.

[162]*Ibid.* 202.

[163]H. Müller, "Mythos als Elementarform religiöser Rede im Alten Orient und im Alten Testament," *Neue Zeitschrift für Systematische Theologie und Religionsphilosophie* 37/1 (1995)14.

[164]Jaspert, *TLZ* 115 (1990) 182 n. 70. Hübner, *TLZ* 120/1 (1995) 6 points out that Dilthey influenced Bultmann more than Heidegger did, but this is not the impression given by most literature on Bultmann.

sessment of Bultmann's thought, even if preliminary assessments can and must be made.[165]

The need for continued discussion of Bultmann is especially evident in such a fundamental question as his epistemology, in which, where historical study is involved, it is often difficult to separate the theoretical rationale that informs historical reconstruction from the amassed data allegedly justifying the theoretical rationale.

Nevertheless, in the wake of R. Johnson's groundbreaking work,[166] largely supported by M. Evang,[167] which demonstrates Bultmann's heavy indebtedness to Marburg neo-Kantianism, it is now possible to understand Bultmann's New Testament interpretation in relation to its epistemological roots with considerable precision and clarity. We have shown above that Bultmann's work is "historical" only in a limited sense. Johnson takes us a step closer to valid assessment of Bultmann by demonstrating that the antinomies of existence as worked out by Heidegger, in some creative combination with Barthian "dialectical" theology, should no longer provide the primary background against which Bultmann is read.[168] Bultmann must be viewed, not so much as a Pauline-Lutheran existentialist, but as a respondent to Kant[169] and, more particularly, a faithful adherent to the intellectual mindset characteristic of the neo-Kantian philosophy in which he was schooled.[170]

[165]Cf. Macquarrie, *HeyJ* 37/3 (1996) 348–359; Harrisville and Sundberg, *The Bible in Modern Culture*, 239–248; Thiselton, *New Horizons in Hermeneutics*, 454f.

[166]*The Origins of Demythologizing*, for the most part supported by the findings of Evang, *Rudolf Bultmann in seiner Frühzeit*; see e.g. 284. C. Garrett, "The Development of Rudolf Bultmann's Views of Christology and Revelation: 1903–1930," shows that Johnson has a "defective understanding of [Bultmann's teacher] Wilhelm Herrmann" (6) which results in "confusion" (44) at points in his explication of Bultmann's thought. Garrett's criticisms do not affect Johnson's central argument. For a shorter version of Johnson's reading of Bultmann see his "Rudolf Bultmann," *Critical Issues in Modern Religion*, R. Johnson et al., ²1990, 24–52.

[167]*Rudolf Bultmann in seiner Frühzeit*; 1988, 284.

[168]Here Garrett (n. 166) is in full agreement with Johnson.

[169]Cf. R. Friedman, "Kierkegaard: First Existentialist or Last Kantian?" *RelS* 18 (1982) 159–170. Friedman argues that Kierkegaard's celebrated leap of faith is his "response to a problem which is essentially Kantian in origin and structure" (159). O. Bayer likewise stresses Bultmann's Kantian ties: *Neue Zeitschrift für Systematische Theologie und Religionsphilosophie* 34/2 (1992) 117–120.

[170]Cf. Johnson, "Rudolf Bultmann," *Critical Issues in Modern Religion*, 49 n. 11: By Marburg Neo-Kantians Johnson refers to philosophers Hermann Cohen and Paul Natorp and theologian Wilhelm Hermann. "Their radical extension of Kant's logical idealism led them to repudiate sense data as a given for knowledge ... For them, the so-called 'objects' of knowledge were actually the 'objectified' constructs of reason ...

True, Johnson may underestimate the impact of Bultmann's Lutheran roots,[171] or may not distinguish sufficiently between formally neo-Kantian themes in Bultmann and to the direct influence of W. Herrmann.[172] He may slightly misunderstand Bultmann's concept of religion.[173] His statement that P. Natorp's relationship to Husserl lacks systematic exploration is belied by Kern's study, among others.[174] Still, Johnson seems to have produced "the definitive work on the subject"[175] and "in broad terms ... is utterly right in his insistence on the extent of the influence of neo-Kantian thought on Bultmann."[176] To the findings of Johnson, Garrett, and Thiselton, moreover, one may add the much earlier and overlooked work of Duncan cited above in chapter four.

A considerable body of scholarship now exists which encourages New Testament theology to reflect on its basic aims and methods in light of the fact that a long-term pacesetter of this "historical" discipline arrived at findings that were largely predictable given the prescriptive epistemology that he was taught and embraced. It is all the more important to press this point since numerous recent studies of Bultmann conveniently pass over Johnson's findings.

2. "Historical" grid

If the "historical" component underlying Bultmann's New Testament theology is largely constituted by his allegiance to an epistemological framework, rather than to empirical observation as might be expected of a "historian," what was the framework, and what difference did it make? We may consider briefly first the framework and then its primary effect.

Evang has aptly synthesized Johnson's work on Bultmann showing his "systematic deontologizing of reason."[177]

Bultmann consistently follows this Neo-Kantian terminology in his theological writing."

[171]R. Morgan, review of Johnson, *The Origins of Demythologizing*, *Th* 78 (1975) 488.

[172]Thiselton, *The Two Horizons*, 208; cf. Garrett, "The Development of Rudolf Bultmann's Views of Christology and Revelation: 1903–1930." On Herrmann and Bultmann cf. also Rupp, *Culture Protestantism*, 35.

[173]Evang, *Rudolf Bultmann in seiner Frühzeit*, 324 n. 135.

[174]Cf. Johnson, *The Origins of Demythologizing*, 38 n. 2, and I. Kern, *Husserl und Kant*, 1964, especially 321-373.

[175]Morgan, *Th* 78 (1975) 488.

[176]Thiselton, *The Two Horizons*, 208.

[177]Johnson, *The Origins of Demythologizing*, 79f. To deontologize reason is to drive a wedge between what is known (which is always a mental construct) and what is real.

Right in the center of [Bultmann's] thought stands from the very outset the conviction of the autonomy of reason—and its limitation to the "immanent" world, which in comparison with neo-Kantianism means its ontological relativization. Believing and knowing, religious and scientific perception, religion and culture stand in a relation to each other that must be called "dialectical." This relation is characterized by a primordial opposition and by the intentional termination of this opposition in the life of the individual under the primacy of religious reality grasped beyond reason. Bultmann increasingly made use of the rigid neo-Kantian schema ... of objectifying reason functioning according to fixed laws. Increasingly, on the other hand, he made use of category of experience [*Erleben*[178]]—taken over from [Wilhelm] Hermann and becoming a buzz word in Bultmann's time. Through it he sees described—not only from the standpoint of theology— the transrational horizon within which human existence can factually seek (cf. "wistful longing" [*Sehnsucht*]) and find the fulfillment appropriate to it.[179]

Several inferences may be drawn from Evang's summary of Bultmann's epistemology.

1. Reason lays hold only of what is this-worldly. This automatically casts a pall over the "theology" of New Testament writers who claim to possess and offer saving knowledge of transcendence mediated through a gospel calling attention to earthly and historical phenomena. As Meding puts it: "Bultmann works out the critical meaning of God-talk against a proclamation that seeks God in nature, history, and myth."[180] "Myth," in Meding's view, extends to such matters as descent from and ascension into heaven, belief in spirits and demons, miracles, and eschatology.[181] "Historical" thinking eliminates such matters from "theological" interpretation on epistemological grounds. This severely circumscribes from the outset the shape that a "New Testament theology" will take.

2. Bultmann's epistemology does not derive from either his historical inquiry (he was simply taught it in university and developed it as he grew older) or his theology (though this was undoubtedly a contributing factor). It is rather a matter of a rigid prefabricated intellectual construct functioning as a sieve through which historical data are poured. Much of importance to the ancient writers is strained out. "Kant's insistence that knowledge include knowledge of the senses,"

---

[178]Evang, *Rudolf Bultmann in seiner Frühzeit*, 282, points out that some neo-Kantians preferred the word "feeling" [*Gefühl*], which they took over directly from Schleiermacher.

[179]Evang, *Rudolf Bultmann in seiner Frühzeit*, 287.

[180]*TZ* 53/3 (1997) 202.

[181]*Ibid.* 200.

for instance, "has been systematically rejected by the Neo-Kantians."[182] In 1908 Bultmann wrote in a letter: "We must have the courage to conceive of the sensual world as mere appearance."[183] This has grave implications for Bultmann's interpretation of writers who speak in the sensually rich terms of gospel narrative and relate items they saw, heard, and touched to living transcendence (cf. e.g. 1 John 1:1–3).

3. Whereas New Testament writers commonly speak of the "trans-rational horizon" confronting humans as heaven (or eternity, or God's kingdom), and of God bringing this horizon into history via his own presence through creation and redemption, for Bultmann that horizon is rather individual experience, in which fulfillment is encountered in contradistinction to data accessible to rational faculties. "Revelation" is therefore primarily about self-understanding and not about events or verities played out exterior to the self and offering themselves to be known and internalized by the cognizant subject. Bultmann's extreme stress on "what concerns me" rather than what God did in Jesus quite outside the believing individual was a major reason why most of Bultmann's students pulled away from their teacher at this point.[184]

The point is that Bultmann as a historian works within the parameters of a philosophy that is not necessarily well suited for application to the biblical data from which he seeks to educe a theology. For those who hold that the relation of reason and revelation is not so antithetical—and this includes of course salvation historical thinkers like Albertz and Goppelt—that is already sufficient ground for calling in question both historical and theological aspects of Bultmann's "New Testament theology."

But the effects of his epistemology are no less striking. Primary among them is the redemptive function of knowing, or rather non-knowing, for Bultmann. Writers frequently call attention to Bultmann's conviction that "radical demythologization is the consistent application of the Pauline-Lutheran doctrine of justification without the works of the law through faith alone to the sphere of knowing."[185] The less one "knows" of putative New Testament facts about Christ's life and redemptive work, the more assured one can be of fidelity to gospel doctrine. In this view "the task of the historian is

---

[182]Johnson, *The Origins of Demythologizing*, 49.

[183]Evang, *Rudolf Bultmann in seiner Frühzeit*, 285.

[184]Harrisville and Sundberg, *The Bible in Modern Culture*, 234f.

[185]Klein, *ZTK* 94/2 (1997) 194; cf. Grässer, *ZTK* 91/3 (1994) 284; Harrisville and Sundberg, *The Bible in Modern Culture*, 235, 245f.

... to prove that God cannot be proved!"[186] The exclamation point is well advised, since it underscores the difference between New Testament writers who call attention to historical phenomena, not to "prove God" but to mediate saving knowledge of him, and Bultmann, who sees his mission as undermining confidence in precisely those phenomena. Perhaps Bultmann is right in this. But his warrant needs to be seen as a function of the philosophy he brings to his exegetical discussions, not the result of historical inquiry in the normal sense—and certainly not the result of the influence of Heidegger, Barthian theological concern, or Luther. Appeals to Luther here are particularly unconvincing, since like most Christians until recent times he "gave assent to the evangelical histories"[187] while Bultmann affirmed little more than the fact of Jesus' earthly existence. It is inconceivable that Luther would have supported a system like Bultmann's which resulted in flat denial of the resurrection of Jesus from the dead. It is curious that a system offering so little assurance of what did happen declares certainty regarding what did not.

To pursue any farther neo-Kantianism's effects on Bultmann historical and theological work would raise issues that we could not hope to surmount in this study. As a philosophical outlook it "assumed pretty well as many shapes as it had representatives."[188] Even if we left aside other variations of neo-Kantian philosophy and focused only on Marburg neo-Kantianism, we would be faced with writings "difficult and stratospherically abstract."[189] When Ernst Cassirer, "whose work was a summa of Marburg scholarship," studied Kant in Berlin under Georg Simmel in 1894, Simmel advised: "Undoubtedly the best books on Kant are written by Hermann Cohen, but I must confess that I do not understand them."[190] Cohen (1842-1918) is the philosopher who, along with Paul Natorp (1854-1924), exerted considerable influence on Bultmann.[191] It is unnecessary here to come to detailed understand-

---

[186]Harrisville and Sundberg, *The Bible in Modern Culture*, 235.

[187]*Ibid*. 232.

[188]F. Copleston, *A History of Philosophy*, vol. 7, part II, 1965, 134f.

[189]Willey, *Back to Kant*, 104.

[190]*Ibid*. 171f.

[191]Johnson, *The Origins of Demythologizing*, shows this via circumstantial evidence. Definitive documentation is provided by a personal letter from Bultmann to Duncan, reproduced in the latter's "Dr Rudolf Bultmann's Epistemology," Appendix A (accessible in the Cambridge University library). Bultmann writes: "Who were my philosophy teachers? When I began my studies in Tübingen in 1903, I read Kant's writings, and when I continued my studies in Marburg in 1906, I came under the influence of Cohen a.[nd] Natorp, that is, under the influence of neo-Kantianism.

ing of the labyrinthine doctrines of Cohen and Natorp. We can rather move to a summary statement regarding implications of Bultmann's prescriptive epistemology for his *Theologie des Neuen Testaments* with its epochal significance for the discipline.

3. Epistemology and method in New Testament theology

It is no longer seriously debatable whether Bultmann in the end seeks primarily to interpret the historical sources in their own contexts, or whether he rather absolutizes a particular philosophy and then strains the New Testament material through this interpretative grid. It is of course possible that Bultmann's interpretative grid is the paragon of truth which he evidently felt it was. What must be questioned is the cogency of Bultmann's interpretation of the New Testament within this framework. Do the data actually lend themselves to the treatment to which Bultmann's ostensibly historical method systematically subjects them? Not a few scholars have felt compelled to answer in the negative.

True, Bultmann argues that he never sought to lead his readers "to an examination of history," but rather "to a highly personal encounter with history."[192] But due largely to philosophy's decisive influence on Bultmann, we are never quite sure that it is *history* he is leading us to have an encounter with. His epistemological starting point does not sufficiently guard against "the danger that the text will be allowed to say precisely what the modern exegete or theologian wishes."[193] In the end there may be a considerable (and discomfiting) similarity between Bultmann's *Theologie*, on the one hand, and Cohen's *Die Religion der Vernunft aus den Quellen des Judentums* (The Religion of Reason from the Sources of Judaism), in which Cohen clearly sets out systematically to explicate the ancient literary sources in the light of the prior philosophical understanding he brings to them.[194]

It is justified to conclude, then, that Bultmann's *Theologie des Neuen Testaments*, thanks especially to its indebtedness to neo-Kantianism, stands squarely in the heritage of Baur[195] and Wrede. For all three, an

---

Later I became acquainted with phenomenology, and when I met Martin Heidegger in Marburg, about 1924, I was decisively influenced by him." On Cohen see William Kluback, *Hermann Cohen: The Challenge of a Religion of Reason*, 1984.

[192] Bultmann, *Jesus*, 10.

[193] Stanton, *ExpT* 90 (1978-79) 327.

[194] Cohen, *Die Religion der Vernunft aus den Quellen des Judentums*, 1919; see especially 1-12.

[195] As history (in a non-Bultmannian sense) would have it, there is actually a direct causal link of sorts between the Kantian thought of the Tübingen school (cf. Baur) and

epistemological starting point seriously restricts the capacity to take seriously those aspects of the New Testament which do not conform to demands made by their respective philosophical commitments. All three risk obscuring an understanding of the New Testament texts by championing modern understandings of understanding. In Bultmann's case particularly, an amalgam of currently accepted insights from various disciplines, especially Marburg neo-Kantian philosophy, is to a large extent systematically read back into those New Testament statements or sections which can, with some coaxing, bear the weight of such heavy demands. Most of the New Testament, of course, falls short or must be radically reinterpreted.

For the sake of comparison with Albertz and Goppelt, we conclude that Bultmann favors the second of the following options: (1) making the starting point and ultimately arbiter for New Testament theology what the texts say, read as much as possible in their historical setting, inevitably and admittedly as seen by a contemporary, yet sympathetic, interpretative eye; and (2) making the starting point and ultimately arbiter for New Testament theology (a reification of) modern thought, so that the New Testament texts are read only after, and strictly in the light of, philosophical pre-determination of what their statements may be taken to signify. It will be seen that modern salvation historical proponents who interact with Bultmann favor the former option. This is to a large extent what separates them from Bultmann and the "critical orthodox" trajectory which views their outlook as a fallacy.

Bultmann's handling of history

In Chapters 3 and 5 above, we noted that Bultmann's approach constitutes a radical rejection of salvation history in any traditional sense. In preceding sections just above we have called attention to peculiarities in Bultmann's historical method. These arise from philosophical commitments analogous to those found in Baur and Wrede. It has been

that of the Marburg school which in time influenced Bultmann. The philosopher (also theologian) E. Zeller (1814-1908), Baur's pupil and later son-in-law, came to teach at Marburg in 1849, remaining there for some thirteen years. This was time enough for him "to spread the new Kantian gospel and prepare the way for [F.A.] Lange and Cohen" (Willey, *Back to Kant*, 107). It was Lange (1828-1875), along with Zeller one of the early neo-Kantians, who was instrumental in Cohen's being offered the chair of philosophy at Marburg in 1872. Baur and Zeller thereby play some small part in the fact that the young Bultmann would at Marburg "come under the influence," as Bultmann puts it, of Cohen (and Natorp).

argued that Bultmann's concept of history, including the celebrated "Historie-Geschichte" distinction,[196] comes from the Bible itself,[197] but this must been seen as an unlikely possibility. It more likely involves above all "a systematic theological rejection of salvation-historical frameworks as a basis for contemporary theology."[198] This derives, we have seen, primarily from his epistemology.

A pair of brief observations will round out an assessment of Bultmann's "historical" method.

1. Eschatological not historical existence

Bultmann asks the pertinent question of the New Testament: "How will the eschatological-transcendental character of the community, when it comes up against ties to the Jewish people, gain acceptance without the ties to the salvation history being severed?"[199] He speaks in reply of a dialectical relationship between the two:

> The eschatological community is, therefore, not simply the historical descendant and heir of the empirical-historical Israel, but rather heir of the (so to speak) ideal Israel, the people of God. This is what the historical Israel was called to be, but what it in fact never actually was.[200]

Bultmann then goes on to concede, "This contrast to the historical Israel, however, this eschatological interruption of history, signifies not discontinuity, but rather precisely history's continuity."[201] Surprisingly, the implications of this concession, which implies some organic relation between the Old Testament salvation history and New Testament historical existence, are not developed and for his *Theologie des Neuen Testaments* as a whole have "no ramifications."[202] Romans 9–11 as the most historically plausible solution to Bultmann's original question, at least from the New Testament point of view, is not seriously considered,[203] or is radically reinterpreted along lines consistent with Bultmann's broader understanding of Paul.[204] The Old Testament, Bultmann admits, has a salvation historical understanding of God,

---

[196]Cf. Kantzenbach, *Programme*, 220ff.

[197]E.g. A. Malet, *The Thought of Rudolf Bultmann*, 1969, 61–80.

[198]Morgan, *NNTT*, 56. Morgan refers specifically to Käsemann, but Käsemann's position here is one of Bultmannian derivation.

[199]Bultmann, *Theologie des Neuen Testaments*, 66.

[200]*Ibid*. 99.

[201]*Ibid*.

[202]Kraus, *Biblische Theologie*, 191.

[203]For major literature on this problem see *ibid*. n. 106.

[204]Cf. e.g. Bultmann, *Theologie des Neuen Testaments*, 229.

God's acts, and human ability to perceive and receive God's historical self-disclosure, but the New Testament people of God are "a history transcending, eschatological community."[205] This effectively removes them from any horizontal temporal nexus as far as Bultmann is concerned.

2. Non-chronological history and dualistic historiography

In Bultmann's historical method, in keeping with Marburg neo-Kantian thought generally,[206] time in the sense of chronological sequence is not a determinative factor. It is, to be sure, highly important in grasping the objectifiable phenomena, the surface picture, of the New Testament world. But what can be objectified is if anything of negative value for explicating authentic New Testament religious experience. There cannot be, and can never have been, knowledge of God in anything like a cognitive sense.[207] Authentic believing self-understanding stands in a negative relation to all objectifications. This is presumably why Bultmann repeatedly so studiously guides Paul way from any sure knowledge of or interest in the historical Jesus. Bultmann's inherited, primarily epistemological dualism has definite

> ontological [= formal] implications for the understanding of any given ontic [= actual] phenomenon: man, world, or God. It is a dualism which may be extended into historiography: history requires objectifying reason which necessarily demythologizes the past as it integrates all objectifications into a unified causal nexus; history requires existentialist interpretation which inquires into the meaning of a given text for the individual subject.[208]

Bultmann's New Testament theology is consistently informed by a nuanced and sophisticated two-stage historiographical rationale. Decisive for our purposes is the consideration that, while Bultmann claims to be letting the historical sources speak freely at least with regard to the religious experience or self-realization they enshrine, "the concrete

---

[205] *Ibid.* 120; cf. 474.

[206] Cf. W. Werkmeister, "Cassirer's Advance Beyond Neo-Kantianism," *The Philosophy of Ernst Cassirer*, ed. P. Schlipp, 1940, 762.

[207] Cf. Bultmann, *ZTK* 81 (1984) 451 n. 4: "Knowledge of God exists only as existential knowledge. Theoretical knowledge does not comprehend God, but the idea of God." It will be recalled from previous discussion that existential knowledge, or knowledge of "being," is distinct from theoretical knowledge, or "reason," which generates knowledge relating to nature, history, or sensory data rather than to authentic being or existence.

[208] Johnson, *The Origins of Demythologizing*, 75.

possibilities of this self-realization are themselves determined by the *a priori* limits of reason itself."[209] Johnson clarifies this assertion:

> In the tradition of critical philosophy, the object of thought and the nature of thought itself are determined first; the interpretation of individuality and of religion accounts for the "left-overs" which could not find expression within the limits of reason. Natorp and Bultmann are clear and consistent in respecting the critical determination of the laws of consciousness as decisive for the limits and possibilities of religion and man's being as individuality.[210]

This two-stage rationale helps clarify certain otherwise puzzling features of Bultmann's *Theologie des Neuen Testaments*.

First, it goes far toward explaining why a historical fact can never be used to prove or support an article of authentic faith.[211] This is a viable theological assertion, but how far can it be substantiated from biblical sources?

Second, if the decisive interpretative criterion for Bultmann is a predetermined mode of religious self-understanding and not the witness of the texts in their unfolding historical milieux, one might expect to find a tendency to mix later data indiscriminately with earlier. For in this case it would not be a historically visible movement which is being discerned but rather an a-temporal immanent dynamic for which chronology is a mere formality. This possibility does in fact seem to materialize, as seen, for instance, in Bultmann's special pleading at the start of his crucial section on the Hellenistic church "prior to and concurrent with Paul":

> Here we seek to give only a picture, in the greatest breadth possible, of the Christianity that existed prior to as well as alongside of Paul. We will also, however, consider the post-Pauline era when there is need to show theological motives. To be sure, these motives may not be attested in the sources until later (that could be purely accidental); indeed, they perhaps did not become effective until later. But they were inherent in the situation—the entry of Christianity into the Hellenistic world and the problematic that resulted from that entry.[212]

Here Bultmann clearly leaves the door open to mixing data of later times with earlier. This same approach to history is evinced when Bultmann takes up the problem of the pre-Pauline and Pauline church's relationship to Judaism and its attitude toward the Old Tes-

---

[209] *Ibid.* 77.
[210] *Ibid.* 78.
[211] Bultmann, *Theologie des Neuen Testaments*, 27; cf. 301f., 420.
[212] *Ibid.* 67.

tament.[213] Bultmann adduces an array of very late first-century (Barnabas, Clement) and even second-century (Ptolemy, Justin) evidence, noting that possible correct solutions to the problem extend

> far beyond Paul's era, and must do so. For it is clear that all of these possibilities were inherent in that historical situation. Where and how soon they were realized cannot be determined due to the paucity of the sources, and it is not only possible but also probable that later-attested ideas were being carried forward already prior to Paul and then during his own time.[214]

One would have thought that the dearth of sources might lead to a commensurately higher valuation of what Bultmann knows to be early and original—Paul's writings. But one repeatedly encounters a dubious and confusing transposition of documentary evidence over the normally definitive boundaries of decades and even centuries.

Cullmann points to this very problem in another manifestation. He observes how Bultmann treats negatively large portions of the New Testament (e.g. Luke-Acts) because they fail adequately to reflect awareness of authentic existence on which Bultmann places such a high premium. Cullmann objects on historical grounds to this negative treatment:

> The Bultmann school cannot, however, justify this exclusion on the grounds of the chronology of the authorship of the various writings, and in fact it does not attempt to do so. For precisely that writing which is seen as the star witness, so to speak, of the true essence of the kerygma, John's gospel, is deemed also in the Bultmann school to be late; in any case it is placed hardly earlier than Luke's gospel. Then it must, however, at least be asked, whether it. . . is not dubious, that the means of determining the essence of the New Testament message is such that entire books from the early Christian era in their full compass cannot be incorporated, or at best can be incorporated only negatively.[215]

Of course, if for admitted systematic or philosophical reasons Bultmann adopts his position, there may be no necessary objections. But the problematic of an approach to *history* within a New Testament theology which dismisses or radically reinterprets large portions of the available documentary evidence in this fashion is considerable.

Merk's conclusion is if anything understated: Bultmann's reconstruction is "interested only secondarily in the mooring of theology in

---

[213] *Ibid.* 109-123.
[214] *Ibid.* 111.
[215] Cullmann, *Heil als Geschichte*, 5.

the history of early Christianity."[216] It is against the backdrop of such tendencies in Bultmann's *Theologie des Neuen Testaments* that the salvation historical presentations of Albertz and Cullmann are best understood.

Martin Albertz (1882-1956) and New Testament theology

1. Location in the discipline
Martin Albertz's two-volume, four-part, 1475-page treatment of the New Testament[217] seems to date to have enjoyed little if any extended analysis. M. Strege probed Albertz's eschatology,[218] and E. Fascher contributed a perceptive critical review.[219] He criticized Albertz at points, but his final words run: "All of this cannot prevent us from testifying that this work contains a wealth of provocative suggestions for further research. One can only call upon the younger generation to interact with Albertz thoroughly."[220]

Students of New Testament theology did not take up Fascher's suggestion, probably because Albertz's contemporaries were visibly piqued by his prophetic declaration that New Testament theology as the classic Gabler-initiated discipline had run aground.[221] We have already summarized this counterinsurgent critique earlier in the chapter. Albertz was apparently the first[222] to call attention to the developing crisis

---

[216]Merk, *Biblische Theologie des Neuen Testaments in ihrer Anfangszeit*, 256.

[217]See p. 263 n. 2 above.

[218]Strege, "Das Eschatologische als gestaltende Kraft in der Theologie: A. Schweitzer und M. Albertz," 1955 (not accessible to me).

[219]Fascher, "Eine Neuordnung der neutestamentlichen Fachdisziplin?" *TLZ* 83 (1958) 610-618. Also worthwhile is the review of B. Brinkmann in *Scholastik* 33 (1958) 267-272; cf. G. Harder, "Martin Albertz' Beitrag zur neutestamentlichen Einleitungswissenschaft," in *Vom Herrengeheimnis der Wahrheit*, ed. K. Scharf, 1962, 179-195.

[220]Fascher, *TLZ* 83 (1958) 618. One of the few to do this was Harder (previous note).

[221]See here especially Albertz, "Die Krisis der sogenannten neutestamentlichen Theologie," *Zeichen der Zeit* 8 (1954) 370-376; *idem*, "Kerygma und Theologie im Neuen Testament," *ZNW* 46 (1955) 267f.

[222]One should also mention Albertz's early use of form criticism, which merits his addition to the usually-cited triumvirate of Dibelius-Schmidt-Bultmann. Albertz, too, who studied under Gunkel, placed the question from early on: "What does the form critical manner of placing questions," which was in Albertz's student days just coming into full flower in Old Testament studies, "mean for New Testament research?" (*Die Botschaft des Neuen Testaments* I/1, 10-12). Albertz's own earliest answer was *Die synoptischen Streitgespräche*, 1921.

in New Testament theology which Childs and others would later chronicle at length. Albertz's forthrightness, however, may have cost his magnum opus the attention which Fascher said it deserved. What fellow scholars either faintly praised, criticized, or simply ignored was not been taken seriously by the next generation. If twenty five years Hasel could confirm Albertz's allegation that New Testament theology was and had long been in crisis,[223] in 1954 German New Testament scholars were in no mood to put up with Albertz's impugning of both Bultmann and New Testament theology in its historical development. This is seen in W. Eltester's biting comments[224] as well as in Kümmel's review.[225]

Representative effects of this disparagement in subsequent years are seen in (1) Kraus's disposal of Albertz on the strength of a line borrowed from Bultmann;[226] (2) Merk's impatient dismissal of Albertz—relying loyally on Fascher, Kümmel, Bultmann, and Kraus—on unsubstantiated grounds;[227] and (3) Hasel's simplistic characterization of Albertz's entire two volumes which leaves one doubting that he read them.[228] One may well be mystified how, then, R.McL. Wilson could ever have approvingly concluded, with reference to volume II/2 of Albertz's work: "The book may be 'unorthodox' in some ways; but it may also herald the beginning of a new era in which the message of the New Testament will be restored to its rightful place."[229]

---

[223]Hasel, *New Testament Theology*, 9, begins: "New Testament theology today is undeniably in crisis."

[224]Eltester, "Notizen," *ZNW* 45 (1953-54) 276f.

[225]Kümmel, review of Albertz, *Die Botschaft des Neuen Testaments*, I/1 and I/2, *TZ* 10 (1954) 55-60. As a review of only one of two volumes of Albertz's entire New Testament theology, Kümmel's comments have limited validity as a judgment on Albertz's whole presentation. Kümmel complains that Albertz's handling of the New Testament ought not be placed in the hands of students, because a student through reading Albertz's treatment "cannot gain the insight which is indispensable to a theologian into the uncertainty of the historical pains we necessarily take as we seek to grasp the rise and the understanding of the apostolic witness" (60). This only points up the contrast between Albertz and most of his colleagues: he believes that the "message" is primary, accessible, and not to be subordinated prematurely to critical considerations; Kümmel and others tend to equate knowledge of the "message" with expertise in the theories of New Testament criticism.

[226]Kraus, *Biblische Theologie*, 188 n. 87.

[227]Merk, *Biblische Theologie des Neuen Testaments in ihrer Anfangszeit*, 2; 262 n. 167.

[228]Hasel, *New Testament Theology*, 67-69. On the other hand, it is clear that he has read Fascher's review (*TLZ* 83 [1958] 610-618).

[229]R. McL. Wilson, *SJT* 11 (1958) 209.

Our task here, then, is to take a fresh look at Albertz, aware of but not subservient to received opinion about him. We will characterize his general approach to New Testament theology, comment on his epistemology, and comment on the view of history which informs his work. Although it seems that to date no one has called attention to Albertz's handling of the New Testament as a salvation historical one, it will become evident as we proceed that he belongs squarely within this tradition of New Testament theological inquiry.

2. Conception of New Testament theology
Focus on the message

Albertz's general intention is almost exactly opposite to Bultmann's. He calls New Testament theology, seen in its historical development in Germany, back to the historical moorings or reality of its subject matter. Both parts of his New Testament theology restrict themselves "basically to a presentation of the historical state of affairs and its foundation in the sources."[230] New Testament theology will not recover from its crisis so long as it "is exploited, from the outside, on the basis of an autonomous theology with close ties to an autonomous world-view, out of deference to the respective culturally dominant world view."[231] Like the Christian faith itself, New Testament theology has to do ultimately with Jesus, and the discipline has not done justice to its subject, inasmuch as Jesus, in contrast to much New Testament theology,

> directs our attention not to the contingent philosophical fragments which nourished the culture of his time, not to the nuanced distinctions between those who bore testimony to his gospel, not to the history of religion and psychology of religion and all that goes with it, but rather to the gospel, whose object he himself is.[232]

This gospel comes to us in the New Testament as "the message" (*die Botschaft*) which centers on Jesus. It is this multi-textured but unified message in its temporal setting which Albertz seeks to explicate.

Key presuppositions

Four presuppositions are axiomatic in Albertz's presentation of this message. The first concerns what he calls "the historical setting of the

---

[230] Albertz, *Die Botschaft des Neuen Testaments* II/2, 11. Cf. the similarity with Schlatter, *Theologie der Apostel*, 3.

[231] *Zeichen der Zeit* 8 (1954) 374f.

[232] *Ibid.* 375.

message."[233] Albertz portrays the interrelationships between "the message" and world history, the history of religion setting in general, and first century Judaism in particular. He feels that this historical milieu is crucial to an understanding of the New Testament message, but that we must realize that the New Testament writings convey a message which challenges and stands in a certain tension with, if not contradiction to, its historical environs. That is, the New Testament claims to mediate a call to or even judgment of the world around it far more than it admits of reduction to a naturalistically explicable product of its environment. Historical background understood as phenomena in a causal nexus provides the obvious and indispensable preparation for this message but is not itself the message's primary content. This anchors Albertz's analysis of the New Testament squarely in New Testament history, even if it is a history more reminiscent of Eusebius than of Baur, Wrede, or Bultmann.

The second presupposition concerns "the bearers of the message."[234] They, like their Old Testament counterparts, execute their task as and "because God entrusted them with the message."[235] The bearers are John the Baptist (who virtually drops out of Bultmann's presentation), Jesus of Nazareth, and the church. In each of these three cases Albertz discusses the "commission" of the message-bearers, the distinctive features of their message, and finally their "fate." Especially in this last category, one finds observations, at times reminiscent of Bonhoeffer, of noteworthy quality, insight, and power which are not common in a modern New Testament theology.

The third presupposition concerns "the act of God which establishes the message."[236] This is not as for Bultmann an act to be understood solely in terms of individual decision and believing self-understanding. It involves that, but it is more than that. "There is something, therefore, that has happened, God has done something, and this message is now proclaimed."[237] The message is "nothing other than the most reliable possible report of that which has taken place, of the great acts of God."[238] Albertz accepts the veracity of the New Testament resur-

---

[233] *Die Botschaft des Neuen Testaments* II/1, 22-64.

[234] *Ibid.* 64-96.

[235] *Ibid.* 64.

[236] *Ibid.* 96-133.

[237] *Ibid.* 96.

[238] *Ibid.* Is Albertz then somehow a rationalist himself, reducing "the message" to sheer factual data? Hardly: see *Die Botschaft des Neuen Testaments* I/1, 31: "We are dealing here not simply with a historical report which would simply need to be faithfully passed on ..., but rather with the unveiling of the secret of the Christ (Col 1:25-

rection reports, though he does at the same time concede that "resurrection" is "spiritual, eschatological reality."[239]

In contrast to Bultmann, then, Albertz views the New Testament message as being built around (1) Jesus' bodily resurrection; (2) the identity of Jesus "with the Lord" ("The resurrected one is the historical one";[240] "The historical one is the pre-existent one"[241]); and (3) the identity of Jesus "with the biblical Messiah."[242] In connection with (3), Albertz delineates his own salvation historical understanding of the New Testament, on which we will elaborate below. Important for now is that Albertz's New Testament theology is rooted in the conviction that the New Testament witness is inexplicable without reference to transcendent presence and material involvement in the historical process. The New Testament witnesses, too, lived in a world which for many reasons rejected their testimony about Jesus, but they continued to proclaim what they had seen and heard, testifying as well to the Christ's ongoing powerful reality among them. A New Testament theology must be faithful to this conviction of the New Testament writers. "If the witnesses have nothing to attest, they are not witnesses."[243]

The fourth presupposition concerns the "unity and diversity of the message."[244] Albertz finds substantial unity in the sources and feels that most of the diversity of the New Testament can be explained by the different languages in which the message first came to expression, the varying perceptions of the hearers, and the different "commission" and giftedness of the respective New Testament messengers or authors. In general, if one is to attain a proper overall grasp of the variegated New Testament witness, "the decisive reference point" is not that "of New Testament theology of the nineteenth and twentieth centuries."[245] We are not dealing with personalities vying for recognition, or with "the individualized expression of the gospel" by a Peter or Paul.[246] "We are dealing with an objective state of affairs, not with subjective individu-

---

29), with the understanding of the biblical witness, gained from the knowledge of the resurrection, that Jesus is the Christ (Acts 17:11)."

[239] *Ibid.* II/1, 99.
[240] *Ibid.* 117ff.
[241] *Ibid.* 121ff.
[242] *Ibid.* 124ff.
[243] *Ibid.* 96.
[244] *Ibid.* 133-154.
[245] *Ibid.* 147.
[246] *Ibid.*

alistic attempts at interpretation."[247] The "message" may admittedly be proclaimed as gospel in the sense of "the missionary preaching which founded churches"; it may take the form of apocalypse, "especially the revelation of the eschatological secrets of God"; it may take the form of teaching.[248] Albertz does not, then, see monolithic uniformity in the New Testament's presentation of the message. Yet he does conclude that all twenty seven New Testament books can be subsumed under the general heading of the authentic message about Jesus Christ: "Christ remains, also when it comes to the written recorded message, the source, content, and goal of the gospel."[249]

Explicating the message: contra Bultmann

For Bultmann New Testament theology "consists in the unfolding of the ideas in which the Christian faith assures itself of its object, its basis, and its consequences."[250] But there was no "Christian faith" until the advent of the proclamation that set forth Jesus Christ as God's "eschatological salvific act."[251] This proclamation is grounded in early Christian self-understanding,[252] not in Jesus' teaching or preaching, and certainly not in any material "act of God." As a result, New Testament theology is understood as early Christian theologizing, and the monument to this activity is the kerygma as it shapes and is shaped by ongoing early church believing self-understanding and eschatological decision. The historical basis and core, if any, of the kerygma is largely irrelevant, since according to Bultmann those parts of the New Testament (portions of Paul and John) which have truly grasped authentic existence are indifferent to historical grounding, while those parts which do not really grasp authentic existence have fallen prey to an illegitimate striving for security. In an important sense, therefore, New Testament theology tends to become predominantly a descriptive analysis of the "that" (*Dass*) of the ideas of often unknown first and second century religionists. The content, or "what" (*Was*)—what Albertz terms the "historical state of affairs" (*historischer Tatbestand*)—to

---

[247] *Ibid.*

[248] *Ibid.* 148.

[249] *Ibid.* I/1, 298.

[250] Bultmann, *Theologie des Neuen Testaments*, 1f.

[251] *Ibid.*

[252] Cf. *ibid.* 27, where Bultmann clearly implies that the gospel writers imposed their faith on the Jesus-tradition to result in the picture of a messianic Jesus. Faith in Jesus is not grounded in Jesus' own person or historical claims or actions—nor can it be.

which the "that" (*Dass*) refers becomes notoriously vague or even falls out of consideration.

For Albertz, however, "the kerygma, which for Bultmann is merely the presupposition for the theologies of Paul and John, is the actual subject with which the new discipline is concerned."[253] By "new discipline" Albertz refers to the post-Bultmannian New Testament theology which he hoped to see emerge. If Bultmann gives a sophisticated explication of authentic believing self-understanding in neo-Kantian/existentialist terms, Albertz gives a lengthy and complexly organized explication of the same Christian thought, but on a different premise—namely, that the ostensible historical grounding (for Bultmann largely mythical or simply "projected back") of the theological or religious statements of the New Testament is essential to the integrity of those statements. This justifies the attempt to set forth the New Testament data in a manner consistent with what the New Testament writers themselves were convinced of: that God was incarnate in Jesus; that Jesus as Christ is the savior of which the Old Testament testifies;[254] and that the New Testament writings preserve and continue a reflected, authentic recollection of Jesus, whose presence is still real and effectual.

Albertz is concerned, then, that the discipline of New Testament theology set forth the New Testament message understood, not as cognitively groundless believing self-understanding, but as convinced, believing, and ongoing existential[255] response to the acts and words[256] of God whose focal point is Jesus Christ.[257] That is what the New Testament writings are concerned with. That is what gave rise to them, the assurance which undergirds and motivates them. That is their underlying if not overt motif. If the writings which are the object of New Testament theology's scrutiny are thus content-centered, concerned so to speak also with matters of fact or cognitive knowledge and not merely of faith or relational apprehension, how can modern New Testament theology rightly explicate the writings while systematically stripping them of their own fundamental concern? Must this

---

[253] Albertz, *Zeichen der Zeit* 8 (1954) 375.

[254] Cf. Albertz, *Die Botschaft des Neuen Testaments* II/1, 124ff.; II/2, 266.

[255] Cf. especially *ibid.* II/1, 237-244; also 77.

[256] Albertz takes up to some extent the apparent conviction of ancient Jews and Christians that what their Scripture says, God says—a position clearly unacceptable in New Testament criticism at least since Semler. Cf. *ibid.* 16-44.

[257] Cf. *Die Botschaft des Neuen Testaments* I/1, 15: "In terms of content the message is right from the start clearly witness to Christ. Jesus Christ is the originator, the content, and the goal of this mesage."

not result in a distorted presentation of their thought? Albertz thinks so, and his work may be seen as an attempt to redress what he sees as an imbalance in Bultmann's approach. The New Testament message in its fact-faithfulness, not mere ideas or even eschatologically-appraised resolve stripped of all "inauthentic" accretions, forms the core of modern New Testament theology as Albertz wants to see it rebuilt.

Alternative program

Yet Albertz's program is not merely anti-Bultmannian. It is somewhat original in its specific positive thrust. Albertz argues that "the message" of the New Testament writers is the primary impetus and accordingly the primary content of their work; "the theology" admittedly is the communicative vehicle of the message but is secondary to it.

This theology arises immediately along with the proclamation, because the acts of God, which comprise the basis of the proclamation, elicit, right from the start, the doubt of rational humans. These acts form the stone of stumbling for the pious person; indeed, they comprise a distinct temptation for the Christ and his church. These acts ultimately in the third century elicit the all-out assault of the philological and philosophical science of Porphyry.[258]

Albertz's suggestion is that the New Testament itself should be viewed as New Testament theology, not merely the raw material of something patently modern, much different, but going by the same name. That is, the New Testament as it stands already consists largely "in anti-criticism against criticism."[259] After all, it is replete with "proof in the form of testimony, proof based on [the Old Testament] Scripture, proof from the Spirit and from manifestations of power, [and] historical proof," even at points attempting to bolster its claims by appeal to human reason.[260] It comprises, therefore, a sort of critical conceptualization and presentation of the New Testament message viewed in contrast to the myriad factors and forces which would and did militate against the message in the first century.[261] It does not readily admit of further reduction or of radical reinterpretation in the way that New Testament theology in the tradition of Baur–Wrede–Bultmann has consistently attempted.

---

[258]Albertz, *ZNW* 46 (1955) 268.

[259]Cf. especially *Die Botschaft des Neuen Testaments* II/2, 252-272.

[260]*Ibid.*

[261]Cf. *ibid.* I/2, 304: "The apostolic canon, as it is now available to us, is in fact a defense of the church" from the falsification "of the genuine message of Jesus and of Paul."

What Albertz calls "the original Christian theology" began and remained, in the face of various pressures, firmly rooted in its "foundation in the message," in its conviction of "the reliability of God's word," and in the apprehension of "Jesus Christ as the truth."[262] This "original Christian theology" "sees its justification for criticizing in the radical criticism leveled by Jesus Christ and his spirit; it sees its freedom to think creatively in the growing knowledge of the Holy Spirit."[263] Albertz's is indeed a move to return the testimony of the texts to the center of New Testament theology, as Wilson noted.[264]

Summary
Compared to Bultmann Albertz advocates a distinct approach to New Testament theology. Albertz wants to keep theological presentation in closer contact with historical or concrete reality; he reflects an openness to the transcendent which makes his New Testament interpretation look much different from Bultmann's; he tries to let the words and events preserved in the New Testament speak in the current skeptical setting with the piquancy which they evidently carried in their original unfriendly environment. It is not a philosophical truth behind the texts but the christocentric message reflected and preserved in the New Testament texts which New Testament theology ought to expound. Finally, Albertz does not give the impression that his presentation of the New Testament, or a rationale behind it, is the definitive one. Unlike Bultmann his approach does not imply a methodological exclusiveness.

In significant respects Albertz's distinctives vis-à-vis Bultmann link him with Hofmann and Schlatter seen in contrast to Baur and Wrede. It remains now to touch on Albertz's epistemology before exploring more specifically the sense in which his work constitutes a salvation historical outlook.

2. Epistemology
We suggested above that Bultmann, largely for epistemological reasons, makes modern thought the starting point for New Testament theology. Proper understanding of the New Testament is predetermined by philosophical considerations.

Albertz has much to say about New Testament attitudes regarding "knowledge" (*Erkenntnis*). A ground level assertion is that "the mental

---

[262]Albertz, *ZNW* 46 (1955) 268.
[263]*Ibid.*
[264]Wilson, *SJT* 11 (1958) 209.

work which the New Testament sets forth cannot at all be comprehended as a philosophical process of thought."[265] The New Testament,
like the Bible as a whole, stands "irreconcilably opposed to all learning
which takes pride in itself. Because such learning is based on its own
reflection, it strives against the wisdom of God."[266] For Albertz there is
a qualitative distinction between the knowledge which man himself
devises, on the one hand, and that which comes from God, on the
other. This distinction is reminiscent of Barth, but there is no obvious
indication that Albertz relied on Barth for it.[267] Albertz's handling of
the New Testament is much different from Bultmann's, not least due
to his view of (1) that which the New Testament sets forth, and (2)
how it is apprehended.

What is known—the object of knowing

The New Testament conveys a message which "leads back to the God
who does miracles and lets his messengers experience and proclaim
them."[268] Accordingly, "the criterion of what is humanly possible and
probable is here repeatedly surpassed, indeed shattered."[269] The bases of
Albertz's entire handling of the New Testament are the historical-
theological presuppositions "on the basis of scripture" (*von der Schrift
aus*) which emphasize that God can impart and has in various times
and by various means imparted (or revealed) accurate knowledge of
himself to humans.[270] Scripture is a compendium of this knowledge
and reliable guide to the historical phenomena in connection with
which the knowledge arose.

Albertz sees implicit in the New Testament message a consistent
theme, namely that "the divine wisdom shatters the wisdom of
man."[271] The parables, e.g., "distance themselves immeasurably from
rational deliberation"; again and again Jesus' message is "that God,
contrary to expectations, is totally different than that which men in

---

[265] *Die Botschaft des Neuen Testaments* II/1, 16. Cf. II/2, 277.

[266] *Ibid*. I/2, 500. Cf. 140ff.

[267] Cf. *ibid.*, II/1, 12, where Albertz indicates that his pastoral work led him to some
of the same insights at the same time as "the pastor of Saferswil" (Barth), "without
either of his knowing of the other." Both were active later in the Confessing Church,
but Albertz's presence in Germany eventuated in a lengthy imprisonment from which
Barth's location in Basle spared him.

[268] *Ibid*. 13.

[269] *Ibid*.

[270] *Ibid*. 16–44.

[271] *Ibid*. 86. Cf. II/1, 115.

their cleverness imagine."[272] Jesus' teaching and proclamation comprise "the overturning of [merely folk, human, or conventional] wisdom."[273] Albertz concludes: "Intrinsic [to grasping the New Testament message] is that all of Jesus' wisdom sayings seek to be understood as revelation and speech of a divine wisdom which transcends and inverts human wisdom."[274] Paul in Romans 1 sees that a "gospel of self-affirmation" exists "against the gospel of self-denial," resulting in "reason bereft of God." Man "is given over to his degenerate reason."[275]

Albertz takes such observations from Jesus and Paul and applies them to reason in the modern age. The result is that, while Bultmann tends to interpret material in such a way as to accommodate it to a set modern viewpoint, Albertz thinks that modern reason (or its self-assurance), like its ancient forerunner, must in important respects be shattered before the New Testament message can really be apprehended.

The reason for this is surely to be found in Albertz's view of just what sort of knowledge the New Testament message imparts, a knowledge which at various points transcends or conflicts with much human thought.[276] For Albertz as for the writer of Hebrews, "the self-glorification of reason"[277] is definitively checked by Jesus Christ[278] and the New Testament message. God in his glory "admits of no rationalization, ethicization, and humanization."[279] This God is most clearly apprehended, not by means of autonomous human reason's constructs,

---

[272] *Ibid.* I/1, 94.

[273] *Ibid.* 82–102.

[274] *Ibid.* 102.

[275] *Ibid.*

[276] Cf. *ibid.* I/2, 99: "It pleased God to bring about an admittedly very peculiar way of salvation." Cf. *ibid.* 124; II/1, 112ff.

[277] *Ibid.* I/2, 418. Albertz speaks here of the general tone of Hebrews seen in contrast to that of 4 Maccabees, in which the question is treated "whether pious reason is master of the passions." Fourth Maccabees' answer is positive. Hebrews in contrast indicates that "the self-glorification of reason is taken captive under the worship of the heavenly Christ." True knowledge, this implies, is not that which commends itself to human philosophy as such, but that which is rooted in the Christologically oriented truth of Scripture.

[278] Cf. Albertz's remarks on John (*ibid.* II/1. 187, whose presentation makes clear "that this Christ is God, that in an absolute sense all salvation and knowledge have their existence in him. All this salvation and knowledge are linked to him and transmitted now through him. He is, therefore, ever more than what can be expressed about him." Contrary to Bultmann, however, he is not less.

[279] *Ibid.* II/2, 245.

but by means of God's own self-disclosure through the Scriptural message and the one who both epitomizes and fulfills it,[280] Jesus Christ.

How it is known—the process of knowing
From a Bultmannian perspective Albertz's approach is invalid, for it
implies that knowledge of God which is at least partially cognitive is
possible. We have already seen that much post-Kantian philosophy
rules this out. Albertz (and apparently much of the New Testament)
has erroneously construed God in such a way that he is at man's disposal. That is, Albertz would have salvation come in close conjunction
with accurate cognitive (in addition to relational) knowledge, which
for Bultmann is tantamount to salvation by works.

Albertz, however, citing 1 Corinthians 15, notes that "it was not
the achievement of the disciples and their imagination that they saw
the Lord, but rather the work of God." That is, "God caused Jesus,
after death and burial, to be seen by the first witnesses as the resurrected one." Both 1 Corinthians and the broader New Testament
testimony on this point exclude "the initiative of man"; "the one who
is manifested, or who manifests himself, is not at man's disposal."[281] For
Bultmann, who views reports of the acts of God as myth to be de-
coded, faith in these acts is disastrous, because "knowledge" of them is
an illicit objectification. It is ultimately mental fabrication of grounds
for belief which authentic faith does not need and must not cling to.
Valid faith is authentic decision in the face of the unknown, unknowable, and even untrue (e.g. "believing" affirmation that Jesus Christ is
risen, when Jesus the man remains quite dead).

Albertz, however, here resembling Hofmann and Schlatter, finds the
historical data of the New Testament quite inexplicable apart from
literal acts of God.[282] Thus, from this perspective, he is not fabricating a
conceptual apparatus by which persons many somehow save themselves through generating redemptive truth. He is rather availing
himself of the divinely-given means by which knowledge of and devo-
tion to God through Jesus Christ are possible on a New Testament
model: affirmation (including cognitive) of and personal commitment
to the Jesus whom God by literal acts has shown to be the divine son
and savior.

Albertz regards the New Testament message as presenting knowledge of God (which for Albertz includes both cognition, and

---

[280] *Ibid.* II/1, 75.
[281] Albertz, *Die Botschaft des Neuen Testaments* II/1, 101.
[282] E.g. *ibid.* 88; I/2, 484.

existential response, or obedience, to what and who is cognized) in a three-fold light. (1) God initiates it and is the ground for it; such knowledge "originates in God."[283] (2) God's spirit, too, is active in revealing God's wisdom, a wisdom which defies human reason[284]: "This wisdom is eschatological, *heilsgeschichtlich*, originating in the cross, therefore not dialectical. It is not, therefore, attainable by human achievement, but rather only by the [Holy] Spirit."[285] (3) Finally, Jesus Christ "is the light of the world and the only basis of knowledge for the knowledge of God."[286] Thus God conceived in trinitarian terms can and does reveal himself to those wishing to receive him—albeit on his terms. Any subject-object distance is overcome by virtue of the fact that knowledge of God is not seen as man's grasp of inanimate object: the knowing subject (man) is simultaneously apprehended by him who is being known (God).[287]

From the human point of view, the New Testament message is known in an important sense by means of "a complete rethinking."[288] Central to the message is the cross—but the cross means (1) "rejection rather than election," (2) "disgrace instead of praise before God and man," and (3) "desertion by God and related to it abandonment to the juridical wrath of God itself."[289] It is nevertheless this cross through which comes the call to discipleship, which "calls to decision, that one may himself also learn to bear the cross."[290] The New Testament message is apprehended only in conjunction with "a total rethinking in the sense that until now all of one's life was egocentrically oriented and that now all of life must be oriented theocentrically and christocentrically."[291] For Albertz as for Bultmann, existential involvement or decision plays a decisive role. The difference is that cognitive knowledge or objectification for Bultmann has a negative function in relation to faith. What is known can have no part of what is believed. For Albertz the two are combined; a certain (if never complete)

---

[283] *Ibid.* I/2, 126.

[284] Cf. *ibid.* II/2, 52, 282f.; cf. 96: "The aphoristic wisdom of the Old Testament is life-wisdom. The lament of Job is suffering-wisdom. The wisdom of the New Testament is death-wisdom. This death-wisdom has its deepest basis in the foolishness of the cross ..."

[285] *Ibid.* I/2, 127. Cf. I/1, 301.

[286] *Ibid.* I/2, 397.

[287] *Ibid.* II/2, 55, 87, 144, 151, 270. Cf. Chapter 1 above on Hofmann.

[288] *Ibid.* II/1, 277.

[289] *Ibid.*

[290] *Ibid.*

[291] *Ibid.*

apprehension of facts or truth relating to God and his acts attends personal relationship to him.

Conclusion

Epistemologically speaking Albertz's formal starting point is not modern thought as such but the New Testament witness. He holds that God has acted and spoken in such a way that persons have perceived it. He argues this on grounds that go beyond, but are based on, historical considerations, not primarily philosophical ones. The New Testament is not an infallible chronicle from heaven; nevertheless, "God's word becomes accessible via human speech."[292] And still more fundamental: "God's word is written down, and Scripture serves to actualize it."[293]

The upshot is that Albertz's largely implicit theory of both the possible content of knowledge and the mode of knowing is to a large extent based on the historically plausible witness of the New Testament texts. Whereas Bultmann's epistemology encourages a presentation of the New Testament material which will bring it into line with modern knowledge and a particular theory of that knowledge, Albertz challenges or even rejects modern knowledge as such, though it would be mistaken to see only a negative relationship between the New Testament message and human understanding. This, he claims, is how the New Testament message encountered its ancient conceptual milieu, and this is how it must be set forth now if a historically faithful representation of ancient knowledge and faith is the goal.

3. Approach to history
Salvation historical outlook

In a sense Albertz's handling of the New Testament from the start "deals, in Leopold Ranke's sense, with a segment of world history, with an elucidation of the most significant events of the reign of the Roman Caesars."[294] Yet the New Testament material, which was not actually "created" by the church but rather collected, often under eyewitness control, and faithfully passed on,[295] contained much which was inherently offensive to persons of its day. Had the proclamation

---

[292] *Ibid.* I/1, 33.

[293] *Ibid.* 38. Albertz refers here to the Old Testament but the same holds true of his understanding of the New (cf. *ibid.* 44), though he concedes "the unwritten character of the early gospel" (*ibid.* 40f.).

[294] *Ibid.* 14. Cf. II/1, 11, 127.

[295] *Ibid.* I/1, 297f.

come as myth in the sense of being only ostensibly historical, it would have been much more tolerable, as other religions of that syncretistic and pluralistic religious world were.[296] But the New Testament message comprises "a fundamental repudiation of myth and a clear anti-gnostic affirmation of history."[297] Thus "offensive" is an apt epithet for this message and its vehicle, "a history which is thoroughly offensive to human reason."[298] We see here something of Albertz's epistemology being reflected in his assessment of New Testament history. This history is played out as part of general history, yet in it God achieves his particular aims, often quite visibly. For example, while "the execution of Christ is an act in the general context of the history of religions," it nevertheless in the same context "signifies. . . the actual salvation historical turning point."[299]

This statement alerts us to Albertz's salvation historical perspective. New Testament history "is more than mere history" in the historicistic or positivistic sense of the term.[300] Albertz holds, not merely as an article of faith but as a matter of fact, that all history stands in a subordinate relation to the reality which gives rise to the New Testament message:

> The gospel begins before the creation of the world. It is established and determined by God and has its goal and termination only in eternity. It deals not only with history past but also, in the power of Jesus Christ's resurrection, with contemporary history ... The witness of the gospels terminates in the majestic past, present, and future encompassing "I am" of God's appearance in Christ.[301]

It is evident from this statement as well as from other features of his work already noted that Albertz's approach to history resembles that of Hofmann and Schlatter (neither of whom, however, Albertz ever cites). While Albertz's approach to New Testament theology seems until now not to have been recognized as a salvation historical one, it is surely within this heritage of New Testament theology that he is most accurately identified. We must now try to describe some ways in which Albertz's work admits of such identification.

---

[296] Cf. *ibid.* II/1, 22-45.
[297] *Ibid.* I/1, 298.
[298] *Ibid.*
[299] *Ibid.* II/2, 53.
[300] *Ibid.* I/1, 299.
[301] *Ibid.* 299f. Cf. II/1, 190.

Conception of salvation history

Neither the noun "Heilsgeschichte" nor the adjective "heilsgeschichtliche" are overly common in Albertz's four volumes on the New
Testament. In the *locus classicus* on salvation history in the entire 1475-
page treatment, he explains why. Referring to "Christ and the revelatory occurrence," Albertz states:

> I avoid the term *Heilsgeschichte*. *Heilsgeschichte* is certainly a salvific occur-
> rence, but not in the sense that it could somehow be fit into the frame of
> history as the nineteenth century thought it should be. We can only speak
> of *Heilsgeschichte* when we are aware that this is a figurative and imprecise
> term which encompasses pre-history and post-history at the same time. It
> begins, therefore, with the pre-existence of Christ and does not cease with
> the post-existence of Christ. It allows that even within the times accessible
> to (as it is termed) critical history, we are not dealing merely with "his-
> tory." After all, the gospel in all of the New Testament is accompanied by
> miracles, which do not accommodate themselves to the nineteenth century
> conception of history. If we, therefore, put it in the language of the nine-
> teenth century: "*Heilsgeschichte* always encompasses myth, too. Myth is the
> beginning, middle, and end of *Heilsgeschichte*." But in saying this I speak
> falsely. For the message [of the New Testament] and myth are mutually ex-
> cluding opposites ... If we regard "myth" with Hermann Gunkel as a
> history of the gods, then we can only say, the entire so-called *Heilsgeschichte*
> is myth, for it consistently deals with God—to be sure, not with gods, but
> still with God—and with God's dealings with gods and with men. From
> the point of view of the New Testament *Heilsgeschichte* actually deals with a
> victory by Christ over the powers hostile to God. That is the actual content
> of this peculiar *Heilsgeschichte*. It is, then, good if we entirely avoid this ex-
> pression and use a word which makes things to some extent clear:
> revelatory occurrence. It is evident that this occurrence enters into the his-
> tory which Ranke in his world history describes, but that it does so from
> start to finish in the form of revelation, which is therefore a force not acces-
> sible to critical historical investigation.[302]

Three observations are in order based on this statement and related
discussion above.

1. The New Testament does in fact point to a salvation history, Albertz implies, but not one which nineteenth century historiographical
premises and techniques can cope with or allow for. Albertz is close to
Schlatter in arguing that within history there are features inexplicable
by means of post-Enlightenment historical criticism. This is especially
the case in biblical history. Part and parcel of the gospel is the so-called

---

[302] *Ibid.* II/1, 127f.

miraculous, and the potential for coming to grips successfully with it exists only where the miraculous is not a priori rejected, as for instance in Bultmann or in "the nineteenth century conception of history" generally.

2. Albertz's remarks foreshadow more recent ones by Kraus: both see the limitations of the term salvation history, both avoid or qualify their use of it—yet both would answer no (though for different reasons) to Kraus' rhetorical question: Do the terminological problems related to the word mean "that the concept which salvation history denotes is invalidated?"[303] Albertz suggests the term "revelatory occurrence" as a replacement.

3. Albertz's statement above fits in with a related one in which, speaking of election, he terms history "only the realization" of the eternal intention, "the becoming visible of God's revelation which was theretofore invisible."[304] This compares closely with Hofmann's characterization of the kingdom of God. It seems fair to suggest that Albertz resembles Hofmann in that both understand salvation history, as it relates to New Testament theology, as the affected-by-the-transcendent historical course of events of which Scripture speaks. Or again, he bears comparison with Schlatter, as both seek to combine insights of formal criticism with the inescapable fact of transcendent involvement in history. Neither Albertz nor Schlatter was a biblical inerrantist, and neither excommunicated himself from the scholarly communities of his day. (Whether their communities tended to excommunicate them is another question.) Yet both felt that critical techniques ought to be the servants of the reality of the New Testament message, not its sovereign lord. To Albertz it is clear that the New Testament message shattered human paradigms of (purely rationalistic) understanding from the start; why should it now since the Enlightenment be thought possible or necessary to reduce the New Testament to rationalistically conceivable or verifiable dimensions?

Summary

Albertz's approach to New Testament theology, not least due to his approach to history, essentially turns Bultmann's on its head. The latter tends to use history as required to make it of service to Bultman's theological aims. This results partially from the way he sets up the problematic of history versus theology in his New Testament theology:

---

[303]Kraus, *Biblische Theologie*, 253.
[304]Albertz, *Die Botschaft des Neuen Testaments* II/1, 259.

Either the New Testament writings can be interrogated as "sources" which the historian interprets in order to reconstruct from them a picture of early Christianity as a phenomenon of the historical past; or the reconstruction serves the interpretation of the writings of the New Testament under the presupposition that they have something to say to the present.[305]

Albertz's approach to history makes it clear that this is a false alternative. Albertz does indeed want to interrogate the sources closely to gain a picture of what he calls the "historical state of affairs" reflected in the New Testament. But, not sharing Bultmann's assumption that facts of the past can in no way be binding on the present, Albertz holds open the possibility that the living reality proclaimed by New Testament messengers—for whom also the Christ event was a thing of the past—can also be experienced in the present. This may violate modernist historiography, but Albertz thinks it leads to the most convincing explication of the data. Again, and as a result, Albertz shares Bultmann's conviction that the New Testament writings have something to say to the present. What they have to say, however, must be drawn directly from the New Testament sources taken as they stand. Demythologization has calamitous effects both historically and theologically.

Albertz's understanding of salvation history amounts to an overarching view of reality, animated by the dynamic reality of the New Testament message and its living center the Christ. Within this overarching reality, whose testimonial pillars include the historical-theological verities conveyed by Scripture, and whose opposite ends run into time unimaginable, biblical and all history is unfolding. Just as Kant admitted that if pure reason could not solve "all the questions to which it itself gave birth," it would have to be rejected as he conceived it,[306] Albertz holds that the extremely well attested "revelatory occurrence" giving rise to the New Testament explodes all a priori approaches to the data. Bultmann undeniably explicates the New Testament data with firm preconvictions of what *can* and *cannot* have happened; Albertz approaches the data asking what *did* happen, what was its significance then, and what are the implications now? His is a studied attempt to let modern thought be informed dialogically by the New Testament's historical witness rather than to suppress that witness by undue confidence in a too-narrow segment of modern thought.

---

[305] Bultmann, *Theologie des Neuen Testaments,* 599.
[306] Kant, *Critique of Pure Reason,* 10.

Goppelt[307] and New Testament theology

1. Conception
"Historically" grounded

New Testament theology in Goppelt's view must grow out of a rigorous and comprehensive understanding of New Testament history. Thus Kümmel could write, with only a few qualifications, that volume one of Goppelt's *Theologie des Neuen Testaments* "is presently the best and most reliable scientific presentation of Jesus' proclamation and effectiveness."[308] Two of Goppelt's critically acclaimed monographs[309] on New Testament and related history show that he adopts a historically responsible approach toward all available ancient data, biblical or extra-biblical.[310]

At the same time it is worthwhile to note the contrast between Goppelt's approach to history and that of many of his colleagues. Historical criticism as often practiced implies a distinct worldview, to which the New Testament data must be made to conform. We have seen this tendency repeatedly in Baur, Wrede, and Bultmann. Goppelt, however, states: "Salvation historical research seeks, in making use of modern research methods, to eliminate their historico-ideological background as much as possible."[311] That is, Goppelt recognizes the usefulness and validity of "modern means of research,"[312] but he insists that the data themselves must have a voice in shaping the tools which are applied to them—if the goal is to attain to the message that the texts convey, not merely to subordinate the texts to previously crystal-

---

[307]For biographical information, as well as an assessment of Goppelt's contribution to New Testament studies, see E. Lohse, "Das Neue Testament als apostolische Urkunde," *KD* 21 (1975) 85-98.

[308]Kümmel, *TRu* 41 (1976) 315.

[309]I.e. *Christentum und Judentum im ersten und zweiten Jahrhundert* and *Apostolic and Post–Apostolic Times*.

[310]Offering caveats on Goppelt's historical method in *Apostolic and Post–Apostolic Times*, however, is Kümmel, "Das Urchristentum," *TRu* 48 (1983) 104-106. Criticizing Goppelt's handling of Jesus in *Theologie des Neuen Testaments* is A. Lindemann, "Jesus in der Theologie des Neuen Testaments," *Jesus Christus in Historie und Theologie*, ed. G. Strecker, 1975, 48f.

[311]Goppelt, *Christentum und Judentum im ersten und zweiten Jahrhundert*, 12. Goppelt's lengthy analysis of the history of New Testament theology and his constant pitting of rival positions against each other in his *Theologie des Neuen Testaments* are means by which the "historico-ideological background" of various schools of criticism may be recognized and corrected.

[312]*Ibid.*

lized modern conviction. Goppelt reckons with criticism of historical
criticism from the outset.

His intention, however, is not merely to critique but to construct.
His alternative is set forth as he describes the hermeneutical starting
point of his New Testament theology.

Tri-polar hermeneutical base and result

Goppelt's *Theologie des Neuen Testaments* emerges from a reading of the
New Testament which incorporates three distinct components.[313]
There is (1) "the principle of historical-critical study of Scripture," the
familiar Troeltschian trinity of "criticism, analogy, and correlation."[314]
But Goppelt refuses to elevate this to the unrivalled arbiter of the
meaning of the New Testament. For equal to this is importance for
Goppelt is (2) the "self-understanding of the New Testament,"[315]
which Goppelt wishes to bring into a critical dialogue with (1).
Emerging from this dialogue is what we may call (3) New Testament
theology. (3) is not categorically distinct from (2)—in fact Goppelt's
hope is that (3) will represent an accurate, relevant articulation of (2)
which will with greater or lesser accuracy set forth (2) in a context
which does justice to both (2) itself and to (1). Goppelt explains:

> It is just as illegitimate to subject the New Testament's understanding to the
> static conceptual presuppositions of modernity as it is to confront mankind
> and society today simply with the "letter" of New Testament statements.
> Both parties, the New Testament and modern man, must rather be brought
> into a critical dialogue with each other.[316]

Out of this dialogue, and only when reciprocal openness between
the New Testament and modern thought obtains, "may we attain to
an understanding of New Testament statements so that they become
audible as ultimate demand and promise."[317]

We detect in Goppelt what we may term a tri-polar hermeneutical
base. Goppelt makes it clear that this base cannot somehow be set out
prescriptively in all its specifics prior to handling the New Testament
itself;[318] this would be to fall into the error of Baur, Wrede, and
Bultmann. These are rather the generally necessary parameters of open

[313] *Ibid.* 50.
[314] *Ibid.*
[315] *Ibid.*
[316] *Ibid.* 17f.
[317] *Ibid.* 18
[318] *Ibid.* 50.

inquiry without which New Testament theology loses either its critical character or its actual, true-to-the-text contemporary relevance. And in Goppelt's view New Testament theology which loses sight of either of these has lost sight of its true raison d'être, for it is presenting the New Testament in a context which is foreign to its own content, intent, or both.

The dialogue just noted eventually reaches, in the case of a particular New Testament theologian, a tentative conclusion which must suffice given the present state of research and thought. This is when talk of "a New Testament theology" [(3) above] becomes possible.

> As conclusion to the intended critical dialogue we seek to gain a historically-critically reflected and at the same time factually understandable picture of New Testament theology in its breadth of variation, a picture which can substantiate what it portrays.[319]

Or again:

> The goal of a "theology of the New Testament" is, on the basis of the individual writings or groups of writings [in the New Testament], to organize and arrange by subject the related pictures of Jesus' ministry or of the earliest church's proclamation and teaching.[320]

This indicates the nature and result of Goppelt's tri-polar approach. Historical-critical methods and their underlying rationale, theological apprehension of the text's message consonant with the text's own claims, and a resulting overall portrait of the New Testament are three interlocking components. Each is informed by and in some ways limited by the other two. A New Testament theology is a digest and presentation of the New Testament data within this framework.

Summary

If we compare Goppelt and Bultmann, we see that their approaches to New Testament theology differ markedly. This would be all the more evident if we could compare their exegetical work and results at specific junctures. This is not feasible here. Nevertheless, we can see at the methodological level that Goppelt wishes to remain at all points in touch with New Testament history; we suggested above that this is of secondary concern for Bultmann. Goppelt wishes to avoid inadequate handling of the data and therefore carries on his discussion in overt openness both to the text and to appraisals of the same data by other

---

[319] *Ibid.*
[320] *Ibid.* 17.

schools. By comparison, Bultmann tends to elevate his peculiar understanding of the New Testament message over that message, and over
non-Bultmannian understandings of it, with the help of a methodologically exclusive procedure. Goppelt's goal is to produce a plausible
overall picture of the New Testament which will do justice to both
the historical-critically and theologically relevant aspects of the texts.
Bultmann finds rather disunity to be integral to the New Testament
documents as a whole; his application of historical-critical method
renders theological interpretation problematic because it is leaves intact
such a small portion of the message the texts convey. Both Goppelt
and Bultmann take pains to orient themselves with reference to the
history of New Testament theology as they see it, but they see the
discipline through significantly different eyes. By implication and by
his own admission, Goppelt identifies, like Albertz, with the fundamental concerns and at times even solutions of Hofmann[321] and
Schlatter.[322]

At the same time it should be pointed out that Goppelt's relationship to older advocates of salvation historical perspectives is not
unambiguous. His review of Albertz's *Die Botschaft des Neuen Testaments* calls attention to this ambiguity.[323] Goppelt stresses that Albertz
"comes from the group of the 'confessing church' associated with K.
Barth."[324] He grants that Albertz correctly counteracts Bultmann (and
Dibelius) and that he does not lose sight of the New Testament's place
in the church. "Yet one cannot concur with Albertz."[325] Goppelt
charges that Albertz neglects the historical context of the New Testament message and tries to present the New Testament as a "system."[326]
He criticizes him, too, for not interacting openly enough with New
Testament criticism,[327] even though, Goppelt concedes, Albertz's
knowledge of it is clearly reflected in his presentation.

---

[321]Goppelt's ties to Hofmann are seen most clearly in *Typos* and again in *Theologie
des Neuen Testaments*, 45f.; cf. 376 n. 18.

[322]Aside from remarks on Schlatter in *Theologie des Neuen Testaments*, 47ff., see also
the following citations of Schlatter's works or views: 52, 71, 78, 83, 180 n. 7, 189,
195, 198, 199 n. 8, 369, 376 n. 18, 423 n. 21, 454, 465, 470, 529, 531f., 545f., 602.
Cf. Goppelt, *Christologie und Ethik*, 14 with n. 6.

[323]Goppelt, review of Albertz, *Die Botschaft des Neuen Testaments*, vols. 1 and 2,
Evangelisch-Lutherische Kirchenzeitung 13 (1959) 222f.

[324]*Ibid.* 222.

[325]*Ibid.* 223.

[326]*Ibid.*

[327]Cf. Eltester, *ZNW* 45 (1953-54) 276.

If, as Goppelt concludes, Albertz's *Die Botschaft des Neuen Testaments* "should not be overlooked to the extent that it often is,"[328] why does Goppelt ignore it in his own subsequent work? Does Albertz really strive to construct a system from the New Testament by downplaying the historical milieu? Albertz cites this very weakness in the work of his teacher Harnack and in B. Weiss, J.J. Holtzmann, and H. Weinel; he expressly sets out to overcome it in his New Testament theology.[329] Our reading of Albertz indicates that Goppelt is off the mark in his critique.[330] Also questionable, or at least inconsistent, is the criticism of Albertz for not citing pertinent critical literature—it will be recalled that Schlatter was denounced for the same reason although his familiarity with the state of criticism and exegetical debate is now known to have been extensive.[331] How wide a spectrum of New Testament criticism does one find Bultmann interacting with, and why does Goppelt not take him to task for his nearsightedness as he does Albertz?

Goppelt's break with Albertz and the questions it raises about the nature of Goppelt's own salvation historical perspective should be borne in mind as we proceed now to consider Goppelt's epistemology. This will clarify Goppelt's approach to New Testament theology, his relation to Bultmann, and his only limited agreement with the salvation historical perspective as articulated by others before him.

2. Epistemology
Epistemologically, in broad terms Goppelt resembles Hofmann and other salvation historical proponents. All aim to reformulate in the contemporary context the message of the New Testament in a way consistent with the New Testament's own self-understanding, not with a rationalistic worldview inimical to a large portion of the New Testament's contents. But tension comes into view when Goppelt is compared with Schlatter. We will show below that he emulates Schlatter's hermeneutical method but introduces an epistemological dualism unacceptable to Schlatter. Inasmuch as Hofmann, Cullmann, and Albertz all tend to share Schlatter's position at this point, Goppelt's

---

[328]Goppelt, *Evangelisch-Lutherische Kirchenzeitung* 13 (1959) 223.

[329]Albertz, *Die Botschaft des Neuen Testaments*, II/I, 11f.

[330]A fairer appraisal of Albertz, one which commends him at some of the points which Goppelt attacks, is Brinkmann, *Scholastik* 33 (1958) 267-272.

[331]One should also note the *Sitz im Leben* of Albertz's work at the opening of *Die Botschaft des Neuen Testaments*: Berlin (Albertz writes from the eastern sector) and Europe are in ruins; libraries (and Albertz's personal notes) are scattered or burned up; Albertz is not long out of prison. Under such circumstances how much documented scholarly dialogue could one reasonably expect?

epistemology marks him as something of an anomaly within the salvation historical context in which he locates himself.

Integrating "historical inquiry" and "theological understanding"

From our discussion of Schlatter in Chapter 2 it is clear that for Schlatter historical knowledge gained by critical means must be apprehended in a theologically sympathetic manner. Bare facts wrenched out of their theological context are not necessarily facts at all. History and revelation (or theology) are not mutually exclusive. Schlatter was an early advocate of a hermeneutic which sought to do justice not only to the claims of modern historical thinking but also to those of the text.

Here Goppelt is in full harmony with Schlatter. He states programatically, e.g., that one can "only comprehend the appearance of Jesus in a manner which *integrates historical inquiry and theological understanding.*"[332] Goppelt elaborates: "The question of Jesus' appearance remains constantly dependent on historical research to a considerable extent. It is, however, decisively determined by theological understanding in its overall outcome."[333]

These statements reflect what we have already shown: for Goppelt New Testament theology cannot do its task adequately solely by means of positivistic or historicistic methodology.[334] The message of the New Testament comes to the fore only if the New Testament texts' own claims are at least provisionally shielded from the sometimes devastating and arbitrary inroads of "contemporary thought."[335] A Troeltschian or Bultmannian worldview can effectively preclude an objective and balanced understanding of the New Testament's claims.

So far, then, Goppelt and Schlatter stand on common ground.

Faith and knowledge separated?

It appears, however, that Goppelt works with a Kantian conception of faith and knowledge, in this sense: what is known is distinct from what is believed; conversely, what is believed is not knowledge. He appears in his reading of the New Testament systematically to separate that

---

[332]Goppelt, *Christologie und Ethik*, 16 (Goppelt's emphasis). Goppelt is speaking of Jesus' post-resurrection appearances.

[333]*Ibid.* 17.

[334]Cf. also e.g. Goppelt, *Theologie des Neuen Testaments*, 272: re the passion story it is evident "that here historical questions are again and again dependent on theological understanding."

[335]Cf. Goppelt, *Christologie und Ethik*, 79f.

which the New Testament writers knew and that which they believed. Let us examine some examples.

Goppelt writes: "According to both the Easter stories and the kerygma the *goal* of the [post-resurrection] *appearances* is nothing other than what it was during Jesus' earthly days: not knowledge, but *faith*."[336] Now few would deny that from the New Testament's point of view Jesus' post- as well as pre-resurrection ministry had as a goal the creating of faith. But was this faith separate from knowledge? Goppelt seems to indicate that this is the case; he does not say "not only knowledge but also faith" but "not … but." Similarly, in another context, but dealing with the same matter of what Jesus conveyed to his followers after the resurrection, Goppelt claims: "The disciples did not receive information about him, but actually encountered him personally."[337]

Now Goppelt states, surely correctly, that Jesus encountered his disciples in the resurrection appearances "as *person* in the *full sense*, i.e. *bodily* in the language of the New Testament."[338] Again, this is not a particularly controversial assertion. However, Goppelt goes on to state that for Paul "body" is "essentially what we call 'person,'" while at the same time "in the Lucan and Johannine Easter stories, elements of the materialistic Greek concept of body have moved in."[339] Goppelt's remarks here seem to go rather far in the direction of separating the historical, material reality of Jesus' appearances—which Luke and John are at pains to stress, and which it could be argued Paul did not deny—from their theological or relational import. Thus elsewhere Goppelt states: "The materializing of the bodily aspect which occurs later in levels of the tradition and which makes a recognition through sense perception possible … contradicts the essence of the appearances."[340]

Clearly we see here a separation of what is known cognitively (in this case nothing) from that which is believed in (in this case a "person" whom some identified with Jesus). Faith and knowledge are split. The distinction Goppelt introduces here is significant, for it involves

---

[336] *Ibid.* 94 (Goppelt's emphasis).

[337] Goppelt, *Apostolic and Post–Apostolic Times*, 19.

[338] Goppelt, *Christologie und Ethik*, 94 (Goppelt's emphasis). Cf. *Theologie des Neuen Testaments*, 284.

[339] Goppelt, *Christologie und Ethik*, 94f. Cf. 95 n. 37.

[340] Goppelt, *Apostolic and Post–Apostolic Times*, 19 n. 21.

the very essence of the Easter message, and *"the Easter proclamation"* in turn *"is the starting point of New Testament theology.* "[341]

This same distinction seems to be operative in Goppelt's programmatic assertion: "Jesus does not signify for Paul a witness to God in history, as the prophets did in the Old Testament or as the martyrs and the rabbis did in Judaism. Paul sees Jesus rather *as personal salvific event* : in his death and resurrection God has intervened eschatologically in history."[342] Once again we may accept the basic soundness of Goppelt's observation but still question whether Paul would have countenanced a "not ... but" conceptualization of Jesus as "witness to God in history" and "as personal salvific event," respectively. What is the substance of Paul's personal experience of Jesus, or of God through Jesus? Is Paul's experience ultimately bereft of any necessary factual content? Goppelt says that the content of Pauline faith is *"Christ, or God himself,"*[343] that the gospel is never portrayed in terms of its content but rather its personal subject.[344] Verses like Romans 10:9 or 1 Thessalonians 4:14 must not deter one from realizing that "the salvific events, which are repeatedly designated with a description of faith's content through a *hoti* (that), *were not meant as facts which had to be regarded as true* ; they are meant rather to designate God or Christ more precisely."[345]

This comprises something of a de-factualizing of New Testament faith in favor of a relational emphasis. The question here is whether Goppelt's position rightly represents the (here Pauline) texts which he wishes accurately to explicate. Goppelt seems actually to be somewhat in line with Bultmann's conception of faith and knowledge; the difference is only that Goppelt's "faith" affirms a larger amount of the New Testament's contents which Bultmann's more caustic criticism and more iconoclastic "faith" dispense with.

Finally, Goppelt says, faith "brings ... knowledge with it."[346] But it is obviously not "knowledge" in the cognitive sense of which Goppelt

---

[341] Goppelt, *Theologie des Neuen Testaments*, 56 (Goppelt's emphasis). Cf. *Christologie und Ethik*, 100: "Perhaps it must be said today, formulated rather exaggeratedly: God comes to us ultmately, or he vanishes from our sight, with Easter."

[342] Goppelt, *Theologie des Neuen Testaments*, 435.

[343] *Ibid.* 456 (Goppelt's emphasis).

[344] *Ibid.* 457. D.R. de Lacey rightly observes: Goppelt "tends at times to present the issues in the form of misleading antitheses, when the issue might well be both-and" (review of Goppelt, *Theologie des Neuen Testaments*, volumes 1 and 2, *Themelios* 9 [1984] 30).

[345] Goppelt, *Theologie des Neuen Testaments*, 457 (Goppelt's emphasis).

[346] *Ibid.* 464.

speaks; it is the sort of "knowledge of God" to which "the Spirit of God" leads.[347] One thinks here of M. Hengel's statement: "There is no historical proof for the truth of faith. The certainty of faith has a different quality from historical knowledge."[348] Is this Goppelt's view, too? It does in fact seem to be. This is not necessarily criticism of Goppelt, for this is a common view today. The question is, how does Goppelt's stance relate to the salvation historical perspective as others have articulated it? And how does it relate to the convictions of the New Testament writers whom he claims to represent? Goppelt seems consistently to be concerned with the question: "How can this tradition, which is at the same time historical and kerygmatic, be appropriated in faith without faith becoming the affirmation of historical assertions?"[349] Do Paul and later salvation historical interpreters really reflect an aversion to affirming facts as part of confessing faith? We may arrive at an answer by examining Schlatter.[350]

Clearly Schlatter holds that Paul's "knowledge" was not other than but concurrent with his "faith." The two are in fact merely different aspects of Paul's (and the Christian's) entire consciousness of reality and therefore of God.

True, according to Schlatter Paul rejects "that selfish striving with which man attempts to raise his own thought to God's level."[351] He rejects a thinking which by itself aspires to move from earth to heaven. He "rejects the demand for a knowledge which serves merely the enhancement of one's own life."[352] There is such a thing as misguided or arrogant knowledge in Paul as Schlatter reads him. In all of this Schlatter and Goppelt represent comparable understandings.

---

[347] *Ibid.* 451. This is to be sure Goppelt's interpretation of Paul's remarks in 1 Corinthians, but in general it seems fair to say that for Goppelt, here as elsewhere, "the basic features" at least of Paul's views are "also binding for us" (Goppelt, *Christologie und Ethik*, 186). Lohse remarks (*KD* 21 [1975] 97) that "in all his studies Goppelt seeks ... to establish an orientation primarily from Paul's theology."

[348] Hengel, *The Atonement*, 1981, 48.

[349] Goppelt, *Christologie und Ethik*, 96. Cf. *Theologie des Neuen Testaments*, 183: Re the synoptic traditions, "faith means ... not trust in a miracle worker, but trust in God's self-revelation through Jesus." But do the synoptics imply that this "trust" through Jesus was legitimate in the case of those who refused to acknowledge who he was in terms of a "miracle worker"?

[350] The following discussion draws on works whose conclusions are in turn latent in Schlatter's first monograph, *Der Glaube im Neuen Testament*, 1885. Cf. the reprint of this work (⁶1982), e.g. 141f., 216, 388ff., 493f.

[351] Schlatter, *Die Theologie der Apostel*, 259.

[352] *Ibid.* 260.

They would also at first glance seem to agree that, both for Paul and for the believers he nurtured, "their connection with the Christ arises not through intellectual achievement but through faith, and ... all knowledge which is necessary for this is the gift of God."[353] But one notes here Schlatter's hint that "knowledge," like faith, can be and is imparted by God. So then, while the Spirit seems for Goppelt's Paul to enable a knowledge which is relational but not cognitive, Schlatter sees knowledge of God in Paul and being both-and:

> Since the Spirit in his essence is the knowing one, who searches out all that is in God, he becomes effective also in us [i.e. Paul and others who follow Jesus] as the creator of knowledge. The result is that a knowledge can arise in us through the Spirit being given to us, a knowledge which really conforms with God's thoughts right down to the last eschatological purpose.[354]

For Schlatter knowledge of or about God, on the one hand, and faith in (or relationship with) God, on the other, are not perceived as standing in the sort of antithetical relationship in which Goppelt appears to cast them.

Elsewhere Schlatter states that two phrases describe the relationship which obtains between faith and cognitive perception (*Erkennen*). These are: "We must know in order to believe," and we must "believe in order to know."[355] Goppelt, in line with Anselm and Schleiermacher,[356] would seem to have no quarrel with the second. But with his consistent deemphasis of the content of faith, Goppelt would seem to bracket or even reject the first phrase. At least he seems to sever necessary connecting lines between them. This may explain why Guthrie observes that "it is not precisely clear what historical significance Goppelt attaches to the Easter event."[357] Similarly, de Lacey notes that "sometimes Goppelt is not clear as to what he considers to be authentic or why."[358] Maurer comments that for Goppelt the empty tomb itself is "merely an ambiguous sign."[359] Kümmel criticizes Goppelt for trying to use the New Testament birth narratives without taking a stand on whether they are factual or not.[360]

---

[353] *Ibid.* 259.

[354] *Ibid.* 258.

[355] Schlatter, *Das christliche Dogma*, 112.

[356] *Ibid.* 569 n. 77.

[357] Guthrie, *JETS* 26 (1983) 240.

[358] De Lacey, *Themelios* 9 (1984) 30.

[359] Maurer, *TZ* 32 (1976) 108. Cf. Holtz, *TLZ* 101 (1976) 429.

[360] Kümmel, *TRu* 41 (1976) 315.

Now it is true that also for Schlatter, as for Goppelt, "As believers we do not base our involvement with God on the fruits of our knowledge"; "faith liberates us from the condition of our knowledge."[361] This statement comports with the position of Hengel and Goppelt seen earlier. In the same vein Schlatter states: "Knowing never replaces faith."[362] "Whoever draws near to God only with the intellect remains far from him."[363] Schlatter by no means rationalizes faith.

At the same time, Christianity in Schlatter's view was from earliest times based on "shared certainties."[364] The New Testament knows of a God who "makes himself the content of our knowing," so that we "know ... him who made us and under whose authority we stand."[365] Faith for Schlatter denotes the highest level of "knowing": "now we ourselves think that which God shows us, and we ourselves know what God says to us."[366] Nowhere does Schlatter imply that such knowledge of God comprises "an unbounded knowledge of God";[367] nowhere does he lose sight of the fact that human knowledge alone is not yet saving faith. He also realizes that it is finally impossible to describe (because even Scripture does not divulge) extensive particulars regarding the "event" or "process" by which "the consciousness of God makes its entrance in man."[368] Nevertheless, for Schlatter this event or process "possesses the certainty of fact."[369]

A considerable gap exists between Goppelt's knowledge-faith dichotomy and Schlatter's position that "the same principles that shape all our intellectual labor apply to our thinking which concerns itself with God."[370] Morgan correctly states that Schlatter "considered dogma to be no less 'knowledge' than the results of historical investigation."[371] Leaving aside here the fact that Morgan's use of "dogma" begs the very question which Schlatter's epistemological monism[372]

---

[361]Schlatter, *Das christliche Dogma*, 569 n. 78.

[362]*Ibid.* 108.

[363]*Ibid.* 103.

[364]*PTNT*, 158; *NNTT*, 206.

[365]Schlatter, *Das christliche Dogma*, 102.

[366]*Ibid.* 94.

[367]*Ibid.* 101.

[368]*Ibid.* 100.

[369]*Ibid.*

[370]*Ibid.* 99.

[371]Morgan, *NNTT*, 31.

[372]Not an absolute monism, to be sure: Schlatter does distinguish between faith and knowledge. But his distinction does not in the Kantian tradition tend to deny one in order to make room for the other. The Kantian move defines faith *negatively* in terms of what is lacking to it, i.e. cognitive support. Faith becomes the "incomplete prelimi-

raises, we may simply observe that Goppelt's implicit disagreement with Schlatter's position places Goppelt in a somewhat more distant relationship to him than Goppelt seems to realize or admit.

Conclusion

We conclude that Goppelt's New Testament theology reflects an epistemological dualism at points which is common in the Baur-Wrede-Bultmann heritage but absent from earlier representatives of the salvation historical perspective. He basically accepts, at least in some cases, the Kantian tenet that faith (theological assertions) and facts (cognitive knowledge) lie in two different realms.

One of the distinctives of the salvation historical perspective in Hofmann, Schlatter, and Albertz is that they each, in various ways, interpret the New Testament as if this tenet were not binding. They insist it is belied by compelling biblical testimony. The salvation historical perspective has affirmed repeatedly that God has acted in history, that persons have not only by faith but in fact known and been known by this God, and that God's acts include his self-revelation to man, a revelation which is theologically effectual in large measure because it has been, not only relationally, but also cognitively, apprehended and affirmed. If Goppelt can bracket the question of what early Christians "knew" by asserting simply that and what they believed, Schlatter can insist: "A consciousness that has no more certainties is blind."[373]

True, Goppelt leaves no doubt that New Testament history "is definitely to be understood as the response to that which was and had been ordained by God, and only secondly as a product of the faith and thought of the disciples under the influence of their environment."[374]

---

nary stage of knowledge" (Schlatter, *Die Furcht vor dem Denken*, [2]1917, 56f.). Schlatter (cf. his *Der Glaube im Neuen Testament*) thinks that faith is to be *positively* distinguished from knowledge: this distinction lies "in this: the idea which is believed enters completely into our act of living, implants itself in us as our own possession, and thereby becomes the motive of our will" (*Die Furcht vor dem Denken*, 56f.). Schlatter's approach can be termed monistic, then, not absolutely, but in the sense that he dispenses with the classic Platonic-Kantian ontological and therefore epistemological dualism. For Schlatter things known and things "believed" may stand in a harmonious mutually conditioning unity, not necessarily in an antithetical tension.

[373]Schlatter, *Das christliche Dogma*, 119. Cf. Schlatter, *Zur Theologie*, 265: "All kinds of knowledge without certainty: that would be a fiasco, fragmented diversity without unity ... A mightily inspiring certainty without knowledge: that would be a person sunk in the depths of himself."

[374]Goppelt, *Apostolic and Post-Apostolic Times*, 15.

This statement distances him from the Baur-Wrede-Bultmann heritage. Was this "response," however, merely theologically imperative and relationally effectual, or must it also be regarded as historically compelling because what was affirmed in faith had a compelling basis in fact? If it is true on the one hand that the New Testament's often "schematic and fragmentary" descriptions and accounts "largely conform to the historical events,"[375] it is also true on the other hand that Goppelt tends to drive a wedge between "demonstrable knowledge" and "faith."[376]

Does Goppelt's salvation historical perspective, then, comprise a departure, not just epistemologically, but also materially, from earlier New Testament theologies written from this viewpoint? Examination of his view of history will be necessary to address this question with assurance.

3. Understanding of history

Goppelt's *Theologie des Neuen Testaments* offers above all a running dialogue with and alternative to Bultmann. Goppelt's disagreement with him is nowhere more concisely formulated than when he defines "the most vulnerable spot in Bultmann's hermeneutical starting point" as "the broken relationship to the Old Testament, the elimination of the salvation historical self-understanding of the New Testament and a corresponding attitude toward revelation and history ..."[377] In contrast to Bultmann's view of largely negative Old Testament-New Testament link and corresponding handling of history, Goppelt sets forth his salvation historical approach. This approach, however, is for Goppelt associated directly with his understanding of (especially Pauline) typology. A first step toward clearer definition of Goppelt's salvation historical outlook is to examine his explanation of typology and how it relates to history. After this we will point out how this approach to history is reflected in his *Theologie des Neuen Testaments*. Lastly we will compare and contrast Goppelt's approach to history with that of both Baur-Wrede-Bultmann and other proponents of salvation historical perspectives.

---

[375] Goppelt, *Theologie des Neuen Testaments*, 329. This citation applies specifically to the passages in Acts which recount the missionary expansion of the early church, but they are typical of similar remarks Goppelt makes regularly in his *Theologie des Neuen Testaments*.

[376] *Ibid.* 287.

[377] Goppelt, *Typos*, 262.

Typological approach

M. Karlberg writes that "the cogency of Goppelt's redemptive histori-cal construction of Biblical typology founders on his uncritical adoption of a neo-orthodox conception of history and theology."[378] Without here passing judgment on this "neo-orthodox conception" or on whether Goppelt's construction "founders,"[379] we may affirm that Karlberg has rightly discerned a nodal point of Goppelt's approach to New Testament history (with implications for Old Testament history as well).

The nodal point is that salvation history for Goppelt is only very loosely connected with real historical events. This position is related to his epistemology but from Goppelt's point of view follows more di-rectly perhaps from his conception of typology. Goppelt has in mind typology as set forth by Paul (and also by Jesus[380]); "the typological outlook [permeates] the apostle's entire understanding of Scripture" and thus "defines the shape of" his whole theology.[381] This remains true despite the small number of passages in which typology as Gop-pelt defines it comes into view.[382]

According to Goppelt, types "are not historical analogies."[383] Pauline typology is, to be sure, "dependent to some extent on the historicity of its starting point."[384] Goppelt's ambivalence at this point is, how-ever, underscored by his contrasting assertion that Pauline typology is "independent to a considerable extent from the historicity of the Old Testament presentation of history."[385] Types' relationship to history (the course of past events) is that they comprise "a self-revelation [of God] which voices itself in historical events that are conveyed by ver-bal revelation and laid hold of by the witness of faith."[386] It appears that for Goppelt God's self-manifestation is only incidentally tied to his-

---

[378]Karlberg, review of Goppelt, *Typos, JETS* 26 (1983) 493.

[379]Endorsing Goppelt's *Typos* with few reservations is E. Ellis in the preface to the English translation, 1982, ix-xx. On the other hand, R. Davidson's *Typology in Scrip-ture*, 1981, appears successfully to have challenged most of Goppelt's substantive conclusions regarding typology; cf. especially 53ff.; 421ff.

[380]Goppelt, *Typos*, 286f. The German edition, [2]1969, is cited here and below.

[381]*Ibid.* 281.

[382]*Ibid.* 280.

[383]*Ibid.* 276. But see Davidson, *Typology in Scripture*, 421: "The historical reality of the OT types does not appear to be optional (*pace* Goppelt) ..."

[384]Goppelt, *Typos*, 289.

[385]Goppelt, *Theologie des Neuen Testaments*, 384.

[386]*Typos*, 290f.

tory; there is ultimately something of a mutual exclusion of the revelatory from the mere historical and vice versa.

This observation is confirmed by Goppelt's statement that a type is "an act of God in demonstrating his grace and in judgments related to ultimate salvation, not the general occurrence in creation and history."[387] This undoubtedly bespeaks a faith-history dichotomy. In the same vein, for Paul salvation history is "not given by means of historical continuity but rather by God's plan of salvation which he comprehends in faith."[388] Paul's knowledge of this continuity is accordingly styled "faith knowledge."[389] When Paul explicates a type,

> he does not desire to offer historical examples, or cite a Scriptural proof from a holy document, or develop a construction which implies a theology of history. He seeks rather to disclose a correlation which God placed in history and permitted to be recorded for the community of faith in Scripture ... This correlation is intended to let the community understand its situation in faith.[390]

The only sense in which Goppelt permits talk of a salvation historical perspective is in terms of this manner of typological understanding of Old and New Testament history, and by implication of history generally.

Is Karlberg correct, then, in terming Goppelt's typological understanding "relational and anthropocentric"?[391] There is at least a kernel of truth in the statement. If Paul's focus is "actually not the course of all that happens but rather God's redemptive plan, not the continuity of history but the faithfulness of God,"[392] it is evident that by "history" in New Testament theology we are dealing with something which functions strictly "without tying itself to historical processes and developments."[393] Attention is necessarily focused on and even limited to a relational human perception of and response to God's grace in contrast to—not in dependence on—any historically concrete means by which the grace is ostensibly mediated or on which it is based.

Goppelt concludes:

---

[387] *Ibid.* 273.
[388] *Ibid.* 275.
[389] *Ibid.*
[390] *Ibid.* 276.
[391] Karlberg, *JETS* 26 (1983) 492.
[392] Goppelt, *Typos*, 297f.
[393] *Ibid.* 290.

One could term *Heilsgeschichte* that correlation of occurrence within history, fixed only by God's redemptive plan and election, which is announced through verbal revelation and becomes visible for the apostle in faith on the basis of its object, i.e. on the basis of Christ.[394]

In a sense this definition of salvation history conforms generally to that of many others who have used the term. However it is clear that Goppelt by "correlation of occurrence" is not referring in any definitive sense to historical events. He refers rather to the relational transaction which obtains in some undefined relationship to events, to "an occurrence between God and man."[395] Such an occurrence relates to "the salvation which appeared in Christ ..., which is testified to by Scripture and proleptically depicts a corresponding occurrence in the end time."[396] Far from Goppelt's salvation historical perspective looking back, then, on concrete historical events (or word-event complexes) which were in God's purpose instrumental in mediating salvation to biblical figures, Goppelt's approach largely cuts necessary ties between biblical events and the biblical interpretation of them. Only the latter is constitutive for theological thought.

The really vital "event" for Goppelt becomes if anything not a *past* one, upon which the New Testament looks back and from which it makes application, but a *future* or *eschatological* one which is naturally out of the range of critical fire. This leaves it also, however, out of the range of critical confirmation. Accordingly, Goppelt's types and their eschatological referents lose a large degree of demonstrable contact with the real world of the past and present about which biblical typology, on the surface anyway, is concerned to speak. The question Goppelt begs is, how revelatory are events which did not happen, be the faith ever so sincere which a Paul or Jesus placed in God who ostensibly stands behind them? And is it really so self-evident that biblical writers like Paul considered the historicity of types to be separable from their theological meaning?

The point is neither to critique nor to affirm Goppelt's typological understanding;[397] our goal is merely to highlight what for our purposes is one of its major features. There is a real history-theology dialectic

---

[394] *Ibid.* 298.

[395] *Ibid.* 273.

[396] *Ibid.*

[397] It is only fair, however, to point out Davidson's conclusion that Goppelt "attempts to uncover the main features of New Testament typology, but these are largely pre-determined by the a priori definition of typology which he brings to the NT text" (*Typology in Scripture*, 55).

which at times approaches the point of being an antithesis. As we look now to his *Theologie des Neuen Testaments* we will try to establish to what extent a similar tendency is at work.

Salvation history in Goppelt's Theologie des Neuen Testaments
Undoubtedly Goppelt wishes to maintain contact with history to a greater extent than Bultmann. He holds that "we miss right from the start the meaning of Jesus' ministry if we sever it from the dialogue with Israel and make it to an abstract message to mankind, as largely occurred e.g. in Bultmann."[398]

Goppelt shows concern for the historically concrete when he states, here defying an ethical assumption found at times in the Baur-Wrede-Bultmann heritage, that "Jesus' redemptive ministry seeks the renewal not only of the inner attitude and the ethical-religious relationship but also of bodily-historical existence."[399] Holtz praises Goppelt's handling of Jesus because "here ... the historicality of God's act in the history of Jesus is taken very seriously."[400] It would be false to see Goppelt's *Theologie des Neuen Testaments* as having a willfully cavalier attitude toward history. The New Testament sources in their development of the Jesus traditions are "*basically accurate* "[401] in their faithfulness to the New Testament history (history, to be sure, in Goppelt's sense of the term), and Goppelt must be given credit for taking those sources in their historical contexts seriously.

At the same time, it is clear that the history-theology tension already noted persists in Goppelt's *Theologie des Neuen Testaments*.

For Goppelt the Old Testament-New Testament link, which he understands primarily in terms of what he sees as Pauline typology, is fundamental for New Testament theology. But what is the nature of this link? Against Cullmann, Pannenberg, and Bultmann, respectively, Goppelt protests:

> When Paul brings the Christ event together with the Old Testament, he has in view, in my opinion, neither a salvation historical or universal-historical overall view, nor solely a mythically circumscribed call to decision, but rather *the correspondence between the event of promise and the event of fulfillment.*[402]

[398] Goppelt, *Theologie des Neuen Testaments*, 76.
[399] *Ibid.* 188.
[400] Holtz, *TLZ* 101 (1976) 429.
[401] Goppelt, *Theologie des Neuen Testaments*, 327 (emphasis Goppelt's).
[402] *Ibid.* 387f. (emphasis Goppelt's).

So then, for all of Goppelt's talk of salvation history, it is not a historical process (in terms of concrete empirical past reality) which he
has in mind.[403] As Holtz points out, the "historicality of God's act in
history" is central for Goppelt—but this leaves undefined the link between "historicality" and the concrete historical reality presumably
attendant upon it.

Goppelt leaves no doubt that salvation history is

> precisely not a historical continuum which stands out historically from the
> rest of history, whether through its miraculous character or through de-
> monstrable continuity. *Heilsgeschichte* is, then, rather a succession of
> historical events which finally are characterized and related to each other
> exclusively in this: that through them the ultimate self-proclamation of God
> in Jesus is prepared, and that Jesus fundamentally identified himself with
> them in that sense.[404]

It can hardly be overstressed, then, that for Goppelt (as for Goppelt's Paul) salvation history is "a continuity of the link between God
and man in history."[405] It does not involve a concrete historical corre-
spondence between Old and New Testament events or phenomena.
Even Luke's presentation of New Testament history assumes a "*continuity*" which is "*the material realization of the redemptive plan, not a
historically connected development.*"[406] Whereas previous advocates of a
salvation historical perspective would indeed want to hold such "realization" in close proximity to "a historically connected development,"
Goppelt constantly drives a solid wedge between the two.

Conclusion

We may accordingly note that Goppelt's salvation historical approach
departs, not only epistemologically, but also materially, from the salvation historical perspective of Hofmann, Schlatter, and Albertz. A major
basic epistemological disagreement with Schlatter has already been
outlined. In a sense Goppelt is on firmer ground in adducing Hofmann
as an ideological forerunner, but it is not at all clear that Hofmann's
New Testament theology (or hermeneutic) is reconcilable with the
basic features of Goppelt's. Granted that Hofmann is no inerrantist or
even biblicist and that he does not defend the "historical" basis of

---

[403] Cf. *ibid.* 388: "Thus Paul does not understand *Heilsgeschichte* as historical process..."
[404] *Ibid.* 82.
[405] *Ibid.* 444.
[406] *Ibid.* 610. The continuity of Acts is, then, "not that of a historical development"
(*ibid.* 690).

every biblical utterance. It is still fair to surmise that Hofmann would take a dim view of Goppelt's studied refusal to link New Testament *Heil* with knowledge of certain facts related to concrete *Geschichte*. From Hofmann's New Testament theological point of view, we might say that Goppelt's salvation history amounts to a *Heilsgeschichtlichkeitsgeschichte*—a history of salvific historicality. That is, Goppelt is willing to speak of salvation history only in terms of historicality (Geschichtlichkeit) in the somewhat existentialist sense of man's authentic faith response in history. His *Theologie des Neuen Testaments* treats salvation history as the history of the relationship between God and man. This is in itself certainly a Hofmannian aspiration. Yet Goppelt's faith-fact dualism hardly squares with Hofmann's more realist epistemological underpinnings.

Albertz occupies somewhat common ground in relation to Goppelt. It is ironic that Goppelt criticizes Albertz for unfolding the New Testament message "as the word that goes out into the world from above."[407] True, Albertz in essence defends the New Testament from some of the more caustic critical modes of analysis and in this sense might be seen as setting forth Barthian "vertical from above" theological constructs. Goppelt exaggerates, however, in his charge that Albertz disregards history. Are Albertz's repeated self-identifications with von Ranke total self-deception? Albertz would inquire of Goppelt what the essence of the latter's *Theologie des Neuen Testaments* is if, as seems to be the case, the salvation history which is at the heart of his New Testament theology has only a relational-confessional, not also a concrete historical, content? Is it not rather for Goppelt that the message comes "vertically from above," since the ties between fact and faith, history and redemptive understanding, are stretched to the breaking point?

One need only peruse Goppelt's *Theologie des Neuen Testaments* to see that he distances himself repeatedly from Baur-Wrede-Bultmann. His exegesis often takes its point of departure from a conclusion which Bultmann has reached. Formally, and exegetically at many junctures, Goppelt offers a skillful rebuttals of and alternatives to the Baur-Wrede-Bultmann line of questioning. Nevertheless, from the salvation historical perspective as Hofmann, Schlatter, Albertz, and others have articulated it, Goppelt's *Theologie des Neuen Testaments* may be regarded as a Trojan horse in the salvation historical camp. The history of New Testament theology, especially as we have seen it in Chapters 1 and 2

---

[407] Goppelt, *Evangelisch-Lutherische Kirchenzeitung* 13 (1959) 223.

as well as in the present chapter, suggests that theological reconstructions of the New Testament which either (1) minimize the relevance of, or (2) bracket the question of the historical or factual justification for the New Testament's theological assertions run a serious risk. If plausible cognitive bases cannot be adduced which ground, complement, and thus to some extent justify the New Testament's faith assertions, those assertions understandably will not long stand the inroads of criticism.

The salvation historical perspective maintained its identity, such as it was, prior to Goppelt not least by its refusal to abide by what it saw as an unsuitable prescriptive epistemology, or in Thielicke's terms a Cartesian methodology. Goppelt's *Theologie des Neuen Testaments* appears to play into the hands of this methodology. It distances itself from earlier salvation historical formulations to the extent that a faith-knowledge dichotomy, and a corresponding approach to typology, salvation history, and ultimately New Testament theology, hold sway.

Conclusion

"Until the 1980s, all that happened in the field of New Testament theology remained in the shadow of Bultmann."[408] That shadow of historical skepticism and ahistorical belief was a storm cloud wreaking havoc on salvation historical formulations. Cullmann's synthesis met widespread approbation for a time but could not be sustained against the combined gales of Bultmann's opposition in the 40s and 50s and the collapse of the Biblical Theology Movement in the 60s. The crochety-sounding Albertz, publishing from the marginalized eastern sector of Berlin and passing from the scene as Bultmann's popularity reached its zenith, received little notice. Goppelt never finished his New Testament theology, and by the time the posthumous and partial edition appeared, Bultmannians occupied nearly all chairs of New Testament in German universities, historically the dominant center of New Testament theological discussion. Goppelt was clearer regarding what he rejected (Bultmann, and, strangely, Bultmann's antipode Jeremias) than what he supported; his putatively positive salvation historical proposal was vitiated by a dualism that left him a no-man's land between Bultmann's ahistorical historiography and the critical realism that has to varying degrees marked salvation historical New

---

[408]Räisänen, *Beyond New Testament Theology*, 6.

Testament theologians since Hofmann. Salvation historical approaches appeared to be dead in the water when they drew attention at all.

This scenario might be of merely historical interest were it not for the fact that in some ways Bultmann sunk his own ship, too. In his wake many spoke of "crisis," a fragmented stasis that characterizes the discipline of New Testament theology to the present hour. We will speak of this more in the Epilogue below. For now we simply note that Bultmann's success in convincing at least two generations to forget about Cullmann and salvation history did not translate into a sustainable positive synthesis to replace the one he scuttled. From that standpoint, the counterinsurgent alternatives of Cullmann, Albertz, and Goppelt are still on the discussion table, even if currently pushed off to the side.

It may seem surprising that Cullmann's name is virtually absent from our analysis of Albertz and Goppelt. Of course comparisons could be made. But it is significant that their New Testament theologies can hardly be said to take their bearings from Cullmann's work to any significant degree.[409] To refute or circumvent Cullmann is not necessarily to have disproved or even seriously impugned the workability of the presentations of Albertz and Goppelt.

Related to this is a striking lack of collaboration, or even mutual awareness, between Albertz and Goppelt. It is fair to say that the New Testament theology of each is constructed independently of the other. There is not even much of a conscious positive connection with Hofmann and Schlatter except in Goppelt's case, and he seems ultimately to depart from their position as much as he adopts it.

While we may speak loosely, then, of a salvation historical approach in the Bultmann era and thereafter, advocates of it have arrived at

---

[409]This holds true as well for the American evangelical G.E. Ladd's *A Theology of the New Testament*, 1974, a New Testament theology attempting to tap into a salvation historical modus operandi. Ladd admittedly cites Cullmann in this work dozens of times. About one-fourth of these citations, however, are merely bibliographical references. Six times Ladd registers disagreement with Cullmann (21, 96, 144, 209, 390, 560). Most often he cites Cullmann's *Christology* to support exegetical points. While Ladd reflect Cullmannian insights, a comparable perspective was already intrinsic to the American evangelical tradition of which Ladd was part: see e.g. J.G. Machen, "History and Faith," *Princeton Theological Review* 13 (1915) 337: "The centre and core of the Bible is history. Everything else that the Bible contains is fitted into an historical framework and leads up to an historical climax. The Bible is primarily a record of events." Ladd was not solely dependent on Cullmann for his salvation historical outlook, which has more affinities with covenant theology and the work of G. Vos, *Biblical Theology: Old and New Testaments*.

comparable positions from distinctly different backgrounds and convictions and with no interdependence resembling a formal school. This convergence of outlook may bespeak a certain integrity of method, the results of an extended thought experiment being verified by independent means.

We have confirmed in the latter half of the 20th century the continuing presence of the same bifurcation within New Testament theology which we established in Chapter 1 starting with Baur-Hofmann. The split is identifiable when the conflicting answers to three key questions are weighed: 1. What is New Testament theology? 2. What epistemological stance is reflected? 3. What view of history is employed or implied? In broad terms Bultmann locates himself in the same "critical orthodox" tradition as Baur and Wrede. In a looser sense, mainly in the way they relate to Scripture and critical orthodoxy, respectively, rather than in the way they emulate or borrow from each other, Albertz and Goppelt follow in a heritage stretching back in time through Schlatter to Hofmann. Goppelt's distinctives mark him as something of a *tertium quid*. Yet he belongs to, and is the most recent advocate for, the salvation historical perspective that the disciplinary hegemony viewed as a fallacy as the 20th century drew to a close.

Epilogue

The Salvation History Fallacy?

In some ways our study of salvation historical alternatives to "critical orthodoxy" stands on its own as a rediscovery of significant labor unjustly forgotten. Simply to be aware of these overlooked chapters in the history of thought is to learn from past example. Some may even receive direction for present challenges. For it appears that salvation historical scholarship has generally produced an intellectually, to say nothing of theologically, cogent rendering of the New Testament's teaching, despite approaching it in a manner at points rather different from critical orthodox practitioners, whose view of things gradually became de rigueur. Judging from impressive past salvation historical formulations, analogous perspectives are likely to continue to find their supporters in days ahead.

Beyond this, there are several more specific suggestive inferences to be drawn in view of the colorful recent history of New Testament studies.

The late 20th century saw fragmentation in New Testament studies across the board. In the wake of the (overstated but real) "crisis" heralded in the 1960s the dominance of Bultmann's New Testament theology gradually faded, though no single work has yet replaced it. New Testament theology seemed to languish, as scholars abandoned anything resembling a theological and sometimes even synthetic approach to the New Testament. In many cases they simply turned to other matters: the new perspective on Paul; the third quest for the historical Jesus; the theologies of individual New Testament writers; new textual finds and historical backgrounds; hermeneutical initiatives growing out of literary theory, social-scientific methods, gender studies, or political concerns. Traditional historical-critical interpretation maintained a healthy if slightly less monopolistic existence. Where theological interest was in evidence, some New Testament scholars moved in the direction of a "theological interpretation of Scripture" less concerned with historical issues than has traditionally been true of

New Testament theology as a discipline.[1] A subtext of this already complex, largely disintegrative scenario was the ubiquitous dynamic of "modern" scholarship running up against "postmodern" calls for radical change.[2]

The last third of the century, then, was not a propitious time to articulate a unified synthesis of New Testament teaching however defined. "Academic," "social," and "evangelical" trends, or combinations thereof, arose and sometimes conflicted.[3] Salvation historical New Testament theology did not fare particularly well and to many seemed to have little future prospect, as the rapidly fading memory of Cullmann and Goppelt noted earlier suggests.

Yet New Testament theology in broad terms seems so far to be weathering this period of breakup, or reformation, or reconfiguration, or disappearance—only time will tell what we should have called it. Notable New Testament theologies cropped up in the 1990s. Räisänen reports on "significant works" by J. Gnilka, G. Caird, G. Strecker, P. Stuhlmacher, and H. Hübner.[4] But each of these studies tends to amount to a variation of former approaches rather than to break truly new ground. None adopts a salvation historical outlook in the historic sense traced by this study. A quarter century ago G. Trompf prophesied that "macro-historical ideas" would meet increasing resistance in "first world" scholarship as the 20th century drew to a close; by the early 1990s B. Hinze could speak confidently of "the end of salvation history," drawing on P. Hodgson in support.[5] Hinze's pronouncement had been anticipated two decades earlier.[6] Salvation historical approaches, it seems, are widely adjudged to be irretrievably passé.

Yet there are grounds for supposing this prognostication to be excessively dour. Our study suggests that salvation historical alternatives to "critical orthodoxy" will continue to find supporters in light of a number of considerations.

---

[1] Examples of a sizable literature would include Watson, *Text and Truth*; S. Fowl, *Engaging Scripture*, 1998.

[2] This clash is explored in Adam, *Making Sense of New Testament Theology*. See also S. Moore, *Poststructuralism and the New Testament*, 1994; D. Patte, *Ethics of Biblical Interpretation*, 1995.

[3] See Bray, *Biblical Interpretation*, 467–583.

[4] *Beyond New Testament Theology*, xiii, 115–133.

[5] G. Trompf, "The Future of Macro–Historical Ideas," *Soundings* 62 (1979) 70–89; Hinze, "The End of Salvation History," *Horizons* 18/2 (1991) 227–245.

[6] See F. Hesse, *Abschied von der Heilsgeschichte*, 1971. But note the reply by R. Schmitt, *Abschied von der Heilsgeschichte?*, 1982.

Firstly, there is a future for salvation historical approaches because successive critical orthodox hegemonies have been pulled down by internal differences between competing schools of thought. Systems like Bultmann's rise and have their day but are gradually undermined by the same historicistic tools that were used to build them. This "live by the sword, die by the sword" dynamic explains the rise and fall of the successive syntheses we have examined, each of which has claimed not so much to improve on its predecessor as to negate and supplant it. True, decline of successive critical orthodox programs does not in itself speak for a salvation historical alternative. But neither does the agreement of a trio of critical reconstructions that salvation history is a fallacy constitute a three-fold refutation of it, since by their own logic either Baur, Wrede, or Bultmann is fundamentally mistaken, and all could be. The cyclic nature and ephemeral force of the hegemonic syntheses we have traced counsel caution in declaring undying allegiance to the one currently receiving the most press or the next one to appear fronted by the biggest name. Since salvation historical outlooks have proved to be an engine generating constructive dissent to frequently misplaced historical critical certainties, it is reasonable to surmise that they will, and by rights should, continue to play a similar role in times ahead.

Secondly, there is the matter of modernity's eclipse along with postmodernity's limited staying power. The former indicates that the hegemonic forces that made monolithic critical orthodox New Testament theology viable no longer compel anything like unified assent. The latter suggests that we are in a period of flux capable of supporting little agreement except that the older hegemonies were mistaken. In other words, postmodernity's raison d'être is parasitic on modernity's dominance. But the longer that dominance recedes, the more postmodern approaches will become the hegemonic benchmark to be surpassed. Then they will be subject to undermining by the same deconstructive impulses that originally fueled their rise to prominence. This presents on ongoing opportunity for salvation historical New Testament theology. It critiqued undue faith in modernism all along, yet not by clambering onto the postmodern bandwagon, heeding the wisdom of G. Marsden: those who "reject the naturalistic biases in the academy would be foolish to do so in the name of postmodern relativism."[7] If an overstated Kantian perspectivalism is the mother of postmodern relativism, salvation historical thinkers who have worked

---

[7] *The Outrageous Idea of Christian Scholarship*, 1997, 30.

out realist alternatives point one way forward for constructive engagement with biblical sources in the current climate.

Thirdly, there is the inherent power of what we may term gospel
witness. A notable feature of a number of salvation historical writers
has been the testimony of their work, and not seldom their lives, to
the truths, as they saw it, of the redemptive message they claimed to
find in the biblical sources. Readers of Schlatter's short biography,[8] for
example, are often moved by the spiritual conviction it reflects and the
way that his prodigious scholarly labors are of a piece with classic
Christian confession. It is hard to read impassively Albertz's prefatory,
personal, and pastoral comments introducing *Die Botschaft des Neuen
Testaments* II/1.[9] Critical orthodox scholarship has become a missionary movement with its own high priests (e.g. Baur, Wrede, and
Bultmann), Scriptures (e.g. treatises by Spinoza, Reimarus, Strauss,
Troeltsch and others[10]), and orthodoxies. Its leading lights and their
literary productions have grounded universities and moved people to
devote their lives to the high calling of making known the putative
post-Christian truth. Their core claim has been that creedal Christianity was substantially mistaken all along and that the only intellectually
honest response is radical recasting of the Christian religion in conformity with post-Enlightenment conviction—if indeed there is to be any

---

[8]W. Neuer, *Adolf Schlatter*, 1995.

[9]A sample is worth reproducing: "This book is dedicated to the young brethren of
the Confessing Church. I was united with them in my office as leader of the Office of
Theological Examination of the Confessing Church in Berlin-Brandenburg. I was all
the closer to these brethren, whose status was illegal from the start, in that performance
of my ministry resulted in the loss of my freedom [i.e. he was imprisoned] as well as
my ordination, withdrawn by a bogus ecclesiastical authority. This book's dedication
bears two names. [One is Erich Klapproth, the other is] Ilse Fredrichsdorff ... When
the church struggle began she was a young girl belonging to the Confessing Church
congregation Nicolai–Melancthon in Spandau. Through our congregation she came to
take up theological study. She studied in our theological college and in Basle with Karl
Barth. She became curate of the only truly evangelical confessional school that could
be established under the Third Reich, the school for non-Aryan Christian children
who were no longer permitted to attend the public school. During the war she remained in congregations northeast of Berlin, in that region where the last battle prior
to Berlin was waged. She was so much in demand for her pastoral skills that the major
of the troop emplacements behind which lay the villages she served repeatedly re-
quested her aid among the troops. Later she led the displaced congregations with the
word of God, went back to the hunger zone as much as possible, and, after she had
buried hundreds of the thousands who perished, succumbed herself to starvation" (*Die
Botschaft des Neuen Testaments* II/1, 13f.).

[10]Conveniently anthologized, and lionized, in G. Dawes, ed., *The Historical Jesus
Quest*, 1999.

justification for religion in the "modern" world at all. Many find this inspirational and follow the critical orthodox lead. But corresponding to this have been salvation historical thinkers, who in distinct but harmonious fashion have not found it necessary to overthrow the substance of Christian faith in order to preserve intellectual rigor. Those who do not automatically blanch at the spectacle of university professors continuing to uphold classic Christian belief may find both intellectual and theological light in older salvation historical writers, to the extent that their memory is not buried beneath the kind of triumphalist historiography that has tended to characterize accounts of New Testament scholarship over the last few hundred years.[11] To summarize, the substance of what salvation historical thinkers claim to find in Scripture, and the force of their testimony to it, is likely to encourage others to continue in trails they have blazed.

Fourthly, and briefly, is the two-fold methodological advantage of salvation historical approaches over critical orthodox ones. From Hofmann to Goppelt, salvation historical outlooks show promise in two vital areas: conceiving a positive connection between Old and New Testaments, and proposing a positive role for New Testament theology in systematic theology and even ethics. Of course in pre-Enlightenment New Testament interpretation both of these features were secure. The New Testament was thought to join with the Old in testifying to a movement of divine initiative stretching back in time to Abraham and beyond, and forward to an eternity of judgment and salvation; the Testaments could accordingly be read in close conjunction with each other. There is one Bible, not two. And because Scripture was God's word its contents, rightly interpreted, could fund both theological and ethical reflection in direct ways. Both of these convictions were jettisoned increasingly as the 19th century progressed. Salvation historical interpretation did not join in with what became first a popular and eventually an obligatory convention. Those seeking ways to hold the two Testaments together or to make exegesis fruitful for theology and ethics[12] will likely continue to find guidance

---

[11]Exemplified, in some ways, by W. Baird's two volumes (*History of New Testament Research*, 1992–2002). In his view implementation of the historical-critical method has been the glory of the discipline. There is little recognition of the attendant loss for Christian theology over the centuries he chronicles. See R. Yarbrough, "A Milestone in the History New Testament Research: Review Essay," *Journal of the Evangelical Theological Society* 46/2 (2003) 299–308.

[12]Schlatter's exegetical interests led naturally into his *Die christliche Ethik*, ³1929. Roman Catholic writers like Schelkle and Schnackenburg who are generally supportive of some sort of salvation historical approach have likewise made their exegesis

in an orientation that never found it necessary to abandon such use of Scripture in the first place.

Fifthly, as many concede, "New Testament scholarship should serve the end of Christian theology and education."[13] New Testament theology is needed to provide "a solid synthesis of what exegetes have discovered" for pastors and others seeking "material for their own reflections and constructions."[14] This is particularly true in realms which now harbor the majority of the world's Christian population: developing nations.[15] Christianity is no longer predominantly either Western or white; as Andrew Walls notes, "The third Christian millennium dawns with the center of gravity of Christianity moving strongly southward, towards Africa, Latin America, and parts of Asia."[16] New Testament theology has a role to play in the establishment and sustenance of life and thought in those areas that continue to embrace the Christian gospel. Under critical orthodox auspices New Testament theology has served largely to justify the increasingly negative regard for the Christian message that marked the "progress" of modern thought in the Western university. But where regard for Scripture is positive, theological study of the New Testament will find little point in assimilating handbooks on how to demythologize what readers have already knowledgeably received as God's gospel. This is particularly true in regions under hostile religious dominance (like many Muslim nations), where study of Scripture proceeds keenly aware of non-Christian religious polemic against the Bible's historical and theological veracity. This polemic is fueled in no small measure by Western scholarship in the critical orthodox mode. It is reasonable to suppose that the growing Christian population will find resources to reply in salvation historical scholarship. This should encourage its growth both in developing nations and in Western enclaves concerned to nourish and affirm, not undercut, Christian communities in developing lands, who often face lethal resistance from hostile majority populations. To put it bluntly, "first world" Christians who take seri-

profitable for ethics. This has not been true of the critical orthodox scholars we examined. See volume three of Schelkle's *Theology of the New Testament,* entitled *Morality*; Schnackenburg, *The Moral Teaching of the New Testament,* 1965.

[13]Räisänen, *Beyond New Testament Theology,* 1. Räisänen himself however calls for a program that many would view as more subversive than supportive of such ends.

[14]*Ibid.*

[15]See Philip Jenkins, *The Next Christendom: The Coming of Global Christianity,* 2002. See also R. Yarbrough, "The Last and Next Christendom: Implications for Interpreting the Bible," *Themelios* (forthcoming).

[16]In P. Brierley & H. Wraight, *Atlas of World Christianity,* 1998, 11.

ously their responsibility to help brethren exposed to marginalization and persecution will find the most help, not in scholarship that anti-Christian apologists consult themselves, but in approaches that model rigorous yet gospel-friendly renderings of the history and theology of the early church. Salvation historical writings are by no means the sole resource here, but they are a leading one when it comes to the synthetic task of New Testament theology.

Sixthly, some will not wish to discount a possible impetus behind salvation historical readings arising from divine grace. Lying at the center of salvation historical understanding is its effective (if often hidden or ambiguous) working, not only in olden times but also presently. Biblical writers testify that this grace abounds where human need is greatest. A common post-Enlightenment view is that such need neither abounds nor exists; "the forgiveness of sins" affirmed in the Apostles' Creed need loom no larger in the critical exegete's thinking than other outmoded convictions like the virgin birth of Christ, his bodily resurrection, or the Trinity. But salvation historical thought is bound to affirm the existence of something like what came to be called original sin, along with its unpleasant consequences. On this view there is indeed need for grace to dispel what human hardness, however urbanely brilliant and well-meaning, has established. "If we claim to be without sin, we deceive ourselves and the truth is not in us" (1 John 1:8). "Do you see a man wise in his own eyes? There is more hope for a fool than for him" (Prov 26:12).

The history of redemption that grounds God's free yet costly grace has met its most studied and sustained opposition ever recorded as a result of critical orthodox syntheses arising since Enlightenment times. Precisely such opposition could imply dire need and accordingly a situation fit for divine response. Unless and until that response takes the form of the kind of development that leads to the virtual eradication of Christian presence—as took place, e.g., in much of modern Turkey and North Africa where Christianity once flourished—there is hope for a fresh infusion of grace. To the extent that New Testament theology informs belief and proclamation of the New Testament's offer of pardon and new orientation through faith in Christ, salvation historical approaches have a role to play in holding the door open to verities affirmed by New Testament writers that many at present admittedly find no interest in affirming—and may even labor assiduously to discredit.

H. Reventlow, whose work has done much to demonstrate the value of rethinking biblical scholarship's vicissitudes, writes wisely, "If we are critical of our forefathers and have objections to the results of their research, the first step must be to <u>assess them in the circumstances in which they lived.</u> That will protect us from condemning them."[17] We have not sought to condemn salvation historical New Testament theologies—critical orthodoxy had already performed that task—but to understand. Perhaps our study will enable more discerning appropriation of the past and less thoughtless commendation of the present. Both could be salubrious in a discipline that appears both fraught with difficulties and ripe for resurgence.

---

[17]"Bedingungen und Voraussetzungen der Bibelkritik in Deutschland in der Periode des zweiten Reiches und bevor. Der Fall Heinrich Julius Holtzmann," ed. W. Müller & H. Schulz, *Theologie als Aufklärung*, 1992, 283.

Bibliography

Abbagnano, N. "Positivism." *The Encyclopedia of Philosophy.* Ed. P. Edwards. London/New York 1972. 414–419.

Abramowski, R. "Vom Streit um das Alte Testament." *Theologische Rundschau* 9 (1937) 65–93.

Ackroyd, P. "History and Theology in the Writings of the Chronicler." *Concordia Theological Monthly* 38 (1967) 501–515.

Adam, A. *Making Sense of New Testament Theology: "Modern" Problems and Prospects.* Studies in American Biblical Hermeneutics 11. Macon 1995.

Addinall, P. "Why Read the Bible?" *Expository Times* 105 (1994) 136–140.

Albertz, M. *Die Botschaft des Neuen Testaments.* 2 vols. in 4 pts. Zollikon–Zürich 1947–1957.

_____. "Kerygma und Theologie im Neuen Testament." *Theologische Literaturzeitung* 81 (1956) 341–344 (= *Zeitschrift für die neutestamentliche Wissenschaft* 46 [1955] 267–268).

_____. "Die Krisis der sogenannten neutestamentlichen Theologie." *Zeichen der Zeit* 8 (1954) 370–376.

_____. Review of new ed. of J. Calvin, *Auslegung des Propheten Jesaja. Theologische Literaturzeitung* 76 (1953) 472–73.

Albrektson, B. *History and the Gods.* Lund 1967.

Albright, W.F. "The Ancient Near East and the Religion of Israel." *Journal of Biblical Literature* 59 (1940) 85–112.

_____. "Bultmann's History and Eschatology." *Journal of Biblical Literature* 77 (1958) 244–248.

____. "Return to Biblical Theology." *Christian Century* 75 (1958) 1328–1331.

Alexander, T. & B. Rosner, eds. *New Dictionary of Biblical Theology.* Leicester/Grand Rapids 2000.

Allen, E.L. "The Limits of Biblical Theology." *Journal of Bible and Religion* 25 (1957) 13–18.

Allen, Leonard. "From Dogmatik to Glaubenslehre: Ernst Troeltsch and the Task of Theology." *Fides et Historia* 12/2 (1980) 37–60.

Althaus, P. "Adolf Schlatters Wort an die heutige Theologie." *Zeitschrift für die systematische Theologie* 21 (1950) 95–109.

_____. "Die Gestalt dieser Welt und die Sünde. Ein Beitrag zur Theologie der Geschichte." *Zeitschrift für die systematische Theologie* 9 (1932) 319–338.

Amit, Y. *History and Ideology: An Introduction to Historiography in the Hebrew Bible.* Trans. Y. Lotan. Sheffield 1999.

Anderson, B.W. *Contours of Old Testament Theology.* Minneapolis 1999.

_____. "Myth and Biblical Tradition." *Theology Today* 27 (1970–71) 44–62.

_____. "The New Heilsgeschichte." *Interpretation* 19 (1965) 337–341.

_____, ed. *The Old Testament and Christian Faith.* New York 1963.

_____. "The Problem of Old Testament History." *The London Quarterly and Holburn Review* 190 (1965) 5–11.

_____. Review of B. Childs, *Biblical Theology in Crisis. Religion in Life* 39 (1970) 608–609.

Arnold, M. "Interview d'Oscar Cullmann." *Foi et Vie* 92/1 (1993) 9–17.

Auberlen, C.A. *The Divine Revelation.* Trans. A.B. Paton. Edinburgh 1867.

Aulén, G. *Christus Victor.* Trans. A. Herbert. London 1970.

Aune, D.E. "The Words of God Interpreting the Deeds of God." *Interpretation* 29 (1975) 424–427.

Avis, P. "Karl Barth: The Reluctant Virtuoso." *Theology* 85 (1983) 164–171.

Baab, O. "Old Testament Theology: Its Possibility and Methodology." *The Study of the Bible Today and Tomorrow.* Ed. H.R. Willoughby. Chicago 1947. 401–418.

Bailer, A. *Das systematische Prinzip in der Theologie Adolf Schlatters.* Arbeiten zur Theologie. II. Reihe. Band 12. Stuttgart 1968.

Baillie, D.M. *God Was in Christ.* London ²1955.

Bainton, R. "Patristic Christianity." In R.C. Dentan, ed., *The Idea of History in the Ancient Near East.* London 1955. 215–236.

Baird, W. *History of New Testament Research.* Vol. 1: *From Deism to Tübingen.* Vol. 2: *From Jonathan Edwards to Rudolf Bultmann.* Minneapolis 1992–2002.

Baird, W.R., Jr. "Current Trends in New Testament Study." *Journal of Religion* 39 (1959) 137–153.

Baker, D.L. *Two Testaments, One Bible.* Leicester 1976.

Balla, P. *Challenges to New Testament Theology.* WUNT 2/95. Tübingen 1997.

Balthasar, H. von. *The Theology of Karl Barth.* Trans. J. Drury. New York/Chicago/San Francisco 1971.

Barbour, R. "The Bible—Word of God?" *Biblical Studies.* Ed. J.R. McKay. London 1976. 28–42, 199–200.

_____. *Traditio–Historical Criticism of the Gospels.* London 1972.

Barnett, P. *Jesus and the Logic of History.* Grand Rapids 1997.

Barr, J. *The Bible in the Modern World.* London ²1969.

_____. "Biblical theology." *The Interpreter's Dictionary of the Bible. Supplementary volume.* Ed. K. Krim. New York/Nashville 1976. 104–111.

_____. *Biblical Words for Time.* London 19812.

_____. *The Concept of Biblical Theology.* Minneapolis 1999.

_____. "Evaluation, Commitment, and Objectivity in Biblical Theology." *Reading the Bible in the Global Village.* Ed. H. Räisänen *et al.* Atlanta 2000. 125–152.

_____. *Holy Scripture.* Oxford 1983.

_____. *Old and New in Interpretation.* London ²1982.

_____. "The Problem of Old Testament Theology and the History of Religion." *Canadian Journal of Theology* 3 (1957) 141–149.

_____. "Recent Biblical Theologies. VI. Gerhard von Rad's *Theologie des Alten Testaments*." *Expository Times* 73 (1961–62) 142–146.

_____. "Revelation in History." *The Interpreter's Dictionary of the Bible. Supplementary volume*. Ed. K. Krim. New York/Nashville 1976. 746–749.

_____. "Revelation through History in the Old Testament and in Modern Theology." *Interpretation* 17 (1963) 193–205.

_____. *The Scope and Authority of the Bible*. London 1980.

_____. *The Semantics of Biblical Language*. London 1961.

_____. "Story and History in Biblical Theology." *Journal of Religion* 56 (1976) 1–17.

_____. "Trends and Prospects in Biblical Theology." *Journal of Theological Studies* [new series] 25 (1974) 265–282.

_____. "Wilhelm Vischer and Allegory." *Understanding Poets and Prophets*. Ed. A.G. Auld. Sheffield 1993. 38–60.

Barrett, C.K. "Quomodo historia conscribenda sit." *New Testament Studies* 28 (1982) 303–320.

_____. Review of R. Bultmann, *Theologie des Neuen Testaments*, 3. Lieferung. *Journal of Theological Studies* [new series] 5 (1954) 260–262.

_____. "What Is New Testament Theology?" *Horizons in Biblical Theology* 3 (1981) 1–22.

Barth, C. "Grundprobleme einer Theologie des Alten Testaments." *Evangelische Theologie* 23 (1963) 342–272.

Barth, K. "Der christliche Glaube und die Geschichte." *Schweizerische Theologische Zeitschrift* (1912) 1–18, 49–72.

_____. *Protestant Theology in the Nineteenth Century*. Trans. B. Cozens, J. Bowen, *et al*. London 1972.

_____. *Der Römerbrief*. München ²1922.

Barth, M. "Die Methode von Bultmanns Theologie des Neuen Testaments." *Theologische Zeitschrift* 11 (1955) 1–27.

_____. Review of Bultmann, *Theologie des Neuen Testaments*, vol. 2. *Journal of Religion* 37 (1957) 46–48.

_____. "Whither Biblical Theology." *Interpretation* 25 (1971) 350–354.

Barton, J. "Gerhard von Rad on the World–View of Israel." *Journal of Theological Studies* [new series] 35 (1984) 301–323.

_____. "Old Testament Theology." *Beginning Old Testament Study*. Ed. J. Rogerson. London 1983. 90–112.

Bartsch, H.W. "Anmerkungen zu O. Cullmann: *Christus und die Zeit*." *Kerygma und Mythos*. Vol. 2. Ed. H.W. Bartsch. Hamburg–Volksdorf 1952. 36–38.

Bauer, W. *Orthodoxy and Heresy in Earliest Christianity*. Philadelphia 1971 (German 1934).

Baumgärtel, F. "Zur Frage der theologischen Deutung des Alten Testaments." *Zeitschrift für systematische Theologie* 15 (1938) 136–162.

_____. *Verheissung. Zur Frage des evangelischen Verständnisses des Alten Testaments.* Gütersloh 1952.

Baur, F.C. (See also under Hodgson.)

_____. *Lehrbuch der christlichen Dogmengeschichte.* Darmstadt 1979 (rpt. of ³1868).

_____. *Vorlesungen über neutestamentliche Theologie.* Ed. F.F. Baur. Leipzig 1864.

Bayer, H.F. & R. Yarbrough, "O. Cullmanns progressiv–heilsgeschichtliche Konzeption." *Glaube und Geschichte: Heilsgeschichte als Thema der Theologie.* Ed. H. Stadelmann. Giessen/Basel, Wuppertal 1986. 319–347.

Bayer, O. "Entmythologisierung? Christliche Theologie zwischen Metaphysik und Mythologie im Blick auf Rudolf Bultmann." *Neue Zeitschrift für Systematische Theologie und Religionsphilosophie* 34/2 (1992) 109–124.

Beale, D. *In Pursuit of Purity: American Fundamentalism since 1850.* Greenville 1986.

Beasley–Murray, G.R. *Jesus and the Future.* London 1954.

Bebbington, D. *Patterns in History.* Leicester 1979.

Behm, J. *Heilsgeschichtliche und religionsgeschichtliche Betrachtung des Neuen Testaments.* Zeit- und Streitfragen des Glaubens, der Weltanschauung und Bibelforschung 15. Berlin 1922.

Beisser, F. "Luthers Urteil über die 'Vernunft.'" *Theologische Beiträge* 15 (1984) 150–162.

Beker, J. "Biblical Theology in a Time of Confusion." *Theology Today* 25 (1968–69) 185–194.

_____. "Reflections on Biblical Theology." *Interpretation* 24 (1970) 303–320.

Bellis, A. & J. Kaminsky, eds. *Jews, Christians and the Theology of the Hebrew Scriptures.* Atlanta 2000.

Bengsch, A. *Heilsgeschichte und Heilswissen. Eine Untersuchung zur Struktur und Entfaltung des theologischen Denkens im Werk "Adversus Haereses" des Hl. Irenäus von Lyon.* Leipzig 1957.

Bernoulli, C.A. *Die wissenschaftliche und die kirchliche Methode in der Theologie.* Frieburg/Leipzig/Tübingen 1897.

Bernstein, R. *Beyond Objectivism and Relativism: Science, Hermeneutics, and Praxis.* Oxford 1983.

Bertram, G. "Die Aufgabe einer Theologie beider Testamente." *Kirche im Angriff* 12 (1936) 416–427.

_____. "Neutestamentliche Religionsgeschichte und Theologie." *Deutsche Evangelische Erziehung* 46 (1935) 355–362.

Bettenson, H., ed. *The Early Christian Fathers.* London 1956.

Betz, O. "History of Biblical Theology." *The Interpreter's Dictionary of the Bible.* Ed. G.A. Buttrick, *et al.* Vol. 1. New York/Nashville 1962. 432–437.

_____. "The Problem of Variety and Unity in the New Testament." *Horizons in Biblical Theology* 2 (1980) 3–14.

Bickert, R. "Die Geschichte und das Handeln Jahwes." *Textgemäss.* Ed. E. Gunneweg & O. Kaiser. E. Würthwein Festschrift. Göttingen 1979. 9–27.

Bierberg, R. Review of R. Bultmann, *Theologie des Neuen Testaments*. *Catholic Biblical Quarterly* 15 (1953) 382–386.

Birch, B. "Old Testament Theology: Its Task and Future." *Horizons in Biblical Theology* 6 (1984) iii–viii.

Black, D. & D. Dockery, eds. *Interpreting the New Testament: Essays on Methods and Issues*. Nashville 2001.

Black, M. *A Survey of Christological Thought 1872–1972*. Croall Centenary Lecture. Edinburgh n.d.

Bland, K. "Interpretation, History of: early rabbinic." *The Interpreter's Dictionary of the Bible. Supplementary volume*. Ed. K. Krim. New York/Nashville 1976. 446–448.

Blank, J. "Geschichte und Heilsgeschichte." *Wort und Wahrheit* 23 (1968) 116–127.

Bockmühl, K. *The Challenge of Marxism*. Leicester 1980.

_____, ed. *Die Aktualität der Theologie Adolf Schlatters*. Giessen: Brunnen, 1988.

_____. "Die Wende im Spätwerk Karl Barths." *Theologische Beiträge* 14 (1983) 180–188.

Boers, H. *What Is New Testament Theology?* Philadelphia 1979.

Boman, T. *Das hebräische Denken im Vergleich mit dem griechischen*. Göttingen ⁵1968.

Borsch, F.H. Review of L. Goppelt, *Theology of the New Testament*, vol. 1. *Interpretation* 37 (1983) 80–82.

Bourke, J. "A Survey of Biblical Theology." *Life of the Spirit* 18 (1963) 51–68.

Bowman, J.W. "From Schweitzer to Bultmann." *Theology Today* 11 (1954) 160–178.

Bowman, R.A. "Old Testament Research between the Great Wars." *The Study of the Bible Today and Tomorrow*. Ed. H.R. Willoughby. Chicago 1947. 3–31.

Braaten, C. *History and Hermeneutics*. London 1966.

Brandenburg, A. "Der Zeit- und Geschichtsbegriff bei Karl Barth." *Theologie und Glaube* 45 (1955) 337–378.

Branton, J. "Our Present Situation in Biblical Theology." *Religion in Life* 26 (1956–57) 5–18.

Braun, D. "Heil als Geschichte : Zu Oscar Cullmanns neuem Buch." *Evangelische Theologie* 27 (1967) 57–76.

Braun, H. "Die Problematik einer Theologie des Neuen Testaments." *Zeitschrift für Theologie und Kirche*. Beiheft 2 (1961) 3–18 (= *Das Problem der Theologie des Neuen Testaments*. Ed. G. Strecker. Darmstadt 1975. 405–424).

Bray, G. *Biblical Interpretation Past and Present*. Downers Grove/Leicester 1996.

Brettler, M. "Biblical History and Jewish Biblical Theology." *Journal of Religion* 77/4 (1997) 563–583.

Brezger, R. *Das Schrifttum von Professor D.A. Schlatter*. Beiträge zur Förderung christlicher Theologie 40/2. Gütersloh n.d.

Brierley, P. & H. Wraight. *Atlas of World Christianity*. Nashville 1998.

Bright, J. *The Authority of the Old Testament*. London 1967.

Brinkmann, B. Review of M. Albertz, *Die Botschaft des Neuen Testaments*. *Scholastik* 33 (1958) 267–272.

Bromiley, G. *Historical Theology*. Edinburgh 1978.

Brown, C. "History and the Believer." *History, Criticism and Faith*. Ed. C. Brown. Leicester 1976. 147–216.

_____. *Jesus in European Protestant Thought 1778–1860*. Grand Rapids 1988.

Brown, R.M. "Is There a 'Biblical Theology'?" *Religion in Life* 26 (1956–57) 31–39.

Brox, N. "Worttheologie und Biblische Theologie." *Bibel und Liturgie* 38 (1964–65) 12–16.

Bruce, F.F. "The History of New Testament Study." *New Testament Interpretation*. Ed. I. H. Marshall. Grand Rapids 1978. 21–59.

_____. "Salvation History in the New Testament." *Man and His Salvation*. S.G.F. Brandon Festschrift. Ed. E.J. Sharpe & J.R. Hinnells. Manchester 1973. 75–90.

Brückner, M. "Die neuen Darstellungen der neutestamentlichen Theologie." *Theologische Rundschau* 16 (1913) 363–386, 415–436.

Brueggemann, W. "A Convergence in Recent Old Testament Theologies." *Journal for the Study of the Old Testament* 18 (1980) 2–18.

_____. "James Barr on Old Testament Theology: A Review of *The Concept of Biblical Theology*: An Old Testament Perspective." *Horizons in Biblical Theology* 22 (2000) 58–74.

_____. *Theology of the Old Testament: Testimony, Dispute, Advocacy*. Minneapolis 1997.

Buchheim, K. *Der historische Christus: Geschichtswissenschaftliche Überlegungen zum Neuen Testament*. München 1974.

Büchsel, F. *Theologie des Neuen Testaments: Geschichte des Wortes Gottes im Neuen Testament*. Gütersloh [2]1937.

Bultmann, R. "Autobiographical Reflections of Rudolf Bultmann." *The Theology of Rudolf Bultmann*. Ed. C.W. Kegley. London 1966. xix–xxv.

_____. *Glauben und Verstehen*. Vol 1. Tübingen 1933.

_____. "Heilsgeschichte und Geschichte. Zu O. Cullmann, Christus und die Zeit." *Das Problem der Theologie des Neuen Testaments*. Ed. G. Strecker. Darmstadt 1975. 296–308 (=*Theologische Literaturzeitung* 73 [1948] 659–666).

_____. "History and Eschatology in the New Testament." *New Testament Studies* 1 (1954) 5–16.

_____. *Jesus*. Berlin 1929.

_____. *Primitive Christianity in its Contemporary Setting*. Trans. R. Fuller. New York 1956.

_____. "Das Problem einer theologischen Exegese des Neuen Testaments." *Das Problem der Theologie des Neuen Testaments*. Ed. G. Strecker. Darmstadt 1975. 249–277.

_____. *Theologie des Neuen Testaments.* Uni–Taschenbücher 630. Tübingen ⁸1980.

Burrows, M. "The Task of Biblical Theology." *Journal of Bible and Religion* 14 (1946) 13–15.

Busch, E. *Karl Barth.* London 1965.

Byrne, J. *Religion and the Enlightenment: From Descartes to Kant.* Louisville 1996.

Cairns, D. "A Reappraisal of Bultmann's Theology." *Religious Studies* 17 (1981) 469–485.

Calhoun, D. *Princeton Seminary.* 2 volumes. Edinburgh/Carlisle 1994–1996.

Callahan, J.F. *Four Views of Time in Ancient Philosophy.* Cambridge, MA 1948.

Campenhausen, H. von. "Die Entstehung der Heilsgeschichte. Der Aufbau des christlichen Geschichtsbildes in der Theologie des ersten und zweiten Jahrhunderts." *Saeculum* 21 (1970) 189–212.

_____. "Irenäus und das Neue Testament." *Theologische Literaturzeitung* 90 (1965) 2–8.

Carson, D. "New Testament Theology." *Dictionary of the Later New Testament and Its Development.* Ed. R. Martin & P. Davids. Downers Grove/Leicester 1997. 796–814.

_____. "Redaction Criticism: On the Legitimacy and Illegitimacy of a Literary Tool." *Scripture and Truth.* Ed. D. Carson and J. Woodbridge. Grand Rapids 1983. 119–142, 376–381.

Catchpole, D. Review of G. Ladd, *A Theology of the New Testament. Theology* 79 (1976) 126–127.

Catechism of the Catholic Church. Liguori, MO 1994.

Cavert, S. Review of G. Ladd, *A Theology of the New Testament. Religion in Life* 44 (1975) 249–250.

Chadwick, H. "The Bible and Historical Study." *The Churchman* 67 (1946) 179–186.

Chapman, M. "Religion, Ethics and the History of Religion School." *Scottish Journal of Theology* 46 (1993) 43–78.

Charlot, J. *New Testament Disunity.* New York 1970.

Childs, B. *Biblical Theology in Crisis.* Philadelphia 1970.

_____. *Biblical Theology of the Old and New Testament.* Minneapolis 1993.

_____. "Is Biblical Theology Still Possible?" Public lecture in Cambridge University, November 28, 1984.

_____. "Some Reflections on the Search for a Biblical Theology." *Horizons in Biblical Theology* 4 (1982) 1–12.

Christ, F., ed. *Oikonomia: Heilsgeschichte als Thema der Theologie.* Hamburg 1967.

Clayton, J.P., ed. *Ernst Troeltsch and the Future of Theology.* Cambridge, 1976.

Clements, R. *A Century of Old Testament Study.* Guildford/London 1976.

_____. "Messianic Prophecy or Messianic History." *Horizons in Biblical Theology* 1 (1979) 87–104.

_____. "The Problem of Old Testament Theology." *The London Quarterly and Holburn Review* 190 (1965) 11–17.

_____. "The Study of the Old Testament." *Nineteenth Century Religious Thought in the West.* Ed. Ninian Smart *et al.* Vol. 3. Cambridge UK 1985. 109–141.

_____. "Theodorus C. Vriezen. *An Outline of Old Testament Theology.*" *Contemporary Old Testament Theologians.* Ed. R. Laurin. Valley Forge, PA 1970. 121–140.

Clemons, J.T. "Critics and Criticism of Salvation History." *Religion in Life* 41 (1972) 89–100.

Clines, D.J.A. "Possibilities and Priorities of Biblical Interpretation in an International Perspective." *Biblical Interpretation* 1 (1993) 67–87.

Coggins, R.J. "History and Story in Old Testament Study." *Journal for the Study of the Old Testament* 11 (1970) 36–46.

Cohen, H. *Die Religion der Vernunft aus den Quellen des Judentums.* Leipzig 1919.

Collins, J.J. "The 'Historical' Character of the Old Testament in Recent Old Testament Theology." *Catholic Biblical Quarterly* 41 (1979) 185–204.

Conzelmann, H. "Fragen an Gerhard von Rad." *Evangelische Theologie* 24 (1964) 113–125.

_____. *An Outline of the Theology of the New Testament.* Trans. J. Bowden. London 1969.

Copleston, F. *A History of Philosophy.* Vol. 7. Pt. 2. New York 1965.

Craig, C.T. "Biblical Theology and the Rise of Historicism." *Journal of Biblical Literature* 62 (1943) 281–294.

_____. "Current Trends in New Testament Study." *Journal of Biblical Literature* 57 (1938) 359–375.

Craigie, P. "The Role and Relevance of Biblical Research." *Journal for the Study of the Old Testament* 18 (1980) 19–31.

Cremer, D. "Protestant Theology in Early Weimar Germany: Barth, Tillich, and Bultmann." *Journal of the History of Ideas* 56 (1995) 289–307.

Cremer, H. *Glaube, Schrift und heilige Geschichte.* Gütersloh 1896.

Crenshaw, J. *Gerhard von Rad.* Waco 1978.

_____. "Gerhard von Rad *(1901–1971)*." *Historical Handbook of Major Biblical Interpreters.* Ed. D. McKim. Downers Grove 1998. 526–530.

Cross, F.L. *The Early Christian Fathers.* London 1960.

Crüsemann, F. "Tendenzen der alttestamentlichen Wissenschaft zwischen 1933 and 1945." *Wort und Dienst* 20 (1989) 79–103.

Cullmann, O. "An Autobiographical Sketch." Trans. T. Tyce. *Scottish Journal of Theology* 14 (1961) 228–233.

_____. *Christ and Time.* Trans. F. Filson. Rev. ed. Philadelphia 1964.

_____. *The Christology of the New Testament.* Trans. S. Guthrie and C. Hall. London 1959.

_____. "The Connection of Primal Events and End Events with the New Testament Redemptive History." *The Old Testament and Christian Faith.* Ed. B. Anderson. Trans. L. Gaston and B. Anderson. New York 1963. 115–123.

_____. *The Earliest Christian Confessions*. Trans. J. Reid. London 1949.

_____. *The Early Church*. London 1956.

_____. "Gottes Heilsplan in der Weltgeschichte: Heil in Christus als Problem für die Gegenwart." *Evangelische Kommentare* 12 (1974) 730–733.

_____. *Heil als Geschichte*. Tübingen 1965 (Eng. trans. *Salvation in History*. London 1967).

_____. *The New Testament*. Trans. D. Pardee. London 1968.

_____. "The Relevance of Redemptive History." *Soli Deo Gloria*. W.C. Robinson Festschrift. Ed. J.M. Richards. Trans. J.A. Hare. Richmond 1968. 9–22.

_____. *Vorträge und Aufsätze 1925–1962*. Ed. K. Fröhlich. Tübingen/Zürich 1966.

_____. "Zur Frage der Erforschung der neutestamentlichen Christologie." *Kerygma und Dogma* 1 (1955) 133–141.

Cwiekowski, F. "Biblical Theology as Historical Theology." *Catholic Biblical Quarterly* 24 (1962) 404–411.

Dahl, N. "Die Theologie des Neuen Testaments." *Theologische Rundschau* 22 (1954) 21–49.

Daniélou, J. "The New Testament and the Theology of History." *Texte und Untersuchungen* 73 [*Studia Evangelica* I] 1959.

D'Arcy, M.C. *The Sense of History*. London 1959.

Davidson, R. "Faith and History in the Old Testament." *Expository Times* 77 (1965–66) 100–104.

Davidson, R.M. *Typology in Scripture*. Andrews Univ. Seminary Doctoral Dissertation Series. Vol. II. Berien Springs, MI 1981.

Davies, R.H. "Gerhard von Rad, *Old Testament Theology*." *Contemporary Old Testament Theologians*. Ed. R. Laurin. Valley Forge, PA 1970. 63–89.

Dawes, G., ed. *The Historical Jesus Quest*. Leiden/Louisville 1999.

De Lacey, D.R. Review of Goppelt, *Theologie des Neuen Testaments*, vols. 1 and 2, *Themelios* 9 (1984) 30.

Delling, G. *Das Zeitverständnis des neuen Testaments*. Gütersloh 1940.

Dentan, R.C., ed. *The Idea of History in the Ancient Near East*. London 1955.

_____. *Preface to Old Testament Theology*. New York ²1963.

Despland, M. *Kant on History and Religion*. Montreal/London 1973.

Dessauer, P. *Der Anfang und das Ende: Eine theologische und religiöse Betrachtung zur Heilsgeschichte*. Leipzig 1939.

DeVries, S. *Yesterday, Today, and Tomorrow: Time and History in the Old Testament*. Grand Rapids 1975.

Dibelius, M. *Geschichtliche und übergeschichtliche Religion im Christentum*. Göttingen 1925.

Dietrich, D.J. & M.J. Himes. *The Legacy of the Tübingen School: the Relevance of Nineteenth-Century Theology for the Twenty-First Century*. New York 1997.

Dillistone, F.W. *C.H. Dodd: Interpreter of the New Testament*. Grand Rapids 1977.

Dinkler, E. "Bibelkritik II. NT." *Religion in Geschichte und Gegenwart*. Vol. 1. ³1957. 1188–1190.

_____. "Earliest Christianity." *The Idea of History in the Ancient Near East*. London 1955. 169–214.

_____. "Existentialist Interpretation of the New Testament." *Journal of Religion* 32 (1952) 87–96.

Dintaman, S.F. *Creative Grace: Faith and History in the Theology of Adolf Schlatter*. New York 1993.

Dobschütz, E. von. "Der Historiker und das Neue Testament." *Zeitschrift für die neutestamentliche Wissenschaft* 32 (1933) 42–52.

_____. "Zeit und Raum im Denken des Urchristentums." *Journal of Biblical Literature* 41 (1922) 212–223.

Dodd, C.H. *The Apostolic Preaching and its Developments*. London 1970 (1936).

_____. *The Bible Today*. London 1946.

_____. *History and the Gospel*. London 1938.

_____. "Thirty Years of New Testament Study." *Religion in Life* 19 (1950) 323–333.

Donahue, J. "The Changing Shape of New Testament Theology." *Theological Studies* 50/2 (1989) 314–335.

Dorman, T.M. "Cullmann, Oscar *(b. 1902)*." *Historical Handbook of Major Biblical Interpreters*. Ed. D. McKim. Downers Grove 1998. 467–471.

_____. "The Hermeneutics of Oscar Cullmann." Ph.D. dissertation, Fuller Theological Seminary. 1983.

Drescher, H.G. "Das Problem der Geschichte bei E. Troeltsch." *Zeitschrift für Theologie und Kirche* 57 (1960) 186–230.

Duncan, C.H. "Dr Rudolf Bultmann's Epistemology: An Examination of the Epistemological Presuppositions in his Theology." Ph.D. dissertation, Cambridge University, 1959.

Dunn, J. "Demythologizing—The Problem of Myth in the New Testament." *New Testament Interpretation*. Ed. I.H. Marshall. Grand Rapids 1977. 285–307.

_____. *Unity and Diversity in the New Testament*. London 1977.

_____ & J. Mackey. *New Testament Theology in Dialogue*. London 1987.

Dymale, H.R. "The Theology of Adolf Schlatter with Special Reference to his Understanding of History." Ph.D. dissertation, University of Iowa, 1966.

Ebeling, G. *The Problem of Historicity*. Philadelphia 1967.

_____. *Word and Faith*. London 1963.

Egg, G. *Adolf Schlatters Position, gezeigt an seiner Matthäusinterpretation*. Arbeiten zur Theologie. III. Reihe. Band 14. Stuttgart 1968.

Ehrman, B. *The New Testament: A Historical Introduction to the Early Christian Writings*. New York/Oxford 1997.

Eichrodt, W. "Hat die alttestamentliche Theologie noch selbständige Bedeutung innerhalb der alttestamentlichen Wissenschaft?" *Zeitschrift für die alttestamentliche Wissenschaft* 6 (1929) 83–91.

_____. "Offenbarung und Geschichte im Alten Testament." *Theologische Zeitschrift* 4 (1948) 321–331.

_____. *Theologie des Alten Testaments.* Vol. 1. Stuttgart ⁵1957.

_____. *Theology of the Old Testament.* Trans. J. Baker. 2 vols. London 1961, 1967.

_____. "Zur Frage der theologischen Exegese des Alten Testaments." *Theologische Blätter* 17 (1938) 73–87.

Eissfeldt, O. "Israelitisch–jüdische Religionsgeschichte und alttestamentliche Theologie." *Zeitschrift für die alttestamentliche Wissenschaft* 3 (1926) 1–12.

_____. "Otto Procksch." *Kleine Schriften.* Vol. 3. Ed. R. Sellheim & F. Maass. Tübingen 1966. 131.

Ellis, E. "Dating the New Testament." *New Testament Studies* 26 (1980) 487–502.

_____. "Die Datierung des Neuen Testaments." *Theologische Zeitschrift* 42 (1986) 409–430.

Eltester, W. "Notizen." *Zeitschrift für die neutestamentliche Wissenschaft* 45 (1953–54) 276–277.

_____. Review of R. Bultmann, *Theologie des Neuen Testaments,* vol. 1. *Zeitschrift für die neutestamentliche Wissenschaft* 43 (1950–51) 275–277.

Epp, E.J. & G.W. McRae, eds. *The New Testament and Its Modern Interpreters.* Philadelphia/Atlanta 1989.

Ernst, J. *Herr der Geschichte.* Stuttgart 1978.

Eslinger, R.L. "Historicity and Historicality: A Comparision of Carl Michalson and Oscar Cullmann." Ph.D. dissertation, Boston University, 1970.

Evang, M. *Rudolf Bultmann in seiner Frühzeit.* BHT 74. Tübingen 1988.

Fangmeier, J. "Heilsgeschichte? Einige Marginalien, besonders zum Gespräch zwischen Karl Barth und Oscar Cullmann." *Geschichte und Zukunft.* Ed. J. Fangmeier & M. Geiger. Zürich 1967. 5–27.

Fascher, E. "Eine Neuordnung der neutestamentlichen Fachdisziplin?" *Theologische Literaturzeitung* 83 (1958) 609–618.

Feine, P. *Theologie des Neuen Testaments.* Berlin ⁸1953.

Felber, S. *Wilhelm Vischer als Ausleger der Heiligen Schrift. Eine Untersuchung zum Christuszeugnis des Alten Testaments.* Göttingen 1999.

Fenton, J. "The Post–Liberal Theology of Christ without Myth." *Journal of Religion* 43 (1963) 93–104.

_____. "Recent Biblical Theologies. II. Rudolf Bultmann's *Theology of the New Testament.*" *Expository Times* 73 (1961–62) 8–11.

Filson, F. "Method in Studying Biblical History." *Journal of Biblical Literature* 69 (1950) 1–18.

Fisch, H. "Ruth and the Structure of Covenant History." *Vetus Testamentum* 32 (1982) 425–437.

Fischer, D.H. *Historians' Fallacies.* New York 1970.

Fischer, H. "Natürliche Theologie im Wandel." *Zeitschrift für Theologie und Kirche* 80 (1983) 85–102.

Fisher, P. "The Triumph of the Irrational in Postenlightenment Theology." *Andrews University Seminary Studies* 37 (1999) 5–22.

Flechsenhaar, G. *Das Geschichtsproblem in der Theologie Johannes von Hofmanns.* Giessen 1935.

Flückiger, F. "Heilsgeschichte und Weltgeschichte." *Evangelische Theologie* 18 (1958) 37–47.

Fohrer, G. "Remarks on Modern Interpretations of the Prophets." *Journal of Biblical Literature* 80 (1961) 309–319.

_____. Review of H.–J. Kraus, *Geschichte der historisch–kritischen Erforschung des Alten Testaments,* ²1969. *Theologische Literaturzeitung* 99 (1974) 502–503.

_____. *Theologische Grundstrukturen des Alten Testaments.* Berlin 1972.

_____. "Die zeitliche und überzeitliche Bedeutung des Alten Testaments." *Evangelische Theologie* 9 (1949) 447–460.

Fowl, S. *Engaging Scripture.* Oxford 1998.

Fosdick, H.E. *The Living of These Days.* New York 1956.

Freedman, D.N. "The Biblical Idea of History." *Interpretation* 21 (1967) 32–49.

Frei, H. *The Eclipse of Biblical Narrative.* New Haven/London 1974.

Fresenius, W. "Geschichte und Historie." *Evangelische Theologie* 27 (1967) 624–627.

Friedman, R. "Kierkegaard: First Existentialist or Last Kantian?" *Religious Studies* 18 (1982) 159–170.

Friedrich, G. "'Begriffsgeschichtliche' Untersuchungen im Theologischen Wörterbuch zum Neuen Testament." *Auf das Wort kommt es an.* Ed. J. Friedrich. Göttingen 1978. 524–550.

_____. "Die Problematik eines Theologischen Wörterbuchs zum Neuen Testament." Texte und Untersuchungen 73 (1959 [= *Studia Evangelica* I]). 481–486.

Frik, H. "Was bewegt der Fundamentalismus?" Review of J. Barr, *Fundamentalismus. Evangelische Theologie* 43 (1983) 484–486.

Fröhlich, K. "Die Mitte des Neuen Testaments: Oscar Cullmanns Beitrag zur Theologie der Gegenwart." *Oikonomia.* Ed. F. Christ. Hamburg 1967. 203–219.

Fuller, R.H. "New Testament Theology." *The New Testament and Its Modern Interpreters.* Ed. E.J. Epp & G.W. McRae. Philadelphia 1989. 565–584.

_____. "Some Further Reflections on *Heilsgeschichte.*" *Union Seminary Quarterly Review* 22 (1967) 93–103.

Funk, R. *Honest to Jesus: Jesus for a New Millenium.* San Francisco 1996.

_____. "The Watershed of the American Biblical Tradition: The Chicago School, First Phase, 1892–1920." *Journal of Biblical Literature* 95 (1976) 4–22.

Furnish, V.P. "The Historical Criticism of the New Testament: A Survey of Origins." *Bulletin of the John Rylands Library* 56 (1974) 336–370.

Galloway, A. *Wolfhart Pannenburg.* London 1973.

Garrett, C.R. "The Development of Rudolf Bultmann's Views of Christology and Revelation: 1903–1930." PhD. dissertation, Sheffield University, 1979.

Gasque, W. "The Promise of Adolf Schlatter." *Evangelical Review of Theology* 4 (1980) 20–30.

Geisser, M. "Mysterium Salutis." *Theologische Zeitschrift* 32 (1976) 159–166.

Georgi, D. "Rudolf Bultmann's Theology of the New Testament Revisited." *Bultmann, Retrospect and Prospect. The Centenary Symposium at Wellesley.* Ed. E. Hobbs. HThS 35. Philadelphia 1985. 75–87.

Gerrish, B. "Errors and Insights in the Understanding of Revelation: A Provisional Response." *Journal of Religion* 78 (1998) 64–88.

Gese, H. "Erwägungen zur Einheit der biblischen Theologie." *Zeitschrift für Theologie und Kirche* 67 (1970) 417–436.

_____. "Geschichtliches Denken im Alten Orient und im Alten Testament." *Zeitschrift für Theologie und Kirche* 55 (1958) 127–145.

_____. *Zur biblischen Theologie.* Tübingen 1983.

Gilkey, L. "Cosmology, Ontology, and the Travail of Biblical Language." *Journal of Religion* 41 (1961) 194–205.

_____. "The Roles of the 'Descriptive' or 'Historical' and of the 'Normative' in Our Work." *Criterion* 20 (1981) 10–17.

Glover, W.B. *Evangelical Nonconformists and Higher Criticism in the Nineteenth Century.* London 1954.

Gnuse, R. "Authority of the Scriptures: Quest for a Norm." *Biblical Theology Bulletin* 13 (1983) 59–66.

_____. *Heilsgeschichte as a Model for Biblical Theology.* Lanham/New York/London 1989.

Goetz, S. & C. Blomberg, "The Burden of Proof." *Journal for the Study of the New Testament* 11 (1981) 39–63.

Gogarten, F. *Demythologizing and History.* London 1955.

Goldingay, J. *Approaches to Old Testament Interpretation.* Leicester 1981.

_____. "Diversity and Unity in Old Testament Theology." *Vetus Testamentum* 34 (1984) 153–168.

_____. "'That you may know that Jahweh is God': A Study in the Relationship between Theology and Historical Truth in the Old Testament." *Tyndale Bulletin* 23 (1972) 58–93.

_____. *Theological Diversity and the Authority of the Old Testament.* Grand Rapids 1987.

Goppelt, L. *Apostolic and Post–Apostolic Times.* Trans. R. Guelich. Grand Rapids 1980.

_____. "Die Authorität der Heiligen Schrift und die Bibelkritik." *Wort Gottes und Bekenntnis.* Sonderdruck zur Rüstzeit der 15. ordentlichen Landessynode in Loccum. Pattensen 1954.

_____. *Christentum und Judentum im ersten und zweiten Jahrhundert.* Gütersloh 1954.

_____. *Christologie und Ethik.* Göttingen 1968.

_____. "Der Ertrag einer Epoche. Vier Darstellungen der Theologie des Neuen Testaments." *Lutherische Monatshefte* 11 (1972) 96–98.

_____. "The Existence of the Early Church in History according to Apostolic and Early Catholic Thought." *Current Issues in New Testament Interpretation.* Ed. W. Klassen & G. Snyder. London 1962. 193–209.

_____. "Heilsoffenbarung und Geschichte nach der Offenbarung des Johannes." *Theologische Literaturzeitung* 77 (1952) 513–522.

_____. "Das hermeneutische Problem in der gegenwärtigen neutestamentlichen Wissenschaft." *Amtsblatt der evangelisch–lutherischen Kirche in Thüringen* 9 (1956) 103–105.

_____. Review of M. Albertz, *Die Botschaft des Neuen Testaments. Evangelisch–Lutherische Kirchenzeitung* 13 (1959) 222–223.

_____. Review of O. Cullmann, *Heil als Geschichte. Theologische Zeitschrift* 22 (1966) 51–56.

_____. *Theologie des Neuen Testaments.* 2 vols. Göttingen ³1981.

_____. *Typos.* Darmstadt ²1969.

Gorman, J. *The Expression of Historical Knowledge.* Edinburgh 1982.

Gorringe, T. "In Defence of the Identification: Scripture as Word of God." *Scottish Journal of Theology* 32 (1979) 303–318.

Gottwald, N. "W. Eichrodt, *Theology of the Old Testament.*" *Contemporary Old Testament Theologians.* Ed. R. Laurin. Valley Forge, PA 1970. 23–62.

Grabbe, L., ed. *Can a "History of Israel" Be Written?* Sheffield 1997.

Grässer, E. *Albert Schweitzer als Theologe.* Beiträge zur historischen Theologie 60. Tübingen 1979.

_____. "Offene Fragen im Umkreis einer biblischen Theologie." *Zeitschrift für Theologie und Kirche* 77 (1980) 200–221.

_____. *Das Problem der Parusieverzögerung.* Berlin/New York ³1977.

_____. "Notwendigkeit und Möglichkeiten heutiger Bultmannrezeption." *Zeitschrift für Theologie und Kirche* 91 (1994) 272–284.

_____. "Rudolf Bultmann zum Gedächtnis." *Zeitschrift für die neutestamentliche Wissenschaft* 75 (1984) 1.

Grant, F.C. Review of R. Bultmann, *Theologie des Neuen Testaments. Journal of Biblical Literature* 69 (1950) 69–73; 71 (1952) 52–53; 73 (1954) 51–53.

Grant, R.M. "'Development' in Early Christian Doctrine." *Journal of Religion* 39 (1959) 120–128.

Green, B. "The Foundations of New Testament Theology." *Interpreting the New Testament: Essays on Methods and Issues.* Ed. D. Black & D. Dockery. Nashville 2001. 481–505.

Greig, A.J. "A Critical Note on the Origin of the Term Heilsgeschichte." *Expository Times* 87 (1976) 118–119.

_____. "Geschichte and Heilsgeschichte in Old Testament Interpretation with particular reference to the work of Gerhard von Rad." Ph.D. dissertation, Edinburgh University, 1974.

_____. "Some Formative Aspects in the Development of Gerhard von Rad's Idea of History." *Andrews University Seminary Studies* 16 (1978) 313–331.

Greschat, M., ed. *Theologen des Protestantismus im 19. und 20. Jahrhundert I.* Stuttgart *et al.* 1978.

Gressmann, H. "Die Aufgaben der alttestamentlichen Forschung." *Zeitschrift für die alttestamentliche Wissenschaft* 1 (1924) 1–33.

Griffen, D.R. "Relativism, Divine Causation, and Biblical Theology." *Encounter* 36 (1975) 342–360.

Gritsch, E.W. "William Dilthey and the Interpretation of History." *Lutheran Quarterly* 15 (1963) 58–69.

Grudem, W. "Scripture's Self–Attestation and the Problem of Formulating a Doctrine of Scripture." *Scripture and Truth.* Ed. D. Carson & J. Woodbridge. Grand Rapids 1983. 15–59, 359–368.

Guelich, R., ed. *Unity and Diversity in New Testament Theology.* G.E. Ladd Festschrift. Grand Rapids 1978.

Güting, E. "Zu den Voraussetzungen des systematischen Denkens Adolf Schlatters." *Neue Zeitschrift für systematische Theologie* 15 (1973) 132–147.

Güttgemans, E. "Linguistisch–literaturwissenschaftliche Grundlegung einer neutestamentlichen Theologie." *Linguistica Biblica* 13/14 (1972) 2–18.

_____. "Literatur zur Neutestamentlichen Theologie." *Verkündigung und Forschung* 12 (1967) 38–87.

Guthrie, D. *New Testament Theology.* Downers Grove 1981.

_____. Review of L. Goppelt, *Theology of the New Testament,* vol. 1. *Journal of the Evangelical Theological Society* 26 (1983) 238–240.

Gwynne, P. *Special Divine Action: Key Issues in the Contemporary Debate (1965–1995).* Rome 1996.

Gyllenberg, R. "Die Unmöglichkeit einer Theologie des Alten Testaments." *Abhandlungen der Herder–Gesellschaft und des Herder–Instituts zu Riga* 6 (1938) 64–68.

Haacker, K. "Biblische Theologie und historische Kritik." *Theologische Beiträge* 8 (1977) 223–226.

_____. *Neutestamentliche Wissenschaft.* Wuppertal 1981.

_____, et al. *Biblische Theologie heute.* Biblisch–theologische Studien 1. Neukirchen–Vluyn 1977.

Hafemann, S. J. "Baur, F(erdinand) C(hristian) (*1792–1860*)." *Historical Handbook of Major Biblical Interpreters.* Ed. D.K. McKim. Downers Grove/Leicester 1998. 285–289.

Hagenbach, K.R. *A Text-book of the History of Doctrines.* 2 vols. Trans. H.B. Smith. New York 1861–1862.

_____. *History of the Church in the Eighteenth and Nineteenth Centuries.* Vol. 2. Trans. J.F. Hurst. London 1870.

Hall, David R. *The Gospel Framework: Fiction or Fact?* Carlisle, 1997.

Harbesmeier, G. "Die Theologie Rudolf Bultmanns und die Philosophie." *Zeit und Geschichte: Denkausgabe zu Rudolf Bultmann zum 80. Geburtstag.* Ed. E. Dinkler. Tübingen 1964. 467–475.

Harder, G. "Martin Albertz' Beitrag zur neutestamentlichen Einleitungswissenschaft." In *Vom Herrengeheimnis der Wahrheit.* Ed. K. Scharf. Fs. Heinrich Vogel. Berlin/Stuttgart 1962. 179–195.

Haroutonian, J. "The Bible and the Word of God: The Importance of Biblical Theology." *Interpretation* 1 (1947) 291–308.

Harrington, D. "The Reception of Walter Bauer's *Orthodoxy and Heresy in Earliest Christianity* During the Last Decade." *Harvard Theological Review* 73 (1980) 289–298.

Harrington, W.J. *The Path of Biblical Theology.* Dublin 1973.

Harris, H. *David Friedrich Strauss and his Theology.* Cambridge 1973.

_____. *The Tübingen School.* Oxford 1975.

Harrisville, R.A. "Von Hofmann, Johann Christian Konrad (*1810–1877*)." *Historical Handbook of Major Biblical Interpreters.* Ed. D.K. McKim. Downers Grove/Leicester 1998. 376–380.

_____ and Walter Sundberg. *The Bible in Modern Culture: Theology and Historical-Critical Method from Spinoza to Käsemann.* Grand Rapids ²2002.

Hart, T. "A Capacity for Ambiguity? The Barth-Bultmann Debate Revisited." *Tyndale Bulletin* 44 (1993) 289–305.

_____, ed. *The Dictionary of Historical Theology.* Grand Rapids/Carlisle 2000.

Harvey, A.E. *Jesus and the Constraints of History.* London 1967.

Harvey, V. *The Historian and the Believer.* London 1967.

_____. "The Pathos of Liberal Theology." *Journal of Religion* 56 (1976) 382–391.

Hasel, G. "Biblical Theology: Then, Now, and Tomorrow." *Horizons in Biblical Theology* 4 (1982) 61–93.

_____. "A Decade of Old Testament Theology: Retrospect and Prospect." *Zeitschrift für die alttestamentliche Wissenschaft* 93 (1981) 165–183.

_____. *New Testament Theology: Basic Issues in the Current Debate.* Grand Rapids 1978.

_____. *Old Testament Theology: Basic Issues in the Current Debate.* Rev. ed. Grand Rapids 1975.

_____. "The Problem of History in Old Testament Theology." *Andrews University Seminary Studies* 8 (1970) 32–46.

_____. "The Relationship between Biblical Theology and Systematic Theology." *Trinity Journal* NS 5 (1984) 113–127.

Haussleiter, J., ed. *Grundlinien der Theologie Joh. Christ. K. v. Hofmanns in seiner eigenen Darstellung.* Leipzig 1910.

Hayes, J. & F. Prussner. *Old Testament Theology. Its History and Development.* Atlanta/London 1985.

Haynes, Stephen R. "Between the Times: German Theology and the Weimar Zeitgeist." *Soundings* 79 (1991) 9–44.

Hebblewaithe, B. "'True' and 'False' in Christology." *The Philosophical Frontiers of Theology.* Ed. B. Hebblewaithe & S. Sutherland. Cambridge 1982. 227–238.

Heick, O. "Recent German New Testament Studies, 1933–37." *Lutheran Church Quarterly* 11 (1938) 159–176.

Heinisch, P. *Theologie des Neuen Testaments: Die heilige Schrift des Alten Testaments übersetzt und erklärt.* Ergänzungsband I. Bonn 1940.

Heintz, J.-G. "In Memoriam: Professeur Edmond Jacob (1.XI.1909–17.I.1998)." *Zeitschrift für die alttestamentliche Wissenschaft* 110 (1998) 485–488.

Hellbardt, H. "Die Auslegung des AT als theologische Diziplin." *Theologische Blätter* 16 (1937) 129–143.

Helm, P. "Faith, Evidence, and the Scriptures." *Scripture and Truth.* Ed. D. Carson and J. Woodbridge. Grand Rapids 1983. 299–320, 411.

Hemer, C. Review of H. Staudinger, *The Trustworthiness of the Gospels. Themelios* 9 (1983) 29.

Hemer, J. *Karl Barth.* Westminster, MD 1962.

Hengel, M. *The Atonement.* Trans. J. Bowden. Philadelphia 1981.

_____. "Kerygma oder Geschichte?" *Theologische Quartalschrift* 151 (1971) 323–336.

_____. "Neutestamentliche Wege und Holzwege." *Evangelische Kommentare* 3 (1970) 112–114.

_____. *Zur urchristlichen Geschichtsschreibung.* Stuttgart 1979.

Herberg, W. "Faith as Heilsgeschichte: The Meaning of Redemptive History in Human Existence." *The Christian Scholar* 39 (1956) 25–31.

_____. *Faith Enacted as History.* Ed. B. Anderson. Philadelphia 1976.

Herion, G. "The Role of Historical Narrative in Biblical Thought: The Tendencies Underlying Old Testament Historiography." *Journal for the Study of the Old Testament* 21 (1981) 25–57.

Hermesmann, H.-G. *Zeit und Heil. Oscar Cullmanns Theologie der Heilsgeschichte.* Paderborn 1979.

Herrmann, R. *Bibel und Hermeneutik. Gesammelte und nachgelassene Werke.* Vol. 3. Ed. H. Beintker, *et al.* Göttingen 1971.

Herrmann, S. *Time and History.* Trans. J. Blevins. Nashville 1981.

Herrmann, W. Review of E. Troeltsch, *Die Bedeutung der Geschichtlichkeit Jesu für den Glauben.* Reprinted in *Zeitschrift für Theologie und Kirche* 57 (1960) 231–237.

Hesse, F. *Abschied von der Heilsgeschichte.* Theologische Studien 108. Zürich 1971.

Hessen, J. *Griechische oder biblische Theologie? Das Problem der Hellenisierung des Christentums in neuer Beleuchtung.* München/Basel ²1962.

Hester, C. "Gedanken zu Ferdinand Christian Baurs Entwicklung als Historiker anhand zwei unbekannter Breife." *Zeitschrift für Kirchengeschichte* 84 (1973) 249–269.

Higgins, A.J.B. "The Growth of New Testament Theology." *Scottish Journal of Theology* 6 (1953) 275–286.

_____. Review of G. Ladd, *Theology of the New Testament. Scottish Journal of Theology* 30 (1977) 389–391.

Hill, D. *Greek Words and Hebrew Meanings.* Society for New Testament Studies Monograph Series 5. Cambridge 1967.

Himes, M. J. *Ongoing Incarnation: Johann Möhler and the Beginnings of Modern Ecclesiology.* New York 1997.

Hinze, B. "The End of Salvation History." *Horizons* 18/2 (1991) 227–245.

Hirschberger, J. *Kleine Philosophiegeschichte.* Freiburg/Basel/Wien [18]1983.

Hobbs, E. C., ed. *Bultmann, Retrospect and Prospect. The Centenary Symposium at Wellesley.* HThS 35. Philadelphia 1985.

Hodgson, P. C. "Alienation and Reconciliation in Hegelian and Post–Hegelian Perspective." *Modern Theology* 2 (1985) 42–63.

_____, ed. and trans. *Ferdinand Christian Baur on the Writing of Church History.* New York 1968.

_____. "Hegel's Approach to Religion: The Dialectic of Speculation and Phenomenology." *Journal of Religion* 64 (1984) 158–172.

Hofmann, J.C.K. von. *Die heilige Schrift neuen Testaments zusammenhängend untersucht.* 11 vols. Nördlingen [2]1869–1886.

_____. *Interpreting the Bible.* Trans. C. Preus. Minneapolis 1959.

_____. *Der Schriftbeweis.* 2 vols. in 3 pts. Nördlingen [2]1857, [2]1859, [2]1860.

_____. *Weissagung und Erfüllung im alten und im neuen Testamente.* 2 vols. Nördlingen 1841, 1844.

Hogan, T. "The Quest for the Historical Essence of Ernst Troeltsch." *Pacifica* 7 (1994) 295–307.

Holmström, F. *Das eschatologische Denken der Gegenwart. Drei Etappen der theologischen Entwicklung des zwangstigsten Jahrhunderts.* Trans. H. Kruska. Gütersloh 1936.

Holtz, T. Review of L. Goppelt, *Theologie des Neuen Testaments,* vols. 1 and 2. *Theologische Literaturzeitung* 101 (1976) 424–430; 105 (1980) 599–602.

Holtzmann, H.J. *Lehrbuch der Neutestamentlichen Theologie.* 2 vols. Freiburg/Leipzig 1897.

_____. Review of A. Schlatter, *Die Theologie des Neuen Testaments. Theologische Literaturzeitung* 35 (1910) 299–303.

Hordern, W. *A Layman's Guide to Protestant Theology.* New York/London 1968.

Hoskyns, E. & N. Davey. *The Riddle of the New Testament.* London [2]1936.

House, P. *Old Testament Theology.* Downers Grove 1998.

Hübner, H. "Biblische Theologie und Theologie des Neuen Testaments. Eine programmatische Skizze." *Kerygma und Dogma* 27 (1981) 2–19.

_____. Review of H. Seebass, *Der Gott der ganzen Bibel. Theologische Literaturzeitung* 109 (1984) 538–540.

_____. "Rudolf Bultmanns Her-Kunft und Hin-Kunft. Zur neueren Bultmann-Literatur." *Theologische Literaturzeitng* 120/1 (1995) 3–22.

_____. *Schrift und Theologie: Eine Untersuchung zur Theologie Joh. Chr. K. von Hofmanns.* München 1956.

Hünermann, P. *Der Durchbruch geschichtlichen Denkens im 19. Jahrhundert.* Freiburg/Basel/Wien 1967.

Hughes, H.D. "Salvation–History as Hermeneutic." *Evangelical Quarterly* 48 (1976) 79–89.

Huizinga, J. *Im Bann der Geschichte.* Basel 1943.

Hummel, H. "Biblical or Dogmatic Theology?" *Concordia Journal* 7 (1981) 191–200.

Hunter, A.M. *Interpreting the New Testament 1900–1950.* London 1951.

_____. *Introducing New Testament Theology.* London/Philadelphia 1958.

_____. *The Unity of the New Testament.* London 1943.

Hurtado, L. "Christ-Devotion in the First Two Centuries: Reflections and a Proposal." *Toronto Journal of Theology* 12/1 (1996) 17–33.

Irenaeus, St. *Proof of the Apostolic Preaching.* Ancient Christian Writers 16. Trans. and annotated by J.P. Smith. London 1952.

Irwin, W.A. "The Interpretation of the Old Testament." *Zeitschrift für die alttestamentlichen Wissenschaft* 21 (1950) 1–10.

_____. "The Reviving Theology of the Old Testament." *Journal of Religion* 25 (1945) 235–246.

_____. "A Still Small Voice ... Said, What Are You Doing Here?" *Journal of Biblical Literature* 78 (1959) 1–12.

Ittel, G.W. "Die Hauptgedanken der 'religionsgeschichtlichen Schule.'" *Zeitschrift für Religons- und Geistesgeshichte* 10 (1958) 61–78.

Jacob, E. *Grundfragen Alttestamentlicher Theologie.* Franz Delitzch Vorlesungen 1965. Stuttgart 1970.

_____. *Theology of the Old Testament.* Trans. A. Heathcote & P. Allcock. London 1958.

Jaesche, W. *Die Suche nach den eschatologischen Wurzeln der Geschichtsphilosophie.* Beiträge zur evangelischen Theologie 76. München 1976.

Jaspert, B. "Sachkritik und Widerstand: das Beispiel Rudolf Bultmanns." *Theologische Literaturzeitung* 115 (1990) 161–182.

Jeremias, J. *Neutestamentliche Theologie. Erster Teil. Die Verkündigung Jesu.* Gütersloh 1971.

Johnson, L.T. *Religious Experience in Earliest Christianity. A Missing Dimension in New Testament Studies.* Minneapolis 1998.

Johnson, R.A. *The Origins of Demythologizing: Philosophy and Historiography in the Theology of Rudolf Bultmann.* Studies in the History of Religions (supplements to *Numen*) XXVIII. Leiden 1974.

_____. "Rudolf Bultmann." *Critical Issues in Modern Religion.* Ed. R. Johnson *et al.* Englewood Cliffs, NJ [2]1990. 24–52.

Johnston, P.I. "Reu Reconsidered: The Concept of Heilsgeschichte in the Hermeneutic of J.M. Reu and J.C.K. von Hofmann." *Concordia Journal* 18/4 (October 1992) 339-360.

Jonas, J. "Is Faith Still Possible? Memories of Rudolf Bultmann and Reflections on the Philosophical Aspects of His Work." *Harvard Theological Review* 75 (1982) 1–23.

Jones, D.R. "History and Tradition in Old Testament Studies." *Scottish Journal of Theology* 17 (1964) 211–225.

Jordan, J. "Zur Hofmann Bibliographie." *Beiträge zur bayerischen Kirchengeschichte* 28 (1922) 129–153.

Kähler, M. *Geschichte der protestantischen Dogmatik im 19. Jahrhundert.* Theologische Bücherei 16. München 1962.

_____. *The So–Called Historical Jesus and the Historic, Biblical Christ.* Trans. and ed. C.E. Braaten. Philadelphia 1970.

Käsemann, E. "The Problem of a New Testament Theology." *New Testament Studies* 19 (1973) 235–245.

_____. "Was ich als deutscher Theologe in fünfzig Jahren verlernte." *Kirchliche Konflikte.* Vol. 1. Göttingen 1982. 233–244.

Kaiser, W. *Toward an Old Testament Theology.* Grand Rapids 1978.

Kant, I. *Der Streit der Fakultäten.* Ed. K. Reich. Hamburg 1959.

_____. *Fundamental Principles of the Metaphysics of Ethics.* Trans. T.K. Abbott. London [10]1946.

_____. *Immanuel Kant's Critique of Pure Reason.* Trans. N.K. Smith. London 1950.

_____. *On History.* Trans. L. Beck, R. Anchor & E. Fachenheim. Indianapolis 1980.

_____. *Religion within the Limits of Reason Alone.* Trans. T.H. Greene & J. Hudson. New York 1960.

Kantzenbach, F. W. "Biblizismus und Bekenntnisfrage." *... und fragten nach Jesus.* Ed. U. Meckert, G. Ott, and B. Satlow. Berlin 1964. 287–304.

_____. *Die Erlanger Theologie. Grundlinien ihrer Entwicklung im Rahmen der Geschichte der theologischen Fakultät, 1743–1877.* München 1960.

_____. *Programme der Theologie.* München [2]1978.

Karlberg, M. "Justification in Redemptive History." *Westminster Journal of Theology* 43 (1981) 213–246.

_____. Review of L. Goppelt, *Typos. Journal of the Evangelical Theological Society* 26 (1983) 490–493.

Kattenbusch, F. *Die deutsche evangelische Theologie seit Schleiermacher.* Giessen [5]1926.

Katz, P. "Bedeutung und Vermittlung von Hebräischkenntnissen zum Verständnis des Neuen Testaments." *Zeitschrift für die alttestamentliche Wissenschaft* 104 (1992) 412–427.

Kaufman, G. "The *Imago Dei* as Man's Historicity." *Journal of Religion* 36 (1956) 157–168.

_____. "On the Meaning of 'Act of God.'" *Harvard Theological Review* 61 (1968) 175–201.

Keck, L. "Problems of a New Testament Theology: A Critique of Alan Richardson's *An Introduction to New Testament Theology.*" *Novum Testamentum* 7 (1964) 217–241.

Keller–Hüschmenger, M. "Das Problem der Gewissheit bei J. Chr. K. von Hofmann im Rahmen der 'Erlanger Schule.'" *Gedenkschrift für D. Werner Elert.* Beiträge zur historischen und systematische Theologie. Berlin 1955. 288–295.

Kelsey, D. *The Uses of Scripture in Recent Theology*. Philadelphia 1975.

Kern, I. *Husserl und Kant. Eine Untersuchung über Husserls Verhältnis zu Kant und zum Neukantianismus*. The Hague 1964.

Kindt, Irmgard. *Der Gedanke der Einheit. Adolf Schlatters Theologie und ihre historischen Voraussetzungen*. Stuttgart 1978.

King, W. L. "Some Ambiguities in Biblical Theology." *Religion in Life* 28 (1957–58) 95–104.

Kippenberg, H. & B. Luchesi. *Religionswissenschaft und Kulturkritik. Beiträge zur Konferenz The History of Religions and Critique of Culture in the Days of Gerardus van der Leeuw (1890–1950)*. Marburg 1991.

Kittel, G., et al. *Ein Lehrer der Kirche. Worte des Gedenkens an D. Adolf Schlatter*. Stuttgart 1938.

Kittel, R. "Die Zukunft der alttestamentlichen Wissenschaft." *Zeitschrift für die alttestamentliche Wissenschaft* 39 (1921) 84–99.

Klein, G. "Bibel und Heilsgeschichte. Die Fragwürdigkeit einer Idee." *Zeitschrift für die neutestamentliche Wissenschaft* 62 (1971) 1–47.

_____. "Rudolf Bultmann: ein unerledigtes Vermächtnis." *Zeitschrit für Theologie und Kirche* 94/2 (1997) 177–201.

Kluback, W. *Hermann Cohen: The Challenge of a Religion of Reason*. Brown Judaic Studies 53. Chico, CA: Scholars, 1984.

Koch, K. *The Rediscovery of Apocalyptic*. London 1972.

_____. "Die heilsgeschichtliche Dimension der Theologie." *Theologische Berichte* 8 (1979) 135–188.

Köberle, A. "Evangelium und Natur. Zur Theologie von A. Schlatter." *Evangelische Kommentare* 10 (1977) 539–541.

Köberle, J. "Heilsgeschichtliche und religionsgeschichtliche Betrachtungsweise des Alten Testaments." *Neue kirchliche Zeitschrift* 17 (1906) 200–222.

König, E. *Theologie des Alten Testaments*. Stuttgart 1922.

Köpf, U. "Ferdinand Christian Baur als Begründer einer konsequent historischen Theologie." *Zeitschrift für Theologie und Kirche* 89/4 (1992) 440–461.

Köppel, Urs. *Das deuteronomistische Geschichtswerk und seine Quellen*. Europäische Hochschulschriften. Vol. 122. Bern 1979.

Köstenberger, A. "Preface: The Reception of Schlatter's New Testament Theology 1909–23." In Adolf Schlatter. *The Theology of the Apostles*. Trans. A. Köstenberger. Grand Rapids 1999. 9-22.

Koester, H. *Introduction to the New Testament*. 2 vols. Philadelphia 1982.

Kraeling, E. *The Old Testament since the Reformation*. London 1955.

Kraus, H.–J. *Die Biblische Theologie*. Neukirchen–Vluyn 1970.

_____. *Geschichte der historisch–kritischen Erforschung des Alten Testaments*. Neukirchen–Vluyn 1956, ³1982.

Kühlwein, J. *Geschichte in den Psalmen*. Stuttgart 1973.

Kühn, U. "Bemühungen um eine Rückgewinnung des Bekenntnisses." *Bekenntnis und Einheit der Kirche*. Ed. M. Brecht & R. Schwarz. Stuttgart 1980. 393–413.

Kümmel, W.G. "Einführung zum Neudruck von *Vorlesungen über neutesta-mentliche Theologie*." *Heilsgeschehen und Geschichte*. Vol. 2. Ed. E. Grässer & O. Merk. Marburg 1978. 101–116.

_____. "Ein Jahrzehnt Jesusforschung (1965–1975)." *Theologische Rundschau* 41 (1976) 295–363.

_____. "Heilsgeschichte im Neuen Testament?" *Heilsgeschehen und Geschichte*. Vol. 2. Ed. E. Grässer & O. Merk. 157–176.

_____. *Introduction to the New Testament*. Nashville 1975.

_____. "Jesusforschung seit 1965: Nachträge 1975–1980." *Theologische Rund-schau* 47 (1982) 350–383.

_____. *Das Neue Testament im 20. Jahrhundert: Ein Forschungsbericht*. Stuttgart 1970.

_____. *The New Testament: The History of the Investigation of its Problems*. Nash-ville 1972.

_____. Review of M. Albertz, *Die Botschaft des Neuen Testaments*. *Theologische Zeitschrift* 10 (1954) 55–60.

_____. *The Theology of the New Testament According to its Major Witnesses*. Nashville 1973.

_____. "Das Urchristentum." *Theologische Rundschau* 48 (1983) 101–128.

Kuhn, T.S. *The Structure of Scientific Revolutions*. Chicago [2]1970.

Ladd, G.E. "Biblical Theology, History, and Revelation." *Review and Exposi-tor* 54 (1957) 195–204.

_____. "History and Theology in Biblical Exegesis." *Interpretation* 20 (1966) 54–64.

_____. "The Modern Problem of Biblical Scholarship." *Bethel Seminary Quar-terly* 5 (1957) 10–20.

_____. *The New Testament and Criticism*. Grand Rapids 1967.

_____. *The Presence of the Future: The Eschatology of Biblical Realism*. London 1974.

_____. "The Problem of History in Contemporary New Testament Interpre-tation." *Texte und Untersuchungen* 103 (1968 [=*Studia Evangelica* V]). 88–100.

_____. "Revelation 20 and the Millennium." *Review and Expositor* 57 (1960) 167–175.

_____. Review of R. Bultmann, *Theologie des Neuen Testaments*, vol. 2. *West-minster Theological Journal* 18 (1956) 210–215.

_____. "The Role of Jesus in Bultmann's Theology." *Scottish Journal of Theol-ogy* 18 (1965) 57–68.

_____. "The Search for Perspective." *Interpretation* 25 (1971) 41–62.

_____. *A Theology of the New Testament*. Grand Rapids 1974.

_____. "What Does Bultmann Understand by the Acts of God?" *Bulletin of the Evangelical Theological Society* 5 (1962) 91–97.

Lambert, W.G. "Destiny and Divine Intervention in Babylon and Israel." *Oudtestamentische Studiën* 17 (1972) 65–72.

_____. "*History and the Gods* : A Review Article." *Orientalia* 39 (1970) 170–177.

Lange, D. "Was ist verantwortliche Rede von Gott?" *Zeitschrift für Theologie und Kirche* 94/4 (1997) 510–531.

Laurin, R.B., ed. *Contemporary Old Testament Theologians.* Valley Forge 1970.

_____. "Edmund Jacob, *Theology of the Old Testament.*" *Contemporary Old Testament Theologians.* Ed. R.B. Laurin. Valley Forge 1970.

Lawson, J. *The Biblical Theology of St. Irenaeus.* London 1948.

Lazenby, H. "Revelation in History in the Theologies of Charles Hodge and Karl Barth." Ph.D. dissertation, University of Aberdeen, 1982.

Leary, A.P. "Biblical Theology and History." *Church Quarterly Review* 157 (1956) 402–414.

Leipoldt, J. Review of A. Schlatter, *Die Theologie des Neuen Testaments,* vols. 1 and 2. *Theologisches Literaturblatt* 30 (1909) 363–366; 31 (1910) 27–30.

Leith, J. *Crisis in the Church: The Plight of Theological Education.* Louisville 1997.

Lemche, N.P. "On the Problem of Studying Israelite History Apropos Abraham Malamat's View of Historical Research." *Biblische Notizen* 24 (1984) 94–124.

_____. "Geschichte und Heilsgeschichte: Mehrere 'Aspekte' der biblischen Theologie." *Scandanavian Journal of the Old Testament* 2 (1989) 114–135.

Lemke, W.E. "Revelation through History in Recent Biblical Theology: A Critical Appraisal." *Interpretation* 36 (1982) 34–46.

Leo, P. "Revelation and History in J.C.K. von Hofmann." *Lutheran Quarterly* 10 (1958) 195-216.

Lessing, E. "Die Bedeutung der Heilsgeschichte in der ökumenischen Diskussion." *Evangelische Theologie* 44 (1984) 227–240.

Lessing, G.E. *Lessings sämmtliche Werke.* Ed. R. Gosche. Berlin 1882.

Leuenberger, R. "Adolf Schlatter und die 'atheistischen Methoden in der Theologie.'" *Reformatio* 15 (1966) 291–299.

Levenson, J. *The Hebrew Bible, the Old Testament, and Historical Criticism.* Louisville 1993.

Lichtenberger, F. *History of German Theology in the Nineteenth Century.* Trans. W. Hastie. Edinburgh 1889.

Liebing, H. "Historisch–kritische Theologie. Zum 100. Todestag Ferdinand Christian Baurs am 2. Dezember 1960." *Zeitschrift für Theologie und Kirche* 57 (1960) 302–317.

Lindblom, J. "Zur Frage der Eigenart der alttestamentlichen Religion." *Werden und Wesen des Alten Testaments. Zeitschrift für die alttestamentliche Wissenschaft* Beiheft 66. Ed. P. Volz, F. Stummer & J Hempel. Berlin 1936. 128–137.

Lindemann, A. "Jesus in der Theologie des Neuen Testaments." *Jesus Christus in Historie und Theologie.* Ed. G. Strecker. Tübingen 1975. 27–57.

Löwith, K. *Meaning in History.* Chicago 1949.

Lohse, E. *Grundriss der neutestamentlichen Theologie.* Stuttgart/Berlin/Köln/Mainz 1974.

_____. "Das Neue Testament als apostolische Urkunde." *Kerygma und Dogma* 21 (1975) 85–98.

Long, B. "Letting Rival Gods Be Rivals: Biblical Theology in a Postmodern Age." *Problems in Biblical Theology: Essays in Honor of Rolf Knierem.* H. Sun, *et al.*, eds. Grand Rapids/Cambridge 1997. 222–233.

Long, V. *The Art of Biblical History.* Grand Rapids 1994.

Lose, D. "The Historical Jesus and the So-Called Crisis of Christology." *Dialog* 37/1 (1998) 38–45.

Lotz, W. *Das Alte Testament und die Wissenschaft.* Leipzig 1905.

Lowe, J. "The Recovery of the Theological Interpretation of the Bible." *The Interpretation of the Bible.* Ed. C.W. Dugmore. London 1944. 108–122.

Luck, U. "Die Theologie des Jakobusbriefes." *ZTK* 81 (1984) 1–30.

Lüdemann, G., ed. "Das Wissenschaftsverständnis der Religionsgeschichtlichen Schule im Rahmen des Kulturprotestantismus." *Kulturprotestantismus.* Ed. K. Müller. Gütersloh 1992. 78–107.

_____, ed. *Die "Religionsgeschichte Schule." Facetten eines theologischen Umbruchs.* Frankfurt am Main 1996.

_____. "Die religionsgeschichtliche Schule." *Theologie in Göttingen. Eine Vorlesungsreihe.* Ed. B. Moeller. Göttingen 1987. 325–361.

Lührmann, D. "Rudolf Bultmann and the History of Religion School." *Text and Logos. The Humanistic Interpretation of Scripture.* Ed. T. Jennings, Jr. Atlanta 1990. 3–14.

Lütgert, W. *Adolf Schlatter als Theologe innerhalb des geistigen Lebens seiner Zeit.* Beiträge zur Förderung christlicher Theologie 37. Gütersloh 1932.

_____. *Die Religion des deutschen Idealismus und ihr Ende.* 3 vols. Gütersloh 1923–1925.

Luick, W. "The Ambiguity of Kantian Faith." *Scottish Journal of Theology* 36 (1983) 339–346.

Luz, U. "Geschichte/Geschichtsschreibung/Geschichtsphilosophie. IV. Neues Testament." *Theologisches Realencyclopädie* 12. Berlin/New York 1984. 595–604.

_____. *Das Geschichtsverständnis des Paulus.* München 1968.

Lyman, M. "The Unity of the Bible." *Journal of Bible and Religion* 14 (1946) 5–12.

Machen, J.G. *Christianity and Liberalism.* New York 1923.

_____. "History and Faith." *Princeton Theological Review* 13 (1915) 337–351.

Macquarrie, J. *Twentienth Century Religious Thought.* Rev. ed. London 1971.

Maier, G. *Biblical Hermeneutics.* Trans. R. Yarbrough. Wheaton 1994.

Malamat, A. "Die Frühgeschichte Israels—eine methodologische Studie." *Theologische Zeitschrift* 39 (1983) 1–16.

Malet, A. *The Thought of Rudolf Bultmann.* Shannon, Ireland 1969.

Mandelbaum, M. "Historicism." *The Encyclopedia of Philosophy.* Ed. P. Edwards. London/New York 1972.

Manson, T.W. "The Failure of Liberalism to Interpret the Bible as the Word of God." *The Interpretation of the Bible.* Ed. C.W. Dugmore. London 1944. 92–107.

_____. Review of R. Bultmann, *Theologie des Neuen Testaments*, pts. 1 and 2. *Journal of Theological Studies* 50 (1949) 202–206; *Journal of Theological Studies* [new series] 3 (1952) 246–250.

Manson, W. *Jesus and the Christian.* London 1967.

Markus, R. "Pleroma and Fulfillment: The Significance of History in St. Irenaeus' Opposition to the Gnostics." *Vigiliae christianae* 8 (1954) 193–224.

Marsden, G. *The Outrageous Idea of Christian Scholarship.* New York/Oxford 1997.

Marsh, J. *The Fulness of Time.* London 1952.

Marshall, I.H. *I Believe in the Historical Jesus.* Grand Rapids 1977.

_____. "New Testament Theology." *The Theological Educator* 9 (Spring 1979) 47–64.

_____. "Some Aspects of the Biblical View of History." *Faith and Thought* 110 (1983) 54–68.

Marshall, J.S. "History in the Aristotelian Vein." *Anglican Theological Review* 32 (1950) 245–256.

Martens, E. "Walther Eichrodt *(1890–1978)*." *Historical Handbook of Major Biblical Interpreters.* Ed. D. McKim. Downers Grove 1998. 482–487.

Martin, J.P. "A Hermeneutical Gem." Review of O. Cullmann, *Heil als Geschichte. Interpretation* 20 (1966) 340–346.

Mason, D.R. "Can We Speculate on How God Acts?" *Journal of Religion* 57 (1977) 16–32.

Maurer, C. Review of L. Goppelt, *Theologie des Neuen Testaments. Theologische Zeitschrift* 32 (1976) 107–108; 33 (1977) 47–48.

McCormack, B. "Historical-criticism and Dogmatic Interest in Karl Barth's Theological Exegesis of the New Testament." *Lutheran Quarterly* n.s. 5 (1991) 211–225.

_____. "Revelation and History in Transfoundationalist Perspective: Karl Barth's Theological Epistemology in Conversation with a Schleiermacherian Tradition." *Journal of Religion* 78 (1998) 18–37.

McCown, C.C. "Climate and Religion in Palestine." *Journal of Religion* 7 (1927) 520–539.

_____. "The Current Plight of Biblical Scholarship." *Journal of Biblical Literature* 75 (1956) 12–18.

_____. "In History or Beyond History"? *Harvard Theological Review* 38 (1945) 151–175.

McIntire, C.T., ed. *Herbert Butterfield: Writings on Christianity and History.* New York 1979.

McIntyre, John. *The Christian Doctrine of History.* Grand Rapids 1957.

McKane, W. *A Late Harvest: Reflections on the Old Testament.* Edinburgh 1995.

McKenzie, D. "Kant and Protestant Theology." *Encounter* 43 (1982) 157–167.

McKenzie, J.L. Review of R. Bultmann, *Theologie des Neuen Testaments*. *Catholic Biblical Quarterly* 16 (1954) 250–253.

_____. "Problems of Hermeneutics in Roman Catholic Exegesis." *Journal of Biblical Literature* 77 (1958) 197–204.

McKim, D.K., ed. *Historical Handbook of Major Biblical Interpreters*. Downers Grove/Leicester 1998.

Meding, W. von. "Rudolf Bultmanns Widerstand gegen die Mythologisierung der christlichen Verkündigung." *Theologische Zeitschrift* 53/3 (1997) 195–215.

Meinhold, P. "Geschehen und Deutung im Ersten Clemensbrief." *Zeitschrift für Kirchengeschichte* 58 (1939) 82–129.

Merk, O. "Biblische Theologie II. Neues Testament. *Theologische Realenzyklopädie* 6. Berlin/New York 1980. 455–477.

_____. *Biblische Theologie des Neuen Testaments in ihrer Anfangszeit*. Marburger Theologische Studien 9. Marburg 1972.

_____. "Gapler, Johann Philipp (1753–1826)." *Theologische Realenzyklopädie* 12. Berlin/New York 1984. 1–3.

_____. "Theologie des Neuen Testaments und Biblische Theologie." *Bilanz und Perspektiven gegenwärtiger Auslegung des Neuen Testaments*. Ed. F. Horn. BZNW 75. Berlin/New York 1995. 112–143.

Merz, G. *Das bayerische Luthertum*. München 1955.

Meyer–Wieck, Karl. "Das Wirklichkeitsverständnis Adolf Schlatters." University of Münster dissertation, 1970.

Michalson, G.E. "Bultmann's Metaphysical Dualism." *Religion in Life* 44 (1975) 454–461.

Michel, O. "Probleme der neutestamentlichen Theologie." *Deutsche Theologie* (1942) 20–30.

_____. Review of R. Bultmann, *Theologie des Neuen Testaments*. *Theologische Literaturzeitung* 75 (1950) 29–32; 79 (1954) 146–149.

Milburn, R.L.P. *Early Christian Interpretation of History*. 1952 Bampton Lectures. London 1954.

Miller, E.L. "Salvation History: Pannenberg's Critique of Cullmann." *The Iliff Review* 37 (1980) 21–25.

Miller, J.M. *The Old Testament and the Historian*. London 1976.

Miller, M.B. "Restoring the Story." *Word and World* 3 (1983) 284–293.

Minear, P. Review of O. Cullmann, *Christ and Time*. *Journal of Biblical Literature* 70 (1951) 51–53.

_____. "Wanted: A Biblical Theology." *Theology Today* 1 (1944) 47–58.

Mitton, C.L. Review of G. Ladd, *A Theology of the New Testament*. *Expository Times* 87 (1975–76) 66–67.

Möller, G. "Föderalismus und Geschichtsbetrachtung im 17. und 18. Jahrhundert." *Zeitschrift für Kirchengeschichte* 50 (1931) 393–440.

Moessner, D. "Oscar Cullman: Scholar of Early Christianity, Doctor of the Contemporary Church. The Significance of His Contribution." *Theologische Zeitschrift* 48/2 (1992) 238–242.

Moltmann, J. "Exegese und Eschatologie der Geschichte." *Evangelische Theologie* 22 (1962) 31–66.

Momliagno, A.D. *Essays in Ancient and Modern Historiography*. Oxford 1977.

Mommsen, T.E. "Petrarch's Conception of the 'Dark Ages.'" *Medieval and Renaissance Studies*. Ed. E.F. Rice. Ithaca, NY 1959. 106–129.

Montgomery, J.W. "Where Is History Going?" *Religion in Life* 33 (1963–64) 238–255.

Moore, S. *Poststructuralism and the New Testament*. Minneapolis 1994.

Morgan, R. "Baur, F.C. (1792–1860)." *The Dictionary of Historical Theology*. Ed. T. Hart. Carlisle/Grand Rapids 2000. 58–59.

"Ernst Troeltsch and the dialectical theology." *Ernst Troeltsch and the Future of Theology*. Ed. J.P. Clayton. Cambridge 1976. 33–77.

_____. "Ferdinand Christian Baur." *Nineteenth Century Thought in the West*. Ed. Ninian Smart, *et al*. Vol. 1. Cambridge UK 1985. 261–289

_____. "Gabler's Bicentenary." "*Expository Times* 98 (1986–87) 164–168.

_____. *The Nature of New Testament Theology*. Studies in Biblical Theology (second series) 25. Naperville, IL 1973.

_____. "Some recent works on Troeltsch." *Religious Studies Review* 17 (1991) 327–331.

_____. "Re-Reading Wrede." *Expository Times* 108 (1996–97) 207–210.

_____. Rev. of R. Johnson, *Origins of Demythologizing*. *Theology* 78 (1975) 487–488.

_____. Rev. of G. Strecker, *Theologie des Neuen Testaments*. *Journal of Theological Studies* 50 (1999) 743–746.

_____. "Theology, New Testament." *Anchor Bible Dictionary* 6. New York *et al*. 1992. 473–483.

_____, and Pye, Michael, eds. *Ernst Troeltsch: Writings on Theology and Religion*. Louisville 1990.

Moule, C.F.D. "The Borderlands of Ontology in the New Testament." *The Philosophical Frontiers of Theology*. Ed. B. Hebblethwaite and S. Sutherland. Cambridge 1982. 1–11.

_____. "The Christ of Experience and the Christ of History." *Theology* 81 (1978) 164–172.

_____. Review of A. Richardson, *An Introduction to the Theology of the New Testament*. *Journal of Theological Studies* [new series] 10 (1959) 373–376.

Müller, G. "Die Erlanger Theologische Fakultät und Wilhelm Löhe im Jahr 1849." In *Dem Wort gehorsam*. Ed. W. Anderson, *et al*. München 1973. 242–254.

Müller, H.M. *Kulturprotestantismus. Beiträge zu einer Gestalt des modernen Christentums*. Gütersloh 1992.

Müller, H.-P. "Entmythologisierung und Altes Testament." *Neue Zeitschrift für Systematische Theologie und Religionsphilosophie* 35/1 (1993) 1–27.

Müller, K. "Geschichte, Heilsgeschichte und Gesetz." *Literatur und Religion des Frühjudentums*. Würzburg 1973. 73–105.

_____. "Die religionsgeschichtliche Methode. Erwägungen zu ihrem Verständnis und zur Praxis ihrer Vollzüge an neutestamentlichen Texten." *Biblische Zeitschrift* 29 (1985) 161–192.

Müller, P.–G. "Altes Testament, Israel und das Judentum in der Theologie Rudolf Bultmanns." *Kontinuität und Einheit.* Ed. P.–G. Müller & W. Stenger. Freiburg/Basel/Wien 1981. 439–472.

_____. *Der Traditionsprozess im Neuen Testament. Kommunikations–analytische Studien zur Versprachlichung des Jesus–phänomens.* Freiburg/Basel/Wien 1982.

Müller, W. & H. Schulz. *Theologie als Aufklärung.* Fs. G. Hornig. Würzburg 1992.

Müller–Fahrenholz, G. *Heilsgeschichte zwischen Ideologie und Prophetie. Profile und Kritik heilsgeschichtlicher Theorien in der ökumenischen Bewegung zwischen 1948 und 1968.* Freiburg/Basel/Wien 1974.

Müller–Lauter, W. "Konsequenzen des Historismus in der Philosophie der Gegenwart." *Zeitschrift für Theologie und Kirche* 59 (1962) 226–255.

Muller, R. *Post-Reformation Reformed Dogmatics.* Grand Rapids 1987–93.

Murdock, W. A. "History and Revelation in Jewish Apocalypticism." *Interpretation* 21 (1971) 167–187.

Murphy, R. "Questions Concerning Biblical Theology." *Biblical Theological Bulletin* 30/3 (2000) 81–89.

_____. "Reflections on a Critical Biblical Theology." *Problems in Biblical Theology: Essays in Honor of Rolf Knierem.* H. Sun, *et al.*, eds. Grand Rapids/ Cambridge 1997. 265–274.

Murrmann-Kahl, M. *Die entzauberte Heilsgeschichte: Der Historismus erobert die Theologie 1880–1920.* Gütersloh 1992.

Neill, S. *Jesus Through Many Eyes.* Philadelphia 1976.

_____ & Tom Wright. *The Interpretation of the New Testament 1861–1986.* Oxford ²1988.

Neuer, W. *Adolf Schlatter: A Biography of Germany's Premier Biblical Theologian.* Trans. R. Yarbrough. Grand Rapids 1995.

_____. *Adolf Schlatter. Ein Leben für Theologie und Kirche.* Stuttgart 1996.

_____. "Der Idealismus und die Erweckung in Schlatters Jugend." *Zeitschrift für die Kirchengeschichte* 96 (1985) 62-72.

_____. *Der Zusammenhang von Dogmatik und Ethik bei Adolf Schlatter.* Giessen/ Basel 1986.

Neugebauer, F. "Wer war Adolf Schlatter?" *Theologische Literaturzeitung* 122/9 (1997) 770–782.

Newton, R.J., Jr. "The Method of Biblical Theology in Cullmann, Barth, and Bultmann." Ph.D. dissertation, Columbia University, 1959.

Nicol, I.G. "Event and Interpretation. O. Cullmann's Conception of Salvation History." *Theology* 77 (1974) 14–21.

Niebuhr, R. *Faith and History: A Comparison of Christian and Modern Views of History.* London 1949.

Nineham, D. Review of R. Bultmann, *Theology of the New Testament*, vol. 1. *Expository Times* 64 (1952–53) 97–98; 66 (1954–55) 15–19; 67 (1955–56) 97–98.

Nissen, A. "Tora und Geschichte im Spätjudentum." *New Testament Studies* 9 (1967) 274–277.

Noack, B. *Spätjudentum und Heilsgeschichte*. Franz Delitzsch–Vorlesungen 1968. Stuttgart 1971.

Noll, M. *Between Faith and Criticism. Evangelicals, Scholarship, and the Bible in America*. Grand Rapids ²1991.

North, C. "Bibliography of Works in Theology and History: Studies in the Philosophy of History." *History and Theory* 12 (1973) 57–140.

North, Christopher. *The Old Testament Interpretation of History*. London 1946.

———. "Old Testament Theology and the History of Hebrew Religion." *Scottish Journal of Theology* 2 (1949) 113–126.

Noth, M. "Das Geschichtsverständnis der alttestamentlichen Apokalyptik." *Gesammelte Studien zum Alten Testament*. München 1957. 248–273.

———. "Die Historisierung des Mythos im Alten Testament." *Christentum und Wissenschaft* 4 (1928) 265–272, 301–309.

O'Collins, G. *Foundations of Theology*. Chicago 1971.

Oestborn, G. *Yahweh's Words and Deeds. A Preliminary Study into the Old Testament Presentation of History*. Uppsala/Wiesbaden 1951.

Ogden, S. "What Sense Does It Make to Say 'God Acts in History'?" *Journal of Religion* 43 (1963) 1–19.

Ogilvie, R. *Latin and Greek: A History of the Influence of the Classics on English Life from 1600–1918*. Hamden, CT 1964.

Ogletree, T.W. *Christian Faith and History. A Critical Comparison of Ernst Troeltsch and Karl Barth*. New York 1965.

Ollenburger, B.C. "Biblical Theology: Situating the Discipline." *Understanding the Word*. Ed. J.T. Butler, E.W. Conrad & B.C. Ollenburger. B.W. Anderson Fs. JSOT Supp. Series 37. Sheffield 1985. 37–62.

Ollenburger, B., E. Martens & G. Hasel, eds. *The Flowering of Old Testament Theology*. Winona Lake, IN 1992.

Oosterzee, J. van. *The Theology of the New Testament*. Trans. M.J. Evans. London 1882.

Osborn, E. *The Beginning of Christian Philosophy*. Cambridge 1981.

Ott, H. *Geschichte und Heilsgeschichte in der Theologie Rudolf Bultmanns*. Beiträge zur historischen Theologie 19. Tübingen 1955.

———. "Glaube und Vernunft." *Theologische Literaturzeitung* 92 (1967) 401–414.

Palmer, H. *The Logic of Gospel Criticism*. London 1968.

Palmer, M.F. "Can the Historian Invalidate Gospel Statements? Some Notes on Dialectical Theology." *Downside Review* 95 (1977) 11–18.

Pannenberg, W. "Glaube und Wirklichkeit im Denken Gerhard von Rads." *Gerhard von Rad: Seine Bedeutung für die Theologie*. H.W. Wolff, R. Rendtorff & W. Pannenberg. München 1973. 37–54, 57–58.

_____, ed. *Revelation as History*. Trans. K. Granskou. New York 1968.

_____. "The Significance of Christianity in the Philosophy of Hegel." *The Idea of God and Human Freedom*. Trans. R.A. Wilson. Philadelphia 1973.

_____. *Theology and the Kingdom of God*. Ed. R.J. Neuhaus. Philadelphia 1969.

_____. *Theology and the Philosophy of Science*. Trans. F. McDonagh. London 1976.

Parsons, G. "Reforming the Tradition: A Forgotten Dimension of Liberal Protestantism." *Religion* 13 (1983) 257–271.

Patte, D. *Ethics of Biblical Interpretation*. Louisville 1995.

Paulsen, H. "Traditionsgeschichtliche Methode und religionsgeschichtliche Schule." *Zeitschrift für Theologie und Kirche* 75 (1978) 20–55.

Paulus, R. "Zum Problem 'Glaube und Geschichte.'" *Zeitschrift für Theologie und Kirche* 7 (1926) 378–399.

Payne, J.B. *The Theology of the Older Testament*. Grand Rapids 1962.

Perrin, N. "Jesus and the Theology of the New Testament." *Journal of Religion* 64 (1984) 413–431.

Peter, J. "Salvation History as a Model for Theological Thought." *Scottish Journal of Theology* 23 (1970) 1–12.

Pfeiffer, R.H. "Facts and Faith in Biblical History." *Journal of Biblical Literature* 70 (1951) 1–14.

Phythian–Adams, W. "The Foundations of Biblical Theology." *Church Quarterly Review* 269 (Oct.–Dec. 1942) 1–24.

_____. "Shadow and Substance: The Meaning of Salvation History." *Interpretation* 1 (1947) 419–435.

Piper, O. "Biblical Theology and Systematic Theology." *Journal of Bible and Religion* 25 (1957) 106–111.

_____. "Christology and History." *Theology Today* 19 (1962) 324–340.

_____. *God in History*. New York 1939.

_____. "The Nature of the Gospels according to Justin Martyr." *Journal of Religion* 41 (1961) 155–168.

_____. *Recent Developments in German Protestantism*. London 1934.

Pittenger, W.N. "Biblical Religion and Biblical Theology." *Journal of Bible and Religion* 13 (1945) 179–183.

Plantinga, A. "Two (or More) Kinds of Scripture Scholarship." *Modern Theology* 14/2 (1998) 243–278.

Pokorny, P. "Probleme biblischer Theologie." *Theologische Literaturzeitung* 106 (1981) 1–9.

Porteous, N.W. "Old Testament Theology." *The Old Testament and Modern Study*. Ed. H.H. Rowley. Oxford 1951. 311–345.

_____. "A Question of Perspective." *Wort–Gebot–Glaube*. Ed. H.–J. Stoebe, et al. W. Eichrodt Festschrift. Zürich 1970. 117–131.

_____. "The Theology of the Old Testament." *Peake's Commentary on the Bible*. Ed. M. Black & H.H. Rowley. 2nd rev. ed. London 1962.

Porter, F.C. "Crucial Problems in Biblical Theology." *Journal of Religion* 1 (1921) 78–81.

Porter, S.E., ed. *Handbook to Exegesis of the New Testament.* Leiden/New York/Köln 1997.

Pottner, M. "Die Einheit von Sachkritik und Selbstkritik." *Zeitschrift für Theologie und Kirche* 91/4 (1994) 396-423.

Press, G.A. "History and the Development of the Idea of History in Antiquity." *History and Theory* 16 (1977) 280–296.

Preston, R.H., ed. *Theology and Change.* A. Richardson Festschrift. London 1975.

Preus, C. "The Contemporary Relevance of Von Hofmann's Hermeneutical Principles." *Interpretation* 4 (1950) 311–321.

Procksch, O. "Die Geschichte als Glaubensinhalt." *Neue kirchliche Zeitschrift* 36 (1925) 485–499.

_____. "Hofmanns Geschichtsauffassung." *Evangelisch–Lutherische Kirchenzeitung* 43 (1910) 1034–1038.

_____. "Otto Procksch." *Die Religionswissenschaft der Gegenwart in Selbstdarstellungen.* Vol. 2. Ed. E. Stange. Leipzig 1926. 161–194.

_____. *Theologie des Alten Testaments.* Gütersloh 1950.

_____. "Ziele und Grenzen der Exegese." *Neue kirchliche Zeitschrift* 36 (1925) 715–730.

Prümm, K. *Gnosis an der Wurzel des Christentums?* Salzburg 1972.

Quigley, M.A. "Ernst Troeltsch and the Historical Absolute." *Heythrop Journal* 24 (1983) 19–37.

Rad, G. von. *Gesammelte Studien zum Alten Testament.* München 1958.

_____. "G. von Rad über G. von Rad." *Probleme biblischer Theologie.* Ed. H.W. Wolff. G. von Rad Festschrift. München 1971. 659–661.

_____. "Grundprobleme einer biblischen Theologie des Alten Testaments." *Theologische Literaturzeitung* 69 (1943) 225–234.

_____. "Kritische Vorarbeiten zu einer Theologie des Alten Testaments." *Theologie und Liturgie.* Ed. L. Henning. München 1952. 11–34.

_____. "Offene Fragen im Umkreis einer Theologie des Alten Testaments." *Theologische Literaturzeitung* 88 (1963) 401–416.

_____. *Old Testament Theology.* 2 vols. Trans. D. Stalker. Edinburgh 1962, 1965.

Räisänen, H. *Beyond New Testament Theology: A Story and a Programme.* London ²2000.

_____. "Biblical Critics in the Global Village." *Reading the Bible in the Global Village.* H. Räisänen *et al.* Atlanta 2000. 9–28, 153–166.

_____. "The 'Effective History' of the Bible: A Challenge to Biblical Scholarship." *Scottish Journal of Theology* 45 (1992) 303–324.

Ramm, Bernard. *After Fundamentalism.* San Francisco 1983.

Ramsey, G.W. *The Quest for the Historical Israel.* Atlanta 1981.

Ramsey, I.T. "History and the Gospels: Some Philosophical Reflections." *Texte und Untersuchungen* 88 (1964 [= *Studia Evangelica* III]). 201–217.

Rasmusson, A. "Historicizing the Historicist: Ernst Troeltsch and Recent Mennonite Theology." *The Wisdom of the Cross*. Ed. S. Hauerwas *et al.* Grand Rapids/Cambridge UK 1999. 213–248.

Redeker, M. *Schleiermacher: Life and Thought*. Trans. J. Wallhauser. Philadelphia 1973.

Reicke, B. "Einheitlichkeit oder verschiedene 'Lehrbegriffe' in der neutestamentlichen Theologie?" *Theologische Zeitschrift* 9 (1953) 401–415.

Reischle, M. "Historische und dogmatische Methode der Theologie." *Theologische Rundschau* 4 (1901) 261–275, 305–324.

Reisner, E. "Hermeneutik und historische Vernunft." *Zeitschrift für Theologie und Kirche* 49 (1952) 223–238.

Rendtorff, R. "Approaches to Old Testament Theology." *Problems in Biblical Theology: Essays in Honor of Rolf Knierem*. H. Sun, *et al.*, eds. Grand Rapids/Cambridge 1997. 13–26.

Rengstorf, K.H. "Adolf Schlatter." *Tendenzen der Theologie im 20. Jahrhundert*. Ed. H.J. Schultz. Stuttgart 1967. 56–61.

Rese, M. Review of P. Wells, *James Barr and the Bible*. *Theologische Zeitschrift* 38 (1982) 116–117.

Reumann, J. *Variety and Unity in New Testament Thought*. Oxford *et al.* 1991.

Reuss, E. *Die Geschichte der heiligen Schriften Neuen Testaments*. Braunschweig ⁶1887.

Reventlow, H. "Aus der Arbeit der Projectgruppe "Biblische Theologie" der wissenschaftlichen Gesellschaft für Theologie." *Theologische Zeitschrift* 39 (1983) 65–67.

_____. *The Authority of the Bible and Rise of the Modern World*. Trans. J. Bowden. Philadelphia 1985.

_____. "Bedingungen und Voraussetzungen der Bibelkritik in Deutschland in der Periode des zweiten Reiches und bevor. Der Fall Heinrich Julius Holtzmann." Ed. W. Müller & H. Schulz. *Theologie als Aufklärung*. Fs. G. Hornig. Würzburg 1992. 264–283.

_____. *Hauptprobleme der alttestamentlichen Theologie im 20. Jahrhundert*. Erträge der Forschung. Band 173. Darmstadt 1982.

_____, W. Sparn, & J. Woodbridge, eds. *Historische Kritik und biblischer Kanon in der deutschen Aufklärung*. Wiesbaden 1988.

Richardson, A. *An Introduction to the Theology of the New Testament*. London 1958.

_____. *History, Sacred and Profane*. Philadelphia 1964.

_____. "What Is New Testament Theology?" *Texte und Untersuchungen* 112 (1969 [= *Studia Evangelica* VI]). 455–465.

Ridderbos, H. *Redemptive History and the New Testament Scriptures*. Trans. H. De Jongste. Revised by R. Gaffin, Jr. Phillipsburg 1988 (= *Heilsgeschiedenis en Heilige Schrift*. Kampen 1955).

Rieger, H.-M. *Adolf Schlatters Rechtfertigungslehre und die Möglichkeit ökumenischer Verständigung*. Stuttgart 2000.

Riesenfeld, H. "Biblische Theologie und biblische Religionsgeschichte. II. NT." *Religion in Geschichte und Gegenwart.* Vol. 1. ³1957. 1259–1262.

Riesner, R. "Der Ursprung der Jesus–Überlieferung." *Theologische Zeitschrift* 38 (1982) 493–513.

Roberts, R.C. *Rudolf Bultmann's Theology: A Critical Interpretation.* Grand Rapids 1976.

Roberts, R.H. "Eternity and Time in the Theology of Karl Barth." Ph.D. dissertation, University of Edinburgh, 1975.

Roberts, T.A. *History and Christian Apologetic.* London 1960.

———. "Some Presuppositions of Gospel Criticism." Texte und Untersuchungen 73 (1959 [= *Studia Evangelica* I]). 66–78.

Robertson, P. "The Outlook for Biblical Theology." *Toward a Theology for the Future.* Ed. D. Wells & C. Pinnock. Carol Stream, IL 1971. 65–91.

Robinson, H. *The History of Israel.* London ²1964.

———, ed. *Record and Revelation.* Oxford 1938.

———. *Redemption and Revelation in the Actuality of History.* London 1942.

———. *Religious Ideas of the Old Testament.* London 1956.

Robinson, J.A.T. *Redating the New Testament.* Philadelphia 1976.

Robinson, J.M., ed. *The Beginnings of Dialectical Theology.* Volume 1. Trans. K. Crim & L. De Grazia. Richmond 1968.

———. "The Future of New Testament Theology." *Religious Studies Review* 2 (1976) 17–23.

Robinson, N.H.G. "Barth or Bultmann?" *Religious Studies* 14 (1978) 275–290.

———. Review of R. Bultmann, *Theology of the New Testament,* vols. 1 and 2. *New Testament Studies* 4 (1958) 339–343.

Rodd, C.S. Review of L. Goppelt, *Theology of the New Testament,* vol. 1. *Expository Times* 94 (1983) 163.

Rogerson, J. "Geschichte und Altes Testament im 19. Jahrhundert." *Biblische Notizen* 22 (1983) 126–138.

———. *Old Testament Criticism in the Nineteenth Century. England and Germany.* Philadelphia 1985.

Rollmann, H. "From Baur to Wrede: The Quest for a Historical Method." *Studies in Religion/Sciences religieuses* 17/4 (1988) 443–454.

———. "Theologie und Religionsgeschichte." *Zeitschrift für Theologie und Kirche* 80 (1983) 69–84.

———. "Wrede, William (1859–1906)." *Historical Handbook of Major Biblical Interpreters.* Ed. D.K. McKim. Downers Grove/Leicester 1998. 394–398.

Rowley, H.H. *The Relevance of Apocalyptic.* London ²1952.

———. "The Unity of the Old Testament." *Bulletin of the John Rylands Library of Manchester* 29 (1946) 326–358.

Runzo, J. "Relativism and Absolutism in Bultmann's Demythologizing Hermeneutic." *Scottish Journal of Theology* 32 (1979) 401–419.

Rupp, G. *Culture Protestantism in German Liberal Theology at the Turn of the Twentieth Century.* Missoula 1975.

Russell, D.S. *Apocalyptic: Ancient and Modern.* London 1978.

Rust, E. *The Christian Understanding of History.* Lutterworth Library 30. London 1947.

_____. *Towards a Theological Understanding of History.* New York 1963.

Rust, H. *Kant und das Erbe des Protestantismus.* Gotha 1928.

Saebø, M. "Johann Philipp Gablers Bedeutung für die Biblische Theologie." *Zeitschrift für die alttestamentliche Wissenschaft* 99 (1987) 1–16.

Sanders, E. P. *Paul.* Oxford/New York 1991.

_____. *Paul and Palestinian Judaism.* Philadelphia/London 1977.

Sandys–Wunsch, J. "G. T. Zachariae's Contribution to Biblical Theology." *Zeitschrift für die alttestamentliche Wissenschaft* 92 (1980) 1–23.

_____. "On the Theory and Practice of Biblical Interpretation." *Journal for the Study of the Old Testament* 3 (1977) 66–74.

_____, & L. Eldredge. "J. P. Gabler and the Distinction between Biblical and Dogmatic Theology: Translation, Commentary, and Discussion of His Originality." *Scottish Journal of Theology* 33 (1980) 133–158.

Sasson, J. "On Choosing Models for Recreating Israelite Pre–Monarchic History." *Journal for the Study of the Old Testament* 21 (1981) 3–24.

Satterthwaite, P. "Biblical History." *New Dictionary of Biblical Theology.* Ed. T. Alexander & B. Rosner. Leicester/Downers Grove 2000. 43–51.

Sauer, E. *Das Morgenrot der Welterlösung.* Wuppertal–Barmen 1937.

_____. *Der Triumph des Gekreuzigten.* Wuppertal–Barmen 1937.

_____. *Vom Adel des Menschen.* Gütersloh 1940.

_____. *Zweck und Ziel der Menschenschöpfung.* Berlin–Steglitz 1931.

Schäfer, P. "Zur Geschichtsauffassung des rabbinischen Judentums." *Studien zur Geschichte und Theologie des rabbinischen Judentums.* Leiden 1978. 23–44.

Schaff, P. *Germany; Its Universities, Theology, and Religion.* Edinburgh 1857.

Scheffczyk, L. "Biblische und dogmatische Theologie." *Trierer theologische Zeitschrift* 67 (1958) 193–209.

Schelkle, K.H. *Theology of the New Testament.* 4 vols. Trans. W.A. Jurgens. Collegeville 1971–78.

Schlatter, A. "Adolf Schlatter." *Die Religionswissenschaft der Gegenwart in Selbstdarstellungen.* Vol. 1. Ed. E. Stange. Leipzig 1925. 145–169.

_____. "The Attitude of German Protestant Theology to the Bible." *Constructive Quarterly* 2 (1914) 99–110.

_____. *Der Aufstieg der evangelischen Kirche von der Reformation zur Gegenwart.* Bethel bei Bielefeld 1931.

_____. "Die Bedeutung der Methode für die theologische Arbeit." *Theologischer Literaturbericht* 31 (1908) 5–8. (For translation and commentary see entry under Yarbrough below.)

_____. *Das christliche Dogma.* Stuttgart ²1923.

_____. *The Church in the New Testament Period.* Trans. P. Levertoff. London 1961.

_____. *Erlebtes.* Berlin ⁵1929.

_____. *Der Evangelist Johannes.* Stuttgart ⁴1975.

_____. *Der Evangelist Matthäus.* Stuttgart 1948.

_____. *Die christliche Ethik.* Stuttgart ³1929·

_____. *Die Furcht vor dem Denken.* Gütersloh ²1917.

_____. *Die Geschichte des Christus.* Stuttgart ³1977.

_____. "Der Glaube an die Bibel." *Heilige Anliegen der Kirche.* Stuttgart 1896. 34–46.

_____. *Der Glaube im Neuen Testament.* Tübingen ⁶1982 (= ⁴1927).

_____. "Die heilige Geschichte und der Glaube." *Heilige Anliegen der Kirche.* Stuttgart 1896. 22–33.

_____. "Karl Barth's *Epistle to the Romans.*" *The Beginnings of Dialectical Theology.* Ed. J. Robinson. Trans. K. Crim & L. De Grazia. Richmond 1968. 121–125.

_____. *Die philosophische Arbeit seit Cartesius nach ihrem ethischen und religiösen Ertrag.* Beiträge zur Förderung christlicher Theologie 10. Gütersloh 1906.

_____. *Rückblick auf meine Lebensarbeit.* Stuttgart ²1977.

_____. *Die Theologie der Apostel.* Stuttgart ²1922.

_____. *Wohin? Eine Frage an unsere Schule und unsere Kirche.* Bethel bei Bielefeld 1929.

_____. *Zur Theologie des Neuen Testaments und zur Dogmatik: Kleine Schriften.* Ed. U. Luck. Theologische Bücherei 41. München 1969.

Schlaudraff, K.–H. *"Heil als Geschichte"? Die Frage nach dem heilsgeschichtlichen Denken, dargestellt anhand der Konzeption Oscar Cullmanns.* Beiträge zur Geschichte der biblischen Exegese 29. Tübingen 1988.

Schmid, C. *Biblical Theology of the New Testament.* Trans. G.H. Venables. Edinburgh 1870.

_____. "Über das Interesse und den Stand der biblischen Theologie des Neuen Testaments in unserer Zeit." *Tübinger Zeitschrift für Theologie* 4 (1838) 125–160.

Schmid, Heinrich. *The Doctrinal Theology of the Lutheran Church.* Trans. C.A. Hay & H.E. Jabobs. Philadelphia 1876.

Schmid, J. Review of O. Merk, *Biblische Theologie des Neuen Testaments in ihrer Anfangszeit. Biblische Zeitschrift* 19 (1975) 266–268.

Schmid, J.H. *Erkenntnis des geschichtlichen Christus bei Martin Kähler und bei Adolf Schlatter. Theologische Zeitschrift* Sonderband V. Basel 1978.

Schmidt, H.H. *Altorientalische Welt in alttestamentlicher Theologie.* Zürich 1974.

Schmidt, W.H. "'Theologie des Alten Testaments' vor und nach Gerhard von Rad." *Verkündigung und Forschung* 17 (1972) 1–25.

Schmithals, W. "Bultmann, Rudolf (1884–1976)." *Theologische Realenzyklopädie* 7. Berlin/New York 1981. 387–396.

_____. *Die Apokalyptik.* Göttingen 1973.

_____. "Zum Problem der Entmythologisierung bei Rudolf Bultmann." *Zeitschrift für Theologie und Kirche* 92/2 (1995) 166–206.

Schmitt, R. *Abschied von der Heilsgeschichte?* Europäische Hochschulschriften. Reihe XXIII, Band 195. Frankfurt am Main/Bern 1982.

Schnabel, E. *Inspiration und Offenbarung: die Lehre vom Ursprung und Wesen der Bibel.* Wuppertal/Giessen 1986.

Schnackenburg, R. "Darstellungen der Neutestamentlichen Theologie." *Biblische Zeitschrift* 19 (1975) 268–276.

_____. *The Moral Teaching of the New Testament.* New York 1965.

Schnädelbach, H. *Philosophy in Germany 1831–1933.* Trans. E. Matthews. Cambridge 1984.

Schnelle, U. *The History and Theology of the New Testament Writings.* Minneapolis 1998.

Schofield, J. "Otto Procksch, *Theology of the Old Testament.*" *Contemporary Old Testament Theologians.* Ed. R. Laurin. Valley Forge, PA 1970. 91–120.

Scholder, K. "Baur, Ferdinand Christian (1792–1860)." *Theologische Realenzyklopädie* 5. Berlin/New York 1980. 352–359.

_____. *The Birth of Modern Critical Theology: Origins and Problems of Biblical Criticism in the Seventeenth Century.* Trans. J. Bowden. London/Philadelphia 1990.

Schreiber, J. "William Wrede als Aufklärer." *Theologie als Aufklärung.* Ed. W. Müller & H. Schulz. Würzburg 1992. 285–297.

Schrenk, G. *Gottesreich und Bund im älteren Protestantismus vornehmlich bei Johannes Coccejus.* Darmstadt 1967 (= 1923).

Schrodt, P. "Can One Speak of 'Dogma' in the New Testament?" Texte und Untersuchungen 112 (1969 [= *Studia Evangelica* VI]). 473–477.

Schroven, B. *Theologie des Alten Testaments zwischen Anpassung und Widerspruch. Christologische Auslegung zwischen den Weltkriegen.* Neukirchen-Vluyn 1995.

Schrupp, E. "Die Heilsgeschichte wieder entdecken." *idea–spektrum* 7/7 (1984) 16–17.

Schubert, K. "Geschichte und Heilsgeschichte." *Kairos* 15 (1973) 89–101.

Schweitzer, A. *The Mysticism of Paul the Apostle.* Trans. F.C. Burkitt & W. Montgomery. London 1956.

_____. *Out of My Life and Thought.* Trans. C.T. Campion. New York 1933.

_____. *The Quest of the Historical Jesus.* Trans. W. Montgomery. London ²1948.

Schweizer, E. Review of O. Cullmann, *Heil als Geschichte.* *Theologische Literaturzeitung* 92 (1967) 904–909.

Scroggs, R. "Can New Testament Theology Be Saved? The Threat of Contextualisms." *Union Seminary Quarterly Review* 42 (1988) 17–31.

Scruton, R. *Kant.* Oxford 1982.

Seebass, H. "Der Beitrag des Alten Testaments zum Entwurf einer biblischen Theologie." *Wort und Dienst* 8 (1965) 20–41.

_____. "Biblische Theologie." *Verkündigung und Forschung* 27 (1982) 28–45.

Segalla, G. "Dieci anni di Teologia (Biblica) del Nuovo Testamento (1985–1995) tra la ricerca di un' unità teologico-biblica e la deriva verso una pluralità storico-religiosa." *Teologia* 21 (1996) 67–127.

Sekine, M. "Vom Verstehen der Heilsgeschichte. Das Grundproblem der alttestamentlichen Theologie." *Zeitschrift für die alttestamentliche Wissenschaft* 75 (1963) 145–154.

Senft, C. *Wahrhaftigkeit und Wahrheit: Die Theologie des 19. Jahrhunderts zwischen Orthodoxie und Aufklärung.* Tübingen 1956.

Shiner, L. *The Secularization of History: An Introduction to the Theology of Friedrich Gogarten.* Nashville 1966.

Sierszyn, A. *Die Bibel im Griff? Historisch–kritische Denkweise und biblische Theologie.* Wuppertal 1978.

Smart, J. D. "The Death and Rebirth of Old Testament Theology." *Journal of Religion* 23 (1943) 1–11, 124–136.

_____. "The Need for a Biblical Theology." *Religion in Life* 26 (1956–57) 22–30.

_____. *The Past, Present, and Future of Biblical Theology.* Philadelphia 1979.

_____. *The Strange Silence of the Bible in the Church.* London 1970.

Smend, R. "Otto Eissfeldt 1887–1973." *Understanding Poets and Prophets.* Ed. A.G. Auld. Sheffield 1993. 318–335.

_____. "Johann Philipp Gablers Begründung der biblischen Theologie." *Evangelische Theologie* 22 (1962) 345–357.

_____. "Überlieferung und Geschichte." *Zu Tradition und Theologie im Alten Testament.* Ed. O. Steck. Biblisch–Theologische Studien 2. 1978. 9–26.

Smith, N.K. *A Commentary to Kant's "Critique of Pure Reason".* London 1979 (= ²1923).

Söding, T. "Inmitten der Theologie des Neuen Testaments. Zu den Voraussetzungen und Zielen neutestamentlicher Exegese." *New Testament Studies* 42 (1996) 161–184.

Soggin, J.A. "Alttestamentliche Glaubenzeugnisse und geschichtliche Wirklichkeit." *Theologische Zeitschrift* 17 (1961) 385–398.

_____. "Geschichte, Historie und Heilsgeschichte." *Theologische Literaturzeitung* 89 (1964) 721–736.

_____. "God and History in Biblical Thought." *Old Testament and Oriental Studies.* Rome 1975. 59–66.

Sontag, F.E. "Is God Really in History?" *Religion in Life* 15 (1979) 379–390.

_____. "Philosophy and Biblical Theology: A Prologue." *Religion in Life* 33 (1963–64) 224–237.

Spener, P.J. *Pia Desideria.* Trans. T. Tappert. Philadelphia 1964.

Spriggs, D. *Two Old Testament Theologies.* Studies in Biblical Theology (second series) 30. London 1974.

Stade, B. "Über die Aufgaben der biblischen Theologie des Alten Testaments." *Zeitschrift für Theologie und Kirche* 3 (1893) 31–51.

Stadelmann, H., ed. *Epochen der Heilsgeschichte.* Wuppertal 1984.

_____, ed. *Glaube und Geschichte: Heilsgeschichte als Thema der Theologie.* Giessen/Basel/Wuppertal 1986.

Stählin, L. *Kant, Lotze, and Ritschl.* Trans. D.W. Simon. Edinburgh 1889.

Stärk, W. "Willy Stärk." *Die Religionswissenschaft der Gegenwart in Selbstdarstellungen.* Vol. 5. Ed. E. Stange. Leipzig 1929. 159–206.

_____. "Religionsgeschichte und Religionsphilosophie in ihrer Bedeutung für die biblische Theologie des Alten Testaments." *Zeitschrift für Theologie und Kirche* 31 (1923–24) 289–300.

Stakemeier, E. "Zur heilsgeschichtlichen Orientierung der Fundamentaltheologie nach dem Zweiten Vaticanum." *Catholica* 21/2 (1967) 101–126.

Stanton, G. "Biblical Classics: XII. Rudolf Bultmann: *Jesus and the Word.*" *Expository Times* 90 (1978–79) 324–328.

Staudinger, H. "The Resurrection of Jesus Christ as Saving Event and as 'Object' of Historical Research." *Scottish Journal of Theology* 36 (1983) 309–326.

Stauffer, E. *New Testament Theology.* Trans. J. Marsh. London 1955.

_____. "Der Stand der neutestamentlichen Forschung." *Theologie und Liturgie.* Ed. L. Henning. München 1952. 35–105.

Steck, K. *Die Idee der Heilsgeschichte.* Theologische Studien 56. Zollikon 1959.

Stegemann, E. "Zwischen religionsgeschichtlicher Rekonstruktion und theologischer Interpretation." *Theologische Zeitschrift* 55/2-3 (1999) 137–155.

Stegner, W. "Recent Religious/Political Developments in a New Testament Theological Perspective." *Asbury Theological Journal* 45/2 (1990) 73–81.

Stendahl, K. "The Bible as a Classic and the Bible as Holy Scripture." *Journal of Biblical Literature* 103 (1984) 3–10.

_____. "Biblical Theology, Contemporary." *The Interpreter's Dictionary of the Bible.* Ed. G.A. Buttrick, *et al.* Vol. 1. New York/Nashville 1962. 418–432.

Steuernagel, C. "Alttestamentliche Theologie und alttestamentliche Religionsgeschichte." *Zeitschrift für die alttestamentliche Wissenschaft* Beiheft 41 (1925) 266–273.

Stonehouse, N. Review of R. Bultmann, *Theologie des Neuen Testaments*, pt. 1. *Westminster Journal of Theology* 15 (1953) 147–156.

Strange, John. "Heilsgeschichte und Geschichte: Ein Aspekt der biblischen Theologie." *Scandanavian Journal of the Old Testament* 2 (1989) 100–113.

_____. "Replik an Niels Peter Lemche." *Scandanavian Journal of the Old Testament* 2 (1989) 136–139.

Strauss, D.F. *The Life of Jesus Critically Examined.* Ed. Peter C. Hodgson. Trans. George Eliot. Philadelphia 1972.

Strecker, G. "'Biblische Theologie'? Kritische Bermerkungen zu den Entwürfen von H. Gese und P. Stuhlmacher." *Kirche.* Ed. G. Strecker & D. Lührmann. G. Bornkamm Festschrift. Tübingen 1980. 425–445.

_____, ed. *Das Problem der Theologie der Neuen Testaments.* Wege der Forschung 367. Darmstadt 1975.

_____. "Das Problem der Theologie des Neuen Testaments." *Das Problem der Theologie des Neuen Testaments.* Ed. G. Strecker. Darmstadt 1975. 1–31.

_____. *Theologie des Neuen Testaments.* Ed. F. Horn. Berlin/New York 1996.

_____. "William Wrede." *Zeitschrift für Theologie und Kirche* 57 (1960) 67–91.

Strege, M. "Das Eschatologische als gestaltende Kraft in der Theologie: A. Schweitzer und M. Albertz." Doctoral dissertation, 1955.

Stroh, H. "Das Erbe Schlatters für unsere Zeit." *Für Arbeit und Besinnung* 32 (1978) 466–474.

Strunk, W. "The Theology of Adolf Schlatter." *The Lutheran Church Quarterly* 11 (1938) 395–402.

Stuhlmacher, P. "Adolf Schlatter als Bibelausleger." *Zeitschrift für Theologie und Kirche* Beiheft 4 (1978) 81–111.

———. "Adolf Schlatter als Paulusausleger—ein Versuch." *Theologische Beiträge* 20/4 (1989) 176–190.

———. "Adolf Schlatter's Interpretation of Scripture." *New Testament Studies* 24 (1978) 433–446.

———, ed. *Das Evangelium und die Evangelien.* Tübingen 1983.

———. *How to Do Biblical Theology.* Allison Park PA 1995.

———. *Historical Criticism and Theological Interpretation of Scripture.* Philadelphia 1977.

———. "… in verrosteten Angeln." *Zeitschrift für Theologie und Kirche* 77 (1980) 222–238.

———. *Jesus of Nazareth, Christ of Faith.* Trans. S. Schatzmann. Peabody 1993.

———. *Vom Verstehen des Neuen Testaments.* Grundrisse zum Neuen Testament 6. Göttingen 1979.

Stupperich, R. "Adolf Schlatters Berufungen." *Zeitschrift für Theologie und Kirche* (1979) 100–117.

———, ed. "Briefe Karl Holls an Adolf Schlatter." *Zeitschrift für Theologie und Kirche* 64 (1967) 169–240.

Sun, H., *et al.*, eds. *Problems in Biblical Theology: Essays in Honor of Rolf Knierem.* Grand Rapids/Cambridge 1997.

Sutton, C. *The German Tradition in Philosophy.* London 1974.

Swarat, U. "Die heilsgeschichtliche Konzeption Johannes Chr. K. von Hofmanns." *Glaube und Geschichte: Heilsgeschichte als Thema der Theologie.* Ed. H. Stadelmann. Giessen/Basel/Wuppertal 1986. 211–239.

Sykes, N. "Some Recent Conceptions of Historiography and their Significance for Christian Apologetic." *Journal of Theological Studies* 50 (1949) 24–37.

———, & J.P. Clayton. *Christ, Faith and History.* Cambridge 1972.

Tångberg, K. "Linguistics and Theology: An attempt to analyze and evaluate James Barr's argumentation in *The Semantics of Biblical Language* and *Biblical Words for Time.*" *The Bible Translator* 24 (1973) 301–310.

Taylor, V. Review of R. Bultmann, *Theology of the New Testament*, vol. 1. *Scottish Journal of Theology* 6 (1953) 197–199.

Teeple, H. *The Historical Approach to the Bible.* Evanston 1982.

Thielicke, H. *The Evangelical Faith.* Vol. 1: *Prolegomena. The Relationship of Theology to Modern Thought Forms.* Trans. G. Bromiley. Grand Rapids 1974.

———. *Geschichte und Existenz.* Gütersloh [2]1964.

———. *Modern Faith and Thought.* Trans. G. Bromiley. Grand Rapids 1990.

_____. "Wahrheit und Verstehen." *Zeitschrift für Theologie und Kirche* 62 (1965) 114–135.

Thiselton, A.C. "Knowledge, Myth and Corporate Memory." *Belief in the Church: The Corporate Nature of Faith*. London 1981. 45–78.

_____. *New Horizons in Hermeneutics*. Grand Rapids 1992.

_____. "The New Hermeneutic." *New Testament Interpretation*. Ed. I.H. Marshall. Grand Rapids 1977. 308–333.

_____. *The Two Horizons*. Grand Rapids 1980.

Thorson, W. "Thinking about Thinking." *Crux* 20/1 (1984) 22–32.

Thurneysen, E. "Schrift und Offenbarung." *Das Problem der Theologie des Neuen Testaments*. Ed. G. Strecker. Darmstadt 1975. 214–248.

Tiililä, O. "Über die heilsgeschichtliche Schriftauslegung." *Gedenkschrift für D. Werner Elert*. Ed. F. Hübner, E. Kinder, and W. Maurer. Beiträge zur historischen und systematischen Theologie. Berlin 1955. 283–287.

Tödt, H.E. "Ernst Troeltsch." *Tendenzen der Theologie im 20. Jahrhundert*. Ed. H.J. Schultz. Stuttgart 1967. 93–98.

Tooman, W. "The Origin and Development of Heilsgeschichte in Conservative Biblical Theology with Special Attention to the Problem of Revelation and History." MA thesis, Trinity Evangelical Divinity School, 1994.

Torrance, T.F. *Reality and Evangelical Theology*. Philadelphia 1982.

Tracy, T. "Enacting God: Ogden and Kaufman on God's Mighty Acts." *Journal of Religion* 64 (1984) 20–36.

Trillhaas, W. "Vom geschichtlichen Denken in der Theologie." *Theologische Literaturzeitung* 80 (1955) 513–522.

Troeltsch, E. *The Absoluteness of Christianity and the History of Religion*. Trans. D. Reid. Richmond 1971.

_____. "The dogmatics of the 'Religionsgeschichtliche Schule.'" *American Journal of Theology* 17 (1913) 1–21.

_____. "Historical and Dogmatic Method in Theology." *The Historical Jesus Quest*. Ed. G. Dawes. Leiden–Louisville 1999. 29–53.

_____. "Historiography." *Encyclopedia of Religion and Ethics*. Ed. J. Hastings. New York 1922. 716–723.

Trompf, G.W. "The Future of Macro–Historical Ideas." *Soundings* 62 (1979) 70–89.

_____. *The Idea of Historical Recurrence in Western Thought*. Berkeley 1979.

_____. "Notions of Historical Recurrence in Classical Hebrew Historiography." *Vetus Testamentum* Supplement XXX. Leiden 1979. 213–229.

Turner, H.E.W. *History and the Gospels*. London 1962.

Unnik, W.C. van. "Der Ausdruck 'in den letzten Zeiten' bei Irenaeus." *Novum Testamentum* Supplement VI. Leiden 1962. 293–304.

Van Asselt, W.J. *The Federal Theology of Johannes Cocceus (1603–1669)*. Trans. R.A. Blacketer. Leiden 2001.

Vawter, B. Review of R. Bultmann, *Theologie des Neuen Testaments*, ³1958. *Catholic Biblical Quarterly* 21 (1959) 399–400.

_____. Review of B. Childs, *Biblical Theology in Crisis*. *Biblica* 52 (1971) 567–570.

Vercruysse, O. "History in the New Testament and in Hinduism." Texte und Untersuchungen 112 (1969 [*Studia Evangelica* VI]). 571–574.

Vischer, W. *Das Christuszeugnis des Alten Testaments*. Beiträge aus der Arbeit der v. Bodelschwinghschen Anstalten in Bielefeld–Bethel 30. 1985

_____. *The Witness of the Old Testament to Christ*. London 1949.

Vögtle, A. "Oscar Cullmann." *Tendenzen der Theologie im 20. Jahrhundert*. Ed. H.J. Schulz. Stuttgart 1966. 488–493.

Vorländer, H. *Die Entstehungszeit des jehowistischen Geschichtswerk*. Frankfurt am Main 1978.

Vos, G. *Biblical Theology: Old and New Testaments*. Grand Rapids 1948.

Vriezen, T. *An Outline of Old Testament Theology*. London 1958.

Wach, J. "Die Geschichtsphilosophie des 19. Jahrhunderts und die Theologie der Geschichte." *Historische Zeitschrift* 142 (1930) 1–15.

Wagner, B.S. "'Biblische Theologien' und 'Biblische Theologie.'" *Theologische Literaturzeitung* 103 (1978) 785–798.

Wagner, S. *Franz Delitzsch: Leben und Werk*. Beiträge zur evangelischen Theologie 80. München 1978.

Walker, R. *Die Heilsgeschichte im ersten Evangelium*. Forschungen zur Religion und Literatur des Alten und Neuen Testaments 91. Göttingen 1967.

Wallace, D. "Historicism and Biblical Theology." Texte und Untersuchungen 88 (1964 [*Studia Evangelica* III]). 223–227.

_____. "Oscar Cullmann." *Creative Minds in Contemporary Theology*. Ed. P. Hughes. Grand Rapids 1966. 163–202.

Wallace, P. "The Foundations of Reformed Biblical Theology: The Development of Old Testament Theology at Old Princeton." *Westminster Theological Journal* 59/1 (1997) 41–69.

Walldorf, J. *Realistische Philosophie. Der philosophische Entwurf Adolf Schlatters*. Göttingen 1999.

Wallis, G. "Geschichte, Überlieferung, Überlieferungsgeschichte." *Geschichte und Überlieferung*. Stuttgart 1968. 109–128.

Walsh, W. H. *Philosophy of History*. Rev. ed. New York 1967.

Wapler, P. *Johannes v. Hofmann*. Leipzig 1914.

Ward, Benedicta. *Miracles and the Medieval Mind*. London 1982.

Ward, W. "New Testament Theology: Retrospect and Prospect." *Review and Expositor* 78 (1981) 153–168.

_____. "Towards a Biblical Theology." *Review and Expositor* 74 (1977) 371–387.

Watson, F. *Text and Truth: Redefining Biblical Theology*. Grand Rapids 1997.

Waubke, H.-G. *Die Pharisäer in der protestantischen Bibelwissenschaft des 19. Jahrhunderts*. BHT 107. Tübingen 1998.

Weder, H. "Wunder Jesu und Wundergeschichten." *Verkündigung und Forschung* 29 (1984) 25–49.

Weinel, H. *Biblische Theologie des Neuen Testaments*. Tübingen [3]1921.

Weippert, M. "Fragen des israelitischen Geschichtsbewusstseins." *Vetus Testamentum* 23 (1973) 415–442.

Weiser, A. "Jesus und die neutestamentliche Theologie. Zur Frage nach dem Einheitsgrund des Neuen Testaments." *Zeitschrift für die neutestamentliche Wissenschaft* 87 (1996) 146–164.

Weiss, B. *Lehrbuch der biblischen Theologie des Neuen Testaments.* Berlin ²1873.

Weiss, Roberto. *The Renaissance Discovery of Classical Antiquity.* Oxford 1969.

Welch, C. *Protestant Theology in the Nineteenth Century.* Vol. 1: *1799–1870.* New Haven/London 1972.

Wells, P. *James Barr and the Bible: Critique of a New Liberalism.* Edinburgh 1980.

Wendebourg, E.W. "Die heilsgeschichtliche Theologie J.C. v. Hofmanns in ihrem Verhältnis zur romantischen Weltanschauung." *Zeitschrift für Theologie und Kirche* 52 (1955) 64–104.

_____. "Die heilsgeschichtliche Theologie Joh. Chr. K. von Hofmanns kritisch untersucht als Beitrag zur Klärung des Problems der 'Heilsgeschichte.'" University of Göttingen dissertation 1953.

Wendland, H.–D. *Geschichtsanschauung und Geschichtsbewusstsein im Neuen Testament.* Göttingen 1938.

Wennemer, K. "Zur Frage einer heilsgeschichtlichen Theologie." *Scholastik* 29 (1954) 73–79.

Werkmeister, W. "Cassirer's Advance Beyond Neo–Kantianism." *The Philosophy of Ernst Cassirer.* Ed. P. Schilpp. Evanston 1949. 757–798.

Werner, M. *The Formation of Christian Dogma.* Trans. S.G.F. Brandon. London 1957.

Westermann, C. "The Old Testament's Understanding of History in Relation to that of the Enlightenment." In *Understanding the Word.* Ed. J.T. Butler, E. W. Conrad, and Ollenburger. Fs. B.W. Anderson. JSOT Supp. Series 37. Sheffield 1985. 37–62.

_____. *Theologie des Alten Testaments in Grundzügen.* Grundrisse zum Alten Testament 6. Göttingen 1978.

_____. *What Does the Old Testament Say About God?* Ed. F. Golka. Atlanta 1979.

Weth, C. *Die Heilsgeschichte. Ihr universeller und individueller Sinn in der offenbarungsgeschichtlichen Theologie des 19. Jahrhunderts.* München 1931.

Wiefel, W. "Zur Würdigung William Wredes." *Zeitschrift für Religions– und Geistesgeschichte* 23 (1971) 60–83.

Wieman, H. "Divine Creativity in History." *Religion in Life* 33 (1964) 52–65.

Wilch, C. *Time and Event.* Leiden 1969.

Wilder, A.N. "New Testament Studies, 1920–1950: Reminiscences of a Changing Discipline." *Journal of Religion* 64 (1984) 432–451.

_____. "New Testament Theology in Transition." *The Study of the Bible Today and Tomorrow.* Ed. H. Willoughby. Chicago 1947. 419–436.

_____. Review of R. Bultmann, *Theology of the New Testament,* vol. 1. *Journal of Religion* 32 (1952) 128–130.

Wiles, M. "In what sense is Christianity a 'historical' religion?" *Theology* 81 (1978) 4–14.

Willey, T. *Back to Kant: The Revival of Kantianism in German Social and Historical Thought, 1860–1914.* Detroit 1978.

Williams, B. "Descartes, René." *The Encyclopedia of Philosophy.* Ed. P. Edwards. London/New York 1972. 344–354.

Williams, M. "Crossing Lessing's Ditch." *God and Man: Perspectives on Christianity in the 20th Century.* Ed. M. Bauman. Hillsdale, MI 1995. 103–126.

Wilson, R.McL. Review of M. Albertz, *Die Botschaft des Neuen Testaments.* *Scottish Journal of Theology* 11 (1958) 208–209.

Windisch, H. "Zwei neue Darstellungen der neutestamentlichen Theologie (zu Schlatter und Feine)." *Zeitschrift für wissenschaftliche Theologie* 52 (1910) 193–231.

Wink, W. *The Bible in Human Transformation.* Philadelphia 1973.

Winter, P. Review of R. Bultmann, *Theologie des Neuen Testaments,* [3]1958. *New Testament Studies* 6 (1959–60) 174–177.

Wolff, H.W. "The Understanding of History in the Old Testament Prophets." *Essays on Old Testament Hermeneutics.* Richmond 1963. 336–355.

_____, R. Rendtorff & W. Pannenberg. *Gerhard von Rad: Seine Bedeutung für die Theologie.* München 1973.

Wood, F.F. "The Contribution of the Bible to the History of Religion." *Journal of Biblical Religion* 47 (1928) 1–19.

Wood, G.H. "The Present Position of New Testament Theology: Retrospect and Prospect." *New Testatment Studies* 4 (1957–58) 169–182.

Wrede, W. *Die Entstehung der Schriften des Neuen Testaments.* Tübingen 1907.

_____. *Das Messiasgeheimnis in den Evangelien.* Göttingen 1901. ET *The Messianic Secret.* Trans. J.C.G. Greig. Cambridge/London 1971.

_____. "The Tasks and Methods of 'New Testament Theology.'" Trans. R. Morgan. *The Nature of New Testament Theology.* Studies in Biblical Theology (second series) 25. Naperville, IL 1973.

_____. *Vorträge und Studien.* Tübingen 1907.

Wright, G.E. *God Who Acts.* London 1952.

_____. "Reflections Concerning Old Testament Theology." *Studia Biblica et Semitica.* T.H.C. Vriezen Festschrift. Wageningen 1966. 376–388.

Wright, N.T. Review of H. Räisänen, *Beyond New Testament Theology. Journal of Theological Studies* 43 (1992) 626–630.

Würthwein, E. "Zur Theologie des Alten Testaments." *Theologische Rundschau* 36 (1971) 185–208.

Wyman, W.E., Jr. "Revelation and the Doctrine of Faith: Historical Revelation within the Limits of Historical Consciousness." *Journal of Religion* 78 (1998) 38–63.

Yamauchi, E. *Pre-Christian Gnosticism.* Grand Rapids [2]1983.

Yarbrough, R. "Adolf Schlatter." *Biblical Interpreters of the Twentieth Century: A Selection of Evangelical Voices.* Ed. Walter Elwell & J.D. Weaver. Grand Rapids 1999. 59–72.

_____. "Adolf Schlatter." *The Dictionary of Historical Theology*. Ed. T. Hart. Carlisle 2000. 505–507.

_____. "Adolf Schlatter." *Historical Handbook of Major Bible Interpreters*. Ed. D. McKim. Downers Grove 1998. 518-522.

_____. "Adolf Schlatter's 'The Significance of Method for Theological Work': Translation and Commentary." *The Southern Baptist Journal of Theology* 1/2 (Summer 1997) 64-76.

———. "A Milestone in the History of New Testament Research: Review Essay." *Journal of the Evangelical Theological Society* 46/2 (2003) 299-308.

_____. Review of Karl-Heinz Schlaudraff, *"Heil als Geschichte"? Die Frage nach dem heilsgeschichtlichen Denken, dargestellt anhand der Konzeption Oscar Cullmanns*. *Critical Review of Books in Religion* (1990) 234-236.

_____. "Schlatter Reception Then and Now: His New Testament Theology." Adolf Schlatter, *The Theology of the Apostles*. Trans. A. Köstenberger. Grand Rapids 1999. 417-431. (= *The Southern Baptist Journal of Theology* 3/1 [Spring 1999] 52-65).

Young, E.J. *The Study of Old Testament Theology Today*. London 1958.

Zahl, P. "A New Source for Understanding German Theology: Käsemann, Bultmann, and the New Perspective on Paul." *Sewanee Theological Review* 39/4 (1996) 413–422.

Zahn, T. *Grundriss der Neutestamentlichen Theologie*. Leipzig 1928.

Zimmerli, W. "Biblische Theologie. I." *Theologische Realenzyklopädie* 6. Berlin/New York 1980. 426–455.

_____. *Grundriss der alttestamentlichen Theologie*. Stuttgart 1972.

Zwanger, H. "Kritischer müssten mir die Historisch–Kritischen sein!" *Evangelische Theologie* 43 (1983) 370–389.

Index of Authors

Index of Biblical References

CARTESIAN
NON-CARTESIAN
HEGELIAN
KANTIAN
NEO-KANTIAN
noumenal
phenomenal